THE NENE OUTFALL.

This Plate Engraved at the Expence of the late H. I Adrane Esq.r and intended to have been dedicated to him can now unfortunately only be Inscribed to his Memory.

Published by R Walker Bridge Foot, Wisbech 1849.

THE HISTORY

OF

WISBECH,

AND

THE FENS.

BY NEIL WALKER,

AND

THOMAS CRADDOCK.

"I descended the mountain and entered a plain level country, which took me a month to travel over, and then I came to the sea side."

ARABIAN TALES.

WISBECH:
PUBLISHED BY RICHARD WALKER, BRIDGE-FOOT.
AND MAY BE HAD OF ALL BOOKSELLERS.

1849.

PREFACE.

LIKE every other principle of human nature, history is undergoing its revolution. The idea formerly attached to this word was that of a kind of public biography of kings and nobles, so written as to inspire a sort of reverence for the divine right and hereditary wisdom. The battles in which these heroes fought were described by particular scenes, in which kings had cloven the sculls of their antagonists with a battle axe, or had fought with the pertinacity of some of those knights which inspired the emulation of Don Quixote. Effusions of blood were the commodity which was at the historian's command; and these he used so lavishly, that history bade fair to become an antagonistic course of surgery, since a regular course of surgery teaches how to heal wounds, but history only told how they were made. The people have now grown well tired of such pictures. They were forgotten in battles where they fell in thousands, and in tournaments which their hands had covered with silken tents, and with the brilliant manufactures which shone from the shoulders of the queen of beauty; and where they had arrayed the steeds in cloth of gold. It was forgotten who had built the castle where the petty lord played his ill-natured tyrannies or the cathedral, towering, like a glorious dream, from earth to heaven. How the progress was made from slavery to liberty,—how the art of spinning and weaving progressed from coarse serge and hempen cloth to silks and velvets,—how the arts of design grew from such rude materials as were the only implements, and the only ideas of the Britons and the Saxons,—or the church, rudely constructed of rough-hewn stone, with arrow-headed doors, and windows stuffed with reeds, grew to the magnificence of Ely and Peterborough and Lincoln cathedrals,—have been passed over, and we are left to grope in the most uncertain manner after the most interesting of events. Though much had been prepared beforehand, it remained for Sir Walter Scott to awaken this sleep of history. In reanimating the past,—a devotee of kings and nobles himself,—he interested his readers less in his favorite characters than in the poor slaves that administered to their lusts and their caprices. He was obliged, by the power of his genius, to draw his pictures faithfully from human nature; and, in drawing these pictures, he naturally stole into his readers' hearts by the sympathies inseparable from mankind in his character of brotherhood and blood. But, more than all, his novel of "*Ivanhoe*" awakened the interest of the French historians. They had been led to consider that the conquest of England was accomplished in a month and a single battle. But they found here a novel, descriptive of the era of Richard I., teeming with Saxon character and Saxon bitterness against their Norman foes. They had believed the Saxon spirit completely crushed long before. They were aroused, and the result was, Thierry's *History of the Norman Conquest*, in which it was shown that the real struggle was of several years' duration; and that the Saxon spirit continued to bite at the Norman yoke for three centuries afterwards. This was the first contribution to the history of the people. It has been succeeded by the *History of Civilization*, of Guizot, drawn chiefly from forgotten laws and customs. But the spirit is awaked: the people are now to have their historians as well as their rulers. Macaulay has made a bold attempt at realizing the demands of the age in his *History of England*; and he will be succeeded by others who are diligently searching Corporation records, acts of Parliament, old diaries, letters, and other materials, which the Camden, and Percy societies, and the Archæological institutes are gathering together for the future historians of the manners, customs, arts, and industry of the people. To these materials, local histories will necessarily contribute much; since he who writes a history of a town cannot be dazzled with brighter ideas than the shop or the council chamber affords him. His history is essentially a history of the people. Their trade, their improvements, their buildings, their opinions, and their habits, are the memorials which he seeks to gather together; and when some adequate spirit shall arise to blend and fuse these various materials, extracting the characteristic, and rejecting the redundant, a history of the country will be produced worthy of the great nation it will commemorate.

This work was projected in October, 1845; and, though only consisting of fourteen numbers, it has been prolonged to December 1849. Such an unreasonable delay seems to require some explanation, and yet only a very inadequate one can be given; so that the indulgence of the subscribers must be solicited, and the concluding number relied on as our chief apology. We have been often asked, with somewhat of impatience, when the work would be finished; and some had begun to suspect that it would never be completed. Having received all kinds of ungenerous surmises, we can only say that we deserved them the more from the very generous manner with which the work has been supported from the beginning. The lukewarmness has not been with the public, but with us, and we willingly quit so ungracious a part of our confession for the more agreeable task of thanking those patrons who have contributed plates to the work. To Messrs. William and Daniel Peckover, and to Mrs. Shewell, we owe the three plates presenting views of different portions of the Brink, which Messrs. William and Algernon Peckover have so much contributed to ornament. To Mr. Algernon Peckover we are indebted for the view of the British School—a valuable institution, which was erected and is chiefly supported by the liberality of himself and his brother. From the Vicar—the Rev. Henry Fardell—we obtained the plates of the Vicarage, and the Chapel of the Church Cemetery. The Rev. W. G. Townley gave the interior of his own church, which is otherwise so largely indebted to his generosity. Dr. Whitsed appropriately contributed the Wharf View, of which he laid the foundation while he was mayor in 1845. Mr. Robert Dawbarn gave us the view of the Port, looking eastward—a view which, like most of the former, had never been previously engraved. Our last acknowledgment must be made to the dead. Mr. Adeane sent us the cost of a plate at the commencement of the work, making no choice of subject. The one to which his name is attached was selected, and would have been submitted for his approval, had not his sudden death removed not only an earnest patron of all liberal measures from the county, but a warm-hearted and generous friend to mankind in general.

It is usual to make a preface the apology for the book. Most books contain some hasty opinions, which, written under excitement, are regretted in cooler moments; and the preface is commonly the point of acknowledgment or defence. We may have been as guilty as others; but, if so, we must abide the fate of rash opinions without crouching. During the progress of the work, some of the most important measures that ever came before the Corporation of Wisbech have been discussed and decided. Railways, and other projects of drainage and navigation, which must ultimately have a great influence on the prosperity of the town, have been selected, and money to the extent of several thousands of pounds has been spent in opposing measures, which, to other minds, presented the prospect of much enduring benefit and prosperity.

We must not omit, however, to thank this body for the very liberal manner with which they complied with our request to make extracts from the records. The whole of their papers were opened to us, and every facility afforded for investigating them. We have availed ourselves largely of this permission, and have preferred giving the records in their own orthography to modernising them, as Col. Watson has done. The records do not contain much of other than local value; but they not only commence at an earlier date than usual, but have only one or two intervals in their succession.

To the other persons who have aided us, we also beg to render our acknowledgments. From Mr. Tycho Wing we received a variety of the most important and interesting documents on the Nene Outfall Improvement, and the drainage of the Fens in general, of which we have largely availed ourselves. To Mr. A. Peckover we are indebted for the interesting account of the Friends' Society in Wisbech, and for other suggestions; and from Mr. W. Peckover we have received help on one or two occasions. The Rev. W. G. Townley furnished us with information and documents on the history and description of Upwell and Welney. To the Rev. Mr. Pike we owe the account of the Baptists, to the Rev. W. Holmes of the Independents, to the Rev. Mr. Reynoldson of the class of Dissenters of which he is minister. Mr. Lefever also opened his curious antiquarian volumes to us, from which we derived considerable assistance.

December 1849.

LIST OF SUBSCRIBERS.

Abbott, Mrs.
Abbott, Mr. J.
Adams, Mr. R.
Adams, Mr. W.
Adeane, H. J., Esq.
Agar Thomas, Esq., Crowland
Allix, J. P., Esq.
Andrews, Mr. H. J.
Anderson, Mr. J.
Arblington, Mr., Wimblington
Ash, Rev. —, Tyd St. Mary
Ashworth, Mr. T.
Aveling, Rev. T., Stoke Newington

Bedford, His Grace the Duke of
Bagnall, Mr. John
Bays, Mr. W. P., 2 copies
Batterham, Mr. J.
Batterham, Mr. R.
Batterham, Mr., Terrington St. John's
Barley, Mr. J. G.
Batterbee, Mr. W.
Bailey, Mr.
Bouttell, Mr. T. H.
Bellamy, J., Esq.
Bellamy, Mr. E., March
Bell, Mr. Wm.
Bell Mr., Bourn
Bennett, Rev. E. L., Rector of Long Sutton
Bennett, Mr. R.
Bennett Mr. H., Whittlesea
Berry, Mr., Nordelph
Beart, Mr. M., Upwell
Blunt Mr. J., Whittlesea
Boon, Mr. J.
Boon, Mr. C., Walpole St. Andrew's
Bothway, Mr. R., Wisbech St. Mary's
Boucher, C., Esq., 2 copies
Bodger, Mr. E.
Boughen, Mr. H., Lamb Inn, Ely
Boyce Mr., Whittlesea
Bradley, Mr. S., Gorefield
Brewin, Mr. John
Brown, Mr. J., Peartree Hills
Briggs, Mr. L.
Broadbent, Mr., Watlington
Broughton, J., Esq., Peterborough
Brookshaw, Mr., London
Blencowe, Rev. E. E., West Walton
Blanchard, Mr. V.
Blazley, Mr. K.
Buckley, Mr. J. S
Bugg, Mr. W. N., Spalding
Burdock, Mr. T., Dog and Double
Burgess, Mr. J.
Burman, Smith, Esq.
Burnham, J. Esq., Whittlesea
Burroughs, Mr. E. J.
Burrell, Mr. E. London

Callow, — Esq., Castor Mills
Campion, Mr. S., Littleworth Drove
Catling, Mr., Ely
Cave, Mr. T. C., Littleport
Chamberlin, Mr. J. H.
Chadwick, J. N., Esq., Lynn
Childers, J. W., Esq., M.P.
Chapman, Mr. C., Upwell
Clarke, Mr. R.
Clarke, Mr. R. Y., London
Clare, Mr. W. Y., Edmonton
Clare, Mr. W.
Claxton, J., Esq , Ely
Climenson, Mr., Upwell
Cole, Mr. E. F., Long Sutton
Collins, G. D., Esq.
Congreve, Mr. Daniel, Crowland
Congreve, Mr. David, Market Deeping
Cooper, Mr. R., Gedney Hill
Coop, Mr., Fleet
Copeman, P., Esq., Long Sutton
Cornwell, Mr. C., Cambridge
Cox, Joseph, Esq., 2 copies
Cox, Mr. J. B.
Creak, Mr. J.
Cripps, Mr. J.
Cross, Mr. John
Cross, Mr. S. M.
Cunnington, Mr. T.
Cutlack, Mr. W., Littleport

Danford, Mr. F., Parson Drove
Dawbarn, T., Esq.
Dawbarn, Mr. Robert, 2 copies
Dawbarn, Mr. William, 2 copies
Dawbarn, Mr. George, 2 copies
Dawbarn, Mr. Richard
Dawbarn, Mr. Henry
Denshire Col., Baston Park, near Deeping
Dean, Captain, Ramsey
Dieppe, Mr. W. D.
Dover, H., Esq., Caston, Norfolk
Dow, Miss A. G. Elm
Dowson, Mr. J.,

Drake, Mr., Whittlesea
Dodsworth, Rev. Joseph, Bourn

Ely, Right Rev. the Lord Bishop of
Elvidge, Mr. J. E.
Elmer, Mr, Nordelph
Elsum, Mr., Walsoken
Elsey, Mr. G. W.
England, W., Esq., M.D.
English Brothers & Harrison, Messrs
Evans, H. R. Esq., Ely
Ewen, Mr. C., Tyd St. Giles
Exley, W., Esq.

Fardell, Rev. Henry, M.A., Vicar, 20 copies
Fawssett, F., Esq.
Fawssett, T., Esq.
Fellowes, E., Esq., Ramsey
Ffolkes, Sir W. B., Hillington Hall
Foster, G. W., Esq.
Foster, Mr. F., Newton
Fountain, Mr. I.
Firth, Mr., Louth
Francis, Mr. J., London
Freeman Mr. C., Crowland
Frusher, T. Esq., Elm
Fryer, J. R., Esq., Crow Hall, Downham
Fryer, T., Esq., Chatteris
Fryer, J., Esq., Chatteris
Fryer, D., Esq., Charteris
Fulcher, Mr. J.
Fraser, J. E., Esq.

Gathercole, Rev. M., Chatteris
Gardiner, Mr. J.
Gatliffe, Mr.
Gay, W., Esq.
Giddens, Mr. C. B., Walpole St. Andrew's
Giddens, Mr. J., Walpole St. Andrew's
Goddard, Mrs. A., 2 copies
Gomm, Mr. W., Britannia Assurance Office, London, 2 copies
Gray, Mr. R., Spalding
Green, Mr., Upwell
Green Mr. J., Lynn
Ground, Mr. E.
Ground, Mr. D., Whittlesea
Grounds, Mrs S.
Groom, Mr. Joseph
Gurney D., Esq., Lynn

H. M. Tidal Harbors' Commissioners
Hall, Rev. Thomas, M.A., Prebendary of St. Paul's, London
Hall, Rev. G., Ely
Halford, T., Esq., London
Hankinson, Rev. H., Walpole St. Andrew's
Harrison, Mr. John
Harrison, Mr. M.
Hampson, Mr. J.
Handley, Mr. Jno., West Walton
Healey, Mr. A. W.
Hill, Mr. R.
Hill, Mr. J., Tilney
Hill, Mr. Willm., Elm

Hiscox, Mr. J.
Hollingworth, Mrs.
Hollingworth, Mr. J., Tid St. Giles
Holmes, Rev. T. P.
Heys, Mr. J., Gedney Hill
Huddlestone, Rev. G., Upwell, 2 copies
Hunt, W., Esq., Littleworth Drove

Ibberson, O., Esq., Ramsey
Ingram, Mr. John

Jackson, Rev. J., Elm
Jackson, Rev. H., Leverington
Jackson, Rev. F., Parson Drove
Jackson, Hugh, Esq., 3 copies
Jackson, Edwd., Esq., 3 copies
Jackson, W. G. Esq., 3 copies
Jackson, Fras., Esq.
Jarvis, Messrs. L. W. and Son, Lynn
Jealous, Mr. J., Parson Drove
Jecks, W., Esq., Trowse
Jennings, Mr. George, Jun.
Johnson, Rev. R., Hilgay
Johnson, Mr. Eleazer
Johnson, Mr. Benjamin
Johnson, Mr. Thos., Ely
Johnson, —, Esq., Holbeach
Johnston, Robert, Esq.
Johnson, Mr. R., Murrow
Johnson, Mr. T., Parson Drove
Johnson, Mr. Saml., St. Edmund's
Jones, Mr. James, Ramsey

Keed, Mr. J., Lynn
Key, — Esq., Holbeach
Kendal, Mr. C. J., Fordham
Kilham, Mr. Richard, Tyd St. Mary's
Kilham, Mr. W., Tyd Gote
King, Rev. R. J.,
Kingerley, Mr. G., Parson Drove

Lamb, Mr. J., Whittlesea
Lawrence, J., Esq., Elton, Hunts.
Lawson, Mr. John
Leach, H., Esq.
Lefevre, G. M., Esq , 2 copies
Lewin, Mr., Leverington
Life, Mr. R. C.
Lilley, John, Esq.
Lilley, F. J., Esq
Limer, Mr. J.
Little, J , Esq , Littleport
Livett, Mr. Z., Whittlesea
Louth, Mr. Joseph

Maclean, J. H., Esq.
Macdonald, Mr. J. T.
Major, Rev. R. J., King's College, London
Mantegani, Mr. A.
Marfleet Mr., Crowland
Marshall, W., Esq., Leith
Marshall, Mr. G.
Martin, Mr. M., Parson Drove
Maudesley, Mr. S., Ramsey
Medworth, Mr. H.

Medworth, Mr. J. T., West Walton
Metcalfe, Mrs. E., Aylmer Hall, Tilney
Metcalfe, C., Sen., Esq.
Martin, Mr., Littleport
Maxwell, Mr., Thorney
Mills, Mr. A.
Mills, Esq., Holbeach
Moor, Rev. W. G., Aslackby
Moore, W., Esq., Em
Moore, Rev. A. Walpole St. Peter's
Morton, Henry, Esq
Mortlock, W. Esq., Cambridge
Moss, Mr. J. Walsoken
Moules, Mr., John
Murley, Mr. J., Walsoken
Moyse, W., Esq., Lynn

Neal, Mr. T.
Newsham, Mr. W., Murrow
Nichols, Mr. J., Parson Drove
Nichols, Mr. S., Wisbech St. Mary's
Noble, Mr. J., Boston

Oldham, Mr W. T.
Ollard, W., Esq.

Pollyn, Mr., Tilney
Pate, W., Esq., Spalding
Pate, R. F., Esq.
Parkis, Rev. J., Rector of Hilgay
Parker, W., Esq., Hansthorpe House
Pattrick, Mr. Thos.
Peterborough, Right Rev. Lord Bishop of
Pestling, Mr. Thos.
Peck, Mr. John, Parson Drove
Peck, Mr. Joseph, Wisbech St. Mary's
Peck, Mr. W., Newton
Peckover, W., Esq., 2 copies
Peckover, D., Esq., Woodhall
Peckover, A., Esq., 3 copies
Peake, —, Esq., Stagsholt
Pearson, —, Esq., Ely
Peyton, Sir Henry, Bart.
Peyton, Rev. Algernon, Doddington
Phillips, E., Esq., 2 copies
Phillips, Mr. W., Peterborough
Pitcher R., Esq., Lynn
Place, Mr. C. M.
Pollard, Mr. W.
Pooley, Mr. H., Jun.
Pope, Mr. John
Porter, Mr., Watlington
Porter, Mr., Downham

Quincey, Mr., Elm

Ratcliff, Mr. J.
Reeve, Mr. Walter, 2 copies
Reeve, Mr. William
Reed, Mr. George
Reed, T. L., Esq., Downham
Reed, Mr., Whittlesea
Reynoldson, Rev. R.
Robinson, Miss
Rodgers A., Esq., Morton

Rose, Mr. A., Ramsey
Roope, Mr. William
Rowell, Mr., Upwell
Rumball, Mr. Josiah
Russell, Mr. Peter
Rich, Mr., Downham
Richardson, Mr. J. S., Gedney
Ringham, Mr. William, Tid St. Giles
Ruston, Mr. Alfred, Chatteris

Scrimshaw, Mr. W., Murrow
Self, Mr, Robert
Sharp, Mr. T.
Sheppard, James, Esq., London
Shepherd, Mr. Benjamin
Shepperson, Mr. R., March
Simmons, Mr. J., Bishopgate St., London
Semen, Mr. Jun., St. John's
Shewell, Mrs., Rushmere
Sloate, Mr. William
Smith, H., Esq., Cambridge
Smith, J., Esq., March
Smith, J., Esq., Ramsey
Smith, Mr. J., Upwell
Smith, Mrs. E.
Smith, Mr. Theophilus
Smith, Mr. William
Smith, C., Esq., Whittlesea
Smith, Mr. J., Tyd St. Giles
Southwell, Mr. F. C.
Southwell, Mr. A.
Sparke, Rev. J. H., Rector of Leverington
Sparke, Rev. E. B., Vicar of Littleport
Spence, Mr. H., Lynn
Spikings, Mr. W., West Walton
Springfield, Miss E.
Springfield, Mr. William
Stafforth W., Esq., Ramsey
Stannard Mrs., Rippingale
Stear, T., Esq.
Stevens, W., Esq.
Steadman, Mr., Whittlesey
Strong, Rev. W., Standground
Swaine, Mrs.

Taylor, Mr. John
Taylor, Mr. Wm., Lynn
Thompson, Rev. G. H. W., Master of the Grammar School
Tuck, Mr R., Nordelph
Thompson, Mr. William
Townley, Rev. W. G., Beaupre Hall
Townley, Mrs., Beaupre Hall
Townley, R. G., Esq., M.P., Fulbourn
Tibenham, Mr. William
Topp, Mr. G., Newton
Tuck, Mr., Gedney Hill
Tuck, Mr., Salterslode

Ulyatt, Mr. John, Parson Drove
Ulyatt, Miss, Parson Drove
Usill, James, Esq.
Usill, Harley Matthew, Esq.
Utting, Mr. F. J.
Ulyatt, Mr. A., West Walton

Veall, Mr. J. R.
Voss, Miss
Vipan, Thos., Esq., Sutton, Isle
Vipan, W., Esq., Mepal

Waites, Mr., Yaxley
Wales, R., Esq.
Walker, J., Esq., New York, U.S.
Waddington, Mr. T.
Ward, R., Esq.
Ward, G. A., Esq.
Ward, H. W., Esq., 2 copies
Ward, Mr. Perry, Walsoken
Ward, Mr. R., Emneth
Wardale, Mr. George
Wardale, Mr. C. B., Houndsditch, London
Ward, W. F., Esq.
Waters Rev., Rippingale
Weatherhead, J. R., Esq
Weight, Mr. C. D., Parson Drove
Welley, Rev. E., Folkingham
Westwood, Mr., Ely
Whitley, Mr. James, Jun.
Whitsed, J., Esq., M.D., 2 copies
Whitwell, Mr. John
Wherry, Mr. R.
Watson, T. S., Esq.
Watford, Mr. W.
Whittaker, Mr., Outwell
Wilson P., Esq., Lynn
Wilton, Mr. J., Peterborough
Wilkinson, Mr. John
Wright, Charles, Esq., Boston
Whisler, Mr., Magdalen
Williamson, Mr. C., Wisbech St. Mary's
West, Mr. James, Tyd Fen

Young, Mr. Richard

LIST OF PLATES.

HISTORY

OF

WISBECH AND THE FENS.

SECTION I.—THE FENS.

CHAPTER I.

PHYSICAL CHARACTERISTICS.

WHOEVER examines the map of England with attention will soon perceive that it is divided into three districts or natural provinces. The extreme west is occupied by mountains, rocky coasts, and mines. A line drawn from Carlisle to Dorchester, will pretty well define this division, in which mining, quarrying stone, and smelting ore, are the principal employments of its inhabitants. The middle district which will include the portion marked by a line drawn from North Shields to Brighton, will comprise a country full of gentle elevations, whose common slope is eastward, and whose population is employed in a mixture of manufactures and agriculture. The remaining portion has neither mountains nor hills; its poor elevations are termed wolds, and these gradually sink into the low marshes which occupy much of the coast of this division, giving it somewhat the appearance of that ocean, of which it seems recently to have been the bed: here the people are entirely agricultural.

England may, therefore, be said to resemble the roof of a house, sinking gradually from the ridge to the eave. It follows as a consequence of this formation of outline, that the principal rivers of the country take their course and fall into the sea that washes the east coast, by considerable estuaries,—the Humber, the Wash, and the Thames. While the west is thus comparatively devoid of large outfalls, the east, by their predominance, has become a series of plains and marshes; and, were it not for the Severn, which is the drain of the west as far as the Malverns, England would be almost entirely drained by the rivers which discharge their contents into the North Sea.[1]

The rivers of the Humber extend from Westmoreland to Leicestershire; those of the Wash occupy less extent of country, and proceed nearly parallel with each other into the heart of the kingdom, taking Lincolnshire for their extreme northern boundary, and divided by the Buckinghamshire hills from the valley of the Thames; which river, proceeding nearly due east and west, drains the southern division of England.

This physical constitution of the country has produced its natural effects upon the manners and arts of the inhabitants, according as the mines, the coal-fields, or the arable plains predominate. But it is that division, drained by the waters which fall into the Wash with which we are concerned. We shall, accordingly, confine ourselves to those physical particulars connected with the history or present state of that part of it bordering on the sea, which is called the Fens.

All the rivers we have named are marked at their outfalls by a certain extent of marshy ground. In the outfalls of the Thames and Humber this is inconsiderable, but in the outfall of the Wash it becomes very predominant; which is

(1) Scotland will be found to present the same general characteristics as England. All its considerable rivers flow through the friths of Forth, Tay, Murray, and Dornock, into the German Ocean; while in the west is the Clyde alone. The marshes, however, which lie at the outfalls of the English rivers, are wanting in the Scotch streams.

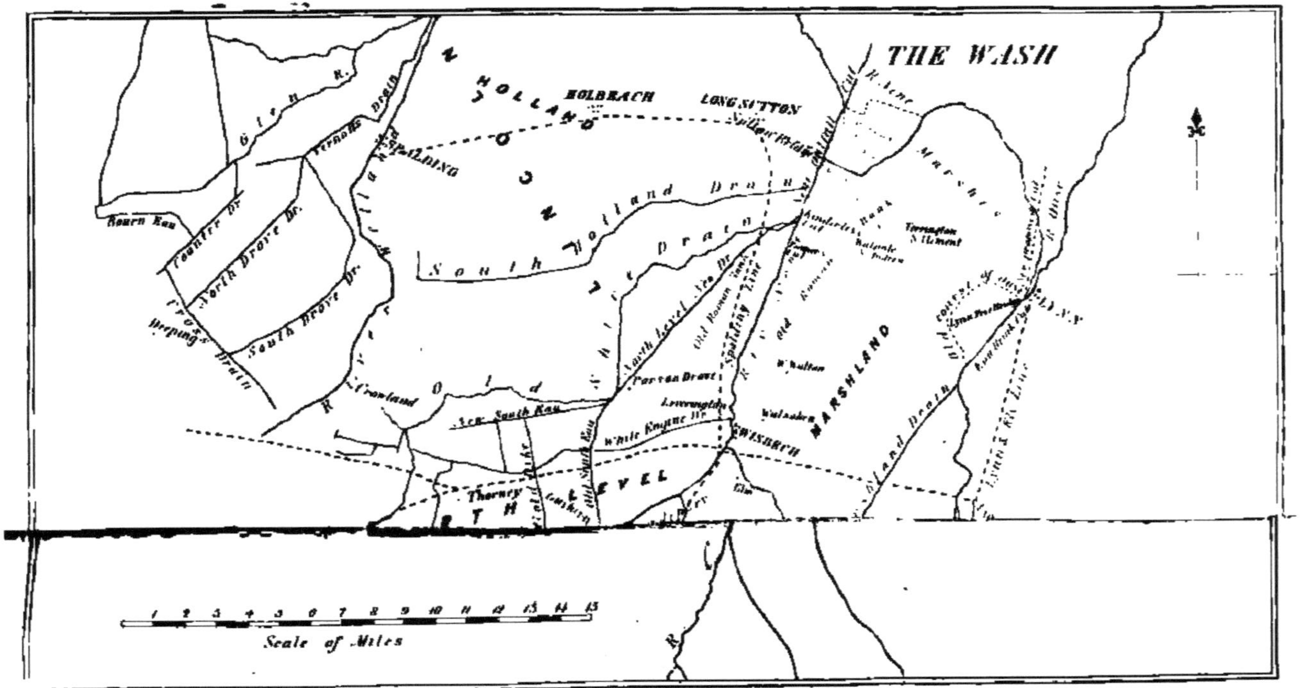

Published by R. Walker, Bridge Foot

probably owing to the moderate heights from which its rivers are derived, and the consequent slow stream with which they discharge their waters. There has, accordingly, accumulated around the coast of the Wash an extent of morass unknown in the vicinity of violent rivers.

In the Thames and Humber we see valleys extending almost into the sea: while the valley of the Nene is lost thirty miles before it falls into the sea, that of the Ouse extends no further than St. Ives, and the river runs a course afterwards of fifty miles between that town and Lynn; and the valleys of the Glen and Welland terminate on the borders of Lincolnshire. We, therefore, find these rivers all seeking a common outlet over lands which are no higher than their beds, and, consequently, only prevented by embankments from distributing themselves over the soil. When it is considered how great an extent of country these rivers drain, and what bodies of water are at all times discharged through their mouths, we shall hardly be surprised that all the exertions of science and ingenuity have scarcely been sufficient to keep the fen from relapsing into the general morass from which it seems to have been originally derived. The extent of country which the Wash drains includes the entire counties of Cambridge, Huntingdon, Bedford, Northampton, and Rutland, nearly one-half of Norfolk, one-third of Suffolk, one-half of Buckingham, three-fourths of Lincolnshire, and a small part of Leicestershire; comprising altogether about five thousand square miles.[1]

All these counties may be said to be contained in one large basin or system of valleys, bounded by inconsiderable elevations. The chalk hills of Norfolk, extending a distance of eighty miles, from Hunstanton to Royston, are its eastern boundaries.[2] These hills are successively interrupted by the lateral rivers, Nar, Stoke, Ouse Parva, Lark, and Cam. From Royston the valley sweeps in a south-west direction to Tring at the foot of the Chiltern Hills, and from thence to

(1) Geography of Great Britain. (2) Ibid.

Mapledurham, a distance of sixty-five miles.[1] The western boundaries of the basin are not well defined. It passes the Roman Camp, near Cottesford Heath, and runs for some distance along the line of the Grand Union Canal till it comes to Bosworth Tunnel. Thence it proceeds near Oakham along the base of the heights of Belvoir, and through Wellingore to the west of Lincoln. Taking almost the line of Ermine-street, it is turned by the wolds in the north of Lincolnshire towards the east, and leaving Louth to the north, where it again enters the chalk, it melts into the low fens to the east of Alford.

The Fens comprise about the sixth part of this extensive valley, bordering the sea-coast from Barton-on-the-Humber to Lynn. In the north of Lincolnshire they do not extend more than four or five miles inland; but in the south of that county they are twenty miles wide; and from Lynn to Peterborough, which is the broadest part, they are thirty miles across. They maintain this width for some miles further south, and then, arrested by the oolitic elevations of Huntingdon and Cambridge, terminate a few miles south of Ely. The whole length of the tract is about one hundred and thirty miles; and with the exception of the Lincolnshire wolds to the north, and a few hills which penetrate into the south and south-west, the whole fen has nearly one level, often beneath that of the sea, especially about its middle and southern parts. Its original condition we may, from these elementary facts, readily conceive. The water falling over so extensive an area as we have traced, from elevations too small to impel it onward, would naturally be arrested in a marsh whose lowest point was about midway between the sea and its inland borders. The result was a large freshwater estuary; which, for many ages, was probably the sole characteristic of the whole fen.[2]

(1) Geography of Great Britain.

(2) Sedgwick conjectures that the passage of the sea over the clayey bottom of the fens caused deep fissures, into which the rivers fell. He says, "we have an evidence that the beds of our river, so to speak, made the rivers, and not the rivers the beds in which they flow."—*Lecture delivered at Norwich.*

The rivers which are the present water-drains to this district, are principally the Witham, Welland, Nene, and Ouse. As fen rivers, the Witham and Welland transport inconsiderable quantities of fresh water to the sea; the more important sewers of the district being the Ouse and Nene,—both of which rise in the same county, and, after taking directions nearly at right angles, discharge themselves within a few miles of each other.

The course of the Ouse is the most tortuous of any river in the island.[1] It proceeds from two branches; the main one of which rises near Gretworth, ten miles W.N.W. of Buckingham, "on a gentle rising ground full of bubbling fountains."[2] At Buckingham, which town it nearly surrounds, the level of the canal is two hundred and sixty-four feet eleven inches.[3] Buckingham is about eighty miles direct distance from Lynn, which gives a descent of $3\frac{1}{3}$ feet per mile; but, from the exceedingly irregular course of this river, it is probable its average fall is less than half this amount per mile; and even this small amount, as we shall afterwards show, is nearly all expended by the time it reaches the fen. After leaving Buckingham, it proceeds north as far as Sharnbrook; then taking a southern direction for about fifteen miles, arrives at Bedford. It now proceeds directly east, but soon turning north it passes Huntingdon, and goes thence nearly due east till it receives the Cam near Streatham. The rest of its course past Ely is north to Lynn.

In this course of eighty miles from Buckingham, it passes over about one hundred and sixty miles;[4] a longer course than any other river in the kingdom, if we cut off such large estuaries as those of Severn, Thames, and Humber.[5] It, however, has no romantic scenery to boast; and mere length is the only point of competition which it can claim against its rival rivers.

(1) Geography of Great Britain. (2) Badeslade. (3) Geography of Great Britain. (4) Badeslade.

(5) Geography of Great Britain.—"Longer than Humber, long as Severn, and wanting not ten miles of the length of Thames."—*Badeslade:* But Badeslade calculates the Thames to the Nore, and the Severn to the Bristol Channel.

The sources of the Nene are two springs, one north the other south of Daventry.[1] One rises at Catesby, on the east side of the water-shed of the Anby Hills.[2] Its course is east to Northampton,[3] "where it meeteth with the second head from Naseby-field, where there be two springs twenty yards asunder, the one of which maketh the head of Avon falling westward to Warwick and so to Severn, the other this brook."[4] At Northampton the Nene becomes navigable at an elevation of one hundred and ninety-seven feet ten inches.[5] The direct distance of Northampton to the outfall at the sea is about sixty miles; but the course of the river is nearly, if not quite, one hundred miles. The distance of sixty miles, gives a fall of 3⅓ feet per mile—the same as the Ouse; but, from the more direct course of the Nene, the actual fall of the river is probably six inches per mile greater than that of the Ouse. Though, like the Ouse, almost all this fall is spent by the time it arrives at the fen, yet, it maintains a declivity superior to the latter river throughout that region;[6] and, therefore, a better and more complete drainage has been effected in the division which it drains than in that of the Ouse. From Northampton it proceeds north-east to Higham Ferrars; then, with many windings past Oundle,[7] it runs

(1) "The several villages of Naseby, Draughton, West Haddon, Fawsley, and Staverton, contend for the honor of its [the Nene's] source, but it is now pretty generally admitted that the north branch springs from Chapel Well, at Naseby, and the western from Hartwell, near Staverton."—*Beauties of England and Wales, vol. ix, page* 39.

(2) Geography of Great Britain.

(3) Near Northampton is the centre or heart of England, where from one hill arise three rivers running different ways,—the Cherwell, south; the Leame, (soon after received by another Aufonia [Avon] making towards the Severn) west; and this [the Nene] east.—*Camden.*

(4) Atkins's Report.

(5) Bradshaw's Canal Map.—Geography of Great Britain.

(6) Rennie's Letter on the Middle Level, 1842.

(7) "The river of *Avon* so windeth about the town [Oundle] that it almost insulateth it." —*Leland's It.*, vol. i., p. 4. The Nene is often called by Camden and other old writers Aufona [Avon], a British name for a river, and applied indiscriminately. Tacitus calls the Nene Antona, [Annals, xii, 31] which Camden conjectures is a corruption of text. "What this river Antona was, nobody has told us: Lipsius, the sun of our age, has dispelled this darkness, or I myself am in a cloud. He directs us to Northampton, and I suppose Antona crept into Tacitus instead of Aufona, on which Northampton stands."—*Camden.* Murphy follows Camden in his translation of Tacitus; but he has confounded the Antona with the Avon.—See *Murphy's Tacitus*, vol. ii., p. 194, Valpy, 1830.

due north to Wandsford, and, turning east, passes on to Peterborough, "bringing with it the waters of many brooks and rivers of more than twenty heads."[1] These, however, are all derived from the north-western slopes of Northamptonshire: the rivers receives scarcely any affluent in its whole course on the right side, as the high lands of Huntingdon present their steepest side to the Nene; so that all the drainage runs down the longer slope into the Ouse.[2] In the course of its route to Peterborough, the Northampton and Peterborough Railway, which runs along its valley, crosses it several times. At Peterborough it enters the Fens, being chiefly conducted through this region by four artificial cuts, so that its original channels are, in some cases, hardly traceable. With the exception of a bend at Guyhirn and another at Wisbech, its course to the sea is now nearly a line of thirty miles, entering the Wash by the fourth artificial cut, about three miles below Sutton Bridge.

The Great Level, as the plain has been well denominated through which these rivers flow, may be divided into the moory, the peaty, and the marshy. The moory division comprises the largest portion of the fen, and is characterised by a black soil chiefly composed of decayed vegetable matter. A few feet under this there is, fortunately, a stratum of clay, without which the soil would be barren; but, by being intermixed with the top soil and well drained, the moor becomes exceedingly productive. It lies too low, however, to secure a complete drainage in every part; and, although two hundred years and immense sums of money have been expended on it, there remains much to be done before this portion of the fen can be said to be secure in the hands of the agriculturist.

The peaty division is intermixed with the moory, of which it seems to be merely the lowest undrainable part,—too cold and watery to be brought into cultivation. It varies in extent according to these circumstances, and every improve-

(1) Atkins's Report. (2) Geography of Great Britain.

ment in drainage of course diminishes it. In yealding, however almost inexhaustible supplies of fuel, it has performed a purpose almost better than that of cultivation, especially where wood and coal are only to be procured from a distance. To this peat of the fen we may reasonably attribute the cause of its first settlement; for it would have been impossible to inhabit so dreary a region in ages when little or no communication was carried on between town and town, without a home supply of all the necessaries of life.

The third, or marshy division, is that part skirting the coast, extending sometimes to nine or ten miles inland. The whole district comprised between Lynn and Wisbech is of this nature; and it is not only the highest but often the richest part of the fen. Its greatest fault is the absence of clay; but there is in the best parts of it such a mixture of sea and land vegetable and animal matter as makes it very healthful to vegetation. In some cases, not frequent, the silt predominates in such large portions as to sterilise the mass.

This must be considered only the outline of the present character of the fen surface. In examining its subterranean structure, we obsevre a variety of evidences that its present differs materially from its ancient state. The condition which it has assumed during the historical era, seems to extend very little beyond that period, if, indeed, it be not more recent; and we have a variety of evidence of prior operations which have marked as successive epochs the whole region comprised within the bounds we have described as the Great Level.

The surface of the whole fen is, as we have stated, either turfy, moory, or marshy; but, on penetrating a few feet beneath the moory surface, we uniformly come to a second moor, containing prostrate trees, whose tap roots are fixed in a substratum of clay. This may be described as the general characteristic of the country,—subject, of course, to local variations. Sometimes more than one stratum of clay, moor, and trees, is found; sometimes oak is found alone;

and sometimes only firs. In other cases, moor and clay, without trees, are the substratum.

But that the stratum of trees is pretty generally diffused over those parts of the fen which do not border the coast, is shown by daily experience, as well as from the accounts handed down to us from early periods. In the Isle of Axholme—a fen connected with the southern fens by a belt of marsh and fen lands along the coast of Lincolnshire—"the oak trees lie somewhat above three foot in depth, and near the roots, which do still stand as they growed, viz., in firm earth below the moor, and the bodies, for the most part, north-west from the roots; not cut down with axes, but burnt asunder somewhat near the ground, as the ends of them, being somewhat coaled, do manifest."[1] Their numbers and sizes are, sometimes, exceedingly great: "five yards in compass, and sixteen yards long, and some smaller of a greater length, with good quantities of acorns near them; and of small nuts so many, that there have been found no less than two pecks together in some places."[2] In some parts there seem to have been successions of vegetation,—first firs and pine, then oak; and the former, probably from their more rapid growth, are greatly more abundant than the oak. "The fir trees do lie a foot or eighteen inches deeper [than the oak], of which kind there are more than any other, many of them being above xxx. yards in length..... The truth is, that there are so great a number of trees thus overgrown with the moor, through a long time of stagnation by the fresh waters in these parts, that the inhabitants have, for the space of divers years last past, taken up two thousand cart-loads in a year."[3]

The same evidences of former fertility and subsequent destruction, occur in the southern fens. "In Marshland, about a mile westward from Magdalen Bridge, at the setting down of a sluice very lately [about 1660], there was discovered, at xvii. feet deep, divers furze-bushes, as also nut-

(1) Dugdale's History of Embankment and Draining, p. 141. (2) Ibid. (3) Ibid.

trees pressed flat down, with nuts sound and firm lying by them, the bushes and trees standing in solid earth, below the silt which hath been brought up by the inundations of the sea."[1]

At Salter's Lode, one of the lowest parts of the Level, we have evidence of moor at upwards of sixteen feet depth; but it does not appear that any other vegetable remains were found. In digging to erect the sluice there, "the silt was observed to be ten feet deep, and next below that three feet thickness of firm moor, then bluish gault (which the workmen judged to have been silt originally, because, being dry, it not only crumbled like it, but had the roots of reeds in it), then below it moor of three feet thickness, much firmer and clearer than the other; and, lastly, whitish clay, which is supposed to have been the very natural and bottom soil at the first."[2]

At Whittlesey, near the inland extremity of the Fens, we learn, "that, digging through the moor, at eight feet deep they came to a perfect soil, and swathes of grass lying thereon as they were first mowed."[3]

At Bardney, near Boston, we find the occurrence of moor and forest thus described: "Bodian sands, near Bardney, lie about three feet and a half below the adjacent lands: they consist of a thin bed of sand upon a bed of strong blue clay, full of large coggles or stones; on which bed was found a great number of oak, yew, and alder roots and trees which had grown thereon. The soil on each side is moory, and full of subterranean wood to three and a half feet thick. The oak roots stand upon the sand and tap-root into the clay; some of the trees are five feet in diameter at the bole, and more than ten feet from out to out at the root."[4] At the same place we are told that enormous oaks have been found, and, amongst others, one which was ninety feet long and four feet square, containing fourteen hundred and forty solid feet

(1) Dugdale, p. 171. (2) Ibid, p. 177. (3) Ibid.

(4) Edwards's Survey of the Witham, 1769.

of timber. It was found three feet below the surface, lying upon clay and gravel, and covered with peat.[1]

In the moors about Littleport, Manea, and Chatteris, the finding of trees in the subsoil is an occurrence so common as to be unnoticed. The trees are in a condition sufficient to serve for various purposes, such as gates, posts, and fences, or even for masts and keels of ships.[2] Sometimes a kind of decomposition seems to have been partly effected, but they are generally sound, and even greatly hardened by their burial.

In addition to these various testimonies we have that of J. C. de Serra, who visited Sutton, near Alford, on the Lincolnshire coast, in 1796, for the purpose of determining the epoch of these forest remains, and the agency by which they had been destroyed. At Sutton, it appears, a denudation of coast had been effected by the sea, by which a number of islets of moor, visible only at the lowest ebbs of the year, had been exposed with strata of trees and other vegetables. De Serra represents them as consisting "almost entirely of roots, trunks, branches, and leaves of trees and shrubs, intermixed with some leaves of aquatic plants. The remains of these trees were still standing on their roots, while the trunks of the greater part lay scattered on the ground in every direction. The bark of trees and roots appeared generally as fresh as when they were growing, in that of the branches particularly, of which a great quantity was found; even the thin silver membranes of the outer skin were discernible. * * The soil to which the trees are fixed, and in which they grew, is a soft greasy clay; but, for many inches above the surface, the soil is composed of rotten leaves, scarcely distinguishable to the eye."[3] After enumerating the general dispersion of similar forests over the entire substratum of the Fens, particularly in Hatfield Chase and Axholme, and to sixty miles south, De Serra

(1) Thompson's History of Boston.

(2) De la Pryme, in Philosophical Transactions, quoted by Phillips, Treatise on Geology, vol. ii., p. 39.

(3) Philosophical Transactions, 1799.

continues: "Little doubt can be entertained of the moory islets of Sutton being a part of the extensive and subterraneous stratum, which, by some inroad of the sea, has there been stripped of its covering of soil."[1]

There can be no doubt that the remains of the Fens grew, in most instances, on the spots where they are found, as the accounts we have given assure us. The roots are generally firmly fixed in the ground, and "do still stand as they growed."[2]

The general depths at which these remains are found differ from two feet to about twenty.[3] Those found near the coast mostly lie at lower depths than those found further inland; and the distance from the sea seems to be, in some measure, proportional to their depth.[4] We have seen that in Marshland, at the depth of seventeen feet, furze-bushes and nut trees have been found. Marshland, at present, averages only five feet elevation above low water at spring tides.[5] As

(1) De Luc, in a letter to Dr. Rennie, observes:—"The history of peat-bogs along the sea-coasts, is a subject in geology which has much engaged my attention. Along the Elbe and elsewhere, submarine peat may frequently be seen. It has glided under the water, where there is a declivity, from the continental soil, on which are large peat-moors; nay, it appears, that though covered with the muddy sediment of the river, or the sea-sand, it does not cease to move forward under them. Along the coasts of Lincoln the same phenomenon may be observed. This I conceive to be a flowing of peat from the land under the water of the sea." —*Rennie's Essays on Peat Moss*, page 405. It has often been conjectured that large bodies of peat-moss may thus glide from higher to lower levels. Valleys are supposed to have thus been filled with the peat grown on mountain-sides; and the moss so often found at the bottom of beep lakes, may owe its origin to the growth of their shallow shores—as at Ulleswater—sliding imperceptibly to the lower levels of the lake. But, on the shore at Sutton, the forest does not seem to be lower than the level at which it is found inland; consequently there could be no gliding under the sea, unless we arbitrarily suppose an order of circumstances to suit such a theory. The shore levels of the Fens now are considerably above those inland; consequently, under similar circumstances, the moss would glide landward, instead of seaward, as De Luc supposes.

(2) Dugdale, pp. 141, 171.—Elstobb, pp. 27, 32, 99.—De Serra, Phil. Trans. 1799.

(3) The superstratum of clay, or soil, is uniformly thickest in the parts adjacent to the sea, or the outfalls of the rivers, and gradually decreases in thickness as it recedes from them. Near Skirbeck church the clay is fifteen feet thick; at Bardney the peat-moor is within a foot of the surface; and in many parts of the East Fen, the upper stratum disappears, and the peat-moor is at top.—*Thompson's History of Boston*, p. 286.

(4) At Sutton, where De Serra saw the islets, the moor, similar to that in which the trees were embedded, was found, in digging a well, to be nineteen feet deep.—See *De la Beche, Geological Manual*, p. 152.

(5) *Walker's Report on the Middle Level*, 1842; whose datum is zero on the tide-guage at Freebridge, Lynn; one foot above datum being low-water mark, as ascertained in May and June in that year.

these tides rise to the average height of twenty-three feet in the Wash,[1] and even higher in the contracted channels of the rivers, the height of water against the banks of this fen must be, certainly, sometimes upwards of twenty feet. We have, thus, a flood-tide in the vicinity of this substratum of bushes, thirty-two feet above the level on which they grew,—a state of things impossible to have existed together.

The lowest level in the vicinity of Whittlesey Mere, is 6.75 feet above low-water at Lynn.[2] The swathes of grass were found there at eight feet depth. This would give them a depression of only 1.25 foot beneath low-water mark, at a distance of twenty-six miles from the sea. High-water, in the channels of rivers to seaward, would thus, occasionally, be twenty-three or twenty-four feet above the level of this soil; which, even at such a distance, must have caused an unembanked fen to be constantly drowned.

In the Mepal and Littleport Fens the trees occur at from three to five feet depth.[3] The lowest level of these fens is 6.25 above low-water mark at Lynn. These remains, accordingly, average about two feet above low-water mark; but the same circumstances, which we have noticed in the two instances enumerated, must have operated here. It would have been impossible for trees, shrubs, or bushes, to flourish at such a depth, so near to a sea unembanked and liable to rise twenty feet above them. It is certain, that instead of a forest-bearing country, such a constitution of things would have precipitated the waters of the Wash over the whole fen, and converted it into a salt-water estuary, or rather an estuary alternating between salt and fresh water, as is supposed to have been the case with the Weald in Kent and Sussex.

It would be no unreasonable conjecture to suppose that the Wash itself has been produced from a submerged fen.

(1) Geography of Great Britian.—The Chart of Lynn and Boston Deeps gives twenty-three feet rise on Long-sand, which is only covered at one-fifth flood.

(2) Walker's Report. (3) Elstobb, p. 99.

Could the present soil be bared to the clay, which seems to have been the original surface of the fen, and the banks which withhold the sea be removed, the whole extent would be suddenly deluged to depths varying from four or five to thirty feet. Now this is a depth greater than two-thirds of the Wash:[1] or, otherwise, if the bed of the Wash were suddenly raised as many feet as this original clay is sunk below the level of high-water mark, two-thirds of this bed would be converted into dry land, leaving only Lynn and Boston Deeps as separate estuaries, the one of the Ouse and Nene, the other of the Witham and Welland.[2]

After we are satisfied, notwithstanding the depth at which these remains are found, that they really grew on the spots where they are lying, the only further inquiry seems to be the period at which they flourished, and the cause of their destruction. Various opinions have been entertained on the former of these questions, as evidence is generally wanting which can fix the era with precision. Some have contended that they were contemporary with an earlier period than the peopling of the island. But, if that were the case, we should in no instance find any remains of human utensils with them, or any marks of the operation of labor upon them. Such negative proof of antiquity has been assailed by the following statements. Referring to the substratum of fen-moor, we are told that "it is generally about a foot thick; upon and within it are found stags' horns, warlike instruments, and other remains of the ancient inhabitants; and, upon its surface, several canoes of a peculiar form and construction have been discovered."[3] This, however, is a general state-

(1) Chart of Lynn and Boston Deeps.

(2) De la Beche has remarked: "If the British islands were elevated one hundred fathoms above the level of the ocean, and thus joined to the continent of Europe, they would be surrounded by an extensive area of flat land; for the fall from the coast to the new sea-coast would be, generally, so gradual as to present to the eye one great plain."—*Researches in Theoretic Geology*, p. 189. De la Beche illustrates his remarks with a map, showing the quantity of sea which such an elevation would convert into dry land. The whole bed of the German Ocean and English Channel would be thus lifted above high-water mark, and parts of the Atlantic Ocean to the extent of two hundred miles seaward.

(3) Thompson's History of Boston.

ment, and therefore not entitled to so much consideration as the following: "About xx. years since," says Dugdale, "in the moors, at Thurne, (near five foot in depth,) was found a ladder of firr, of a large substance, with about xl. staves, which were xxxiii. inches asunder; but so rotten, that it could not be gotten up whole. And in Haxey Carr, at the like depth, a hedge with stakes and bindings."[1] We find a more curious circumstance recorded by Dr. Rennie: "In June, 1747, the body of a woman was found six feet deep in a peat-moor, in the Isle of Axholme, in Lincolnshire. The antique sandals on her feet showed she had been buried there for many ages; yet her nails and hair were as fresh as any person's living. Her skin was soft, of a tawny color. It stretched like a piece of doe-leather, and was as strong."[2] This case might have been a burial. The evidence of human bodies is always to be suspected, unless under extraordinary circumstances. But, even if otherwise, neither of the above-cited cases confirm the contemporary existence of forest and inhabitants, even in the parts where they occurred. The ladder, the hedge, and the body, were all found in the moor. Now the moor, or peat, must have been a subsequent growth to forest, and may have been even ages afterwards: the forest seems only a preliminary of the peat-moss, which it has generally preceded.[3]

There is a further testimony which has been adduced in proof of these forests having been contemporary with an inhabited country, which seems more serious. The wood is frequently charred, and has often been evidently felled by burning. Dugdale, in a quotation already given, speaks of the oaks being "burned asunder," not cut down with axes, "as the ends of them being coaled do manifest." The same authority informs us, that "in 1653 there was a fir pole taken up, thirty-six yards long, lying near the root, which stood as it grew, having been *burnt*, not hewn down."[4]

(1) History of Embankment and Draining, p. 141. (2) Essays, p. 520.
(3) Rennie on Peat-Moss, p. 358.
(4) History of Embankment and Draining.

Though it be most rational to attribute such an operation to some kind of inhabitants, yet it is not necessary to the effect. The forests of America are frequently fired in autumn, and, though this has generally been attributed to the carelessness of Indians or settlers, yet it has been shown that nature herself is often her own incendiary. The rank grass that borders the forest, dried by the warm summer, is reduced almost to the state of tinder which a sheet of lightning readily sets on fire, and thus spreads, in a short time, a conflagration over a hundred miles. It is not contended that the burnt wood of the Fens has resulted from such a cause; but it is not enough, while there are such and other causes capable of producing the effects appealed to, to attribute them, without especial evidence, to either such case or the work of men.

But we have another and more direct statement to produce, which, if it be thoroughly proved, must certainly assure us that the parts in which it is observed were inhabited while it remained forest. Dugdale, in speaking of the Great Level, says; "Great numbers of trees, of several kinds, have been found, most of oak and fir, and few of them *severed* from their roots."[1] This testimony is strengthened by another authority, who informs us, that "in the survey of the lands in Sutton and Mepal levels, at the bottoms and sides of many of the drains made therein, I observed multitudes of roots of large trees, standing as they had grown, at the depth of about three feet under the present moorish soil; from which the bodies had, manifestly, been *sawed* off; and some of which I then saw lying at a small distance from their roots, at the same depth as before mentioned; and I was credibly informed that great numbers had been and were still found *severed*, and lying in the like manner."[2] In an account of Hatfield Chase, on the Humber,—a fen similarly circumstanced to those of the south, and, doubtless,

(1) History of Embankment and Draining, p. 171.

(2) Elstobb's History of the Bedford Level, p. 99.

their contemporary in former as in present condition, we learn, that "many of the trees, and especially the fir-trees, have been burnt, sometimes quite through, others *chopped, squared, bored through*, or split, with large wooden wedges and stones in them, and broken axe-heads, somewhat like sacrificing axes in shape; and this at depths, and under circumstances, which exclude all supposition of their being touched since the destruction of the forest."[1] The same account furnishes us with the further testimony, "that on the confines of this low country, between Burningham and Bramley, in Lincolnshire, are several great hills of loose sand; under which, as they are yearly worn and blown away, are discovered many roots of large firs, with the marks of the axe as fresh upon them as if they had been cut down only a few weeks."[2] Near a large root in Hatfield, coins of the Roman emperors have been found; and, among other evidences of former contemporary population, "the very ground at the bottom of the river was found, in some places, to lie in ridges and furrows; thereby showing that it had been ploughed and tilled in former days."[3] The conclusion, which these facts naturally lead to, is, that portions of the fen-forests have been destroyed since they have been inhabited. This is scarcely open to dispute, against the facts which have been produced; but it may reasonably be doubted, whether the whole fen has been thus reduced since the period at which this destruction is generally fixed—the Roman invasion. Mr. De la Pryme, indeed, thinks, "the Romans were the destroyers of *all* the great woods and forests that are now found underground, in the bottoms of moors and bogs;"[4] and this "conclusion," says Phillips, "has been generally adopted by geologists."[5]

(1) *Phillips's Treatise on Geology*, vol. ii, p. 39,—whose summary is derived from an account in the *Phil. Trans.* written by the Rev. A. De la Pryme, 1701.

(2) Ibid. (3) Ibid, p. 40. (4) *Hutton's Abridgement Phil. Trans.* quoted by Phillips.

(5) *Treatise on Geology*, vol. ii, p. 41. See also *Elstobb's Hist. Bed. Level*, p. 101, who arrives at the same result, arguing from the deforesting which Cæsar resorted to in the country of Memapii, whom he attempted to reduce, as huntsmen unearth foxes, by cutting away the cover they have sought for shelter. See also *Lyell's Prin. Geol.* b. 3, c. 13.

The opinion of Dr. De Serra is very different. Disregarding the marks of an inhabited country which have been shown, he thinks that "the stratum of soil, sixteen feet thick, [at Sutton] placed above the decayed trees, seems to remove the epoch of their destruction far beyond the reach of any historical knowledge;"[1] and, following this idea, he shows that in the points of elevation above the sea, and in structure of soil, Flanders bears an exact resemblance to England. In Flanders too, the same kind of submerged forest occurs. "These two countries, then," he says, "are certainly coeval; and whatever proves that maritime Flanders has been for many ages out of the sea, must, in my opinion, prove also that the forest we are speaking of was, long before that time, destroyed and buried under a stratum of soil. Now, it seems proved, from historical records carefully collected by several earned members of the Brussels Academy, that no material change has happened in the lowermost part of maritime Flanders during the last two thousand years. I am, therefore, inclined to suppose the original catastrophe which buried this peat to be of very ancient date."[2]

Another authority, again, supposes that the Romans found this country a sea-marsh, and that the forest, moor, and top-soil have been produced since that period;—the forest by Roman draining and planting—the peat by subsequent decay between that time and the Norman conquest,—and the present moor by the drainage since Henry III.[3]

So many different conclusions from men of judgment only declare the weakness of the evidence on which their decisions are founded, and no fresh light has succeeded the times in which their accounts were written to make us speak with greater confidence. The marks of the axe, which would certainly prove the trees to have been contemporary with inhabitants, are, on the whole, very rare in the southern fens, where the trees generally bear evident tokens of having been borne down by some common convulsion,—to which, rather

(1) Phil. Trans. (2) Ibid. (3) Thompson's History of Boston, pp. 276, 280.

than to the Romans, we would attribute the prostration of this fen. What this cause might be, it now becomes us to consider.

The presence of subterranean forests in fens is by no means uncommon,—indeed, it is one of the most usual circumstances of their existence; and every part of Europe, where fens abound, furnishes similar facts to those we have produced from the east-coast fens.[1] In Flanders,[2] on the shores of the friths of Tay and Forth,[3] the coasts of Normandy,[4] and in the peats of Ireland,[5] we find the same kind of trees; and the circumstances under which they are found are nearly similar—occurring, not unfrequently, yards below low-water,[6] and generally in the vicinity of the sea.

Almost all the theories proposed for deciding the cause of such phenomena, have merged in that which attributes it to a general or partial depression of the land. Phillips, following a notion of De Luc, suggests that the trees may have been drifted;[7] but this theory has received such repeated contradiction, that it is not tenable, except for particular cases. Dr. Fleming, with more argument, supposes, "that the waste of the coast has opened to the sea some secluded valley of peat, which, originally full of moisture like a sponge, was raised thereby above the tide-level, but, on loss of its sea-ward barrier, was drained, and sunk considerably."[8] De Serra, before mentioned, observes, "that the force of subsidence, suddenly acting by means of some earthquake, seems to me the most probable cause;"[9] and he has been

(1) "De Luc ascertained that the very site of the aboriginal forests of Hircinia, Semana, Ardennes, and several others, are now occupied by mosses and fens; and a great part of these changes has, with much probability, been attributed to the strict orders given by Severus, and other emperors, to destroy all the wood in the conquered provinces."—*Lyell's Principles of Geology*, vol. iii. p. 203, 4th ed.

(2) De Serra. (3) De la Beche, Manual of Geology, p. 153. (4) Ibid.

(5) Lyell's Prin. Geology, vol. iii., p. 201. Phillips observes "that it is common in Ireland to find trees in the place and attitude of growth, rooted in peat seven feet thick."—*Treatise*, vol. ii., p. 37.

(6) Phillips's Treatise, vol. ii., p. 32. (7) Ibid.

(8) Quoted by Phillips in *Treatise*, vol. ii., p. 33, from *Quarterly Journal of Science*, 1830.

(9) Philosophical Transactions.

followed by eminent modern geologists. "That there has been a change in the relative levels of land and water since these trees were planted," says De la Beche, "cannot be doubted. From the subsidences sometimes caused by earthquakes, we may presume that Great Britain, with the Shetland Isles, Hebrides, and North of France, have subsided."[1] Lyell, however, who always shrinks from convulsive movements in the earth, is inclined to more peaceful changes; and De la Beche seems rather so hesitate at his own opinion, when he says, "the absence of marine remains seems to show that the forests were not suddenly overwhelmed by the sea; for, had this been the case, some vestiges of its former presence must have appeared."[2] "We must hesitate," says Lyell, "before we call to our aid the action of earthquakes to explain what have been termed submarine forests. I have already hinted that the explanation of some of these may be sought in the encroachment of the sea in estuaries, and the varying level of the tides, at different periods, on the same parts of our coasts.[3]"

This careful idea was anticipated by Elstobb; who, rather in an unsatisfactory manner, supposes there to have been no change of level in the Fens, but that the waters found their way to sea over the original bottom, with more facility than they do now, elevated from ten to eighteen feet above it.[4] The latter condition having, according to his theory, been produced by the means taken to prevent it;[5] and, consequently, "there can be no need to have recourse to such violent and perpetual causes of earthquakes, the violence of which it does not appear this happy country has ever been considerably affected with."[6]

(1) Manual of Geology, p. 156. (2) Ibid.

(3) *Principles*, vol. iii., p. 27. He says, further on, "we should endeavor to find a solution of the problem by reference to any cause rather than an earthquake." Yet, it is more difficult to reconcile the observed facts with common alterations, denudations, and other mutations of coast—which he hints as his opinion of the operating cause—than even with such a phenomenon as an earthquake.

(4) History of the Bedford Level, pp. 35, 246. (5) Ibid, pp. 44, 250. (6) Ibid, p. 18.

We shall only add another authority, who, not unlike Elstobb, thinks we may see, in the artificial operations which have been carried on here, some reason for the low level of the ancient lands, and the deposit of peat and earth above them. "The soil of Holland, which had been longer inclosed in banks than Friesland, is on a lower level. The same explanation applies to the fact—well known near Lynn—that the land that had been regained since the Roman sea-banks were made is on a higher level and of greater value than that which was enclosed by the Romans; and, outside of 'Marshland,' as their tract is called, the new foreshores are sometimes higher."[1]

All these opinions are founded on generalization; the tract affords no direct evidence which may be said to favor any one of them; nor are there any analogies to strengthen the few arguments which can be produced in their favor—as the fens of other countries are as difficult in giving information on their former state as our own. The only analogy which seems to yield any light upon the subject, is the fact of the gradual rise of part of the Swedish continent, at the average rate of forty inches per century.[2] In Italy, the same operation has been carried on in the Bay of Baiæ, where there has been first a subsidence of the land twenty feet, and then as much of re-elevation; but, as this has been, probably, the work of an earthquake, it is to Sweden we would rather look for a glimmer of light upon this difficult problem which the substratum of the fens has afforded inquirers. It was long doubted—even by geologists partial to regular and quiet operations of nature—whether parts of Sweden were actually being elevated. But it was suspected, more than a

(1) *Treatise on Geology*, by Phillips, vol. ii., p. 35. This fact may be observed on most of the Roman and later inclosures. The land on the inland side of the bank, going from Walton to Walpole, is about four feet lower than on the river side. The next enclosure, about a mile nearer the water, is as high above its outer enclosure; so that the land nearest the river, of which this large space was formerly a part, is twelve feet or more above the first inclosure.

(2) *Lyell's Prin. Geol.*, vol. ii., p. 346. "In the northern part of the Gulf of Bothnia, it is as much as four feet in a century."—*De la Beche: How to observe.*

hundred years ago,[1] that an alteration of level was being effected, either in the sea or land. Observations, the work of time, have since fully proved that the land is really rising at rates varying between the north of Europe and Stockholm—at the latter place the rise being imperceptible. If a fact of this kind could be established with regard to the Fens—the fact of subsidence not of elevation—it would at once account for the phenomena which the whole tract exhibits. We know there must have been elevatory causes to lift the substratum of clay out of the water, either gradual or violent—and may we not as reasonably believe that it was afterwards subject to a slight depression; probably going on for several ages, but never sufficient to immerse it again in the sea. The first consequence of such a depression would be, the decay of the outfalls of the rivers; when, instead of making way to the sea, the fresh waters would gradually spread over the wide plain which was sinking beneath them. The growth of peat is thus easily accounted for; there being all the circumstances necessary for its production,—stagnant water, and, probably, a low temperature, and the forest, which, if not necessary, is its general accompaniment.[2]

It were useless to prolong such theoretical views; but there is one circumstance which we have hitherto omitted to notice, but which is one of the most striking facts connected with these forests—the direction in which they lie. From every account, this seems to be uniform in the southern fens, the heads pointing from the roots south east.[3] This circumstance, if there were no other, seems fatal to the idea of the woods having been cut by the Romans. But, on the other

(1) *Lyell's Prin.*, vol. ii., p. 331. Celsius, the Swedish naturalist, at the beginning of last century, "expressed his opinion, that the waters of the Baltic and Northern Ocean were gradually subsiding," from the circumstance of what were once known to be sunken rocks, were, in his time, above water.

(2) Rennie on Peat Moss, pp. 243, 259, 368.

(3) According to Dugdale, the heads of the trees in the Isle of Axholme are north-west from their roots; while in the morasses of the Netherlands and Germany, according to Verstegan and De Luc, the prostration is towards north-east. The same direction was observed by De la Pryme in the forests of Hatfield Chase, before alluded to. See *Phillip's Teratise*, vol. ii, pp. 39, 41.

hand, it rather increases the difficulty of accounting for the destruction of the country by gradual subsidence. It would seem to imply a sudden rush of water over the whole land, as the operating cause; and yet, had such been the case, would it not have left behind it some marks of such a catastrophe?[1] The general character of this fact leaves us scarcely any room to give the destruction of these woods to human agents; and all that the former arguments on the subject prove, is only, in our opinion, that inhabitants were contemporary with some parts of the forest: but there does not seem to have been sufficient attention paid to the particular trees marked with axes, or otherwise bearing records of population, to decide whether they were of contemporary or subsequent growth to the most ancient parts of these fens. Though a great reverse of physical constitution deprived the fens of their wood, we are not to declare that this wood was all destroyed at once, unless we can prove it by means such as De Serra and De la Beche favor. If it was accomplished by means of a gradual subsidence of land,—this might be going on for several ages, and parts of the fen might be in a state of forest, while other parts had actually been, perhaps, centuries under water. The direction in which they lie seems to intimate that the cause of their destruction was constant, however variable it might be in time. But, on the whole, though there is a clue to the means of their overthrow in this uniformity of their prostration, yet it only makes us more unwilling to acknowledge that all the methods hitherto proposed to solve the question are alike unsatisfactory.[2]

We proceed to the production of the fen next after these woods—the turf moors. These, we have shown, are co-exten-

(1) De Luc attributes the direction of the submarine forest at Bremevorde to the prevalent winds and rains from the S.W.—*Phillips's Treatise.*

(2) From the facts adduced by Lyell.—*Principles*, vol. iii., p. 201,—it appears not unreasonable to attribute this general direction of the trees to an overthrow by a gale of wind, and the subsequent formation of peat to the obstruction their prostrate trunks presented to the drainage of the land. In this case the cause must have been sudden, but it need not have been universal. Do the trees on which the marks of axes are found lie in the same direction as the generality of the forest?

sive with the forests, and the very production of this substance gives us an insight into some of the characteristics of the fens during the period that they were forming. It is very probable that it was never covered with water deeper than a few feet, and that it was mostly a quaking bog, blown up with water which filled it like a sponge. Had the water been deep, moss could not have flourished; for, though it is sometimes found at the bottom of deep lakes, nothing affords a surer evidence that the lake has been a subsidence since the formation of peat.[1]

We are also certain that the water which covered the fen was not derived from the sea. There is, indeed, a species of peat named *marine moss* or *braack torf* as the Dutch call it, in whose country it prevails; but the peat universally found in the fens bears none of the characteristics of this substance.[2] That it was formed in fresh water, derived from the rivers, is thus certain; and the outfalls must have, necessarily, been obstructed against their discharge. The Romans, probably, found these fens in this condition of a peat-bog, with the outfalls of all the rivers barricaded against the discharge of the upland waters, when they undertook the embankment of this tract, if that work was really effected by them.

That the water was also stagnant, and not liable to be affected by winds, is as evident; since, without these conditions. moss will not grow.[3] But moss being found over the whole fen, assures us that the water which covered it was, by some means, secure against the agitation of the winds. This could not have been effected where there was depth of water; for in this case, it must, over such a wide area, have been in

(1) The shallow ends of lakes, as Derwentwater, Ullswater, are frequently converted into peat; but in their depths, where these are great, it is never found as a living moss.—See *Phillips's Treatise* vol. ii. p. 35.

(2) These are a congeries of *marine* as well as other aquatic plants; always the presence of some salt, and often large quantities; a blue flame and hissing sound when burning, which is produced on it with difficulty. "It always communicates a livid death-like hue to the countenance, and a sickly squeamish feeling, sometimes fainting and syncope when burnt in a close room."—*Rennie's Essay on Peat Moss*, p. 646.

(3) Rennie's Essays, p. 249.

almost continual agitation at the surface. The water must, therefore, have been stagnant as well as shallow,—perhaps so shallow, in the first instance, as not to rise to a greater height than the trees which obstructed its passage seaward; and the trunks of these trees preventing the current which the winds tended to create, would so favor the growth of peat, as well as, probably, afford the water part of that antiseptic property, which is necessary for the first growth of the substance.[1]

It is certain that the country was inhabited while the fen was in this state, as the frequent finding of utensils, coins, and other remains of population, in the moor, demonstrates.[2] None of these, however, that we are aware of, have been shown to belong to a very advanced age.[3]

We have said that the first operation of the gradual depression of such a tract of land as the Fens, would be felt in the outfalls of its rivers. As this is a circumstance which has been the common cause of expense and solicitude since the drainage of the Fens was first projected, we shall now give a short examination to the conformation of coast, or peculiarity of estuary, which has so often thrown silty barriers between the inland waters and the sea.

A little inspection of the map of the North Sea or German Ocean, as it is sometimes called, will show the reader that its form is rather that of a large bay, than an ocean. He will also see that the southern half of the British shores presents but few salient points to the sea; but is rather composed of curved lines, intimating the presence of materials easily eroded by the action of water; and strongly contrasted with the opposite shore of Norway, where sharp rugged promontories, deep inlets, and a number of jagged islands, intimate

(1) *Rennie's Essays*, p. 252. "Forests have furnished materials for peat in many places But they are not, in themselves, the *cause* of it. There must be *stagnant* water, and that water, by some AS YET UNKNOWN CAUSE, must have an antiseptic quality."—*De Luc to Dr. Rennie.*

(2) In the Museum at Wisbech is a large paddle (?) found in the moor at Chatteris.

(3) *Wells's History of the Bedford Level*, vol. i., p. 42, mentions the finding of spears, shields, and military weapons in the Middle Level; but he neither enumerates the apparent age of the weapons, nor the strata in which they were found.

that the sea is resisted by those rocky materials that belong to the primary formations. Into this sea the great tide-wave of the Atlantic passes by separate channels. Divided by the projecting coast of Ireland into two parts, one proceeds up the English Channel, and passes by the Straits of Dover into the narrowest part of the sea as far as the Thames; while the other sweeps round the north of Scotland, and, by the great channel between Duncansby Head, in Scotland, and Soter Island, in Norway, passes southerly till it meets the tide which flowed up the English Channel. In this course, the northern wave, which is the greatest wave of the sea, is obstructed by no considerable promontory in its course southwards, except that part of the Scottish coast projecting eastward from the Frith of Murray, and terminating near Kinnaird's Head. This projection serves as a jetty to the tide-wave, preserving the coast from erosive action as far south as the Tyne, where the wave again meets the shore. From this point it passes along the coast of Yorkshire, which, inclining eastward, is constantly abraded by this tidal wave from the north.[1] For thirty miles along this coast, from Kilnsea to Bridlington, the waste of coast is two yards and a quarter per annum.[2] The coast of Lincolnshire is also subjected, in a less degree, to the same kind of waste, being partly protected by Spurn Point;[3] and the Norfolk coast, from Cromer to Yarmouth, is gradually being washed into the bed of the sea. All this matter is swept by the currents of the ocean, and transported, some to its depths,—but the greater part is taken up by the tides that enter the mouths of the rivers, and thrown down as soon as the current is

(1) Lyell's Prin. Geol., vol. 2, p. 22.

(2) *Phillips's Treatise*. vol. ii, p. 6. The mean height of this wasting cliff being taken at only ten yards, the total quantity of fine sediment, coarse sand, pebbles, and boulders falling into the sea in one year equals 1,188, 000 cubic yards.—*Ibid.*

(3) The following, from *Leland's Itinerary*, exemplifies the encroachment of the sea on this coast:—" Skegnesse, sumtyme a great haven toun. Mr. Paynelle say'd unto me, that he could prove that there was ons an haven and a toun, waullid, having also a castille. The olde toune is clene consumid and eten up with the se. Part of a chirch of it stode a late. For old Skegnes is now builded a pore new thing. * * At low waters appere yet manifest tokens of old buildings."—Vol. vii, p. 152.

slackened or delayed by the obstacles with which it there meets. A great part of the waste of the cliffs of Yorkshire is thus transported up the Humber:[1] the remainder is carried forward by the tidal current that sets along the coast of Lincolnshire, and, gathering fresh matter as it proceeds, it sinks into the mouth of the Wash, whose conformation seems as well adapted as it can be to receive and deposit the sediment of such a current. The entrance of this bay, which is its narrowest part, receives the flood in a strong stream which spreads over an increased space, and, entering the mouths of its rivers, soon deposits its contents. The outer coasts of this bay act as a kind of warping to the sea, and it is probable that a very small proportion of the sediment which the flood holds in suspension on entering the Wash, returns with the ebb. It is not surprising, therefore, that we should find this estuary choked with sand-banks, and even its river-channels so uncertain as in a few years to shift sometimes several miles. Indeed, with the exception of one broad channel running through the centre of the Wash, with an average depth of ten fathoms, the rest of the surface is only a series of sands dry at low water, and shallows of one or two fathoms.[2]

Into this bay the fen rivers discharge themselves, and from this bay they derive the principal sediment which they hold in suspension. This consists of very fine silt, composed chiefly of particles of flint and limestone, but containing likewise clay and animal matter. The weightier particles of sand are deposited before the tide enters the rivers, but it carries enormous quantities of the minute silt to the very extremity of its flow. Now, the laws of suspension and deposit are pretty well ascertained to depend upon the fineness of the material transported, and the force of the current by which it is carried along. When, therefore, a current

(1) Phillips.

(2) Boston Deeps average about five fathoms. They are separated from Lynn Deeps by Roger Sand and Long Sand, most part of which is dry at low water. The last part of the bay, or rather the north part of the Norfolk coast, as far out as the Docking Shoal, is principally composed of low flats, probably deposited from the sediment of the Wash driven by its rivers seaward.—*Chart.*

meets obstructions, the material held by it in suspension instantly begins to deposit. The power that causes the current of the tide to throw down its silt, may either be a widening of the channel of a river, or an abrupt rise of its bed, or angular bends in its course, or the pressure of fresh water gradually increasing as the tide proceeds inland.[1] This last is the most variable of the opponents of the tide, depending chiefly on the quantity of recent rains fallen.[2] In every tide that enters a river there is an intermediate state between flow and ebb, which, entering the river about four hours after flood, traverses every part of the space travelled by the tidal current, and is called, popularly, "still-water," and proceeds to greater or less extent according to the opposition of the freshes.[3] This pause in the flow of the tide continues about a quarter of an hour, and, consequently, extends over about a mile of channel when the average progress of the tide is four miles per hour. During this interval silt is freely deposited, but the returning current of the ebb, which sets in immediately after, generally removes it, and returns, even more loaded than the flow, to sea. In some cases, however, although the ebb current always runs longer than the flow, and, therefore, the tendency of every river is to keep itself open,[4] this rule is not preserved; but, from the predominance of some of the impediments we have named, the deposit of

(1) "When the flood-tide takes place in rivers of sufficient depth, the first operation of the tide appears to be that of a wedge, elevating the fresh water from its inferior specific gravity to a higher level. The flood gradually opposes greater resistance to the outflow of the river, and in the end succeeds in damming it up."—*De la Beche, Geological Manual*, p. 88, 2nd edition.

(2) "If the seasons are wet, the rivers, having a greater quantity of water in them, run to seaward with great velocity, and, of consequence, drive the silt further out;—on the other hand, if the seasons are dry, and the tides stronger from the effects of wind or other causes, the silt, of course, is driven less powerfully outwards, and settles nearer to their mouths, which chokes them up, and prevents their free discharge from the fens."—*Rennie's Report on Wildmore Fen.*

(3) The freshes of the Nene are sometimes so great as to make little appreciable tide at Wisbech; while, at other times, when there are no freshes, the high springs are sensible at the Dog and Doublet Bridge, twenty-seven miles inland: over this space, then, the final point of neutralization must, of course, travel.

(4) "In the estuary of the Thames, and in the Gironde, the tide flows five hours, and ebbs seven."—*Lyell's Principles*, bk. ii, ch. 8. At Wisbech the flow is about four hours and the ebb eight.

the flood is not all carried away by the ebb. In this case bars are formed, which, if neglected, grow in time to the extent of stopping up the outfall, and producing in the channel at tide-flood that extraordinary rush of water called *Eager.*[1] The existence of a bar of this kind has also a tendency to lift the whole bed of the river by prolonging itself inland, till, in time, a navigable tidal channel is reduced almost to stagnant water.

There is, besides, in every river which discharges either much natural sediment or silt derived from the sea into which it flows, a tendency to form a bar in some particular part of its seaward channel, where the opposite marine and river currents meet. This bar is often a serious injury to the navigation of the river, ; and none of the rivers of the Wash are without it. That of the Nene is about ten miles below Sutton Bridge; and, although the channel has nine fathoms depth at low water in parts inland of the bar, it has only a depth of one fathom and a half over this impediment.[2]

So many obstructions, liable and real, to the ready discharge of the body of waters, which we have described as falling over the basin of the Wash, have exercised the ingenuity and perseverance of many generations. The great difficulty to be overcome is, to give a complete outfall to rivers whose fall from the uplands is too gradual to impart any force to their streams; and which, for twenty or thirty miles from their deltas, does not average more than three or four inches per mile.[3] The mouths of the rivers are, thus, so obstructed by

(1) We have had an illustration of this fact at Wisbech. On the opening of the Nene Outfall, in 1830, the *Eager*, which had formerly preceded every tide, vanished. It was formed among the obstructions and shallows at the mouth of the river, and used to come rushing on to Wisbech, raising the water there suddenly from one to four or five feet. When this Cut was completed, and the shallows cut through, it accordingly ceased,—the tides ran higher—and the ebb has since been more rapid and scouring. Old Ralph Thoresby, who appeared to have visited Wisbech about 1680, thus notices the *Eager*, at that time: "This morning, before we left Wisbech, I had the sight of an *Hygre* or *Eager*, a most terrible flush of water, that came up the river with such violence that it sunk a coal-vessel in the town, and such a terrible noise, that all the dogs in it did snarl and bite at the rolling waves, as though they would swallow up the river, the sight of which (having never seen the like before) much affected me, each wave surmounting the other with extraordinary violence!"—*Diary* vol. i. p. 12.

(2) Chart of the Wash.

(3) This small fall, or even no fall at all, as rivers approach the sea, is no detriment to

the tides, sands, and silts of the Wash, that, to use the quaint language of Colonel Dodson, they "do beat back our freshes into our bosoms, when they are poasting to the embraces of their mother, the sea."[1] Yet, to secure an efficient outfall, these rivers ought to have enough cleansing power in them to scour the silty deposit which the tidal current leaves behind; and, though this has been accomplished, in some instances, for a series of years,—yet, the character of the tract and the configuration of coast, have made it a work of almost insuperable difficulty, which the greatest engineers have only been able to mitigate, not remove.

This has been effected by means of cuts, embankments, mills, and sluices, variously constructed and directed. But the results have, hitherto, been so unsatisfactory, that we find writers—in vain attempts to account for deficiency—arguing against every principle which has been brought forward; some discovering the faults of the country in straight cuts,[2] some in mills, some in embankments,[3] and some in sluices.[4] But the main evil may certainly be traced rather to natural than artificial causes; and in the fact of such a large body of fresh water having so little impulse to carry it forward, and so many impediments to overcome,—while the sea gains power as the freshes lose it,—we may see most of the disadvantages to which the Fens are liable. The artifices that have been used to encounter these difficulties, only, by their failure, show that even science has not resources sufficient to overcome them.

The embankments of the Fens are as characteristic of the country as any of its natural features. As they are the means by which the beds of rivers may be lifted above the levels they drain, they have been the chief resources of engineers to obtain a grinding current through these low provinces. The discharge of water which they effect, is

their rapid discharge of water, provided they have a good impulse of back waters; but this is the needful power that is so deficient in the fen rivers.—See *Ox. Ency.*, vol. vi, p. 150, Art. *Rivers*, and *Phil. Trans.* vol. lxix.

(1) Dodson's Design, &c. (2) Lord Gorges, Wells. (3) Elstobb. (4) Badeslade.

found to be proportional to their distance asunder, and the stream they are intended to carry. The fixing this point with precision has been a constant trial and dispute with engineers; some contending for wide meadows to allow the waters to bed in, and some holding the contrary opinion of nearly uniform and narrow river channels. The latter opinion has gained most advocates in modern practice. One effect of embankments, however, is to lift the beds of the rivers they confine. The sediment, whether derived from the uplands or sea, which an unembanked river spreads over wide meadows, is, in rivers which are embanked, partly deposited in their beds; and this, accumulating continually, lifts them above the lands they drain.[1] In an elevated country this increased height of the beds of the rivers only requires a greater security of the banks; but, in the Fens, it becomes a serious evil: the weak stream becomes weaker, till at length a complete stoppage of outfall is effected, and the waters, instead of tending seaward, return to the lower parts of the level, and deluge half the waste.

Although there is thus so much danger of the whole of this tract returning to its original state of water and bog, yet the coast is gaining accessions daily, and becoming more habitable. The sea is constantly receding from its parts on the Wash,[2] which would, before this, have been left inland, had not the deposit been kept in subordination by artificial means. Elstobb makes the "river's end,"—as he calls the mouth of the Nene,—at twenty-three miles and a half below Peterborough, or four miles and a half below Wisbech, when he wrote his history;[3] but it has receded seven miles and

(1) *Lyell's Prin.*, vol. i., p. 277. The Po is an eminent example. There are records of its having deserted its channel five times before it was embanked; since, however, that work has been accomplished, it has lifted its bed considerably, and now "traverses the plains on the top of high mounds, like waters of an aqueduct; and at Ferrara its surface has become more elevated than the roofs of the houses."—*Ibid.* See also *De la Beche: Geol. Manual*, p. 62.

(2) That this was the case when Leland wrote at the beginning of the seventeenth century, appears evident from the following notice of Wainfleet: "It hath been a very good Toune, and yn it 2 paroche churches. Shippiletes cam in *hominem memoria* up to the schole. The haven now decayith."—*Itinerary*, vol. vii., p. 182.

(3) *Elstobb's Hist. Bed. Level*, p. 93, published after his death in 1793.

a half, the mouth now being twelve miles below Wisbech. The low marshes which the waters overran between this point and the present mouth of the river, stretching from a quarter of a mile to two miles in breadth, have all been enclosed and embanked; and the sands extending further into the Wash are gradually becoming elevated above the level of the tides.

This, however, has not been wholly accomplished by natural means. That which would take fifty or more years to effect without assistance, is completed in eight or ten years by warping. The tide-water, thickened with the waste of coast and the transported sediment of the rivers, overflows the wide flat plains which skirt the seaward parts of the rivers, and in the course of a summer—when restrained by some simple impediment from returning rapidly into its channels—will raise the soil from six inches to two or three feet.[1] This matter, which is not simple sand, but a rich nutritious soil composed of argillaceous and siliceous earths, with portions of marine salt and animal matter,—is fit for cultivation as soon as it is enclosed, and produces excellent crops. It is to be borne in mind, also, that it is some of the highest land in the Fens, being, in some cases, eighteen feet above the land first enclosed, which sinks step by step as the embankments separate the three or four enclosures to which the washes have been subjected.

It is this constant accession of matter, with the difficulties of the country before detailed, that produce the anxiety and expense of keeping open the outfalls of the rivers. The natural tendency of the waters of the Wash is, as we have shown, to heap sand upon sand, until effectual barriers are raised between the discharge of the fresh waters and the sea; consequently, the whole fen, if left to itself for a period of years—its rivers allowed to deposit—its drains to grow up—and its outfalls unimproved,—would become a turf or bog marsh, or shallow freshwater mere; and many ages of natural

(1) In enclosing the marshes of the Wash, faggots, fixed to the ground with stakes, are used to hold up the waters of the tide till they have deposited their contents.

deposit would scarcely be able to lift it sufficiently to become cultivable land.[1] The system of drainage which is adopted, is only an anticipation of nature; or, rather, forcing her to accomplish the work she would only naturally perform after she had raised the soil some twenty or thirty feet. Art has thus been able to complete what, unaided by art, many generations alone would have been able to do; and we see a land full of produce which nature has hardly brought out of its aquatic state.[2]

(1) The sediment which the upland waters transport to the sea by the fen rivers is scarcely appreciable. We, therefore, find the washes of Morton's Leam and the Bedford River remain at the present day with hardly any accession of matter. The winter floods never appear to leave any deposit behind—or the smallest possible. We speak, however, only from hasty observation; some well-conducted experiments on the fresh water and tidal water, at different points of the Ouse, Nene, and Welland, would be a useful accession to our knowledge of fen rivers; and might lead to some important facts relative to fen drainage.

(2) For an account of the Geology of the district see Appendix.

CHAPTER II.

POLITICAL HISTORY.

THE history of the Fens may be divided into two parts—its political and its local history. Previous to the reign of Henry III., we know scarcely anything of these regions, only through the political events of which they became the arena; while, subsequently to that reign, we find them almost unconnected with the general history of the country, and exclusively occupied in drainage, sewerage, and the efforts of generation after generation to reclaim their wastes. The only interruption of this natural separation which occurs in their history, is the early erection of those great sea embankments which are called Roman; but we have elsewhere given our reasons for supposing they may be rather considered as a military work, than part of a system of agricultural drainage.

Little is known of any part of Britain before the Roman invasion; and even long subsequent to that event, our knowledge is rather circumstantial than direct. We gather more information from coins, pottery, the remains of walls, arches, and pavements, than from the chronicles of the oldest British historians, or the contemporary writers of Rome. Our knowledge of the arts and social history of the ancient inhabitants of this country—which is necessarily very imperfect—is mostly derived from this source: but such investigation must always be accompanied with difficulty, especially where the remains are rude. We require not only to know the people, but the age to which a trinket or an utensil belongs; and when, as in the Roman invasion, a highly civilised race introduce themselves among a very barbarous one, we are sure that ages must elapse before the civilisation will have progressed far enough to alter the arts, manners, and ideas of barbarian society. But, at the same time, portions of that society will, within a very short period of its connection with civilisation, evince a progressive improvement. When, therefore, our knowledge depends wholly on the relics which a people leave behind them, buried in their tombs, or lost by accident, it requires a very delicate discrimination to pronounce upon their antiquity. The rudest forms of ancient British art were doubtless practised for more than a century after the Romans settled here; and utensils, as different in their workmanship as China ware from Delft pottery, may have been produced by the same race of people, in the same age. The mere finding, therefore, of rude fragments, the work of most unskilful hands, is not always to be assumed as proofs of an age anterior to the landing of Cæsar.

We shall not encounter much of this kind of difficulty in the Fens, as very few remains of any kind have been found here. On the borders of the high country several very coarse implements and military weapons, belonging, apparently, to a very distant age, have been found, which are generally considered British: but nothing of the kind, referable to such remote periods, seem to have been found in the middle fens. At Somersham, in 1757, several human skeletons, "with the iron sword, spear, and umbo of a shield, an earthenware urn, and glass vase," were found,[1] which Dr. Stukely refers to some British king resident and buried there. Several celts, arrows, beads, bones, &c., were found at Eye, near Peterborough, in 1721;[2] and in the Witham a curious British shield was dug up, some years since, which has been referred to British artists after they had received Roman instruction.[3]

(1) Gough's additions to Camden. (2) Ibid.
(3) Pictorial History of England, v. i., p. 133,—where the shield is engraved.

But the most interesting and perhaps most authentic relic of this early period, was a canoe, found in Deeping Fen, in 1839, This was of oak, hollowed out of a single tree, and of the extraordinary length of forty-six feet. Its head was three feet across, and its stern five feet eight inches, and four feet deep. A keel ran along the bottom, and its sides were hollowed out towards the stern. Eight ribs crossed the bottom, serving at once to strengthen the canoe and affording firm foothold to the rowers.[1]

Such scanty relics, derived only from the borders of the Fens, would certainly lead us to infer that the country was only very thinly populated during the ages the Britons held possession of their own land. Had the fen been a vast wood, as many authors would lead us to believe, we ought, doubtless, to find some remains of inhabitants in the parts where we find remains of these woods—at any rate, in the same proportion that such remains are found in other parts of England. We are told by Cæsar that a British town was nothing more than a thick wood, fortified with a ditch and rampart, to serve as a place of retreat against the incursion of their enemies;[2] and in such recesses, other authors inform us, they performed the most sacred rites of their religion.[3] Nothing, therefore, could have been a safer retreat for the half-defeated Britons, after the landing of Cæsar, or a more certain spot of habitation before his arrival, had these Fens been in this condition

(1) For this account we are indebted to Algernon Peckover, Esq., who has also furnished a drawing, which we regret we did not receive early enough to have engraved. We are also indebted to the same gentleman for the following additional particulars: "The canoe is of oak, and was found last spring [1839] about three feet below the surface of the land, filled with clay, and appears to have rested on cross timbers, which had broken down with the weight. There was not any iron or tools of any kind; the only things found were about fifty small stones about an inch and a half in diameter. It was sound at the bottom, but the sides were partly decayed; the bottom is about seven inches thick at the wide end, and five inches thick at the other; there are ribs left for strength, and the log must have contained at least 650 cubic feet." This is the largest British canoe of which we have seen any account. There is a similar one, in every particular of shape and workmanship, in the British Museum; but its length is only thirty-four feet four inches. It was found in a creek at North Stoke, in the River Arun, in Sussex. It has been engraved in the 26th vol. of Archæologia, and in the Pict. Hist. of England, vol. i., p. 102.

(2) Commentaries, b. v., c. 17.

(3) Speaking of the Druids, Lucan says—

"They haunt the lonely coverts of the grove."—*Pharsalia.*

And Tacitus speaks of "the religious groves dedicated to superstition."—Annals, b. xiv. c. 39.

of forest. But we have a testimony which, if not quite direct, is sufficient to give us a strong inclination to believe this country was then, as it has ever subsequently been, a land of marshes.

The irruption of the Romans into this country was not
A.C. 55. wholy unresisted: but, like all uncivilised forces against forces inured to war and trained in its principles, the inhabitants could only make an ineffectual resistance, which was afterwards weakened by the desertion and treachery of various tribes. We learn, particularly, that the Coritani, a tribe that inhabited the eastern coast south of the Humber, and which had arrived in Britain some ages previously, from a country which the Britons called the "Land of Marshes,"[1] were thus treacherous to their countrymen. This base conduct facilitated the loss of England, if it did not achieve it; and we learn that, even ages afterwards, the Britons cherished a contempt or hatred for the race.[2] This feeling was by no means diminished when, at a subsequent age, they went over to the Saxons as readily as they had done to the Romans. We think their situation on the east coast south of the Humber, makes it reasonable to suppose that what inhabitants were in the Fens were of this race; and their original country—the Land of Marshes—seems to mark them more particularly as a people likely to settle here,—not because it was a forest, but a marsh similar to the land they came from. The Isle of Ely has been generally included in the country of the Iceni. But, not only are the exact limits of the Isle, at this period, very imperfectly known—except that they were much smaller than at present,—but the arbitrary division of counties very ill accords with the ancient division of provinces. The separations of rude nations are, mostly, such natural barriers as mountains, rivers, and marshes; and, therefore, it is probable that, as the Coritani occupied the marshes of Lincolnshire, such a tract—naturally only one plain—would not

(1) Thierry's History of the Norman Conquest, v. i., p. 6.—The Corraniaid from Pwyll (perhaps Poland).—Sharon Turner's Anglo-Saxons, v. i., p. 15.

(2) Ibid, p. 24.

likely be divided with any other race; and that, therefore, all the marsh lands on the east coast belonged to one country. The country of the Coritani included a wide tract to the west of Lincolnshire, as well as that county; but, as the sea-coasts were commonly the first points of settlement, the more internal tribes were probably the posterity of the Coritani of the Fens.

The proofs which attest the state of the Fens during the sway of the Romans, are very few and incomplete. Though there are many evidences of towns having been erected and occupied during the Roman period on the borders of the Fens, not one place, which may be said to be within their limits, can be proved beyond the Saxon era. Neither Wisbech, Lynn, Boston, Spalding, nor Ely, appear to have been in existence previous to the seventh century. There are not wanting indisputable remains, however, to attest the presence of this remarkable people; and works, which, if fully proved to belong to their labors, will make this part of England the chief scene of their peaceful achievments.

At March, on the road between that town and Wisbech, urns containing burnt bones, and a pot containing 160 Roman denarii[1] of all the emperors from Vespasian to Antoninus Pius, were found in 1730.[2] Another parcel of the lower empire was found at Elm,[3] and also an altar twenty-one inches high. An urn, with brass coins, was found at March, in 1713, near a tumulus; and, at the same place, foundations of buildings have been discovered.[4] Coins at Chatteris; coins and Roman foundations at Gedney and Sutton St. Edmunds;[5] urns and coins near Whaplode Drove and Fleet;[6] Roman cisterns and coins at Spalding;[7] and vessels and urns near Moulton,[8] have been found; and, though there are no sufficient remains, either in extent or character, in any one

(1) It may be useful to some readers unacquainted with Roman coinage, to be informed that a denarius was valued at 10lbs of brass, and that from every pound of silver 100 denarii were coined.

(2) Gale's Letters, p. 163. (3) Gough, from Bell's Letter to Bloomfield, 1713.

(4) Gough, from Stukely. (5) Ibid. (6) Ibid.

(7) Phil. Trans. No. 279.—Stukely, p. 127. (8) Gough's additions to Camden.

spot, to induce us to believe that the Romans occupied any place that could come under the description of a Roman town, or even a station or fort, in these parts, yet so many different remains, in such distant situations in the Fens, quite establish their settlement here.[1]

It is also worthy of remark, that no remains—except at Chatteris, which lies near the high country—have been found in the middle and southern fens; we may, therefore, conclude that they were in a very depopulated state,—probably more so than any other part of the Level. The region in which Roman remains have been mostly found, it will be seen, is towards the coast, and in the neighborhood of these extraordinary works called Roman embankments.

But, we are naturally asked, whether these great works were really performed by the Romans; for, if so, we want no further evidence to establish the fact of the Fens having been an important province of their authority. In the absence of any historical record, the inquiry, at this time of day, is attended with more than ordinary difficulty. We have generally pretty well preserved proof of Roman works in their well-known methods of construction, and proficiency in art and architecture; but, in the instance of these embankments —to which neither art nor architecture can be applied—we are reduced to the common traditions of the country,—the knowledge that similar works were performed in the low countries of Holland and Belgium during the Roman dominion there, —a passage in Tacitus,—and the comparative tranquillity which appears to have prevailed in England during the Roman period. These are almost the sole authorities for appropriating to the Romans these very important labors.

The traditions of the country, which universally attribute the embankment of the Fens to the Romans, have probably been transmitted from very remote times; and in the absence

(1) Mr. Reynolds, arguing on the distances between Durolipous and Durobrivum, as set forth in Antoninus' Itinerary, and the circumstance of *Dur* being in each name, and somewhat appropriate to fenny places, considers them to be respectively Ramsey and West Lynn, instead of Cambridge and Castor (Northamptonshire), as they are generally considered; and the same authority supposes Boston to be the Ancient Causennæ, instead of Ancaster, as it is described to be by every other author.

of better authenticated evidence, are important. The evidence derived from Holland and Belgium is only indirect. That the inhabitants of these countries had raised embankments to protect their lands, even thus early, against the incursions of the sea, is certain;[1] and, rather from this circumstance, and that the Romans were possessed of these countries before they obtained England, the notion has perhaps been derived, that a colony of Belgians were transported from their own country to instruct the fenmen in the art of embankment, and to superintend their labors.

The passage in Tacitus has rather been adduced as a witness for the Romans, by Dugdale,[2] in the absence of better argument than from any particular force in itself. Galgacus, in order to inspirit his followers against their invaders, tells them that "they [the Romans,] wear out our limbs and bodies in cleaning woods *and draining marshes*."[3] "In sylvis et paludibus emuniendis," are the words which Tacitus uses; which Dugdale, with perhaps a nearer approach to the truth, reads, "in clearing the woods and banking the fens."[4] But we think the passage has, in each instance, been unworthily strained from its meaning. The reading seems to be, rather in *fortifying marshes*; and this would fully answer the Latin text, and, at the same time, apply to the condition of the country, and to the most probable cause of the embankment of the Fens, as other circumstances, which we shall presently advert to, seem to indicate.

It is certain the Romans had a good knowledge of the art of draining. They had, in their own country, and almost under the walls of Rome, a wide marsh, of which they had undertaken the drainage in 592, A.U.C., or upwards of one hundred years previous to their landing in England.[5] Upon the

(1) Grattan's Hist. Netherlands.

(2) Hist, Emb. pp. 16, 174.

(3) Life of Agricola, c. xxxi.—Murphy's Translation. (4) Hist. Emb. p. 16.

(5) Livy,—contents of the lost bk. 46—Dugdale, p. 16. Some idea of the difficulty of draining marshes, whose level is nearly the level of the sea, may be obtained from the fact, that two consuls, three emperors, one king, and fifteen popes, have attempted, with various success, to drain this marsh; and that, at the present day, a few years of neglect would reduce it to a state of infection and sterility. See Eustace's Classical Tour, v. ii.. p. 292.

conquest of any country, as soon as their legions began to be idle, they immediately looked for labors suitable for them; and in this way formed their celebrated camps, roads, military walls, and forts. "Neither," says Dugdale, speaking of their draining, "is this employment thought too mean for the legions, though consisting of free men: for the Roman and Italian infantry, as well accustomed to the spade and basket, as to the sword and buckler, used to be their own pioneers in their daily intrenchments; neither work they for their own safety only in time of danger, but for the common good also in time of peace."[1]

The tranquillity which England seems to have enjoyed during its subjection to Rome, perhaps goes as far as any argument to prove the embankments Roman. The Saxons, who came after them, had inhabited the marshy and fenny shores of the Baltic, and were not unacquainted with embankments. The Frisians, for instance, are described as inhabiting a complete flat on the western shores of Sleswick, often inundated by the ocean, which was only kept from overwhelming it by *artificial mounds*.[2] But the Saxons, while in England, were too turbulent to follow the peaceful occupations; and their kingdoms shifted from conqueror to conqueror so readily, that we cannot suppose a work that would employ much time, labor, and security, could have been effected during so confused a period. The Romans, on the contrary, had a large army here, which they generally employed in works of public utility, when their military operations were at rest. They held the island nearly four hundred years; and certainly completed other important works for the benefit of the country,

But, if the Romans embanked the Fens, wherefore was it done?—was it for agricultural or political purposes?—was the country so populated that such waste lands had become valuable?—or had the social system so far progressed that the outlay of labor on such a swamp was calculated to be overpaid by its after-productiveness? These questions, which

(1) Hist. Embankment. (2) Turner's Anglo-Saxons, v. i., p. 125.

G

naturally suggest themselves, can now only be answered by argument or conjecture. We cannot think it could have been for agricultural purposes, since the conquerors had allowed the Pontine Marshes, almost at the gates of their city, to remain five hundred years undrained, while the state was so over-populated that it had to procure its corn from Egypt and Sicily.[1] Besides, we know that Britain could only have been very thinly populated before the Roman invasion. Savage and half-civilised life is unfavorable to the increase of population; and agriculture was almost unknown to the Britons. There must, therefore, have been a superfluity of land all over the kingdom awaiting the hand of the agriculturist; so that it was very unlikely that he should resort to a waste of stagnant meres, bogs, and salt marshes.

This is confirmed by considering how large a tract of country is required to support a nation whose food is almost solely the produce of the chase and a few flocks and herds. The red men of America, who still pursue this mode of life, occupy plains, now only supporting thousands, which, in a civilised state, would yield food for millions. The quantity of population in England at these early periods, has long been an interesting problem with historians; but no data sufficiently accurate remain to give us any satisfactory result. Turner, however, from comparisons formed from the Doomsday Book, concludes the Anglo-Saxon population of the country in the time of Edward the Confessor, to have rather exceeded two millions.[2] It is not unreasonable to suppose this amount to have been double what it was during most part of the Roman domination. Can we, therefore, suppose that the million and a quarter of people—as we will call them—with thirty millions of acres in the country to support them, should have raised fifty miles of laborious embankment to secure a few additional thousands of acres of boggy land?—or that this addition would have been adequate to support what, we will say, ten millions of available acres could not? It seems an idle idea.

(1) Livy, b. ii. p. 34. (2) Hist. Anglo-Saxons, v. ii.

Taking these considerations into view, we think there must have been some political reason for the work; and we can only conceive this to have been either to subdue the defences of a refractory people, or to gain surer points for driving back the Saxon marauder by defending the shore; or perhaps, as some have suggested, merely to employ the Roman soldiers.

The Fens were, in after ages, found a very powerful defence against more than one tyrant; and may not Britain have been subject to revolts during the four hundred years it was held by the Romans? In such case, the marshes would be places likely to be chosen by a people deprived of the command of any fortified place. We know, indeed, of one revolt—that led on by Carausius—by which a mere soldier of fortune was able, for seven years, to usurp the imperial power in this country, and to whom works of drainage here are attributed.[1] The quick-sighted Roman would see the necessity of securing the natural advantages of such a position and holding it himself; and, for this purpose, what could he do more effectually than turn back the ocean from its marshes and make causeys over its moory swamps?

It is, furthermore, well known that, in the latter days of the Roman empire, the conquerors of the world began to show that their power was decaying, by erecting artificial defences instead of trusting to those invincible soldiers who had won so much and held their conquests so long. The barbarians were not backward in discovering in this apparent strength, the signs of weakness. In the third century they began to swarm the boundaries of all the empire; and the east coast of this country first began to be infested by those Saxon pirates who finally triumphed over half Europe.[2] It was called "the Saxon Shore; and Palgrave, arguing from this distinguishing name, believes these people had already fixed themselves in this part of the country.[3] The Romans

(1) See Stukeley's Carausius.

(2) Turner's Anglo-Saxons, Wheaton's History of the Northmen.

(3) "Is it not reasonable to assume that the Saxons had already fixed themselves in some portion of the district? For it is a strange anomalous practice to name a country, not from its inhabitants, but from its enemies."—*Rise and Progress of the English Constitution.*

kept a fleet and built forts of protection at various places; but it does not appear upon record that any forts were built in these parts. Stukely, indeed, conjectures that there were such erected at Boston, Spalding, and Wisbech; but the only argument for such a conjecture seems the eligibility of the places for defending this part of the coast. But, it may be asked, how could the embankment of the Fens be a defence against the Saxons, if there were no forts or military stations to watch the coast? We do not suppose, if they were really erected as defences against the Saxons, that military stations would be wanting. The Romans, doubtless, erected the usual conveniences for their soldiers; but sixteen or eighteen hundred years are long enough to sweep away all traces of such works in such a country. The forts would, perhaps, be small and numerous, as every part of the coast presented the same facility for landing; and, when all traces of the great forts at Dover, Richborough, Yarmouth, and other places, are entirely swept away, it is unreasonable to expect to find them here.[1] By embanking the Fens they not only made a military rampart from which they could withstand the enemy at advantage, but they removed the chances of these marauders obtaining a footing in the country by means of these Fens, where they would, probably, have been as powerful and unmanageable as the Menasians and Frisians were found to be by Cæsar.[2] The poverty of men has often been more difficult to conquer than their affluence, Many of the Saxons came from countries little different from these marshes; they were, consequently, inured to the character of such places, and had they once obtained possession here, might have made it their first permanent settlement in these islands. We contend, too, that the only interpretation which can be put upon the brief passages in which the Roman writers seem to allude to these works, is, that they were forti-

(1) The great northern wall first erected by Agricola was, like the embankments of the Fens, of earth; that afterwards built by Severus was, however, of stone. It was commanded by thirty-seven forts placed at such distances as one could alarm another. Something of the same kind must, we should suppose, have been part of the defences of the Fens.

(2) Commentaries, b. iii., c. 29, 30.

fications. We have given the passage in Tacitus which is supposed to refer to them; and another in Herodian's "Life of Severus," is even more directly to the point. Speaking of that Emperor, he says: "He took care to make causeys over the Fens, that his soldiers might stand on firm ground, and with ease passing over them, fight on the dry land."[1] We, therefore, conclude that these embankments are likely to have been part of the military defences, of the Saxon Shore.[2]

The third political purpose for which we have suggested the embankments may have been formed, was the employment of the Roman soldiers. These celebrated legions who were subject to revolts, and who, in the latter days of the empire, used to raise up emperors at will, were often politically employed in national works to preserve them from constructing treasons. We do not, however, regard this as so likely a reason as the former.

This embankment extends from Lynn, and follows pretty generally the present line of coast, at a distance from the shore varying from three-quarters of a mile to two miles. It runs southwardly from Lynn to Wisbech, at which point, following the estuary, it turns north, and rounding the Foss-dyke in the same manner, may be traced for a considerable distance along the Lincolnshire coast. Much of this embankment remains entire, and has been the model for later works of the kind, few of which have equalled it in bold construction. In the neighborhood of Wisbech the remains are singularly perfect; and by their distance from the present watercourses, show how much country has been gained, and what an alteration has come over the face of it since these were the barriers to an arm of the sea rather than a river. The extreme banks—about midway of which is the present

(1) Life of Severus, b. iii.

(2) The defence of this shore was considered so important, that not only were forts erected along the coast northward from Sussex, but a fleet was kept, and an officer appointed to the chief command of the defences, called "Count of the Saxon Shore." He had a court, consisting of a principal officer, two auditors, master of prisons, three secretaries, a registrar, clerks of appeal, sergeants, and other officers. A similar superintendent to the Count was appointed to the Picts' Wall.

channel of the Nene—are a mile and a quarter asunder, just below Wisbech.[1]

Among the other ancient works of the Fens, the Tumuli which have been thrown up in several parts, must be included. None of them, unfortunately, seem to have been examined by adequate authorities, so we are in doubt to what people they may be attributed. It seems to have been the habit of northern and barbarous nations, after they had interred their most celebrated warriors and their kings, to heap large mounds of earth over them—the rudest and most permanent of all monuments. The Britons used this mode of sepulture before the Roman invasion,[2] and the Saxons[3] and Danes[4] after them;[5] but, as each of these people had peculiar arts, their barrows are readily known by their contents. Unless, therefore, the contents of the Fen barrows were examined, so as to ascertain, if possible, by which of these people they were raised, we cannot come to any conclusion on the probable period of their erection. The Romans never resorted to this method of burial;[6] but so many implements and articles, evidently of Roman construction, are found in the barrows scattered over England, that there is no doubt many were raised during the period of Roman occupation. There are no less than six in the neighborhood of Wisbech, not one of which, we believe, has ever been opened.[7] These barrows are all of the circular

(1) At a Sessions of Sewers, held at Wisbech in 1437, it was presented: "that the sea-bank, beginning at Tyddegote, and extending to Bevy's Cross, in Wisbech, ought to be fifty feet in height, (viz. from the first sloping thereof unto the crest), and in breadth at top, six feet."—*Dugdale*, p. 319.

(2) Pict. Hist. of England, vol. i. p. 131. (3) Leland.

(4) Adolph Cypri, quoted by Dugdale.

(5) "The funeral pile," says Tacitus, speaking of the Germans, "is neither strewed with garments, nor enriched with fragrant spices. The arms of the deceased are committed to the flames, and sometimes his horse. A mound of turf is raised to his memory."—*Manners of the Germans*, c. 27, *Murphy's Translation*.

(6) The single exception is the circumstance noticed by Dugdale, p. 174, of Germanicus raising a mound over the bones of Varus' legion. "A monument to the memory of the dead was raised with turf."—See Tacitus Annals, b. i., c. 61, 62. Dugdale quotes the "Life of Agricola" for the passage, which is an error; and seems to infer from it that the Romans were in the habit of interring their dead in this manner, which does not appear to be the case.

(7) There are, apparently, two in Walsoken, two in Leverington, and two in Walpole.

kind, and it is remarkable that they are in the immediate vicinity of the Roman banks.[1]

The other works attributed to the Romans in the Fens are the Car-dyke and Po-dyke. These have been considered catchwater canals to take off the upland downfall without spreading it over the plain,—a system of protection to the Fens which has been revived of late years by one of the most eminent of drainage engineers. Others contend these rivers were for the purpose of navigation, and had no connection with drainage, which is, perhaps, not an improbable opinion, as the Car-dyke is exceedingly ill constructed for conveying water to the sea, but well constructed for communicating between great Roman towns. The remains are yet very discernible. It was originally forty miles long, sixty feet broad, and had on each side a broad flat bank.[2] It appears first near the southern extremity of the Isle of Ely, and runs north, commencing at Waterbeach, if not Cambridge.[3] It runs along the edge of Chaff Fen, and along the present channel of the Ouse from Aldreth to Earith. Thence it proceeds, along the course of the West Water, by Benwick.[4] It takes a westerly direction to Peterborough, and, skirting the edge of the Northamptonshire and Lincolnshire fens, terminates in the Witham, near Lincoln. This extensive cut has employed the researches of various antiquarians, who having no authority or date for the work, have endeavored to extract from its name evidence of both. Dr. Stukely at first thought it to have been made under the direction of Catus Decianus, the Procurator in Nero's time, and supposed that in the neighboring places,—Catesbridge, Catwick, Catley, Cathorpe, &c.,—he found the name of this governor;[5] but he afterwards attributed it to a work of Agricola, begun in

(1) Gough, in his additions to Camden, thinks that what are taken for tumuli, may, in many instances, have been raised for boundary marks. Siculus Flaccus tells us that ashes, potsherds, broken glass, burnt bones, chalk, or plaster, used to be put under boundary marks; and other writers say little hillocks of earth, called *botontines*, were placed on bounds. "So that," says Gough, "I am apt to think most of the tumuli and round hillocks we see scattered up and down the country, were raised for this purpose, and that ashes, coals, potsherds &c., would be found under them, if they were searched."—*Additions to Camden.*

(2) Beauties of England and Wales, v. ix., p. 526.

(3) Stukely. (4) Gough's additions to Camden. (5) Itin. i., p. 8.

the northern parts of Britain, and continued by Adrian, and that Carausius scoured it, and continued it from Peterborough to Cambridge;[1] and from the latter he derives its name. But it has been, on good foundation, described to signify nothing in its name but Fen-dyke.[2]

We have more perfect information respecting the only remainder work which the Romans seem to have constructed in this province,—their roads, or causeys. The first object of a conqueror who seeks to establish himself in the country he subdues, is is to give facility to communication. This was so well understood by the Romans, that almost the first works they attempted, after settlement in a country, were to make causeways to the extremities, "to have their marches in a straight line, and to employ the people;"[3] and every country, where their sway endured for any time, bears evidence still of the extent and stability of their works. England possesses several of these roads, known by the names of Ermine Street, the Foss Way, Ryknild Street, and others; some of which, as Watling Street, which goes from Dover to Chester, are supposed to have been originally British. These principal roads had branches, and such branches are the only constructions of the kind which seem to have crossed the fens. The most direct of these passed from Downham, through Charke, to the high grounds about March, and then, by Eldenhall, to Whittlesea and Peterborough; whence it was continued to Caister, a celebrated Roman station.[4] This road, "of about three feet thickness, and sixty feet broad," is now covered with moor, in some places three, in others five feet thick.[5] Dr. Stukeley supposes a branch of this road passed, by way of Upwell and Elm, to Wisbech, and thence into Lincolnshire, by Spalding and Sleaford. "Nor is this unlikely," says the Bishop of Cloyne, "as the care of the Romans was such, in the latter times of the empire, to secure the sea-coasts, that we find forts and roads evidently con-

(1) Gough, from Palæog. Brit., ii., 37; and Hist. Carausius.
(2) Salmon's New Survey of England. (3) Isidore.
(4) Lyson's Mag. Brit., v. ii., p. 47. Communication by the Bishop of Cloyne.
(5) Dugdale, p. 174.

structed, with this sole view, along the whole east shore of the island: and it is by no means probable, that the line would be interrupted in this part of the coast only, and the troops obliged, upon any alarm, to make a considerable *detour* without reason."[1] Another road crossed the fen from the north-east coast of Norfolk to St. David's, going by Littleport and Ely, and by the east end of Grunty Fen to Streatham, becoming invisible, probably from the top growth of moor, when it drops into the fen. It re-appears at Denny, and thence takes its way through the southern part of the county.

These are all the works which can be attributed to the Romans in the Fens, and they constitute almost its sole antiquities, if we except the religious foundations. They will always rank among the most praiseworthy remains which the Roman nation left behind it in Britain; for, whether they are considered as works of a civil or military kind, it cannot be denied that they have contributed to the reclaiming of the wastes among which they were raised.[2]

From the arrival of the Romans to that of the
A.D. Saxons—a space of four hundred years,—we learn no
449. further of this part of the country; and it is only after two hundred years more, that we obtain any notice of

(1) Lyson's Mag. Brit., v. ii., p. 47.

(2) This notion, however, is strenuously denied by Elstobb, who blames the Roman embankment for all the subsequent overflowing and drowning of the Fens.

it among the many events which, meantime, had changed the whole character of the land. The Saxons had established themselves in England;—from being marauders they had become citizens and agriculturists;—the Roman laws had given place to the old customs of the race of Sakai;—the Roman arts had been supplanted by rude structures and coarse manufacture;—men, luxurious and attached to delicacies, had been succeeded by men coarse in their appetites and rough in their manners;—the Christian faith had been introduced;—and Saxon kings sat on the eight thrones of England.

A.D. 652. One of these—Anna, king of the East Angles,—had a daughter, whom he loved "passing well." It was the early period of Saxon conversion to Christianity; and the people were vehement either in rejection or in adoption of a religion which confounded all their former customs. Etheldreda, the daughter of Anna, became—probably through the influence of enthusiastic teachers—an early convert to the new faith; and her character, tending to melancholy, induced her to make a resolution, almost in early youth, to dedicate herself to God.[1] This resolve, however, received several interruptions before it was accomplished; for, by the account of her historians, she was not only the daughter of a king, but beautiful; and though cold, according to Bede, to the interests and passions of this world, she inflamed the heart of one of the prince-vassals of her father, named Tonbert. Tonbert ruled over the South Girvii, or Fenmen;[2] and, though a subject of the king of the East Angles, he appears to have been an independent prince in these territories.[3] The king favored the wishes of Tonbert;

(1) Bentham's Hist. of Ely Cathedral. (2) Dugdale, p. 180.

(3) The Saxon kings were eight in number: but Camden reckons thirty-four provinces on this side the Humber. As far as the researches of historians have been able to penetrate, some of these appear to have been held by direct feudal tenure, some feudal and hereditary. The governors were called *Baldormen*, which the old Saxon histories and charters express by *Princeps* and *Duces*. They were the principal nobility of the times, and had place, together with the bishops, in the great councils of the nation. There were two provinces of this kind in East Anglia, called North and South Girvii, the latter comprising the district, or rather part of it now called the Isle of Ely.—See *Bentham's Ely*.

and his happiness would have encountered few obstacles had not Etheldreda herself—mindful of the vows and resolutions of former days—looked with less delight upon him than a young prince and a lover expected. For some time she remained firm and constant to her early resolution, but her father at length prevailed on her to renounce her secretly-formed design, and she was married to Tonbert in 652, A D. On this marriage she had the Isle of Ely settled on her in dower.[1] But, though married, this inflexible saint, writes the old historian with exultation, maintained her chastity; and when, at the end of three years, Tonbert died, her marriage-portion, the Isle of Ely,—which seems to have been most, if not all, her husband's possession—became the sole property of this rigid woman.

Having now opportunity to fulfil the design she had so long conceived, and being enriched with worldly possessions, she left her immediate concerns in charge of her servant Ovin—the same whose cross is preserved in Ely Cathedral—and departed for the Isle. "Affecting the place, both in the difficulty of access to it, as also that it was in the nature of a wilderness, severed from the pleasures of the world, she there settled herself, taking to her company certain persons with whom she had contracted friendship for religion's sake."[2] Etheldreda doubtless conceived that she had now freed herself entirely of the temptations of society, and that she would be allowed to pass the remainder of her days in the tranquillities of prayer and contemplation. But, alas for human resolves and professions! She had not been more than five years in her solitary region, when her father being dead, her uncle Ethelwold had ascended his throne. In those times the stability of a monarch depended less on the unity of his subjects than the alliance of other powers. Prince Egfrid, of Northumberland, had either seen Etheldreda or heard of her

(1) Bentham—Dugdale—who both derived their facts from the M.S. Liber Eliensis. It appears from this incident that though Tonbert was a noble in the court of Anna, his possession was at his own disposal.

(2) Dugdale.

beauty, or perhaps the fame of her piety had reached a court where Christianity had triumphed over every obstacle, and, desiring to marry her, obtained the important influence of the new king of East Anglia. Ethelwold, anxious to secure the protection of such a prince, did all in his power to draw Etheldreda out of the Isle, and make her princess of Northumberland. His endeavours succeeded, and the lady was again married. But, "though she continued his consort twelve years, she remained glorious in the perpetual integrity of virginity," says Bede.[1] The future history of Etheldreda partakes of the legendary character which belongs to most of the heroes or heroines of the Catholic church. Her chroniclers relate how she fled her court and took refuge in the monastery of Coldingham; how Egfrid, inconsolable for her loss, pursued her,—and how she, resolving to be no more enticed into the world she despised, left Coldingham for the greater security of Ely. Egfrid, they relate, was near overtaking her by the way, when she ascended a great hill; a flood of rain came, and so completely insulated the hill, that Etheldreda was miraculously preserved till her pursuers, wearied with waiting for her, departed. We are also gravely assured, that water gushed from the rock to slake her thirst; that her staff, "old and long withered," being stuck in the ground, was not only "clothed with a new green bark, but budded with verdant branches and leaves;"[2] and that she finally reached Ely, founded the monastery, and became its first abbess.[3] Here her exemplary conduct gained her converts daily. To deny the reasonable requests of nature, and

(1) Hist. Eccles. Bede seems to have considered Etheldreda a miracle of piety, and bestows upon her all the adulation of a Catholic suppliant to his saint. "Let Virgil," says he, "sing of wars, I celebrate the gifts of peace. My verses are of chastity, not of the adulterous Helen. I will chaunt heavenly blessings, not the battles of miserable Troy."

(2) Dugdale, from Liber Eliensis. These, with other particulars of Etheldreda's life, are sculptured in Ely Cathedral on the bases of eight niches, which in a peculiar manner swell from the centre of the elegant shafts from which the fan-roof of the lantern springs.

(3) Ibid. "That zeer Egfridus, King Oswy is sone, spousede seint Etheldreda, that was to forehoond ywedded to oerl Todbertus. Theiy hue were twyes yspousede and bisiliche ywowed to cossis and clippinges and fleschlich lykynge, yet hue left clene mayde and was departed fro Egfridus, and wente to the Abbey of Elig and was ymaad Abbesse there, and dude many fayre miracles and grete."—*Hygden's Polychronicon.*

to seem to be bereft of the common feelings of humanity, were in those days the passports to fame in this life and canonisation afterwards. Both these were secured by Etheldreda. Her austerities are extolled by Bede and her other chroniclers as examples to an age of austerity. "From her first entrance on her office she never wore any linen, but only woollen garments; she usually ate once a day, except on greater festivals, or in time of sickness; and if her health permitted, she never returned to bed after matins, which were held at midnight, but continued her prayers in the church till break of day."[1]

We have thus briefly related the principal incidents in the life of Etheldreda, as it is to the peculiar manner in which the Isle was appropriated to her, and by her consigned to the head of her monastery, that the privileges and jurisdiction which it enjoyed till 1836 are referred. It possessed a distinction from most of the other possessions of the church, in consisting, not only of estates and domains, but of a jurisdiction, in which all but supreme power could be exercised; blending thus—somewhat in the manner of some of the old church-powers on the continent, as at Liege and Wartzburg,—the temporal with the spiritual jurisdiction, where the bishop was more a baron than a priest. In conferring her dominion on her church, Etheldreda seems to have made a complete gift, retaining nothing and subtracting nothing; and in a national assembly, which has been interpreted
A.D. into the Synod of Herutford:[2] "It was decreed by all
673. the great men of England, as well secular as ecclesiastical, that the Isle of Ely, which the holy virgin Etheldreda had possessed as her dower, and had now dedicated to the service of God, should not for the time to come suffer any diminution of its liberty, either by the king or the bishop of the diocese."[3] Though, subsequently, much of the property of this domain got dissipated and appropriated to lay propri-

(1) Bede. Hist. Eccles. (2) Bentham.

(3) Non de Rege nec de Episcopo libertas loci diminueretur, vel in posterum confringeretur.—*Liber Eliensis.*

etors,—partly by confiscations, partly by the expenses of restoration after the disasters which subsequently befel the cathedral at Ely and its priests, and partly in alienations of priests to their dependents,—yet the Isle never entirely lost the liberties which it at this time secured: and though it was afterwards celebrated for a rebellious priesthood, and for being the harbour of rebellion, it obtained, even from the monarchs it defied, the confirmation of its privileges.

The habit of settling in solitary places, generated by a desire of seclusion from the world, was an early passion of the Catholic church. It was first manifested, like almost every other growth of Catholicism, in the East; whose inhabitants, by a certain force and heat of character, have carried every principle they have adopted to extravagance. Pliny records the existence of a colony of misanthropes, who lived on the borders of the Dead Sea,—"associates of the palm-tree, who had been perpetuated through thousands of ages without women and without property."[1] It does not appear, however, that their asceticism arose from any religious feeling, but purely from some singular caprice, or fancied disagreement with society. The voluntary banishment of the early Christians was from very different motives. It manifested itself first in Egypt; and in a country, the one half of which was totally unfit for cities or societies of men, the passion for solitude was easy to indulge. Various motives have been assigned to the exiles; some fancying they were copyers of the prophets,[2]—others observing in the scenery and climate of the East sufficient motive for the acts of these hermits,[3]—and some believing they fled from persecution.[4] Whatever might be its source, monacism became popular. The common people soon began to revere the voluntary severities which these men suffered. Their hard food and harder beds, their constrained attitudes and short interrupted rest, their haggard looks and constant prayer, made them not only

(1) Hist. Nat., v. xv. Gibbon's Decline and Fall, c. xxxvii. Waddington's Hist. of Church, c. xix, s. 1.
(2) Gibbon, c. 37. Dugdale.
(3) Waddington, c. xix, s. 1. (4) Camden's Brit., p. 555.

appear examples of faith and penitence, but induced their worshippers to heap wealth upon them in proportion as they professed to despise it, and to lay before them the gratifications of the world—distinctions and obedience—in proportion as they declared both to be evil and unworthy machinations. "My vow of poverty," exclaims a Benedictine abbott, "has given me a hundred thousand crowns a year; my vow of obedience has raised me to the rank of a sovereign prince."[1]

When Etheldreda chose the solitude of the Fens for her residence, the same passion was manifesting itself in the first struggles of Christianity in England. To deny everything,—wealth, distinction, society, friendship, affection,—in order to gain everything, was the popular tenet. Thus the most severe lives were passed in the most inhospitable places. Those regions, which seemed destined to long depopulation, or to be only inhabited by the meanest of mankind, became for this reason the select spots to which religious votaries retired. There, in emaciating offices, their lives were spent.[2]

The foundation of Etheldreda had been preceded by a similar one at Peterborough, in 655, by King Wolfere, in compunction for having slain his sons for their profession of Christianity;[3] and, in 716, another abbey, more immediately in the midst of fens and swamps than any of the former, was founded at Crowland, in celebration of the austere and self-denying life of St Guthlac, who had there passed many inhospitable years, tempted and assailed—if we may believe the monkish author of his life—by the most terrible demons, who claimed Crowland as an island of their own.[4] These foundations succeeded so rapidly that they soon became nur-

(1) Gibbon, c. xxxvii, note 56.

(2) It may be for peace, as well as for solitude, that the religious of this island chose the Fens of Lincolnshire and Cambridgeshire for their retirement. "At the time when these Abbeys [Peterboro', Ely, Crowland, Thorney,] were respectively founded, Christianity was not universally adopted in the island, and its disciples were exposed to opposition and danger. Hence places were chosen which might either escape notice, or be difficult of approach to marauding and piratical enemies."—*Britton's Hist. and Antiq. of Peterboro' Cathedral,—Preface.*

(3) Gunton's Hist. of Peterborough Cathedral, p. 5.

(4) "St. Guthlac was once hurried away from his cell by demons, and carried by violence to the very gates of hell, into which they threatened to cast him, for invading their own island of Crowland."—*Gough's Collections for Leicestershire.*

series of other establishments; and Peterborough Monastery had hardly been built fifty years when a company of monks, under the protection of its abbot, established themselves at Thorney,[1] and were the commencement of a religious house there. A few miles from Crowland, a pious woman, named Pega, had so invested the place of her residence with sanctity, by a life of devotion, that a hermitage and church were built there by the flourishing monks of Crowland, and the place called Pega's-kirk or church, and now known as Peakirk.

Thus three monasteries and two other religious foundations, destined to much opulence in after ages, were founded within a few miles of each other, in what must be considered the most miserable part of the kingdom. The history of these buildings becomes, henceforth, the history of the Fens; for a great part of the property of these parts, by grants from kings and bequests, soon became appropriated to the uses of these churches. We have shown how the jurisdiction of the Isle of Ely had been consigned to the abbey by Etheldreda; and the possessions of Peterborough consisted mostly of property within the same region—waters, meres, fens, weirs, and lands;[2] and those of Crowland of the like kind, with common-rights and fisheries.[3]

These religious houses soon increased in wealth, and became endowed with especial privileges. Ely, almost immediately after its foundation, had obtained the right of choosing its own bishop; and, therefore, it became, in some measure, an independent diocese, though nominally included in that of the Bishop of the East Angles.[4] It was decreed that the Abbot of Peterborough should be "chiefest of all abbots on this side the river Thames, and should have the first place in all conventions;"[5] and that those who were too infirm to make a pilgrimage to Rome might, by visiting Peterborough, obtain the same absolution.[6] Crowland was repeatedly enriched by the donations of kings and nobles.[7]

(1) Gunton, p. 5. (2) Charta of King Wolfere. (3) Hist. Crowland.

(4) Bentham's Ely. (5) Gunton, p. 6. (6) Ibid.

(7) Witlaff, King of Mercia, in his charter to Croyland, among other donations, enumerates the following. "I give also for the holy service of the altar my scarlet cloak which was

We learn little of these monasteries for a hundred and fifty years, except these particulars, and the deaths and elections of their abbots. Meanwhile, the grants and privileges they were obtaining were gradually raising them from poverty to wealth, and much of the riches of the country were accumulated in their treasuries. The church already aspired to the highest luxuries in its services,—for the impressions of pomp are, in certain stages of society, more powerful than the impressions of faith. The chalices, altars, candlesticks, and crucifixes of the mass, were seldom of meaner metals than silver, and often of gold, when the scarcity of these metals was a hundred times greater than at present.

The island at this period appears to have been comparatively tranquil, or only disturbed by the occasional disputes of petty kings. The whole country had now long forgotten the ceremonies of Thor; and, proportionably to its peacefulness, the church increased in proselytes and enthusiasts. The old pirates of the "hazy ocean," as they called the North Sea,[1] had settled into quiet herdsmen and ploughmen—the fatters of cattle and growers of corn—instead of seizing both these produce from the industrious hands which reared them. Opulence and the peaceful arts seem to have been progressing, and the nation was in the road to as much prosperity as these early ages afforded, when the whole was swept into ruin by the same cause as had altered its character two hundred years before.

A.D. 866. The most disastrous period in the history of the churches in the Fens, and indeed of the country generally, may be dated from 866. The asylum, which the founders of the abbeys in the Fens so long obtained, received at this period such a check from the ravages of the

used at my coronation, and to the sacred ornaments of the church my gold veil, on which is sewed the sacking of Troy, to be suspended from the wall on my anniversary (if it please). I give also to the refectory my jug, gilt on every part of the exterior, and engraved with hunters and dragons fighting, and internally impressed at the four corners with the sign of the cross, which in my trouble I am accustomed to invoke. Also my table-horn, that the old men of the monastery may drink from it at holy festivals, and speak well of me, and sometimes remember the soul of the giver, Witlaff."—*Monasticon Anglicanum.*

(1) Turner's Anglo-Saxons, v. i.

Danes, as neither before nor since has befallen Christianity in England. With a rancour, which requires a short explanation, these pirates selected the religious buildings and their inhabitants for their principal spoil and destruction.

The Saxons and Danes are mere distinctions in name. Both came originally from the same countries; and in religion, habits, and language, were essentially one people. The difference is a mere difference of time. The Saxons were the pirates of their country in the fourth and fifth centuries; and the Danes—who came not from Denmark only, but from all the countries on the Baltic—in the ninth century. But, in the mean time, the Saxons had forgotten their country, and, more than that, their country's gods. Christianity had not yet established itself in the north; there the followers of Thor and Odin still gloried in their Paganism. Charlemagne, indeed, during his conquests in Germany, had forced many Northmen to be baptised; but this had been accompanied with too much severity to have any other effect than that of embittering the converts against Christianity and all its disciples. It was the lingering recollection of this tyranny which is supposed to have induced the Danes, in their incursions to England and France, to select the religious houses for their prey.[1] That the Saxons were their brethren—the offspring of almost the same country—only infuriated them the more against those whom they only now beheld as bastards and renegades[2] from the faith of their old warriors and traditions. "They were particularly fond of the blood of priests," says Thierry, "and the gold taken from the churches; and would lodge their horses in the chapels of palaces."[3]

There was doubtless another motive, not less powerful than that of hatred, which induced the Danes to plunder the churches of the eastern coasts of England. Their incursions in countries nearer to their own had been successful. They had pushed their way into the north of Germany, the Nether-

(1) Wheaton's Hist. of Northmen. Hume, c. ii. (2) Thierry.

(3) Hist. Norman Conquest. Capella regis equos suos stabulant.—*Chron. Herman.*

lands, and Normandy, and had reaped immense treasure. Every year fresh swarms embarked on these expeditions, and every year fresh countries were required to satisfy their avarice. The coasts of England were, therefore, reached and devastated, because they lay conveniently for it; and the churches, from generally possessing more plunderable wealth than any other public establishments, were naturally selected as a first object.

With such inducements, and prepared for new achievements, the men "who never slept under a smoky roof, or drained their drinking-horn at a cottage fire,"[1] took their arrows and lances, and, committing themselves to the deep, steered for the eastern coasts of England. The ships, or "steeds of the ocean," as they called them,[2] in which they embarked, would have frightened a modern sailor, acquainted with the storms and currents of the ocean; for they were frequently hollowed out of the trunks of trees, and could be carried on men's shoulders.[3] But the resolution of their crews was prepared for difficulties; they even seemed to hope for danger; and often preferred embarking in tempests, because it was then their victims would be most unguarded,[4]—singing at such seasons, with recklesss bravado: "The force of the storm is a help to the arms of our rowers, the hurricane is in our service, for it carries us the way we would go."[5]

A.D. 870. Though they had landed several years previous, both in the south and north of England, it was not till the year 870 that we have any record that they penetrated the Fens. After ravaging the northern parts of Lincolnshire,—seizing their booty and departing to their ships,—they sailed south; and so terrible had they made themselves, that the serfs and inhabitants, at the rumour of

(1) Yalinga Saga. (2) Turner.

(3) Wheaton's Northmen, p. 142. These habits are only a repetition of the habits of the Anglo-Saxons. "They traversed the ocean in boats," says Turner, "formed of osiers, and covered with skins sewed together."—*Hist. Anglo-Saxons*, v. i, p. 3.

(4) Turner. (5) Thierry.

their approach, quitted their towns and habitations, and fled with their slender stock of moveables to the monasteries, or the less passable parts of the Fen. They would force the Saxons to prepare food for them,—and, after they had eaten it, often slew their hosts, set fire to their houses, and departed.[1] But the first prey, and as a means of securing the rest, they were most covetous of obtaining horses: for these they would often promise an exemption of plunder,[2]—and, mounting them, dive into the midland parts of the kingdom, carry off their spoil, or charge the inhabitants with their cavalry, as the unskilful Saxons threw themselves between their enemies and their possessions in order of battle.

It was about Michaelmas, 870, when the Danes entered Kesteven. The description of their ravages had preceded them, and Earl Algar of Hoyland [Holland] had mustered some forces, and obtained two hundred more from the monastery of Crowland, commanded by Toli, who, though a lay-brother of the monastery, had formerly been a soldier. These were afterwards increased by the family and dependents of Morcar, Lord of Brun, and five hundred men under the governor of Lincoln, who had sworn by the holy host to die in defence of their country and the faith of Christ.[3] In a short time, by these and other supplies, they mustered nearly three thousand men.[4] By speedily uniting and attacking the advances of the Danes, they gained a partial victory on the feast of St. Lawrence, slaying, in the course of the engagement, three Danish kings,[5] and chasing the rest of the army to its entrenchments. But the main body of the Danes had been on an excursion of plunder, and came up in the night, loaded with booty, and a multitude of women and children. The news of this reinforcement spread a panic through the ranks of the Fenmen, who, though victorious, seem to have earned their victory with difficulty; and, fearing to encounter such increased numbers, many deserted in

(1) Hen. Hunt. Hist.—Pictorial England, v. i, p. 178. (2) Pictorial England.
(3) Ingulf. (4) Turner, v. i, p. 230. from Ingulf.
(5) These were sea-kings, a title claimed by every leader of a piratical squadron.

the night. Algar, however, and his compatriots, resolved to stand their ground, and drew up the remainder of their army in good order. Toli, with five hundred men under him, occupied the right; Oscott, the sheriff of Lincoln, commanded the left; and Algar himself led the centre. The Northmen, having buried their kings at early dawn, left some detachments to guard their camp and plunder, and hastened forward, under four kings and eight earls, to the encounter. The English had formed themselves into a wedge. Though severely reduced by their losses and unskilful at the bow, in which the Danes so greatly excelled,[1] they withstood for some time the charge of the whole Danish army, warding off the arrows with their shields, and resisting the cavalry, which the Danes had stolen from them in their forays, with their pikes.[2] In this manner they were able to continue unbroken and resolute the whole day,—when evening coming on, the Danes, who had spent their darts, exhausted their cavalry, and wearied their whole army, had recourse to a common artifice of barbarian warfare, and by feigning a flight drew the Saxons in a disorderly manner from their position. Their leaders strove to prevent this movement, which they saw was only a desperate effort to draw the Fenmen into the open field, where the character of their warfare gave the pirates many advantages. But the Saxon soldiers impetuous and desiring revenge, rushed forward, despite their commanders. The Danes, having enticed them to some distance, turned upon them suddenly in the midst of this pell-mell pursuit—and rallying and forming, which they knew so well how to accomplish on the instant, overpowered the Christians (says Ingulfus) without difficulty, and put almost all to the sword. Two or three of the common men, youths of Sutton and Gedney—the only fugitives who escaped this battle, by secreting themselves in a neighbouring wood—carried the news to Crowland. But the approach of the Danish army was already intimated to the monks by the villages which they fired in their progress. After the first

(1) Hist. Northmen. (2) Ingulf.

consternation was subsided, the monks thought only of securing their valuables, and buried their altar-piece and plate in the well of the cloister.[1] The abbot dispatched what treasures, and relics, and chartas he thought most valuable, with St. Guthlac's body, his psalter, and his whip, by boats, in the care of about thirty monks, across the neighbouring waters to Ancarig Wood (Thorney); and remaining himself, with a few old monks and children, he arrayed himself in sacred vestments, went into the church, and performed high mass. The Pagans arrived just as the communion was ended. Their leader, probably incensed to find the principal booty had escaped, rushed upon the abbot at the altar, and slew him there, while his followers beheaded the monks who were assisting. After interrogating and torturing the rest of the house, they slew all, broke open the tombs, swept all the bones in a heap, and set fire to the building. "We have sung the mass of lances—it began at the rising of the sun,"[2] was their sarcastic expression after committing such horrors. At the end of three days they departed with their plunder and cattle towards Peterborough, or, as it was then called, Meadhamstead.[3]

Here they found a different reception to that which they had received at Crowland. The gates of the monastery were shut against them, and the monks and country people were armed and ready to receive them.[4] The Danes, however, were also prepared. They assailed the gates and fastenings; and, with their archers and engines, they soon made a breach in the walls,[5] and forced their way into the monastery. In the course of this assault, however, a stone cast from the tower gave a mortal wound to the brother of the Danish general Hubba,[6]—who, doubly enraged at the loss, urged his men forward, bore down every opposition, broke into the church, and slew without mercy. But the havoc had yet only begun. When the inmates of the convent had been slain with their abbot, they fell upon everything sacred or

(1) Hist. of Crowland. (2) Thierry. (3) Ingulf—Dugdale.
(4) Gunton's Hist. Peterborough Cathedral. (5) Turner, v. i, p. 234. (6) Gunton.

venerable about the edifice. "Its monuments were demolished,—altars broken down,—a goodly library set on fire,—chartas, evidences, writings to a great number, all torn in pieces."[1] Everything belonging to Christian worship was alike demolished by these barbarous pirates, except such valuables as they could transport to their ships. These they piled on waggons, and departed: but as they were passing the Nene,[2] part of their booty, the load of two waggons, was overturned at the left of the stone bridge, into a fathomless whirlpool.[3]

They now proceeded towards Huntingdon and Cambridge, in order to unite with another body of their countrymen, who, under Inguar, was ravaging the southern parts of East Anglia. The Isle of Ely had yet been unvisited; for, at this early period, it was the most insulated of all the fens. Only boats or shallow vessels were able to reach the convent of Etheldreda; but the Danes were prepared for emergencies, and they soon contrived to visit the monastery of Ely as they had visited the monasteries of Crowland and Meadhamstead.

On their incursions abroad the Danes prepared themselves with small boats, drawing little water, in order to sail up creeks and shallow inlets.[4] The Isle was secure enough from inland enemies, but extremely open to enemies like the Danes, to whom water was more congenial than land, for it was, as it were, completely open to seaward.[5] The celebrity and riches of the place had reached the ears of the Danes; who, accordingly, entered their ships, sailed into the mouth of one of its rivers,[6] and soon gained the low plain out of which the town and cathedral of Ely rise with peculiar magnificence, enhanced by the foggy and watery fen which stretches, a vast waste seething with vapor, beneath it. Here

(1) Gunton. (2) Ibid. (3) Turner's Anglo-Saxons, v. i., p. 234.

(4) Hist. Northmen.—Hume.

(5) "The depth of water encompassing this Isle extended nearly to the sea."—*Dugdale*, p. 181.

(6) Bentham.—Dugdale. This must have been the Great Ouse; and they must, therefore, have passed Wisbech on their way to the monastery of Ely, as at this period, no other river discharging itself into the Wash would afford the facility. The Ouse, by Lynn, was only the small Brandon river running between Norfolk and Suffolk.

they landed without opposition;[1] and the inhabitants in this secluded island appear to have had so little intercourse with the world beyond the meres and marshes, or they put so much trust in the natural defences of their situation, that, although several noble refugees had fled thither for safety, they were unaware of the landing of the Danes; and their alarm seems to have been incited by the first depredations they experienced. They were not long, however, in mustering a troop of resolute men; the refugees joined them, and inspired them to battle, in which the robbers suffered so vigorous a repulse that they hastily retreated to their ships and departed.[2] The islanders thought they had escaped with credit; but none could congratutate themselves safely on the defeat of such foes. Those who escaped only summoned fresh tribes of their countrymen, magnifying, probably, the wealth of the monastery, or the booty of the island; for a much greater number of soldiers, headed by one of their kings, formed the second expedition to the Isle.[3] The islanders again united, and defended their property resolutely for some time; but after a bloody fight, in which they lost many men, they were totally routed, and the Danes halted only at the doors of the monastery.

It seems almost surprising that a few foreigners—for they must have been few in comparison with the population they robbed—should so easily have pursued their depredations, notwithstanding the forces that were brought against them. We may be sure the Saxons,—fighting for their homes, their families, their treasures, and their lives,—would contend with the utmost determination, especially against a foe which seems to have known nothing of mercy. They, doubtless, did all they were able to defend themselves, but their peaceful occupations seem to have completely destroyed their former warlike manners, and left them far inferior to the Danes in all that pertains to the art and experience of war.

(1) Liber Eliensis. (2) Bentham's Hist. of Ely Cathedral.

(3) Liber Eliensis. The coincidence of time and other concomitant circumstances render it highly probable that this king was Hubba, who has that title given him by several ancient writers.—*Bentham's Hist. of Ely Cathedral.*

The same riotous scene and carnage, which had been performed at Peterborough and Crowland, were perpetrated at Ely, with the additional barbarity of murdering the nuns as well as the monks. The cathedral was deluged with their blood, and the massacres of the long sword were succeeded by the demolitions of the pickaxe, and the pickaxe by the brand. They set the town and church on fire, and departed to their ships, loaded with more than common wealth; for nothing had been removed from the monastery, which had been enriched with the wealth of the surrounding country, brought thither by the simple countrymen, who believed its sanctity would make it a place of peculiar security.[1]

The Danes had accomplished their work so effectually, that for some time—for years—the churches they had destroyed lay in ruins. A few monks returned to Crowland, and, by selling some of the jewels they had saved, managed to repair a corner of their church, gather a small company together, and elect a fresh abbot. They were not, however, allowed to pursue their work in peace. The King of Mercia was beleaguered with Danes, and fighting for his crown and life. He required money and lands to induce his soldiers to grapple with such formidable enemies, and seized for that purpose all the jewels the Crowland monks had saved from the wreck, and appropriated the lands and revenues of the church to himself, his crown, and his mercenary soldiers.[2] Peterborough was used in the same manner, the king seizing all the lands belonging to it between Stamford, Huntingdon, and Wisbech,[3] and "it lay buried in its own ruins the space of ninety and six years, no abbot, monk, government, or religion, there professed in all that time, that is to be found in story."[4] The Isle of Ely, though not within his dominions, Borhead also appropriated to his own service;[5] and the

(1) Bentham. (2) Ibid.
(3) Britton, Hist. Peterborough Cath., p. 8.—Gunton, p. 243. (4) Gunton.
(5) Ingulphus. "Borrhedus Rex—totem Helyensem Insulam fisco suo applicavit." "That is to say," says Bentham, "he took it as an Escheat, and annexed it to his crown. We are to understand this not of the lands, but of the jurisdiction, in the same sense as when our kings formerly granted whole counties, in which grants the government of them only, and the profits thence arising, are understood."—Hist. Ely Cath.

church remained some years in ruins, before eight of the clerks, according to the "Book of Ely," repaired to their former dwelling, and, having restored the *porches* of the church, commenced divine service there. Supported perhaps by oblations from the people, they continued to exercise the duties of their faith till the restoration of this and other churches by King Edgar. In the mean time the Danes had dethroned Borhead, and were now masters of the territory which had been especially afflicted by their arms—the countries of the West Saxons under Alfred, and of the Britons in Wales and Cornwall, being the only parts of England they did not possess.[1]

The subsequent history of the Danes—their defeats by Alfred—their oath on the bracelet of Odin and the cross of Christ to preserve a peace which they broke almost the hour afterwards—and their final defeat, and Alfred's resolution to divide the kingdom between himself and Guthrum, in order to re-people with Danes the countries the Danes had depopulated[2]—belong to the general history of the country. In this division the Fens were all appropriated to the Danish dominion;[3] and the example of Guthrum—or Godrun, as modern historians call him[4]—who embraced Christianity, was followed by many of his Pagan dependents. "Several Danes," says Thierry, "in consideration of grants of land, took the title and office of perpetual defenders of the churches they had burned:"[5] and, subsequently, Odo, an old pirate chief, who late in life had received baptism, became Archbishop of Canterbury;[6] so violently does success alter the opinions and manners of mankind.

A.D. 970. It was not till the reign of Edgar that the monasteries in the Fens obtained a thorough restoration of their former uses, or any reasonable part of their revenues. What Borhead had seized by force, not from his enemies but his subjects, succeeding kings never thought of

(1) Hist. of Northmen—Hume, c. ii. (2) Hume—Turner, p. 246

(3) All the east side of the island, as far as the Humber, was surrendered to the Danes. —Pictorial England, p. 150.

(4) Wheaton—Thierry. (5) Hist. Norman Conquest. (6) Ibid.

restoring till the reign of Edgar, who, placed on the throne by monks, and secured there by their influence, was especially liberal to churches and monasteries. Peterborough was indebted to him for the restoration it now underwent; and on consideration of sixty hides of land, £100 in money, and one crucifix of gold, "beautified with marvellous work and filled with reliques,"[1] he restored the jurisdiction of the Isle of Ely, and its properties;[2] and this, as his charta expresses it was not done "privately and in a corner, but in the most public manner and under the canopy of heaven."[3]

A.D. 974. On this happy restoration the Abbot Birthnod, who had succeeded to so much temporal as well as spiritual jurisdiction, determined to set out the bounds of his power: as, in former times, this limit seems to have been disputed. Deputing, therefore, the business to Leo, one of his monks, this officer procured a meeting of the chief inhabitants of the Isle and adjoining counties, in which the bounds of the territory and possessions of the church were settled, and afterwards confirmed by King Edgar.[4] As a lasting and indisputable mark, he "caused that large and deep ditch to be cut through the main body of the Fen, which was then called by the name of Abbot's-delf, to the

(1) Dugdale.

(2) Monasticon Anglicanum, p. 92, Edgar surrendered "the whole district of the Isle of Ely, 20 hides of land within the same, all at that time parcel of the royal estate and subject to his treasury, with all the appurtenances thereto belonging, with the dignity and soke of the two Hundreds within the Isle, and five Hundreds in Wicklaw within the province of the East Angles, [Plomesgate, Wilford, Thridling, Carleford, Colnes, and Loes Hundreds in Suffolk] with the power and authority of trying all causes, also the fines and forfeitures for transgression of the laws in all secular causes in all the lands and manors that do now belong to the Monastery, or that shall hereafter belong to it, either by purchase, gift, or other lawful acquisition; also the fourth part of the profits of the county of Grantaceaster, [Cambridge] and also the villages of Meldeburn, Earmingaford, and Northwold, and 10,000 eels, part of the royal revenues due from the village of Wyllan:—for the endowment of the monastery at Ely, for the maintenance and support of the monks, and to supply them with necessary food and clothing. This is the substance of King Edgar's charta, which is now and ever since that time hath been the ground of that temporal power given to the Church of Ely, and to this day vested in the Bishop, though it is certain it had originally been given by St. Etheldreda, but on the destruction of the monastery by the Danes was resumed by the crown, and after a hundred years restored again to the Church by King Edgar."—Bentham.

(3) Non clam in angulo, sed sub divo palam evidentissime.

(4) Dugdale, from Liber Eliensis.

end it might remain as a boundary in that deep mud and water."[1]

During this time the presence of the Danes in this country was ill relished by the inhabitants. On the one side the lofty bearing and hard tasks of masters possessed of property acquired by violence,—and on the other a people who had been long enough in the land to claim their possessions as a right, not a conquest,—could only for some ages be productive of ill will between the Danes and Saxons. The Danes were likewise, it appears, too conscious of the power by which they had gained their footing in England, and by many kinds of insolence made the inhabitants miserable. Wherever they were quartered—and it appears that bands of mercenaries were quartered on the thanes and franklins[2]—they made their landlords not only provide them sumptuously, but also perform the most degrading offices, and punished resistance with stripes, or even death.[3] So much to provoke at length induced the king to cleanse the land of them by a simultaneous and secret massacre. This policy, in every respect so cowardly and wanton, only served to desolate the country afresh. Swarms came over with King Sweyn, from Denmark; and having their natural desire for plunder provoked by the murder of their countrymen, they seem to have exercised all their ferocity on the poor Saxons. This vengeance was now, however, rather directed to the cities and opulent inhabitants than to the churches. The Northmen, since their first invasion, had been converted to Christianity by Olaf Trygvason, who had not hesitated to use torture, fire, and sword against them;[4] but they seem to have more generally respected religious establishments on this visit than heretofore, notwithstanding

A.D. 1002.

(1) Bentham. "And these," says the Liber Eliensis, "are the limits of the Isle, viz. from Cotingelade to Littleport, or to Abbot's Delph, seven miles in length—and from Chirche mere to Stretham mere, four miles in breadth: but the boundaries of the two hundreds that of ancient time belonged to Ely are known to be of greater extent, viz., from the middle of the bridge at Tyd to Upwere, and from Bishop's Delf to the river near Burgh [Peterborough] called the Nen."

(2) Hume—Wheaton.

(3) Pict, England, p. 177.

(4) Sturleson's Heims-kringla.

the provocation they had received, and the swarms that came to plunder and destroy. The monastry of St. Pega, in Lincolnshire, was burnt; but the usual method was to demand a certain sum, and time was sometimes allowed for payment. A thousand marks were demanded of Crowland to be paid in a set time, on pain of burning the abbey; which sum was, accordingly, paid in three months. A heavy rain had laid the country more deeply under water than usual; and this additional security had induced such members, in their general distress, to seek the asylum of such a spot as Crowland, that "the choir was filled with monks, the rest of the church with priests and clerks, the whole abbey with laity, and the churchyard day and night with women and children. The strongest of the men watched among the reeds and elders along the rivers."[1] This sort of sanctuary did not suit the purpose of the Dane; and he was continually threatening the abbot for harboring so many people.[2] The predatory warfare of the Danes continued fifteen years, and was only finally quelled by Canute assuming the crown.

This king, who sought to conciliate his new subjects rather than exasperate them, founded new monasteries, gave the old ones gifts in return for the riches or the ornaments of which his subjects had formerly divested them, and paid many of them visits on state occasions of the church. These pleasing flatteries to the people—often the means of rivetting slavery more tightly—have been preserved in tradition Two or three of these relate to the monasteries of the Fens, which he appears to have visited several times. Ely was especially honored with his presence; and its abbot, Leofsin, was one of his three chancellors.[3] Canute generally spent the "Feast of the Purification of the Virgin" at Ely; and at this time Leofsin entered on his office.[4] Once as he was journeying thither with his queen and nobles—there being no access to the Isle but by water—as the king drew nigh land, he stood

(1) Gough's Hist. Crowland. (2) Ibid.

(3) At this time there were three chancellors, each of which held his office four months per year.

(4) Liber Eliensis.

up in the vessel and "commanded the mariners to make what haste they could to a little port, but to go steadily; and, fixing his eyes on the church which stood on high on the top of the rock, he heard a pleasant voice on every side, where, listening further the nearer he approached to land he perceived it was the monks then singing in the quire, and with shrill voices performing their divine offices; he commanded all the rest that were in the next ships to him, and, exhorting them to sing with him, became so transported that, expressing this joy of his heart, he presently composed and sang this hymn:[1]

"Merrie sungen the munchen binnen Ely,
Tha Cnut, ching, reu ther by.
Roweth cnihtes nær the land,
And here we thes munches sæng."[2]

Canute on this occasion confirmed the liberties of the church, offering the charta himself upon the altar of St. Etheldreda.[3]

On another occasion, when the king attended the same feast, a severe frost had frozen the fen, but not sufficiently to make it safe to travel over; so that being prevented using a boat, the king, "sorrowful and much troubled,"[4] was induced to employ a sledge. The passage he was about to attempt was by Soham Mere, but he appears to have been surrounded,

(1) Dugdale, p. 184.

(2) This is a very celebrated Saxon relict. Almost every writer who has traced our early literature has quoted this rude fragment. Palgrave says the king was navigating the Nenne, which has been followed by many subsequent authors; but we think it is not necessary to suppose the king was navigating any river at all, but merely the overflowing fen; or, if any, it must have been the Ouse, as we believe no authority has before placed the Nene in the vicinity of Ely.

Cheerful sang the monks in Ely,
When Canute the king was passing by,
Row to the shore, knights, said the king,
And let us hear these churchmen sing.

This would suppose a wide body of water stretching to the foot of the cathedral, and not a river. "All the other stanzas have been lost," says Palgrave, "and we may regret that we possess no further specimen of this composition, which entitles Canute to rank among the royal authors of England."—Hist. England, v. i., p. 320. Thierry adduces the above, among other things, as a proof of Canute's craft in endeavoring to give his conquest the air of a native despotism.—Hist. Norman Conquest, b. iii., p. 317. "This verse," says Strutt, "with the rest of song, was afterwards sung in the churches in commemoration of this extraordinary fact."—Herda, v. i.

(3) Bentham. (4) Dugdale.

by rather weak-hearted courtiers. None of them were willing to adventure with the king, and he had to ask, among a crowd of Isle-men, for a leader to show him the way. A stout native, named Brithmer, offered his services, which the king accepted, and set off, "all that beheld him admiring his boldness."[1] Both arrived safely at Ely, where the king kept the usual festival. Canute "used frequently to speak of this adventure, and in telling the story would pleasantly observe the lucky circumstance of having such a lusty fellow for his guide, as it made him quite easy, and satisfied that he himself, who was but of moderate stature, and withal vigorous and active, might safely venture where he had such a guide to lead the way."[2] Brithmer, for this service, was rewarded with freedom of body and possessions.[3]

By such acts it is easy to suppose that Canute would gain the rude approbation of the populace, though he did not cease to be a hard task-master to them.[4] By cultivating their native tongue, visiting the shrines of their saints, and rebuilding the churches his countrymen had destroyed, he made the Saxons not only tolerate but almost approve his despotism; and some public works which he constructed are as honorable to him as his pilgrimage to Rome with a wallet on his back, and a pilgrim's staff in his hand.[5] One of these, which passed through the Fens, is still called King's Delph, and formed a causey of communication between the abbeys of Ramsey and Peterborough. It has been the cause of some controversy with antiquarians. The occasion of the work, and the appearance of the country about it, is thus described by Camden: "These places, lying in a lower ground, and for many months under water, and the soil in some places as it were floating on the surface of the water, are much infested by the thick air and offensive vapor of the meers and fens. Here that clear lake, called Whittles-mere, well stocked with fish, extends itself for six miles in length, and three in breadth, in a very fenny part of the country;

(1) Dugdale. (2) Ibid. (3) Bentham, p. 95.
(4) Thierry. (5) Pict. Eng.

but the inhabitants reckon the thickness of the air is compensated by the advantages of the fishery, the plentiful pasturage, and the quantity of turf so fit for firing. King Canute ordered the fen to be parcelled out among the several towns upon it by Turkill the Dane, who divided it in such a manner that each town had such a proportion of fen for its own use as each town had firm land abutting on the opposite fen. He ordained that no township should dig or mow, without leave, in the fen belonging to another, and that they should all have a common right of pasturage, *i. e.*, horn under horn, in order to maintain peace and harmony among them."[1]

When the sons and servants of Canute, sent for from Peterborough to Ramsey, were crossing this lake, "a most violent storm arose, with a whirlwind, as they were cheerfully sailing along amusing themselves with singing, and enveloped them on every side, so that they absolutely despaired of their lives or assistance. But the mercy of the Almighty did not quite fail them, nor suffer the dreadful gulph to swallow them up, but mercifully by his providence delived some of them from those raging waves, and permitted the rest, according to the secret workings of his righteous judgment, to pass out of this frail life in the midst of those waves. When the report of their danger reached the king's ears, fear and trembling fell on him; but after he had recovered himself, by the advice of his nobles and friends, to prevent for the future any misfortunes occasioned by this raging element, he caused a dyke to be marked out by his soldiers and servants with their daggers and swords on the adjoining marshes, between Ramsey and Whittlesey, and afterwards cleaned by labourers; whence, as we learn from the credible testimony of our predecessors, some of the neighbouring inhabitants give that dyke the name of Swerdesdelfe, from its having been marked out with swords, and others will have it called Cnut's-delffe, after the king."[2] It is commonly called, at present, Steed's-

(1) Britannia. (2) Ibid.

dyke, and is accounted the boundary between Huntingdonshire and Cambridgeshire.[1]

A.D. 1066. We have now brought the narrative of fen transactions to an important period—the Norman Conquest; which succeeded, in the course of two short reigns, the facts last related. In this contest the Fens became an important asylum; especially that part of them which is more immediately attached to Wisbech—the Isle of Ely. This little spot was repeatedly the centre of refuge and hope during the misfortunes of the periods which we now approach. Nature had so fenced it about with quagmires and waters, that it was sure to be the first place of retreat when danger prevailed. Here, as in a fortress, the resolute patriot could long defy his enemy; or escape, when close pressed, to those wide acres of reed or osier forests, with which the shallower parts of the marsh were overspread. In these defiles the most experienced found himself at fault. It was impossible to pursue a fugitive over ground that sunk beneath the feet, or tottered as the horseman trod over it, or subsided into wide bogs which neither man, nor horse, nor boat, could traverse. In the loftier and firmer ground, however, where a substratum of gravel or upheaved chalk had provided a surer foundation for the habitations of the fenmen, they could hold, as it were, the keep of the fortress; and, from such an elevation as Ely, trace for miles the approach of any hostile force over the passes of the Fens. At this period, too, we should remember, that few or no castles had been erected in England. These were the introduction of the Normans; and seem, in their construction, to indicate a people who obtained

(1) King's-delfe occurs in records before Canute's time. Camden afterwards distinguishes it from that made by his order. Edgar, in his charta to the church of Peterborough [*Saxon Chron.*] makes it the bounds of his donation; and delf is rather a ditch or channel than a raised causey. "The delphe, as moche as stands in —— Hundred, is yn the shyre of Huntyngdune and a little part of it in Normancros Hundred in the same shire; and it is totally to speke of in Huntyngdonshyre; and if there be any part of the delph over the Nene longinge to Thorney, it is no grete thing."—*Leland's Itin.*, v. iv., p. 48. The road here mentioned might probably be the work of some abbot of this rich monastery, like that from Deeping to Spalding, made by Egelric, abbot of Peterborough and Bishop of Durham, 1008, and called from him Elrichrode, *q. d.* Egelric's Road.—*Ingulf.*—*Gough's Additions to Camden.*

by stealing, and held by force. When, therefore, one portion of a country—as a fen or a mountain defile—was less exposed to military inroad and control than another, there the weaker party was sure to assemble in times of difficulty.

The Fens had, as we have shown, obtained a celebrity of this kind during the Danish invasion; and the fenmen of those ages, as far as we can trace their character, seem to have been a race whose subjection it was difficult both to attain and to hold. Dugdale calls them "a rude and almost barbarous sort of lazy and beggarly people."[1] And Camden is not more courteous when he describes them as "a set of people rough and uncultivated as the soil itself, envious of others whom they call upland men, devoted to feeding of cattle, fishing, and fowling, and usually marching about on a sort of stilts like giants."[2] Both these characters, though drawn five or six hundred years later than the Norman period, would lead us to expect men who were very unlikely to submit to violent changes. Their remote situation and solitary habits would render them as averse to any change in the government, as they were afterwards found averse to changing their fruitless land into cultivation. It is men of this kind, who, with no notion and no wish for alteration, whose position gives them more natural security than their neighbours, and, consequently, more independence of powerful parties, who have been found the last to be conquered in every country where their conquest has been attempted. What the rock and defile were to the mountaineer, the reed-field and mere were to the fenmen—his home, the source of his subsistence, and his defence in seasons of oppression or misfortune.

The conquest of England by William the First, though generally considered the sudden result of the battle of Hastings, has been demonstrated to have been the lingering

(1) Hist. Embankment, p. 171.

(2) Britannia.—The Landes-men of the south of France, who inhabit the undrained marshes of the Adour, which bear a similar character to those formerly in the Fens, use stilts for passing over the boggy ground, and herding and driving their cattle from pasture to pasture.

work of seven years, and only accomplished at the edge of the sword,—in some parts by extermination, in others by tortures, and in all by confiscation and dreadful punishments. The English fought for their homes with desperation; for the policy of William was to dispossess wherever he subdued, and reward his hungry followers with the ancient estates of the old thanes and franklins of the country. Such a policy, the most wicked and heartless of all policy, was sure to embitter, to a deadly extent, the people on whom it was exercised. And all the records we derive from these times show that this bitter warfare of life and death was the only warfare known between the Normans and the Saxons. The latter, however, were continually the losers. The Normans had more of the tact of war than the English; and their rewards were so abundant that their armies, however despoiled, were quickly repaired by the new swarms that joined the Conqueror from his continental territory. The English were chased from one asylum to another; and so unsparing was their enemy, that more than ordinary opposition and treachery—if that could be called treachery which was exercised to preserve country and home—was followed almost by depopulation. This had been the case in the north, where some successes of the inhabitants had been revenged by such cruelties, that the wasting of the country is represented by the old chroniclers as extending to every living thing, from man to beast.[1]

At length the power of the Normans began to predominate so greatly that the event of the contest became daily more manifest. The Saxon cowered down in despair,—sometimes selling himself and family to perpetual slavery for a meal,[2]—or flew to the highways and the woods and turned robber, consoling himself that he did but retake his own.[3]

In two or three spots, however, fugitives still survived. Those who had been lucky enough to foresee somewhat of the

(1) Thierry. "Ab homine usque ad pecus periit."—*Alured Beverley.*
(2) Roger de Hovedon. (3) Thierry.

events that followed, or had eluded the separate columns in which the Normans marched to devastate the country, had fled, some to the mountains, some to the forests, but the most considerable and formidable number had taken shelter in the impassable marshes of the eastern coast—in the Isle of Ely and the Fens. Here many became robbers and pirates, and were accused in the king's proclamation of violating the public peace and morals by following an infamous profession.[1]

Historians are not agreed upon the precise date at which the Isle of Ely became properly a Camp of Refuge. Some, indeed, comprise in its history the whole period from the invasion, in 1066, to the final subjection of the kingdom, seven years afterwards; while others include in the year 1071 the whole of the political transactions which made this spot, at that time, the last hope of England. Both are, perhaps, somewhat right. There is no doubt that, from the very beginning of William's warfare in the country, the marshes and the Isle of Ely had been sought as a refuge; but it was only after the unexampled fury which had been exercised in the northern counties, and which almost persuaded the nation they had got an inveterate enemy of the human race for a ruler, instead of a human being, that the Isle became the general rallying spot of bishops, abbots, earls, chiefs deprived of their inheritances,[2] and the noblest of the disaffected in the country,—that is, the noblest of the Saxon race.

Such a spot was, indeed, well suited to defend them. The force of the Normans consisted in cavalry and heavy-armed foot; that of the Saxons of foot-soldiers only. It was on their cavalry that the Normans chiefly relied, either to waste a country and hunt down its inhabitants, or to charge in battle; and, by their rapid and masterly evolutions, they, in every instance, prevailed against a people armed even with the almost invincible weapons of despair. But, in these marshes, though they might succeed in entering by the few passes that led into them, such forces could be of no avail.

(1) Thierry, v. i., p. 390. (2) Ingulf.

The Saxons had here the same advantage that the Guerilla has in his mountains. While they traversed the meres and rivers in small vessels, or ferried in flat-bottomed boats the overflowed shallows, the Normans dare not set foot on the treacherous soil. The refugees could communicate in every direction without being waylaid, and as they strengthened in numbers they commenced a harassing warfare by land and sea, which the Normans called piracy and robbery.[1]

In the former part of William's invasion, the church had shown less resentment to him than any other part of the state, for it had been generally respected; and, while all others were plundered, it was spared. But this spoil had only been reserved; and, having seized most other possessions in the kingdom, the Conqueror now began to lay his hands on the property of the church. The resentment of the ecclesiastics was thus as confirmed as the rest of the Saxon population.

Among the distinguished personages who now successively quitted their lofty stations, or were rudely expelled from them, and sought the Fens for protection, were Egelric bishop of Lindisfarne; Sithric, the head of a rich convent in Devonshire; Frithric, the abbot of St. Albans; Stigand, the deposed archbishop of Canterbury; Egelwin, bishop of Durham; and Earls Edwin and Morcar, brothers-in-law of Harold, and who were so celebrated in the history of these times. These distinguished personages, by adding greatly to the confidence of the Saxons, were so much the more disagreeable to the Normans, who reproached them with uniting themselves to a set of land and water robbers, and degrading the holy church by an infamous example.[2] Some of the insurgent ecclesiastics had, indeed, always held the Normans cheaply. It was Frithric who felled the wood on the lands of his abbey, and laid it across the way William had to pass in proceeding to London after the battle of Hastings, and who so intrepidly told him that he had but done his duty, in

(1) Piratæ maris et latrones regionis.—*Monasticon Anglicanum.*
(2) William of Malmesbury.

thus preventing, as far as he could, the entrance into the country of an enemy to the Saxon race.[1] It was, however, the last and most serious aggression on the Saxons—the falsifying their Scriptures, which Lanfranc had done,[2] and the violating their relics and shrines—which caused Frithric to desert his convent and seek the Camp of Refuge. William, indeed, had promised reparation for this and other injuries, and swore on the relics of St. Alban to observe the ancient Saxon laws;[3] but they were the promises and oaths of expediency. Persecution followed faster than reform, so that Frithric, assembling his monks in the chapel of his convent, and showing them the situation of their country, said:—"My brethren, my friends, the time has come when, as Scripture saith, we must fly from our persecutors and wander from city to city."[4] With this farewell, he departed to end his days in the Isle of Ely.[5]

William now seriously set about dislodging this formidable conspiracy: but first he tried artful measures. They had succeeded so well in several former instances, that he hoped to allure these refugees into a snare, and thus destroy them without hazard. Earls Morcar and Edwin, the favorites and the hopes of the Saxon race, were, for that reason, peculiarly hateful to him; and, although the Conqueror had betrayed them twice before, Morcar was again duped into confidence. He was induced by promises to quit Ely and repair to William; but, as soon as he was out of the defences of the Isle, he was seized, ironed, and put in a fortress, where he endured perpetual imprisonment. This treachery fully persuaded the camp at Ely what they were to expect, and they prepared themselves accordingly. Earl Edwin, indeed, quitted the Isle to seek assistance and set his brother free; but he was basely betrayed, and died fighting against superior numbers.[6] He left a sister, named Lucy, behind him; whom, in order to give a seeming title to the confiscated estates of the brothers, William gave in marriage to his nephew, Ivo

(1) Speed's Chron., p. 417. (2) Thierry. (3) Speed's Chron., p. 418.
(4) M. Paris. (5) Speed—Thierry. (6) Oderic Vitalis.—Thierry.

Tailbois,[1] a ruffian Anjouan, who made himself hated by all sort of cruelties and injuries. But a more important character was about to resent his oppressions. and become the defender of the Saxon.

Lord Hereward was the son of Leofric, Lord of Brunne, (Bourn), in Lincolnshire. He was tall and handsome; but, from his youth he had displayed such ungovernable passions, that his hand was raised against every one, and every one's hand against him. Unless he triumphed in his wrestling and other sports with the youth of his age, he would draw his sword and extort a confession of his superiority; and even to his parents his conduct was so fierce and disobedient that, upon the representations of his father Leofric, King Edward had sentenced him to banishment.[2]

Hereward left his home, and visited various parts of England, and afterwards crossed the sea to Flanders, where his dominant disposition, which had now ripened into bravery, made him a celebrated man.[3] He was in Flanders when the events which caused so many to take refuge in the Isle of Ely, were enacted. There he learnt from English emigrants, who had fled thither to avoid the calamities of their country, that his father was dead,—that his fortune had, like so many others, been confiscated by the Norman, and bestowed on Ivo Tailbois,[4]— and that his mother had been driven away from her home and was suffering in poverty. This news, so well calculated to awaken the spirit of a meaner man, decided Hereward at once to return home and seek the redress of a warrior. There he arrived secretly; and gathering about him a company of former friends and relations, he at once proceeded to dispossess the Normans who occupied his birthright. This he seems to have accomplished without difficulty; but the foreigner had already gained so much strength in the country that Hereward found he should not complete his work till he had made himself feared by the counts,

(1) Monas. Angli., p. 306.
(2) Turner's Anglo-Saxons, v. ii., p. 140.—Dugdale, p. 188.
(3) Turner. (4) Bentham's Ely.—Gunton's Peterborough, p. 262.

barons, and governors who either held lands or were placed over the towns and fortresses in his vicinity. In this object he also succeeded by carrying on a warfare of attacks and surprises which harassed when it did not weaken the enemy. These were conducted with such skill and success that he soon found himself, not only master of his own territories, but gradually gaining reputation among the Saxons as the last and most successful of their champions.[1]

It cannot be supposed that Hereward, practising such successful skirmishes in the vicinity of the Camp of Refuge, and in the same cause, could long remain unknown to those warriors. They heard of his exploits, and anxious to secure the advantage of such a leader, sent a request that he would join them at Ely. Hereward complied, taking with him all his companions: having first, as an indispensable part of a commander, been made a knight according to the forms of Saxon warriorship.

The Norman soldiers had now long been posted at all the usual outlets of the Isle, especially to the east and west, which, by way of Aldreth and Soham, were the principal causeys into the Fens. But this force, intended to intercept all provisions and resources, had been unable to prevent either. William, therefore, resolved to attempt a passage into the Isle, and take it, like a castle, by assault. For this purpose he assembled his whole army at Aldrede, and causing wood, stone, faggots, and trees to be brought, he ordered them to be "fastened together underneath with cow-hides."[2] They appear to have intended this as a raft; and, in order to make it more buoyant, they attached to it the skins of beasts "filled with wind like bladders."[3] The king, to incite his followers onward, promised the first who should enter and do some harm to the defenders should have whatever he demanded "of any man's therein."[4] But, trusting too much to the ricketty construction they had put together, and pressing on it in great numbers, "being greedy of the gold and silver," says Dugdale, "whereof they supposed store to be in

(1) Thierry. (2) Dugdale, p. 186. (3) Ibid. (4) Ibid.

the Isle, many of the foremost were drowned, their bridge sunk, and those in the midst became swallowed up in the depth of the fen; but of those that were hindmost, a few, throwing away their weapons, made shift by the mud to escape;"[1] but only one man got into the Isle alive.

William retired in disappointment from the assault, and seemed inclined to treat for peace; but his followers, who expected more from battle than from compromise, dissuaded him; and, while he hung in doubt whether to come to treaty or endeavour to penetrate the fen, Ivo Tailbois, either more superstitious than the rest, or a better master of the character and prejudices of the times, proposed the aid of a witch,[2] who, by her diabolical skill, would soon, he said, destroy the strength of the Isle. Any art that will drive out the cowards from their island, said the courtiers, ought to be employed and rewarded. William seems to have listened to this advice, though with some shame, as he had the old woman "privately sent for, that it might not be talked about."[3] He now re-assembled his scattered army, and besetting all corners of the Fens, raised new fortifications, and, enforcing strictest guard, prepared once more to reduce this stubborn corner to subjection.

Having gathered a quantity of materials together for making causeys over the Fens, he engaged a great number of fishermen, who, by their manner of life, were best adapted to aid him. Assembling them at Cotinglade, he caused them to transport his materials, and "raise hills and heaps on this side Aldrey, whereon to fight." Hereward did not let these works proceed unmolested. Coloring his head and beard red, and otherwise disguising himself, he took a boat, and personating one of the fishermen, appeared as earnest as the rest, "using all show of diligence;" but, before evening, he had managed to fire the materials which were brought, destroy the forts they had erected, and committing other depredations, "killing and drowning divers," he secured his escape.[4]

(1) Hist. Emb. (2) Dugdale—Thierry—Bentham. (3) Dugdale. (4) Ibid.

These discomfitures incensed the Conqueror: he caused strictest watch to be kept by day and by night; and, on the western side of the Isle, raised a causey three thousand paces long over the meres, and covered with flags and rushes,[1] and mounds on which were placed warlike engines. While this work was proceeding, the powers of the sorceress were called in to intercept with her spells the interruptions of the Saxon. She was placed, in great state, on a high wooden tower at the head of the work.[2] Here, by aid of speeches and spells, she hoped to appropriate to herself the diabolical power by which it was supposed the Saxons had so long triumphed. As, however, she was beginning her third spell, Hereward and his followers, at a favorable opportunity, set fire to the reed growing all around the works; which, "by help of the wind, spread itself no less than two furlongs, and making a horrible noise of crackling among the willows and such like vegetables, did so affright the assailants, that they hasted away as fast as they could; but, being troubled with the smoke, could not tell which way to betake themselves."[3]

The witch was killed among the rest; and the king, says Dugdale, narrowly escaped. An arrow penetrated his target, and he retreated to his tent in no very satisfied mood, telling his courtiers he was only wounded by their evil counsels in persuading him to put trust in a deceiving sorceress.

The celebrity of these and other exploits kept circulating through the country; and, notwithstanding the vigilance of the Normans, Saxons from all parts still continued to resort to the Camp. But in those times of insecurity, agricultural operations were only inadequately performed, and in some parts had ceased altogether. A scarcity of provisions had, in consequence, begun to manifest itself; and the monks, alarmed at the increasing calls upon their stores, began to wish they were rid of the intruders, even though submission to the Conqueror should be the consequence.[4] This feeling was not diminished when the king, incensed at the loss of men he had sustained to no purpose, had resolved on confis-

(1) Thierry. (2) Ibid. (3) Dugdale, p. 190. (4) Bentham.

cating all the possessions of the abbey which lay without the Isle, as a donative and fief to his soldiers. The monks, accordingly, consulted privately together, and it was determined to yield up the Isle, as far as they were able, to William, provided he restored the church all its possessions, and left them unmolested in their offices. But they had to go subtilely to work to effect this. The Camp was thronged with warriors whose spirits were raised by their success; and Hereward—himself a host—it were fruitless to attempt to entice to base purposes. They endeavored at first to corrupt the soldiery, but these men, attached to their masters, or perhaps more ardently to the cause, gave no ear to the counsel.[1] The Abbot, therefore, and a few monks departed secretly from Ely, and coming before the king at Warwick, tendered their obedience, and promised to be faithful in future. The offer was accepted; and two Norman chiefs, Guilbert de Clare and Guillaume de Garenne, became pledges for the monks.[2] The Abbot, in a private audience, gave William every information on the state of the Isle, and the best means of bringing it into subjection, promising all his aid to effect the work. This treachery had well-nigh met its reward. Hereward heard of the proceedings of the monks with all the indignation of a brave man; and, on the first impulse of his passion, resolved to fire the church and town;[3] but, at the earnest entreaty of one of the monks, who had some control over him, he desisted. The king, in the mean time, had again encamped at his old situation at Aldrey, and gave orders for perfecting the causeys, forts, and engines, that had been destroyed in former attempts. The preliminary labor was exceedingly great; for they were obliged to traverse moors, and bogs, and shallow waters overgrown with reeds and sedge, which intercepted the view, and occasioned their work to be often endangered with deep pools and quagmires.[4]

The summer passed away before the defences were completed, and William had to bear a winter campaign, when

(1) Bentham. (2) Thierry. (3) Dugdale. (4) Bentham.

"the inclemency of the weather added much to the hardships of the soldiers, and tempted them to frequent mutinies and desertions." The causey, however, was at length completed; and the army marched onward, but found difficulties from some deep waters which lay between them and the firm land. Boats were now to be fetched from a distance and dragged through the Fens, in order to carry the soldiers on a floating bridge. The Islanders were not unprepared to dispute the passage, having thrown up a strong intrenchment, and annoying them from a distance with "a variety of missive weapons and stones."[1] At length the military genius of the king prevailed, and the Isle surrendered at discretion.

In this conflict a thousand Saxons were slain;[2] but Hereward still retained his independence; and, yielding only at extremities, retired to those parts of the fen where the enemy found it dangerous to follow him.[3] He gained some ships, which he had placed on the seaward side of the Isle to guard it, and sailed into "a large and spacious meer, called Wide, not far from Welle, in regard there were free passages out of it."[4] Here he stayed awhile, and, with his soldiers, pillaged the country of which the Norman had possessed himself.

But the king gaining ground every day, he was soon obliged to quit his retreat; and, at last, driven to greater extremities, he had to part with his horse, and lest he should fall into the hands of the enemy, "and some mean fellow should boast that he had taken him," he killed him and went towards the northern part of the country.[5]

Driven thus from post to post, there was little further hope for either him or his cause. He resolved, however, though nearly single-handed, to exert the remains of his power against the Norman usurpation. Deprived of the command of an army, he once more found himself the outlaw, whose only care was his own life, and this he little valued unless he could make it tormenting to the foe. His daring now displayed itself in a more vigorous and desperate manner, and

(1) Bentham. (2) Stow.—Speed says "a thousand of the common sort."—*Chron.*
(3) Thierry. (4) Dugdale. (5) Ibid.

sometimes he encountered peril so close at hand as to seem almost fool-hardy. The sagacious captain—as the continuator of Ingulphus calls him—would almost have earned his name for bravery and patriotism after every other sword had submitted to the conqueror. One other anecdote of these exploits will serve to mark the character of them. He had quitted the Isle, and had arrived in the low lands of Lincolnshire—the scene of his first adventures. In his neighbourhood was a Norman fort, which was daily supplied by some Saxon fishermen with the produce of their nets. Getting into company with these countrymen, and perhaps disclosing to them in confidence who he was, he persuaded them to conceal himself and a few companions in their boats, and proceed to the fort as usual. The fishermen covered their guests with straw, and carried their fish to the fort, where the chief and his soldiers received the food, prepared their repast, and went to partake of it in their tents. When they were all occupied with their meal, Hereward and his followers started up at a signal, and the unsuspicious Normans, taken unawares, were almost entirely slaughtered, with little resistance.[1] "This *coup de main*," says Thierry, "was not the last exploit of the great captain of the English guerillas: he visited several other places with his band recruited afresh, and, wherever he went, laid similar ambushes for the foreign soldiers—unwilling, says a writer of that day, that his countrymen should be unavenged."[2]

He afterwards was constrained to submit; but whether by treaty or in consequence of some sort of reverence which William professed for bravery, he was not only spared indignities, but permitted to enjoy his inheritance. His character may be gathered from these exploits, to which one chronicler adds that "he was not cruel to his enemies"—a virtue the more noble since it was so rare in that age of cruelties.

The Saxons were long in forgetting the struggles of the Isle of Ely; which was not only one of the most formidable conspiracies against the government of William, from the

(1) Thierry (2) His. Norm. Conq., v. ii., p. 59.

strength of the country and the high characters engaged in it, but it was the last stand that, for any length of time, was made against the Norman power. The adventures of Hereward were favorite tales with the people; and the remains of a wooden fort, called Hereward's castle,[1] and entrenchments of turf and grass, for many years afterwards were held as holy spots where the liberty of England was last contested and lost.

In order to preserve so dangerous a tract from the like rebellion in future, William erected various strongholds in the dangerous and prominent parts of the Fens. The most celebrated and durable of these edifices was a castle at Wisbech, which was three times rebuilt in different styles, and only finally demolished in 1816, about seven centuries and a half after its first erection.[2]

The monks at Ely met with a proper reward for their base conduct. On pretence of guarding the Isle, William sent forty men-at-arms to the convent, whom he obliged the monks to support with a certain quantity of money and provisions, which were every morning distributed by the cellarist in the chapter-house.[3] Fearing this was only the preliminary to greater exactions, the monks offered seven hundred marks to be reinstated in the king's favor, and hold on their possessions;[4] and the money was paid to the royal viscount at Cambridge.[5] The viscount, considering their bad repute

(1) M. Paris.

(2) "Castellum in loco qui Wisseberum dicitur, a fundamentis ererit."—*M. Paris.* "He built the castle at Wisbech, against which they in the Isle raised another of timber and turffes, and called according to the name of their captain Hereward."—*Speed's Chron.*, p. 419.

(3) Thierry.

(4) "To be freed of the incumbrance of the forty men-at-arms," says Thierry; but this careful historian seems to have erred in this instance, as almost all others concur in representing the monks as well pleased with their soldiers, and the thousand marks as being a peace-offering between the king and the monks. Some represent the thousand marks as having been offered at Warwick, when the Abbot and monks first made overtures to the Conqueror. Indeed, there is strange confusion in the dates and sequence of these transactions; and the length of the siege is variously comprised in one year and seven.

(5) "Howsoever the monks of Ely kept their promise with William for betraying the Isle, he, contrariwise, brake his for their preservation and peace; for by no means their prayers would enter his ears till the sound of seven hundred marks had opened the way."—*Speed's Chron.*,—p. 419.

with the king, knew any tyranny he might exercise would rather be approved than censured by his master; so he commanded the silver to be carefully weighed, and finding a drachm deficient,[1] he accused the monks of fraud against the king, and procured a fine of three hundred marks more to be levied for the offence.[1] The money had been gathered together with great difficulty; valuable and necessary articles—crosses, altars, shrines, chalices, patens, cups, gold and silver dishes, a rich image of the virgin,—the ornaments of their church had been sold;[3] but they sacrificed willingly, as they expected to hold more permanent possessions in return. But not satisfied with this sum, William sent a commission down to the monastery, who appropriated all the remaining valuables,[4] and surveyed the lands of the abbey, in order to divide them into fiefs.[5] These accumulated misfortunes reduced the monks to despair; but they excited no sympathy—they had been their own betrayers, and their church, as they said, "once fairest among the daughters of Jerusalem, now oppressed and degraded," was allowed for a long time to suffer on.[6]

The Isle became, in subsequent reigns, an asylum for the oppressed or rebellious; but it never again rose into the importance which the establishment of the Camp of Refuge gave it: and though it was several times besieged, the events are not important enough to supersede the history of the Drainage, from which the rapid incidents we have sketched have already perhaps too long delayed us.

(1) Speed says "a groat."—*Chron.*, p. 419.
(2) Stow.—Speed says "a thousand more."
(3) Stephenson's Continuation of Bentham, p. 57.—Speed, p. 419.
(4) "Quidquid optimum in ornamentis et in aliis rebus."—*Anglia Sacra.*
(5) Thierry. (6) Ibid, v. ii., p. 67.

CHAPTER III.

HISTORY OF THE DRAINAGE.

THE Charta of King Wolfere to the Abbey of Peterborough, which bears date 664, makes the first mention of the Fens. In setting out the bounds of the property with which he endowed the abbey, Wolfere says: "Directly through the main Fen to Esendic, and from Esendic to the place which they eall Fethermute; thence to Cuggedic, ten miles distant; thence to Raggewilc, five miles, to the principal stream which goeth to Elme and Wisebeche: thence for the space of three miles up the said principal stream to Trockenholt; thence winding through the immense fen to Dereford, in length twenty miles; and from thence to Gatecross, by a beautiful water named Bardanea, six miles to Paccalade. Then through the middle of many stagnant waters and immense marshes to Huntingdonshire."[1] There are no signs of drainage or cultivation in the language of this bequest; which, so far as we can interpret its dead names, appears to embrace much of the Fens now included in the North and Middle Levels. If we had no other inference, we might suppose that such an extensive tract, in the single gift of a king, could not be in a cultivated state; as the cultivated or cultivable parts of the country were too valuable to be given up in such wholesale proportions, when kings were numerous and their territories small. The possessions of monasteries at

(1) Monasticon Anglicanum, p. 64.

such early periods were generally confined; it was only with their age and their success that these establishments became rich. King Wolfere's fens were probably unproductive in everything except fish and wild fowl; and he endeavored in the extent of his donation to make up for its barrenness. This is the earliest charta relating to Fen monasteries, and it is singular that Wisbech and Elm are mentioned in it—giving these places the earliest date of any place at present inhabited in the Fens.

It appears, however, evident, from other authority, that parts at least of the Fens had been drained during the Saxon era. Turketyl, an officer of King Edred, who had renounced the sword for the pastoral staff, and, having become abbot of the ruin which the Danes left behind them at Crowland, set about repairing the edifice and increasing the value of its landed property. His successors followed in his steps. Ingulphus, speaking of Egelric, says: "In dry years he tilled the Fens in four places, at the four corners of them, and for three or four years had the increase of an hundred fold of what seed soever he sowed. Amongst which that fen at Tadwarthar was the most fruitful; the monastery being so much enriched by these plentiful crops, that the whole country thereabouts was supplied therewith."[1] Yet Crowland was always represented by the old writers as one of the most dismal parts of the Fens; and William of Malmesbury, speaking of it about one hundred and fifty years afterwards, says that there was no access to the monastery without boats, there being no path further than to the gate of the abbey. These accounts can only be reconciled by believing that the fens which Abbot Egelric cultivated were only a small quantity of the higher parts; for it is evident, from the mention of "four places," that there was no common cultivation. The land was probably at some distance from the monastery, and perhaps on the borders of the high country where, as appears from the charta, much of the estate of the abbey was situate.

(1) Hist. Emb. p 210.

If, therefore, any draining was effected by Egelric, it was only of that partial kind, which, in the more elevated lands, had, perhaps, always been practised by the church.

But, it appears that not only parts of the Crowland estates were, at an early period, converted into ploughed land, but that the adjacent parts of Holland, bordering the north side of Crowland, were, as early as the reign of Henry II., under some kind of drainage. Dugdale, on the authority of a manuscript history of Crowland, mentions that the inhabitants of Holland "had drained their marshes and converted them to good and fertile arable land, whereof each town had their proper portion." From this it would seem that a drainage had been, at any rate, partly effected; and that a tax, or perhaps sort of service from different towns, had been the means of its completion; and that the rescued lands were shared between these towns and the great proprietors of the soil. Dugdale goes on to say that this conversion of marsh into arable land had produced a deficiency of pasture. We may, therefore, infer that the lands so gained were not very swampy, but had, before drainage, been summer lands, and, as such, used for pasturing cattle, and perhaps for gathering hay. There appears to have been some dispute between these proprietors of the drained lands and the monks of Crowland, whose fen pastures lay annexed them. We are not told the particulars of this dispute; but, "bearing themselves not a little on their strength and wealth," and taking advantage of the death of Henry II., some of the opulent proprietors seized upon the neighbouring pastures of the "poor monks of Crowland," having ploughed up so much of their land that they had not enough left to pasture their cattle.

In order more effectually to prosecute their purpose, they combined against the monastery, with the Prior of Spalding, and met in the recreant prior's barn, and sometimes in the church at Holbeach, and there, it appears, concerted a regular plan to seize and appropriate the pastures. It was the habit of the abbot to "keep up his marshes"[1] about Rogation

(1) We suppose this expresses the same idea as "laying land down" at present.

week; and for that purpose he caused proclamation to be made on the bridge at Spalding, that the men of Holland and others should keep their cattle from the meadows. This mandate was the signal for the conspirators to make their seizure; and, instead of obeying the proclamation, they drove in more cattle than usual. On this, the servants of the abbey impounded the cattle; but the conspirators, gathering strength to the number of three thousand, entered the marsh armed as it had been to battle. The abbot met them at a place called Asendic—the bounds of Crowland Fen—and would have made peace with them, for he feared they meant to destroy the abbey. But they refused compromise, "answered him scornfully, and passing through the midst of the fen, shared it amongst themselves, according to the situation of their towns: and, having so done, pitched tents, and made huts on every side the abbey, wherein they placed guards of armed men, to keep each part thereof; and, likewise, digged turf, cut down a great part of the wood and aldergroves of Crowland, and burnt them; depastured their meadows, and carried away the hay, with divers other violence, by the space of fifteen days."[1] The abbot, thus beset, made his complaint to the king's justices, who sent force to his relief, and summoned the ringleaders before them. The result was a five years' suit, in which the abbot prevailed, and some of the offenders, we are told, were imprisoned for the offence at Northampton and Rockingham.[2]

This outbreak gives us a little insight into the rights of property, and manner of holding it in the Fens at this early period. The right of pasture and the right of gathering hay were, apparently, distinct; for, while the abbot of Crowland appears, by the above controversy, to have had the latter privilege exclusively, the right of pasturage was enjoyed in common.

Ingulphus notices that Richard de Rullos, chamberlain to William the Conqueror, who, by marriage, became Lord of Deeping, enlarged his town by diverting the waters of the

(1) Dugdale, p. 211. (2) Ibid

Welland; "and in the meadows, which before were deep lakes and drowned fens, by excluding the river he made them fruitful fields, and as good ground as could be wished: nay, the very pits and bogs he thereby made a garden of pleasure.[1]"

We may infer, from these and other facts, that a partial system of drainage had been commenced by the more opulent proprietors of the church: but how was it affected? Was it by main drains and tributaries,—or by such tributaries as were merely convenient for the estate of the proprietor who undertook? We think that the latter system would be the first resorted to; for, in such early efforts, only that land which required the least labor and contrivance to effect its drainage, would be undertaken. A system of drainage would have required too much combination for ages like these; and we have already learnt, by the detail of the operations of the Camp of Refuge, that the Isle of Ely had never experienced any general amelioration at the Norman conquest. Indeed, the earliest account we receive of any drainage, that seems supported by law or public control, is in the reign of Henry III., when, for the first time, we meet with accounts of parties who came before courts to dispute upon their liabilities to repair and uphold certain drains and sewers. But we are sure that the Fens must, before this, have been intersected with canals and drains. Had we no other evidence, this would be certain from the following passage from Matthew Paris: "In the year 1256 William, Bishop of Ely, and Hugh, Abbot of Ramsey, came to an agreement upon a controversy betwixt them, touching the bounds of their fens; whereof in these our times a wonder happened; for whereas, as anciently, time out of mind, they were neither accessible for man or beast, affording only deep mud, with sedge and reeds; and possest by birds; (yea much more by devils, as appeareth in the life of St. Guthlac, who, finding it a place of horror and great solitude, began to inhabit there,)

(1) Hist. Crowland.

is now changed into delightful meadows and arable ground; and what, therefore, doth not produce corn or hay, doth bring forth sedge, turf, and other fuel, very useful to the borderers, which occasioned much dispute and contention betwixt them that were the most ancient inhabitants in those parts, nay, quarrels and fighting, touching the bounds of such fruitful lands."[1] It is difficult to infer from this passage whether the alteration he so much applauds had been completed in his own life-time, or whether he drew his notions of the ancient Fens from ancient writings. The mention made of St. Guthlac would almost persuade us that the latter is the case; and yet, had the Fens been drained long before, and been made fit for arable cultivation, how is it that he says, " in these our times a wonder happened "?[2] The particular mention also of the borderers and the most ancient inhabitants, would lead us to believe the change had been effected almost in the lifetime of the writer.

Previously, therefore, to Henry III., we only blunder among conjectures and circumstances so imperfectly joined that they hardly produce a satisfactory idea. But, in that reign, the disputes which the regulations of drainage produce yield us an imperfect light on the subject. But before we go into these controversies, it will be proper that we adjourn ourselves to Romney Marsh in Kent—the parent fen from whence emanated the ordinances which were afterwards held law in matters of drainage dispute.

Romney Marsh, like the marshes of the eastern fens, had been embanked by the Romans;[3] and from that time to the reign of Henry III., its history is almost unknown. It appears, however, that previous to our first hearing of the proceedings in 1250, towards the draining of this marsh, that like our Fens it had been put under a sort of drainage or supervision, which was entrusted to twenty-four jurats chosen by the commonalty of the marsh.[4] These had "the

(1) Annals, M. Paris—Dugdale, p. 358.
(2) De quo marisco hoc mirum nostris accidit temporibus.
(3) Dugdale, p. 16. (4) Ibid, p. 29.

conservation of the marsh and sea-banks,"[1] and levied sums and distresses upon those properties, according to "ancient and approved customs, and the proportions more or less which each man had therein" for the repair of banks, and for the "safeguard and defence of all the country against the sea."[2] On this ancient custom, or common law, the subsequent statute laws of Romney Marsh appear to have been founded.

In the reign of Henry III., however,—and often before,—the invidious office of jurat had occasioned the resistance of the landowners to any distraint being made on their lands for the repair of banks, in which the sheriff had sided with the Marshmen, and had made replevin of the distresses levied by the jurats. In this dilemma the jurats appealed to the king, who reprimanded the sheriff and confirmed the distresses. The dispute, however, had got to such a head, that the jurats were unable to levy distress, and consequent neglect ensued; so that it was not till the sea broke through the embankments and overflowed the marsh, that the matter was again referred to the king, who sent Henry de Bathe—"a famous justice itinerant of the that time,"—to examine the state of the parties, and "to provide for the security and defence of the marsh."[3] A council of the commonalty of the marsh was accordingly called together; and, upon the judgment of "honest and lawful men of the bailiwick," six ordinances were agreed to, which became afterwards the standard regulations of all the marshes of England.[4]

(1) Dugdale, p. 17. (2) Ibid. (3) Ibid, p. 18.

(4) These ordinances were substantially:—I. That there should be twelve men chosen, in addition to the twenty-four jurats, who should measure the banks and lands liable to be flooded, set off portions along the banks portionate to the liable lands, which each proprietor was to keep in repair. II. The jurats on danger on breach of banks, to assemble and declare "to whom the defence of the same should be assigned, and within what time repaired." III. The bailiff of the marsh to give notice to liable parties, and if they neglected to repair within a specified time, the bailiff to repair them himself, and the liable party to pay the bailiff, by distraint or otherwise, double his expense. IV. In case land is held in partnership, and one partner neglects to repair his portion, the neglected portion to be repaired by the other partners, who are to hold his lands till double levy is paid as before. V. Should all the partners neglect, the bailiff to act as in ordinance III. VI. All the lands to be kept against the violence of the sea and the floods of fresh water, "as anciently had been accustomed."—*Dugdale*, p. 19.

These laws received, from time to time, various additions and confirmations, as circumstances required; and, in the reign of Henry VI., "having considered the great damage and losses which often happened by the excessive rising of waters in divers parts of the realm," an act was passed "to make and ordain necessary and convenable statutes and ordinances for the salvation and conservation of the sea-banks and marshes, and the parts adjoining, according to the laws and customs of Romney Marsh."[1]

What were the first methods pursued in order to drain the Fens of Cambridgeshire, is hopeless to attempt to ascertain. That they were almost without method, is most probable,—desultory efforts, according to the wealth or enterprise of the proprietor. There is one alteration, however, which we can trace in the Fens, which gives a little light even on this subject, though it only manifests the slovenly manner which marked the proceedings of early engineering—if that name be appropriate to such proceedings. It is well demonstrated that the two principal rivers of the Fens—the Ouse and the Nene—formely took courses to the sea very different from their present routes. Indeed, there was anciently only one great river that discharged the Fen waters into the wash—the Nene and Welland being merely tributaries to it; and this river, instead of making its way sideways to its outfall, as it does now by Lynn, proceeded to the direct and central outfall by Wisbech.[2]

(1) 6 Henry VI., c. 65.—It was not only ordered that all the low grounds between Thane, in Kent, and Pensey in Sussex, should be guided by the Romney Marsh laws, but they also now became a pattern and example to all the like places of the whole realme whereby to be governed."—*Lambard's Perambulations of Kent.*

(2) Dugdale, pp. 299, 175, Badeslade, pp. 6. 16, Elstobb, pp. 79, 83. Atkins's Report.—The arguments which have been adduced by Dugdale and others to prove that this was the case, are as conclusive as they can be. They are:—I. The sea-banks from Well to Wisbech, showing the existence, at some former period, of a large and important river in that direction. II. The passage in the Red Book of Thorney; which says that "Wisbech Castle is founded [situated] upon the banks of the famous river which is called Wellstream" ["super flumen illud famosum, quod Wellstream appellatur"]; and speaks further of a stream derived from marshes, springs, and rivers, which, by a long mouth, is discharged in the great sea, near Wisbech. III. The commission of 21 Edward I., whereby Marshland men, complainingof the injury which the altered course of the waters had done their province, it was ordered that

But, were all other evidence wanting, we might reasonably have suspected that Wisbech had at one time been the principal outfall of the Fens, from the conformation of its estuary. We find estuaries are mostly a measure of the waters they discharge; and the estuary of Wisbech, even at the present day, is broader than those of either Lynn or Fossdyke. It now presents a stumped appearance, in consequence of the inclosures which have been effected by the retiring of the waters.[1]

The original course of the Ouse seems to have been the same as at present, as far as Littleport, where a small portion of fen, of about two miles, only separated it from the Little Ouse or Brandon River, which fell by Lynn.[2] Instead of its present course, it ran nearly in the same direction as the Old Croft River; and at about six miles north-west of Littleport, it formed the division of the Isle and Marshland; passing by Welney, Upwell, Outwell, and Elm, nearly in the track of the present Canal, to Wisbech. The Nene entered the Fens by two branches; one tending northerly and passing by Crowland, the other taking its course through Whittlesey, Ramsey, and Ugg Meres, uniting with the Ouse at Upwell.

"the fresh waters should have their due and ancient course to the sea."—*Dugdale*, p. 246.—*Badeslade*, p. 6. IV. To these may be added the presentiment in the reign of Edward III., where is mentioned "the stream of the water called Wellenhee, which had wont to run towards the sea-bank of Walsokne." V. The testimony—as valuable as any—afforded by King Wolfere's charta to Peterborough, before alluded to, wherein he mentions "the principal water which runs to Elme and to Wisebeche" ["Magistram aquam quæ ducit ad Elme et ad Wisebeche."] There is also various evidence to testify that the waters of the Fens did not at first fall by Marshland, and that there was no water from Littleport Chair to Rebeck, which would wholly prevent all discharge by Lynn, except the waters derived from the small rivers of Stoke and Brandon.—See Dugdale, pp. 395-6.

(1) If the Wash is a submerged fen—as the existence of more, even under its marshes, seems to indicate—there could originally have been only one main channel for all the rivers that now seperately fall into it—the Witham, Welland, Nene, and Ouse. This main channel must have been the Ouse, and the rest of the rivers its tributaries, uniting with it perhaps nearly at the present points of discharge. The removing of the Wash only beyond Hunstanton Point would be sufficient to produce this condition in the outfall.

(2) "The Great Ouse which, in conjunction with the Nene, formerly discharged itself into the sea by Wisbech, after vainly endeavoring to force its waters again in that direction, became so circuitous, and approached the Little Ouse so nearly, and created such damage by its floods, that at last, in 1292, the inhabitants, in order to save themselves, cut through the narrow space which separated the latter from it at Littleport Chair, and thus uniting their waters they both proceeded to discharge themselves into the sea below Lynn."—*Sir John Rennie's Report*, 1840.

This alteration in the course of the Ouse was effected by merely cutting a drain about two miles and a half long, at Littleport Chair, where we have said the Great and Little Ouse approached each other to within that short distance; and thus diverting into the narrow channel of the Little Ouse—the drain of about one hundred and fifty thousand acres—the waters of the Great Ouse—which altogether drain nearly two millions of acres—and, thereby, forcing the latter from the central outfall at Wisbech to the lateral outfall at Lynn. There were still left the waters of the Nene and West Water for the outfall at Wisbech. But if there had been a tendency in that outfall to decay while all the waters of the Fens passed through it, it will not be marvelled at if, when the principal waters were taken from it, the poor remainder were found insufficient to wash back the deposit of the tides. It is generally allowed that this great mistake was the cause of most of the ensuing disasters which befel the Fens.[1] It is obviously a part of natural operations that rivers running through the same system of valleys should unite before falling into the sea: we see this in almost every river in the world, till sometimes, as in the Amazon or Oronoco, the channel that conveys the water at length into the sea, is the united flood of hundreds of tributaries. This system of combination is obviously the law which secures a deep and good outfall to rivers; for if those tributaries had each a separate mouth, the opposing currents of the ocean would soon, by causing them to deposit their sediment in their outfalls, dam them up, and arrest all free discharge. In the Amazon this law is so perfectly performed, that the fresh river-water drives the ocean-water before it for the space of nearly fifty miles out to sea. Yet, in the instance of these Fens, where the ocean level is frequently above the land, and where, consequently, this rule of combination was most required to keep the outfalls clear, this law was defied, and instead of increasing the combination of water, and producing a powerful seaward current, the stream that descended

(1) Dugdale, p. 299.—Badeslade, pp. 15, 16, 17.

through one mouth was frittered away into three, and thus the power of the sea encouraged to arrest the muddy stream and cause deposit, and the power of the rivers that should have encountered this opposition of the sea, was materially diminished, if not entirely neutralised. And yet the effect—the obstructions of outfall in consequence of this principal fault of the Fens—was wondered at and debated for several centuries.

The period at which this error was committed is unknown, except that it was previous to the year 1292; for in that year the inhabitants of Marshland procured a commission from Edward I. for taking into consideration what ought to be done for restoring the waters of Outwell—as they were called—to their ancient course.[1] The Little Ouse—that had only been used to carry off the poor stream that fell from a few hills in Norfolk—was now overloaded with the waters of almost all the Fens and the six counties beyond them. The channel of the river was found too narrow; the flood in consequence acted on the Marshland banks, and the waters, being thus impeded by an unfit outfall, fell back upon the upper parts of Marshland—while the sea, acting upon the lower banks, broke through and reduced those parts to the same extremity. When it is remembered that this was the alteration of a current of a river into the channel of another of the twelfth of its volume, without having made any preparation for the change, but left the old drains, lodes, gotes, and dikes, all as they were cut and built when they were intended to drain by Wisbech, the confusion of overriding and overflowing waters may be imagined. The complaints and presentments during the reigns of the three Edwards are indicative of this work of havoc over all the Fen; and in order to allay some of the evil, the Commission, which the men of Marshland had procured from Edward I., and which sat at Outwell, ordered that three dams should be made:—one at Outwell Bridge, another at Little Lode Bridge, and a third

(1) Dugdale, p. 300.—Badeslade, p. 6.

in Fendike Lane, both in Upwell.[1] The object of these dams was to prevent the waters of the Ouse, which descended to the sea by the West Water, and the waters of the Nene from Peterborough, which joined the West Water at Benwick, from falling to sea by Lynn, and to force them again into their old channel by Elm and Wisbech. By this means the track of country drained would, perhaps, have been pretty equally divided between the outfalls of Lynn and Wisbech. The Marshland-men, drowned by land floods and impoverished with embankment repairs, eagerly seized on the opportunity of driving the waters again by Wisbech, and before any order had been issued by the Sheriff, "or any Bailiff of the Hundred," made the dams at once. But now ensued certain difficulties. The outfall at Wisbech, partly by former neglects and partly by this diversion of the outfall, had become so thoroughly silted up that no stream could force its way through the sands. To this was added the interruption of navigation, passing by Upwell to Outwell, which the dams of course arrested. In this difficulty some boats broke one of the dams, forced a passage, and another commission was called.[2] For many years afterwards this state of things continued—complaints, presentments, and commissions following each other, but apparently without effect, though merchants, as they said, "were hindered from passing with their ships, boats, and other vessels," from Lynn to Yaxley, Holme, and other places, as they "had been wont to do."[3] At length, in the year 1329, the state of navigation and obstruction induced a serious investigation. There had lived at Coldham, some years previously, Walter de Langton, Bishop of Coventry and Lichfield, who, "by his power and greatness," says Dugdale, had made a dam at Outwell, with earth and sand, to drain his own land.[4] A presentment, twenty-eight years afterwards, was exhibited to the justices itinerant, complaining of the stoppage, and showing that in

(1) Badeslade's History of Lynn, p. 6.—Dugdale's History of Draining, p. 300.

(2) Dugdale, p. 300. (3) Ibid, p. 301.

(4) "By his power, say some, but I rather think by the appointment of those justices," (who had ordered the three dams at Outwell).—*Badeslade*.

consequence of this obstruction the lands, meadows, pastures, and marshes of Thorney and Borough Fens were overflowed to the damage of £300 per annum, and no navigable vessels could pass from Peterborough to Lynn, though corn, wool, and other commodities had previously been regularly conveyed by water to that haven, and victuals and other necessaries returned to Northamptonshire and Huntingdonshire.

This presentment led to a controversy of some duration, which may be termed the great fight between the parties who favored the old or new system of drainage, and was the question which decided whether the river of Wisbech or Lynn was to be the main drain and outfall of those Fens which were afterwards comprised into one system under the name of the Bedford Level. The importance of the question induced the parties to ratify it at a high tribunal. It was, therefore, agreed that the shireeves of Norfolk, Cambridgeshire, Huntingdonshire, Lincolnshire, and Northamptonshire, all of which counties were affected by the dam at Outwell, should each summon twelve "honest and lawful men, whereby the truth might be better known, to appear before the king."[1]

For some time nothing was effected. Whether by the tricks of interested parties, or other causes, the forms of the law were slighted, and no decision was come to on either side. Some of the shireeves summoned jurors, some did not, complaining for their neglect that they had not received their writs in time. The king, who seems to have been by some means interested in this business, and appears to have supported the party who were for continuing the dam, issued a precept for carrying the former process and inquisition to the Exchequer. The preamble stated that the men of Marshland had complained that a great part of their country was "lost and destroyed by the inundation of the salt waters, as also of the fresh, by reason that the said waters and sewers *had not their right course*, and that King Edward the First, passing that way, had taken notice thereof."[2] It went on to say that

(1) Dugdale, p. 302. (2) Ibid.

an inquest held upon the matter had decided that a dam at Outwell was the only way to preserve these parts; but that after the dam had been made, some persons, "for their own particular advantage," had represented that the obstruction "had been made to their damage." The king, therefore, wishing for the truth between these rival parties, now required that the proceedings of the former inquisition might be laid before him, and that every person concerned in the matter should be summoned by proclamation to appear to make complaint or to answer to it.

Writs were in consequence re-issued to the sheriffs who had failed to summon the twelve jurors, calling upon them to summon twenty-three instead of twelve; and, in the interim, the king dispatched his writ of certiorari to the Treasurer and Chamberlain of the Exchequer, commanding them to send him the inquisition which had been taken when the dam was adjudged necessary to be made. But the documents were not to be found: upon which the king ordered that the sheriffs of the interested counties should issue a proclamation that all who were concerned should attend the king upon a certain day—the 15th of Holy Trinity—and make their complaints and proposals. The sheriff of Norfolk returned, that he had made the proclamation, "and found no man gainsaying or finding fault with that dam, but that the said passage was as commodious as it had wont to be."

It is to be borne in mind that the Marshland or Norfolk party were the persons who first proposed and afterwards made the dam; for, although the heir of Walter de Langton is the person cited as the defendant in the case, yet this seems more for form's sake than any serious consideration that the dam was made for the sole benefit of Coldham Manor. The inhabitants of the opposite part of the Fen—Thorney, and the parts adjacent to Peterborough and Huntingdon—espoused the opposite side, and we shall soon see what arguments they produced for annihilating the obstruction.

In the meantime Edward Peverell, the proprietor of Coldham, died, and his wife, having succeeded to the estate, was summoned to answer to the complaint. But, on the day appointed, neither the defendant, nor the Marshland-men, nor the men of Cambridge, Norfolk, or Suffolk, made their appearance. Thus lightly were what are now considered important and primary duties in operation of the law then regarded. The inquisition was, however, afterwards taken.

In the complaint it was stated that "those men who had occasion to go with ships and other vessels, laden with goods and merchandise, from Holme, Yaxley, and other parts thereabouts, unto the port of Bishop's Lenne in Norfolk, as also such as had a mind to return directly from thence to Peterborough could not pass with their ships and vessels, as anciently before that stop was so made they had used to do; but were forced to go a long way about, viz., by Old Wellenhee, and Lyttleport, (which in going to and fro is fifty miles and more), whereby corn, timber, wool, reed, turf, stone, and other commodities, were the dearer; and so likewise were fish, herrings, and other victuals, by reason of that circuit, to the damage of the inhabitants of Norfolke £200 every year."[1] They also showed that the stop had been made in the king's soil, and it was the common passage for ships and boats, and a common fishing for all the neighbourhood. The complainants of Lincoln showed that the dam had materially damaged the lands about Crowland. The South Eau Dyke, running between the latter place and Tyd, through which the fresh waters descending from the fens and upper countries "used to pass unto the sea by raising the crest no more than two feet," was now scarcely able to carry the waters with a crest of fifteen feet; and that before the dam was made the agistment of every acre of land in those parts was only a halfpenny, it was now fourpence; and that eleven thousand acres of moor and marsh ground in Holland Fen were drowned.

They also represented that two thousand acres of meadow, moor, and fen, belonging to Crowland, were overflowed, "so

(1) Dugdale, p. 304.

that the possessions of the monastery would not suffice to maintain the house unless the number of monks were lessened, and that by means thereof *the king in times of vacancy did lose the benefit which might accrue to him thereby.*"[1] Other fens in the same parts were represented in the same miserable condition, and that the navigation, by being forced round by Littleport, damaged the king and his liege people of those parts a thousand marks yearly.

The jurors of Cambridge showed that all the lands betwixt Fen Drayton and Benwick and Outwell, being about thirty miles square, were yearly drowned since the obstruction had been made to the damage of £200 per year, while Coldham was represented to be worth £40 per year more by the alteration.

The jurors of Huntingdon showed that the fens of Mustcote and others, thirty miles long and ten broad, were overflowed; so that the lords of those fens and their tenants, as also the commoners in them, did totally lose benefits to the damage of six hundred marks a year.

The evidence of all these parties, which does not appear to have been met with counter statements of sufficient force to overset them, finally prevailed, and procured the condemnation of the dam, which was ordered to be pulled down forthwith. "They decreed that the dam, so raised to the hurt of the king, and nuisance of all the persons before mentioned, and whatever else was of nuisance in this behalf, should be taken away."[2] This was in the year 1331.

This decision may be considered one of the most important to the Fens of any that ever was brought to a court of fen legislators. It decided, as we have hinted, the future history of the Fens; for, by altering the ancient and natural course of the waters, diverting all the drains and sewers, and making Lynn the principal outlet to the waters, the old system of drainage had to be entirely renovated; and at the present day scarcely any of the old sewers remain which were prin-

(1) Dugdale, p. 304. (2) Ibid, p. 306.

cipal drains while the chief outfall was at Wisbech. It is true that the course of the river had been altered many years before the removal of this dam. But the violent departure from an established system had brought the usual disruption in its train, and the pitiful state of the country—alleviated in a partial manner for some time after the change—seems on the whole to have been reduced to a state even worse than its previous condition, when the Wisbech outfall was so impeded as to drive the waters back in the Fen, instead of allowing them to pass to sea. Marshland seems to have especially suffered by the change. We have good evidence of this from the decision of the inquisition at Outwell, in 1292, when the three dams were ordered to be made, in order to send a considerable body of the waters again to their old outfall at Wisbech; and it is very evident, that though this court came to this decision, the opposition of the country was so great against their verdict that the executive dare not put it in force. The bishop of Coventry did the work for them, and twenty-eight years afterwards, as we have seen, the dam was removed, and Lynn was triumphant.

This change of nature for art, and making three outfalls where one only was intended, may be considered the primary cause of most of the subsequent experiments and disappointments which Fen-drainage has produced. It was the original cause of that disastrous state of the Fen which preceded the undertaking of the Adventurers and the Bedford Level Corporation. To the present day this mistake has been only partially removed; the first evil remains, and must certainly remain, till some great system is adopted that shall blend the three outfalls of Lynn, Wisbech, and Spalding, into one.[1]

We find, by the foregoing inquisition, that Lynn had become a port and granary for the Fens, and that one of the principal objections to the dam at Outwell was the stoppage

(1) There are indeed four outfalls to the four rivers—Lynn, Wisbech, Spalding, and Boston; and it was one of the rational schemes of Kinderley, to relieve the drainage by reducing these four outfalls to two—carrying the Wisbech river to Lynn outfall, and the Spalding river to Boston.

it caused to the vessels which supplied not only the Fens, but Peterborough, and the internal counties. We also find that the Fens about Crowland, Deeping, Burgh, Spalding, Fen Drayton, Benwick, and the Fens of Huntingdon and Northampton, were all represented as more or less drowned, by reason of the dam; while Coldham, which lies in as low a part of the Fen as any of these places, was represented as of increased value, to the amount of £40 by the year. This is not very clear; especially as, under the constitution of things created by the dam, all the waters of these Fens must have passed by Coldham. Coldham, indeed, was protected by embankment; but, in that case, we can hardly see how it could have been £40 a year more valuable by reason of the upland waters running northwards of it to Wisbech, instead of southwards to Lynn.

Marshland seems soon again to have felt the effects of the change; for, two years afterwards, we find Walsoken, Emneth, and West Walton, petitioning the king for an alleviation of his subsidy of a fifteenth, in consequence of their losses from overflowed lands and tempests during the winter. They succeeded in obtaining a remission of £8 out of £60.[1] The following year was not more propitious. "In the winter of this year, [1334] the sea was so outrageous, that it brake the banks in sundry places, drowned many cattle, and spoiled a great quantity of corn."[2]

So serious, indeed, were the calamities of this year to Marshland, that there was an inquisition held upon the state of the country, at which the following facts were elicited:—Tilney was overflowed with sea water for the space of seven days, by which the sown corn, and the winter corn and hay, and "a hundred muttons, and sixty ewes, to the damage of £300, were destroyed. The charge in repair and maintenance of one mile of bank, from Clenchwarton to Wigenhall, was eightpence per perch. Within the compass of sixty years past one parish church with the parsonage, a manor-

(1) Dugdale, p. 255. (2) Ibid.

house, twenty messuages, and a hundred acres of land were utterly lost."

Walpole had received the same kind of visitation; for, within thirty years then last past, they lost for ever one parish church, twenty messuages, and three hundred acres of land. Three hundred acres, sown with winter corn, were also represented as being drowned, in consequence of the waters being diverted to sea by Lynn. The damage to every acre is estimated at forty pence, and in the following years twelve pence per acre from the same cause.

West Walton and Walsoken suffered in a similar manner from this storm. We have the same record of broken banks, and their yearly and particular cost, as in the other instances, and the overflowing of the waters. Only eighty acres were lost "by the raging of the sea" in Walton, but the parish had been subject to disasters of this kind; for at the same time it is recorded that in 1327 seven messuages and one hundred and forty acres and a half—in 1316 thirteen messuages and one hundred and sixty acres—and in 1308 twelve messuages and one hundred and twenty acres—were all lost.[1] In gutters, pipes, sewers, and bridges, they spent £40 yearly, of which three drains, "one towards the sea and two towards the fen," cost twenty shillings.

The representation of these various disasters had a proper effect upon the king, who having received a parliamentary subsidy of a tenth and a fifteenth, the towns we have enumerated set forth the details of their situation, "by which they represented their extraordinary losses by the before-specified inundations; desiring that the assessment might not extend to any other of their goods and chattels than what they had remaining after these their disasters:" the king, tenderly commiserating their condition, made a considerable remission of their taxes.[2]

(1) Dugdale, p. 256.

(2) "Tilney was taxed at £10; Walpole at £16 8*s.*; Walsokne at £12; West Walton, with the hamlet, at £16 2*s.*; Wigenhall at £13 4*s.*; and Terrington at £16 9*s.* 6*d.*"—*Dugdale*, p. 257.

Marshland was not yet reconciled to the changed route of the waters. The destruction of the dam at Outwell had poured almost the whole contents of the fen-floods into the small and narrow channel, six perches wide, which bounded the eastern side of that district. The broken banks, and flooded lands, and destroyed crops, which we have narrated, were some of the fruits of this change. It is no wonder, therefore, that we still find the inhabitants of that fated fen, in 1362,[1] petitioning the king upon the state of their country, and the cause of it,—representing "that whereas the river going to Lenne had used to run between banks distant twelve perches asunder,[2] but was now a full mile in breadth, they humbly petitioned that the river might be confined to its ancient bounds, and in such sort as it was before the boisterous floods had carried away the banks and the country so surrounded."[3]

Lynn, however, that had obtained increased importance and more internal communication with the country by the changed outfall, and had received one of the principal rivers in the kingdom for its service, was not likely to promote such a petition. We therefore find that town giving a counter-representation to that of the Marshlanders, and showing that the river ought not to be narrowed, for not only the existence of Lynn as a port depended upon it, but nine counties would receive material damage thereby.[4] Marshland, in despair, sent again to the king, imploring his assistance, "considering the sudden mischief and destruction which might happen by one hour's neglect, the whole country being in danger of irrevocable drowning."

These repeated applications do not appear to have introduced any change in the state of the country; and, notwithstanding the remission in their subsidies which the drowned districts had obtained in 1334, the tax-gatherers levied the original amount about nine years afterwards, and the sheriff

(1) Dugdale.—Badeslade says 1342.

(2) "The channel, not long before, was six poles wide."—*Dugdale*, p. 395.

(3) Dugdale, p. 261.—Badeslade, p. 7. (4) Ibid.

had attempted to levy arrears "of that old fifteen, whereof by the king's special direction they were to have abatement." They again, therefore, appealed to the crown, and set forth another catalogue of losses so great and expenses so constant, as gives us a very woful, but doubtless correct, idea of the state of the country at that time. There had been a fearful tempest in the year 1337, in which Marshland shared its usual fate. Sixteen hundred and seventy acres, beside messuages, were "drowned and for ever lost. Lest, therefore," say the petitioners, "in regard of their disabilities to bear so great a burden, they should be compelled to leave the country," they implore some remission of their fifteenth, which in the whole amounted to £205 7s.[1] The king remitted a third of the amount.[2]

In the same year another effort was made by the south side of Wisbech and the towns of Elm and Well to send part of the fresh waters back to their ancient outfall at Wisbech, by stopping up Well Creek, which crossed Marshland from Outwell, and carried into the Ouse part of the waters of the Nene and West Water. A causey from Gongested Lake to the Creek, and from the Creek to March Ditch, was a further part of the plan. It was to be executed by an agistment of twopence per acre on the lands of Wisbech, Elm, and Welle. This scheme was opposed by the north side of Wisbech, with Tyd, Leverington, and Newton, on the plea that the water which fell through the Creek to the Ouse would thereby be driven on their banks, and break them, and destroy the adjacent country. The opposition was augmented by the aid of the abbot of St. Edmund'sbury, who claimed a right of fishery in the Creek by an ancient grant of King Canute.[3] "In case they should proceed," argues the attorney-

(1) This subsidy was thus distributed:—Wigenhall £37; Walpole £35 10*s.*; Tilney £30; West Walton £23; Walsoken £26 8*s.*; Terrington £40 9*s.*; and Emneth £13.

(2) Dugdale, pp. 258—60.

(3) The Creek is an artificial cut; and this specification of a grant of a fishery shows us that drainage had commenced in this part of the Fens as early as the reign of that monarch. We do not know but it also proves that the course of the Ouse by Wisbech had, as early as that date, been altered; as the Creek, whether intended for navigation, or drainage, would have the effect of carrying part of the waters of the Nene to Lynn, instead of allowing them to pass by Wisbech.

advocate of this churchman, "the abbot would totally lose the benefit of his fishery, to the damage of the king himself, because that the profit thereof with the benefit of the other lands belonging to that abbey, being of the said king's patronage, ought to belong unto the crown in the time of every vacancy." An inquisition was, therefore, ordered to be held on the subject at the Castle at Wisbech, which appears to have left the matter without alteration, as we hear no further of their proceedings.[1]

The petition of 1362 by the inhabitants of Marshland to Edward III., imploring him to force the sewers to confine Lynn river in its ancient channel, had produced no effect, but the accession of a new monarch, in 1377, infused fresh hopes into the Marshlanders; for, soon after Richard II. came to the throne, the same petition against the breadth and violence of Lynn river, which had been presented to Edward III. in 1362, was presented to Richard, with the addition "that the river, by its extraordinary breadth after the banks on one side were worn away, had so great a power on the banks on the other side, that all the towns in those parts were frequently overflowed."[2] The remedy proposed was to restrict the width from forty perches to sixteen perches, and to straighten the river; which, they said, would be a secure, lasting and perpetual defence to all the banks and all the lands. It was ordered by the justices to be done; and we find, by a petition of the Marshlanders two hundred and fifty years afterwards, that it was done with good success.[3]

In 1378 a new bank was ordered to be made at Elm, for the purpose of preservation and safeguard to three hundred acres of land in Elm, and for stopping the salt water; for which purpose it is specified that an acre of land must be bought, valued at 56*s*. 8*d*.; and another acre at 46*s*. 8*d*.; "and of John Waltersea one acre, valued at 20*s*. and no more, because it was low ground."[4]

(1) Dugdale, p. 307. (2) Ibid, p. 261. (3) Badeslade, p. 8.
(4) Dugdale, p. 315.

The provisions against floods and drownings, which the courts of sewers continually made, seem to have been very insufficient; and the great change in the courses of all the fen drainage, caused by removing the outfall to Lynn, was only remedied gradually by repeated complaints, the effect of repeated drownings. The value of the fen lands we may see by the above extract from the proceedings of one of those courts; but we are not able to compare it with the value of other lands in the kingdom at this period, as there is no general fact that can be relied on. The average rate at which land was let in the fourteenth century is reckoned to have been about fourpence per acre, and the average price of wheat was four shillings and sixpence per quarter; but the average production was not much more than twelve bushels per acre.[1] At the present day land is about five times the value of its produce, and the produce three and a half times the value of its rental. At this rate of calculation the land here enumerated would have been worth thirty-three shillings and ninepence per acre; which will be found not greatly different from the value above quoted. Perhaps the fen land was not much below the average value of land in the kingdom; and that of Elm is so advantageously situated as scarcely to be included with the general fen. Still, much of it must have been in a precarious state; for, in 1392, Elm complains that their old sewers were so silted up that their lands were under water, "which did so impoverish the townsmen that many of them were constrained to seek new habitations, and the rest likely to do so, except some speedy remedy were applied thereto."[2]

At a Sessions of Sewers at Wisbech, in 1437, it was presented that "the landholders in the Old Market, at Wysebeche, did use, time out of mind, to repair, maintain, and new-make a certain sea-bank from Bevyse Crosse unto the great bridge of Wysebeche, on the west part of the river

(1) *Cullum's History of Hawstead*, quoted in *Pictorial History of England*, v. i., p. 839.

(2) Dugdale, p. 302.

Wyse aforesaid, viz., every man against his own land."[1] The presentment goes on to say, that "no one should cast dung, or anything else, into the river, nor make stamps, nor lay sege-reeks, nor dung-hills, from Guyhirne to the sea, upon the brink thereof, whereby the current of the water might be straightened or stopped." At the same time, we learn that the river at Wisbech had become so silted up, that it was impossible to use it for drainage purposes, notwithstanding such ordinances for its preservation as the one above quoted. "The water of Oldfield in Elm," says one of the presentments of this Sessions, "ought to run into the river of Wysebeche at Bevyse; but, by reason that the river of Wysebeche had for many years past been filled up with silt and sand brought in by the sea tides, that it could have no passage there." It was, therefore, ordered that the waters should be conveyed by sewers "to a pipe lying under the river of Wysebeche, called Coldham Pipe, and thence to the flood-gate in Leverington, called Dieugard, and thence to the sea."[2]

The above extract would lead us to suppose that the chief obstructions to the drainage lay in the town of Wisbech, and not far below the town, as they have done in more recent times. But we must remember that the Dieugard floodgate, though in Leverington, was at that time nearer the sea than any of the present drainage sluices—the sea at this date being seven or eight miles further inland than at present. The miserable condition which had fallen upon the Wisbech river, since the "principal waters," as old King Wolfere calls the river, had been abstracted, had driven the proprietors of those lands which were still obliged to use it, to the extremity of making a pipe or culvert under it, in order to convey their waters to a point lower down, and, by consequence, freer of obstruction. In this state it is somewhat surprising that the river was retained at all. With the

(1) The mention here of *great* bridge would seem to imply that there were one or more other bridges at this time in Wisbech; and "the west part of the river of Wyse" is so particular an epithet, that it is reasonable to suppose that there was an east or some other branch of the river of Wyse. Sometimes Dugdale calls it the river Use.

(2) Dugdale, p. 324.

waters on one side conveyed to sea by the Welland, most of the drainage on the other side carried to Lynn, and the remainder passed by culverts under it, little seems left but the tides, whose action, unless somewhat checked by fresh waters, must soon have silted all up. We need not be surprised if the condition of the river grew worse and worse, and that Wisbech, though originally better situated than Lynn for trade and shipping, should have been almost lost sight of during the whole of these periods, while Lynn, which had been enriched by the misfortunes of Wisbech, had long since grown commercial and opulent.

It does not require much knowledge of the early history of the Fens to discover whence the great errors originated, which led the Fenmen from year to year to complain of banks broken "by the outrageousness of the sea," low lands flooded by thousands of acres with fresh water, channels that could not discharge the waters they had gathered together, and sewers and drains "stopped up and filled with reeds, haffs, and other vegetables." Most, if not all these misfortunes, originally induced by great errors, were perpetuated by little ones. The blind adherence to the Romney Marsh Laws went far to keep disorder disorderly. "And when by necessity it shall happen," says the second clause of these statutes, "by occasion whereof it may be requisite to withstand or resist the danger and violence of the sea, in repairing the banks, the twenty-four Jurats shall meet together, and view the place of danger, and consider to whom the defence of the same shall be assigned, and within what time to be repaired."[1] The effect of this law was to cripple every useful exertion, and leave to indolence, short-sightedness, or avarice, the welfare of a whole province. It appears, by the proceedings of the meetings of these Jurats, or Commission of Sewers, that hardly anything was done to keep up the embankments and cleanse the water courses, till the work was forced upon the liable parties by losses and drownings,—sometimes so sudden

(1) Dugdale, p. 19.

and violent that, as we have seen, churches and messuages were washed down, and lands, by a thousand acres at a time, lost for ever. Hardly any man kept his proportion of drainage-works in repair till he was threatened with the penalties of the law by a court of sewers; and the conservators of the country being everybody in it, or every owner of land in it, no one considered himself responsible, or would do more than was actually forced upon him. Besides, every transfer of property entailed a new allotment of sewers to be cleansed and banks repaired; and when a landholder knew, that however careful and diligent he might be to keep his drainage in order, the carelessness of his neighbour, no less than his own, might drown his land and spoil his crop, there was no incentive to obey, except at the very extremity of the law. It is no wonder, then, that we find the history of the country, from Henry III. to James I., a mere summoning of landed proprietors to repair and cleanse. No new and enlarged system of relieving the country by a general drainage, no thought of going farther than the poor limits of their allotments, seems to have dawned on the fen-landholders. The duty they performed, too, was performed with exceeding ill-will: they litigated about cleansing a dike of its "reeds and haffs," and about filling the gap of an embankment which had drowned their own land, and hundreds of acres besides—the property of their neighbours.[1]

But there were, among these short-sighted and slovenly protectors of the country, some who saw farther, and understood more of what was really required for its preservation. Among these must be reckoned Bishop Morton, who, in the reign of Henry VII., executed the most extensive work of which we have any record previous to the undertaking by the Earl of Bedford. This was a Leam, or new channel for the Nene, from Standground to Guyhirn. The Nene wandered through the Fens by three or four different channels; part of it being diverted to Lynn, part of it carried into the

(1) In some instances, these laws are still the only rule, or rather common law, for preserving fen-works.

Welland, and the rest working with difficulty, and as it were up-hill, to Wisbech, or to its outfall below it. As soon as the river entered the Fens it was divided into branches, and turned to the left and to the right,—some of its waters skirting the edge of Northamptonshire, some the borders of Huntingdonshire,—the latter losing itself for a time in the great meres, or chain of fresh-water lakes, called Whittlesey, Ramsey, and Ugg,—the former passing almost to Crowland, and from thence into the Welland to Fossdyke. In this rambling course, the southern and principal branch described half a circle, turning into the direct seaward line again at Guyhirn. Now, it seems to have occurred to Bishop Morton, that much of the flooding to which that part of the Fen dependent on this branch of the Nene was subject,[1] was owing to this rambling of the river, or the neglect which had ensued upon the alterations it had suffered, and that if a straight cut were made, as a kind of chord to this segment of a circle, the waters would be carried with more fall, less impediment, and by a shorter distance, to their outfall. He had the means and the spirit to carry out this idea, and accordingly made the channel, twelve miles long, which bears his name, from Standground Steafe to Guyhirn, forty feet wide, and four or more feet deep;[2] and so eager was he in prosecuting this undertaking, that it is said he built a tower of brick, "to the end he might see his workmen afar off in the Level, and give such directions as were requisite."[3] Bishop Morton executed this Leam sometime between 1478 and 1486, if, as is generally supposed, he planned and completed the work during the time he held the Bishoprick of Ely. His life was chequered with the stormy complexion of the times, in the political affairs of which he was a conspicuous character.[4] His

(1) "By the way flooding many thousands of acres."—*Dugdale*, p. 372.

(2) Dugdale.

(3) *Sir C. Edmonds's Report*, 1618; who states that part of the tower was then standing. In a copy of *Badeslade*, which formerly belonged to J. Edes, Esq., of this town, now to Mr. Lefever, is the following M. S. note: "How often have I been asked whereabout the Tower stood. Answer.—Where the ferry-house is, or a little higher up.—J. E., 1801."

(4) It was he whom Richard III. addressed at that famous council in the Tower, which Shakspere, Sir Thomas More, and the tragedy which concluded it, have made immortal.

fen-work, which appears to have been the first of any importance, or tending to any enlarged system of draining, has not escaped censure. The effect of the cut at first, however, appears to have been very satisfactory; for Atkins informs us that Wisbech Fens were made good sheep-pastures in consequence, and "then was the fall of the waters in Wisbech so great, as no man would venture under the bridge with a boat, but by veering through."[1]

Eighty years afterwards we find these good effects had perished; for, at a Session of Sewers held in 1570, it was presented, and the following order issued:—"That the sewer called the New Leam, from Knar Lake to Standground, being so grown up that no water can pass in dry years, to the utter decay of Wisbech River, be diked thirty feet wide and six feet deep:" and, further,—"That the great river of Wisebeche being greatly decayed, raised, and silted up, by reason of the flowing and ebbing of the salt water; for preservation, therefore, of the whole hundred, that a sluice be made in the said river of Wisebeche, or any other place that shall take profit by it, and to be made (i.e. the river) in breadth sixty feet, and depth ten feet, from Guyhirn to the sea."[2]

It is not surprising that Morton's Leam should so soon have fallen into decay, when its shallowness, and the carelessness with which such works were then regarded, are con-

"'My lord,' said Richard to Morton, 'you have very good strawberries in your garden in Holborne; I request you let us have a mess of them.' 'Gladly, my lord,' returned Morton, 'would to God I had some better thing as ready to your pleasure as that.' And then, withal, in all haste he sent his servant for a mess of strawberries." An hour or two afterwards he was arrested by the Protector, and confined in the Tower; while his coadjutor, Hastings, was beheaded on a log of wood in the Tower yard. Morton subsequently obtained his liberty and became a torment to Richard, who offered 1000 marks in money, and 100 marks a year in land, for his apprehension.—[*Supplement to Bentham.*] He became the confidant and principal minister of Henry VII., who advanced him to the see of Canterbury; and he promoted those political events which, in the reign of Henry VII., secured the peace of the kingdom and the safety of the crown. He died at Knowle, in Kent, in 1501.

(1) *Report*, 1618. Elstobb expresses a doubt whether this Leam was ever completely executed, as about thirty years afterwards the old channels of the Nene were presented as requiring scouring. We cannot see any reason why such an argument should infringe upon the credit of Morton's Leam, which was independent of those branches of the Nene, and only received their waters; the branches indeed would be as liable to grow up after the construction of the Leam as before, unless they had been properly deepened and scoured at first to adapt them to the Leam.—See *History Bedford Level*, p. 137—40.

(2) Dugdale, p. 340.

sidered. It appears to have been dug only four feet deep, and though even this slight depth is represented at first as being highly beneficial, we may easily see how soon a drain so insufficiently constructed would accomplish its own ruin. In this instance we see its width was ordered to be narrowed ten feet—thirty feet instead of forty—and its depth increased two feet. Whether this was accomplished,—or, if accomplished, what was its effect,—we do not learn.

Elstobb seems to imagine, from the early decay of Morton's Leam, that the waters of the north and south branches of the Nene, which were intended to be brought into one channel at Guyhirn, did not find their way into the Leam, as was intended. He also blames its construction, in being too narrow and too shallow.[1] The contemporary Commission of Sewers entertained a different opinion of the former fault, as they made it narrower and deeper, instead of broader and deeper, as they would have done had they been of Elstobb's opinion.

In 1546, the old complaint of the injury which the alteration of the Ouse from Wisbech outfall to that of Lynn had caused, was revived. This alteration must, at this period, have been made nearly if not quite three hundred years, and possibly much longer, and yet its effects upon the eastern part of the fen were, if we may trust the representations at this time, as hurtful as ever. "There are yearly drowned," says the presentment, "within the towns of Upwell and Outwell, eight thousand acres of marsh and pasture grounds over and besides the great damage unto four several infields in the same parishes, to the number of sixteen hundred acres, and to the houses of the inhabitants of the same parish to the number of three hundred households, were not the same fields and houses defended by great banks, dikes, and crests, made for their safeguard, to the great impoverishing of the inhabitants." The cause of this inundation is thus attributed,—"forasmuch as the most part of the water of the great Ee sometimes was conveyed unto the north seas by

(1) History Bedford Level, pp. 143—6.

Wisebeche,—but now the water being forced to take in a manner his full and whole course contrariwise from his natural and most ready fall at Wisebeche;" for while the old river, and the relieving lodes, called Great Cross, Crekelode, and New Leam, which communicated with it, reached Wisbech by running ten, six and a half, and five and a half miles, they had now to travel respectively thirty-three, twenty-eight, forty-seven, and twenty-seven miles. "The decay of which several sewers, with the rivers, lodes, and drains, from them extending unto Wisebeche, they say be the chief and special occasion of the drowning as well of the said marsh and pasture in Upwell and Outwell, as of the whole country of Marshland, and Wigenhall adjoining, and in continuance of time, as they think in their consciences, will utterly drown the said parishes and the country of Marshland—unless a great part of the fresh waters be conveyed unto the north seas by the town of Wisebeche, in manner and form aforetime used."[1]

Memorial after memorial, each tending to show the abject and dangerous state of the country, are all the notices we receive of its condition during these times. The natural decay and distress of the country was sometimes aggravated by wanton mischiefs; and poor Marshland, which had been suffering for so many generations, and complaining so loudly of the sea on one side and the fresh waters on the other, and appealing alternately from Wisbech to Lynn, and from the commissioners to the king,—had to bear the additional distress of having its banks breached by the "wickedness of some people," so that the inhabitants had been put to "extreme danger and costs," and much people in consequence "drowned in their beds within their houses." That this was a repeated crime, is evident from the fact that an act was passed making it felony to cut the Podike—the principal embankment, or, as Dugdale expresses it, "the rind and uttermost part" of the province.

(2) Dugdale, p. 332.

So these northern portions of the fen continued to struggle till 1613, when the calamities which had so often before afflicted them, broke over them with redoubled fury. An inscription, formerly on the east wall of Wisbech church, but now obliterated or removed, recorded that it happened on the feast of All Saints, late in the night, "through the violence of a north-east wind meeting with a spring-tide, and overflowed all Marshland, with this town of Wisebeche, both on the north side and the south."[1] In this distress the people of the town of Terrington fled to "the church for refuge; some to hay-stacks; some to the baulks of the houses, till they were near famished; poor women leaving their children swimming in their beds, till good people, adventuring their lives, went up to the breast in the water to fetch them out at the windows: whereof Mr. Brown, the minister, did fetch divers to the church upon his back: and had it not pleased God to move the hearts of the mayor and aldermen of King's Lynn with compassion, who sent beer and victual thither by boat, many had perished; which boats came the direct way over the soil from Lynne to Terinton."[2]

This destructive flood caused a commission to be appointed to survey the losses, and provide for avoiding them in future. In their report they said that Terrington, "being a frontier town, was very ingeniously fortified, not only with banks of extraordinary height and thickness; but with two mighty brick walls, armed and defended with piles of woodshooves, and other devises, of as much hope as the wit of man according to the abilities of the people could invent."[3] But, notwithstanding this defence, a new bank of "extraordinary

(1) The presentment which followed this calamity gives us some particulars of its devastation, from which it appears that four miles of the sea-embankment at Terrington were borne away,—1876 sheep, 120 great beast, 480 acres sowed, valued at thirty shillings per acre, were lost in Terrington, besides hay, corn in barns, 13 dwelling houses "ruinated and wasted," and 142 impaired to the value of £1000. All the other towns in Marshland suffered greatly, though not to the same extent as Terrington. Walton suffered to the extent of £850, Walsoken 1328; and the total loss to Marshland was estimated at £35,834,—a very large sum for those days.

(2) Dugdale, p. 277. (3) Ibid, p. 281.

scantling" was recommended to be raised nearer to the town by six hundred yards.

Marshland, in its despair, again blamed Lynn river for its disaster, and sought again, by petition, to convey some of the waters, which had overwhelmed the Fens so often, by the Wisbech outfall to sea. "The mayor and townsmen of Lynn, being made acquainted with their petition, seemed to stand indifferent."[1] The petition was presented to the Lords of the Privy Council, and so far attended to that a special commission was summoned, which seems to have done nothing, or rather contemplated a further injury to Marshland, by the erection of a sluice in the Wisbech river, near the Horse-shoe; upon which the Marshlanders again petitioned the Board, "imploring their care for the safety of that country, and intimating that the erection of that sluice would be an apparent overthrow thereof." Wearied, at last, with unredressed grievances,—their banks borne away almost as fast as they were raised, and their province almost a mere,—the Marshlanders petitioned, that the high country might "contribute with them towards the charge of their banks sustaining, which the lords thought but just."[2]

The system by which the drainage of the Fens had been hitherto maintained, at length began to betoken alteration. Its deficiencies grew more and more glaring—its effects more and more destructive. It had arrived at that point, when either some enlarged plan must be adopted, or the country abandoned to inundation and ruin. The blunder of turning the waters from Wisbech to Lynn had preserved the southern fens from certain waste at the expense of Marshland, but the reaction of this improper step was only more felt as it was more experienced, and there was a daily danger of the whole relapsing into that succession of island and mere, reed-pleck and willow-wood, which had been its characteristics before drainage commenced. The dissolution of the monasteries is appealed to as the final cause of this ruinous condition of

(1) Sir C. Edmonds's Report. (2) Dugdale, p. 281.

the Fens, and that event may indeed have contributed to it. "The total drowning of the Great Level," says Dugdale, "hath for the most part been occasioned by the neglect of putting the laws of sewers in due execution in these latter times, and that before the dissolution of the monasteries by King Henry VIII., the passages for the water were kept with cleansing and the banks with better repair, chiefly through the care and cost of those religious houses."[1]

There is doubtless good reason for this statement. While every landed proprietor in the Fens had to be his own engineer and his own embanker, that property would be best preserved which was in the most opulent and trustworthy hands. Many monasteries and religious houses, comprising Crowland, Peterborough, Ramsey, Thorney, Ely, Denny, Spinney, Chatteris, Peakirk, Deeping, Spalding, Mirmound, Thirlinge in Upwell, and Isleham, were situated in the Fens, and possessed manors, towns, lordships, and fisheries therein; besides others, as Dereham, situated on the borders, which had similar properties. These houses, doubtless, exercised a wholesome and conservative influence on the drainage, and kept their possessions in a fit condition for affording revenue. Being all comprised in the boundaries of the Fens, and mostly situated in the neighbourhood of their estates, they had a constant superintendence of them, and though we often meet the names of churchmen in the earlier presentments, their neglects are never accompanied with such pitiful complaints as are made by the appellants during the period at which we have arrived.

But it is to the method of drainage pursued that we must look for the cause of that ultimate condition of almost hopeless ruin which the Fens presented before drainage was followed as a system, not a convenience. Under its Commission of Sewers we have already shown that everything was done by piecemeal, and mostly inadequately; while this court, the only court indeed that possessed any power over

(1) History Draining, p. 375.

drainage, was so loosely constituted, that it was only in the reign of James I., when the most important part of its jurisdiction was about to be surrendered to more adequate hands, that its power to construct new drains and other works was recognised.

The wretched state of the Fens had roused these habitual sleepers to a sense of their condition, and they had in consequence ordered the erection of certain new works for the purpose of conveying the waters to Lynn with greater dispatch. The parties, however, who were called on to contribute to the work, framed three objections to it. I. That the Commissioners had no power to make new banks, drains, or sluices, where there had been none before. II. That they might not tax the inhabitants in general, but only on presentment charge every man in particular according to his portion of land. III. That they had no power to imprison refractory persons.[1] The question came finally before the Attorney General and the twelve Judges, who "in their wisdoms finding that it could neither stand with law nor common reason, that in cases of such great consequence the law can be so void of providence as to restrain the Commission of Sewers from making of new works to withstand the fury of the waters," they found a verdict for the Commissioners, recognising their power of making, erecting, repairing, and assessing.

The opinion of the Attorney General was to the same effect. "The ancient drains," he says, "cannot now possibly (were they never so well maintained) drain the country, because their conveyance (whilst they were in use) was into the sea running out at Wisebeche, from whence the sea is now departed, so that there is now no way to carry these waters to the sea but by Lynn haven, to which therefore these works are made to carry them. * * I am of opinion," he proceeds, "that the law of sewers lately made for these new works is warranted by the Commission of Sewers * * and though it may seem still within the power of the

(1) Dugdale, p. 371.

Commission to maintain the old sewers, yet the Commissioners cannot now enforce the maintenance of them when they are no longer indeed sewers; nor benefit nor damage can arise by them, for sewers are made and maintained for the land, and not the land for the sewers."[1]

This was a step forward, but ruin had preceded it; and it was now hardly possible to retrieve the lost ground by any modification of the old means. Nearly four hundred years had gone by since the alteration of outfall from Wisbech to Lynn had been effected, which this court was now arousing itself to carry out. But, in the meantime, the drains and lodes, cut to convey the waters by Wisbech, had silted or grown up, and no new channels had been formed to effect the conveyance of the water by Lynn. Those lodes which refused to turn their water in the new course, were left to themselves, and became useless, or so treated that they served merely to carry a portion of the waters off the fen in the most flooded seasons. Well might the Fenmen believe that a law which had been asleep for four hundred years, was scarcely at liberty to awake at all. There had been warning enough, and outcry enough; Marshland, which was only defended against the slight floods of the Brandon and Stoke rivers, aroused by broken embankments, flooded lands, and a drowned or ruined population, had been calling out for assistance and pointing to the evil for three hundred years, but it was unregarded. Elm, Walsoken, and Upwell, had done the same, by presenting their drains choked with reed, and their rivers choked with silt; showing at the same time that they were all laid in the direction of Wisbech, and that they were ruined in consequence of having to discharge by an outfall now more than thirty miles distant from some of them, instead of by their natural outfall, from three or four to ten miles distant. Wisbech seems to have been singularly inert. There was neither complaint, nor support, nor opposition, (apparently) from that quarter. She seems neither to have favored her own interest nor the interest of her enemies.

(1) Dugdale, p. 372.

Lynn, on the contrary, exerted itself both in and out of court to retain its stolen outfall, even while the land-floods which the change had caused beat upon its walls, and all the country in its vicinity was changed into a pool.

So much indifference in the Commission of Sewers shows that the little recognised power which they possessed was exercised rather mechanically than with a comprehensive spirit. They seem to have regarded the Fens as a hopeless trust, which must sooner or later revert to their original waters,—and that they were only its conservators, and often seemed impatient ones, so long as that time was delayed. They provided, or rather imposed, fines against hogs rooting into banks,[1] or driving of cattle over them,[2] and pronounced denunciations against rats and conies;[3] yet all enlarged plans for carrying the waters away with such speed as to render such precautions only half as necessary, seem never to have been entertained.

Even when some important subject was brought forward, we have seen how carelessly they went to work, and either passed resolutions which they seldom provided means to enforce, or heard complaint upon complaint without making adequate efforts to ameliorate them. By the number of presentments which were made at almost every session of which we retain reports, we ascertain that it was only at the last extremity that the courts were generally held, when the whole drainage and embankment of a district were in such a condition as to require immediate repair, in order to save the country. But even this tardy method of legislature was not always resorted to, and often the only summons which called this indolent court together was deluges that laid thousands of acres under water. And then the shameful neglect which had produced this state of the country was no further inquired into than just to ascertain the liabilities of parties; and having portioned off the drains and embankments, and discriminated bit by bit who ought to repair, and who had

(1) Dugdale, 290—4, *et seq.* (2) Ibid, p. 265—75. (3) Ibid.

neglected to repair, the court separated with as much apparent satisfaction as if they had raised the land from its swamps and floods.

Acting upon the before-mentioned decision of the Judges upon the power of the Commission of Sewers to make new drains, as well as to maintain old ones, "which being notyfyed and publiquely read in soe great an assembly of Commissioners and inhabitants of the country as hath seldome been seene togeather att any one tyme before," a Commission which sat subsequently at Huntingdon in 1616, proceeded over the whole of the Fen, to make more decided alterations than had yet been done. Their commission set forth that "certayne selfe-conceited wilfull and overweening persons, out of theyre own singularity and perverse disposicions, noe lesse dangerously threatening the iminent ruyne of those parts by spurning against the authority and proceedings of those by whose prudence, care, industry, and diligence, such outrages were wont to bee prevented, avoyded, or suppressed,"[1] had been overruled by the law, and that they were authorised to punish such "stubborn and perverse persons." Having thus become somewhat independent of the country for which they legislated, they re-enacted the law for two new drains, to convey the Ouse from Harrimere to Littleport Chair, which had been enacted seven years previously, and had been prosecuted "even untill the workes were disturbed and hindred by a few quarrellous and contentious and refractory persons making question of the power of the Commissioners."[2] Other works were ordered; especially that the Nenne and Welland be sufficiently "roaded, rooked, hooked, haffed, scowered, and cleansed from side to side to the old breadth and bottom thrice every year; and that noe person should make any dames, wayes, gravells, wares, slamps, slakes, flakes, herdells, cradgings, or other annoyances over the river."

This, however, was rather the struggle of the dying than the commencement of a new birth. These efforts had

(1) History Bedford Level, Appendix, p. 43. (2) Ibid.

been preceded by two schemes, each having for its object a system rather than a medley of drainage. The first proposal was in 1577, but the scheme,—crude, ill-compacted, and partial,—worthily fell to the ground. It was succeeded by one of more importance in 1605. In that year, Mr. Richard Atkins, of Outwell,—"a person whose observations on these fenny grounds were very notable,"[1]—was directed to try the soil of the Fens "with an augur eleven feet long," on the skirts of Morton's Leam, from Standground to Guyhirn. These observations revealed nothing but a moory subsoil; and the like searches were made, with the like results, from Earith Bridge to Plawlis Were. "At the head of Mr. Skipwith's ground all vile moor by the whole tract."[2] This work was carried on apparently with sufficient energy to anticipate a prosperous result. A Commission was appointed to hear and satisfy the claims of those who, "having no respect to the general good," would be likely to oppose a general drainage, and their report was, that "they concluded with one consent that this work of a drainage was feasible, and without any peril to any haven or county." A particular view was taken of the whole Level, and a report made on the state of it, and what cuts, banks, sluices, and clows, would be necessary, and the true content of the fens to be rescued, obtained by a survey of William Hayward. In the particular view, it was noticed that the descent of the Nene into the Ouse at Salter's Lode was ten feet from the soil of the Fens to low-water mark, and that defects of breadth and depth were found in most of the drains and lodes depending on the Nene.

Being thus somewhat prepared, the Commissioners sat at Wisbech to make a final agreement with the Undertakers, who were four persons, of whom Sir John Popham, Lord Chief Justice of England, seems to have been chief controller and director. In the specifications it was agreed that the work was to be completed in seven years, and that, among other alterations, the Ouse was to be brought directly from Earith to Salter's Lode, and the Nene from Peterborough to

(1) Dugdale, p. 378. (2) Ibid, p. 379.

Wisbech; and that the recompense was to be 130,000 acres, "to be taken out of the worst sort of every particular fen proportionably,"—the whole number of acres to be drained being 307,242. The king (James I.) took great interest in the proceedings, and wrote "from Theobald's" commending the endeavours of the Undertakers, and their progress, and enjoined them to give himself and the council notice of "any mutinous speeches which might be raised concerning this business, so generally intended for the public good."[1]

Under such favorable auspices, "upon Wednesday [August 7th, 1605], about eight of the clock, the work began in the presence of Mr. Hunt (the engineer), who cast the first spit the wrong way." This was ominous: and though the cut, which was then commenced, was completed, and has since been called Popham's Eau, the undertaking soon suffered a defeat. The great proportion of land which was to be allotted on the completion of the work, alarmed the Fenmen, many of whom now vowed that their lands were good lands, and required no drainage; that they would sustain losses and hindrances by the contemplated works; and they petitioned that they might be excluded both their benefits and their costs. A Commission was appointed to examine into these murmurs, which ended in favor of the Undertakers; and in the answer of the Commission to the Council it was stated that "whereas an objection had been made of much prejudice that might redound to the poor by such draining; they had information by persons of good credit, that in several places of recovered grounds, within the Isle of Ely, &c., such as before that time had lived upon alms, having no help but by fishing and fowling, and such poor means, out of the common fens while they lay drowned, were since come to good and supportable estates."[2]

In the bill, which subsequently came before Parliament—in order to allay the opposition which the Undertakers had already encountered, and give the highest authority to their labors—various alterations were made: the time, instead of

(1) Dugdale, p. 384. (2) Ibid, p. 385.

seven years, was increased to ten; and, instead of 130,000 acres reward, 112,000 acres were to be the remuneration, which were to pay fourpence per acre tithe for ever. The works which were to be done and the privileges to be granted were nearly the same as were afterwards granted to the Bedford Level Adventurers. But the bill was defeated in Parliament upon the third reading.[1]

A bill, however, for the drainage of Waldersey, undertaken by three individuals, was passed,—so attached were the men of those days, as of the present, to insulated schemes, rather than bold and comprehensive ones. This work was completed, and Waldersey remained under the system of drainage then established till 1829, when an act was passed for the further improvement of the district.[2]

The works which seemed so well begun under Lord Popham, were now, for five years, no more heard of. The king had shown an extreme bias for the undertaking; but opponents in Parliament, and "the opposition which divers perverse-spirited people made thereto, by bringing turbulent suits in law, as well against the Commissioners as those whom they employed therein, and making of libellous songs to disparage the work,"[3] set the matter at rest for the present.

(1) Wells's Hist. Bedford Level, v. i., p. 89. (2) Ibid, p. 91.

(3) *Dugdale*, p. 391.—This author quotes one of these, called "*The Powte's Complaint*," a few stanzas of which will somewhat illustrate the spirit of the times:

"Come brethren of the water, and let us all assemble,
To treat upon this matter, which makes us quake and tremble;
For we shall rue it, if't be true, that the Fens be undertaken,
And where we feed in Fen and reed, they'll feed both beef and bacon.

"They'll sow both beans and oats, where never man yet thought it,
Where men did row in boats, ere undertakers bought it:
But, Ceres, thou behold us now, let wild oats be their venture,
Oh let the frogs and miry bogs destroy where they do enter.

* * * *

"Away with boats and rudders, farewell both boots and skatches,
No need of one nor th'other, men now make better matches;
Stilt-makers all and tanners shall complain of this disaster;
For they will make each muddy lake, for Essex calves a pasture.

The Sewers again, after their old manner, assumed the government of the Fens; and for some time it appeared probable that the schemes which had been entertained would not be returned to again. The Lords of the Council had assumed some management of fen affairs, and had sent several imperative orders to the Commissioners, one of which was to erect a sluice at the Horse-shoe, Wisbech, and to ditch that river and make it sixty feet wide from the Horse-shoe to Guyhirn Cross.

The Commissioners themselves had, as we have seen, attempted on their own responsibility—which the law confirmed—to erect some new and necessary works. But the alarm which had seized the Fenmen at the contemplation of turning swamps into pasture, began to taint these authorities likewise. They had fallen out with one another; and while part espoused the new principles that were springing up, and were advocates for thorough improvements, the rest were for doing nothing, but holding the Romney Marsh laws to the letter. Eleven had declared themselves of the latter party—inspiring the Fenmen, who had already arisen, almost to insurgency against drainage; and had even succeeded in procuring an order of council to stop all proceedings. The remaining party applied to the same authorities, and by better or truer representations, showing that their decision was likely to be disastrous to the country, a reversion of the order was procured. The division, however, which existed

"Wherefore let us intreat our ancient winter nurses,
To shew their power so great as t' help to drain their purses;
And send us good old Captain Flood to lead us out to battle,
Then Twopenny Jack, with skales on 's back, will drive out all the cattle.

"This noble Captain yet was never known to fail us,
But did the conquest get of all that did assail us;
His furious rage who could assuage? but, to the world's great wonder,
He bears down banks, and breaks their cranks and whirlygigs asunder.

* * * *

"Great Neptune, (God of seas!) this work must need provoke thee,
They mean thee to disease and with fen-water choak thee:
But with thy mace, do thou deface, and quite confound this matter,
And send thy sands, to make dry lands, when they shall want fresh water."

in the Commission as a body was too complete to admit of reconciliation; and, at length, the Council, on a petition of the Commission to have an independent person nominated to make a general survey of the Fens and report upon their condition, appointed Sir Clement Edmonds.

Sir Clement spent seven days, accompanied by the Commission, in viewing the principal rivers and sewers of the country. From his report we learn that "the Ouse is a goodly faire river throughout, and from Ely downwards runneth with such a current that it is absolutely the best sewer in all that country."[1] The West Water was represented as running contrary to its proper course, filling the Ouse instead of relieving it. "Wisbech river," he says, "wanteth much depth, and is grown up and choaked with silt, not only below Wisbech but above also, insomuch as I was informed that the bottom was six foot higher than it was before."[2] And he also states that a sluice, which had been formerly erected at the Horseshoe, "stood not seven days, but was broken and blown up by the tide." He represents Wisbech to be quarrelling with the upland men about cleansing the river and outfall,—Wisbech contending that the uplands ought to contribute to the scouring of a river which drains their lands, and the upland men producing precedents against contributing. In consequence of these neglects and disputes the country about Crowland and Thorney, though in former times firm and good ground, had become "a mere Lerna, surrounded with water, and serving only for fish and foule * * which overcharge of water doth not only cause the like overflowing in the upland country, to their infinite loss and disadvantage upon occasion of floods and swellings of waters, but the Islanders themselves are in like danger, as well for those parts whereof they make use, as for their cattell and their own safety, out of fear whereof they oftentimes upon the swelling of the waters ring their bells backwards, as they do in other places when the towne is in danger of fire." From the survey of the Nene Sir Clement went to that of the Wel-

(1) Report. (2) Ibid.

land, which he found a very fair open and clean river down as far as Crowland; but at Spalding the water was less than half a foot deep, and beyond it had become so silted up that navigators "were forced at the time of this view, and in sight of all the company, to carry their boats by cart the space of three or four miles to a place called Fossdyke, (where great ships lay at anchor,) for want of a current at low water to carry them down the channel." Sir Clement concludes his report with this solid but bitter reflection on the construction of works of public benefit: "He that will do any good in serving must do it against the will of such as shall have profit by it."

About the same time, (1618,) a report upon the state of the Fens was made by Mr. Atkins, of Outwell, whose account is only a corroboration of that of Sir Clement Edmonds. Speaking of Wisbech, he says: "Thither of old resorted ships and vessels of great burden; but the sea still forsaking the Isle hath made the whole passage betweene Wisbech and the Washes high marshes and sands, and by the decay of the river the channel or outfall so shallow and weak, as poor people often go over it on foot bare-legged, under the knee." He ascribes this neglect solely to the passiveness and idleness of the Wisbech people, whom he represents as "one while saying they cared not if their towne were a dry towne, another while thinking to keep it as a standing pool."

The effect of these reports was to bestir the Lords of the Council; another undertaking to drain the whole country was set on foot, with the Earl of Arundel at its head; and, in 1619, a scheme, similar in plan to that which had been proposed by Lord Popham in 1605, was commenced, so far as engagement and proposition could commence such a work.[1]

(1) These proposals were:—I. Of all the King's Majesty's lands drowned with fresh or salt water, which we shall recover and make dry, the fee-farm rent of fourpence an acre over and above all rents or revenues now in being or coming to his Majesty. II. Of all the Prince's Highness's lands the like contract respectively. III. Of all the subjects' lands which are so drowned or surrounded all the year, to have two third parts. IV. And all those lands which are by half the year's space, or more than half the year, drowned, to have one half. And we hope, by God's grace, to drain a great part of the said Fens, and all, or most part, within three years after the contracts made with his Majesty and his subjects."—*Badeslade's Hist. Navigation of King's Lynn*, p. 31.

There was one part of the scheme now proposed which differed from the former and from all subsequent ones, which makes us the more regret it was not more successful. It was proposed to "begin their work at the sea by opening the outfalls of the Nene and Welland, and to make the same navigable to Spalding and Wisbech, which would draw the waters into their true and natural channel."[1]

The demands being made proportional to the amount of fen to be drained afford us another comparative example of the state of the country.[2] Needham Fen and the lands on the north side of Wisbech appear to have been in the worst condition, and wholly surrounded or overflowed winter and summer, for of these the maximum demand of two-thirds was made. Those of the second class, or lands dry for some period during the year, of which one half was demanded, were, among others, Thorney, Upwell and Outwell, Ramsey and Downham, Wade Fen, and the fens between Welney river and Welney causey. The best-conditioned of the Fens were some of those of the South Level; for, of Hunney Fen, only one tenth was demanded; one eighth of Sutton and Haddenham Fens, and those in the vicinity of Waterbeach and Denny; and one sixth of Soham Fen. From these facts we may be sure that the drainage of the South Level was at that time superior to any other part of the Level, and that the Ouse had then as much advantage over the Nene, as the Nene surpasses the Ouse at the present day. Unfortunately, this plan was defeated; but not directly from the opposition of the inhabitants, as in the former case, but from the scruples of the Commission, who either fearing the loss of their own power, or, more probably, grown warm with party feelings and disappointments, looked with an evil eye on those who sought to outstrip their own tardy movements. They argued that they had no power to take away any man's land without some clear profit having accrued to that man's

(1) Dugdale, p. 401.

(2) "In recompense whereof we do make our particular demands of parts and shares out of the particular fens within the Level, so far forth as we can get knowledge of them, having little instruction or information from the owners or dwellers there, who rather endeavour to conceal the whole from us,"—*Badeslade*, p. 34.

property; and also that the means which were meant to apply for rescuing the country should be laid before them. But the Adventurers argued that the means ought not to be pressed until their agreement with the country was made perfect and sure.[1] The king, however, interfered, and some more conciliating regulations being introduced, an agreement was concluded: but the Undertakers did not proceed; and though ordered to begin, and keep the country no longer in suspense, or desist altogether, they seem to have been so thwarted in their proposals, and foresaw so many difficulties of prejudice as well as of nature to overcome, that they adhered to the last advice. The king was more determined, and declaring "that for the honor of his kingdom he would not any longer suffer these countries to be abandoned to the will of the waters, nor to let them lie waste and unprofitable,"[2] he undertook the work himself, and obtained an allotment of 120,000 acres as his reward. But the royal adventurer, who had so impatiently regarded the delay of his subjects, fell into the same error himself, and never commenced anything. The Continent was at this time desolated by the Thirty Years' War, and the Elector Palatine, the son-in-law of James, was destined by it to experience the severest reverses. These domestic rather than political cares are supposed to have diverted James from his undertaking.

There was thus another interruption of the projected drainage. But these futile attempts were not without effect. They directed attention to the Level. Men, who at first treated drainage as a fancy never to be realised, began after a time to consider whether such a work was really possible; and when they had convinced themselves of the possibility, they began to convince themselves gradually of the use and the recompense it would afford. In this way, the process by which most great undertakings are facilitated, the work gained advocates and partisans with every failure, and we need not be surprised after a few more years to see it starting up again with re-invigorated spirit.

(1) Badeslade, p. 32. (2) Sir C. Vermuyden.

CHAPTER IV.

THE BEDFORD LEVEL.

1629.

AT this time there was in England a Dutchman named Cornelius Vermuyden, who was well acquainted with fenny countries, and had been now some years employed in draining a marsh, similar to the Level of the Fens, called Hatfield Chase. This he finally accomplished, so that land not worth sixpence per acre per annum was, after draining, worth ten shillings per acre.[1] To this man the promoters of Fen drainage applied, and, wishing him to undertake the whole work, offered him 90,000 acres. He asked an additional 5000 acres. "But the Commissioners being unwilling to enlarge the number of acres unto him, and the country by their several petitions showing much unwillingness that any contract should be made with an alien born, or any other stranger,"[2] the negotiation dropped, and a new treaty was entered on with the Earl of Bedford, to whom, they readily offered the 95,000 acres.[3] The agreement is incorporated in a Law of Sewers, made at Lynn in 1630, called the Lynn Law, which is celebrated for having, as Badeslade says, "given life to the undertaking." By this

(1) Dugdale, p. 145. (2) Lynn Law.—*Cole's Bedford Level Laws.*

(3) "I took several views thereof (the Fens,) went away, returned, and reviewed the same, took advice of the experienced men of the low countries, and from time to time did study how to contrive that work for the best advantage."—*Sir C. Vermuyden's Discourse.*

law the 95,000 acres were to be divided into three parts; 43,000 to be appropriated to the construction of works, 40,000 to the support of them, and 12,000 allotted to the crown, for certain royal favors to be "vouchsafed to this poor distressed part of his country, which can receive no help or relief but by his royal hand in giving life to this law."[1] The Earl was to commence immediately, and finish his work in six years.

The accession of the Earl of Bedford seems, however, to have been more satisfactory to the country than the other Adventurers, who had made attempts at this work, and failed. "He," says one of his historians, "of whom all men thought well, would, by being able to make them think well of each other, reconcile their jarring interests."[2] But, whether through misgivings of the success of the work, or alarm at its probable expense, or by an union of authority to weaken the hostility which the Fenmen yet manifested to the undertaking, the Earl did not begin till he had associated himself with thirteen gentlemen, who were to raise money for carrying on the works proportionally to the number of shares each took,—each share being 4000 acres.[3] An agreement was drawn up, called the indenture of fourteen parts, in which the shares are recited, and each participant agrees to spend £500 per share.

1630. The work was now begun in earnest: the king was favorable, and everything promised a happy termination. In the third year of the work a Charta of Incorporation was granted, which recited that "hereafter, as it was hoped, in those places which lately presented nothing to the eyes of the beholder but great waters and a few reeds thinly scattered here and there,—under the Divine mercy, might be seen pleasant pastures of cattle and kyne, and many houses belonging to the inhabitants."[4]

The good assurance and independence which the Charta gave the Adventurers, doubtless helped them forward; and

(1) Lynn Law. (2) Cole's Historic Account, p. 23. (3) Badeslade.
(4) Charta.—*Cole's Bedford Level Laws.*

in three years after this incorporation they had executed most of their works, and were about to demand an acknowledgment of the Court of Sewers that they had fulfilled their contract. The works completed for this purpose were:—

1. The Old Bedford River, extending from Earith to Salter's Lode, being seventy feet wide and twenty-one miles long. This river had been projected by the first Adventurers, and runs in a direct line from the point at which the Ouse enters the Fen to the point at which it enters Marshland. In this course the Ouse describes a very irregular figure, running some part of the way nearly at right angles with its former course; which is apparent enough from the fact that the Bedford River makes the same point of the Fen in twenty-one miles that the Ouse does in thirty-two miles. This cut had become the more necessary since the West Water, which was originally a slaker to the Ouse from Earith in its original course by Wisbech, had, since the alteration and decay of that outfall, been gradually growing up, notwithstanding the effects of repeated presentments to preserve it.

2. Their second work was Sam's Cut, from Feltwell to the Ouse, twenty feet broad and six miles long.

3. A cut, called Sandell's Cut, to drain Burnt Fen, two miles long.

4. Bevill's Leam, from Whittlesey Mere to Guyhirn, forty feet wide and ten miles long. This cut was to serve the same purpose as Morton's Leam, commencing at a different and farther point in the Fen. Morton's Leam was at the same time newly thrown out.

5. Peakirk Drain, ten miles long and seventeen feet broad.

6. New South Eau, from Crowland to Clow's Cross.

7. Shire Drain (re-excavated), from Clow's Cross to Tyd.

The last three works, all situated to the north of Morton's Leam, formed a kind of system of canals, whose object was to relieve the Nene, and for many miles to supersede the use of it. We have shown that at this time the drainage dependent on the Nene was in a more disastrous state than any other part of the Level. It is not, therefore, surprising that the

Adventurers should have spent extra pains in works to relieve the fens which it traverses. The above formed altogether about fifty miles of drains in the portion of the Level drained by the Nene, while they formed only about thirty miles in that part drained by the Ouse,—an evidence, if more were wanting, of the neglected state of the northern compared with the southern Fens; since, although the Nene now only drained about one-third, and the Ouse two-thirds of the Fen, yet it was found necessary to protect the former with twenty miles more of drainage works than the latter.

The Adventurers also made several sluices, and "above all," says Dugdale, they made "that great stone sluice below Wisbech, at the Horseshoe, to hold the tide out of Morton's Leam, which cost above £8000."

1637. Having completed so much at the cost of about £100,000,[1] nothing remained for the Adventurers but to claim their recompense; and at a Session of Sewers, held at St. Ives, on the 13th of October, 1637, the Fen was adjudged to be drained according to the intent and purport of the Lynn Law; the claims of the undertakers were allowed, and their portions set out.

But, by some unfortunate disposition of events, the favor and aid which King Charles I. had bestowed upon the undertaking at its commencement were suddenly changed. His charta had been given in all confidence, and was full of privileges. Now, however, this regard was converted into something like hate, if we may trust to the way in which he treated the Adventurers. We need hardly repeat that the works had all along been viewed with distrust by a large and powerful party in the Fens; but while the king and court were favorable, their petitions against the Adventurers, which were frequent and angry, were disregarded. But, in whatever spirit dictated, they were now entertained, and a Commission, composed of officers and servants of the crown, was sent to Huntingdon, to traverse, says Cole, what the St. Ives

(1) Vermuyden's Discourse.

Law had done six months before.[1] The Lord Treasurer wrote to this Commission, prescribing what they were to do; and the king himself, three days after, wrote, declaring that he was perfectly satisfied that the Earl of Bedford had not drained the country, and offered himself to be the undertaker. Previous, however, to the receipt of this letter, the Commission had adjudged the whole drainage to be incomplete; and that the Earl and his companions, not having performed their contract, were not entitled to the recompense that had been awarded them. "And with scandalous adulations," says Cole, "extolling His Majesty's great goodness in offering to undertake the work, they most meanly accepted his proposals, with a free-will offering of 57,000 acres more, for his princely care of this distressed country."[2] They further imposed a tax of thirty shillings an acre on the 95,000 acres adjudged to the Adventurers, and at a subsequent session at Wisbech a tax, varying from six shillings and eightpence to forty shillings an acre, was laid on all the lands drained by the Nene, for completing what the Earl of Bedford had failed to effect, "that the said Fens might by sufficient drainage be made as well winter as summer grounds."[3]

Three causes have been assigned for this enigmatical behaviour of the king. Charles was at that time in the beginning of his difficulties: he was laboring to obtain money by any

(1) *Historical Account of Bedford Level*, p. 26.—"If in so serious a subject gravity did not peculiarly belong to the manner of treating it, one might be indulged a smile at the idea of the first interview of these court judges; those who had figured together in a drawing-room or the embroidery of a court, now met together for the first time in an alehouse in the country, as the tools to be employed in committing an act of the highest oppression and injustice."—*Cole.*

(2) Historical Account prefixed to Bedford Level Laws.

(3) *Dugdale.*—This imposition of a tax upon undrained land was merely a formal proceeding in law to transfer the powers of property from its legitimate owners, who were generally unwilling to facilitate improvements, to other parties. The tax was laid by the Commission of Sewers, but seldom or never paid; the government, therefore, transferred the power of levying the tax to a company who undertook the drainage, for which it was first laid; and in default of payment—which always happened—the company were empowered to seize a certain portion of the lands drained. In this way the right of property in the Fens was transferred from its original owners to the adventurers and participants who undertook its drainage. The tax at this time laid on the Fens—which affords us a comparative estimate of their state—was, 30s. per acre for Deeping Fen; 20s. for Waldersey and Coldham; 6s. 8d. for Needham; 40s. for the marshes of South Holland and Marshland; Marshland Fen, Wisbech North Side, Newton, and Tyd, 20s., 10s., and 6s. 8d., according to quality.

means; and being somewhat unscrupulous, and tending to despotism in his character, the Fens, it is thought, presented to him a golden prospect,—especially as so much was accomplished towards complete drainage. Another attributed reason is that the Earl of Bedford was attached to the popular party, and the king, whose resentments were more steady than his favors, is conceived to have taken a dislike to the whole matter on account of one man. A third reason assigned is that, in the adjudication of lands by the St. Ives Law, no mention was made of the 12,000 acres which had been promised to the king; and as money was the first difficulty of Charles, and led ultimately to his downfall, this is not unlikely to be the case.

The contract with the Earl of Bedford had been to make the lands summer lands; but if we examine the nature of the works executed, it is much to be doubted whether even this condition was fulfilled. There was only one considerable drain made in an extent of fen twenty miles long, and nearly as many broad, yet 95,000 acres had been assigned for what had been done; and the country, dissatisfied at the prospect of drainage, was doubly dissatisfied at such a completion. The appeals of the Fenmen may, therefore, have really influenced the king, and his motives may have been purer and more just than some of his detractors have been willing to believe.

1639. King Charles I. must now be considered the Undertaker, and he began his work with some spirit, promising to make the Fens winter as well as summer lands.[1] Forty thousand acres were assigned to the Earl of Bedford as a recompense for his labors, instead of the former amount, and the king's portion was duly allotted in the different fens; but "no lands were to be taken till the work was done, and judgment formed upon a winter's experience."[2]

The king appears to have seen some glorious vision in this

(1) Lands, it may not be unnecessary to state, are called summer lands when they can be used as pasture during the summer months though overflowed in winter. Winter lands are those which are not habitually overflowed in winter, but can be used for winter cropping and seeding.

(2) Dugdale.

undertaking, and to have entertained some hopes of repairing by it the losses he was sustaining in every part of his legislature.[1] He formed romantic notions of success before he had accomplished anything; for Dugdale informs us that he intended to "enrich these countries by several new plantations, and ample privileges; amongst which, his royal intentions, that of building an eminent town in the midst of the Level, at a little village called Manea, and to have called it Charlemont, was one; the design whereof he drew himself, intending to have made a navigable stream from thence to the river Ouse."[2]

In order to accomplish this Utopian undertaking he began or completed the bank on the south side of Morton's Leam, extending from Peterborough to Wisbech, and began a bank on the north of the Leam. He caused a new river, sixty feet wide, to be cut from the Horseshoe, Wisbech, two miles and a half seaward, and he erected a sluice at the outfall of Shire Drain.

1649. But the troubles of the king accumulated daily, and he soon forgot, in the turmoil of events which will never be forgotten, his fen engagements, and for some years all that had been done was left to grow up and decay; till the death of Charles afforded William, son of Francis Earl of Bedford, who was now dead, an opportunity to assume in fen affairs the same position his father had done.

The guide, under whose directions the first Earl of Bedford and King Charles had executed their works, was Vermuyden; who, although rejected as an Undertaker, had become in reality the principal contriver of all that had been done. He had written his *Discourse on the Fens* as an instruction to King Charles; and the Company, now about to enter on a fresh scheme of drainage were, by the instrumentality of Vermuyden, ultimately to carry out the principles detailed

(1) "His now majesty taking consideration thereof, and foreseeing that these lands being a continent of 400,000 acres, which being made winter grounds would be an unexpected benefit to the commonwealth of £600,000 per annum and upwards, and a great and certain revenue to all parties interested."—*Sir C. Vermuyden's Discourse.*

(2) History of Embankment, p. 414.

in that *Discourse.* We shall, therefore, give a brief account of that work.

Vermuyden lays down his principles in a small space; they are chiefly these four:—1. That the rivers be carried on the highest grounds where possibly they may be. 2. That the drains be laid in the lowest grounds. 3. That there be receptacles for the waters to bed on in all times of extremity; "otherwise the work might bee put to an impossibility and a continual hazard of inundation." 4. That the river-water and the downfall be kept asunder, and brought to the fall severally.

Of these principles the receptacles have encountered the most virulent opposition. They are stubbornly defended by their author, who either somewhat doubted their efficiency, or he deemed such a singular principle needed more than ordinary explanation; or, as is not improbable, he prided himself on this peculiar method of draining an overflowed fen.

The river Glen, he says, drowns Deeping Fen, because its banks are placed too closely together; but, as a relief to the banks when the floods run high in the river, two slakers are opened by which the waters are let out into the fen: "therefore, if the waters should be kept within the banks as they now are without slakers, they would run over and break them. * * These slakers, then, are made to keep the banks from breaking, which is no otherwise than an issue in a corrupt body, where there is neglect to take away the occasion by a known remedy." Had the banks been placed at four times the distance, this occasion would have been prevented, the high-riding floods would have been confined and got away without drowning the fen. "I resolve," he says, "to imitate nature in the upland countries; for, between the hills, there are meadows, and on each side pasture grounds or plough lands."

Vermuyden has left two memorable examples of this principle in the Fens;—the one Whittlesey Wash, or receptacle for the Nene; and the other the Wash extending all along the Bedford River, and varying in width from a hundred yards to three-fourths of a mile.

It was a further part of the plan of Vermuyden to unite the Nene and Welland, and pour their waters in one body through the outfall of the former river. "To make sure work, I advise to bring the aforesaid rivers [Nene and Welland] into one, that they may (in time) gain themselves a natural channel, which will be far better than to leave them to sundry outfalls, which, in future ages (as it is conceived), will reduce the work into an uncertainty again, by reason of the daily great increase of the salt marshes, and the sands of the sea."

This principle appears so rational—and, as we shall have occasion to show, so natural—that it can only be in consequence of the interests it would revolutionise that it has never been resorted to on a larger scale than the blending of the Nene and Welland.

The works he proposed for improving the Middle Level,—for he had already divided the Level into North, Middle, and South,—were two main embankments: one on the south of Morton's Leam, from Standground to Guyhirn, partly raised by Charles I.; and the other the whole length of the Bedford River (twenty-one miles), from Earith to Salter's Lode. The embankment of the Nene, or Morton's Leam, by confining their waters, will make them, he says, "grind their own outfalls, especially the lower ends thereof," an error which may be excused in Vermuyden, since his successors pursued it so blindly for so many generations. Fen rivers will not grind their outfalls till their channels are freed of all obstruction; in fact, till they have little left to grind.

These are the principal points in Vermuyden's discourse; and to him the Earl of Bedford, after he had facilitated his own movements, applied. The Earl had entered into the feverish politics of the day; and, first supporting the parliament, he turned afterwards to the king, who, somewhat suspicious of his sincerity, received him with coldness. He afterwards again returned to the ranks of the Parliamentarians, who now, like the king, suspected him; and thus forced out of public life, he had only the more leisure and inclination to become the leader of the new undertaking to restore the Fens.

1649. The Earl having mustered some confederates, the measure was speedily introduced into parliament, and the Commission of Huntingdon, which had reversed the St. Ives Law, was declared null and void. Two questions—First: Whether the work was feasible?—Second: Whether it would, if feasible, redound to the benefit of the Commonwealth?—were answered in the affirmative, notwithstanding upwards of forty petitions were presented against the measure; and within four months of the death of the king the bill was passed.

This act gives the Undertakers nearly the same powers as had formerly been invested in the hands of their predecessors by the Lynn Law; but in its preamble it specifies, in rather decided terms, the expectations which the Commonwealth entertained of the measure. "Whereas the Great Level * * if drained, may be improved and made profitable, and of great advantage to the Commonwealth and to the particular owners, communers, and inhabitants, and be fit to bear coleseed and rapeseed in great abundance, which is of singular use to make soap and oils within this nation, to the advancement of the trade of clothing and spinning of wool, and much of it will be improved into good pasture for feeding and breeding of cattle, and of tillage to be sown with corn and grain, and for hemp and flax in great quantity for making all sorts of linen cloth and cordage for shipping, within this nation; which will increase manufactures, commerce, and trading at home and abroad, will relieve the poor by setting them in work, and will many other ways redound to the great advantage and strengthening of the nation."[1]

The Level at this date appears to have been in a state hardly better than it had been before 1626. The works had

(1) Pretended Act, passed May 29th, 1649.

all been suffered to decay; the rivers, cut at such vast expense, were choked with weed. Many of the lands of the original Adventurers had been seized either by mortgagees, assignees, or creditors; and much was totally abandoned.[1]

The first act of the Participants was to re-engage Vermuyden, who, already in possession of much fen-property, had the most experience of the necessities of the district, as well as a competent knowledge of the subject. There was, however, much negociation and replication before Vermuyden and the Company could agree. He proposed for his recompense to become a joint adventurer with the Company on the guarantee of 4000 acres and £1000, which they seemed willing to allow him, but not on such favorable conditions as Vermuyden thought himself entitled to demand, and for some time there was a kind of conflict between him and the Company—sometimes Vermuyden rejecting the propositions of the Company,—sometimes the Company rejecting the proposals of Vermuyden. But the Company were evidently out of their depth: they were unwilling to grant Vermuyden's demands, and yet could not find another individual who could do so well.

Pecuniary matters distracted them even more than these preliminary disputes. At a meeting on the 11th of October, 1649, it appeared that £450 were due to the workmen; and the clerks of the works, as we should call them now, write "that, for want of money to pay the workmen, they fall into mutinies, and seize upon the officers and threaten to carry them away and cut them in pieces, in case they have not speedy payment."[2]

A final settlement had not yet been made with Vermuyden; and in November two opponents, each ready to undertake parts of the drainage, offered themselves to the Company. Vermuyden had grown peevish or disgusted with the wavering proceedings of the Company, and, as he said, "utterly discleymed to medle or have anything to doe with

(1) Wells, p. 157. (2) Ibid, p. 179.

the dreyning of the fennes." Perhaps he was certain his terms would prevail at last.

In the meantime, Sir Edward Patheriche had offered to drain the fen between the Bedford River and the Welland for £3900 less than Vermuyden's estimate; and this advantage, weighed with the ill-will which many bore to Vermuyden, so prevailed, that on the vote whether Patheriche or Vermuyden should be director, twelve declared for the former and two for the latter.

Patheriche was, of course, chosen, and, from that time, a kind of warfare commenced between him and his opponent; for in the minutes of the Company's meetings we find the following entry: "Sir C. Vermuyden offers to demonstrate to the Earl of Bedford, &c., that Sir Edward Patheriche his designe is destructive to the work of dreyning in divers particulars."[1]

Whether the design of Patheriche was destructive or not he had ventured rashly on a work he did not understand. He made no sign of beginning; and, in little more than a month after he was chosen, his opponent was called in and a final agreement, probably on his own terms, was made between him and the Company. The decision is thus recorded: "24th January, 1650.—A draught of articles of agreement between the Company and Sir Cornelius Vermuyden, touching his being director of the worke of dreyning, was read, and, upon the reading thereof, assented unto and agreed upon, as well by the Company as by Sir Cornelius Vermuyden."[2]

To the division of the Level into North, Middle, and South, according to the rule he laid down in his *Discourse*, he now adhered. The embankment of Morton's Leam he placed as the northern boundary of the Middle Level; and the embankment of the Bedford River as its southern boundary; the fens beyond these embankments being respectively the North and South Levels, in each of which he executed a kind of system of drainage independent of exterior works.

(1) Wells, p. 192. (2) Ibid.

The North Level, which had engaged so much of the attention of the first Adventurers, received no material additions from the Company. Their labors here were principally scouring the drains already made, and the completion of boundary embankments; especially that on the northern side of Morton's Leam wash, and another completing the external defence of the North Level on the west, from Peakirk to Brotherhouse.

In the Middle Level, which had been neglected by the original Adventurers, they constructed their principal works. The Forty-foot, or Vermuyden's Drain, was cut from the Nene beyond Ramsey Mere to the Old Bedford, which it entered at a right angle. It was designed to carry off the waters of the Old Nene by a more direct and easier passage, and thus preserve the Fens, which that river was in the habit of drowning, from Huntingdon to Upwell. Moor's Drain, which connected Bevill's Leam with the Old Nene. The Sixteen-foot,—a drain running parallel with the Old Bedford for eleven miles, at six miles west of it,—designed to carry away the waters of the fen extending between March and Welney. This drain discharged itself at a right angle into Popham's Eau. Tongs Drain,—a cut from Nordelph which entered the Ouse, about a mile above Stow Bridge,—whose design was to give the Nene floods an opportunity of discharge into the Ouse, when the high-riding waters of the southern drains of that river over-rode the Nene waters, whose natural discharge was at Salter's Lode.

In the South Level the principal work,—and, indeed, the principal work ever excavated in the Fens,—was the New Bedford River, or Hundred-foot. This river, which is of the same length as the Old Bedford and nearly parallel with it, is placed at the average distance of half a mile east of the old river, and like it, is designed to carry away the upland waters without distributing them over the fen. Between these rivers Vermuyden raised no embankment, so that in times of flood this space was overflowed, and there his waters "bedded," as he calls it. The New Bedford was designed as the main artery of the Fens in which tide and flood were to circulate; and, in order to secure this condition, he erected Denver Sluice across the Ouse at the point where it re-entered that river, thus forcing the tide that formerly flowed up the Ouse to work its way up the New Bedford.[1] St. John's Eau,—a drain of similar character to the Tongs,—was the only other great work connected with the South Level.

All the drains we have enumerated, with others of minor importance, he made finally to discharge themselves into the Ouse, at about eleven miles south of Lynn, between Denver and Nordelph. Here Popham's Eau, Well Creek, the New Bedford, and the Old Bedford, poured their floods together into the Ouse, forming by their junction the most important and unmanageable part of the whole Level, the difficulties of which the Tongs and St. John's Eau were intended to mitigate. We shall have frequent occasion to draw attention to this point of the Ouse.

1651. These works, with others, having been put in progress, in about twelve months the Company thought themselves entitled to apply for the adjudication of their remuneration, and a meeting for that purpose was called at Peterborough, and met in the "Minster Church."[2] After various adjournments 58,200 acres were adjudged, or the proportional part of the land recovered; their labors in the South Level not being yet considered entitled to remuneration, as scarcely any works had yet been there completed.

There is some little difficulty in this adjudication. Only 58,000 acres are adjudged out of 83,000, thus leaving 25,000 unawarded; though, according to the tenor of this judgment, the principal works ought to have been done.[3] At any rate the unfinished works are said to be contained in the South

(1) Elstobb, p. 195.

(2) Bedford Level Records.—The reader will not be startled when he learns this was during the period of the Commonwealth.

(3) The Earl's agreement specified that an award might be made when 30,000 acres were adjudged to be drained; but then the award was only to be proportionably made out of this portion.—*Pretended Act.*

Level, and yet the only great work which was made for relieving the South Level—the New Bedford River—had been completed.[1] St. John's Eau, indeed, was not made;[2] but this was so unsatisfactory after it was finished, that it would hardly have induced the Commission to make a grant of 25,000 acres as its reward. On the whole we must conclude that only a few of the works were yet finished. There were, doubtless, many in progress which had encumbered the finances of the Adventurers, and the Commissioners felt themselves warranted, on the mortgage of these incomplete works, to make the above award as an encouragement to the Company to finish what they had begun in the same spirit. The enormous outlays necessary for these works, which, after all, were a problem whether they would ever realise their expenses, might well damp the spirits of some of their experimenters. The Undertakers had been significantly styled Adventurers, and it is probable that no wild speculation of our day seems more unworthy pursuit than these men appeared to some of their contemporaries, while spending their money on a country which was little better than a bog. In our own age speculation excites no wonder. Pursuits that seem hunting the rainbow often, indeed, turn up the pot of gold; but in those days the prudence of speculation was always doubted, because very little understood: commerce had not familiarised the people to those generalships of trade where, by a rapid movement or a striking manœuvre, a fortune, like a battle, may be won.

1653. The works were continued with spirit immediately after the adjudication, and they were facilitated in the scarcity of labor by the employment of Scotch prisoners taken in the battle of Dunbar, and Dutch prisoners taken in Blake's victory off the Isle of Portland. Fifteen hundred of these were employed, and their aid had become the more welcome from the reluctance of general laborers to work for the Com-

(1) "In the year 1650 or 1651 the New Bedford or Hundred-foot River was cut."—*Elstobb*, p. 219.

(2) "They, anno 1653, cut Downham Eau, alias St. John's Eau."—*Elstobb*, p. 215.

pany. They made such good speed that, in 1652, the Company claimed the residue of their bounty. The Lords Commissioners came from London, were escorted into the Level by a troop, surveyed the works, and at Ely Vermuyden was called upon to give an account of his performances. He there describes the works he had completed in the South Level, but first adverts to the flourishing state of the other Levels, which, he says, " are so far improved, that there are about 40,000 acres soune with cole seede, wheate, and other winter graine, besides innumerable quantityes of sheepe, cattle, and other stocke, where never had byn any before." The work on which Vermuyden chiefly expatiates is the New Bedford River, whose service he estimates higher than some of his successors have done. No other works than a few slight embankments of its little rivers are described. The Level, as Elstobb and Badeslade argue, was probably in a flourishing condition compared with the North and Middle Levels;[1] and the works enumerated, though small in comparison with those completed in the other Levels, were probably sufficient for rendering it as dry and productive as any part of the Fen. At any rate the Lords Commissioners were satisfied: the land was adjudged to the Company, and thanksgiving for the completion of the undertaking was offered up in Ely Cathedral.[2]

The works of Vermuyden display sundry errors of judgment, and others which may, perhaps, be attributed to the difficulties of his position. Part of the system of draining the Fens which he pursued was prescribed to him by former designs, but the principal features were his own, and have excited various degrees of feeling against him. The making of the Old Bedford River had been entertained as long as the improvement of the Fen; for, nearly forty years previous to

(1) " When any flood happeneth, it cometh by wind catches and runneth over but some part of our grounds, and continues not long so we are never hurtfully surrounded: but conceive and find these grounds to be bettered thereby, and in our fens, time out of mind, have been kept many horses, colts, and young cattle all winter time, &c."—*Feltwell Petition against the Adventurers*. Like petitions were sent from Lakenheath, Methwold, Northwold, and other places in the South Level.

(2) Wells, p. 277.

the employment of Vermuyden, and in the first undertaking under Lord Popham, it was provided that the river Ouse should be conveyed "from some place at or near Earith bridg unto such place between Salter's Lode and Mayden Lode as the undertakers shall think fit."[1]

Before we consider the parts of his plan which have been most condemned, it will be only doing justice to Vermuyden, as well as to later engineers, to state the public difficulties he had to surmount,—some of which were peculiar to him: some have operated upon every masterly work which has been executed in the Fens. Though the animosity against disturbing an old system of drainage, which has degenerated into drowning, is violent and headstrong even at the present day,—in Vermuyden's time it was evidently much more difficult to manage and to conquer. Opposition is now generally satisfied with its moral power; but, against Vermuyden's works, it often rose into menaces that endangered his operations, and sometimes threatened the lives of those concerned in them. These works were executed among a rude and barbarous people, who had no examples of former success to mitigate their angry feelings, and, indeed, derived their subsistence from the very desolation of the country. They could be little grateful to men who were come among them to take away the fish and fowl on which they lived, and introduce a new race and a new nature into the land—or rather the water—of their birth. Vermuyden, too, was a foreigner; a misfortune which evidently induced even his coadjutors to regard him with a sort of aversion, and inclined them to estimate his talents at the lowest ratio; and, though they employed him, there was never that confidential understanding between them which should exist between the engineer and the undertakers in a work of such magnitude and importance as the first general draining of the Fens.

It was also the peculiar disadvantage of Vermuyden that he wrought upon a country where there had been only the most crude and unsystematic drainage; where, in fact, he

(1) Dugdale, p. 383.

could learn as little from former errors as if the country had never been drained at all. He had, therefore, as it were, to penetrate a sea without a chart,—there were no warnings of former wreck,—and that science, which varies with localities and can only be gained by years, sometimes by centuries of experience, had, in his case, to be learned suddenly and applied at once.

Whatever may be urged against Vermuyden, it cannot be denied that he partially effected an important drainage; and that since his era the land has never been that forlorn abandoned waste it was before. The feature of his works which excited the most acrimony was the leaving of washes along his great rivers; but this had been tried for sixteen years along Morton's Leam, before it was adopted along the Bedford rivers, and it was considered satisfactory or it would never have been permitted by a company so jealous of their director as the Participants were of Vermuyden. His errors may have been expensive, and we may see now how, for less outlay, a more efficient drainage might have been secured; but even this knowledge must be considered theoretical; for, in such a country, it is almost impossible to calculate the disturbing causes which may drive an apparently regular design into eccentricity. We must consider that not only Vermuyden, but all who have since operated on the Fens, have been in error,—if error consists in an unsufficient drainage of the country. The most successful have been those who have sought out obstructions in the mouths of the rivers, and carried on their works, less by inland drains, than through sand marshes and tidal bars. But let us remember how much opposition this idea—now so much respected—encountered from wise men while it was only an idea; and how much it still encounters, even while there are examples of its good effects. There is no doubt that part of the defects of Vermuyden resulted from restricted means. He was commanded to produce an effectual drainage; but he was to do it against a host of conflicting interests. He was only to expend a certain sum about it; he could not command means according to the work; and yet he was to make his means accord with an entire drainage. Now, it is demonstrably impossible in any natural operation to make materials perform more than the laws which control them permit. It is impossible to load a cord that will only bear ten tons with eleven tons, or to make a pillar of stone support a weight disproportioned to its height and diameter. Yet when we command a certain work to be performed that will take a quantity of labor indicated, we will say, by 8, and yet provide funds sufficient for creating a quantity of labor indicated by 6, we do as foolishly as when we load a cord beyond its strength or a pillar beyond its capability. That Vermuyden was cramped by these inadequate means is too evident. Money was the constant cry; laborers were unpaid;[1] and at last the Company resorted to the questionable means of employing Dutch and Scotch prisoners, because they could not induce laborers to work for them, who were not sure of getting their hire after they had earned it. There was another impediment which the engineer had to surmount, not less difficult than the former. He was not allowed to look on the country as if it were a waste without inhabitants or vested interests in it, and to adopt the best and shortest means of getting over its difficulties on broad and natural principles, independent of everything but its condition. He was told that there were towns all around it, each of which expected an accession of trade and prosperity without giving up any present interest or control. He was to do the best that could be done; but he was to respect the ancient watercourses and navigations. He was to drive the floods away; but he was to make no new discharges for his waters, however inconvenient or crosswise his present outfall might be; and if he attempted to infringe on these ancient rights, he must expect all the disheartening opposition of men who were ready to do anything to support their selfish conve-

(1) "In 1650 a petition was presented to the Company by upwards of five hundred laborers, praying the payment of £5000 then in arrear to them, and which, it appeared, continued unpaid."—*Wells*, p. 228.

niences. If these things are not actually expressed, the conduct of his opponents—and even of his coadjutors—prove them to have operated as blindly in the days of Vermuyden as they have in our own times. Had he been permitted to seek out the most commodious point to get rid of the waters he had with so much pains accumulated, it is very probable he would neither have resorted to sluices nor receptacles, for a proper outfall would have been sufficient to drain his rivers as fast as the floods filled them. But whoever looks on the Fens and compares their outfalls with their levels, will see that—by the influence of this load of vested interest, brought on first by resorting to convenience rather than science—the rivers are obliged, as it were, to climb in order to gain the sea; and the principal quantity of water is discharged at the most distant point from its accumulation, which it gains only by a crosswise and crooked route, at the sacrifice of fall and speed, and the encouragement of sands and bars at its outfall.

There is also another and material injury to great undertakings which has been generally thrown in the way of fen engineers. This is, when the controlling power by which great works are conducted, allow many incompetent minds to impede, according to their prejudices, schemes which are the result of education, experience, and invention. The ill consequences which have resulted from this cause, cannot be calculated; and were it not that there are advantages as well as disadvantages in such a system, there would be little hope for a full and well arranged system of drainage in the Fens.

Some time before the last adjudication at Ely, the Earl of Bedford—either from suspicion of the general efficacy of Vermuyden's system, or some motive that has not transpired—obtained the consent of the Company that John Bavents Westerdyke, an eminent Dutch engineer, should be solicited to come over and give his opinion on the works of Vermuyden. This opinion was anything but favorable to Vermuyden; for Westerdyke condemned, in decided terms, the grand principle of leaving washes to his rivers, in which Vermuyden put so much reliance. "If the banks," says

Westerdyke, "from Peterborough to Guyhirn unto Wisbech had been set out at a convenient distance one from the other, and one fair cut made for the waters to pass in, much money might thereby have been saved and the work had been far better, which is to be doubted must yet be done at last; for experience will show that waters kept in a body pass swiftly and mend their channel, but divided and dispersed pass away very slowly, and in time lose their channel."[1] Dodson follows Westerdyke; he had been employed under Vermuyden, but is no more merciful on that account. "That small neck of river at Guyhirn, too hard to be found by such a sea of freshes between those banks and Whittlesey, that the waters grope the way to finde that small quil to creep out at;" and further, "if the wind blows hard almost in any point, when the floods are within the great wash of the Bedford River, the banks are in great danger of being lost or blown up; for it maketh so rough a sea that it washes and undermines the banks."[2] Edmund Scotton, whose opinions date two years previous to Dodson, writes to the same effect, arguing for deep narrow channels; and showing that washes encourage violent waves "which whinder the banks to pieces."[3] Badeslade, who is a violent opposer of the Bedford River in every particular, and has labored through folio after folio to prove its absurdity, says of Vermuyden that "he ran counter to all the known rules of draining."[4]

These opinions, so decidedly against the system of Vermuyden, are too uniform to be treated as the mere effects of party spirit. They all point to his receptacles—the principle he advanced so boldly in his *Discourse*, and introduced so extensively in his practice—as the major error of his system. But this was evidently a favorite feature with Vermuyden,—he believed it to be original, and from that cause he cherished it with extraordinary fondness. He saw in it a remedy

(1) A Brief of the Observations and Advice of John B. Westerdyke, 1650.

(2) Design for a perfect Draining of the Bedford Level, 1664.

(3) A desperate and dangerous Design discovered concerning the Fen Countries.

(4) History of the Navigation of King's Lynn, 1725.

against such drownings as Deeping Fens had been subjected to, where the drains being swollen with water which the outfall could not discharge quickly enough, the waters were again let into the fen to save the embankments; and he also saw in it the resource of nature where, in the higher parts of the country, the rivers overflow an extent of meadow, instead of being driven forward with violence by precipitous shores. But modern experience condemns this system as having entailed upon the Fens not only its own bad principle, but encouraged a series of other errors to support it. The contemporaries of Vermuyden were not less severe upon it. We have shown how Westerdyke, Scotton, and Dodson viewed it; and thus Vermuyden is left without a defender. But we shall see by a slight examination that his contemporaries condemned his works on principles very different from modern writers. By the latter he is blamed for not opening the outfalls of his rivers, and thus, by allowing the waters a free seaward passage, remove them as quickly from the rivers as the drains supplied them. But the former never speak of outfalls,—they seem to have had no idea of their beneficial operation; but insist on narrow channels, in order to drive the floods more violently forward. "Let rivers," says Scotton, "be made large and deep, with high banks near on each side. These banks being made high, and but a small distance between, will be a shelter to the water that shall run betwixt them, so that the wind will have no power to raise violent waves against these banks to tear them as the others set at a distance."[1] Westerdyke's remedy is not very different: "That the unrestrained overflowing of the rivers is the principle cause of the surrounding of this level, and this being apparently the disease, therefore the confining these rivers within sufficient banks must consequently in reason be the cure: and the drains must be made for the downfall waters, and they must have sluices at their outfalls." We have had sufficient proofs in our own day of the sound principles on which Vermuyden is condemned for not opening his outfalls

(1) *A desperate and dangerous Design, &c.*, quoted by Badeslade.

by modern engineers; but we are inclined to dispute the soundness of the evidence on which his contemporaries pronounced their verdict. He did not use his receptacles till his rivers were filled to overflowing with water; and at that period it may be doubted whether it was not more prudent to mitigate the force of the stream than to allow it to gain weight, strength, and friction, when controlled by the weaker portions of the embankments only. For it is not necessary to state to those acquainted with embankments that the general principles of their construction cause their strength to diminish in the inverse proportion as the height and power of the water increases. When, therefore, the outfall presented all the stoppages of vast immoveable sands against the discharging stream, it is most probable that the inland embankments would have yielded under the system of narrow and deep rivers, and the fen have suffered more wofully than it does under the system of receptacles. These considerations seem to us to plead somewhat in favor of Vermuyden; and when the character of his work as well as the character of his age are rightly balanced, we are almost ready to excuse his errors in recollecting whence they sprung.

The government which recognised the completion of the works of the Company, and established it by law, was that of Oliver Cromwell. The Restoration followed quickly afterwards, and then all the laws which had been enacted during the Commonwealth were declared null and void, unless they obtained a re-enactment under the government of Charles. This was peculiarly unfortunate for the drainage. It had been pushed onward against the wills of a great part of the Fenmen; they were anxious to see their waters again instead of their new lands, and eagerly seized the opportunity of a null and void law to destroy the works raised with so much pains and outlay.[1] Another difficulty occurred in the claims which the old Adventurers, whose works had been usurped by Charles I., instituted against the new Adventurers. They

(1) Wells.

now made claims and declared interests to a great amount, till the new Adventurers saw most of their reward in danger of being snatched from them at the very moment of its partition. These varied difficulties were not got over without long negotiation and much prudence and patience; but, at length, a settlement was agreed on effectual enough to induce parliament to raise the Company to a Corporation, and fix its properties and its regulation on a secure basis. This act, which is called the "General Act," was passed July 27th, 1663.[1]

(1) This act recites that the Corporation shall consist of one governor and six bailiffs, who shall each hold at least 400 acres of the 95,000 acres; twenty conservators who shall each hold at least 200 acres; and a commonality who shall possess 100 acres or more of the 95,000. The governor, bailiffs, and conservators, may lay taxes to support the works, and are constituted a Commission of Sewers for maintaining and preserving of works, with whom no other Commission of Sewers are to intermeddle; 83,000 acres are invested in the Corporation and 10,000 in the Crown. The Corporation can erect new works within or without the Level; and if 8,000 acres are drowned for twelve months, the Commission may tax the 95,000 acres for their recovery, and sequester for non-payment.

CHAPTER V.

SOUTH LEVEL.

PERHAPS the work which has engaged the most acrimonious feeling of all Vermuyden's operations is Denver Sluice. This was resisted from the beginning, and has never ceased to excite angry and bitter crimination. Westerdyke condemned it, and all the South Level confirmed whatever argument was brought against it.

In order thoroughly to comprehend the nature of this obstruction we must consider its situation. We have said that the part of the fen near Denver is where most of the great drains and rivers join; but, in order to understand this junction, we must confine our notice to the three principal rivers of that part of the Fens,—the Ouse, the Bedford, and Well Creek. The Ouse runs due north for some miles before it approaches Well Creek, which runs due east; and these rivers, one running north and the other east, meet near Denver. It need not be said that by this union they form a right angle: but nearly at this point of junction, and dividing this right angle into two equal parts, the Bedford River also joins the Ouse. It was found, however, after this last river had been cut, that in consequence of flowing through higher lands on a higher bed than the Ouse, and its much greater fall than that river, being only little more than half the length of it between the same points, its waters, in floods, turned up the Ouse and back upon the South Level, instead of flowing down to Lynn. There was only one apparent remedy for this fault, which was to place a sluice across the Ouse just above its junction, so as to force the waters to their outfall, instead of allowing them to flow backward on their source. But there was another river, as we have shown, flowing from the west, and joining the Ouse at the same point as the Bedford. If, therefore, the Ouse were sluiced at Denver, and the Bedford waters were prevented re-flowing into the South Level, they might force themselves on the Middle Level by Well Creek, and lay those fens under water. To remedy this, another sluice was put across Well Creek, called Salter's Lode Sluice, and thus these two main channels, one of the South Level, the other of the Middle Level, were effectually defended against the overflow of the Bedford or upland waters. There was no course, therefore, for the freshes now to take but directly forward to Lynn, and of course there was no direction for the tide to take but that up the Bedford River, instead of its old course up the Ouse.

1649. Lynn and Cambridge were among the first who complained of Denver Sluice; the former on account of the scour which they feared would be taken from their harbour by stopping the tide twenty miles below its ancient flow, and the latter on account of the injury they supposed would result to the navigation of the river, and the "prejudice that would thereby befal to a great part of the whole nation by the stoppage of the general commerce at Sturbridge fair."[1] That there was a prejudice to the navigation in consequence of the sluice is not to be denied. It was deposited at the time when Lynn and Cambridge were combining together for its removal, that ships trading between Lynn and Newcastle for salt and coals had, before Denver Sluice was erected, been in the habit of making fifteen and sometimes eighteen voyages per year, but that "all the vessels that belong to the rivers cannot now carry up above eight of those

(1) Cambridge Petition, Badeslade, p. 51.

voyages in a year, so that the price of freight and commodities is now at Cambridge raised near upon one half part."[1] Lynn represented her roads and channel as having grown up so that two fathoms water had diminished to two feet; that the tides had abated from five to three hours' flow, occasioned, she said, by the "sluices that are built fifteen or sixteen miles above Lynn, which doth not only stop the outlet of the river that extends forty miles above the sluices, but stops the free passage of the tide of flood which comes out of the sea."[2] The higher parts of the river were represented to be in the same decaying state, "where boats and barges usually passed in the old adjacent river beyond Ely, grass and fodder is now mown and cut."[3] At length Lynn introduced a bill into Parliament for removing the sluice; which was supported by petitions from Marshland, Mildenhall, Stoke, Brandon, &c., and by a host of witnesses to prove the injurious nature of the sluice; but the influence of Lynn was insufficient against the Bedford Level Company;—the bill was thrown out.

We have already described the situation of this sluice, and of that at Salter's Lode, which is similarly circumstanced, and the facts applicable to the one may be applied to the other. We have shown that the rivers between which the Bedford River flows, and to which these sluices are attached, form a right angle. Now, the bed of the Bedford River was then eight feet higher than the bed of the Ouse and Well Creek, so that of these three rivers, joined almost at one point, two were almost eight feet lower than the other. It had, therefore, become necessary to provide other means of draining the Ouse and Well Creek than by Salter's Lode and Denver Sluices, as those rivers would otherwise have been obliged to wait their discharge till their waters had swollen to a level with the waters of the Bedford; or, in other words, till they had flooded themselves to a depth of eight feet. But, meantime, while this head of water was accumulating in the rivers, their dependent lands must have been gradually drowning, and many lands might be perished

(1) Badeslade, p. 56. (2) Ibid, p. 60. (3) Ibid, p. 62.

before they could be released of their waters. To relieve this difficulty two sub-drains were cut,—one on the south side of Denver Sluice, and the other to the west of Salter's Lode,—one of which—St. John's Eau—re-entered the Ouse at Stow, about five miles nearer Lynn; and the other—the Tongs Drain—at three miles and a half from Salter's Lode. By this means the head of water of the Bedford was avoided, for at the point where this second junction was formed the bed of the river and drains more nearly corresponded. But this kind of patchwork was soon found to be fertile in mistake. The loss of scouring water which the portion of the Ouse suffered, from Denver to Stow, caused that channel to silt up, "till its bottom became to be on a hanging level with the bottom of the Bedford River, *i.e.*, it silted and grew up in a little time eight or ten feet;"[1] and at length one of the rivers—St. John's Eau—became so silted up that its outlet was lost and abandoned.[2] Thus these complicated means for the relief of the South Level became in the end ruinous to it, and instead of being subject to partial floodings, the result of "wind-catches," many of the lands in this Level were now habitually drowned.

To remove these evils, restore the South Level, scour out their harbour, and benefit navigation,—Lynn had uniformly insisted that it only required the removal of Denver Sluice, and restoring the Level to the same condition as before the works of the Adventurers. They never reflected that nature, no less than art, had been meanwhile changing the relations of the fen,—that their river had been enlarging in one part and silting up in another,—that the channel of their outfall kept varying,—and that if the fen on the whole was relieved of its waters more quickly and more completely than before the works of the Adventurers, (as was undoubtedly the case,) their harbour, except by the counteraction of natural causes, could not by possibility have been deteriorated, but improved, by the scour of a greater force and greater quantity of fresh water.

(1) Badeslade, p. 84. (2) Badeslade—Elstobb.

1713. Things were in this state when natural causes performed what Lynn had been so long anxious to force on the Company. High tides and strong freshes, conspiring together, undermined the sluice, and finally blew it up, so that the tides again reverted to their old channel up the Ouse. Those who had so long prayed for this destruction were now rejoicing in the expectation of all the benefits they had prophesied. Denver Sluice was removed, the Ouse was opened to the tide, and Lynn, anticipating a deeper and readier discharge from an increased indraught of water, had soon to lament the very work it had spoken so confidently upon and petitioned for so often. It must be remembered that a dam of eight feet had been formed in the channel at Denver; the channel beyond the sluice had greatly grown up, and at Earith a sluice still standing turned the highland scour down the Bedford. Instead, therefore, of the Ouse realising its anticipated benefit, the ebb of the Bedford River now turned up the old channel; and thus the South Level became a kind of receptacle to the Bedford River, and was not only drowned by its own floods, but it became drowned by all the floods of the high lands beyond the Fens and of the Middle Level also. This happened to such an extent that during a land flood in 1720, the Bedford waters turned up the Ouse for twenty-one days together, without intermission.[1]

The Ouse began gradually to silt up to a great extent—at one time it deposited as much as four feet in three weeks[2]—which tended to hold up the waters with which the Bedford was daily drowning the South Level. Lynn sent out surveys, and remonstrated with the Adventurers, in vain. Ruin seemed to be making a gradual but certain prey of half the fen; and a contemporary authority says, that the lands were

(1) Badeslade. The advocates for the removal of Denver Sluice had still one point left, which their strongest partisan thus states:—"This mischief would have been prevented if, as soon as Denver Sluice fell, the Adventurers had taken up the sluices at the Hermitage, and given the stream its old course by Harrimere and Ely to Denver, and then the freshes incorporating with the tides, they would jointly have drove out the sand, and borne down all before them to sea."—*Badeslade*, p. 87.

(2) Badeslade.

drowned "to such a depth that the sun cannot exhale the waters, nor dry them up; and from Haddenham Hills, in our view of the Fens, we observed they were all to the south and east bright, excepting here and there a reed or sallow-bush, and some small tract of grounds which appeared above the water."[1]

Many remedies were proposed to counteract these miserable effects. Colonel Armstrong, under the protection or direction of Lynn, proposed an entire restoration of the old Ouse, by deepening, and removing obstructions; but his scheme was not likely to be entertained by a body that had spent so much in altering the course of the Ouse, and constructing the Bedford River. The South Level, sickened at length with delay, became as clamorous for the re-erection of Denver Sluice as it had been formerly for its removal. It was only, however, after repeated applications, that the Corporation was induced to rebuild the sluice, which was done by Labelye in 1750,—a century after its first construction, and thirty-seven years after its demolition.

The evils of Lynn haven still continued, and their favorite panacea having so miserably failed, engineers were induced to turn their attention to another principle. A remedy, both for the haven and the drainage, had already presented itself to inquirers, and had been proposed. It was contended, against those who would have returned to the old course of the Ouse, that the injury to drainage was not altogether at Denver but existed even more forcibly in the lower channel of the river, and at its outfall. The principal obstruction, according to theory, lay in a vast bend which the Ouse made just before it entered the harbour, describing nearly three parts of a circle; and, when actually within three miles of Lynn, running a course of seven miles through broken sands and shallows more than a mile wide. Kinderley, in 1720, first directed attention to this impediment. He contended it was not Denver Sluice that blocked the Ouse, but this broad

(1) Badeslade.

winding arm; and he recommended a straight cut from Eau Brink, where the Ouse first began to bend, to Lynn harbour, thus carrying it to its destination in three miles of direct channel, instead of seven of winding and shifting channel. But Lynn and its advocates had got the notion that this large sandy channel was a benefit to them by the large indraught of tide which it afforded to the harbour, and for many years this fallacy prevailed.[1] Kinderley was followed by others; and although both navigation and drainage were blind to the merits of the scheme, and almost all who had any power exclaimed against it, it yet awakened the country to some suspicion that Denver Sluice was not alone to blame for a deficient drainage.

The idea was renewed in 1750 by the son of Kinderley, who had been consulted on the subject; but Lynn, with remarkable inconsistency, objected that the Eau Brink Cut would tear down its buildings by allowing flood and tide less freedom, though for a hundred years it had been complaining that Denver Sluice was silting up its river. The Fenmen were not less averse to a scheme which would impose another heavy tax upon their lands. Engineers,[2] however, were nearly of one mind in strenuously representing it as the

(1) Badeslade's object is to represent the ill effects of Denver Sluice, and to prove that all the ruin and relapse of the Fens are to be attributed to this stoppage in the Ouse alone. He considered the old encumbered channel, which the Eau Brink Cut has superseded, to be the salvation of Lynn harbour, by the large indraught of water which it took in. His sole remedy, therefore, for Lynn was like that of Col. Armstrong, to throw down all sluices, and to admit the tides and floods into their old water-courses. "That is," says Kinderley, "letting the rivers do as they actually did when they took that course, viz., drown the whole country;" and Kinderley has proved himself, both in his opinions and his works, a sound engineer.

(2) Golborne, Governor Pownall, Mylne, Watte, Hudson, Rennie. Against these may be set Smeaton, Hodgkinson, and Sir Thomas Hyde Page. The opinion of the latter may be instanced as the general argument preferred by its opponents against the Eau Brink Cut. "I have already observed," he says, "that I judged the Eau Brink Cut would make no part in a rational plan for a general drainage; and I am of opinion it would be wrong to make any work that should lessen the quantity of water brought in by the tides, too much mischief having already been experienced by Denver Sluice, which stops the tides from passing as they formerly did, the indraught was lessened by that sluice, and Lynn harbour must have suffered a loss of depth. I fear the loss of the great space from Lynn to Germans for a back-water, upon making Eau Brink Cut, would bring after it the loss of Lynn Harbour for ships of the size that now trade there. With regard to the consideration whether a straight line or a curved line is the best for the entrance of a river, I shall only observe, that from the quick rise of the tide at Lynn, nature has there given the curved or crooked line the preference;

most probable method of giving the greatest quantity of permanent relief, and their estimates of its cost are strange documents now we know its actual expense.[1]

The united opinions of so many well-qualified men at length induced the proprietors and sewers to lend a more ready ear to the proposed scheme. The old system of cleansing had been tried to a great extent, at a vast expense, without adequate improvement; there was no hope from Denver now; and the adherents of draining by the old Ouse had fallen into a sad minority. But a greater stimulus to the work was given by the success which had attended a cut of a similar nature which Golborne had made in the seaward channel of the Nene.[2] This cut, now called Kinderley's Cut, from having been first recommended by that engineer, was excavated for a mile and a half through sands and marshes. But the Eau Brink scheme still frightened the more timorous; and it was only the prospect of lands continually deteriorating in value, and liable every winter to be flooded, that at length overcame these nervous oppositions; and a cut from Lynn to St. Germain's began to be the cry. Everything is, after all, accomplished by popularity; and to seize the popular opinion at the proper time is the art of producing effective changes, both in legislature and social improvement. The alteration manifested itself first in the public discussions of public meetings; one opponent after another either became converted or was removed by death; and, in the year 1792, a

the indraught is by the banks in oblique direction gradually checked; and the currents passing alternately from side to side in a wide expanse of river, being also gradually checked in a velocity that otherwise would be dangerous, are certainly governed by a wise law of nature, and the circuitous course is not only beneficial in moderating the velocity of the currents, but the projecting banks at all times afford shelter, and prevent the destructive effects of high waves, which a straight line of some miles, and current of from four to seven miles per hour, or more in the proposed cut, would frequently occasion; and, in my opinion, be far more dangerous to the land owners in general than to the navigation."

(1) "What is £15,000 charge, (which is the sum it has been estimated at, including the lands that are dug through,) compared with the advantages which will follow upon it?"—*Kinderley's Ancient and Present State of Lynn, Wisbech, and Spalding Havens.* The total cost of the cut was near £300,000, just twenty times the original estimate.

(2) This was only part of an enlarged plan of Golborne, and was really executed by others—Elstobb and Dunthorne.

Court of Sewers, hitherto decidedly averse to the measure, came to the resolution—"that the most probable mode of obtaining relief for the country would be by making a new river from Eau Brink to Lynn, through the marshes."[1] This resolution was so ably seconded that, in 1795, an act was passed for the work.[2] But the opponents of the measure had contrived to render even this victory fruitless. The tax appropriated for the works was so inadequate as barely to pay the law expenses; and it was not till five other acts had been passed, and twenty-one years elapsed, that this long-debated work was commenced. It was opened in 1821, and its effect corresponded pretty nearly with the predictions of its engineers, and not at all with the predictions of Lynn and its other opponents. It shortened the course of the old river two miles and a half, and the low-water mark at its upper end shortly after fell between four and five feet, and subsequently two feet more, in consequence of an improvement in the work.[3] The low-water mark continued subsequently to fall until it reached its maximum of seven feet. The drainage sills of Denver Sluice were laid six feet lower, and a correspondent improvement was felt in all the low lands of the Middle and South Levels.[4]

Thus its effects, though less than was anticipated by those who expected a deluge rather than a river, have made a manifest change in the South Level. The tide, that before hardly lifted itself into the Bedford, now penetrates almost to the end of it; that river has deepened considerably; and the channel of the Ouse, formerly so silted below Denver, was speedily cleansed by the increased speed and body of tide that scoured through it. Had the cut been carried into deep water beyond Lynn harbour, its effects would have been much more effective.

(1) Watson's History of Wisbech.

(2) "The expenses of obtaining the first Eau Brink Act, in 1795, were £11,943 13s. 7d." —*Wells.*

(3) Rennie's Report on the Wash. (4) Ibid.

CHAPTER VI.

THE NORTH LEVEL.

THE Middle and South Levels are still somewhat connected in interests; but the North Level has, for nearly a century, been thoroughly separated from them—as far as liability, works, and funds are concerned. The proprietors of Adventurers' lands in the North Level have the same general rights and control at the Board of the Bedford Level Corporation as other proprietors, but in all matters of a financial character their superintendence is confined to their own Level. This separation was confirmed by Act of Parliament in 1753, and arose from the disordered state of the finances of the Corporation, brought about principally by the expenses incurred on account of the North Level, and the difficulty of securing even a moderate drainage of that district. This district, which contains only about one-seventh of the whole quantity of land contained in the three Levels,[1] had loaded the Corporation with a debt of nearly £19,000 for itself alone; while the debt for the other two levels only amounted

(1) "Whereas the taxes, rents, and revenues, arising and payable to the Corporation out of the North Level, are about one-eighth part of the taxes, rents, and revenues arising and payable to the said Corporation out of the whole of the Great Level of the Fens."—*North Level Act.—Cole's Bedford Level Laws.*

to £16,000.[1] The cause of this expense must be looked for in the unwarrantable experiments which had been made with the Nene Outfall some ages before. The lands in this Level had been decaying for several centuries before they were undertaken; for most of the fresh waters having been suddenly diverted from the outfall on which the value of its lands depended, the greatest estuary in the Wash was left to the scour of the least quantity of flood, and thus relinquished almost entirely to the destructive influence of its tides. A natural consequence ensued. There was a continual increase of deposit; and the estuary, instead of a scour, became a warp. Even the sluggish floods which part of the Nene, its only river, sent seaward, could not get away in consequence of this perpetual accumulation of deposit, which lay like an embankment between the sea and the fresh waters, and they were consequently returned back on their fens, flooding all the lands dependent on the Nene. It is no wonder, therefore, that when the first Adventurers undertook the drainage, they demanded a greater proportion of land in the North Level than in either of the others; and that even after many works were completed, it should have been less satisfactory than those lands which poured their floods into a sounder outfall. Whatever was done, there was still the opposition of a choked estuary, and a river below Wisbech which had only been very inadequately altered since it was the discharge of ten times the water it at that time discharged.[2] Their inland works. the only works which the Adventurers and the Company executed, were consequently always unsatisfactory,

(1) The North Level Act, passed in 1753, enumerates the state of the Level at that time; and shows that a debt of £14,300 had been incurred on account of the three levels previously to 1728; that a further debt of £18,913 11*s.* 9*d.*, owing to the Duke of Bedford and the Earl of Lincoln, had been incurred on account of the North Level only since the former date; while £15,940 had been incurred in the same on account of the Middle and South Levels. It thus appears that, out of a debt of £49,153 11*s.* 9*d.*, the sum of £20,713 11*s.* 9*d.* had been incurred on account of the North Level, though this district paid only one-eighth of the taxes of the Level.—*See N. Level Act*, 1753.

(2) The difference of condition brought about by the change of estuary may be conceived, when it is known that upwards of 20,000 acres of what formerly constituted part of this estuary are now enclosed and cultivated. Marshland had to suffer from contrary causes. There the sea usurped the land.

and expensive without reward: the waters on the lands were only mitigated, not removed; and any casualty was sufficient to deluge half the fen between Wisbech, March, and Peterborough. There was one advantage, however, which seemed to promise success to some future bold design; but it required enlarged, not contracted, efforts to carry it out. The drains of the district had never been diverted from their proper course, but were laid in lines corresponding with their outfall, so that the stupid inconvenience, increased expense, loss of fall, and multiplication of frictional difficulties, incurred by the Middle Level drainage in consequence of most of its drains being led to their outfall in circles and right angles, instead of right lines, were not felt in the North Level. But it required many fruitless experiments and vast outlays without result to convince the proprietors that the old inland system of drainage was valueless; and these fruitless experiments and vast outlays were the final cause of the North Level debt and separation between the Levels.[1]

Previous to the passing of the act comprising this separation, attention had been drawn by Charles Kinderley, a conservator of the Level, to the real cause of the deplorable state of the North Level. He showed that the great difficulty and disease of the drainage was not spread over the fen, but confined to a few miles of the estuary, or to the seaward of the river's-end, as it was termed. This notion was not wholly original; but Kinderley made such good use of it, and showed the evil and the means of its removal in so clear a manner, both at Wisbech and at Lynn, that he is entitled to the praise of having first given it so much strength as to make men, who were extremely reluctant to employ new methods, consider it and finally adopt it, though the latter alternative was delayed for sixty years.

Both Bishop Morton and Charles I. attempted to relieve the Nene by cutting to the seaward of Wisbech; and the

(1) Besides this separation from the Middle and South Levels, the North Level is subdivided into five districts, with "power to raise taxes for their several internal drainages."—*Wells*, p. 684.

company, formed under Lord Popham, proposed—as has been related—to begin at the outfall. But the works of the former were imperfect and ineffectual; and the latter never had the opportunity of performing their designs. In 1613, when Marshland had been so deluged by a storm and land-flood, one of the remedies proposed was to carry Wisbech waters to sea by making a new cut "from the Four Gotes over Tid Marsh and Sutton Marshes into a creek called the King's Creek, and then fall into the deep called Lutton Leam, and so to the sea, which is a shorter course for the river by six miles, and hath a much better outfall."[1] This idea of the Jurors of Marshland was confirmed three years afterwards by the report of two Commissioners of Sewers for Norfolk and Lincolnshire, who stated that such a cut as the above "would be the best issue for those [the Wisbech] waters, the river being brought from Peterborough to Guyhirn between sufficient banks, for the better grinding of the outfall; and that the river should be cut straight from the Horseshoe to the Four Gotes."[2] These recommendations were never carried out, nor do they appear to have gained many advocates, before Kinderley, with more penetrating views and a finer knowledge of capability, gave them currency.

It is to be remembered that at this time the river's end, which is now twelve miles below Wisbech, was four miles and a half below the same place. From that point marshes began to swell on each side of it, extending from half a mile to two or three miles wide, among which the river took its course in a very irregular line. During the tide the marshes were covered, but as the waters began to ebb the overflow gradually sunk into the channel. By a singular mistake these large marshes were held to be preservative of the outfall, by discharging their tide into the channel. This channel, having nothing but loose moveable silts and sands to confine

(1) Dugdale, p. 278. (2) Ibid, p. 282.

it, varied continually, sometimes dividing itself into two or three parts;[1] and a gale of wind was sufficient to cause a material difference in its course.[2] It was, therefore, always necessary to engage pilots up to Wisbech, even by vessels in the habit of trading thither; for there was no part of the North Sea more dangerous in rough weather than these sands and uncertain channels, which were the cause of frequent wrecks to the small barges that ventured among them at such seasons.[3]

It was the reflection that these wide shifting sands and marshes, which never allowed the river a deep channel, and always forced it into indirect ones, were the main hindrances to a good drainage, which induced Kinderley in 1721 to propose that the river should be cut in a line through these marshes, and confined by embankments to a comparatively narrow channel. "It was designed," says his son, "for the turning the channel under Shire Drain Sluice, and to keep it there confined. It was to have been two miles in length, and to begin at the river's end, *i.e.*, about four or five miles below Wisbech, the river being so far confined. And it was designed to carry the river so confined two miles further to a place called Peter's Point."[4]

1723. A little consideration will explain the advantages which this plan promised. At Peter's Point—seven miles from Wisbech—there was a fall of five feet seven inches; while the representations of the state of the river at that day show us that much of the intermediate space could

(1) *Kinderley's Ancient and Present State, &c.*, 1753: who states that the channel changed its course a full mile, by degrees from west to east, in two years' time from June, 1721.

(2) "A rage of winds and tides, or an extraordinary time either of drought or rain, will occasion great alterations in it, [the channel,] sometimes for the better and sometimes for the worse, but perhaps mostly for the worse; because even when the back waters are the strongest, and so the most likely to preserve a good channel, they will sometimes scour away the sands in one place, and let them drop in another, where they may be more prejudicial to the channel than before."—*Remarks on Rowsell's Scheme*, quoted by Mr. Wing.

(3) *Considerations on the Drainage of the North Level*, an admirable pamphlet by Tycho Wing, Esq., 1820. Mr. Wing's facts refer to a later date, but they were even more applicable at the date to which we refer.

(4) Ancient and Present State of the Harbours of Lynn, Wisbech, and Spalding, 1753.

have had only a few inches fall.[1] There would, therefore, be an opportunity of lowering the fen drainage, were this cut successfully accomplished, at any rate five or six feet; and such a difference in such a district is often the difference between great productiveness and the entire want of it. So promising a measure was wisely adopted by the Bedford Level Corporation; and a conference having been held with a deputation from Wisbech, a mutual agreement was, apparently settled.[2] Indeed, so perfectly did these parties coincide, that the cut was completed, and a dam was in the course of being made across the old channel to turn the river down the new one, when the whole was upset by a movement at Wisbech.[3] We have shown that it was the prevailing notion of even sensible men at that time, that the marshes which lay at the mouths of the Wash rivers, were the last preservers of the outfall, by taking in a large quantity of tide quickly and running it off slowly; or, in other words, taking it in a foul silty state and returning it to the channel comparatively free of sediment. This was the notion of the Corporations of Lynn and Wisbech, who were each seconded by able advocates;[4] and, though good engineers had shown its fallacy, that which seemed true prevailed over that which was really so. The Corporation of Wisbech, thinking they had unwisely agreed to help their enemies, resolved on an excuse to recall their agreement. They complained that the cut was too narrow, "though it was wider than the river by twenty feet;"[5] and while the dam was being raised across the old channel, they "violently opposed it, and

(1) A century afterwards, according to Mr. Rennie, the fall from Wisbech Bridge to Gunthorpe Sluice, a distance of about six miles, was only six inches—an inch per mile. We have not had an opportunity of consulting the levels at Kinderley's date, but it would be unlikely there would be a much greater difference.

(2) Wells. (3) Kinderley.

(4) "Jan. 9th, 1722.—At a meeting of the Capital Burgesses in their Comon Hall, it was then and there agreed and ordered that the Town Bailiff do take up on the Town Seale £150 towards procuring an Act of Parliament for preventing embanking any salt marshes on either side of Wisbech channel."—*Corporation Records*: to which, by the courtesy of the Corporation and Mr. E. Jackson, we have had unlimited access.

(5) Kinderley.

at length proceeded to the extremity of demolishing the works,[1] and after that obtained an injunction from the Lord Chancellor to put an effectual stop to the making of any further progress therein."[2] A long vexatious law-suit succeeded between the Commission of Sewers, backed by Wisbech, and the Bedford Level Corporation.[3]

1726. This act of dishonesty in Wisbech may be said to have put back the improvement of the North Level for fifty years, as that length of time elapsed before the same kind of exertions were renewed. In the mean time Wisbech exulted in a bad river gradually getting worse, and flattered itself it had saved its port, though every day added fresh dangers to its entrance. The Corporation of the Bedford Level meanwhile returned to their old system, and hoped still to be able to reduce the level of their waters by internal works, and for that purpose they scoured, and altered, and renewed; their principal exertions being directed to the present channel of the Nene, from Guyhirn to Peterborough, which they at this period excavated.[4]

1751. But internal works had been long enough tried, and failed. There was no remedy for the obstructed outfall but its removal. This was still apparent enough, and Nathaniel Kinderley, son of the before-named engineer, wrote his "Ancient and Present State of Lynn, Wisbech, and Spalding Havens," at this time, insisting on some speedy

(1) "June 7th, 1726.—Memorandum. On the day and year above written, at a meeting of ye Capital Burgesses, it was ordered that the Town Bailiffe do pay unto Mr. John Franklin, Clerk of ye Sewers, one hundred and fifty pounds towards defraying part of the expense of demolishing of the Damm or Bank cross Wisbech River, which was erected by Mr. Kinderley, and thereby securing the trade and navigation of the said town."—*Corporation Records.*

(2) Kinderley.

(3) "June 11th, 1727.—At a meeting of the Capital Burgesses at their Hall in Wisbech, it was then and there agreed by them that two hundred pounds shall be paid by the present Town Bailiff towards the discharging the debt incurred by the Commissioners of Sewers in their dispute wth the Adventurers for preservation and the benefit of ye navigation of the port of Wisbech and the country adjacent.

"May 3rd, 1728.—Agreed, that five hundred pounds shall be taken up at interest by the Burgesses, to be applied to the discharging the debt incurred by the Commissioners of Sewers in their dispute, &c."—*Corporation Records.*

(4) It is called Smith's Leam, from Thomas Smith, a conservator of the Bedford Level, under whose superintendence it was cut.

measures of relief to the Level, or the alternative which further neglect must produce of abandoning it to the waters. Speaking of Wisbech river, he says: "As to the present state of this river, it is now so bad that whereas about forty years ago small vessels not without some difficulty might sail up to the town, now they are forced to lie at the Wash-way; and even barges, by which they used to load and unload their vessels at the Wash-way, cannot now pass, but they are forced to use lighters to the river's end. It is a common thing for people in a very dry time to walk over the bottom of the river under the bridge, the river is so shallow. The sands in the Wash-way are grown so high, and are so daily increasing, that it is impossible this outfall should keep open for any long time."[1] He also tells us further that the bed of the river had grown so high by the sands filling it up, that those sluices which used to run out the waters by a natural stream have now two engines, one behind the other, to raise the water from six to eight feet high before it can pass into the river.[2]

1770. But argument and truth had for a long time to speak in vain. The country still submitted twenty years longer to these hindrances, during which the North Level Commissioners—for this fen had now passed from the general Board—were several times admonished by inundations; and in 1763, 1765, 1767, and 1770, breaches to an alarming extent occurred in the north bank of the Nene, flooding the adjacent fen to a ruinous extent, and entailing serious expenses on the Level.[3] These disasters served to revive the project of a cut through the marshes, and the design of Kinderley naturally occurred to the Commissioners. Fifty more years of impeded navigation, diminished trade, and flooded neighbourhoods had somewhat abated the fever

(1) Kinderley, p. 70. (2) Ibid, p. 74.

(3) *Watson's Wisbech*. In the last-named year "so terrible a breach took place, that the whole country for several miles was covered six feet deep upon the average." The repairs of this bank cost £21,405 14*s*. 8*d*. in the thirty years subsequent to this breach.—*Note*, p. 64.

of opposition which Wisbech had manifested so notoriously against the project in 1721. But that which was offered them then as a free gift was now preferred in a less liberal manner. The Corporation of the Bedford Level expressed their intention of promoting the imposition of a tax on all vessels navigating the new cut, at which Wisbech again rallied a determined and more praiseworthy opposition. But the design promised to be of such benefit to the drainage, that the Bedford Level, unwilling to hazard any serious opposition, withdrew the offensive clause, and Wisbech appeared satisfied. The Corporation called in the assistance of John Grundy, Esq., of the County of Lincoln, to give his opinion on the opening of the cut, and to draw up such clauses as he should think necessary for securing the trade and navigation. His report appears to have been favorable to the measure, and a clause for making the navigation free seems to have been all the alteration attempted.[1] The North Level proprietors thereupon undertook the work, an act was obtained, and at £10,000 expense a cut was carried through the green marshes, beginning about five miles below Wisbech, and terminating at a mile and a half length at Gunthorpe Sluice.[2] This was only about half the distance proposed by Kinderley in 1721, but it was sufficient as an experimental proceeding to alter the whole of the drainage system, and throw its energies as violently to the seaward as it had been for some hundreds of years toiling at internal works. It was called, as a testimony in honor of its first proposer, "Kinderley's Cut."[3]

(1) This clause is thus entered in the *Corporation Records:*

"May 21st, 1773.—And be it further enacted and declared by the authority aforesaid.—That all persons navigating vessels between the Town of Wisbech and the sea shall at all times hereafter have the free usage of the said cut to navigate, hale, and tow with man and horses, in, along, and through, in the same manner as they have usually navigated in and through the present channel to and from the town of Wisbech to the Washway, or any part thereof.—Resolved, this day and date above, that two of the Capital Burgesses do immediately go to London, and endeavour to get the above written clause inserted in the bill now depending in Parliament for the opening of Kinderley's Cut."

(2) Watson.

(3) We are indebted for the facts from which the following were drawn to Tycho Wing, Esq., who obtained them from the correspondence of the day and the books of the North

The success of this work may be considered of more importance to the Fens than any single work of drainage since they were first undertaken. It opened new and most extensive fields of operation. Hope again began to be entertained for those parts of the fen which were lying in the condition of morass. Engineers saw at once that, in future, every work intended for great or permanent benefit to the country must be primarily directed seaward, and that inland operations

Level Commissioners. The important results of the cut, and the success of its principle in its subsequent application, make these minute facts important.

As the cut was the first work that had been attempted next the sea, the anxiety about its stability and the care used to preserve it were proportionably great. It was feared it would get too wide at its mouth, and thus expose itself to the wearing influence of heavy waves: to avoid such an effect stone, foot-wharfing, and jetties were ordered to be used; and the dam to be thrown across the old river, on whose stability the consummation of the work depended, was ordered to be formed by two rows of stone 120 feet asunder laid across the channel, each row to be 20 feet wide at the bottom, and to be raised one foot above low-water mark, and proportionally diminished to about four feet wide at top—the intermediate space to be filled with flag or earth.

The Commissioners seem to have been fully aware of the dangerous effects of broad rivers, as all their directions tend to hold the cut in a proper degree of restraint. "Ordered," says one of their minutes, "1000 tons of stone from Wandsford, that the new cut be restrained as much as possible from wearing more than 150 feet wide;" and a further entry says, "Report that the late tides have worn away the sides very wide in some parts where the cut is not stoned or flagged,—are of opinion that the whole success of the cut depends on its not growing too wide." These precautions were not in vain. The progress of the work was often endangered, and required constant vigilance and skill to preserve it. "In making the dam Mr. Elstobb has been obliged to deviate from the intended method of doing it: by such time as he had laid one row of stone across the channel, the spring tides put in and went over the dam with such a head in their flow and re-flow as to pool the ground away so deep on each side the row of stones as to endanger their falling into the holes, which obliged him by every means he could use to stop the tyde waters as quick as possible, which he did by laying a great quantity of sand-bags on the stones, and earth upon them."—[*Extracts of a Letter of the late John Wing, Esq., of Thorney.*]

At first the cut wore very unequally. "From the river and to Buckworth Sluice there was from three to thirteen feet of water; from Buckworth Drain to Gunthorpe Sluice there was from seven to only one foot of water." But the works notwithstanding went on well, as the following extracts manifest: "The cut keeps deepening; the flat against Gunthorpe Sluice is much worn down, and the channel to Peter's Point wears very regular, and keeps a pretty good opening towards the main channel; the tides get much sooner through the cut, and run with great alacrity. .... October 23rd, 1847.—The water has never been known for many years to run so low at Buckworth Sluice and Shire Drain as it does now. .... Below Gunthorpe Sluice the sands grind away to the eastward too wide, which obliges us to make use of stone in particular places. .... There is a good outfall below Peter's Point." The following letter was written eight months after the opening of the cut, and gives a further insight into its working: "We completed [the work] last autumn, so far as to get the cut dug about eight feet deep and to turn the water out of the old channel, and it was much opposed by some of the Wisbech people, and ruin to the whole country was foretold; but to their shame and disappointment the first fresh that came in October last ground the bottom of the channel from twelve to sixteen feet deeper than it was cut, and has lowered the water at Buck-

could only be subordinate to outfall works. Lynn, after as violently and as blindly opposing the Eau Brink Cut as Wisbech opposed Kinderley's Cut, and for as long a period, became, after the success of the latter, almost consenting to the measure. The bill was passed for that work about twenty years after the opening of Kinderley's Cut; and another scheme for enlarging the works in the Nene, by carrying Kinderley's Cut five or six miles further, began to be entertained.

worth Drain and Gunthorpe Sluice about five feet, which has given a complete drainage to the North Level and others draining by Shire Drain. Ships of 200 tons burden have gone to Wisbech, the tide flows more than an hour longer at Wisbech than it had used to do, and the water comes up much clearer." [*Letter from Mr. Wing to Mr. Golborne, Engineer of the Works, April 25th*, 1775.] These documents so well illustrate the proceedings, that we make no other excuse for the following extracts from the same papers: "June 8th, 1775.—We find that nothing but confining the new cut within proper bounds will make it keep its depth below Gunthorpe Sluice, where it goes through the bare sands. .... By the works we have done we have lowered the surface of low water at Wisbech about two feet and a half, which is as low as the bottom of the river there will admit it, there being scarcely six inches of water in some places in that town. .... December 3rd, 1775.—On Friday I was at Kinderley's Cut, and the other works there: the great sand at the south end of the new cut is entirely removed, and the channel has a fine current where the sand-bed lay into the cut which continues very deep, and all the works that have been done to preserve the sides stand very well. .... June 19th, 1776.—The cut cost about five shillings per floor digging, and the leeking the water after it was dug about four feet deep, to get eight feet deep in the marsh, near half as much as the earth cost digging and barrowing: the cut was made a hundred feet wide at top, forty feet at bottom, and eight feet deep, and the earth laid on one side to form a bank towards the sea with a foreland of sixty feet wide. It was said the cut was not made deep enough, but the first fresh that came ground it from seven or eight feet to fifteen or sixteen feet, and it has continued so ever since, and it is worn to about a hundred and sixty feet wide, and answers the purposes of draining beyond the most sanguine expectations, having lowered the low water at Wisbech between four and five feet." The former channel of the river and the wide marshes on its shores were by this work laid bare, and on the survey were found to comprise 7457½ acres, which were vested in the Bedford Level Corporation.

CHAPTER VII.

THE MIDDLE LEVEL.

THE Middle Level contains the most indirect and complex system of drainage of any of the three Levels. It was here principally that those clumsy and ill-constructed works were made by which the outfall was diverted from Wisbech to Lynn. These works, though for a time they gave relief—like a powerful medicine in a threatening disease—yet in the end they left the Fens weaker against the attacks of the sea, and more liable to derangement. A cursory glance at a map of this division will show a tangled network of drains, leams, eaus, and rivers, running almost at random, but mostly at right angles with their outfall and with one another.

1753. The main artery of this Level is the old Nene, which runs a round-about course through Whittlesey, Ugg, and Ramsey Meres, and then by March and Upwell, where it is connected with the Ouse by Popham's Eau and Well Creek. This river, which is the only communication between Northamptonshire and the counties in that direction and Lynn, has always been a principal channel of navigation and a constant matter of dispute between the drainers and the navigators.[1] This will not be surprising when we know

(1) Cole.

that the navigation of this river preceded the drainage of the Fens; and the navigators, by common if not statute law, claim the right to have their communications preserved in all their conveniences, however adverse they may be to draining. Yet they experienced, time after time, the violation of these ancient rights by the drainers. Morton's Leam drew much of the Nene waters away from its original channel, an evil which Vermuyden's Drain greatly increased, so that what had formerly been the principal watercourse of the Middle Level, and the highway of all traffic through the Fens, became gradually so grown up that small vessels were unable to traverse it. Then came the debate of who was to restore these navigations: the drainers were not compelled to keep the Nene open, as the drains they had made to relieve it could be used for the purpose of carrying their waters away, though the policy of allowing it to grow up can only be described as an extremely vicious economy. The navigators appealed to the drainers for redress, since all Acts of Parliament by which the latter persons had become authorised to disturb the ancient drainage or rather drowning of the Fens, provided that navigation should be respected in all its privileges and necessities. But the drainers demurred. Their works, indeed, had contributed to abstract the ancient waters from the Nene, but they showed that navigators had received a tenfold value and convenience for the loss of water of which they complained. They had obtained haling banks for their horses, and a fruitful country to traverse instead of a morass; the production of grain was a hundredfold what it had been when the Nene overflowed with water, which grain the navigators carried between town and town and port and port; population constantly demanding their aid was now spread over a country where it had been almost unknown; all which results of draining had increased the traffic of the navigators to an amazing extent. Things continued in this doubtful and debateable state for some time, till the necessity of some decision caused the opposite parties to meet at Lynn, where they agreed to certain mutual advantages, which were incorporated in an Act of Parliament, passed in 1753, called the "Nene Act."[1] The policy of this law is by tolls laid on the navigation to raise a fund for scouring and deepening the Nene; and, as a preservative against the future encroachments of draining, a clause was introduced which has since been a frequent matter of acrimonious dispute, and some have gone so far as to attribute half the faults of the Middle Level drainage to it alone. "It is further enacted, that the drain called Marshland Cut, or the Tongs Drain, shall not at any time be run, unless upon a breach of bank, or in case of imminent danger thereof, or unless the water in the said rivers[2] be raised more than one foot above the level soil of the lowest lands in the fens."[3] As the Tongs gives three or four feet relief to the Level, this clause, which is still in operation,[4] tends to prevent the fen from being relieved till material mischief has been done to it, and in some cases a ruinous extent of loss incurred. The act, however, did not serve its purposes; a large debt was contracted without chance of liquidation, and the river in consequence of neglect became almost abandoned,[5] when, in 1810, its prospects were partially revived by the passing of an Act for imposing a shilling per acre on certain Middle Level lands, to be expended in deepening and scouring the river.[6]

1795. The remedies which had now for many years been applied to the Fens, consisted merely in cleansing drains when they had become so grown up as to be impassable to the waters; repairing where repairs could hardly remedy; and altering in such a manner that it only made an embarrassed system more embarrassing. Yet these alterations, made at various times and in slight degrees, had entailed great expenses; and, mitigating temporary evils

(1) Cole.

(2) Old Bedford, Forty-foot, &c. (3) Cole's Bedford Level Laws, p. 515.

(4) The recent Middle Level Act has moderated this clause, which may now, indeed, be considered repealed, since the Middle Level Cut has just been opened.—May, 1847.

(5) "A respectable alderman of Lynn facetiously observed, that he regularly attended the River Nene meetings until he saw on his way thither persons making hay in the bed of the river, after which he thought such attendance perfectly unnecessary."—*Wells's History of the Bedford Level*, p. 720.

(6) Wells.

in a temporary manner, left the great demand for a better system of drainage still unfulfilled. Unless a defective system be improved, it gradually gets worse: this fact, which yearly became more clearly demonstrated, seemed to demand an extensive scheme, which by its comprehensiveness should not only relieve all parts of the fen, but render the whole more capable of control, and in a great measure independent of those sudden wet seasons which now reduced the fen to somewhat of its original state. It was with this view that the Eau Brink Cut had been proposed in 1721, and the act for it obtained in 1795. But though so far facilitated, its enemies made it worthless, and the Ouse remained without alteration for twenty years longer. It was, however, at best, but a partial measure, and considered only as a preliminary to more extensive schemes for the complete drainage of the Level. Its promoters had gained a barren victory, but they still hoped to complete their work, and indeed other and more extensive works supplementary to it.

In the year 1800 Mr. Rennie had succeeded in effectually draining the East, West, and Wildmore Fens, having triumphed over the greatest difficulties of silted rivers and fens in a horrible state of neglect and flood. He had for this purpose adopted means now first extensively employed in fen drainage, though not altogether original in idea. He divided the upland from the lowland waters, and carried them separately through the fen. This he had accomplished by drains skirting the fen, called catch-water drains, in which the whole downfall of the higher lands was conveyed away, and by a system of internal drains wholly for the purpose of taking away the fen waters. The rationale of this system is simple enough when it is stated. The water derived from high lands, having a greater fall, runs away with greater impulse than that derived from fen lands. Thus the same rain will have filled the rivers of the high lands while it has not got into the ditches of the fen. When, therefore, the same drains are made for conveying away both streams, as had formerly been the case, the high land waters filled the drains, and of course held the fen waters up in their ditches, and on the low lands; or, in other words, over-rode them, causing them to stagnate at points the most difficult to relieve, because the greatest distance from their outfall.[1] The success of Rennie in carrying out this principle in the Lincolnshire fens, induced the Corporation of the Bedford Level to request him to make a survey of their fens, and form for them a plan of general drainage. But fenmen have seldom been beforehand with their remedies; they have seldom seen peril before they have experienced it; and almost every great work which has been done in the fens has been pressed upon the owners by inundations and losses to an immense extent. Such was the case when Rennie was requested to furnish his report. The previous spring, (1808,) thousands of acres had been overflowed, banks had been breached, sluices had been blown, and damage done to the amount of "at least one million."[2] This then was the exciting cause which elicited one of the most comprehensive reports which has ever been proposed for the relief of the Levels. The plan may be briefly described as insisting on the making of the Eau Brink Cut as a preliminary necessity, and then surrounding the whole fen with catch-water drains. The two Bedford Rivers were to be converted into one by a drain carried through the middle of their Wash, from Mepal to Denver, and the Wash itself thereby drained. A new cut was proposed from Whittlesey Mere, in lieu of the Old Nene and its extensions, and continued thence to the Eau Brink Cut, and a drain carried to the like point from Grunty Fen. These were the principal works to be made; but the extent of the design and the estimated expense of upwards of a million so alarmed those who by an

(1) This principle, though so new in its application, had been promulgated by some of the first attempters of fen drainage. Vermuyden seems to have had a glimpse of it when he says, in his *Discourse*, among other things, it is to be observed "that the river waters and the downfalls be kept asunder and brought to their fall severally." It was even more emphatically insisted on by Lord Gorges, who says: "This is a rule in draining never to be varied from, where it can be done,—that is, to embank all rivers or brook waters, to carry them to their outfalls separate from sock or downfall waters."—*Proposals for Draining, &c.* It was, however reserved for Rennie to put this system into thoroughly successful practice.

(2) Rennie.

unfriendly season had suffered to more than that extent, that this great design was never carried out.

The plan, however, was not forgotten, and at various times parties interested in the country attempted its revival. The Eau Brink Cut had been made, with important results. Still it was felt that other works were required to second the relief it gave, or promised. It was not, however, till 1836 that any definite plan began again to be entertained. Meanwhile Mr. Rennie died, and his son had succeeded to the system and much of the genius of his father. Under the superintendence of Mr. Telford and Mr. (now Sir John) Rennie, the Nene Outfall had been perfected, and bestowed upon the North Level, even at its extremities, a natural drainage, with four inches fall per mile. By this great work a large salt-water marsh, that four years previously was covered with the sea at every tide, was converted into farms; unprofitable wastes were converted into rich agricultural districts; and the crooked and shallow channels of the river exchanged for straight deep cuts, capable of effecting any drainage, and admitting any shipping.

A large portion, amounting to one-third of the whole, of the Middle Level is situated along the borders of the Nene, from which an embankment alone separates it. This portion, in a wretched state of drainage, has to send its floods, that come within a few yards of the Nene, a distance of thirty miles, through crooked and shallow drains, to gain their discharge into the Ouse. The consequence follows that much of the lands are nearly worthless,—the least flood inundates them,—reeds and osiers are their principal crop, varied by quagmires that will not bear the tread of man or animal. The mills which drain this region are not able to effect their duty till the water has often remained so long on the soil as to destroy most of its fertilising properties—dissolving the nutritious salts and manures on which its grasses and its seeds ought to be fed.[1]

(1) "The waters are so raised by the mills which are between Whittlesey Mere and the outfall at sea, that they revert upwards to the Mere, and swell the waters in it and its sur-

Many of the proprietors of this distressed portion of the fen, on the success of the Nene Outfall, and the drainage of the North Level naturally, saw that their own fen was favorably situated for enjoying the same benefits. It lay in the same relation south of the Nene as the Level now naturally drained was to the north, and might by simple works be made to enjoy similar, or nearly similar advantages, if it were drained into the Nene in the same manner as the North Level. There were fertility and prosperity, well-stocked farms and abundance of grain and cropping, north of the Nene,—and morasses, meres, bogs, reed-fields, and sterility south of it; and the sterility of the land south of the Nene seemed convertible into the prosperity of the north, provided similar means were pursued to secure it.

These facts, combined with the drainage of Morton's Leam Wash, and improving the channel between Wisbech and Peterborough, so as to enable small seaborne vessels to visit

rounding fens, which in fact only begin to be drained when the mills to the eastward of the parishes of Farcet, Ramsey, Whittlesey, and March, have discontinued working."—*Considerations, &c.*, a pamphlet by Tycho Wing, Esq., 1840. This pamphlet contains a condensed view of the advantages to be derived from a proper drainage of the Middle Level. From the same pamphlet we extract the following sound remarks: "Nothing is more certain than that water stagnating near the surface of the fen lands for any considerable time greatly injures the roots of growing wheat, thus rendering the corn defective in quantity, and still more in quality. It likewise destroys clover, and all those valuable grasses which strike their roots deep in the ground, and more than this dissolves, and when put in motion by wind or steam engines, carries away with it, the soluble fertilising particles in the soil, from whatever source derived, whether from its natural composition or from manures applied, and thus occasions lasting injury to its productive powers. Hence there can be no doubt that many fen lands, which are usually regarded as well drained by the existing system of engines, do in reality suffer very much from the causes here stated, even when water is seldom or perhaps never seen level with their surface. A striking and familiar testimony to the truth of this remark may be drawn from the dark blood-colored water which is thrown out by mills, whereas in those parts of the North Level where the drainage is by the natural descent to sea, and is tolerably rapid, the water in the drains is colorless and transparent. The truth is, that all the water which cannot be retained by the soil or absorbed by vegetation ought to be drawn off the soil without being suffered to stagnate: then it has no time to dissolve the fertile but soluble matters mixed with the soil: on the contrary, by its slow but uniform filtration and gentle motion through the earth, it communicates and mixes the various substances in that equal manner which is most conducive to fertility. This is accomplished in the fens by a natural drainage when the vent is kept always open in winter, so that every shower of rain which falls in excess on the land begins immediately, and without a moment's delay, to pass gradually away; and the manifest increased fertility of parts of the North Level, which were previously held to be well drained, since the new system of a natural drainage was introduced there, affords an illustration of the nature of this argument, and the strongest confirmation of its truth."

the latter place, induced a public meeting at Peterborough, in 1836, to make certain resolutions, requesting Sir John Rennie " to re-examine the surveys, sections, plans, and estimates, made by his late father and by himself, or by others, with a view of re-adjusting the same according to the altered circumstances of the river by the operation of the Nene Outfall, and of other works subsequent to those surveys, according to the reduction in the value of land, labor, timber, and all materials, since the former estimates were made."[1] The report, which was completed in the course of the following year, affords a variety of valuable facts on the whole district over which the improvements were intended to be distributed. Sir John states the defects in drainage and navigation to be caused by: " First—The irregular, circuitous, and obstructed channel of the river, the defective bridges, the deficiency of banks and forelands, and the want of adaptation and classification in the drains;" and he proceeds to enumerate his method of removing them. The chief purpose of the promoters of this work was to secure a navigation to Peterborough, and inclose Morton's Leam Wash; the third point—that of draining 50,000 acres of the Middle Level—was only half-fearfully adventured on, and stated with hesitation. " Sir John Rennie is desired to consider this question of the Middle Level as distinct from those previously stated, and involving only an incidental result, inasmuch as the landowners in the Middle Level may be generally averse to any interference with their present course of drainage by the Ouse."[2] But this, notwithstanding, became the base of the whole scheme, and in the end was the destruction of it.[3] Its grand natural

(1) Instructions to Sir John Rennie, April, 1835, (2) Ibid.

(3) The means of effecting Peterborough navigation and draining Morton's Leam Wash, do not belong to this branch of our subject; but the plan by which Sir John Rennie proposed to render the passage of the Nene through Wisbech free and unobstructive, may be interesting to many of our readers: " I would recommend, in the first place," says his Report, " that the present old bridge should be removed entirely, together with the adjoining houses on the north and south sides of the river below the bridge. The river, so enlarged, would be more than double its present width; and, as the bottom would be excavated to five feet deeper than the present, the sectional areas, both at high water and low water, would be more than doubled. The old bridge should be replaced by a new one having a single arch of

features, based on the nature of the country, may yet in the end be adopted.

The district which was proposed to be drained was that comprised between the Old Nene and the South or Morton's Leam Bank, extending from Whittlesey Mere west to Guyhirn east. This district contains about 50,000 acres, most of which is in the melancholy condition we have described, and of which Whittlesey, Ugg, and Trundle Meres are but modifications. There are two drains in one line running through the centre of the district—Bevil's Leam and the Twenty-foot—which Sir John proposed to employ as his main channels, by re-excavating them and continuing them from Guyhirn through the centre of Whittlesey Mere to Caldecot, making a branch drain from Pond's Bridge through the southern portion of the fen, and surrounding the whole, from Standground to Ramsey Mere, with a catchwater drain. This plan, simple and comparatively inexpensive, he anticipated would give the fen a natural drainage, and drain Whittlesey Mere. Its advantages over the present system will be best seen by a comparison of facts and distances. The whole cost was estimated at £185,330 for the river Nene, and £120,260 for the Middle Level.

The three extreme points of this fen and the terminations of the proposed drains are Standground, Caldecot Farm, and the end of Monk's Lode, between Sawtry and Wood Walton.

about 150 feet span, which would be more than double the width of the present bridge; proceeding upwards, the channel should be enlarged as far as practicable, leaving sufficient width on both sides for the carriage road, until arriving at about 900 feet above the bridge, where the angles should be taken off entirely, and both sides of the channel from thence downwards through the town should be faced with substantial quay and walls, if required, as nearly perpendicular as practicable; by this means the greatest additional area would be gained at the low water line, which is most desirable, and the adjoining buildings will be effectually preserved against being undermined by the current, a danger to which they are much exposed at present, and always have been requiring annually, at great expense, a large quantity of stone, or other heavy material, to be thrown into this part of the river, which again in a short time is dislodged and deposited in shoals lower down, very much to the injury of the navigation and drainage. It may be a question, well worthy of consideration, whether it would not be advisable to construct a wet dock for the increasing trade of the town on either side of the river, which would have the additional advantage of taking the vessels out of the main channel of the river, and affording an increased facility for the discharge of the upland waters in cases of flood."—*Report*, 1836. The cost of these improvements in Wisbech was estimated at £91,975.

Standground is twenty-three miles direct from Sutton Bridge, twenty-nine from Lynn; Caldecot is twenty-seven miles from Sutton Bridge, thirty-three from Lynn; the end of Monk's Lode is twenty-nine miles from Sutton Bridge, thirty-five from Lynn. There is thus, at all these extreme points, a common saving of six miles direct distance between the proposed outfall and the present outfall, or perhaps rather more, as Sutton Bridge is nearer the outfall of the Nene than Lynn Bridge is to that of the Ouse. But when we trace the proposed lines of drains by which the district was to be drained into the Nene, and the lines of drains by which it is now drained into the Ouse, the advantage of the former becomes much more apparent. The distance of Caldecot by the drainage from Sutton Bridge is twenty-eight miles, thus giving only a mile of deviation from the direct distance by drains already made; while the distance of the same point from Lynn is forty-two miles, or fourteen miles farther, and giving a deviation of no less than nine miles from direct distance, which is spent on a succession of contrary courses and angles, so that none but a drainage having the most absolute fall could succeed.

The levels of these extremities of the fen in their lowest parts average seven feet six inches elevation[1] above low water

(1) These numbers are from Mr. Walker's levels, who states them as follows:—

		Above Datum. Ft.	in.
Low ground south of Ramsey Mere	lowest	7	0
" " " "	average	8	0
North and west of Ramsey Mere	lowest	7	0
" " " "	average	8	0
Whittlesey Mere	lowest	7	9
" "	average	8	6
Washes around Whittlesey Mere, including Yaxley, Stilton, and the adjoining Fen	lowest	11	0
" " " " " " " "	average	11	6
Wood Walton, Connington, Sawtry, Holme, banks of Monk's Lode, Ravely Drain, and New Dyke	lowest	10	0
" " " " " " " "	average	12	0

One foot is to be deducted from the numbers as Mr. Walker's datum is one foot below low water mark on Lynn Bridge.

on Lynn Freebridge, but the general average of the district is about ten feet eight inches above the same point. If, therefore, we apply these numbers to the Ouse at Lynn, and the Nene at Sutton Bridge, the advantage of the latter point strikes us with redoubled force. The Nene, according to Rennie, ebbs five feet eight inches lower than the Ouse;[1] but, according to Walker, it ebbs only three feet six inches lower below Sutton Bridge.[2] Taking, therefore, the latter number, we have an average elevation of eleven feet for the lowest portions of the fen above low water mark in the Nene, and fourteen feet two inches as the general average elevation of the district. Taking the average distance of the district, according to the foregoing numbers, at twenty-six miles from Sutton Bridge and thirty-seven from Lynn, the lowest portions give 2.8 inches fall per mile, and the average of the district four inches per mile, to their present outfall; while, by the Nene, the lowest fens average 5.2 inches, and the general district 6.5 inches fall per mile. These, however, are only numbers gained by a process which cannot be applied in practice. The only way by which we can arrive at a perfect notion of the advantage of draining into the Nene is by applying the above elevations to the actual length of drains which their waters have to traverse. These we have shown are twenty-six miles to Sutton Bridge and thirty-seven to Lynn Bridge, from which we readily find that, allowing eighteen inches fall from the surface of the land to the drain, there are about two inches fall per mile for the lowest portions, and not quite three inches for the average of the district to Lynn, but that there are 3.8 inches for the lowest by Sutton, and 5⅓ inches for the average of the district: in other words, the fen is nearly twice as high above the Nene as it is above the Ouse.[3]

(1) Report, 1839. (2) Report, 1842.

(3) We have made our calculations from Mr. Walker's levels, so that what argument there may be in these numbers is Mr. Walker's own testimony against his own plan. The levels of Sir John Rennie—which we have only had an opportunity of consulting since the above was written—do not agree in every particular with the above, as they are taken from a different datum. We may subjoin the most particular facts relating to this part of the Level.

It might have been supposed that these facts would have been sufficiently intelligible to have made Sir John Rennie's plan at once approved, especially as the casualties of such a country might at the most important time render the smallest advantage invaluable. There was only seven feet and a half fall to be distributed over forty-two miles before it reached its discharge at Lynn. This, it is to be remembered, is taken at low water during a time when there are no floods to lift the level of the outfall. But suppose a flood, in which it would be not unusual for the Ouse to be lifted five feet. This would reduce the fall to two feet and a half, or little more than one foot if we deduct the fall from the soil to the drain, for the forty-two miles by Lynn; but it would, under the same circumstances, give five feet fall for twenty-eight miles by Wisbech: in other words, the waters would lie on the lands in the one case, and be rapidly discharged from them in the other. This seems to be insisted on by Sir J. Rennie,

Sir John Rennie's datum is the cill of the North Level New Sluice; but in order to get the real available fall 3½ feet are to be deducted from his elevations,—2 feet for water on the cill of the Sluice at the date of observation, and 1½ feet for the fall from the surface of the land to the drains:—

	Above Datum.		Dist. from N. Level Sluice.	Fall per Mile.
	Ft.	in.	Miles.	Inches.
Lowest part of Whittlesey Mere	8	6	23	2.6
Principal part of the bed	9 or, 10	0 0	23	3.4
Behind the banks of the Wash at Guyhirn..........	12	6	15½	
Near Whittlesey Dyke	8	6	22½	
Between Yaxley and Stilton Fen ....lowest	11	9	26	4
" " " .... average	12	9		
At Caldecot Dyke.........................lowest	11	3	26½	4½
" " .... average	12	9		
Holme Dyke to Monk's Lode ....lowest	11	6	....	4½
" " " ...., average	12	6		
Near Ravely Drain	12	0	27	4
Ravely Drain to Ramsey Mere.............lowest	10	6	24	3½
" " " " .... average	14	3		5¼
Ramsey Mere to Whittlesey Dyke ....lowest	8	3	18	3½
" " " " .... average	8	8		4

where he explains that "by draining this district into the Nene there would be a fall of two or three inches per mile, during floods, from the lowest parts; whereas, by Mr. Walker's plan by the Ouse, there would be scarcely a fall of one inch per mile, and obtained at a cost of about double."[1]

Notwithstanding such facts, and the disposition which men in such circumstances as the fenmen generally possess to avoid expensive works, and to patronise the most obvious methods, so great a clamour was raised against this plan that it was forejudged before it was examined, and rejected by the Middle Level proprietors, whose lands it did not include, almost from the beginning. The main argument which they used was the disturbance it would effect in the old system of drainage, never reflecting that in fact it was a partial restoration of the old system, or system first pursued in the natural state of the fens, instead of that forced upon them by artificial works.[2] But Sir John Rennie's plan had aroused them as it were from a lethargy. They began to think something was wanted, and resolved to give their consideration to a general drainage of the Level. For this purpose Messrs. Little and Human, superintendents under the Bedford Level Corporation, were employed to devise a general plan, including the drainage of Whittlesey Mere. The plan which these gentlemen recommended was simple enough. They proposed to effect every necessity by scouring the present watercourses,

(1) Rennie's Letter to the Duke of Bedford.

(2) In order to show the sort of arguments which overthrew this scheme we quote some statements of one of its main opponents, made at a meeting at Whittlesey, in 1840:—"The new North Level drainage is a failing measure, and the present plan is devised more to remedy its defects than to improve the Middle Level drainage." He maintained that the Middle Level was better drained than the North, and that "the artificial drainage of low lands has many advantages over natural drainage."—*Newspaper Report.* As if to convict such fallacies, for two months the next winter the Middle Level, with artificial drainage, was under water, and some hundred thousand ponnds' worth of its property destroyed; while the North Level, with natural drainage, hardly suffered. Another person of the same order, at a subsequent meeting at March, contended that the advice of men of science was useless in draining. At the same meeting Tycho Wing, Esq., showed that at that time "the low water at the Tongs was only one foot six inches below the average bed of Whittlesey Mere, while low water at Guyhirn was three feet six inches below the Tongs." That is, there was one foot six inches fall for twenty-four miles to the Tongs, and five feet for thirteen miles to Guyhirn.

uniting Vermuyden's Drain with the Sixteen-foot, and making a new cut, four miles and a half long, from the Old Bedford to Well Creek. By this method the drainage of Whittlesey Mere—a principal and imperative object—would have been effected, as at present, over a course of forty-two miles, or about one-third more distance than by Wisbech, with one-third less fall.[1] But many who rejected the Wisbech scheme with contempt were sanguine in their hopes of this. They seemed to consider drainage as a kind of magnetism, of which Lynn was the attractive pole of the Whittlesey waters, and Wisbech their repellent one. Still there were difficulties to overcome. The employment of men not scientifically educated in engineering had emboldened many others to believe themselves as capable of devising a perfect plan of drainage. Several, therefore, now propagated independent schemes, and each securing his party thought only of hunting the rest out of the field. Under these circumstances, it is not surprising that the scheme of Messrs. Little and Human, though prepared for parliament, did not progress, but was overwhelmed by its opponents, who in turn were swallowed up by one another, and nothing seemed likely to be done.

At this period the country received an admonition which it was obliged to regard. The whole summer of 1841 had been wet, the autumn was not less so, and the winter set in mild with almost continual rain. It was only on the most favored lands that the winter seed could be sown, and by December the Middle Level proprietors began to be alarmed for their property. The rain did not cease during January, but sometimes for four-and-twenty hours together fell in torrents. The effect of this downfall was now manifest enough. Almost all the Middle Level was under water, the rivers were swollen with freshes which could not subside, the mills could not make head against the flood, the water rose to fourteen feet above zero at the Old Bedford Sluice, Denver Sluice was

(1) Down Bevil's Leam, then at a right angle down Whittlesey Dyke, thence at an acute angle into the Old Nene, thence down Popham's Eau, thence at an obtuse angle into the Tongs, thence into the Ouse.

in danger, and banks were torn down by the violence of the torrent. This desolation, sent just at the time when folly most needed such advice, was not unheeded. The proprietors again bestirred themselves, and, tired of their own schemes and their own janglings, they resolved to refer the subject to an educated engineer. A meeting for this purpose was held at Chatteris in April, 1842. Sir John Rennie had shown himself so favorable to draining the northern part of the Level by the Nene that he was at once rejected, and Mr. James Walker was called in, with directions to make the best drainage possible for the Level, but on no account to drain by Wisbech.

1842. In the following August Mr. Walker made his report, in which he introduced a feature before unpractised, and we believe unsuggested, in fen drainage—the separation of navigation from drainage. This he proposed to effect by "draining the whole Middle Level by means of a new straight drain of sufficient capacity, made so low as to be entirely under such of the present rivers and drains as are navigable, these rivers and drains being carried over and across the new drain in cast iron aqueducts for the purposes of navigation and the supply of fresh water for the land and cattle."[1] This new drain was to extend from Caldecot Farm on the west of Whittlesey Mere to the upper end of the Eau Brink Cut, its length being thirty-one miles. The drain was to be level in its whole length, and its expense, with the works which would be required to make it efficient, was estimated at £360,000.[2]

This report was discussed at a meeting at Chatteris in November, 1842; but the enormous expense which it entailed, and the confession which Mr. Walker had been obliged to make, "that there are some low places upon which in high

(1) Report, 1842.

(2) Speaking of this report, Sir John Rennie says:—"It appears to be defective in many of those great principles which the late Mr. Rennie, as well as Kinderley, Armstrong, Smeaton, Brindley, Myine, Telford, and other authorities who preceded him, considered absolutely essential for the combined purposes of navigation and drainage."—*Letter to the Duke of Bedford*, p. 11.

floods water may for a short time stand too near the surface for perfect natural drainage,"[1] induced the meeting to reject the plan by a large majority, and for half a year more the matter slept.

A party, however, determined on having something done had, during these preparations and defeats, been only more firmly organised by their disappointments, and in July they again began to prepare for a new campaign. At this time no single scheme was discussed, but a sort of union was made of portions of the preceding schemes—a third of Mr. Walker's drain being joined to the fourth of Messrs. Little and Human's plan, with bits from those of Messrs. Lawrence and Mylne. Mr. Walker was induced to become sponsor for the design, and notwithstanding the opposition of those who contended there needed no better drainage, and those who adhered to cleansing and deepening the old works, it was carried, and a committee appointed for effecting the preliminaries for introducing it into parliament in 1844. The resolution on the one side was only equalled by the animosity on the other. The Bedford Level Corporation firmly opposed the measure, and means, vigorous if not prudent, appear to have been adopted by the advocates to secure their scheme.

The measure progressed, and the report which was finally adopted, recommended a drain "branching from Popham's Eau near the north end of the Sixteen-foot, and proceeding, as nearly as circumstances will allow, in a direct line to the Ouse, near the upper end of the Eau Brink Cut."[2] This, which may be termed Mr. Walker's portion, was to be seconded by scouring and deepening the present water-courses, so as to be able to lower the water in them to one general uniform level, which was to be three feet ten inches below the present navigation level; and it was expected to defray the expenses of the works by a tax of 1*s.* 6*d.* on drained lands for twenty-three years, and a tax proportioned

(1) Report.

(2) Committee Report, September, 1843.

to the benefit conferred on those at that time undrained.[1] The advantages to be gained by this cut, which is merely prolonging the Sixteen-foot to the Eau Brink, is the avoidance of the channel of the Ouse north of Denver, and it is in principle merely an extension of the Tongs. The course of the Ouse which this drain will avoid is encumbered by several features hurtful to drainage, the principal of which are, an accumulation of silt between Stow and Denver; hards at Shingle Hill and below Magdalen, by which the river bed is lifted seven feet; and a serious bend at Magdalen, which further promotes the other obstructions. These obstructions had altogether made a difference of ten feet between Denver and the Eau Brink Cut, a distance of ten miles, giving a fall of twelve inches per mile in a district whose common fall is less than two inches per mile. The Tongs Drain gave an advantage of three of these feet to the Level, so that the increased advantage to be secured by the new drain, if it be all realised, will be five or six feet, or, if we may trust some of its opponents, only three feet three inches.[2] It is remarkable that this scheme, professedly advocated by Mr. Walker, should, contrary to his former leading principle, have connected navigation and drainage. In his previous measure he had denounced navigation as the bane of drainage; now he encouraged it. "My instructions," he says in 1842, "are to suggest the very best means of effectually improving the drainage of the Middle Level, having a regard to navigation. And this I propose doing by entirely separating navigation from drainage. Both useful in themselves, they have been long united, but have never agreed; and the attempt to reconcile them, and at the same time keep them together, has been the stumbling-block and difficulty of all the schemes I have referred to or know, as well as the great cause of

(1) "Instead of a tax of 1*s*. 6*d*. for twenty-three years, it must be double if not treble that sum for perpetuity."—*Speech of Mr. Gay, April, 1844, at the Bedford Level Corporation Meeting.*

(2) "In Whittlesey Mere the land was seven feet nine inches above zero, that at the end of the cut was four feet six inches, leaving only a fall of three feet three inches, or an inch and a half per mile."—*Mr. Austin, in Committee.*

constant disputes and of nothing useful having been done to relieve the country from the evils which it has suffered."[1] Opinions so decidedly expressed might reasonably be thought permanent; but they were entirely abandoned in this new scheme.[2]

The measure proceeded with difficulty, but on the whole successfully, though opposed by the Bedford interest and the Bedford Level Corporation, and it was finally carried. It may be wondered how parties, who arrayed themselves so strongly against a measure of decided hope, could, with their money and influence, support one with so little of that feature to recommend it as this. It is true it is in a certain degree beneficial, but it may be queried whether it does not entail an evil that will in the end neutralise most of its advantages. The point to be attained in all drainage is to gain the greatest benefit at the least expense. This is manifestly done by securing, if possible, a fall independent of artificial drainage, and the only means to insure this is to make drains in direct lines to the lowest and nearest point. Moreover, these means are of comparatively small value if the final basin that is to receive the drainage be obstructed. We have shown the difference of fall and distance between parts of the Middle Level and Wisbech, so that it seems an idle and fruitless waste of labor and money to carry those waters to Lynn which, in little more than half the space, would secure three times the fall by Wisbech. It was, moreover, shown on the parliamentary investigation that low water in Lynn Deeps is seven feet beneath the zero or low water point in the Eau Brink Cut. Although this fact indicates a considerable impediment in the channel of the river, yet no provision was made to secure these seven feet, and, as in the Nene Outfall, confer on the lowest parts natural drainage. Mr. Walker, on his

(1) Report, 1842.

(2) "Its defects were that instead of separating navigation and drainage, it united them." —*Mr. Austin's Speech in Committee, May*, 1844. "It is impossible to forget the great importance which Mr. Walker attributes to the separation of drainage and navigation, and the total abandonment by this measure of that most important object, and not only its abandonment, but the perpetration of that objection."—*Mr. Merivale, in Committee, June*, 1844.

examination, admitted that one-third of the Middle Level would still be obliged to employ the artificial system, and it may be greatly doubted whether a general resort of the districts to steam drainage would not have imparted more sensible advantages to the Level at less expense.

Since the above was written Mr. Walker, in conjunction with Mr. Burges, has published another report on the Middle Level, in which he endeavours to separate navigation from drainage by a system different from his former one. We have in this report his own opinion of what may be called his own measures, which will be best shown in the following extracts. "The average of the low fens is about eight feet four inches above datum,[1] or about two feet above the navigation level of 1844, which is considered the smallest proper difference between the surface of the soil and the surface of the water, and this in the absence of all flood. *Machinery, therefore, will be indispensable for by far the greater portion of the Middle Level;* the cases where it may not be required being rather exceptions to the general rule. * * It will, with the advantage of the new main drain in the lower district, and the aid of machinery, prevent the future flooding of any of the fens that will take advantage of it; but that the power of wind or steam engines will generally be indispensable, and that the navigation, particularly through the towns, will be prejudiced. There appear, also, great difficulties in the way of extending this plan at any future time, so as still further to improve the drainage of the country, whenever a better outlet to sea may be obtained."[2] In order to remove or moderate the features respecting navigation, which with nearly four feet less water must, in many parts at many times, be wholly impossible, Messrs. Walker and Burges propose to divide the present drains and rivers, setting some apart for navigation and others for drainage, and in the former to lift the waters, in the latter to lower them; thus "leaving the

(1) "Taking zero on Lynn Freebridge as datum, the present navigation level is ten feet two inches above it, and the future level being three feet ten inches less will, therefore, be six feet four inches above zero."—*Report*, 1846.

(2) Report, October, 1846.

rivers that pass through the towns in their present state, without at all deepening them, but raising the navigation standard in them one foot, and deepening some of the other rivers to a greater extent than is proposed by the act. This deepening we propose to be two feet below datum, the bottoms afterwards being level throughout, or on an average three feet below the Parliamentary Plan of 1844, and only sixteen inches lower than was intended for the north or lower end of the Sixteen-foot river. Thus the capability of drainage will be much increased, while the navigation through the rivers will still be preserved:"[1] and he then proceeds to show that by the Parliamentary Plan, by which name he now rather cavalierly designates the scheme he adopted, "the water in the rivers during heavy floods will generally be from one to two feet *above* the surface of the low fens, while, by the suggested modification, the floods will be two feet *under* the level of the same fens."[2] But the additional charge of £100,000, which this alteration would at least entail, caused a speedy rejection of the scheme, which certainly holds out fairer hopes than the received plan.

This is the last great work of drainage which has been undertaken for the relief of the Level, and at this time (September, 1846,) its effects have yet to be tested, as it is now in course of construction. We can only regret that, with such well-authenticated proofs of obstructions at the Lynn outfall, works were not commenced there. The conformation of this country, so situated as to be often under the waters of the ocean which washes its embankments, requires first of all to have its passage free to seaward. With its outfalls blocked up, though its internal drains be ever so open, it is impossible to drain the land; but with its internal drains obstructed, and its outfalls free, it is still possible to obtain a partial drainage. It follows, therefore, that the outfalls are more important than the sewers, yet we find the greatest doubts and reluctance to interfere with the seaward

(1) Report, October, 1846. (2) Ibid.

portions of the main rivers, and with the Ouse this necessary work has scarcely been attempted at all. The Rennies, Rendell, Cubitt, Telford, have shown that the principal hindrances to drainage lie to seaward—that, by carrying the fen rivers to deep water, a more effectual discharge might be procured than by a hundred mere intersections of internal watercourses; and on the last work, whose history we have just detailed, this principle was proclaimed with more assurance, even by Walker himself, than the moderate scheme which he consented to protect. "Whenever," he says, "either by means of a cut across the marshes below Lynn, as proposed by the late Mr. Rennie, or by continuing and straightening the channel, the low water in the Eau Brink Cut shall be lowered, then the natural drainage of every part of the Middle Level may be considered complete."[1] But these facts surely do not need substantiating by any authority. It is clear that the obstruction that should be first removed is that which is felt by every part of a system, not the inconsiderable and partial stoppage which is only felt by a small district of it.

But it may be doubted whether any system of drainage in the Fens can be permanently serviceable, unless it is formed on some enlarged and comprehensive system; some resort to nature and some to art. The Fens are a large basin which, but for drainage, would be generally a standing pool, formed by the washings of the high border lands. The great reservoir into which they discharge their contents is filled with sediment, which every wind and tide throws into the mouths of its rivers. If the Fens were of greater elevation, the force which these elevations would give the fresh waters falling into their outfall, would effectually cleanse whatever the tide and tempests might deposit, and—as in the Rhone, which brings vast quantities of earthy materials from its mountains, —drive the suspended matter forward till it subsided in deep water. But the fen rivers are placed in such peculiar rela-

(1) Report, 1842.

tion to the sea—their force is so nearly balanced by the sea force—that they have no energy to push forward, but become passive and clogged up, unless art brings in its aid to assist them. In these circumstances, whatever force can be imparted to the fen waters requires to be economised and used as effectually as possible. It is clear that the rivers which have the greatest quantity of fresh waters to scour them, have the greatest chance of keeping their channels open, provided those channels are restricted against weakening themselves with breadth. It is, then, an exceeding waste of impoverished means to send the fresh waters of these regions to sea in three or four separate streams, instead of combining them into one stream, and driving them into their receptacle in a firm united body, That this was the original method of nature seems pretty evident from the history of the Great Ouse, which, as we have already shown, discharged itself originally by Wisbech, carrying with it the waters of the Nene and even part of those now discharged by the Welland. Engineers have not been entirely blind to this fact; but the extent of the work and the adverse interests it would involve have made them shrink from any plan which might be considered perfect. Nathaniel Kinderley, in 1751, proposed to blend the outfalls of the Nene and Ouse by a cut from Shire Drain Sluice across Marshland, falling into the Ouse at that point which is now the lower end of the Eau Brink Cut; and, by a like method, he proposed to unite the outfalls of the Witham and Welland by a cut from Fossdyke past Boston, where it united with the Witham and was carried into deep water at Leverton. "The rivers so conjoined," he says, "will be much more strong to rush through the sands and make their way to sea than they can do now separately, as any man in reason may easily conceive."[1] Vermuyden entertained a similar idea of conjoining the fen rivers. "To make sure works, I advise to bring the aforesaid rivers [Nene and Welland] into one, that they may in time gain them-

(1) Ancient and Present State of the Navigations of Lynn, Wisbech, and Spalding.

selves a natural channel, which will be far better than to bring them to sundry outfalls."[1] Colonel Dodson had preceded Kinderley in his idea of bringing the Nene and Ouse together. He says: "As for the river of Wisbech, I carry it in a river through Marshland, from the Horseshoe to the great sluice at German's Bridge, then have I sufficient waterway for all these freshes to the sea, which will force good navigation and maintain the channel winter and summer."[2] The advantages which would accrue from this method of blending the rivers, each engineer represents as very great. But the last and greatest proposal of the kind was brought forward by Sir John Rennie, in 1839, in a plan which, in its design and comprehensive utility, has never been excelled. Instead of dividing the outfalls between Lynn and Boston, he took a more enlarged view; and, as Wisbech lies centrally on the Wash, he proposed to restore part of the ancient system by blending the Ouse, Welland, and Witham into the outfall of the Nene, and driving their accumulated waters to sea in one grand outfall. He proposed to unite the three rivers at that point in the Wash called the "Roaring Middle," leaving them an outfall three miles wide[3] through the centre of Lynn Deeps; and to reclaim the rest of the Wash, of about twelve miles breadth, as far as Wainfleet Harbour on the Lincoln coast, and Gore Point on the Norfolk coast. By these means an accession of 150,000 acres would have been added to the kingdom at the expense of £2,000,000, the land reclaimed being worth £6,000,000, leaving £4,000,000 profit for investment. But, besides this, it promised to draining all the advantages it could possibly receive by artificial means. Sir John Rennie proposed to effect this magnificent work by the usual system of warping and embankment. Now, as half the quantity of land proposed to be enclosed is left dry at low water, and the deepest

(1) Discourse, &c., 1613.

(2) Design for the perfect Drainage, &c., 1665.

(3) Our description is drawn from the plan accompanying Rennie's *Report*,—the details not having been given, we believe, in any other form.

part to be rescued is not more than sixty feet deep, the work will not be thought insuperable when it is borne in mind that parts of the Ouse, in five or six years after the opening of the Eau Brink Cut, warped up twenty-five feet by nature alone.[1] The deepest part of Lynn Deeps—through which the proposed outfall is to be carried and held by barrier banks—is one hundred and fifty-six feet, but it averages not more than about sixty feet,[2] and the major portion of the parts to be enclosed which are under low water mark are not six feet deep.

The great extent of the scheme, and the consequent difficulty of inducing speculators to embark their capital, has delayed, if not wholly prevented, for many years the prosecution of the entire plan. A portion of it, however, lying between the Nene and Ouse, and consisting of about 30,000 acres, has found a company to undertake the work; but these have met with unforseen difficulty. Three applications to parliament have been defeated, and the company were obliged to make large allotments of land and fee with heavy sums various claimants who have asserted rights of frontage to the parts about to be inclosed, in order to secure the recognition of parliament to their fourth application. The act, by these means, was obtained in August, 1846, and the work is thus so far prosperous; but the expenses of their defeats, and other disbursements of the company, have so depressed its prospects that, though there is little doubt of its remuneration, there is much doubt whether it will be so highly lucrative as was at first anticipated. Sir John Rennie anticipates that 10,000 acres will be ready for enclosure and sale in 1860, at a cost of £15 per acre; other 10,000 acres in 1870, at a cost of £25 per acre; and the residue, 10,000 acres, in 1880, at a cost of £30 per acre. But preliminary to this, a cut 400 feet wide at its commencement and four miles long is to be made, in lieu of the present uncertain, shallow, and winding channel of the Ouse, commencing from

(1) Rennie's Report, 1839. (2) Chart of Lynn and Boston Deeps.

the Harbour of Lynn, proceeding through Vinegar Middle into the main channel near the Breast Beacon. By this, says Rennie, "the low water mark during floods will be lowered from four to six feet. The tide also at Lynn will rise an additional height from low to high water of five to six feet."[1] It will also reduce the distance between Lynn Harbour and the sea by two or three miles, and materially lessen the port expenses of buoys, beacons, and pilotage.

The drainage of the Middle and South Levels could scarcely receive a greater boon than this. It promises, as far as the different situations of the Fens with respect to their outfall admit, to confer on the Levels draining by the Ouse the same kind of benefit as the Nene Outfall conferred on the lands draining by that river.

In tracing the works which have either been agitated, begun, or finished in the Fens during this century, we have seen some of the boldest and greatest plans entertained which have ever been conceived for improving such a district. The half of the century is not yet accomplished; yet, during that period, the Eau Brink Cut and the Nene Outfall[2] have been completed, and the Middle Level drainage partially so; and the last-mentioned work, the Norfolk Estuary, is now commenced. Fenmen might be proud of such works, even if they had failed in their principal objects; but the two which have already been tried have been singularly fortunate in this respect. The Eau Brink Cut was only not so satisfactory as the Nene Outfall, because it was not wrought to the same extent; it was not begun with such boldness and finished with such confidence. Had it been carried to sea in the same manner as the Nene Outfall, it is scarcely prediction to say its effects would have been as thoroughly satisfactory. Still there are great and lamentable defects in the Fens, and the same energy which has been manifested for the last fifty years will be

(1) Report, March, 1846.

(1) The Nene Outfall, though properly belonging to the History of the Fens, has had so striking an influence on the trade and prosperity of Wisbech, that we have decided to include its history in the portion of the work devoted to the history of the trade and commerce of the town.

needed, not only to maintain what has been done, but to devise and execute new methods to relieve and rescue lands still more subject to the waters than to the service of man.

The extremities of the Fens are the parts which yet feel the effects of a deficient system in the most grievous manner, and we are sorry that the heavy expenses of one of the great works we have named, chiefly incurred to remedy these portions of the fen, hold out at present very uncertain prospects of fulfilling their purpose. But the extraordinary richness of the land after it has yielded to drainage soon pays the most extravagant expenses, so that in such a country one failure is not likely to prevent the trial of new methods. If land can be raised in a few years from £10 to £70 value per acre, the burden of a small drainage tax is of little moment compared with such manifest benefit. We may notice, however, that the schemes which have uniformly produced the most effect in the Fens, and have been most generally successful, are those which have been directed and controlled by some ostensible head in whom all could confide, and whose knowledge was equal to his task. The first general drainage owed some if not all its success to this principle, and the Nene Outfall was fortunate enough to adopt its leader and adhere to him. The want of success in the late Middle Level scheme may, on the other hand, be attributed to the independent and contrary opinions of the many counteracting and reversing every movement forward: it was a scheme without a head, and it is consequently a great mistake. However, there is valuable wisdom in such errors. The same parties are not likely to commit them again, and before many years have elapsed the proprietors of those fens will, perhaps, have to congratulate one another on some new and successful undertaking.

Engraved by John Mottram.

HISTORY

OF

WISBECH AND THE FENS.

SECTION II.—THE TOWN.

CHAPTER I.

GENERAL HISTORY OF WISBECH.

SO uncertain is our knowledge of the early condition of our island, that we have only accurate information of the existence of twenty-eight towns or cities during the Roman period; while an enumeration dating about the period of the Norman Conquest, makes the number of parish churches 45,011, and that of villages 62,080. As the number of parishes is now about 10,000, and villages about 15,000, this account has all the appearance of fable; but it is generally admitted that nearly every parish and village at present existing may trace itself,—either circumstantially, or by name or document,—to the Saxon period. Wisbech is fortunate in tracing its antiquity in one of the most authentic forms, as a charta of the Saxon king, Wolfere, to the monastery of Peterborough, before alluded to, makes distinct mention of it and Elm, A.D. 664: "The principal river that goethe to Elme and to Wisbeche."

The Romans at this period had left England more than two centuries, but if the great embankments raised in the neighbourhood were the work of the Romans for the purposes of defence, we can hardly doubt that Wisbech derived its origin from being one of the forts of those people. Its position, at the junction of the principal river of the district with the sea, marks it as an especial point of interest, and where the chief force of the Romans would be concentrated for an emergency. Its situation in the fen is peculiar, and corroborates the expediency from which we have supposed it to be derived. All the other towns, and most of the villages of the Fens, are situated on spots of a certain elevation above the surrounding district, which elevation is mostly a kind of wart on the surface of the fen, caused by some denser substratum than usual, as rock or gravel. Ely, Whittlesey, March, Chatteris, and others, are thus situated ; but Wisbech seems to have derived its existence merely from the embankments which lie about it, and at the present day all its older portions are built on the top of older embankments, at an elevation of ten or twelve feet above the level around. Both sides of Timber Market, Church Street, the Market Hill, may be instanced as portions of this original town, while the church, situate at the foot of the embankment, has generally led strangers to believe that it is placed on lower ground than the common level on which the town is built.

This circumstance of the town, or the original town, being situated on embankments, is peculiar, and shows that it has been derived wholly from those artificial constructions. Dr. Stukely supposes that Boston, Spalding, and Wisbech all originated in Roman forts, or that Roman forts were erected at all these places.[1] But his opinion, though valuable, has no firmer argument than conjecture, which seems, in the absence of better authority, to be the most rational method of accounting for the foundations of a town in a spot so

(1) "Beaupre Bell, Esq., in his letters published in *Bib. Top.*, dated 1730, gives the description of the pipes of a Roman aqueduct found at Wisbech, besides several other Roman antiquities."—*Watson's Hist. Wisbech*, p. 112.

unlikely to be selected, except by circumstances more powerful than natural choice.

Many towns trace a kind of genealogy in their names; but as this doubtful heraldry will not carry Wisbech further from the present time than King Wolfere's charta has done, we shall gain little by such an investigation. The Saxons wrote it *Visebec* or *Wisebec*. We have no difficulty in attributing the first syllable to the river Ouse, which is often called the *Wis* and the *Wise*;[1] but it is more uncertain whence the latter syllable *bech* is derived. Col. Watson, with much argument, says: "The latter syllable has commonly, or vulgarly, been considered as taking origin from *beach* of the sea; but may not the termination be found in the Saxon word *bec*, which signifies water or a running river." This interpretation seems the most rational that can be given. Leland uses *beck* in this signification in speaking of Lincolnshire: "The beck or brooke that runneth by the north side of the Abbaye of Bardeney, and within a half quarter of a myle lower runneth into the great Rhe of Lindis, is cawlid Panton Bek. Thys bek riseth yn Hy Lindesey."[2] Hammond's Beck, Poklington Beck, are only other examples of the same use of *beck*, which, in the southern parts of the Fens, has been almost universally softened into *bech* or *beche*. In the *Register of Peterborough* we find *beche* used in a similar sense: in describing Whittlesey Mere, we are told that "upon the east are two other meres called Wellepole and Trendlemere; betwixt which is a narrow stream, containing two furlongs in length, Trendlemere Beche, having in it two fishings." Three other *beches* are mentioned—Selfremere Beche, Trendemere Beche, and Oppebech, all of which are used to express a stream of water connecting one lake with another. There no less than twenty-three different streams or places in the Fens, mentioned by

(1) Dugdale describes a session of Sewers, where he mentions:—"The freeholders of Newton, Tyd, Leverington, and Wisebeche on the north of the *river of Wise*," [p. 307] and he says further, "So long as the outfall of Wisebeche had its perfect being, the whole river of Ouse had there its perfect outfall, from whence the town seemeth to have taken the denomination, viz., Ouse or Wisebeche."—p. 394.

(2) Itinerary.

Dugdale, which end in *beche*;[1] and a number of others which end in *beck*, as Pinchbeck and Skirbeck. These facts point decidedly to the signification of *bech* being a stream of water, and, consequently, that Wisbech signifies the *beche* or *stream* of the Ouse. It has been variously spelt at different periods. Dugdale generally spells it Wisbeche, often Wisebeche, and once Wyssebech, Wisbich, and Wisbidge. In *Doomsday Book* it is written Wisbece; on the Guild Seal, Wysbech; on the Castle Seal, Wisebech; and in the Chartas, Wysbeche. The form in which it is generally written by persons not inhabiting the town, as Wisbeach, nowhere occurs in any of the old forms, and seems to be merely a corruption founded on the assumption that the termination signifies a beach or shore.[2]

But if we can establish the existence of Wisbech so early as 664, we are able to do nothing else. Neither can we ascertain whether Wisbech, though mentioned in the Peterborough Charta, was included in the possessions of that monastery, as the document merely specifies the "river that goes to Elm and to Wisbech" as the eastern limit of these possessions. But all the lands in the Fens had been seized by King Borhead, and had undergone violent changes in the eighth century; and King Edgar, in 970, restored the possessions of the Church to their original owners, in which Wisbech does not appear to be included, for, about thirty years subsequent to this event, Wisbech is named as being

(1) These are: Langbeche, Trendemere beche, Selfremere beche, Trendelmere beche, Oppebeche, Ayxschabeche, Hagbeche, Holbeche, Briggbech, Broadbeche, Warbech, Budbech, Cannesbeche, Chelebeche, Cheseebeche, Dukesbech, Nobeche, Rousebeche, Rebbech, Wisebeche.

(2) It has been argued, with very apparent authority, that Wisbech may have derived its termination from the French term *bouche*. "The name is derived from Ousebeach, being a compound of Ouse and beach, being the beach (from *bouche*, mouth, Fr.) or outfall of the river Ouse."—*Cooke's Topographical Description of Cambridgeshire*. This derivation accounts for the circumstances of situation in a much better manner than the Saxon derivation; but we know the French terms were wholly unused in England before the Norman Conquest, or, at any rate, the reign of Edward the Confessor, and Wisbech we have shown to have had this name some four hundred years previous to that event. Though, therefore, such a derivation is most agreeable to theory, it can hardly be substantiated when we find the Saxon term used in its Saxon sense in the Fens so many years previously.

one of the manors bestowed on the church of Ely by Oswy and Leoflede, when their son Ailwin, afterwards bishop of Elmham, was admitted into the monastery. Great part of these possessions still remain in the hands of that church, under the names of Wisbech Murrow and Wisbech Barton, —the former being appropriated to the Dean and Chapter, the latter, which is considerable, is possessed by the Bishop, —and constitute much of the leasehold and copyhold property now in the town and vicinity.[1]

The *Doomsday Book* affords us more specific facts on the disposition of property in this district, though from the uncertainty of some of the terms used the information is very unsatisfactory. The following are the portions relating to Wisbech:—

" CAMBRIDGESHIRE.

" *Land of the Abbot of Ely in Cestreton Hundred.*

" The Abbot of Ely holds the manor of Wisbece. There are 10 hides of land[2] and 10 caracutes.[3] In the lord's hands 1 hide & 1 virgate, and there are 2 caracutes. There are 15 villeins,[4] of whom each holds 10 acres, and 13 socmen,[5] of 2

(1) " Great part of this estate was assigned to the monks after Ely became a bishop's see, and now belongs to the Dean and Chapter of Ely. The remainder, " Wisbech Barton," was annexed to the see, and is the paramount manor of the hundred. The annual value of this last manor was taken, A.D. 1588, at £142 4s. 10d."—*Watson's History of Wisbech*, p. 116, *Note*.

(2) The quantity of land contained in a hide is very uncertain. Gervase of Tilbury makes it 100 acres. The Malmesbury MS., cited by Spelman, computes it at 96 acres, or 4 vigates each vigate being 24 acres. The history of the foundation of Battle Abbey makes 8 vigates go to a hide. Polydore Virgil makes a hide only 20 acres. " The truth seems to be," says a writer in the *Pictorial History of England*, " that a hide, a yard-land, a knight's fee, &c., contained no certain number of acres, but varied according to different places."

(3) " The caracute was of Norman introduction, and probably nearly corresponded in Norman to hide in Saxon. Its measure is involved in as much uncertainty as that of hide, Bp. Kennett gives instances of its application to quantities of land varying from 60 to as much as 150 acres."—*Pictorial England.*

(4) Villeins are acknowledged to have been the lowest and most numerous description of slaves in the feudal system. They were attached to the land, and could be sold with it as part of its stock or property; or they were attached only to the person of the lord. In the former case they are called *villains regardant*, in the latter, *villains in gross*. Many conjecture them to have been prisoners of war.

(5) Socmen were a higher class of dependents, holding land by a tenure inferior to the military tenure. Tenures in socage are supposed to have been services of a certain or ascertained kind. Blackstone describes this tenure as having "its renders or services ascertained."

hides and a half, which cannot nor are able to remove from all their 8 caracutes. There are 17 cottages, and 2 bondsmen.[1] The fisheries produced 1500 eels; 10 caracutes of pasture for the cattle of the town. In the whole it is and hath been valued at 100 shillings. In the time of King Edward the Confessor at £6. This manor lies and hath lain in the demesne of the church. In the same town two fisheries yielded the abbot 14,000 eels, and at present render 13*s.* 4*d.* The abbot hath soke over all the men of the town.

" *Land of St. Edmund's.* In Wisbece the same abbot hath one fishery which renders 5000 eels.

" *Land of the Church of Crowland.* In Cestreton Hundred. In Wisebece the Abbot of Crowland hath four fisheries rendering 14,000 eels.

" *Land of the Church of Ramsey.* In Norestor Hundred. In Wisbece the Abbot of Ramsey hath eight fisheries, which render 5260 eels.

" *Land of William de Warren.* In Wisbece William hath six fisheries in the Hundred of Ely, rendering 3500 eels and five shillings."[2]

The generality of opinions, which make a hide of land to be about 100 acres, and a caracute about as much, would give about 3000 acres as the amount of this manor. Attached to this quantity there seems to have been thirty menials—a number altogether insufficient for such a quantity of land

(1) These are supposed to have been the same as *villains in gross*, or serfs attached to the person of the lord.

(2) The following is the form in which the above particulars appear in *Doomsday Book:* " Grentebiscire. Terra abbatie de Elyg. In Cestretone Hund. M. Wisbece, tenr. abb. de Ely. Ibi x hide tra. e. x car. In dnio. i hida, & i virg. & ibi su ii car. Ibi xv villi. qsq. x ac. & xii sochi de ii hid. & dim. q. non potuer. nec poss. receder hi. oms. viii car. Ibi xvii cot. & ii servi. De piscar. mill. & q'ngent. anguill. ptu. x car. pasta. ad pec. villæ. Int. tot. val. & valuit c. sol. T. R. E. vi lib. hoc M. jacet & jacuit in dnio. eccle. In ead. villa ii piscat. redd. abbi xiiii mill. anguil. & de psent. xiii sol. & iiii den. Sup. oms. hoes. huj. ville ht. abb. socam.

Terra Sci Eadmundi. In Wisbece ht. isd. abb. i piscatore, redd. v mill. anguill.

Terra Eccle. de Croiland. In Cestredone Hd. In Wisbece ht. abb. de Croilant iiii piscat. redd. iiii x mill. anguill.

Terra Eccle. de Ramesyg. In Norestor Hund. In Wisbece ht. abb. de Ramesi viii piscatores redd. v mill. & cclx anguill.

Terra Willi de Warene. In Wisbece ht. Wills. vi piscatores in Hund. de Ely reddtes. iii mill. angnill. & dim. & v sol."

in the present day. At this time, however, agriculture was in a very subdued condition, and much less labor was employed upon it than at present. The fisheries are the most remarkable part of the document, and inform us circumstantially of the state of the country at this period. Eels seem, indeed, to have been an important part in the produce of Wisbech, and the rank muddy waters which they suggest give no very favorable color to the neighbourhood of the town at this early period. There is no mention made of the Castle, though, if the accounts of its foundation be correct, it must have been built many years previous to the Doomsday survey, which is commonly fixed at A.D. 1085, whereas the Castle at Wisbech was founded, according to the popular accounts, during the rebellion of Hereward, or immediately subsequent to that event, which would fix it at about A.D., 1073. The fact that the abbot had soke over all the men of the town is another feature, and shows that Wisbech was wholly and solely in the hands of the church, and it is probable the services of the men of the town were compounded into certain taxes.

With this wholly inadequate memorial we must be content. There is scarcely any other mention of Wisbech during this and the following periods. Boston on the one side and Lynn on the other became at an early date important from their commercial distinction and their religious establishments; but, although Wisbech appears to have been a greater place at an earlier period than either of them, it lost its importance by losing its river at the very time when the nation was becoming settled, and mercantile intercourse was beginning to make inroads in the passion for arms.

1190. But here, no less than in other towns, we can trace at intervals the gradual slackening of the bonds of the feudal system. The first record of this nature is in the second year of Richard I., when we learn that he granted the tenants of the Manor of Wisbech Barton a freedom or exemption from toll in all fairs or markets throughout England, which his brother John afterwards confirmed.[1] Unfortunately, we do not learn the cause of this royal gift; but we may estimate the value of it from the fact that a considerable part of the royal revenue was derived from the tolls extorted at fairs, though these were sometimes in the hands of the lords of the manor, whether churchmen or laymen. Our modern notions of fairs convey a very inadequate conception of the necessity of these places at these early stages of society. It was on their annual fairs that tradesmen then depended for their supplies; so that much of those taxes which are now laid in the form of customs and excise, were then extorted as tolls at fairs. In the convulsions which succeeded, this privilege appears to have been lost once if not more times, for it was renewed by Henry IV. in 1411, and confirmed by writ of privy seal in the time of Henry V. The inscription on the tomb of Nicholas Sandford, who died in 1638, honors him as the last restorer of the distinction,[2] or of some privilege of the same kind, for it is not clear that the exemption of Richard I. and Nicholas Sandford are identical.

1216. The next event which brings Wisbech into notice is the struggle of the latter years of King John. The Isle of Ely had become an arena where some of the minor events of that period were transacted, and, alternately in the hands of the Barons and the King, it was alternately subjected to ravage and plunder. The Barons at length obtained possession of the whole Isle with the exception of one castle, to which the friends of the King had retreated. Leland thinks this was Ely Castle,[3] but it is not improbable it was the castle at Wisbech, as John himself was at that place shortly afterwards, and it seems to have been attached to his cause; and the town, in consequence, appears to have been rewarded.[4] John had for some time hovered about the

(1) Lyson.

(2) "A patterne for townesmen, whom we may enrole,
For, at his owne charge, this towne he freed from tole."

(3) Lyson, ab Collectanea.

(4) A row of almshouses, that formerly extended along the east boundary of the churchyard, were called King John's Almshouses. These were taken down in 1835, and rebuilt

borders of the Fens—perhaps to drive his rebellious barons from the Land of Marshes; and at Lynn, which had shown him great fidelity by furnishing him with ships and sailors, and raising recruits, he had kept a kind of court, entrusting to the care of those faithful subjects his crown, regalia, and valuable treasures.[1] Though John was considered almost as incapable of gratitude as of any other virtue, yet he seems to have been rather munificent to Lynn, having granted the inhabitants a charta of incorporation; and, to this day, they hold two memorials, a gold cup and sword, which they value as his gifts.[2] His connection with Lynn, however, has engaged more attention from being the last of his miserable life. He left Lynn on the 11th of October, 1216, and was at Wisbech on the 12th, and at Sleaford on the 15th.[3] But, between the departure from Lynn and arrival at Sleaford, an event, which most historians consider as partially, if not wholly, the cause of his death, had deprived him of most of his remaining resources. In crossing the waters of the Wash his treasures, crown,[4] regalia, the great seal, and baggage, were lost, and himself escaped with difficulty.[5] History is not very decided which stream is entitled to the credit of ridding the land of such a scourge. The interruption of three days between John's appearance at Wisbech and Sleaford would seem to intimate that the accident happened some time during this period, and that probably he remained at Wisbech to recover his lost treasures, if possible, and estimate his other losses. In passing from Lynn by Wisbech to Sleaford, it seems hardly possible that John could have taken the waters at any other part than the wide estuary which then came quite up to

near the new Church Cemetery. There is no other authentic information that they were endowed by King John than this significant name, which, though doubtful, is still a probable case.

(1) Richards's History of Lynn. (2) Speed's Chronicle, p. 505.

(3) Richards. Dr. Brady also proves that John came to Wisbech, by original records in the Tower. Some writers say John was at Swinstead on the 11th. On the whole there is not much faith to be placed in particular dates at so remote a period.

(4) "Henry III. was crowned with a plain ring of gold in consequence of this loss."—*Pict. England.*

(5) Speed, p. 505.

Wisbech, and whose breadth may be estimated by the distance between Leverington Bank and the Roman Bank in Walsoken. These will now be found to be about a mile and a half asunder at their narrowest part, and as there was probably only a ford or a ferry over the river in those days, the King would not have come to Wisbech to go to Sleaford, unless the nature of the river had compelled him. Some accounts name the Cross Keys as the point of passage over the river, but this could hardly be the case if the King came to Wisbech, as is generally agreed; besides, the river was there four or five miles wide, and we should suppose wholly unused as a place of transit. Other accounts, which place the accident at Fossdyke, have less reasoning on their side. The King must have safely crossed the widest and most dangerous wash to get to Fossdyke, and no account says that he crossed two washes. Besides, Fossdyke would be out of his way by many miles in passing from Lynn to Sleaford, after he had succeeded in crossing the estuary of the Ouse at Wisbech, or even at the Cross Keys. But M. Paris, who lived in the reign of John, and has written his life, gives the following account, from which it is pretty evident the accident happened at Wisbech:—"Leaving the town of Lynn, which he had greatly distinguished and honored with donations, he attempted to force a passage over the water which is called Well-stream,[1] and there suddenly and irrecoverably lost all his waggons, treasures, costly goods, and regalia. A whirlpool in the middle of the water absorbed all into its depths, with men and horses, so that

(1) "Deinde versus aquilonem iter arripiens in fluvio qui *Welle Stream* dicitur." It is scarcely necessary, from what we have already deduced in the former part of this work, to prove that Well-stream was the Wisbech river. The following corroboration may, however, be interesting. The *Register of Peterborough* and the *Red Book of Thorney* both mention the river under that name. The former notices that the Castle of Wisbech is founded "super flumen illud famosum quod *Welle Streme* appellatur." It is thus that Atkins writes,—"I am come to Wisbech river. Your lordship shall understand that anciently this was an arm of the sea, and the time was when the whole course of the Ouse, as well from Westwater by Great Cross as all such waters as now fall on the east of the Isle with the Ouse from Littleport Chair to Lynn, had their passage by Welney and Welle to the North Seas at Wisbech, and from thence where now the Washes be, in regard whereof writers say King John's people perished in the waters of Welle."—*Atkin's Report*, 1618.

hardly one escaped to announce the misfortune to the King."[1]

Well-stream, we have already shown, was a name for the Great Ouse,—which at that period ran by the Wells past Wisbech to the sea; we are thence inclined to believe that the scene of this historical incident was somewhere near Wisbech, perhaps between Wisbech and Walton Dam, where the estuary branched off to a much greater width.

(1) Shakspere puts the following interpretation of the event into the mouth of the *Bastard*:—

> "I'll tell thee, Hubert, half my power this night,
> Passing these flats, are taken by the tide,
> These Lincoln washes have devoured them;
> Myself, well mounted, hardly have escaped.
> *King John, Act* v., *Scene* 6.

In the *Pictorial History of England*—in which most of the modern historical discoveries and researches are incorporated,—the following is the account of this transaction: "At the beginning of October, marching through Peterborough, he entered the district of Crowland, and plundered and burnt the houses belonging to that celebrated abbey: he then proceeded to the town of Lynn, where he had a depot of provisions and other stores. Here turning his face again toward the north, he marched to Wisbech, and from Wisbech he proceeded to a place called Cross-Keys on the northern side of the Wash. It is not clear why he took that dangerous route, but he resolved to cross the Wash by the sands. At low water this estuary is passable; but it is subject to sudden rises of the tide. John and his army had nearly reached the opposite shore called the Fossdyke, when the returning tide began to roar. Pressing forward in haste and terror, they escaped; but, on looking back, John beheld the carriages and sumpter horses which carried his money, overtaken by the waters; the surge broke furiously over them, and presently they disappeared—carriages, horses, treasures, and men being swallowed up in a whirlpool caused by the impetuous ascent of the tide and the descending currents of the river Welhand."—p. 532. Here the reader will perceive a startling discrepancy; for if John entered the waters of the Cross Keys and had reached the opposite shore of Fossdyke when he was overtaken by the tide, the Wash must have extended beyond Holbeach, and the sands have been about eighteen miles across. The writer has also been evidently misled by mistaking the term Well-stream, used by M. Paris, for the Welland. Camden commits a similar blunder.

1236. In the course of history Wisbech appears to have been three times visited by severe inundations, and much oftener by those of less note, which its situation with respect to the sea and the Fens made particularly disastrous to it. The first of these occurs at the above date, and is thus described by Holinshed: "On the morrow after the feast of St. Martin, and certain days after, the sea burst out with such tides and tempests of wind that the marish countries neare to the same were drowned and overflowen, beside great heards and flocks of cattel that perished. The sea rose continually in flowing for the space of two days and one night without ebbing, by reason of the mighty violence of contrary winds. At Wisbech also, and in villages thereabouts, the people were drowned in great numbers, so that in one village there were buried one hundred corpses in one day." Matthew of Westminster gives nearly the same account, particularising Wisbech and the neighbouring marshes as suffering in an extraordinary degree. "The sea," he tells us, "was raised much higher than usual, and the storm continued eight days, so that of men, small ships, and cattle, a great multitude perished." Seventeen years afterwards, Dugdale merely mentions that there happened "such another woful accident;"[1] about thirty years afterwards, a similar calamity is recorded, by which it is said "the town of Wisbech and the castle were utterly destroyed."

It was at this time that attention first began to be directed to a systematic protection of the Fens by carefully attending to the drains and embankments; and we know not but these serious inundations may have contributed to directing attention to the subject. Indeed, Dugdale expressly mentions, after recording one of the above calamities, that "the King thereupon directed his precepts to the shireeve of this county [Cambridgeshire] requiring him to distrain all those who had lands within the precincts of the old banks in these parts of Wisbech to repair the said banks as they ought to do,

(1) Hist. Embankment, &c., p. 299.

according to the quantity of their holdings."[1] These inundations, he tells us, had been better borne had not "that stream of water called Wallenhee, which had wont to run towards the sea under the sea-bank of Walsokne.... been diverted towards Wigenhall by Well dam, thereby causing the sands to grow to such a height in the channels of the Wisbech river, that no drainage could be effected for the drowned lands.... But these irruptions of the sea as they were casual—viz., when the north or north-east winds accompanied extraordinary spring tides—so they were not frequent, nor did those floods continue so long upon the land as to destroy it by drownings; the stagnation of the fresh waters producing much more damage."

It was about this period, or somewhat subsequent, that those commissions were called and investigations instituted on the Wisbech river, which we have already recorded. The dams at Outwell were made in 1292, and the disputes which ended in an acknowledgment of the change of outfall for the Ouse from Wisbech to Lynn, were commenced. As far as we can trace this controversy, it seems to have been as stoutly disputed as any question that came before men who, habitually averse to enterprise and experiment, seem generally to have felt little with regard to the Fens, and to have adventured less. Wisbech, though so largely interested in this dispute, hardly appears in it: all the country from Crowland to Huntingdon and Marshland brought their grievances to bear upon it; but Wisbech, more highly grieved than either, made no appeal. Had the repeated losses to which the severe inundations of the sea subjected it forced the inhabitants to abandon the place?—or did it stand indifferent to the results? Lynn was already, by reason of the diversion of the waters, carrying on a trade to a considerable amount, which, before the alteration of the Ouse outfall, must in a great measure have belonged to Wisbech, when "of old great ships resorted thither."[2] The investigation proved that

(1) Hist. Embankment, p. 299. (2) Atkins.

corn, wool, and other commodities were carried from Northamptonshire to Lynn, returning with "victual and other necessaries"—that "ships laden with goods and merchandise" traded to the same port from Huntingdonshire, and that the obstruction of forcing the vessels by a more roundabout course to Lynn had the effect of raising the price of corn, timber, wool, reed, turf, stone, fish, herrings, and other commodities and victuals, "to the damage of the inhabitants of Norfolk £200 every year." These statements show a very considerable trade to Lynn, and show a very considerable loss to Wisbech, if we agree, as we must necessarily do, that it was the port for these commodities while it retained the main and only river of the Great Level. Indeed, we find Lynn at this time was in a high state of prosperity, "a city distintinguished for commerce and abundance, the residence of many wealthy Jews, and resorted to by foreign vessels."[1] The distinctions which King John had bestowed upon it, in consequence of the help it had afforded him, would show it to have been a wealthy and flourishing town, had we no other evidence, but we meet with it in connection with most of the commercial relations of these early ages. It was one of the towns to which John addressed his letters, promising, for the encouragement of trade, foreign merchants safety and protection there; and, in levying the *quinzeme*,—a tax generally supposed to be on foreign commerce,[2]—Lynn contributed £651, while London paid only £836. The whole tax yielded about £5000; so that Lynn paid upwards of an eighth of the whole. There is no doubt that much, if not all, this prosperity resulted from the river which it had obtained from Wisbech many years before, and which was at this time confirmed to them by law as an ancient right.

1327. Notwithstanding this great error, and the unfortunate inundations to which the town was now sub-

(1) Pict. England, vol. i, p. 589.

(2) "The *quinzeme* was a duty which was paid by every merchant, whether native or foreign, and merchant was at that time an appellation given to every person who bought and sold, however trifling his dealings might be."—*Thompson's Boston, on authority of Anderson's History of Commerce.*

jected, and which must altogether have greatly reduced it from its former importance, it appears in the reign of Edward III. to have somewhat recovered and resumed some consequence; for we learn that John Hotham, bishop of Ely, obtained a charta for a fair here, to commence on Trinity Eve, and to continue twenty days. At this period there was also a hospital here dedicated to St. John the Baptist, in support of which certain lands and messuages were appropriated.[1] No record remains of the cause of decline of this hospital, or where it was situated, or what estates were appropriated to its support.

1379. This is the period when the Guild, which was to have such an important influence on Wisbech, was established. We reserve to another chapter a more detailed account of this body. The influence which these associations had on the emancipation of society was most important. They may be termed conspiracies against the overwhelming influence of great powers; and, perhaps more materially than any other form of social manners, contributed to erase the more offensive principles of the feudal system.

During all the period comprised between the reign of Henry III. and James I., we meet with repeated notices of the Commission of Sewers held at Wisbech. Indeed, the principal transactions for keeping up the drains and embankments, on which the habitableness and security of the Fens depended, centred in Wisbech. Sometimes these Commissions were held at the Castle, which appears to have been soon rebuilt after its destruction in the inundation of 1260. In 1329 Edward III., "being informed that the banks, ditches, and sewers about Wisebeche, Elme, and Welle, were broken and out of repair," issued a commission to inquire through whose default they became so ruinous, and who were the landholders thereabouts, or had safeguard by

(1) Regist. Episc. Elien. Rex concessit Johanni Francies in feodo certa mess. terr. in Wisbich, nuper amortizat Hospitalis ibidem, per servitia debita. The following masters of this hospital are recorded: 1234, John de Lenna; 1243, John de Weston; 1259, Rad de Islingburgh; 1350, Rad de Ringslade; 1352, Edward Engeho.—*Cole's MSS. Brit. Museum, quoted by Watson.*

the said banks, and to distrain them for their repair according to the proportion of their lands.[1] This was followed by a Session at Wisbech, whereby a remedy was proposed for protecting Wisbech, Elm, and Well, by a causey to be made at Gongested Lake to Well Creek, "and thence unto Marche Dyke, and that the Crike should be wholly stopped up, and that the said towns could not be preserved unless that were done." We have already related the heads of this inquiry, which was opposed by the Abbot of Bury St. Edmund's and the north side of Wisbech.

1340. Another Session of Sewers held at Wisbech this year, which was chiefly occupied with the condition of the drainage of Elm and Well. They ordered a clow of "five feet in breadth and in depth two feet," to be made at Lakebrigge, and another of similar dimensions at Friday Bridge; and also "that no man should dig turfes nor slakkes in the common droves of Elme and Welle for dieving of flax or hemp in the common ditch and sewer, to the nuisance of the commonalty;" and that the great bridge near the church of Elm should be newly repaired and amended.

1353. It was this year presented at meeting of "Justices of Sewers" at Elm, that "a certain bank anciently made for the safeguard of all those lands betwixt the river of Wisebeche and the river of Welle, beginning at the footpath opposite the gate of Wisebeche Castle, was then almost broken and in decay." It was shown that this bank was only four feet high, and that many lands were, consequently, drowned. It was, therefore, ordained to be raised three feet, "so that the whole height thereof might be seven feet, and the thickness thereof at the bottom twenty-two feet, and at the top twelve feet, so that the water of the fen might not any way enter through the same bank."[2] It is on this bank that Timber Market is built; and it now forms the west bank of the Canal and Elm Road as far as Elm Bridge, where it leaves the Canal and forms part of the public road

(1) Dugdale. (2) Ibid.

through that village. This bank was at that time an important protection to Wisbech and Elm, if we may trust the strict orders which were made for protecting it. No one was to dig earth for repairing the bank within twenty perches of it, on pain of 20*s.*; and it was further ordained that neither the lord nor any commoner should depasture any of his cattle on the same bank, except sheep, nor make any drifts with cattle over it, upon penalty of a penny for every beast so driven. It appeared, in the course of this inquiry, that there were 5200 acres on the south side of Wisbech river, and and 2090 more to Well, which were liable to contribute to the repairs of this embankment. The inhabitants of Wisbech were finally ordered to begin upon the repairs; and it appears that their portion extended to "the stone cross near the house of Lepers" which divided Elm and Wisbech.

1437. At a Session of Sewers, held at Wisbech this year, much of the neighbouring fens and marshes came under notice. It seems to have been a long investigation, but not a needless one, if the representation of broken sea and inland banks, confined and grown-up drains, ruined bridges, impassable highways, broken and decayed tunnels, and sluices silted up, call for alteration. We must confine our notice, however, to two or three portions relating to Wisbech. It was ordered that three pipes, "newly made in a certain field called Smalmedows in Wisebeche, being made too large by twelve feet, should be amended .... and that the parson of the church of Wisebeche ought and had used to repair a sewer in Wisebeche beginning at the house of Reginald Rogers in Wisebeche and leading into the same town, and that the town of Wisebeche ought and had used to make a clow in the sewer of Wisebeche at a certain bridge in Newton, near Tytton Gote, for stopping of the water when need required." Wisbech was also presented as being liable to the repair of another bridge in Newton, called Mutcroft. "And they likewise presented that John Everard, Esq., had straightened the common river of Wisebeche with nets and other engines therein placed, to the general nuisance, &c.

.... And for the better safeguard of the town of Wisebeche they did ordain that the bank called Wisebeche Fen-dike should be barred in certain places needful to prevent cattle from passing thereon, and that hassocks should be gotten in the fen and laid at the foot of the bank .... and that a person be appointed to oversee, open, and shut the four gotes of Wisbeche, Leverington, Newton, and Tid St. Giles." Their last ordinance shows in a powerful manner the inadequate character of their proceedings to preserve the fen in any state of security: "And they lastly presented that Thomas Horne, of Okham, in the county of Roteland, ought to repair and maintain upon the bank called Wisebeche Fenn-dyche a certain proportion containing six hundred feet, in respect of 24 acres of land in Wisebeche; and that upon Monday, the feast of St. Wolstan the bishop and confessor, in the 17th year of the said King Henry VI. reign, the same portion of that bank was broken and decayed, and that the dikereeves aforesaid did warn the said Thomas to amend the same: which he refusing to do, the fresh waters made the said breach greater, whereby the portions of the same bank, belonging to Geffrey Lambard and others, adjoining thereto, were also broke and ruined, to the danger of destroying the whole country, 4400 acres in Wisebeche, 4600 acres in Leverington, 1400 acres in Newton, and 2000 acres in Tyd, being thereby at that time overflowed and drowned."[1]

1554. We have a brief record of a very unsatisfactory event—the burning of two persons named William Wolsey and Robert Piggott, inhabitants of Wisbech. They appear to have suffered for adhering to the Protestant religion during the temporary revival of the Catholics in the reign of Queen Mary. They "had been long previously confined at Ely."[2]

1571. This year was remarkable for another of those great storms and inundations to which this low part of the eastern coast has always been subject. It happened in October, and has been described at some length by Holin-

(1) Dugdale. (2) Watson.

shed; who says that "in Norfolk the Cross Keys' Wash house was overthrown; in [Isle of] Ely, Wisbich and all its neighbourhood was flooded some feet deep. .... The sea broke in," he continues, "between Wisbech and Walsoken, and at the Cross Keies, drowning Tilneie and Old Lin, St. Marie, Teding St. Marie, Tid St. Marie, Tid St. John, Waupl e, Walton, Walsoken, Emnie, Jarman's, and Stow Bridge, all being in the space of ten miles: these towns and villages were overflown, that is to say, Wisbech, Guihorne, Parson Drove, and Hobhouse. This Hobhouse being an almshouse, and the water breaking down the walls of it, the wind blew the clothes off from the bed of a poore man and his wife, who being cold, awaked and suddenly stepped out of his bed to reach up his clothes, and slipt up to the bellie in water, and then he thinking himself to be in danger (as he was indeed), and knowing the best waie to escape the danger of the water, he took his wife on his neck and carried her away, and so were both saved. At the same time in Wisbech a tennis place and a bowling allie, walled about with bricke worth £20 by the year to the owner, was quite destroyed by the water." The following particulars of other places on this coast will serve to give a clearer idea of the nature of this flood. "Mumby Chapell, the whole toune was lost, except three houses. A shippe was driven upon an house; the sailors, thinking they had bin upon a rocke, committed themselves to God: and three of the mariners lept out of the shippe, and chaunced to take hold on the house toppe, and so saved themselves: and the wife of the same, lying in childbed, did climbe uppe into the toppe of the house and was also saved by the mariners, her husband and child being both drowned. *Item*, the church was wholly overthrown, except the steeple.... Wentford (Wansford) bridge, being very strong, of eight arches in length, had three of the arches broken and clean carried away.... *Item*, between Hummerstone and Grimsby were lost eleven C sheepe of one Mr. Specers, whose shepherde about mid-day, comming to his wife, asked his dinner, and shee, being more bolde than mannerly, sayd, he should have none of hir; then she chaunced to look toward the marshes where the sheep were, and sawe the water breake in so fiercely, that the sheepe would be lost, if they were not brought from thence, sayd that he was not a good shepherde who would not venture his life for his sheepe, so he went straight to drive them from thence; both he and his sheepe were drowned, and after the water was gone, he was found dead, standing upright in a ditch.... Boorne (Bourn) was overflowed to the midway of the height of the church."

We have now arrived at a date where the Corporation Records will enable us to define our way more clearly. These Records, which commence at 1379 with one entry, dc not follow any consecutive order till 1423, and are then only a yearly account of the orders and expenses of the Guild of the Holy Trinity. The proceedings are of the same character till the dissolution of the Guild in 1549, and the establishment of a corporate body upon its funds and estates. There is a lapse of some years, however, before any regular entries take place, which commence in 1500. From this date, therefore, we shall trust to the documents themselves for such general facts as may be worth preserving—giving generally the form and literal entries rather than their interpretation, reserving only to ourselves such brief illustrations as may seem necessary.

1580. The following singular entry occurs in the Town Records, and shows that the old and unpopular revenue of Purveyance was still in operation, though it had lost much of its ancient extent and offence. The Norman kings had enforced it with all their accustomed severity, taking from the subject whatever they required at their own price, and also impressing his cattle and carriages, and even musicians, goldsmiths, and embroiderers, to their service.[1] It was greatly reduced by the time of the Tudors, and we may, in the following extract, see what spirit it had left in the time of Elizabeth. Still it was yet very offensive. The queen

(1) Thompson's Illustrations of British History.

victualled her navy with it during the early part of her reign, but Oxford and Cambridge were exempt from its exaction to the extent of five miles around.[1] Purveyance was abolished by Charles II.

" *Md.* Yt ys agreed by ye Tenne Men and of others of ye cheyf Hedborowe of ye Towne with the consent of the Justices of the Peace, viz., Sir Henry Weston, Knyght; Mr. Colvile, and the Purveyor, for a quyetus hereafter to be contynued amongest us for the se~vyce of the Quenes Matie wth lambs and calves. Yt they wch hereafter shall kepe a kyne or ewes shall pay for eu~y ewe acording as the se~vyce shall requyre and not otherwise. And he yt shall refuse this order or break the same, to pay and delyvr his calffes or lames acording to ye Quenes pryce; and yff any p'son or p'sons yt kepe kyne or ewes and have no calffes nor lambes to sue, yt then he to pay for eu~y cowe yt he milkes, and for eu~y ewe yt had a lamb, according as the se~vyce shall requyre, as he will abide the pe~ll that shall fall thereupon."[2] In a subsequent entry, five years afterwards, we find a memorandum, " that whereas xxis. viiid. ys wantyng in full paymt for ye paymt of ye Quenes p~vision for calves, &c., yt the Toune Bayley shall pay ye sayd xxjs. viijd. out of ye Toune Stocke, wch sayd s~m shall be repayd again to ye Toune Bayley for and to ye use of ye Toune out of ye next assessment of ye sayd p~vision out of ye sayd money yt shall be assessd for ye p~vision hereafter."[3] And another entry, dated 15th June, 1585, states that " yt ys agreed that every p~rson whin the toune shall pay towards the Quenes majestie p~vision for calves, lambs, and bakon in manner following: For every kowe 1 *ob.*[4]; for every 20 ewes 2*d.*; for every 20 wethers 1*d.*; every swine 1 *ob.*, being above a quarter old; and constables within the watch to collect the same and pay the money to Henry Pulter, gent."[5]

1584. Some years previous to the above date, the plague had been brought into England by the Earl of War-

(1) Hume. (2) Town Records. (3) Ibid. (5) Ibid.
(4) A contraction for obolus, a halfpenny.

wick's emaciated garrison from Havre. We do not hear of its previous progress in this part of the kingdom till the above date, when it appears, by the following entry in the Records of the Corporation, to have broken out at Guyhirn.

"Y^{e} xvth day of December, 1584. Md. Y^{t} y^{e} same day John Robynson, collector, and John Enne, expenditor, yielded y^{e} accompt of all suche s~ms of money by them collected and expended. Vpon examination of y^{e} books and bylls John Robynson was chardged wth vij$^{li.}$ ij$^{s.}$ vj$^{d.}$ by hym collected of sondry y^{e} inhabitants, as by y^{e} books of y^{e} ass~^{ssmt} appeared, wherof John Robynson payd to John Enne vj$^{li.}$ vj$^{s.}$ viij$^{d.}$ and for other chardges iiij$^{s.}$ iiij$^{d.}$ so rem~ in hys hand xj$^{s.}$ vj$^{d.}$ w^{h} was alowed hym for hys payns for collectyng mony for vi weeks assessed to be payd to y^{e} poore at Guyhurne vissyted wth sycknes of y^{e} plage supposed, and John Enne expended to y^{e} poore in Guyhurne, as by hys byll appeared iiij$^{li.}$ xv$^{s.}$ v$^{d.}$ and so rem~ in hys hand xxxi$^{s.}$ vi$^{d.}$ wch was allowed hym for vi weeks servyce in comyng and goyng to p vyde for y^{e} afflycted."[1]

1587. This visitation only preceded the same kind of calamity at Wisbech; but we have no earlier record of it than about three years after the above entry. However, in April, 1587, it had become serious enough to call for energetic proceedings. The town was divided into ten wards, over each of which one of the "Tenne Men," as the old records call the Corporation, was set; and an adequate idea of other proceedings may be drawn from the following entries.

LIST OF WARDS.

"*Tymber warde* 10*s.*[2] From ye begynnyng of ye town vnto ye fyrst style of ye church, cont^{g} all Tymb~ M~kett and ye almeshowsses to ye s^{d} style.

"*Churche warde* 10*s.* All ye almeshowsses and others on bothe sydes of ye Churcheyarde, and all ye Castle dyke to ye g^{t} gate.

(1) Corporation Records.

(2) This sum seems to refer to the weekly expenditure or weekly allowance to the governor of the ward for dispensing to the sick.

"*Castle warde* 5*s*. Alle ye rowe agaynst ye Castle gate, and all Deadman's Lane, wth all ye howses to Swyllynghyrne.[1]

"*Sowth warde* 3*s*. All ye howses in ye bryncke watche on ye south syde of ye gt ryver of Wisbeche.

"*Berton warde* 5*s*. All ye howses on ye north syde of ye sayd Ryu~ in ye bryncke watche.

"*Whyt Crosse*[2] *warde* 6*s*. All from berton lane to ye ponde[3] in ye old M~kett.

"*Olde M~kett warde* 8*s*. All ye olde m~kett to ye Gt Brydge on ye other syde of ye ponde.

"*Shyppe Lane warde* 6*s*. All from ye Gt Brydge next ye gt Ryu~, and all from shyppe lane to ye Towne hall.

"*New M~kett warde* 3*s*. Ye rest of Shippe lane and ye howsses on all ye rowe agaynst ye Crosse.

"*Myll warde* 4*s*. From ye corn~ of Ryc~ Best howsse to ye myll hyll,[4] wth all ye longe m~kett bowthes, and thus ye wardes be ended.

"1587, ye 3 of december. The metyng of ye gou~nours ye day abovesayd where yt was agreed yt all those ix p~sons wch were alowed xijd. a pece at or metyng ye 26 of November, shall thys weeke folowyng have theyre libertye to goe abrode, and eu~y of them except M. Brewster and hys wyffe, & wydowe Thystlethwayt, wch were disobedyent p~sons, to have eu~y of them for releyff for thys weeke vijd. eu~y of them vsing themselves well, and not gyvyng any offence to any inhabitant aft~ warnyng gyven them of yr mysconduct.

"Itm. Yt ys agreed yt all ye rest of ye sycke at Berton being xj p~sons, shall have libertye to come to yr howses, & abyde ther, & eu~y of them to have xijd. a pece for thys weeke folowyng, so yt they doe obey the orders expressed for Robert Kyme, at ye metyng ye 26 of Novembr.

"Itm. yt ys agreed yt eu~y p'son now chardged by ye assessmt made by ye Justyces for ye Sycke and poore yt have

(1) "A field beyond Oldfield, and leading to New Common bridge."—*Watson.*

(2) "In the open space in the North Brink, called the Low, a cross, called White Cross, formerly stood."—*Watson.*

(3) "The pond was filled up in the year 1669."—*Watson.*

(4) Where Mr. Henry Leach's house now stands at the upper end of Hill Street.

payd all ye due wch are by them to be pd shalbe but chardged w^h one haweffe of theys chardges, & y^t Robert Tym shalbe dischardged from hys offyce, & ye bearers also, & eu~y of y^m to have haweffe theyr wages gave more, so y^t they doe helpe to brynge home ye thyngs from Berton, and make clean ye howsse & such thyngs as y^t tyme shalbe apoynted them.

"Orders by ye gouñours ye 7 of november, 1587.

"It. for y^t Edmund wryght hathe abused ye Towne in castyng fylthye clothes into y^e little Ryver, to the annoyaunce of y^e inhabitaunts & euyll ensample, therefore yt ys fully agreed y^t he shalbe p~sently put into y^e howsse of correction, and y^r to remayne on breade & water, tyll yt be thought mete he be released by consent of iiij of y^e gou~nours.

"$M^{d.}$ y^e same day there was delyuered by the Bayley fowrtye shyllyngs of y^e p~fitt of mony gyven to be destrybuted by y^e gou~nours in eu~y of y^e wards.

"Itm, for y^t yt ys knowen y^t Godfrey Smythe, contrary to y^e Justycs orders, & to y^e daunger of hys neyghbours, hathe gone to Berton into the howsses amongest ye infected, & synce hathe gone abrode, beyng warned by ye governours of ye ward wherin he dwelleth, & dothe refuse to obey any good order, therefore yt ys agreed at o^r metyng by all o^r consente y^t ye same Godfrey shalbe imprysoned in the howsse of correction vntyll vj of ye clocke, & in lyke man~ Robert Smythe also, for y^t he dyd accompany ye sayd Godfrey, & also abuse in vyle woords ye deputye of ye same warde.

"1587. The meeting of ye Tenne menne for orders for ye sycke to be sent to Berton, agreed vpon ye ix of october, a^o Reg. Eliz. 29.

"Itm. Y^t a carte be p~pared & cou~ ow~ w^t borde.

"It. Y^t harvey & juxon be ye carters.

"It. Y^t a horse be bowght to carry all necessarys.

"The meeting of ye gouernours ye 21 of november, 1587, for ye releafyng some of those y^t are before sent to Berton.

"Itm. Yt is agreed y^t wyll'm Brewster and his wyffe, wydow Thystlethwaytt, & wydow pylkyngton shalbe sent for to the Towne & placed in ye same howsse wherat Brewster dwelett before, & y^r to remain vntyll o^r next metyng, & eyther of them to have allowed xvj^d. a weeke & to kepe close tyll o^r next metyng or ells not to have any allowaunce.

"Itm. Y^t Robert Kyme shall have libertye to sende forth hys man to gather vp hys debts eu~y day, but only on ye m'kett day & on ye Sabaoth day, & y^t hys wyffe & mayde may for some of theyr necessarye busynesses some tyme goe abroad, having not any com~on recoursse into any men's howsses, and not on ye m'kett day nor on the Sabaoth to goe abrode at all. thys order to contynue to o^r next metyng.

"Itm. The same day John Byrd was absent beyng warned, & also John Stregett ye deputye, & therfore eu~y of them hathe forfeited xij^d.

"1587. At ye metyng of ye governours ye 26 of november.

"Itm. We have agreed y^t eu~y of those p'sons wch are removed from Berton beyng ix persons, shall have eu~y of them xij^d. a pece for thys weke folowyng, so as they doe p'forme all orders wch by them are to be observed, the orders expressed above for Robert Kyme.

"It. We did then agre y^t Wyllm Brewster abouesayd shalbe set in ye stocks vntyll evenyng prayer be sayd, & then y^t he shalbe tyed to one of ye posts of ye M'kett Crosse, & y^t he shall have xx strypes & then delyuered. He was punyshed w^h 4 stryps.

"1587. decimo die decembris.

"The metyng of ye gouñours for ye order of ye sycke ye day abousayd.

Itm. Y^t eu~y gouernour shall brynge in a byll in wryting the names of all & eu~y p'son beyng an howsholder not beyng able to gyve w^thin theyr wards, & of eu~y p'son havyng neede, by reason wherof eu~y p'son y^t are wyllyng to distrybute any releyffe to suche as have nede may be certified, y^t ye poore may be releuied & not goe abrode as usualy heretofore they have done at xts.

"Y^t ye poore shalbe forbydden to goe abroade as heretofore they have done at xts., & not be gyven to at any mans doore, but such as be mynded to gyve eyther to sende yt to them or to gyve yt them selues at yr howses, or to delyu'r yt to ye gou'-nour of eu'y warde & yr minde to whom yt shalbe delyue'd.

"Itm. Yt pylkyngton shall have xijd. eu'y weeke to kepe a boy of Roger lamb deceased.

"Itm. Yt Carter shall have warnyng yt he doe not accept any more to remayne in hys howsse but onely ij besyde hym selffe & hys daughtr.

"Itm. Yt George Williams be talked wtall for hys man.

"Itm. Yt Smyths wyff shall have xijd. eu'y week for ye kepynge of one of lambs chyldren.

"28 die decembris 1587.

"The metyng of ye gou'nours for ye order of ye sycke ye day aforsayd.

"Itm. Yt ye weaver wch goeth about as a Roge be sent to ye Justyce eyther to be sent away or punysshed accordyng to lawe.

"Itm. We doe agre yt wheras Robert Skortred beyng appoynted as gou'nour of Berton warde by reason of sycknes cannott p'forme ye same. Therfore by consent of the gouernours ye day aboue sayd we do appoynt yt Wyllm. Skortred shalbe in hys place, & yt wyllm. day shall execute ye place of a gou'nour in Shyppe warde in ye rome of w. Skortred, vpon payne of conteyned in ye orders.

"Itm. Yt was agreed yt Robert Skortred shall have for the kepyng of Emme Skortred for' one whole yere, kepyng her and dischardgyng ye Toune, p. an. xiiijs. iiijd.

"2 die Janvary 1587. Itm. Yt there be an order taken for to place bothe men & women wch were late visyted in stools convenyent by them selues in ye churche.

"No. For ye towns mare and carte & thyngs at Berton and for ye locks, ye table, & ye bedds.

"5 die Janvaris 1587.[1] Ye metyng of ye gou'nours.

"Itm. Yt was agreed yt whereas ye howsse of James Goodrycke ys suspected to be infected & p'tly fully knowen. Therfore yt the sayd James shall kepe hys howsse & shoppe from henceforth shut vp, & not to suffer any p'sons or p'son

(1) The year at this time began on the 25th of March.

other than of hys owne howsse to come to hym, & y^{t} ye goñuour of y^{t} warde shall carefully ou~see y^{t} he doe not contrary to ye Justices order vntyll o^{r} next metyng, & y^{t} yf he refuse to p'forme y^{e} same order y^{t} then he shalbe comytted to y^{e} howsse of correction.

"1588, 17 die mensis Aprilis. Itm. Yt was agred y^{t} James Goodryche shall have fyve pounds to be payd at y^{e} feast of phylypp & Jacobb 1589, takyng hys howsse for assuraunce for y^{e} $repaym^{t}$ of yt agayne.

"Itm. Y^{t} wyllm herbye & hys wyff shall take all y^{e} stuff owt of y^{r} howsse & lay yt on y^{e} farther syde litle ryver dayly & make fyre in y^{e} howsse."[1]

This visitation seems to have been at its height during the autumn, as we find, from the parish register, that 42 were buried in September and 62 in October; after which the numbers declined to about 20.[2] The average monthly mortality for the ten preceding years was about 5; and the average yearly mortality for the same period was 55. The average yearly mortality for the ten succeeding years was 112. But the mortality for this year, 1587, was 206. Taking the average of these ten preceding and ten succeeding years, we find there died about 2½ in 1587 for 1 during the above period of twenty years. It would thus seem that about 130 were carried off by this disease out of a population which, at a rude estimate, formed by comparison of the births, deaths, and marriages, we compute to have been about 2500.[3]

No part of the system of revenue was more unpopular than that of granting patents to particular persons for the sale of commodities. Of these the patent for the exclusive sale of salt was one of the most unpopular, from being one of the most necessary and general articles of consumption.

(1) Corporation Records, vol. ii. (2) Watson.

(3) Bishop Gunning is said to have caused the inhabitants of Wisbech to be numbered in 1676, and that they were found to be 1705. Upon a comparison, however, of the burials for five years before and five years after this date with the burials five years before 1821 and five years after, when the population amounted to 6515, we find the average to be 157 in the former period, and 141 in the latter. Now the former and greater number cannot be reconciled with one-fourth of the population; neither can we believe that a twelfth of the population died per year. The census of Bishop Gunning is hence necessarily wrong, or a numbering of the male population only, or the population above a certain age.

These patents existed extensively during the reign of Elizabeth, and comprised not only salt, but such articles as ox shin-bones, accidences, aqua vitæ, oil of blubber, &c. Before her death, however, Elizabeth declared all patents null and void. The unpopularity of the salt monoply in Wisbech is shown in the following extract.

"3 Nov. 1593. At y^e metyng of y^e tenne men.... yt was fully agreed by all y^e tenne men.... for and in y^e name of all y^e inhabitants y^t wh~as a cont'versy ys lyke to aryse betwene y^e patentees graunted by her Ma~tie to certayne for y^e bryngyng in of salte, &c., and y^e $inhabit^s$ of Wisbech aforesayd, y^t y^e sayd Towne should be w^tin the grauntt y^t for the defence in lawe of a tryall of y^t controversie so longe as yt is or shalbe complayned upon to be tryed as a matter tending or being to be geñall y^t yt shalbe borne by y^e comon charge of y^e sayd towne, except yt be to be tryed or done against any special man as a pryvate cause, & y^t cause as tending to ye lib~tye of Wisbeche, ye charges of ye same shalbe payd & borne out of the towne stocke, and of ye charge of such as shall deal in the trade of buying and bringing in of salte or any other comoditie whereby ye buyers of ye same use to have dealings in any m~chandise, vitayle, or fyreyng."[1]

We have printed this passage literally, but it will be seen there is a certain obscurity about it; yet, judging from the apparent tenor of the record, and the general feeling manifested at that time by the people of England against these monopolies, we think it may be interpreted as a determination to stand a suit at law against the patentee, depending, perhaps, upon some technical objections which do not appear in this record. The entry seems to intimate that so long as it shall be a general question and the proceedings of the patentee be made against the town generally, the inhabitants shall pay the law expenses by a general contribution; but that, if proceedings shall be made against any individual, his expenses shall be paid out of the town stock, as, in his person, involving a question touching the "lib~tie of Wisbech."

(1) Corporation Records, vol. ii.

It was only late in our history, and on the breaking up of the feudal system which the Normans had so fully developed, that the poor became an object of legislative consideration; and then it was only with threats and severities that the government attempted to improve their circumstances. The dissolution of the monasteries aggravated the evil; but, though various acts were passed by Henry VIII. and Edward VI., for mitigating pauperism, it was only in the reign of Elizabeth that any measure calculated to give real relief to those who, in the language of a statute of Edward VI., were given to "idleness and vagabondry," which, it goes on to say, "is the root of all evil acts and other mischiefs, and the multitude of people given thereto hath always been within this realm very great, and more in number, as it may appear, than in other regions." In 1562, the act was passed for relieving this beggary by an assessment on persons obstinately refusing to contribute to the relief of poverty; this was finally perfected by the act of 1601, which remained in operation until the recent remodelled Poor Law.

We find various notices in the Corporation Records of the early operation of these acts; the first of which, bearing date 1587, is as follows:

"The acc^{t} of the Money bestowed on the Poore
in Año 1587....................tot. 48$^{li.}$ 14$^{s.}$ 9$^{d.}$"

A further entry shows us that the same precautions which had been taken in the time of the Plague were now resorted to to manage and provide for the poor. The ten wards are the same as those adopted during the plague.

"May, 1595. At y^{e} metynge made y^{e} 1st May, y^{e} wardes for y^{e} P'ysshe of Wisbeche St. Peter's by consent of the 10 men of the Bodye Corporate of the Toune and dyvers others of the chyffe Inhabitants were elected and sev~ed into 10 P'ts, to be ov~seen by y^{m} whose names doe followe with ye coadjutors by ye full consent ag^{d} upon, to take ordre for the good gov~ment of the Inhabitants within every several warde & the relief of the Poore within the same, and y^{e} neede to be by y^{m} weekly certifyed to the rest at y^{e} Metynge every

Sabaoth day and after evening prayer, with consent that every of the said gouñours which doth not once every weeke make view of y^{r} ward to forfeit 4$^{d.}$ to the use of the poore, except upon reasonable excuse."

The amount of the poor rate levied at this time seems to have been about £30 per annum, as appears by the following record: "xxix day of February, 1591. M$^{d.}$ y^{t} John warner & wyllm castleton dyd yelde y^{r} accompt, beyng collectors for y^{e} poore appoynted from y^{e} feast of St. Bartholomew thapostle, año dñi 1592, & contynued tyll y^{e} feast of phylypp and Jacobb, 1592, duryng wch tyme they collected as by y^{r} p'ticulars appeare in all xviij$^{li.}$ vij$^{s.}$ iiij$^{d.}$ and they rec~ in y^{t} tyme by order sett down of Mr. Ryots liij$^{s.}$ iiij$^{d.}$ s~m tot. xxj$^{li.}$ xj$^{d.}$ wherof they payd and destrybuted in y^{t} tyme to y^{e} poore in all of y^{e} same money, & by them layd forth of y^{r} own all as by y^{r} accompt appeareth, for y^{e} poore xxj$^{li.}$ xvij$^{s.}$ vij$^{d.}$ so rests due to them xvj$^{s.}$ viij$^{d.}$"

As this is only a collection for nine months, viz., from the 14th of August to the 1st of May, the yearly amount will be more; and in 1594 we find it stated at £32 10*s.* To this sum the following permanent bequests are to be added:

"Januarii 20mo, 1596. A note taken the same day of all such money as is to be distributed yerelie vpon the poore:

Impr^{s}, by the Kinges gifte	iij$^{li.}$ xv$^{s.}$
Itm. by y^{e} gifte of Robt. Beste	iij$^{li.}$ vj$^{s.}$ viij$^{d.}$
Itm. for xx$^{li.}$ geuen by Bartholomew Edwards & his wief, yerelie p'fit	xl$^{s.}$
Itm. by the gifte of Robert Girden	xxxiij$^{s.}$ iiij$^{d.}$
Itm. the gifte of John Strigett	xx$^{s.}$"

Thus making the whole expense of the poor about £45 per annum. It would seem, from the following singular entry, that the rate was a weekly charge upon the inhabitants: "y^{e} xiij day of October 1591. M$^{d.}$ that wheras Wm Skortred hath bargayned and sould to one Wm Styrman gent one geldinge for and in consideration y^{t} he the sayd Wm Styrman his exer., administer or assignes should from henceforth pay

(1) Corporation Records, vol. ii.

& dischardge for and duringe y^e lyfe of the sayd Wm. Skortred all such sumes of mony as at any tyme hereafter ye sayd Wm Skortred shalbe chardged wth for the weakly payment for the collection for the pore of Wisbich, and for the assurance and suertye y^t ye sayd sume may wekly be payd they have desyred to have the same recorded in this book, and for the true payment of the sayd collection ye sayed Wm Styrman doth by these p'sents bynde himself, his exer., and administr, for and during ye lyfe of the sayd Mr Skortred, to be payd wekly for and in consideration of the weekly collection for the pore of Wysbych. wherw^t the sayd Mr Skortred duringe his lyfe shalbe chardged."[1]

The "tenne" seem at this time to have been very cautious of admitting strangers into the town, and very rigorous in expelling those who were likely to become a burden to them: "foweth day of June, 1590. Md. y^t Thom~s Wylson hathe made hys p'myse y^t he wyll dep^te from Wisbech to make hys abode in some other place.

"6 die Augusti, 1591. Md. y^t Robert Snoden, who dyd come from east derh~m, beyng found to abyde in Wisbeche w^t hys wyffe, not beyng of abilitie accordyng to o^r order, hathe made hys faythfull p'myse to dep^te out of ye Towne w^t hys wyffe, chyldren, & all other y^t by hys means come or shall come, before ye xx daye of thys moneth of August, or ells y^t he shalbe sent forth & punyshed."[2]

Nearly a century after we find this jealous exclusion of strangers from the town still adhered to. In January, 1673, it is ordered "that the Towne ballif pay tenn shilings a quarter, beginning at Candelms last past, unto — Wright, for his salery tacking care to giv notis to the Justesses of peace, constabl, and colechtars for the poore, for the better keeping oute poore strangers that shall come to satill hear to be a charge to oure towne, and this salery to be payd so longe as the Burgeses dew aproue of his diligence and no longare."[3]

Occasionally, however, there seems to have been a certain degree of toleration exercised, but only on such guarantees

(1) Corporation Records, vol. ii. (2) Ibid. (3) Ibid.

as the following exhibits: "8 octobris, 1596. Md. y^{t} vpon ye ixth day of October phyllypp Charten & Roger hunt dyd vndertake & p'mysse to be bound to y^{e} inhabitants of wisbech y^{t} one Rychard parker who synce y^{e} feast of thumiliation last dyd come w^{t} his wyffe to wisebech, y^{t} neyther he, hys wyffe, & chyldren, should at any tyme w^{t}in tenne years next be chardgeable to y^{e} towne of wisebech, & y^{t} they should enter bond in x$^{li.}$ w^{t} y^{e} s^{d} Burg^{s} w^{t}in one month next, accordyng to an order made in y^{e} court at wisebech y^{e} 28 of Sept^{r}, Ao Regie xxxiij."

It is perhaps not of much avail to make comparisons between such distant dates as pauperism in Wisbech during the age of Elizabeth and the age of Victoria. But the above rates afford us a kind of parallel on which to found such a comparison. The poor's rate of Wisbech for one year ending Midsummer, 1847, was 4*s.* 6*d.* in the pound, which, on £20,000, which is about the present assessment, amounts to £4500. The above documents give only £32 as the maximum annual collection made in the reign of Elizabeth; and, after estimating money at six times its present value, and population one-fifth of its present number, we leave the proportion of paupers at present four times their proportion at that date.

In the extract which we gave from *Doomsday Book*, it will be seen that "ten caracutes of pasture for the cattle of the town," are mentioned as part of the property attached to the manor. This, which comprises about one third of the whole landed domain mentioned, was probably common; and more recent documents show that this common and common-rights remained pretty large for centuries afterwards. Dugdale mentions that about 1341 "there was a survey made of the marshes about Wisebeche, whereby it was found that the marsh called the Hay-fen, belonging to the manor of Wisbeche, and to the towns of Leverington, Newton, Tyd, Elme, and Welle, within the liberty of Ely, did begin at the Shofe, and continued from thence to the Horseshoe.... to Great Cross, to Merch-ford by the Crike, and to Shrewid Nist, where the said towns ought to common together with their cattle, horn under horn, saving always the bishop his royalty and fishing within the said bounds."[1] These commons became afterwards matters of dispute on various occasions; but we are able to draw only unsatisfactory inferences upon their causes from the notices that remain to us. The following letters and documents show, however, the feelings which these disputes manifested:

"*The true coppye of a lettre sent unto Mr. frances hynde esquyer by Mr. Richard Goderycke one of the quenes ma^ties^ p'vye counsell.*

"I understand their is a matter betwixt the toune of Marche and Wisbyche and other townshippes Tñnts to my lord of Ely for the tythe of a com~on, and because you as a gentylman worshipe and an inhabiter of the toune of Marche I thought good to pray you bothe for yor owne p'te and for yor neighbours to suffer the Inhabiturres of Wisbyche and others of that hundred to enjoue and use their com~on in as large and ample man^r^ as they have done at any tyme heretofore, w^th^out any interruption of you or any other, accordyng to the order y^t^ my sayd lord of Ely tooke wth you for the same at the last assies untill suche tyme that the matter may be heard betwene the seyd p'ties by my seyd lord of Ely and his counsell lerned wth yor good confirmytye herein, all wise men will not only allow & comende, but my selff for the same yor confirmitye shalbe redye at yor request bothe for yor selff and for yor frend at all times hereaft^r^ to do what soeu^r^ shall lye in me, and thus wth my hartye comendacons I bydde you farewell. from my house in london the iiij^th^ of April, 1561. Yo^r^ assured, RICHARD GODERYK.

"To the right worshipfull and my
very frynde F. Hinde esq^er^."[2]

This letter is followed by the following examination, probably taken after the receipt of the above advice from the queen's counsel, and it appears by its address to have been sent to the Bishop.

(1) Hist. Embankment and Draining. (2) Corporation Records.

"The examicon of alexandre cookson, xposer, &c...saithe and eu˜y of them saith upon their conscience as they will aunswere wheresoeu[r] they shalbe called that the last day of aprill being wednysday they rowed from guyhirne together to the com˜on of norwood, and as they landed their they found kylled upon the com˜on in dyu˜s places the nombre of xij shepe and two lambes, that ys to say the first place they came at iij wherof one of them was worowed as seemed & thrust behynd into the belly as yt hadd bene wth a spytte, and the other two warre thrust into the backe wth a pycheforke and sore beaten about the hedd that the braynes came out....Aft[r] whiche the seyd xposer went to seek for Mr. willm bryan's horses y[t] warre of y[e] seyd com˜on of norwood, & whan they culd not fynde them upon the com˜on they went from thence into m˜rche toune to inquyre for Mr. bryan's horses, and as they passed thorowe the toune a lytle of the churche theyr they founde the most p'te of thynhabitants of marche workyng of a menwork, and than he sayd unto them and asked them if any of them culd tell hym of his m[rs] horses, and they asked hym agayne who was his mast[r] and he told them y[t] he was Mr. bryan, smit, and the seyd y[t] they dyd not knowe his m[s] horses nor yet his m[r] and he sayd agayne yes, ye do knowe them, for they went upon the com˜on here the last yeare. And than one stephen stubbe, butcher..wth dyu˜s others to the nombre of vij or viij p'sons spake wth open voyce & sayd that they ware jollye fellowes of wisbyche and sayd y[t] wisbyche men warre upon norwood upon mñday last being the xxviij[th] aprill 1561, & kylled their owne shepe and cut owt their tonges of their hedds, to that ende and purpose that the toune of m˜che shuld be slandered......and to prove that the shepe warre sayff aft[r] the dep˜ture of o[r] neighbours of Wisbyche yor l. shall understand that theyr came ij butchers of cambridge & ij men of wisbyche the same day at nyght about eight of the clocke over the same com˜on of norwood, and sawe the shepe sayff aft[r] o[r] seyd neighbours warre goyne, as they will delay before yor g. l. or ells where, whensoever they shalbe called to depose the same. Thus we have sent their ex~macons unto your l. levehyng god to send them better spyrytte. from wys. [Wysbech] the vij of may, 1561. yor l. Tnñts and bodmen [Tenants and bondmen.]"[1]

The bishop appears to have interfered on behalf of Wisbech in this quarrel, but with little effect, as the following angry letter testifies:

"I am sorrye to heare that ye ar so stowte, so disordered, and so lawlesse people, that neyther the order of me and my counsell can stay you. I understand ye fall to yor olde practyse, please yor selfes in yor owne devises, go contrarye to yor owne agremente, and pynne yor neighbours' cattell. Sithe ye be at that poynte I ensure you what the lawe will gyve me that I intende to use roundelye agaynst you. Say not but that ye have had warnyng. So fare ye well. From downham the viij^th of April. Yo^rs, R. ELY.

"To my Teñnts of doddyngton & m'che."[1]

A further order at a later date gives a slight insight into the custom of these ancient common rights: "9 June, 1612. It was ordered by ye company that if any inhabitant of the towne of Wisbech shall putt any shepe or any cattell uppon the comons contrary to ancient customes heretofore used, wch customes hath been hertofore p'sented at the Sess., viz., no shepe from 25 of may unto the first of november in ord'ye years. That then the burgesses are contented to make trials of the sayd custom against any who shall offend in breaking of the same, and so save harmless the drivers, so far forth as it shall concern them for the driving of shepe."[2]

In 1605 the Gunpowder Plot was discovered; and the celebration of that escape would, of course, be almost a saturnalia afterwards. Accordingly, we find the following year the anniversary thus noticed in the Records: "Nov. 3, 1606, it was agreed that Thomas Sponfer, clerk, should have p^d him by the inhabitants xiij^s iiij^d for and towards the payment of all such p'sons as shall have paynes about ringinge

(1) Corp. Records, v. i. (2) Ibid

the bells the vth of this month." Which seems to intimate that there were no regular ringers at this period.

At different poriods we meet memorandums of fires which have happened in the town; but none seem to have been of a very serious character. Wisbech, indeed, seems to have been very fortunate in this respect; and it may, perhaps, be accounted for in the fact, that while most of the other towns of England were built of wood, the scarcity of that article in the Fens, and the abundance of clay would force the inhabitants to use bricks in larger quantities than in most other towns. The first notice which the Records have preserved of a fire is in 1588: "Yt ys ordered y[t] John Ladd y[e] Town Bayley shall pay to W. Styrman 40[s.] in pte of suche chardges as he layd forthe about y[e] expence bestowed aft[r] y[e] fire in y[e] olde m'kett, w[ch] happened y[e] x of Aprill, on Wednesday at nyght about xij of y[e] clock, & yf all ye x men did not agre to y[e] same y[t] then y[e] sayd W. Styrman to repay yt afterwards." The following, in 1607, seems to have been of a more serious character, if we may judge by the particularity of the record: "18 Aug., 1607. It was ordered & agreed that allowance should be made from the Town for fyve kylderkyns of beare, twoo dozen bread, viij[lb.] of candel, and xj[s.] vj[d.] for watchynge; viij[d.] given to twoo pore women, to Henry Holmes for a dozen of pales vj[d.], which all was expended at the fire late in the old m'kett. Summa 2[li.] 6[s.] 6[d.] More, by the discretion of the town, was allowed the same tyme to certeyne p'sons that wrought at the fyre, viz., to Bloggett's man, in respect he was sore hurt, 2[s.], to Henry Ouen, &c., the same tyme, eu~y of them iiij[d.] It was finally ordered that the Town should p'vided of xxiiij leather buckets, of three large ladders, three new cromes wth ropes maid uppon purpose to the same, and the sayd ropes to be xiij yards in length, of the best Norf[k] hempe, and are to be fastened to the chains of the aforsaid cromes, and Henry Perke to p'vide the forsaid bucketts between this and Halowmass next. It was allowed by consent of the company that Rog[r] Norton should have p[d] him by y[e] Townbayliff in respect his house was pulled down for the p'servation of the rest, at the fire in the old m'kett, $x^{li.}$"

By the tenor of the above extract we may infer that this fire was of rather a serious character, and wholly unprovided for. No other of the same extent seems hinted at in the Records, unless it be the following, in which the character of the sufferers seems to have aggravated the misfortune.

"2 April 1652. At a meetinge the Capitall Burgesses doe order and agree that the Almes howses wch were lately burnt doune shalbe reedified accordinge to the dimensions of the former buildings, and the toune bailiffe is desired to take care thereof and to expedite the same." A general subscription was set on foot for the sufferers, as the Records contain "a note of such monies as was collected in severall tounes within the Isle of Ely for and towards the reliefe of distres poore people wch lost y^r goods at a sudden fyer happening at Wisbech the 23 of March, 1651." In this subscription Wisbech contributed £4 16*s*. 5*d*., and the whole collection amounted to £14 0*s*. 10*d*.

In the following we see the elements of those money disputes which afterwards attained to so serious a character, and in the end brought the son of James to the scaffold.

"22 oct. 1612. It was ordered by consent that Thomas Parke gent. havinge received warrant from the $Commission^{rs}$ of the high country for the levyinge of the fourth of a fifteen through the whole hundred, as also the sum of tenn pounds to be pd out of the lands of y^e Northsyde of the ry^r of Wisbech.... uppon a peine of tenn pounds to be levied uppon his goods and chattells by way of distresse, if it be vnsollvend and not payd to Sir Anthony Wyld.... before the first of November next; it is this p'sent day vppon a meetinge of the whole hundred agreed that the sayd sume shall not be collected vntill there be some conference had with the $Commission^{rs}$ of Northamptonshire, neu~thelesse since the Burgeses do p'myse to the sayd Mr Parke he shall not any ways be indempnifiied but shalbe borne by the town harmlesse for not executing the sayd warrant."

The next commemoration was on the occasion of the return of Charles, Prince of Wales,—afterwards Charles I.,—from Spain. He had, at the suggestion of Buckingham, undertaken a romantic journey to that country in disguise, in order to marry the infanta. James I. looked on this knight-errantry as madness, and even used his tears to persuade "baby Charles" and "Steenie" off it. The rejoicing on their return was perhaps the greater as the marriage was not contracted; for Spain had insisted on various Catholic privileges then almost abhorred by the nation.

"xvi die Oct. 1623. The Baylife appoynted to pay to dyvers parsons for beare, kakes, bread, and bonfyres spent vppon Sunday the xvi of october—to pay to the ringers at the Tryumphes in joy for the prince's comyng home from Spayne. in toto iiij$^{li.}$ viij$^{s.}$ j$^{d.}$

"Itm, more the Baylife paid to 4 watchmen to watch the the toune that night, xvj$^{d.}$

This is soon followed by another commemoration which was less hearty, at any rate less expensive, than the former. "The Baylife hath paid for beare, bread, kakes, pitch-barrels, coales, and fagotts spent at the bone fyres upon Saturday the 2 of Aprill, 1625, when King Charles was proclaymed xxxvj$^{s.}$ iiij$^{d.}$"

Among the various implements of which an inventory was taken shortly after the Corporation was established, several pieces of armour are mentioned, of which we obtain no further notice till the following date, when on some occasion, of which the brevity of the entry only gives us a very faint notion, it appears to have come into use. "11 May, 1626. the baylife [to] pay to Thoms Williams wch he had layd owt for mending and dressing the town armo^{r} at the martial discipline, v$^{s.}$ vij$^{d.}$ The times, however, were approaching when the implements of war unfortunately became in request, and we accordingly now find entries betokening the "shouts of battle and the shock of arms." The civil war had hardly begun, when the following entry occurs, but there seems a sort of anticipation of evil in its brief paragraph. "Secundo

Sep. 1631. The Baylife was appointed to pay unto Webster the cutler, for skowering of the arm^{r}, iij$^{s.}$ iiij$^{d.}$, and to another for tryming one musket vj$^{d.}$"[1]

The next entries concern one of the first causes of the popular outbreak—the levying of ship-money. The writ for this levy still exists among the Corporation papers, but its defaced condition, in consequence of damp, renders it impossible to decipher it. "December 12, 1634. Payd unto Robert Edwards, gent., for moneys expended by him about the Toune Buissnes vppon his journey to London concerning the King's Ma~ties shippinge, viij$^{li.}$ 2$^{s.}$ 4$^{d.}$"[2] This question agitated the country for some years. It was originally only levied upon ports, but became afterwards an excuse for a general tax upon the community. Insidiously and illegally imposed at first, for the pretended purpose of recruiting the navy and protecting the Protestant cause in France—a subject on which Charles knew the majority of his people were united—it would probably have issued in a complete royal control of taxation, had not Hampden and others risen against it. But neither Hampden nor any of the enemies of Charles could have succeeded in organising the people into their spirited resistance, had not the general principles of the nation been averse to the tax. Wisbech, as it appears by the following minute, was among the resistants, though it acted carefully; and, however illegal the imposition, its conduct appears in accordance with the spirit of the constitution: "31 Aug. 1638. The same day the Burgess^{s} did appoint Mr. Marshall to pay out of the 100$^{li.}$ he hath in his hands Tenn pounds unto Mr. Fisher, gen., and Ro. Edwards, gen. for their chardges expended in going to London about the Toune busines to get abatem^{t} for the shippmoney."[3]

The next entries take us into the heat of the civil war:

"duodecimo die July anno dño 1642. At a meetinge the Burgesses did deliver unto Mr. William Fisher.... three new musketts, rests, wormes, skowrers, and bandyleers, to be redelivered to the Burgesses and their successors vpon request

(1) Corporation Records, vol. iv. (2) Ibid. (3) Ibid.

respectively. The same day the Burgesses did also deliver vnto John Wilson and other new muskett wth the rest, worme, skowrer, and bandyleers, to be also re-delivered vpon request.

"Quinto die Aprilis, 1643. M[d.] that I willm dodson, gent. have received of the Burgesses of the toune of Wisbech the sume of one hundred & fyftye pounds w[ch] I doe p~mise to repay to the said Burgesses att the feast of St. John the Baptist next, or sooner, upon receipt of so much money, or a greater sume, for the s'vice of the king and p'liament. I say received the said sume of 150[li.] WILLIAM DODSON.

"Witnessed by Robert Swaine, &c.

"Att a meetinge of the Capitall Burgesses the sayd fyrst day of Aprill, 1643, they did agree to lend the above said sume of 150[li.] to Captan Wm Dodson wth the consent of du~se of the freeholders then p'sent."[1]

There is a similar entry and acknowledgment of a loan of £20 lent to Gregory Gamble on the 17th of April.

Almost all the eastern counties adhered to the Parliament, and were united under the name of the "Eastern Association." Cromwell was an eastern counties' man, and all his instruction in the art of war seems to have been learnt in his native county and its neighbourhood. Lynn, indeed, adhered to the King; but, being surrounded by those who were attached to opposite principles, it was unable to maintain itself, though from the strength of its fortifications it sustained a siege of near three weeks.[2] Wisbech was unprovided with any defences of that kind, and it does not appear to have been the scene of any greater conflict than a mutiny, as we learn from the following entry: "The Burgesses did agree that the Bailiffe shall pay vnto Captayne Richard Lehunt the sume of fyve pounds for a gratuitie, for his paines and care in suppressinge of a mutinye amongst the souldiers & the indangering of the Toune of Wisbech."[3] It was also endeavoured to remedy the natural defencelessness of the town by raising some kind of fortification at the Horseshoe;

(1) Corporation Records, vol. iv. (2) Richards. (3) Corporation Records, vol. iv.

for, as Lincolnshire was generally in the hands of the King, the Parliamentarians seem to have raised intrenchments, or other slight defences, to prevent a sudden attack from that quarter. The castle, as it will be seen, was also put into a state of defence: "31° Octobris, anno dño, 1645. The Capitall Burgesses did agree that the Toune Bailiffe shall pay vnto Mr. William Edwards the sume of seaven pounds, seaventene shillings, and six pence, wch the said W. Edwards did long since pay to Richard Dassell for iron work imployed about the fortyficacons of the toune of Wisbech, by order of Colonell Sr John Palgrave, Barronett. 14th Nov. 1643. To pay Richard Tassell his bill for iron work vsed about the drawbridge at the castle, by the appointm^t^ of Colonell Sr John Palgrave, wch doth amount to ij^li.^ 12^s.^ 6^d.^"[1] The siege of Lynn on the one side and of Crowland on the other seem to have been the nearest approaches that hostilities made to Wisbech. Cromwell, in the earlier part of the war, and before his name became celebrated, appears to have been Captain of these parts. He directed the siege of Crowland, to which Wisbech contributed in the following manner: "xxvij Feb. 1643. The Town Bailiffe shall pay for 2 barrells of beere deliured to the vse of Captaine dodson's suldiers in the tyme of the siege of Crowland, in dischardge of the p'mise made."[2] There is also another record of the lending of armour: "26 March, 1646. the Burgesses by order and comande have deliu^er^ed vnto Maior Ireton for the service of the king and parliam^t^ fower musketts, & three bandileres, two swords wth the hangers."[3] The *King and Parliament* is still the careful and prudent manner of the entry, and shows that the town, without in its corporate capacity espousing either party, held itself subject to the strongest. The town itself was doubtless as divided in its opinions as are the political parties of the present day, and some, indeed, of its inhabitants appear to have transgressed the prudent example of their corporation, for by the journals of the House of Commons we find John Fisher, of Wisbech, was fined for delin-

(1) Corporation Records, vol. iv. (2) Ibid. (3) Ibid.

quency and being in arms against the Parliament; and there is an ordinance for granting pardons to Thomas Wragg and Edward Buckworth, both of the same place, for delinquencies. Fisher was fined a fourth of his estate.[1]

The seven eastern counties were, by an ordinance of parliament charged with a weekly sum of £8435 for the raising of men and supporting the popular cause; of which Cambridgeshire and the Isle of Ely were rated at £783 15*s*. These expenses, with others incidental to the unsettled state of the nation, appear to have been long afterwards felt by the town; and it had some difficulty in releasing itself from its engagements. In the lord's journals is a petition to parliament from the inhabitants and landowners of Wisbech, signed by John Hobart and William Fisher, in which it is stated, that having, in all the taxes on the Eastern Association, paid a moiety more than their neighbours' counties, and having sent a troop of horse for the service of the Parliament, and also having, with others, expended £2000 in the last reducing of Crowland, they prayed to be repaid that sum, and to be exempted from all arrears of taxes, as, in addition to these burdens, the sea-banks had broken and destroyed 14,000 acres of rich ground, carried away their houses, drowned their cattle, and destroyed their hay and corn.[2] We should suppose this petition was successful from the following grateful record. Hobart was colonel of a troop of sixty horse for the defence of the Isle of Ely. "viij° die Maij, 1644. The Town Bailiffe shall pay vnto John Hobarte, Esq., the sume of xx^li. for and in support of his extraordinary paynes, travaile, and expences for the said towne..... The said Bailiffe shall also pay vnto Mr. William Fisher... five pounds, wch he hath expended for the good of the towne."[3]

The civil war was drawing to a close when the following loan was recorded: "7° die Augusti, 1648. At a meetinge of the Burgesses vpon consideracon[4] of a let^r directed vnto them from the Committee for the Eastern Associacon....for

(1) Quoted by Watson. (2) Watson. (3) Corporation Records, vol. iv.

(4) This passage is obscure and doubtful in the Records.

the borrowinge of 250li. vpon the creditt of an ordinance past both howses of Parliamt whereby the charge of maynteyninge the troope of horse raised for the defence of the Isle of Ely is at the reimbursement of the Excise, in course wth interest, the said Burgesses doe agree that the Town Bailiffe shall pay... in that behalfe the sume of 250li. for the purpose aforsaid vpon the affirmt... for the repaymt thereof... wth interest... after the rate of 8li. p. centum p. annum."[1]

The £150 lent to Captain Dodson at the beginning of the war, and which he had engaged to repay to the Burgesses in less than a year, appears, as might be anticipated from the lawless character of the times, to have remained unpaid some years afterwards: "Quinto die Novembris, 1646. At a meetinge of the Burgesses this daye they did agree that Mr. Fervour shall, in their names, commence an accon against Willm. Dodson, gent., for the recovery of the 150li. wch he borrowed of the Burgesses, 5° Aprilis, 1643."[2] We are not informed whether this money was ever repaid; but the Burgesses appear by the following entry some years afterwards—indeed after the Restoration—to have involved themselves in the same kind of liability: "9 May, 1663. This day the Burgesses gave to Sr Jas. Burrell, Kt and Baronett after a suite in Chancery... after a composition and agreemt... fower sev'rall obligations vnder their common seale... for paymt of ... two hundred pounds at fower sev'rall paymts... in discharge of 200li. received... some years since, and in the time of the late vnhappy wars."[3]

During the Protectorate, Wisbech was honored by the presence of Thurloe, Cromwell's chief Secretary of State, who purchased the Castle as his residence, and was elected one of the Capital Burgesses. It was, doubtless, through this connection that, in the parliament which Richard Cromwell summoned, a writ was issued for the burgesses of Wisbech to elect a member. This proceeding, unconstitutional as it may seem, has met with defenders. It is argued that the privilege of sending members to parliament, even so

(1) Corporation Records, vol. iv. (2) Ibid. (3) Ibid.

late as the Commonwealth, was ill defined, and rested chiefly with the arbitrary authority of the sheriff, and that representation was rather considered by towns as a burden than a distinction. However Wisbech, though thus entitled to the honors of a borough, never had a member. The burgesses elected Secretary Thurloe; but being also chosen for Cambridge and Huntingdon, he selected Cambridge as his constituency, and Wisbech was never again allowed this honor.

The following are the only memorandums on this important event in the Town Records:

"3 Jan., 1658. Ordered, that to-morrow betwene the hours of ten and twelve in the morning the p'sent Towne Bayliffe doe cause notice to be given in a publig manner that Thursday, being the 6th of this instant January, betwene the hours of 8 and 11 in the forenoon of the same day, the Burgesses are desired to meete at the Toune hall to choose a Burgesse for this Toune & Burrough in Wisbech to sitting in the Parliam^{t} ensewing.

"x^{h} Jan. 1653. The Toune Bayliffe shall paie vnto Mr. John Frynne, deputy, under sheriffe of the county of Cambridge, for his paynes about electing the Burgesse for Parliam^{t} for this toune & Burrough of Wisbech, the sume of forty shillings."[1]

This was only four months previous to the termination of the Protectorate, and the people were already prepared to receive with extravagant joy the King they had a few years previously hunted out of the kingdom. A rigid and moral government seems, indeed, wholly unsuited for a large country, or at any rate has never lasted long in dominions of extent.

"12 May, 1660. The Towne Bayliffe gyve to the wayts of Lynne for their musick for this day twenty shillings....and that the towne Bayliffe expend vpon the Gent. y^{t} shall joyne wth the Bayliffe in p'claiming Charles the Second, forty shillings."[2] This, with the next extract, shows that Wisbech, no less than other parts of the kingdom, was well satisfied with the new and brilliant fetters it had imposed upon itself. It

(1) Corporation Records, vol. iv. (2) Ibid.

is remarkable, perhaps, that the Stuarts were the only sovereigns whom it was found impossible to teach, even by adversity.

"22 April, 1661. Ordered, that the Toune Bailiffe paye vnto Anthony Balan, Esq., for 2 third parts of a horse and furniture for his ma^{ties} service, the sume of eleven pounds thirteen & fower pence. Ordered, that the Toune Bayliffe expend to morrowe at the coronation of King Charles the Second vpon the poore in bread, forty shillings."[1] The horse and furniture did not long tax the town, for on the following 30th of November we find an order "that Antnony Balan be discharged from the Tounes pt of a horse laid to the militia vpon the Toune of Wisbech & Mr. Balan, forasmuch as Mr. Balan informs the towne that the said horse is now dead of the new descease."[2]

Previous to the reign of Charles I., the coinage of the country was confined to silver, which was not divided lower than pence; but the progress of commerce, and the nicer divisions of value in commodities, had made a smaller coinage, in a metal of less value than silver, absolutely necessary. At first this smaller coinage was in the hands of corporations and private individuals, who made their own half-pence and farthings, pence being coined by the government in silver.

"The tradesmen, at this time, used to keep sorting boxes with several divisions, and when a quantity of any sums or corporation tokens was collected, they took them to be exchanged for silver."[3] The copper coinage was thus at first in the hands of the public, but the government soon adopted this as well as the higher branches of coinage. The following are the records of the corporation coinage, but there were besides these several individual coinages, of which tokens are still existing: "Nov. 20, 1668. The town Balife is ordered to lay oute five or tenn pounds in farthings at London, having them made with the toune armes upon them. Feb. 28th, 1669. Itt is this day ordred that the Toune Ballif and Mr. Richard Harrison dooe lay oute twenty pound in halfpennys,

(1) Corporation Records, vol, iv. (2) Ibid. (3) Ibid.

withe thes motto upon one side, 'a wisbeach halfepen'y,' and one the other side the effeges of the toune seale with the date of the yeare."[1] We do not know that any specimen of either of these coins is yet remaining.

The following discreditable record has been often too faithfully followed: "1st Feb. 1669. Ordered, that the Town Bayliffe be allowed fifty foure shillings and tenn pence which he hath payd to Mr. Erouse on his bill conserning the p'venting the towne of March being made a market towne."[2]

The maintenance of the Isle of Ely troop appears to have been still a general charge upon landed property in 1690, as we learn from a record at that time that "it was agreed that whereas the towne lands in the Isle of Ely is charged with half a horse to forme in the troop, that ther shall be p[d] yearly four pounds... by 40[s.] eu˜y halfe yeare vnto John Marshall... who shall... finde the s[d] horse, and that all the armes and furniture of the horse to be one halfe p[d] for by the Towne Balife."[3]

The occasion of the following celebration is not very apparent:

"Jan. 7th, 1716. Agreed for expence for y[e] day, being a publick thanksgiving, to every solder in arms ½ a pound of tobacco,[4] and a twelvepenny ordinary at Mr. John Sissons, y[e] ensigne, four pounds, not exceeding five, for beer, at y[e] discretion of y[e] Town Bailiff, and for y[e] fire upon y[e] Markitt Hill 15[s.], and for drink 5[s.], there being five men concerned, and for y[e] gaol 10[s.], to be equally divided amongst y[e] prisoners."[5]

"1740. There was a great frost, followed by an untoward summer, which brought on a rise in provisions, with high price of grain; and on Sunday, 29th of June, a mob gathered together near the town entered the same, and broke the corn merchants' windows, siezed about twenty-five lasts of wheat, and forced waggons to carry it off, when they sold the same

(1) Corporation Records, vol. iv. (2) Ibid. (3) Ibid, vol. v.

(4) We have ventured on this interpolation as the record seems imperfect here.

(5) Corporation Records, vol. v.

at four-pence per bushel, and some at one penny; they then levied contributions on the shopkeepers, and collected upwards of £30. This alarming the gentry and richer sort of traders, who at first thought themselves unconcerned, they met on the 1st of July, subscribed nearly £200, and by beat of drum enlisted above five hundred men, with whom they marched to Upwell (the chief rendezvous of the rioters), where they took about forty of them, who, with others taken elsewhere, in all about sixty, were laid in irons, by which means peace was restored."[1]

The following is another of those melancholy perversions of sound sense which, though doubtless adopted at the time as conducive to the prosperity of the town, or as preventing infringements on its prosperity, are only now to be contemplated as wretched delusions, and warnings to those who come after them: "Dec. 26th, 1749. We, the Capital Burgesses, do order our present Town Bailiff to execute certain articles of agreement enter'd into for opposing of an intended bill . . . for draining of Thorney Fen, and to subscribe the sum of ten pounds for carrying on the purposes of the said agreement."[2]

1775. The ports of Lynn, Wisbech, and Boston have always been exceedingly ill-supplied with all fish, excepting such as live among the sands and in the silty channels between them. The Wash being a great inlet filled with such sand-beds,—the washings of the ocean beyond,—is, in a great measure, such a compost as few fish can live in; and it follows that fish are rare in the estuary, and the fisherman's trade more precarious than usual: sea-fish are, consequently, seldomer found at Lynn, Boston, and Wisbech, than in most other ports. To remedy this deficiency,—which is much felt by all classes,—Wisbech, without well consulting the true cause of its bad supply, sought, at this period, to invigorate the trade by offering rewards for an abundant supply, which will be better seen in the annexed copy of a notice printed in 1775: "Wisbech St. Peter's.—

(1) Watson's Wisbech, p. 387. (2) Corporation Records, vol. v.

To all masters of cod-smacks, or other fishing vessels or boats.—The Corporation of Wisbech will give... to the person who shall bring... the greatest quantity of fresh cod, ling, holybut, and scate, between the 25th of March, 1775, and the 25th of March, 1776, a premium of five guineas, provided that no person shall be entitled to this premium unless he shall... have brought one thousand fish, at least, of any one or more of the sorts above mentioned, and provided also that no cod or ling shall be reckoned of sufficient size weighing less than seven pounds, nor any holybut nor scate weighing less than fourteen pounds. To the person who shall, in like manner, bring the next greatest quantity a premium of three guineas, provided that no person shall be entitled to this premium unless he shall within the said time have brought one thousand fish, at least, of the size above described. The bellman to give notice of the arrival of the fish, and the inhabitants to have two hours... to buy what they want, and after that the remainder may be sold to retailers. N.B. The channel of Wisbech river is now in so good a state that the boats may come at all times."[1] The last fact was, doubtless, owing to Kinderley's Cut which had just been opened.

This premium appears only to have been but once merited, and that is twenty-five years after the announcement:

"July 14th, 1800. Ordered that the Town Bailiff do pay to William Russell two guineas as a reward for his having brought into this town the greatest quantity of cod-fish, scate, holybut, &c., in the spring of this present year."[2]

We are now approaching an era with which we are better acquainted, and where events will soon be those which have passed under the personal observation of our contemporaries. But in proportion as events cease to be old they, in a great measure, cease to interest. As this, however, is an evil of which every year will reduce the weight, we shall make no further apology for our subsequent extracts from the Records, which carry generally with them their own chronology and history.

(1) Corporation Records, vol. vi. (2) Ibid, vol. vii.

In 1793 the French war had commenced; the first battle-ground of that memorable conflict, as of most of the modern conflicts of Europe, was Flanders. Our troops had gone there to contend against the army of the Republic of France, ill-supplied with necessaries, and victims to the diseases of the marshes: the country, therefore, by the aid of public meetings, entered into subscriptions to supply the troops "with comfortable articles of extra clothing." But, to the expenses and privations of war, were now to be added those of famine. The harvest of 1795 was almost destroyed by wet; which the Corporation of Wisbech forseeing would press heavily on the most necessitous classes, wisely and in time came to a resolution which is thus entered in the Records: "July 13th. It appearing that there is a strong probability of there being a defective supply of flour in the town and neighbourhood, from the great scarcity of wheat—Resolved, that the Corporation will join with such of the respectable inhabitants of the town as are desirous of promoting so prudent a measure, in purchasing such a quantity of wheat as may be thought necessary for securing a regular supply." A subscription of £105 was raised, which was dispensed in reducing the price of bread to the poor. But this class of persons are always ruled by feeling, never by judgement; and a contemporary observes that "a spirit of discontent was observed to have prevailed in Wisbech for a considerable time, though no serious consequences at first showed themselves; but on a certain market-day a party of laboring bankers paraded the town with drums and fifes, having bread and meat stuck upon poles, to excite the lower classes to tumult and disorder. Their numbers at length increased to that degree that it was necessary to send for the military to quell so turbulent a spirit: in the mean time the house of one of the principal inhabitants,[1] in the centre of the town, was thrown open during the evening of the day in which this licentious spirit was prevalent, for the use of any gentlemen resorting thither, so that it became the general rendez-

(1) That of the late Richard Shepherd, Esq., now occupied by Mrs. A. Usill.

vous for all the loyal and peaceable inhabitants, who assembled to deliberate on measures to be taken for the suppression of these disturbances. Whilst the mob were collected around this spot, one of the gentlemen there assembled observing one man more forward than the rest in exciting his companions to riotous acts, rushed out of the hall door and seizing this ringleader by the collar, in the midst of the crowd, dragged him into the house, and secured him in safe custody; this spirited conduct had the effect to intimidate the rest of the mob, so as to prevent their proceeding to any further acts of riot at that period; several windows were indeed broken, but no particular damage ensued."[1]

Such scenes as these, coupled with the excitement which affairs abroad were daily assuming, appear to have made this period one singularly active; and the great and well-founded terror which the progress of French arms made, caused the whole nation at length to arm in self-defence. A corps of sixty volunteers was organised in Wisbech, in 1797, consisting of the principal tradesmen, which continued embodied till the peace of 1801. In the meantime Wisbech joined in with the general feeling of the kingdom at this time, in contributing one hundred guineas as an aid to government for the prosocution of the war, which, by a minute of the 5th of April, 1798, is entered as "the voluntary contribution of this Corporation."[2] On the disbanding of the volunteers, the Corporation came to the resolution, that as they had hitherto abstained from contributing to their support, they considered it "expedient to discharge the remaining debts of the said corps." But the threatened invasion soon after aroused the country to such exertions that all its former efforts sunk into insignificance. Instead of a corps of sixty men, Wisbech now raised three hundred; and a general feeling, not unmixed with fear, so prevailed over England, that perhaps the invasion would have been more dangerous, had Napoleon prosecuted it, than he found that of Russia to be. "An additional light infantry company was formed at Wisbech in

(1) Watson. (2) Corporation Records, vol. iv.

1807, and with reinforcement from Thorney and Whittlesey, the battalion consisted of six hundred rank and file, and was denominated 'The Third Cambridge Regiment of Voluntary Infantry.' In 1808 an act passed for enabling his Majesty to establish a permanent 'local militia' force, under certain restrictions, for the defence of the realm. By this act, corps of volunteers were allowed to transfer themselves . . . into such local militia. The officers were required to have the same qualifications as the regular militia, and the regiments were to be called out yearly to be trained for twenty-eight days. . . Under this act, most of the volunteers of this district . . . agreed to transfer their services into the local militia, when the Earl of Hardwick formed one regiment for the Isle of Ely consisting of twelve hundred men,[1] and one for the county."[2]

In 1809 a general jubilee was celebrated over the kingdom for the completion of the fiftieth year of the reign of George III. Almost every town having its local military staff, this festival was celebrated with more martial splendor than usual. There was service at Wisbech church, at which the military attended; which was followed by a grand fielding and review, and a ball in the evening.

In 1814 these military scenes ceased with much rejoicing. Peace was secured, or thought to be so, by the abdication of Buonaparte, and all Europe rejoiced in the restoration of what it supposed would be a permanent cessation of hostilities. To celebrate this event there was a grand festival and public dinner on the Market Hill, at Wisbech, followed by rustic sports, and an illumination at night, which is thus recorded in the Corporation minutes: "Resolved, that a general illumination of the town, for celebrating the greatest of political blessings, a secure and lasting peace, do take place on Wednesday, the15th inst. (June). Candles to be lighted at nine o'clock."[3]

(1) Colonel Watson held his commission in this regiment, and was one of its most indefatigable officers.

(2) Watson's Wisbech. (3) Corporation Records, vol. ix.

In 1810 an important proceeding towards the improvement of the town was resolved on and successfully completed. The management of the affairs of the town, though always vested in the Corporation, had, by the increase of property and population, and the alteration of manners, laid its powers open to somewhat of dispute, or, at least, to inconvenience. In order to settle its authority, and give it greater freedom than the old charters had given, it was resolved to apply for an act which should give definition and consistence to their jurisdiction, and, at the same time, provide for those improvements which were becoming necessary and eligible under proper authority. The first resolutions which the Corporation came to, are dated the 8th of January, 1810; which, having incorporated the main principles of a bill for paving, watching, lighting, and cleansing the town, the regulation of the port, the forming a cattle and corn market, and other improvements, they were submitted to a vestry meeting and there laid before the inhabitants. The measure,—though apparently highly called for,—was not very favorably entertained by this assembly; and, on the 18th, the result is thus entered in the Records: "The proposed improvement of the town by paving, not being agreeable to the inhabitants assembled in vestry—Resolved, that the resolutions before entered into... be rescinded." Other resolutions were, however, immediately agreed to, in which the port and markets, and the power to remove buildings and open streets, were incorporated; but, ultimately, the whole bill for "establishing a cattle market,... removing the shambles, paving, cleansing, lighting, and watching the town, removing nuisances, preserving and improving the port and harbor,... and for increasing the duties payable at the port,"[1] were adopted, and the act carried through parliament without opposition.

The following appears to have been one of the applications of this act; from which we infer that the common streets were formerly used during our "Carnival" as general receptacles, and that the present arrangement of the Mart dates

(1) Title of the Act,

so late as 1815. "21st Feb. 1815. The sense of this Hall being that the arrangements of the caravans frequenting the mart is vested, by the late Town Act, in the Capital Burgesses, ordered that such caravans be stationed during the ensuing mart in the Old Market, and that the Town Bailiff do give the necessary directions for... leaving the common streets as free from obstruction as possible."[1]

Public dinners on the Market Hill have been a popular way of celebrating such national events as coronations, at Wisbech. That of George IV., in 1821, seems to have been unusually spirited, and the manner with which it was conducted has been imitated on the two subsequent coronations. The expenses were covered by a public subscription; and the provision included bread, beef, mutton, plum-pudding, and beer, to which field sports were added. Three quarters of a pound of meat, and half a pound of pudding, were estimated for each individual. One ox, two heifers, and fourteen sheep were purchased; about four thousand four hundred penny loaves and thirty one barrels of beer were provided; and the feast was enlivened by twenty-six musicians. "The stewards," says Col. Watson, from whose account we have drawn the the previous particulars, "met at the Town Hall at half past twelve; about one they moved from thence to the Market Hill preceded by the town constables with staves, band of music, and the colors belonging to the Wisbech Battalion of Militia. The tables were all ranged in regular order in the Market Place. An elevated table was prepared for the stewards about the centre. The Town Bailiff presided. More than four thousand three hundred persons... seated themselves at the tables with more than three thousand surrounding spectators. On the first signal of the trumpet the tables were loaded with beef, puddings, and vegetables, on the second, grace was said by the Rev. Dr. Jobson, vicar... After dinner the stewards, escorted by the band, colors, drums, and fifes, conducted the company to the field appointed for rustic sports. The total expenses amounted to

(1) Corporation Records, vol. x.

£296 19*s.* 3*d.*"[1] The great difficulty on such occasions is to make an intermixed multitude conform to order, however strictly enforced. A little incident is sufficient to throw all into confusion, and to produce a disagreeable scene of what was intended to be a pleasing one. The next coronation, celebrated by a similar festival, was that of William IV., in 1831. Every thing was arranged in the same order as that of George IV., and a military precision and regularity was expected. But, unfortunately, the day proved rainy; the torrents which fell just as dinner should have commenced produced a *melée* rather than a banquet. Carvers sat under umbrellas before vacant tables; many dishes never arrived at their destination; and those which got there were scarcely more fortunate—their contents vanished mysteriously, as if they had melted in the rain; and aprons, baskets, pockets, and all sorts of receptacles served, in the confusion, to diminish the prospects of the hungry. The third and last coronation banquet, which happened in 1838, was more fortunate. The day proved fine, and all seemed to vie in their honor of a lady ruler. The decorations of the tables and surrounding houses, which consisted principally of evergreens and flowers, were numerous and tasteful, and the whole scene was orderly and spirited. Nearly 5000 persons are said to have been regaled on this occasion; and the statistics which we subjoin from a report printed at the time, will give an idea of the consumption of the day.[1] The subscriptions for this feast amounted to upwards of £430, and required only a few additional pounds to make up the expenses, which did not exceed £450. Rural sports followed as on the other occasions.

1830. The opening of the Nene Outfall, in 1830, though an event regarded with some misgiving by Wisbech, and wholly uncelebrated, ought not, on that account, to pass

(1) Beef, 264 joints, weighing 4830 lbs. Plum-puddings, 521, each weighing 7 lbs. [These puddings contained the following proportion of ingredients: Flour 1246 lbs., spice 3 lbs., sugar 392 lbs., suet 280 lbs., milk 480 pints, eggs 2450.] 4983 penny loaves; 8992 pints of ale: 16 lbs. of mustard in 294 pots; 56 lbs. of salt in 400 salts; 15 lbs. of tobacco; 1152 pipes; and 1150 yards of cloth for the tables.

unnoticed among the remarkable events of the town. Of all the illuminations which peace or war, or other occasions, have drawn from Wisbech, none have been so worthy of public demonstration as this, when we consider it in its results. But to show how these results disappointed expectation, we find a Corporation entry protesting, after the opening, "that the channel of the Nene Outfall Cut hath not been made of a depth required for the purposes either of drainage or navigation."[1] This protest was speedily doomed to disappointment: the waters ground the channel at every tide and every ebb till the inhabitants of Wisbech were obliged to stone the sides of the river through the town, in order to hold up their buildings. Its results, however, upon the trade and prosperity of the town will be treated in another place.

1832. In 1831 all Europe was visited with the cholera: this dreadful disease, which had originated in the swamps of the Ganges, in 1817, after ravaging all Asia—producing in the hot climates where it originated, speedy and almost certain dissolution—entered Europe by Turkey and the Black Sea, and proceeded regularly, by Russia, Poland, and Prussia, westward. Happily, however, like a great material force, as it kept spreading it lost vigor, and by the time it reached England it was the mere phantom of what it had been in more favorable climates. All the prescribed precautions, however, were used at our ports; but in November it found its way into Sunderland, and quickly spread along the coast. It reached Wisbech and the Isle of Ely about June, 1832, but, fortunately, it assumed here rather more favorable symptoms than in the neighbourhood,—especially Upwell and Northdelph,—and only twenty or thirty persons fell victims to it. A row of ruinous houses on the South Brink, about three-fourths of a mile from the town, were fitted up as a hospital, and other precautions used to prevent the progress of the infection. At that time the ground which has since become the Church Cemetery, was purchased, but not conse-

(1) Corporation Records, vol. xii.

crated; yet, as it was deemed prudent to prevent even a burial where any fear might be entertained of a renewal of the disease, a portion of this ground was parted off, and all who were the victims, or so supposed, lie together in this spot, which is still separated from the rest of the cemetery. At Northdelph, and some other swampy parts of the fen, its ravages were very great, considering the proportion of inhabitants. Indeed, its origin in the delta of the Ganges, among the most pestilential swamps in the world, intimate marshy regions as its peculiar province; and the track it followed through Europe along the swamps of the Don, the Dnieper, the Volga, and the Vistula, shows that imperfect drainage is the great promoter of the disease.

1833. An event somewhat, curious in the peaceful histories of corporations, took place in this year, which ought not, perhaps, to be wholly forgotten. One hundred and thirty-three years previous to this event, the following record appears in the Corporation books: "8th November, 1700.... Ordered, that a small piece of wast ground near the river side of Wisbech, over ag^{t} the new Butter-cross, shall bee fenc'd in by the p'sent Town bayliffe, for a place to lay cobbles in."[1] Nineteen years after this order we find another which came, afterwards, to be almost prophetic: "April 1st, 1719. It was ordered that the Town Bailiff should set a new lock upon the door of the place call'd the coble yard, and if, at any time, he should be disturb'd in the possession of the same, he is order'd to defend the rights of the town."[2] This would almost appear as if those rights had already been disputed. However, the cobble-house seems to have never been wrested from the hands of its first proprietors, nor their title again disputed for a hundred and fourteen years. In the mean time a granary had been erected partly over this yard, which passed eventually into the hands of Mr. Aves, a tradesman of the town. This gentleman had already been concerned in a dispute with the Corporation regarding the Crane, which he had for some

(1) Corporation Records, vol. v. (2) Ibid.

time rented, but which was at length wrested from his hands. To revenge himself, he resolved to erect a crane of his own, and secure, as far as he could, the emoluments derived by the Corporation from this source. It was for this purpose of erecting a crane and warehouse that he had bought the above-named granary. He immediately claimed the cobble-house under it, and proceeded to take forcible possession of it. This the Corporation authorities resisted, and having shown him that he had no claim on this place, they demanded re-possession. Mr. Aves resisted, professed to hold his possession good in law, and firmly defied every attempt at re-possession. The Corporation now had no alternative but to resort to those elementary principles of right, between which all law is but an arbitrator. But Mr. Aves professed to slight these elementary principles as profoundly as he had slighted the law itself; and, like a general in a strong fortification, he determined to resist an army, should it be gathered against him. The Corporation bore no good will to Mr. Aves, who had sought to invade their revenues, and Mr. Aves bore as fixed an antipathy to the Corporation; so that there was not much hope of conciliation between the parties. Under these circumstances, on the 7th of January, 1833, they made the following order: "The Town Bailiff reported to this Hall that Mr. Aves had effected a forcible entrance into the cellar belonging to the Burgesses, beneath the granary near the Stamp, lately purchased by him, and now converted into a crane and warehouse, by breaking a hole through the interior wall of the building, and removed some coggles and other property in custody of the Corporation therefrom—Resolved, that the Harbor-master, taking with him the police officer and other necessary assistance, regain immediate possession of the cellar and premises belonging to the Corporation."[1] Pursuant to this order, the Harbor-master mustered a force of constables, police-officers, and porters, and having obtained the cromes used in fires to rescue property, and other offensive weapons, prepared for the retaking of the disputed premises.

(1) Corporation Records, vol. xii.

On the part of Mr. Aves, a quantity of sharp pointed cobbles, and bludgeons were provided; and he mustered a force of not more than two or three men who, by their position, were able, in an admirable manner, to command the entrance of the cobble-house. For some time both parties watched each others movements in silence; but at length, about half-past twelve, the action commenced by the Harbor-master seeking to force an entrance into the cobble-house with the long spiked crome. This action, which was seconded by his auxiliary forces, was resisted by the defenders, who hurled their sharp-pointed stones so quick that, for a short time, the assailants shrunk from this well-directed volley, and the assailed had the advantage; but the constables, seizing what had been their enemy's ammunition, re-aimed their stones back again in as thick a volley as they had been sent, and, having the advantage of numbers and the long weapons we have named for forcing their way forward, Mr. Aves and his force gradually retired further into the granary. One of the principal defenders being already seriously hurt, the Harbor-master pushed forward, though two of his fingers were broken, and finally gained possession of the cobble-house. The Corporation had three meetings in the course of the day, and, immediately after the battle, they received the report of it, and made the following minute of it in the Records: "One o'clock in the afternoon. The Harbor-master and Mr. Morrison reported that they had procured assistance for the purpose, that the most violent resistance was offered to them in recovering possession of the premises, but that they had effected an entrance, and are now in possession of the cellar and premises belonging to the Corporation; in doing which the Harbor-master had two fingers broken and was otherwise severely bruised, and George Ringrose had his nose broken, and was also severely bruised."

1834. This year an effort was made, which at first had every prospect of success, for materially improving the town, by pulling down the Grammar School and making a new street from the Market Hill to the Lynn Road. For this purpose it was proposed to procure an act, having for its object the "improving of wharfs and quays, rebuilding the bridge, regulating police, better lighting the town, forming the new street, to sell any part of the estates of the Corporation applicable to general purposes, and to make various other alterations and improvements in the town." Though so many other objects are here named, they were all subordinate to the plan of forming the new street on to Lynn Road. The principal of the property, however, which the burgesses would be obliged to purchase for the purpose was bishop's leasehold, and was held for lives. Under such circumstances it became necessary to consult the lease-holder, the bishop, and his agent, before such preliminaries could be arranged as to secure a transfer of the property. At first all these matters were arranged readily. The elderly lady who held the land, which consisted of seventeen acres, finally agreed to part with her interest for £2200 and three rights of way; the bishop expressed himself favorably, and his agent "saw no objection to the principle." Under such a thriving position of affairs the bill progressed, and was read a first time without opposition: but here the interference of the bishop was needed to carry on the bill, "for the rules of house would not admit of the bill being read a second time without his lordship's written consent."[1] This, however, could not now be obtained. The agent opposed the principle of the measure, to which he had hitherto seen no objection, and the bishop faithfully followed his legal adviser. The following minute expresses the principle on which this prevaricating conduct was formed: "7th May. This Hall met in consequence of a communication from the solicitor of the bill, that Mr. Pickering, the solicitor... of the Bishop of Ely, objected to the bill as inimical to the interests of the see, and that the bill could only be allowed to proceed, upon power being reserved to the Bishop, to let the land on either side of the contemplated approach, for building leases for the benefit of the see, Mr. Pickering being decidedly opposed

(1) Corporation Records, vol. xii.

to the sale of the fee simple of the seventeen acres of land to the corporation, for the purposes of the bill."[1] This resolution of the see of Ely, which no representations could move, brought the measure to speedy death, and on the 10th of June it was given up "as a hopeless case."

1835. Royal visits, or even the visits of the near relatives of royalty, have been too unfrequent at Wisbech to be considered otherwise than as events. The present position of the daughter of the Duke of Kent makes, therefore, the following Corporation memorial somewhat interesting: "A deputation was sent to Burghley, where the Princess and her mother were then staying, in September, 1835, to request her permission to present a corporation address on her passing; but the deputation to Burghley having reported that it was communicated to them through Sir John Conroy, . . . that it is an invariable rule . . . not to receive an address on merely passing through a town—Resolved, that a procession be formed to meet their Royal Highnesses on their arrival, and to escort them through the town; and that a very elegant copy (belonging to the Town Bailiff) of the late Col. Watson's *History of Wisbech* (which he had kindly offered) be presented by the Town Bailiff to their Royal Highnesses on the occasion." Which resolution was adopted.

1845. The establishment of railways in England will probably be to the future an event paralleled by no discovery that has been made, except printing. But it has, in some measure, realised its benefits in a far more rapid manner than that supreme discovery did. In fifteen years we have advanced the social system as far as a preceding century has done, and drawn, as it were, the extremities of Europe together. The railways have made what used to be a serious journey no more serious than a morning walk; and to commerce, social inter course, and the knowledge which is drawn from travel and experience, it has given to boys what used formerly to be hardly bestowed on men; it has, in fact, increased human life by increasing the ideas which constitute it, and converted what

(1) Corporation Records, vol. xii.

was formerly mere time into wealth, pleasure, and knowledge. We are now in the situation of those beings who have travelled out of the polar night and emerged into lands of longer day, brighter light, more productions, and pleasanter arts. It becomes us, therefore, in an especial manner, to mark the means by which this great revolutioniser of human kind has linked town by town, and it will always, we may anticipate, be one of the greatest events in local history to note when and how the first railway was established in the precincts of every place.

Though, like every invention tending to alter an established order of things, the railway system was slow at first, it was only slow enough to improve its principles and ensure its results. The first traffic-rail was opened, with misgivings, in 1830; but after the opening of the London and Birmingham Line, in 1836, the system became a certainty; by 1840 it became the grand vehicle of speculation; and, in 1845, it grew into a general madness, rolling into the commercial system like a flood, and threatening to bear all down before it. It was only at this period, when every village in the kingdom was animated with the same enthusiasm and rushing into the scrip market, that Wisbech bestirred itself in the same cause; and this may be said to have arisen less from its own eagerness than the activity of those boundless speculators who were fabricating imaginary lines about her, as if to inclose her in a net of railways. Two years previous to this Peterborough had obtained a railway from Northampton, and Lynn had obtained an act wholly by the assiduity of its inhabitants, for a railway from Ely, in which act a branch from Watlington to Wisbech was included. This latter line can only be denominated a mistake. Its track is through a bare fen; and its termination at Watlington leaves the traveller seven miles from Lynn, and further from Ely. The country, on the contrary, which lies between Wisbech and Lynn, is highly populous, and requires accommodation, there being no less than eight considerable villages in the track, which is only about thirteen miles extent; whereas, by the authorised line, there is not a single village, and Lynn is about five miles further off than it need be. The act authorising this improper line, and the schemes which were propagated in 1845 for making seventeen others, some of which were conceived in as enlightened and accommodating a spirit as the Watlington Branch, at length roused Wisbech to choose her own lines, and hunt the other speculators out of the field. There were three lines proposed from Lynn to Peterborough, but one, which was called the Earl Fitzwilliam's Line, was adopted by Wisbech; several lines were proposed going south, but one proposed by Mr. Day, of St. Ives, and called the Wisbech and St. Ives Line, was the favorite, though it would be difficult to reconcile its adoption with reason or judgment. But how could reason or judgment be expected at a time when all men were speculators? Opinions, on such occasions, are not matters that are weighed in the scale of justice, but by principles of far less disputable decision. Other lines were taken under the protection of the town, but the panic which seized railway speculation in October, 1845, so paralysed the last and most important efforts of their promoters, that hundreds were unable to fulfil the first of parliamentary standing orders.

1846. All the lines adopted by Wisbech—except the St. Ives Line—fell in the first charges of the conflict; the Lynn and Peterborough never appeared in the field; while a line which had been overlooked, or only looked on as harmless or unworthy dispute, crept through the house and was passed without opposition. This line—called the Boston, Stamford, and Birmingham—came afterwards to be better known. In the meanwhile the St. Ives Line, reduced to one opponent and protected by Wisbech, made its progress steadily through parliament; and, having detected a material error in the levels of its opponent, it succeeded in routing it, and finally passed both houses in June, 1846. Immediately on this accomplishment it was purchased by the Eastern Counties' Company at the rate of £4 for every £2 deposit, as an adjunct to their Ely and Peterborough Line, which was opened in January,

1847; and the portion between that line and Wisbech, comprising about nine miles, was immediately commenced. Such good speed was made in the works that, in May, 1847, the line was opened; and thus Wisbech has gained possession of lines of rail communicating with the London and Birmingham Line for the north and west, and the Eastern Counties Line for the east, London, and the south; so that, although other lines may reduce the direct distance between different points, it already possesses communication with all the great thoroughfare lines in the kingdom.[1]

1847. During the present year railway agitation has rather increased than diminished at Wisbech. The Boston, Stamford, and Birmingham Line, which passed so quietly side by side with the St. Ives Line, was doomed this year to become a strong and energetic opponent to it. The St. Ives Line had blended itself in the powerful ranks of the Eastern Counties Line, and the Boston, Stamford, and Birmingham had become incorporated with a company as powerful—the Great Northern. These great companies, therefore, both passing through the country in the same direction, projected lines from Wisbech into Lincolnshire from the same point, and very nearly in the same route. As it was impossible that parliament would permit two such lines, and as the Great Northern wished to confine the Eastern Counties Company to a lower latitude than the latter were content with, this line became a point of conflict between the parties, with Wisbech as the auxiliary of the Eastern Counties Line. The Eastern Counties were first in the field, and had picked out the main line of the district, passing from Wisbech to Sutton, and thence to Holbeach and Spalding, a line describing a considerable curve, but still the curve of population. On the other hand, the Great Northern managed to incorporate a considerable portion of the same district by nearly a direct line, passing from Lynn to Gosberton, across

(1) The traffic by the Wisbech Branch at present is carried on by five London and two Peterborough trains and their returns. There are two trains on Sundays and their returns, and a cattle train on Saturdays.

the Ouse and the two Washes, and communicating with Wisbech by a line from Sutton Bridge. The idea of running a line into the interior of the kingdom, leaving Wisbech nine miles south, was too pleasing to Lynn to be rejected. It was, therefore, taken up with clamour there, and a monster petition, signed by thousands, rather tended to show the intemperance than the strength of their support. On the other hand Wisbech looked coldly on the scheme, or rather her opposition was as dogmatic as the support of Lynn was fervent. But not only Wisbech, but Spalding, was also a decided opponent, and this opposition being feared by the Great Northern, which had the weakness of being more theoretical than practical, that Company saw it would require skilful manœuvring to drive the enemy successfully from his position. One circumstance seemed, under judicious management, capable of gaining the interest of a powerful party in the district, and at the same time of diminishing or diverting the opposition of Wisbech. Sutton Bridge had, ever since its erection, been the constant bane of navigation and drainage. It held up the waters of the fen, and was to vessels, after they had escaped the perils of the sea, often a greater peril than they had found there. This blockade of the district the Great Northern promised to remove, and construct a bridge consonant to the best principles of the age, and fully sufficient both for navigation and drainage. The drainers had now no doubts—anything that would alter Sutton Bridge must benefit them, and they were at once diverted to the ranks of the Great Northern. The Eastern Counties were hardly surprised at this. But Wisbech, its trusty ally, was not to be deluded. A railway over the Nene at Sutton was looked upon here with more horror than any other obstruction could possibly be; and the removal of Sutton Bridge, under such circumstances, began to be prophesied as the virtual ruin of a prosperous town.

An act had been passed in 1846, whereby any railway or other public work, connected with navigable rivers, could not be constructed, unless it were approved by the Lords of the

Admiralty, who founded their reports on the representations of engineers and experienced officers, sent out to ascertain by personal inspection the features of the district. Two of their officers were sent to this district to hear the objections made to the railway interference with the harbors of Lynn, Wisbech, and Spalding; and upon their report it was considered a great part of the success of the adverse lines must depend. The Great Northern party were men of emergency. They had heard themselves rejected by the resolutions of two or three public meetings at Wisbech, and the Eastern Counties' scheme heartily, perhaps blindly, adopted; but they relied on an impression they were now prepared to make on the Admiralty Commission for adequate support to their line. Both the Eastern Counties Company and the Great Northern proposed to construct Docks at Wisbech; but, while the Eastern Counties proposed twelve acres of dock, the Great Northern hardly proposed five. As then the difference between five and twelve, combined with Sutton Bridge, would be the difference between hate and love, a manœuvre must restore the balance, or turn the scale, if they meant to succeed. They immediately sought out some great desideratum of the district. They were not long in gaining one exactly suited to their purpose, which had been proposed before by more than one engineer of eminence, and which had the advantage of being in the town of Wisbech itself, and likely to have ready effect on the Commission. The river in passing through Wisbech makes three almost right angular turns; it is grossly contracted by buildings constructed down to the water's edge; and since the scour caused by the Nene Outfall, these buildings have only been preserved in their situation by enormous quantities of stone thrown at their foundations. The river, in consequence of these obstructions, is held up from three to four feet in the course of a mile. The Great Northern Company took up this fault as their grand manœuvre; and, as docks were demanded by the town, they proposed to convert the present channel into docks and cut a new straight river—uniting with the old river at the Horse Shoe and at the South Brink toll bar—on the north side for drainage and navigation. This scheme would have the advantage of serving two absolutely necessary ends—continue the trade in the town, and preserve the lower channel of the river to a greater extent, by producing a quicker and more complete outfall. Besides this, it would completely overthrow the scheme of the Eastern Counties for constructing docks near the town, as the line of the proposed cut went completely through the centre of the land which had been scheduled for their docks. There was thus, in the scheme, a double advantage to Wisbech, and a signal triumph, if it prevailed, to themselves. But the Eastern Counties Company had so closely wrapped Wisbech in its arms, that no fondling from another nurse would pacify it. It did not want docks in the town; it did not want a straight river at the back; the stagnant waters of the docks would generate infection; it was a scheme impossible to realise; it was not before Parliament.

All these objections, however, were unavailing with the Commissioners; they saw at once the necessity of the work, reported in favor of it, and the Great Northern looked upon its cause as won. But, though they had the finest of parliamentary powers,—though they spared no money nor pains in bringing up witnesses and proving the soundness of their preamble,—and though all these points were neglected or imperfect in the management of the Eastern Counties,—the crossing of the three great rivers of the district finally overthrew them; and the Eastern Counties, like some neglected horse at a St. Leger, found itself winner when the odds had run sadly against it. Wisbech has no reason to be dissatisfied with this conclusion—nor is she. The line from Lynn to Gosberton would have been a rival line to her interests, as Lynn well knew. The bridge at the Wash is virtually condemned by the formation of lines which will leave its traffic a nonentity, or a mere village roadway, while Wisbech has got a line into Lincolnshire securing better points for her interest than that of the Great Northern would have done. As, however, the Great Northern Line from Wisbech to Sutton Bridge passed, and the Great Northern are to have the use of the Eastern Counties rails as far as they need them in Lincolnshire, both parties have in a certain degree been reconciled, though the field being in the hands of the Eastern Counties Company has given them the nominal, perhaps the real, victory. Neither has Wisbech any reason to fear, in this conflict of parties, that she will lose her docks and her new cut.[1] The cut must come, as the readiest work for improving the district; and docks will come as an auxiliary of the cut. It is only from the natural hatred that all men have at the disturbance of an old and venerated system, that Wisbech looks at present with aversion on Town Docks and the North Side Cut. Such weakness is neither very formidable nor very permanent.

(1) The feeling upon this cut in the Admiralty is decided. All their reports, private and public, have called for the suspension of railways, or works in conjunction with railways, which may interfere with its formation, and the Lords have withheld their necessary consent "until the new cut is established."

CHAPTER II.

HISTORY OF THE CASTLE.

THE materials for a history of the Castle are exceedingly meagre. We may, therefore, infer from this circumstance that it has generally been unimportant and unconnected with stirring events. We have already had occasion to detail the events which led to the foundation of this building, or rather the supposed events, for it is exceedingly doubtful whether it was not erected many years after such a mitigation of war, as was called tranquillity, had been restored to the kingdom by William the Conqueror. It is not mentioned in *Doomsday Book*; and it could scarcely have been omitted, had it been in existence when that survey was made. The opinion, therefore, which gives William the Conqueror the credit of erecting a castle of stone here in the last year of his reign, is more probable, or admits of less contradiction than that which attributes the same building to him in an earlier part of his reign. Some say the first building with which he repelled Hereward was constructed of "turfs;" and, if so, it may not have been considered worthy of enumeration in the Doomsday Catalogue, and may only have obtained the lofty name of a castle from a subsequent building of that consequence having been erected on the same spot. The building of "turfs" could have been merely a sort of entrenchment, and by no means worthy of the consideration of a fortress by such a people as the Normans, who so thoroughly despised the wooden churches and mud and thatch-work dwellings of the Saxons. Almost all that is known of its subsequent history is comprised in the following particulars, which we have taken from *Stephenson's Supplement to Bentham's History of Ely Cathedral.*

"The castle is said to have been destroyed by a dreadful inundation in 1236; it appears, however, to have been soon rebuilt, as we meet with the name of a constable, or keeper, of the castle in 1246. The building was kept in repair by certain persons in West Walton, who held their estates by a tenure to that effect. It is probable that this building was dismantled in the reign of Henry II., and it appears that Bishop Morton erected a new one of brick on its site, between 1471, and 1473, from which period it became a palace of the Bishops of Ely. And from 1609, to 1619, Bishop Andrews expended considerable sums upon this, and his other residence.

"When the possessions of the church were sold at the Restoration,[1] Thurloe, afterwards secretary of Oliver Cromwell, purchased the castle, and erected the edifice, apparently after a design by Inigo Jones, and here he resided, when he was chosen to represent the Town of Wisbech in 1658, for then it was intended to have made that a borough town; but it did not take place, and he was returned for Huntingdon.[2] Upon the restoration of Charles II., the castle reverted to the see. From that time the building was leased to several respectable families; among others, to the ancestors of Sigismund Trafford Southwell, Esq., High Sheriff of Norfolk in 1816, who descended from Sir Marmion de Suell, or Southwell in the reign of Edward III. At length Bishop Yorke sold the premises under an act of Parliament to Joseph Medworth, Esq., who pulled down the buildings, and and erected several elegant houses on the site.

(1) Query—Revolution?

(2) Cambridge was the town he represented, not Huntingdon.

"We have no description or graphical representation of the castle before the time of Secretary Thurloe. But the particulars below induce us to suppose that it was a place of strength. In June 1403 the keeper of the arms was paid 3*d.* a day. The walls were rebuilt with rag or rackstone, and a new bridge was erected. In 1404 the draw-bridge (*le Draughtbrigg*) towards the church occurs, and the moat round the ***Julik*** was scoured out. In 1409 new ***Floud Gate***, which cost £30. 3*s.*, and a new water gate, were erected. In 1410 a new ***Pons tractabilis*** towards the church, a chapel within and a bridge without the castle, also a garden and dove house in the castle which let for 6*s.* 8*d.* a year are frequently mentioned; and it is noted that the dove house was totally destroyed in 1513,[1] and that it was walled round and moated. It was also a place of custody for state prisoners at a very early period; for it is recorded that in 1297 Edmund Hastings, of the county of Suffolk, manumised John de Drommon, of Scotland, a prisoner in the Castle, on condition that as soon as possible he should go to King Edward I. then beyond sea, and serve him well and faithfully against the King of France and all his other enemies.[2] In 1314, Robert Wishart, bishop of Glasgow, and the wife of Robert Brus, were prisoners here, and conducted from hence to York.[3] In 1414, Dns Heyle, and other prisoners taken by the Earl of Dorchester, were kept here by permission of Bishop Fordham. In 1476 the prison was repaired. The following dignitaries died here under a charge of conspiracy against the government of Queen Elizabeth: Thomas White, bishop of Lincoln, in 1584; John Fakenham, abbot of Westminster, 1585, after a confinement of twenty-six years; and Thomas Watson, bishop of Lincoln, in 1587, confined here twenty-eight years. All these persons are buried in Wisbech Church.

"The office of constable or keeper of the castle appears to have been always conferred upon a person of distinction, who had his deputy, and held Courts Leet, Baron, and Hundred Courts. The Courts for Wisbech were held in the mote-hall,

(1) Bentham's Notitia. (2) Rymer's Fœdera, v. ii., p. 782. (3) Ibid, vol. iii., p. 496.

and a gallows was erected in Gallows Marsh in 1348. His stipend, in 1301, was 3*s.* 10*d.* a week, the gaoler's 18*d.*, and the Præpositus 10*d.* From 1368 to 1370 the wages were paid to the *janitor*, or porter, *in defectu constabularii.* In 1430 it was 20 marks in silver, or £13 6*s.* 8*d.*, paid in equal quarterly portions, a robe for himself, another for his deputy, or 40*s.* in lieu thereof, 40,000 turfs, 10 cart-loads of hay, 45 quarters 5 bush. of oats, and a sufficient quantity of straw or litter for three horses annually. In 1514 the fee is stated at £26 7*s.* 8*d.*, without specifying particulars. The constable's dwelling was a hall which was new-built of freestone in 1404, near the gates of the castle, and the chambers at the ends of the same, and upon the gates. In one patent, 1443, the houses and chambers called *Le Dungeon* are allotted to the Constable, who was answerable for the safety of the prisoners committed to the gaol. Accordingly, Sir Andrew Oggard, in 1452, and Sir James Hobard, in 1494, were each fined £5. by the justices at Ely, for the escape of felons.

"The names of the following Constables appear on Record:

"1246. Wm. Justice.

[Witness to a charta of Bishop Northwold, dated 1246.—*Bentham's Notitia.*]

"1262. Symon de Dullingham.

[Witness to a grant of Bishop Balsham, 1260.]

"1308. Richard de Halsted.

"1401. Thomas de Braunstone.

[The author of the *Beauties of England*, vol. ii., says this person was an ancestor of the representative for Essex in 1801. His effigy, engraved on brass, still remains in the church of Wisbech, but, according to a print in *Lyson's Magna Britannia*, a great part of the ornamental arch around it is now reaved and gone. Mr. Gough has engraved this memorial from a drawing taken by Mr. Vertue, and corrected it from an impression which Mr. Ord took off the original in its perfect state. The date prefixed to this person's name is the year of his death, which it may be proper to observe, because Mr. Gough has said that Sir John de Rochford was probably the immediate predecessor, whereas he was the successor of Thomas Braunston.]

"1403. Sir John de Rochford.

[In the *Beauties of England* he is styled Lord John, and said to be Constable before 1631. In the *Notitia* he is styled Dns. Johannes Rochfort M. (iles), under the date 1403. And in 1407 we find, Solut: Dno Johanni Rochefort, Constabulario de ultima obligatione Dni: Epi: eidem facta, pro maritagio uxoris suæ £20. The Lady Rochford died in 1409, Sir John in 1410, and Dns. Johans: Colvyll fit Constabularius.]

"1410. Sir John de Colville.

[The grant to Sir Jno. Colville by Bishop Fordham. It is singular that during the life of Sir John, Cardinal Luxumbourg, as perpetual administrator of the Church of Ely, granted the office to Richard Waller, in 1443, upon the death of the said Sir John, who, it appears, outlived his intended successor; for, in 1446, Bishop Bouchier appointed Andrew Oggard, "upon the death of Sir John Colville."—*Notitia.*]

"1446-7. Sir Andrew Oggard.

"1476-7. Sir Thomas Grey.

[Grandson to Bishop Grey.—*Notitia.* John Aspelon was *locum tenens* to Thomas Grey, Esq., et habet expensas pro quodlibet 2*s*. ex antiqua consuetudine. The Præpositus wages were £2.]

"1489. Sir James Hobard.

[Sir James (the patent observes) adtunc armiger, was appointed by Bishop Alcock, in 1489; in 1494 he was fined £5 for the escape of a prisoner, and he is mentioned as constable in 1507.—*Notitia.*]

"1525. Walter and Miles Hubbard.

"1531. Thomas Meggs.

" Sir Richard Cromwell.

[We find mention is made of the name of Master Ric: Crumwell, Knt., Steward of the Manors in Marshland, and Keeper of the house and park at Downham, as Constable, and his fee of £27 13*s*. 5*d*.—*Notitia.* There is no date to the minute, but on reference to *Mr. Noble's History of the Cromwell Family*, no one with the title of Knt. appears so likely to be the person as the great grandfather of the Protector, knighted by Henry VIII., 1540; who, when he had witnessed the prowess of Cromwell, exclaimed "formerly thou wast my Dick, but hereafter thou shalt be my diamond," and, presenting him with a diamond ring, bade him bear such a one in the fore paw of the demi-lion in his crest.—*Fuller's Church History*, p. 370.]

"1605. Wm. Chester. sen., Esq,

[Appointed by Bp. Heton, in 1605, for the lives of Wm. Chester, jun., and Thomas and Geo. Heton, Gentlemen.—*Bentham's Notitia.*]

"1663. Matthias Taylor."[1]

This long extract comprises the principal facts which are known of the castle. "The building," says Watson, "covered two acres of land, and stood in the midst of four other acres, at the boundary of which was a strong wall, and on the outside next the town was a ditch or moat forty feet wide, and there was no way to the castle but by a drawbridge in the west front. This castle was more than once in a state of siege... and for the better and more secret conveying of intelligence at those times between the garrison and their friends... lead pipes were laid within the walls underground, and under the walls and ditch to the outside next... Deadman's Lane, and by the pipes being branched out to all parts

(1) Stephenson's Supplement to Bentham's History of Ely Cathedral.

of the basement story of the building *intelligence* is said to have been conveyed either to or from the garrison."[1]

It appears to have been first used as a palace by the Bishops of Ely about 1483, when Bishop Morton reconstructed it. This eminent person is said to have usually resided here during part of the year.[2] After him, Bishop Alcock, his successor, used it as his residence, and died here in 1500.[3] Though a palace, this castle still continued a prison, and it is not impossible that the Bishop might be

(1) *History of Wisbech*, p. 124. "On digging up the foundation of the castle premises, such pipes or tubes were found in the lower part, about three inches diameter, extending to the moat from the four quarters of the building."—*Ibid.*

(2) Morton lived in that age of the church when it exhibited all the wantonness and recklessness of its corruption. The bishop, however, was a man who saw beyond his age, and whether he is considered as a statesman, a churchman, or a ruler of the Isle of Ely, he is in each position an uncommon man. His public work between Guyhirn and Peterborough we have before spoken of. He strove to re-introduce some discipline into a church that had now long ago outgrown all rule, and issued letters commanding his clergy "not to wear short liripoops of silk, nor gowns open before, nor swords, nor daggers, or embroidered girdles, to be careful of their tonsures, and to keep their hair always so short that every one might see their ears." Like every other man who has had an influence on his age, and has struggled at reforms in natural abuses, he has been inordinately praised and censured. "Lord Bacon represents him as a stern haughty man, odious at court, and more so in the country. Weever says he was a man so well deserving both of the church and commonwealth, that all honors and offices were too little which were conferred upon him. Rapin ascribes his motives in opposing King Richard to revenge, and adds that 'he died detested by the people,' who suspected he was guilty of the oppression which proceeded from the king himself. By the moderate he is styled eminent and wise, an artful and an able politician.—*Carte.* After a deliberate consideration of his history, an impartial judge will allow this Primate to have been learned, prudent, beneficent, and eloquent; the adviser and confidant of Henry VII., and the happy means of stopping the effusion of human blood with which the houses of York and Lancaster had deluged the country."—*Stephenson's Appendix to Bentham's Ely.*

(3) Willis, in his history of cathedrals, says he rebuilt Wisbech Castle of brick; but this is evidently a mistake, if that had been already done, as is generally stated, by Bishop Morton. "Bishop Alcock's sermons," says the continuator of Bentham, "were remarkable for their length: one preached by him before the University continued nearly three hours, to which he himself bears the following testimony, as it is recorded in Wren's M.S. collection: (registr: parv: consistorii Eliensis, called the Black Book,) 'J. Alcock, divina gratia, episcopus Eliensis, prima die dominica, 1488, bonum et blandum sermonem prædicavit, in ecclesia B. Mariæ Cantabrig: qui incepit in hora prima post meridian: et duravit in horam tertiam, et ultra.' The following is from *Bentham's Notitia*:—" Goinge forthe on a tyme into his parke, and seinge there a grate mayny of bulloks, he asked whose they were. His steward answered that they were his, being bought for the findinge of his house. Then he comandyd that they should all be browght together into one place, nere unto the pallase, and calling his servaunts together he distributed all those bullocks among them according as every one had most nede, gyvinge his steward charge to buy fleshe, breade, and beere, to sarve his howse of his fermers, payinge for it as moche as it was worthe, and as they mought aforde it."—*Cat. MSS. Bib. Har.*—*Stephenson's Appendix to Bentham's Ely.*—Bishop Alcock is buried in a sumptuous chapel which he built on the north side of the choir in Ely Cathedral.

holding his court in one part of it while Catholic priests and Jesuits, to the confinement of whom it was assigned, might be walking in chains in another. Col. Watson conjectures that it was used as a prison only during the twenty years' vacancy which occurred in the See of Ely[1] in the reign of Elizabeth, but it appears to have been commonly used for that purpose afterwards, for in the third year of Charles I. we find the Commons congratulating the Crown that it had driven all the "Papists and Jesuists, enemies of church and state, to lurk in dark corners like the sons of darkness," and this was followed by a proclamation ordering a levy upon their estates of two-thirds of their value, and for all priests and jesuists not already banished to be confined in the castle of Wisbech.[2] Watson, Bishop of Lincoln, whom Pugin calls a "faithful witness of the Catholic Church," was confined here about eight years after, having been in confinement near twenty years in some place in or about London. He obtained the Bishopric of Lincoln from Mary in 1557, and immediately applied himself to the recovery of its ancient possessions, and succeeded in procuring plate, vestments, furniture, estates, and got the patronage of above a hundred benefices. But these were all resumed by Elizabeth, whose affection for the Reformation was largely blended with the desire for the riches of which it excused the plunder. Watson was deprived of his See by Elizabeth in 1559, and died in Wisbech castle in 1587.[3]

During the confinement of this prelate in the castle, the prisoners broke into rebellion, "on account of one Father Weston, who pretended to make orders and set up for governor over all the rest;"[4] the majority, however, refused this dictatorship, and asserted that this office had been tendered to Bishop Watson, who had refused as being a distinction "unsuitable to their circumstances, from affliction and confinement." A Catholic priest, to whom the question was referred, decided against the Jesuits.[5]

(1) 1579-1599. (2) Howitt's Visits to Remarkable Places.
(3) Storer's Cathedrals, v. 3. (4) Watson. (5) Ibid.

Among the celebrated prisoners confined here during the reign of Elizabeth, we must not omit Robert Catesby and Francis Tresham—the plotter and counter-plotter of the Gunpowder Treason, as they may be called; for Catesby is generally considered to have been the principal promoter of that famous conspiracy, and Tresham is supposed to have written the letter to Lord Monteagle which, in the end, exploded the scheme. They appear to have been sent here as suspicious characters on the threatened invasion of Spain, when the hopes of the Catholics were high, and conspiracies and treasons frequent, or imagined to be so, which was excuse enough for every kind of persecution. We do not know but the Wisbech confinement of two such characters may have had an important influence in contriving the conspiracy which has made them so notorious.

The frequent residence of the Bishop here appears to have been considered beneficial to the town; and the Corporation Records contain many minutes of presents in money and other necessuries to him, during his residence among them. Bishop Andrews[1] spent £2000 on this and his other residences, and upon his visit here in 1611 we find the following note of a donation to him from the Burgesses. "The company was contented to beystow on the Lord Byshopp the viij day of August next, half a byff, one mutton, and one velle, ij lambs." And the same Bishop, six years afterwards had another gift from the same hands. "17 Oct. 1617. The toune baliefe shall pay into the hands of Mr. Taylor iij$^{li.}$ vj^{s} viij$^{d.}$ to buy certaine foule to p'sent unto my L^{d} of Ely." In 1619 we find "the some of vij$^{li.}$ xvj$^{s.}$ for recognition money" ordered to be paid to the "use of my Lord of Elye," and minute made that "xx stone of the best beef, a veall, and a lambe" be provided, and bestowed upon my Lord of Ely against the assizes. In 1669 a more extraordinary effort than usual was made to gratify his lordship: "The towne balife is ordred to send for a bucke from Exton parke, and

(1) 1609—1619.

give the keper 20*s.*, and send halfe to the Bishop of Ely and the other halfe for the Burgesses and their friends."[1]

The last erection of the castle was by Thurloe, secretary to Oliver Cromwell, who purchased the estate on the sale of church property during the Protectorate. The new building is said to have been designed by Inigo Jones, "upon a model of the Lord Chief Justice Oliver St. John's seat at Long Thorpe, near Peterborough."[2] A painting of this building has been preserved, and is now in the palace at Ely.

After the Restoration the castle appears to have been disused as an episcopal residence and as a prison, and was generally leased to some considerable family. The Southwells had five separate grants of it of twenty-one years each, in the seventeenth and eighteenth centuries. But, either from the decay of the building, or the belief that the property might be made to realise much more to the See by selling the fee simple of its site as building ground, in 1793 the Bishop of Ely procured an act for the sale of this estate, and the appropriation of the monies arising from it to the purchase of other lands, &c., within the diocese of Ely. The castle was accordingly put up to auction in London, and purchased by Mr. Medworth, of Bermondsey, for £1945, and £300 more for the materials. The ground occupied by the castle and premises amounted to about five acres, and Mr. Medworth, immediately after his purchase, commenced one of the most decided improvements which has been privately effected in the town. He removed all the detached offices of the castle, and commenced the erection of what is now called the Crescent. "He also purchased a dwelling-house and premises at a great price, for the purpose of a more easy communication with the Market Place, thereby forming a street from the castle premises into the heart of the town.[3] The Crescent is now extended into a circus... and consists of more than fifty houses... After disposing of the surround-

(1) Corporation Records. (2) Watson.

(3) "The entrance to this street from the Market Place is the freehold property of Mr. Joseph Medworth, of Bermondsey, purchased by him at £400 for the accommodation of the town of Wisbech, A.D., 1793."—*Inscription in Market Street.*

ing ground for the purposes of building, Mr. Medworth retained the residue (consisting of the castle itself with the inclosed garden) in his own possession and occupation, and in the year 1811 offered such reserved portion to the Corporation of Wisbech for £2000."[1] Mr. Medworth's object was to confer a double and material benefit on the town. The Grammar School house was greatly in decay, but by this arrangement the castle might be appropriated for the residence of the master and a school, and the present buildings be removed, and the street continued through across the Old Horse Fair and over the canal to Lynn Road. The offer, however, was not entertained by the Corporation, and thus an opportunity, never to be renewed, was lost for preserving the most interesting building in the town, and at the same time effecting an improvement of the highest character in its streets and approaches. Mr. Medworth, perhaps chagrined at the refusal of his liberal offer, took the castle down in 1816, and fragments of its materials may now be traced in several houses in the Crescent and in the low building which Mr. Medworth erected as his new residence. The four gateways which formed the immediate entrances into the court of the castle, still stand, built into the garden-walls; and two cannon, which formerly defended it, are yet in the castle gardens.

One other interesting relic of the castle remains to be noticed. It is the governor's seal, which is at present in the possession of Chas. R. Colvile, Esq., M. P. for S. Derbyshire, of Duffield Hall, and Lullington in the County of Derby, who kindly furnished an impression for the use of this work, and whose ancestor, Sir John de Colvile, was governor here in 1410. The engraving represents it very faithfully. It is of iron, which, by rusting, has perhaps caused the delineation to assume its present very broken and irregular appearance.

(1) Watson. Half to be paid down and half to be under Corporation bond at interest for twenty years.

CHAPTER III.

HISTORY OF THE GUILD.

THE origin of Guilds is one of those disputed points in history which are not likely to find a satisfactory solution. Their existence is traced to very early periods on our own island, and in Europe generally; but as they cannot be traced to any authentic Roman original, they may be esteemed as purely Gothic institutions. They have been traced to the Anglo-Saxon period, and the name Guild has been considered to signify a fraternity, or company, because every one was *gildare*, *i.e.*, to pay something towards the charge and support of the company. Among the Saxons it was a law that every freeman at twelve or fourteen years of age should find sureties for his honesty, or be committed; upon which certain individuals, consisting of ten families, entered into a company, and became mutually bound for each other. One of the laws of Canute provides that "every one of twelve winters should swear that he will not be a thief, nor the adviser of one." It is from these early benefit societies that Guilds are supposed to be derived. Though Guilds were somewhat common in the Saxon era, their rules are almost wholly unknown till some time after the Norman Conquest, when they assumed different characters,—some being mere trading associations, some religious fraternities, and some societies for mutual

Drawn & Engraved

WISBECH SEALS

Published by H. Walker Bridge Foot Wisbech

benefit, like the Freemasons' and Shepherds' societies of the present day. The Guild at Wisbech, which was termed the Guild of the Holy Trinity, was wholly a religious community, and seems to have been instituted to provide those expensive church ceremonies and officers, such as priests, daily masses, masses for the soul, decorations for the altar, which could only be provided by the poorer classes by mutual small contributions.

The proceedings of the Guild are contained in a thin folio volume. The first entry is dated A.D. 1379; but a period of forty-four years elapses before there is another entry. These entries are in Latin till 1470, when the first English entry occurs.[1] The entries, however, are not wholly in English till 1513.

The officers of the Guild varied as the society increased in wealth. At first they consisted of six persons; and the number of the brethren in 1379 appears to have been sixty-seven, whose payments altogether amounted to £13 14*s.* during that year, though the manner of their payments, or whether they were a certain yearly sum, or ruled by the necessity of the company, is not very clear. The functions of the officers are defined with more certainty. The revenues of the Guild seem at first to have been wholly personal contributions, but they appear to have had also tithes accruing to them, as such are ordered in their minutes to be levied. They also received a certain sum at the entrance of every member, who is called a novice; and, after a time, they had various lands left to them by different members, mostly for a certain number of masses to be said for the soul of the deceased. After this kind of property became of some value, we meet with a Balie to look after their estates among their officers, and from this source our Town Bailiff, of nearly three hundred years, was derived.

(1) Col. Watson took the trouble to translate much of this part of the Records, and has given the substance of the rest in a MS. volume which he presented to the Corporation in 1822. This has greatly facilitated any future investigation of these Records, and with a General Index, made by the Rev. Jeremiah Jackson, A. M., vicar of Elm, commencing where that of Col. Watson terminates, comprising 230 years, and presented to the Corporation in a similar spirit, the whole series of Records are very easy of access.

The first officer of the fraternity, however, was the *Alderman*, who, by various orders we find, was by no means an unconditional magistrate. It is commanded that he "seall no mañr of writynge nor grauntes to be seallyd w^t the com~on seall of the gild, w^tout assent & consent of xij of the most honest men, brethren of the gyld"—that he be attended to church by the brethren—that he sue and recover monies, prosecute for debts, and recover tenths from those who owed them—that no lease of land be granted without his leave—that he go to church and make offering with brethren, &c., at their dead day—"the longe chest shett w^t iij locks, wherof the seid Ald~rman to have one key, and eche of the Chableynes for the tyme beyng a key."[1]

The *Scabina* were generally two in number. Their duty seems to have been to provide the necessaries of the Guild—to buy the wax for the altars, and make all payments in the church, and receive legacies.

The *Clerk*, in 1456, is ordered to make sufficient repairs in the hall—in 1503, to be at the first mass in the morning, when required by the chaplain, and celebrate the first mass in the surplice—in 1511, he is ordered to translate the first statutes—in 1531, it is ordered "that the clerk for the tyme being schall at all tymes giffe tendauñce to the balye vppon resonable requeste for malcyng & writinge of his accompts, uppon payne of xx^s. Also that the clerk of the same Gilde for the tyme beyng shall at all tymes hereaft^r on Trinite sonday aft^r Den^r openlie rede all our anstitucons & olde ordinance, as shall appere by an order to hym maide in Englesse to the audience to them out, that no brother shall come in contempt & faute of knowlegge."[2]

The *Dean* is called Dean of the Church in 1460, and his duties may be collected from the following orders which are scattered over the Records concerning him. In 1423 he is called the Dean before the altar, and he accounted for 3*s*. 6d. for the souls of eleven persons; he is ordered, in 1460, to warn all the brothers and sisters if any brother die, that they

(1) Corporation Records, vol. i. (2) Ibid.

may come and make offering for the soul of the departed. or in default pay 8lbs. of wax; in 1470 it is "orderd y[t] in eu~y principale day after dyn[r] & souper the Deene shall p'clame w[t] an opyn voyce that eu~y man and woma~ shall p~ye devoutely for the soules of all the Bred~en & systers of this Gyld & for all Crysten soules, and to keep sylence while the Gild pr'ste shall sey Grace and *de profundis*, &c., for all Crysten soules." In 1477 he is ordered to keep at the altar of the Holy Trinity, on every Principal Day, four waxes, called tapers. In 1478 he is ordered to demand of persons last admitted the wax which they owe for their admission. In 1537 the brotherhood "will and order by a hole assent of the Jure that eu[r] from hensforth the Dean shall geve monicon to the enguert chosen at the elecon of the balie & other officers of the same enguert to be allway at the recitt of the bales accompts."[1]

One feature of the institution of the Guild was an annual festivity, which forms a prominent object in many of the minutes of their proceedings. The day on which this was yearly held was called the Principal Day, and on that occasion all the old ordinances were read, and services were performed at the church of a more expensive character than usual. In the first entry of the Guild a Hostiliarus is mentioned among the officers; but there are no specific entries from which we can infer his duties, though they were probably attached more particularly to the proceedings of the Principal Day.

These are all the officers which are named in the early proceedings; but as the brother and sisterhood became land proprietors, and otherwise opulent, they elected several other officers, as Scribe, Storekeeper, Server in the Hall, Keeper of

(1) Mann Hutcheson, in his introduction to the Charts, thinks the office of Dean was not ecclesiastical; "but that it might be, and really was, executed by a layman, is clear from a tailor having been elected to it two successive years. We are therefore, of course led to inquire what was the duty incumbent on this officer? but of this difficulty I have not any solution at hand more satisfactory than supposing (which is not impossible) that the Dean, as now at Inverness, in Scotland, superintended the markets, and regulated the prices of provisions."—p. 78.

the Jewels, two Chamberlains, Bailiff, Server in the Kitchen, Porter at the Door, Skyven, and in some of their late proceedings, two Cupbearers and two Aldermen are added. They had also several Priests and a Chaplain.

We do not gain any facts from the Records that explain the peculiar duties of several of these officers, though their names perhaps lead us to infer pretty nearly as to their services. In the following orders we see a portion of the duty of two of them: "1506. We ordeyn that the *Steuard in hall* and *Server apud le kechyn bord* shall see eu˜y broder and sustir fuyd [fed] in the hall upon Trinyte sonday next comyng. And whan the Alderman and his brethrene have dynyd, we wyll that all the pore people then ther p'sent shalbe set at a Tabyll in the seyd hall and fuyd w^t such mete as shalbe left the seid ald˜man & his brethern by the foreseid stuard and server." In 1515 an order relating to one of the same officers occurs: "It is agreed by all the forseid eleaven that the server at the dressing borde shall see the brethern and susters beyng seke svyd of their svce [service] acordyng to their porcon, and that no brodyr nor sust^r beyng in good helth shall have eny s˜vie sent home to theym, but they so beyng absent to depute s'teyn p'sons for them, and to sitt in the hall as a brodyr, and be sved as a brodyr in their absence."[1]

The *Chamberlains* are frequently alluded to; and one of the first orders we meet with is, that they "shall go before all the brethern of this gyld to church in the vigill of the holy Trinytie to evynsong, the next day to messe and evynsonge, and so to c'm home to the halle befor the seid brethern w^t their garlandds and typpe-stavyes in their handds." They are further commanded to "ou˜see and survey almañ repacoñs made and done by the ballyf;"[2] they also each of them held a key of the "large chest" in which the valuables of the Guild were doubtless kept.

The *Chaplain* is ordered, in 1461, to keep the ornaments of the altar, and on every Sunday and double feast to say vespers in the Chapel after the principal vespers said in the

(1) Corporation Records, v. i. (2) Ibid.

quire. He is ordered, in 1469, to pray for the good estate, tranquillity, and peace of all the realm, and for the souls of all those who have entered the fraternity and continued therein, to the honor and laud of Almighty God, on pain of 20*s.* to the use of the Guild. His salary is stated at 6*s.* 4*d.* In 1497 there is an order for the celebration of mass at the altar of the Holy Trinity from the fifth to the seventh hour; and that eight chaplains should celebrate, on certain days, at the altar of the Holy Virgin lately erected.

The *Bailiff* was an important functionary of the Guild. He is first mentioned in 1463 as Balum p. tr˜. and tenement; and in 1468 is named as one who was to direct and manage, and to farm and let all lands and tenements belonging to the Guild. 1470. To have xx[s.] for his salary. 1472. To be assisted by the Alderman in distraining lands and tenements from all persons owing. 1483. Ordered that the Bailiff deliver to the Alderman out of the issues and fines £10 14*s.* 4*d.* to pay the priests their salary. 1514. "We ordeyn that the Ballyf shall make no man[r] of lees of no man[r] of landds and tenements for term of yeers w[t]out thadvyse and councell of the seid ald˜man and chamb˜leyne, but for one yere at the most." 1519. "We ordeyn that the Chamb˜leyne and Ballyfe of this Gyld shall p'vide the next yere iiij tapirrs of wax to brenne all the tyme while grace is seynge, and eche of theym holdyng in their handds a pot of ale of a quarte, and whan grace is endyd the seid ale to be gevyn to the people thare then beyng p'sent, acordyng to the old ordinance." 1531. "From hensforth the Balie shalhaue none allowaunce ou˜ and aboue xij[d.] of eu˜y charge that he schall doo, w[t]out it be seane by the chamb˜leyne for the tyme beyng."[1]

The duties of the *Skyvens*[2] are not very clear. There are, however, two ordinances in which their offices are assigned. 1519. "We wyll and ordeyn that the skyven of this gyld

(1) Corporation Records, v. i.

(2) Col. Watson makes the Skyvens and Scabini the same officials, and says "they were the guardians, governors, or stewards, and had the charge of the goods and effects of the Guild." We do not think the orders given to these officers, under their different names, are hardly reconcileable, and we have accordingly considered them as distinct officers.

the next yere upon the gyld-day before masse, at the fechyng of the seid ald˜man to church, shall p'vyde a competent brekfast for the seid alderman, brethern, and susters of this gyld, and at lest eu˜y one to have drynke if they wyll." 1525. "Yt ys agreyd by this forseid eleaven that the scevens now chosen, and all other scevans heraft[r] to be, shall sufficiently kepe the revell, and bryng in ther mone on the sunday to y[e] ald˜man and hys brethern."[1]

The *Priests* were, of course, an important part of the establishment of so religious a foundation as that of the Holy Trinity. Their duties are frequently set forth. One part, and perhaps the principal feature in the foundation of the Guild, seems to be the establishment of masses for the soul. Orders respecting these, indeed, are met with in every part of the proceedings, and by the special commands regarding them we naturally infer them to have been of principal importance according to the articles on which the Guild was established. In 1472 the Priest's salary is stated at £5 6*s*. 8*d*. 1514. "We ordeyn that one of ower preests that shall sey messe next aftyr the first messe be seid in the seid chapell, that same preest shall sey v messys in the same chapell for eu˜y brodir and sustir by name immediately aftir their ded daye such messis as the frendds of the ded wyll desyer the seid preest to sey." 1517. "We wyll and order that o[r] preests of this gyld shall sey messe in the man[r] followyng, that is to say the first messe to be seid in the chapell of the holy trinytie of Wisbech at vj of the clok, and anod[r] of the seid preests to synge messe by note in the chapell of o[r] blessed lady there at viij of the clok, and anodir of the seid preests to sey messe in the seid chapell of the holy trinytie whan he is disposed. Also, we will & order that all o[r] forseid prests shall alway be redy eu˜y day in their surplessye to help to synge o[r] lady's messe & antem in the seid chapell of o[r] blessid lady, and all other divyne s'vce to be sangyn in the seid chapell and church of Wisbech, in peyn of seche of o[r] seid preests so making defawt, for eu˜y day iiij[d.] to the p'fitt

(1) Corporation Records, v. i.

of this gyld. Also we orden that none of o[r] seid prests shall not go owt of the town the space of a day & a nyght w[t]out lieave of the seid ald'rman, or his depute." In 1513 this order had been disobeyed, and the priest was declared to have "forfett his penaltie." 1524. "We wyll & orden that the morow messe p'ste shall at all tymes kepe ther mores in doing morow messe, and always at the seid messe at tyme convenient shall turn them & p~y for y[e] sowlys by name, as they were wont to do w[th] *de p'fundes* and other orysune aft[r] the old constitucone & ordinanc~ and also the seid morow messe p'ste shall hereaft[r] do evynsong on eu~y sunday & other holydays in the chapell of y[e] tinte whan they begyn complyne. Also, we orden y[t] the seid p'ste & clerk shall alway be redy to begynn our lady's messe at viij of y[e] clok, w[t]owt any ferther delay, and the anthyme in som[r] tyme at 6 of the cloke & in wynt[r] tyme at iij of the clok." In 1533 we find the following instruction: "Ordin, that none of the Gilde pristes from hensforth shall sing at the lektern[1] w[t]out a surplesse, under the payn of eu~y tyme so doing iiij[d.] to be paid of his & their wages so doing." The Catholic church had at this date reached its climax of riches, luxury, indolence, and corruption. D'Aubigne has given a powerful picture of these ages in the preliminary chapters to his *History of the Reformation*, especially the third.

From the orders respecting the brethren, it appears by one made 1423, that each was to have a hood on pain of 2lbs. of wax; that all were to dine together on the Principal Day; 1457—the brethren and sisters were commanded to come into hall on the first and second vespers on Principal Day, and also at the great mass, and there sit with the Alderman at church, according to the ancient laudable custom, on pain of 8lbs. of wax. All were to come to church with a deceased brother or sister to make prayer and offering for their souls, on pain of 1lb. of wax. In 1445 every

(1) "The desk or stand on which the larger books used in the services of the Roman Catholic church are placed."—*Glossary of Architecture* v. i. In the church of Walpole St. Peter a brass lectern is still used. There is one of oak in Leverington church, and a noble one of brass in Peterborough cathedral.

brother is ordered to pay the chaplain 20$^{d.}$ 1515. "No brodyr nor sust^{r} beyng in good helth shall have eny svis sent home to them, but they so beyng absent to depute steyn p'sons for theym, and to sitt in the hall as a brodyr, and be sveid as a brodyr in their absence." In 1489 a brother gave 6*s*. 8*d*. for his admission, to be paid equally in four years.

These orders give us a slight acquaintance with the constitution of this society, which appears to have been similarly constituted to the generality of the religious guilds. Some further extracts from its proceedings will render our acquaintance with it more complete. The following is a translation of the earliest entry in the Records:[1] "2nd Richard II. 1379. Memorandum, that here begins the Book of the Accountants of the Brotherhood of the Holy Trinity. The account of Adam Reynald, the Chaplain, Symon Pokedych, Adam Mareys, Gilbert Grout, the skyvens of the Guild of the Holy Trinity of Wysbech, from Sunday on the feast of the Holy Trinity, in the 2nd year of King Richard II. after the Conquest, to the same Sunday in the 3rd year of King Richard IInd, for one whole year: "Imprimis, in a tenth received for the chaplain. Also in the sum of £4. 5. 8. received of the brotherhood of the said fraternity, from the feast of St. Michael, in the third year of the reign of Richard IInd, to the feast of Saint Michael next following, except the pence which were received of ten novices, for the third time from the nativity of St. John the Baptist next following. Sum £4. 9. Also in the sum of 26*s*. 8*d*. received of sixty-four brethren of the said fraternity, for the purchase of an image of the Holy Trinity: Sum £1. 6. 8. Also in the sum of 46*s*. 8*d*. received of fourteen novices... of each of them 3*s*. 4*d*.:—Sum £2. 6. 8. Also in the sum of £5. 11. 8. received of sixty-seven brethren of the aforesaid fraternity, viz. each of them 20*d*. Sum £5. 11. 8. Total sum £13. 14.

Expended. First they account in a payment made to Mr. Adam Reynald, the officiating chaplain of the said fraternity, for one whole year, viz., from the feast of St. Michael last

(1) We have adopted the translation of Col. Watson before alluded to.

past to the said feast next following, £4 6*s*. 8*d*. Also, they reckon for the purchase of one image of the Holy Trinity, 25*s*. 3*d*.; and they paid to the plaisterers 8*s*.; and for one man's assistance for the said plaisterers for one day 4*d*.; and they paid to John Kingspen, for the removal of the Parclos,[1] with timber and boards and iron nails for the same, and for beer given to the workmen 3*s*. 2¼*d*.; and they gave to John Flaxman for his labor to Walpole for carriage of the tent, 6*d*.; for sand and whitening bought, 12*d*. Sum £1. 18. 3¼. Also they reckon for two pieces of woollen cloth, bought in London, for hoods for the brethren of the said fraternity, with the carriage from London to Wisbech, £5. 6. 8. Also they reckon for bread bought, 3*s*. 6*d*.; for beer bought, 19*s*. 6*d*.; for wine, 2*s*. 7¼*d*.; for beef bought, 3*s*.; for saffron, 1*d*.; for eggs, 4*d*.; for one quart of verjuice, 2*d*.; for fish, 3*d*.; cheese, 13*d*.; for beer given at the fitting of the hall, 4*d*.; for the cook's wages, 6*d*.; as a reward for the brethren at Lynn for their care and labour, 6*s*. 8*d*.; for five minstrels, 10*s*.; for the expense of Nicholas Tynetshalle to Lynn, and for the purchase of apparel for ten dancers, 6*s*. 8*d*.; for iron railings bought for the fitting up of the hall, 6*d*.; and they gave to Robert, son of Thomas, for the hall and ornamenting the same, 3*s*. 4*d*.; and they gave to John Symon for one man to hang up the burial things, 8*d*.; and they paid for a tent, in part payment, 10*s*.; for paper bought for the accountant, one farthing; Sum, £3. 6. 4. Sum of all the expenditure, £14. 17. 10¼.; and so the expenditure exceeds the receipts, £1. 3. 10¼., which was paid by the sixty-seven brethren, viz. each of them 5*d*.; and so remained 1*s*. 11¼*d*., which the said brothers expended in wine before they departed; and so from the account nothing remains. Amen."[2]

This was the initiatory year of the Guild. In order to estimate the value of the above-named articles according to

(1) "An enclosure, screen, or railing, such as may be used to protect a tomb, to separate a chapel from the main body of a church, to form the front of a gallery, or for other similar purposes; it is either of open-work or close."—See *Glossary of Architecture*, vol. i., p. 271, 4th Ed.

(2) Corporation Records, vol. i., translated by Col. Watson.

the present value of money, we shall not be wrong, perhaps, in multiplying the amounts by ten. In 1429 we learn that workmen were employed in repairing the hall after the rate of 4*d.* per day, which would be perhaps about a tenth part of their present wages. The reference to Lynn seems to signify that they constructed their society after the manner of one of the Lynn societies, probably the Holy Trinity, which there, as afterwards at Wisbech, was the most opulent and flourishing of the Guilds. The image of the Holy Trinity was probably for their altar in the church. It would seem, by the notice of the plaisterers, that they had not at this time any hall, but merely fitted up a room for their use. Indeed, it was hardly probable that they should build a hall before they built their society. In 1453 we have an item of 2*s.* 8*d.* for 200 reed for repairing the hall, which, upwards of seventy years after this date, shows that their place of assembly was still of the humblest description. The purchase of the apparel for ten dancers is a curious item, and not very reconcileable with our modern notions of a religious association. But we shall afterwards have to show that their gloomy masses and obits were varied with lighter and more worldly recreations. The items relating to beef, beer, fish, &c., were probably those constituting the annual feast. The following memorandum, enumerating the "necessaries" of the Guild, is interesting:

"Imprimis, 1 crown, silver gilt; also 1 pair of beads of coral; also 9 pair of beads of amber; also 3 pair of beads of jet; 2 pair for three of the silver ones; also 2 pair of beads of coral, with 20 silver; also, hanging over the aforesaid beads of amber, 3 crucifixes, and 3 silver rings; also 1 crucifix; also of single rings, 10 rings; also of double brooches, 9 brooches; also of brooches with stones, 6 brooches; also of single rings with stones, 8 rings; also 1 silver clasp, with 9 pair of silver stomachers; also 1 double crucifix; also 1 stag with a gilt head; also 1 ryn with a stone; and 1 golden Jesu; also 1 chain with a crucifix; also 2 Lambs of God of silver; also 1 gilt brooch, also 1 brooch; also 2 small brooches; also 1 pair of beads of beryll; with a crucifix and an image of the Virgin Mary; also 1 accer, which is called Dowbell W. with a crown; also 1 silver gilt ring; also 4 stones of crystall and a beryll, one branch of corall."[1]

The earlier portion of these Records furnish many particulars of the Principal Day, which, during the latter portion of these entries, seems to have lost some of its festivity, and got into "degenerate times." In 1473 we find an order for the Clerk of the Guild and Dean to get provided against the principal feast certain wax shots and 7 torches, and to buy wax "at Sterbrigefeyre next." The church was especially cared for on this occasion, and the whole fraternity, preceded by the Alderman and the Chamberlains, "with their garlandds and typye stavyes in their hands," went to mass in their cloth hoods. The altar seems also to have been highly decorated. By an order of 1477 a number of ornaments are delivered to the Dean for this purpose, and nine crowns and panel with the jewels are mentioned as portions of the decorations. The provisions for the dinner are not less great. In 1460 it is ordered that this anniversary should be celebrated with bucknard and potage for the first course, with *ancis*, and at the second course one stroke of veal and no more, and for supper pullets and chitterlings. In 1463 this fare was improved upon, for in addition to the bucknard, and the stroke of veal and ancis, they ordered seven bushels of furmenty and six dozen of good beer. Supper is always provided for, and it was more necessary at that time than in these days,[2] when, influenced by an artificial system, it is not unusual to dine at supper time; for then they dined at ten or eleven in the morning, and supped at four in the afternoon. For supper they ordered lamb or mutton, with chickens or pigeons, and that they should have 2*s*. worth of spices, "and

(1) Corporation Records, v. i.

(2) The Normans had a proverb, thus translated, which gives us a notion of their principles of domestic economy:

"To rise at five, to dine at nine
To sup at five, to bed at nine,
Makes a man live to ninety-nine."

if they order any more they shall pay for it out of their own purses." In 1464 the expenses of this feast day amounted to 41*s.* 3*d.*, with two minstrels who were each to have 2*s.*;[1] and, in 1465, to 43*s.* 8½*d.*, of which sum 2*s.* 4*d.* was paid for a calf, 3*s.* 6*d.* for 3 lambs, 3*s.* for 5 porkets, 2*s.* 4*d.* for 44 chickens, and the remainder for honey, spices, cook's stipend, minstrels, &c. Dinner was a long and important meal in this age, and three hours were not unfrequently consumed at it. But the intervals between the courses, which were probably very long, were entertained with various amusements, which the entries of the old Guild lead us to suppose were not wanting at their festivals. We find various notices of the employment of minstrels, who were the usual accompaniments of a respectable entertainment, and the dancers referred to in the first entry probably exhibited themselves between the "potage" and the "stroke of veal," or between the "frumenty" and the "chitterlings." It seems also not unlikely that these hearty ancestors of our Corporation employed occasionally higher amusements than that of minstrels and dancers to cheer the intervals of their solid courses; for, in 1464, there is an order that the Alderman should procure all men and women to give something for the *performances* of the Guild. In 1481 there is an order respecting some revels, and in 1525 the Scevens are ordered hereafter that they shall "sufficiently kepe the revell." The "performances" here mentioned appear to point to the miracle plays or mysteries, which were now in high repute[2] both by the court and in the country. They were often acted on moveable platforms in the public street, and opened the way for those magnificent dramatic productions which have immortalised the age of Elizabeth more than either the Armada or the Reformation. Revels are frequently confounded with

(1) 2*s.* appears to have been a usual payment for minstrels in this age, which was about equal to 20*s.* at present. In John Lord Howard's household book, there is the same charge of 2*s.* "to the mynstrells the same day."—*See Collier's Annals of the Stage*, vol. i.

(2) Voltaire gives the origin of these productions to Gregory Nazianzen. This, however was perhaps only a piece of ingenious malice against the priests. His opinion has, however been followed by those who had neither his feelings nor his prejudices.

these miracle plays, though they designate mummings and buffooneries, so popular and common in this age. The following order seems to refer to this occasion: 1507.... "shall fynd or cause to be foundyn̄ to the alderman and all the brethern and susters of the Gyld on Trenytye sonday next to c^m an honest dynere and supere, and dynere on the monday next after that folowyng w^t an honest repast for the guest at afternone, and the pore people to be set and suy~d at a tabyll in the hall, as it appereth by the ordinance made the last yere past, and that the Scevens shall fynd the light of the seid gyld wel and honorably bettir than it hath ben foundyn in tyme past, in payne of vj^s. viij^d."

The following miscellaneous extracts from these papers either exhibit some peculiar feature of the institution, or are otherwise worthy of preservation.

In 1462 there is an order for letting the hall to eight other Guilds, which at that time appear to have existed in Wisbech. They are the Guild of St. George, Corpus Christi, the Cross, St. Lawrence, St. John the Baptist, St. Peter, St. Thomas, and the Holy Virgin Mary; excepting, however, this brief notice, they have left no further evidence of their existence. Boston at this time certainly had six Guilds,[1] while Lynn had thirty-one.[2] In each of these towns there was a Guild dedicated to St. George, which was a trading Guild; and St. George never having been a very sacred saint, even in England, though the patron saint of the kingdom, would not be likely to be chosen by any Guild whose design was purely religious. It seems, therefore, not improbable, from the above entry, that Wisbech at this period contained one or more trading Guilds, though all their proceedings are lost.

1476. John Cant delivered the common seal. This is the first mention of the Guild Seal, two impressions of which have alone been preserved,[3] and one of these is in a state of

(1) Thompson's History of Boston, p. 72. (2) Richards's Lynn, vol. i., p. 416.

(3) From the best of these impressions we have, by the kindness of John Bellamy, Esq., to whom it belongs, caused our engraving to be made. It is attached to a small deed of release of right in a tenement situate on the castle ditch. The seal is of the exact size of the engraving, which sufficiently explains all its features.

great dilapidation. The use of this seal appears to have been under the subjoined restrictions: 1517. "We orden that the ald'rman of this gyld shall not seall no man^{r} of writinge nor grauntes to be seallyd w^{t} the comon seall of this gild w^{t}out assent & concent of xij of the most honest men, brethern of this gyld."

1477. "Mr. Thomas Barker, one of the executors of the will of Thomas Blower, came in his own proper person before William Gybbe, vicar of Wisbech ... and other co-fraters in the gild hall ... and there granted and in perpetual alms gave to the said gild of the Holy Trinity, to the honor of God omnipotent and the blessed Virgin Mary, for the salvation of the soul of the said Thomas Blower, one new edifice, called the Almshouse, built and situate in the New Market of Wisbech, next the church-yard of the church of St. Peter of Wisbech west, and the common way east." This bequest is thought by Col. Watson to be, perhaps, those almshouses formerly situate on the north-east side of the church, and called King John's almshouses. A messuage, with buildings and appurtenances, was also given to the Guild by John Mass, in perpetual alms for his soul and the souls of his wife and children. This person was a very liberal donor to the Guild, as will appear in the inventory of the estates.

1479. "By way of charity with common consent ordained and chose Henry Pundell to be forgiven his revel during his life, if he diligently performs the office of entertaining strangers in the hall."

The following specimen of land-letting occurs in 1505: "Md. letyn to ferme to Agnes Bonyng and John Bonyng in fen, ix acr iij rods of lond pastur, lyyng in fenlond, for the T~me of xx^{ti} yeer from the fest of Candilmes in the xx^{ti} yere of the reayn of kyng henry the vijth payyng therfor the first yere vij$^{s.}$ and the ij yere viij$^{s.}$ and the iij yere ix$^{s.}$ and the iiij yere x$^{s.}$ and so to pay yerly x$^{s.}$ dueryng the forseid t~me of xx^{ti} yer.

"Also we ord. that Ric. Lowe shall pay for the farme of vij acr. of lond lyyng in the est feld, that he had of the les of

Symond Sylke, from hence forth x$^{s.}$ yerly so long he shall have it in ferme by the space of xxx yeer, and the said Richerd shall bere all man~ of charge of the said vij acr duryng y^{e} said t~me."[1]

Orders respecting the formalities to be observed on the death of any of the fraternity are frequently made; and the observances on that occasion may be gathered from the following particulars: 1509. "We ordeyn that all y^{e} Trinit Prestis shall fechs to churche all bredren & sistres of the Trinit Gilde y^{t} deptitt y^{e} world, under the peyne eche of them so found to fawts xij$^{d.}$ w^{t}out a resonabill excuse. Also to be Dekin & Subdekyn fynally to thos p'sones that be abill to kepe a dirge." 1514. "We ordeyn ij obitts yerly to be kept in the chapell of the holy trinytie w^{t}in the churche of sanct Petyr and Pavle of Wisebech, w^{t} *Placebo*, *dirigie* and messe of Requiem solemly by note for the sowlys of the fyrst founders of this gyld, brethren sowlis, suster benefactours of the same, w^{t} all true cristeyn sowlys, and one of the seid obitts to be kept the monday next after the feast of the holy trinytie next comyng, and that odyr obitt to be kept in the feast of sanct Thomas martyr in crystmes weke next after that folowyng, and then to be deltt at the ij obitts yerely to the preests, clerkks, childern, and belman there being p'sent x$^{s.}$, and to the pore people in almes iij$^{s.}$ iiij$^{d.}$ in money or bred."

"Also we ordeyn to be made at the cost and charge of the seid gyld iij Torchetts of wax, to be borne afore the seid ald~man to churche and fro churche, and to brenne in the hall at the tyme of grace and prayers seynge, and also to be borne befor eny brodyr and suster of this gyld to church at their ded day, and to brenne all tyme of *dirigie* and messe at the cost and charge of the seid gyld, and borne to church at the cost and charge of the ded bodye."

1513. The following, if ever executed, does not appear in the remains which the Guild has left: "We wyll that the clerk of this gyld shall translate all the first statut and ordynance of this gyld owt of lateyn into englysshe, and so to

(1) Corporation Records, vol. i.

publysshe and declare the seid statut and ordyñnce in the halle at the feast of the holy Trinitye at the assignement and comanndment of the seid ald˜man."

"We fynd that Sir Thomas Whyte, preest,[1] hath forfett his penaltie to this gyld, as it more opynly doth appere in the fyrst statut and ordinance of this gyld made and stablesshed by the first begynners of this gyld, for his enlefull departynge out of this fratñytie and gyld w^t^out lycene of the seid ald-man and his brethern.

1515. "The seid eleven[2] is fully agreed to amorteyse Sir John Swynkker for terme of his naturall lyfe in this gyld, in seknes and in helth, gevyng to hym yerely dueryng his naturall lyfe, in seknes and in helth $v^{li.}$ $vj^{s.}$ $viij^{d.}$ and his chambyr, & he be bound to the ald˜man to s'ue the seid gyld as wel as he hath done in tymys past, and not to depart from the seid gyld dueryng his seid lyff naturall but for a p'mo˜con of $x^{li.}$ or aboue, und^r the peyn of $v^{li.}$ $vj^{s.}$ $viij^{d.}$; also the seid eleavn is agreed that the seid Sir John Swynkker shall have yerly from yere to yere, as longe as is in good helth and doth good s'rice, in rewarde above hys seid $v^{li.}$ $vj^{s.}$ $viij^{d.}$ and his chambyr, $xiij^{s.}$ $iiij^{d.}$

1517. "We ordeñ & will that all o^r evidence, charters, Scpte, minyments, Recordds, comon seall, the Sept^s w^t ij typyd staves, shalbe browt unto the seid gild hall of the Holy Trinytie, and there to rest & remayn in the tresr^e howse, in the longe chest there shett w^t iij lokks, wherof the said ald˜man to have one key, and ech of the cha˜bleyns for the tyme beyng a key.

1518. "We the eleav'n will & ordeñ that the M^r of the Trinytie chapell of Walsoken shall Sonday next comynge

(1) Sir, or sire, was a common name given to priests in this age. Chaucer uniformly so designates them:

> "Sire Clerke of Oxenforde," our Hoste said,
> "Ye ride as stille and coy, as doth a maid
> "Were new spoused."—*The Clerk's Prologue.*
> "Sire preest, art thou a vicary,
> "Or art thou a persone?—*Persone's Prologue.*

It was so usually given to priests, that it has crept into acts of parliament. Hence a Sir John came to be a nickname for a priest.—*See Tyrwhitt's Chaucer.*

(2) Jury or Inquest as they sometimes call themselves.

aft[r] the date herof shall befor the ald~man of the gyld and his brethern c'm and shew why . . . this gyld shuld not ent[r] & have a messuage & iij acr. lond late Sir willm Reddyk, p'sone of outwell, for the nowne kepynge of the ppetall obitt of the seid Sir willm Reddyk & his frendds in the church of seynt Peter of Wisebech, acording to the testament & last wyll of the forseid sir will. Reddyk."

1535. The splendour and riches of the church had at this time encountered the dangers of the Reformation, and the overthrow of that wonderful establishment, which was now so generally sought, threatened to tear down all the auxiliary institutions—convents, schools, and guilds—with it. There is a kind of fore-shadow of their fate to be seen in the following admission. Henry had already banished the Papal supremacy, and set up his own—" Fidei defeño," as he is now for the first time called in the Records, " et in terra suprem~ Capite Anglicane Ecclse~"—" Md. that at this day of the gyld ther was amyttid brethern John Zeugge, p'st, & Robt. Martyn, upon condicon that they nor eny of them shall not be disobedient to the alderman for the tyme beyng, nor to have any ap~brious words to hym, nor ageyn the avantage p'fett of the gild, but to make . . . [illegible] for the same ageyn any p'son spekyng ageyn us, or els not [to be admitted.]"[1]

The fallen have few friends. Evil had evidently been spoken of the Guild, and, perhaps, its speedy dissolution threatened; and the brethren feared to admit any person to their society who would be likely to foment the feeling against them, or be disguised enemies, seeking rather their overthrow than to promote the fellowship it had now maintained for a hundred and fifty years. The succeeding entry shows that some efforts had been already made to save their great mother from her humiliation: " Rec xj[s.] and delyv~d to hamond Stephynson & Willm Robtson for ther v'ste to London in defendyng of the Chirch land, wherof was recoveyd of Raff Richerdson, chirch wardyn, by the hand of Alex. Balam,

(1) Corporation Records.

alderman xviij[s.] iiij[d.] of the wich the said alderman hath payd vij[s.]"[1]

From this time the proceedings lose their regularity. There is no entry made after 1540 till 1547, when the Alderman, Bailiffs, two Chamberlains, and most of the other officers are named as elected, and the following memorandum made: "takyn owtt of the Chyst the xxiij day of October xix[s.] for the expynss of the ald~man, &c., when the Cumyssynors sent for the forsaid ald~man & the Chirch wardens to Elye, & rem~ iij[li.] xij[d.]" The last ordinance they made was as follows: "We will & ordeñ y[t] y[e] aldma~ & bayley shall do nothing w[t]out the consent of xij."[2]

The Commissioners here named were those sent in the the beginning of the reign of Edward VI. to inquire into the possessions and uses of all institutions formerly connected with the church, as chantries, colleges, free chapels, schools, and guilds, and the act under which the Commissioners pur sued their inquiries, gave to the king, as forfeited property, all these possessions; but it also gave the commissioners license to re-appropriate the "lands, tenements, and other hereditaments," belonging to any suppressed guild or chantry, "to a school-master or preacher for ever, for and towards keeping of a grammar school or preaching," or for other godly purposes.

The Commissioners appear to have sent certain articles to the Guild, which have not been preserved. The answers, which are contained in the Records, however, supply this deficiency. They are as follows:

"The answer to y[e] articles of y[e] Trinitie gylde of Wisbich acordeyne to ye articles sent by the king's hyghnesse comissioners and deliu~d by Thomas crosse constable, mayd by vs John Austyn, Henry Jo[t]nsn, chirchwardens, Thomas Priest curatt of y[e] townshepe of Wisbiche, w[t]in y[e] countt of cambrig as here aft[r] doth folow by order.

"In primis, i fraternite, or brotherod, founded w[t]in ye churche of sent petres and paull in wisbiche aforsaid, named

(1) Corporation Records. (2) Ibid.

ye trinite gyld. The namys of ye prests or chapleins ther to belongyng as foloweth: Mr Henry Ogle, scolmast, Sir Nicholas myller, Sir Thomas cameron, Sir Robt lynde.

"It. ye said fraternite was founded by steyn devott psons in ye second yere of Kyng Richard ye second, and also confyrmyd be divers of ye Kyng's most noble progenitors, and also lykeways confirmed by ye kyng's hyghtnesse in ye xx yere of his most noble reygne, founded for a free scoll y^er to admatt and bryng up yoyoth, and to preach ye word of god, and to celebratt y^er divine servis, praying for ye kyng's maiestie, and for ye pservation of y^is realme, and to relyffe steyne poore pepull, as more pleynely doth apere by ye foundation.

"Itm, ye said Thomas & ye other to ye fyrst article sayth: y^r is one chapell w^tin ye said toune of Wisbech, at a plac called murow, in ye fenn hend of ye same toune, underneath ye hyghe fendyke, namyd ye chapell of corpus christi, and to ye same y^r is one stypendary prest, whose name ys Robt Yorke.

"It to ye second artycle they say y^t ye said chapell of corpus xti was ther sett & founded nyghe unto ye said hyghe fendyke for one principall cause, y^t is for asmuch as ye said hyghe fendyke beyng in dystanc from ye prish church iiij myles and more, and beyng a very paynefull & noysome way, and comonly also unsound, so y^t ye Inhabitants ther to adyonyng is not abull nethr to ryde nor goe to y^er chirch, and was w^towtt mynd of man, & at this p'sent day is so grettly charged w^t ye fresche waterrs comyng down from ye shyrys of Huntyngton, bedforth, Northamton, lessytur, & ye wat^r of Weylond, so y^t they stand so grettė an hede of ye fresche wat^r yerly agenst ye said hyhe fendyke, ye wch is nott only ye safe defens & p'suacion of ye town of Wisbich, butt also ye p'suation of xiiij towns adioynyng unto ye said toune of Wisbich, & liyng so in ye drainag of ye said hyghe fendyke. To thentent & purpose ye said hyghe fendyke myght be continualy maynteyned & kepte w^t & by ye Inhabytance inhabtyng under ye said hyghe fendyke, not only for ye p'suation of ye said toune of Wisbiche, but also for ye welth and p'svation of ye said xiiij touns therunto adioynyng. The wich is yerly in greate daunger & hassard of brech, oneless aswell y[e] said inhabitans now inhabityng under y[e] said hyghe fendyk, as all others inhabytyng & dwellyng w[t]in any of ye said xiiij touns, wearr nott at all tymes ready at hande as welby nyght as by day at y[e] rysyng of eny floode & suddyn storme (y[t] is yerly in experience) y[t] if ther were lakyng but iiij men all y[e] rest shuld nott be abyll of ther powers to save & p~sue ye said hyght fendyke w[t]out breche; for if any breche shuld chaunce for lacke of man's helpe, as god defend ytt from, y[e] hole inhabitanc of y[e] seid town of Wisbiche, and also y[e] other xiiij tounys ther unto adioynyng, shuld be utterly & clerly undone & dystroyed for ever. In consideration and for that intent & purpose y[e] said hyghe fendyke beyng iiij[er] myles and more from y[e] said p'rche churche of Wisbiche (as is before expressed) myght be contynually and foreu~more ye bett[r] p~sued maynteyned & substancyally kept for y[e] welth & p'svation of y[e] forsaid countre. The said chapell of corpus christi was sett & founded nyghe unto ye said hyghe fen-dyke by ye auncestors of Mr. Ric. everad, w[t] y[e] helpe of y[e] inhabitans ther dwellyng at y[t] tyme, as y[e] inhabitors saith hawyng none other foundation to these but y[t] my lord of Ely and his p~decssors from tyme to tyme hath licensed & p'mit-tyd ye inhabitanc y[er] for y[e] causes be fore mentioned to have a chaplen or prest ther to minist[r] and celebratt to y[em] divine servis as true christen pepull owght to here, to y[e] sustentacion wherof y[t] y[e] inhabitanc myght y[e] bett[r] be in redinesse to gyve theyr attendanc ye more redily. steyn of y[e] inhabitanc of y[e] said hyghe fendyke as is before mentioned beyng dessessed, hath gyvyne to ye said chapell steyne lands to reymeyn from tyme to tyme in y[e] hand of y[e] chapell wardyns, towards y[e] fyndyng of y[e] said prest, as more plenly shall apere her aft.[r]

"It. to ye third article &c., chapell.

"It. to ye iiij article they say y[t] all y[e] pfytt of y[e] seid lond and tenem[ts] belongyng & appteynyg to ye said chapell hayth been & is taken & payed by the said chapell wardens employ-ing & expendyng ye same towards y[e] sustentacion and fyndyng a prest to celebratt divine servis to y^{e} inhabitants.

"It. to ye xij article they say y^{t} ther is nowe at y^{s} day growing upon steyn ground undermeat in messe in ye tenour of ye wiffe of Thomas Raffe, steyn trees, in valow to be sowld iij$^{s.}$ iiij$^{d.}$"[1]

"Upon the inquiry by His Majesty's Commissioners it was satisfactorily ascertained that the Guild had supported a Grammar School... and likewise that a priest or incumbent of a chantry was *in esse*, and that certain piers, jetties, and banks, were also maintained... whereupon the inhabitants of Wisbech lost no opportunity of availing themselves of the before-mentioned statute; and having obtained the good offices of Bishop Gooderick... His Majesty was pleased to restore the possessions of the Guild on payment of a certain sum of money, and to raise the town to a Corporation."[2]

(1) Corporation Records. (2) Watson's Wisbech, p. 168.

CHAPTER IV.

HISTORY OF THE CORPORATION.

THE Guild of Wisbech having conformed to the provisions of the act we have alluded to, by the maintenance of a Grammar School, &c., the inhabitants availed themselves of the opportunity of securing a Charta of Incorporation. Bishop Gooderick appears, as well from the Charta as from the Records, to have been instrumental in gaining this privilege, for which the town paid to the king £260 10*s.* 10*d.*, being the twenty years' purchase[1] of the clear annual value of £14 1*s.* 6¼*d.*[2] The act of King Edward recites, that in consideration of the payment of the above sum, and at the instance of Thomas Bishop of Ely,[3] he has granted that the inhabitants of Wisbech "from henceforth may and shall be in fact and in name one body and one community of themselves for ever incorporated:" it goes on to say that they shall have perpetual succession; shall use a common seal; that all the possessions of the Guild are granted to them with their appurtenances, now extended to the clear annual value of £28 3*s.* 2¼*d.*,[4] "to be

(1) "The estimate given in to the crown doubtless fell far short of the real value of the estates, it being certain that the inhabitants were highly favored. Nor was this singular; the revenues of all the religious fraternities that were suppressed having been calculated very low, some even ten times less than their real value."—*Mann Hutcheson's Introduction to the Charta.*

(2) See Schedule in the Appendix.

(3) The Bishop accommodated the Inhabitants with £30 towards defraying the fees and other expenses.—*Ibid.*

(4) See Schedule.

Drawn by [illegible] Engraved by [illegible]

VIEW OF THE HARBOUR, WISBECH.

holden of us . . . or of our manor of East Greenwich . . . in socage not in capite, viz., by fealty only, instead of all services, rents, and demands whatsoever . . . And further we will . . that the inhabitants there maintaining a household, or so many of them as shall be willing, on the 1st day of November . . may assemble in . . the Common Hall, and there . . nominate and choose ten men of the better, more honest, aud more discreet inhabitants . . there maintaining a family, to the intent . . that the said ten men . . shall have power to graunt and let to farm . . the manors, lands, &c., of the inhabitants for the term of twenty years, or less."[1] Other clauses give the liberty of acquiring other messuages, &c., to the amount of £100 per year; a schoolmaster, with £12 salary, to be provided, and £3 15*s*., the yearly distribution of the late Guild to the poor is to be continued; and that all those banks, shores, and streams, which were maintained by the Guild, are still to be so maintained.

This incorporating act was of the simplest description of these privileges, and approached more nearly the original form of the municipal privilege than any other in the kingdom. Corporations consisted originally neither of a select body, nor a legitimate head. The inhabitants of the town after having procured from the King a Charta, under agreement of a certain yearly sum to be rendered to the crown, and which before had been farmed by the sheriff, or some other crown functionary, became by common agreement, their own legislators. In process of time, when population increased, and the occupations of the people became more divided, the simple form of constituting every inhabitant a part of the Corporation became by mutual consent to be lodged in the hands of a certain number of the principal inhabitants,—say ten,—who were chosen from the whole democratic class beneath them. This was ostensibly the form of the Wisbech Corporation, and it was thus in principle as near as it possibly could be in a civilised state of society to the most primitive form of incorporation. It was a mere

(1) Charta of Edward VI.

selection of ten men from the body of the people for the management of their affairs; though, after a little time, and perhaps from the very commencement, it was found necessary to proceed a step further, by choosing from this select number a more select one as head and director of the rest, who was called the Town Bailiff. Yet this head was not in conformity with the Charta of King Edward, nor was it recognised by the two subsequent Chartas which were granted to the town. In fact, therefore, the incorporation of Wisbech retained a primitive and simple character, with the exception of the elective franchise being subsequently invested in forty-shilling freeholders, till it was superseded by the general act of 1835. The innovations which gradually crept into the older corporations, and which were called privileges—as Mayor, Common Council, Aldermen, Sheriff,—but which Wisbech, either from its insignificance or its poverty, avoided, became in many instances so many vehicles of corruption, and finally reduced the corporate power into a means of the basest tyranny over the town and over the charities by which it should have been enriched.

The earliest entry after the dissolution of the Guild is the following, but whether before or after the incorporating act is uncertain:

"*Wysbeche infra Insul: Elien:*} Md. sold by us Robt. Stregytt & Thom's butcher, Richard Ev~ard, &c., p'is~shers of ye said towne of Wysbiche w^t^ ye consent & assent of all the residue of ye same p'isshe, at london, to ij goldsmythes, about mayday, the thirde yere of ye reign of o^r^ most dreade sovraign lord King Edward the sixt, these p'celle of platt as here aft^r^ p'tic'rs followethe:

"First, a crosse of silu~ & gilt, poz....lxxix oz. et dm
"Itm., a pype of syluer p'cell gilt, poz..xij oz. & dm
"Itm., a pare of saurers of sylu~, poz..xxxvij et dm
"Itm., a shippe of silu~ p'cell gilt, poz..xiij oz.
"Itm., a chalysse w^t^ a patent gilt, poz ..xxx oz.
"Itm., a pype of siluer for the crosse
staff, poz.......................xx oz.

"Sm^{a}, x$^{li.}$ rec. xij oz. & de at iiij$^{s.}$ viij$^{d.}$ y^{e} oz. which amounteth to y^{e} sm^{a} of xlv$^{li.}$ ij$^{s.}$ iiij$^{d.}$,[1] which sm^{a} wth moche more money was employed as p'ticul~ here after followeth:

First, payd for y^{e} costs & charge of xxxvij men sent to lynne to s~ue y^{e} king's ma^{tie} in his affaires in the comocyon tyme agaynst y^{e} rebells in Norff.,[1] for their coats, dubletts, boytes, and other their app'ell, with vj$^{s.}$ viij$^{d.}$ eu~y of them in their purses, as by y^{e} p'ticu~ it may & dothe appere, the sm^{a} off ....xxviij$^{li.}$ ix$^{s.}$ viij$^{d.}$

Itm. paid for makynge of the gayte or slusse at the little Ee, w^{t} bryck, tymber, & workmanshippe for y^{e} same, ..x$^{li.}$ xi$^{s.}$

Itm., paid for certayn repa~cons done upon y^{e} church, iiij$^{li.}$ v$^{s.}$

Itm., paid for leade, tymber, & workmanshippe off the Crosse in the M'kett place ....iiij$^{li.}$ iij$^{s.}$ iiij$^{d.}$

Itm., payd for pavyng of the M~ket place, and for Ragge stone, sand, & workmanshippe of the same, as by the p'ticulers planely doth appere the sm^{a} off ....xvij$^{li.}$ ij$^{s.}$ ij$^{d.}$

Itm., paid for makyng of a banke & a slusse at Keky's myln, to kepe owt the salt wayter fro surroundyng of our comon fermes, and for the p'seracon of the freshe warter for our cattell, as planely appereth by the p'ticulers the sm^{a} off ix$^{li.}$ xij$^{s.}$ iiij$^{d.}$

Sm^{a} x$^{li.}$ off the hole paym^{t} as before wrytyng amounteth to the Sm^{a} of lxxiiij$^{li.}$ v$^{s.}$ vj$^{d.}$ And so our payments and charges excedethe our receytte, as planely appereth by the p'ticulers, the Sm^{a} of xxix$^{li.}$ iij$^{s.}$ ij$^{d.}$."[2]

(1) This was during Kett's rebellion in Norfolk, which happened in 1549, and was headed by Robert Kett, a tanner, and William Kett, a butcher. It was occasioned by the inclosure of the abbey lands, commons, and other waste grounds, whereby the poor were deprived of their ancient and prescriptive pasturages. The rebellion speedily became serious: 16,000 men flocked around the leaders, and several skirmishes ensued, in which, at first, the rebels were victorious. Their battle-song was the following rude rhyme:

"The country gnoffes, Hob, Dick, and Hick,
With clubs and clouted shoon,
Shall fill the vale
Of Dussin's dale
With slaughtered bodies soon."

They were finally routed by the Earl of Warwick; 3500 were killed, and the ringleaders were gibbetted alive, one at Norwich and the other on the steeple of Wymondham church.

(2) There is some ambiguity in this reckoning which we have not ventured to alter—otherwise we have misread the almost illegible writing at this part of the Records.

There is an unaccountable omission of entries for sixteen years subsequent to the incorporation of the town. The first entry, therefore, which has been handed to us is dated 1564, and is as follows:

" Wysbeche, md. 9d. primo die novembris, &c.

" First, we do chuse & appoynte to be baley for the receyt of all the lands and tenements belonging to ye bodye corporate of the toune of wisbeche for this yere to c'me, Richard Best;[1] and we will & ordeyne that he shall lay out no money to no p'son or p'sons, but suche as be ordenarye charges belonging unto y^{e} lands & tenements of y^{e} same toune, without the assent & consent of the tenne men aforesayd, vpon payne off xx$^{s.}$; and y^{e} sayd baley to haue for his stypende or sallerye for this yere xxvj$^{s.}$ viij$^{d.}$

" Also, we will & ordeyne that Mr. Rastall, schoolmaster, ... shall have for his wagies & stipende for this yere xiij$^{li.}$ vj$^{s.}$ viij$^{d.}$

" Itm., we will that vmfrey turner shall haue for his stipende for syngyng & maynteyning of Goddes s'rvyce in the churche for this yere & to do his dutye as heretofore he haith doyne iij$^{li.}$ vj$^{s.}$ viij$^{d.}$

" Itm., we will that philyppe wryght shalbe the wayt of this towne for this yere, and the inhabytaunts of the towne watche to be contrybuters for his wayges to the sme of xxxiij$^{s.}$ iiij$^{d.}$

" Also, we appoynte him to be skavenger for the M~ket Stede, the Corne M~kett, and dead man's layne this yere; and he to have for his paynes towards his lyuyn of the baley of the towne lande x$^{s.}$, and to collecte and gather the deva~cons of the inhabytants chargeable vnto y^{e} same besydes.

" Also we will and ordeyne that theyr shalbe graunted no lease off any lands or tñts belonging to the bodye corporate

(1) The Capital Burgesses elected were Richard Everard, Robert Skortred, Robert Best, Edward Wylks, Edward Storye, Thomas Butcher, a carpenter, William Day, Nicholas Mitchell, Alexander Coxon, and Henry Makeman; unless therefore, there has been a mistake, and Richard has been substituted for Robert, the reader will perceive the Town Bailiff was not a Capital Burgess. This circumstance occurs more than once in the History of the Corporation.

of the towne of wisbyche, aforeseyd to any forenor but onely vnto suche p'son & p'sons as be resy~annt w^th^in ye sayd towne at any tyme hereafter vpon payne of eu~y lease granted to ye contrarye by the said tenne men, they to forfeit for eu~y suche lease xl^s.^

"Also, we do appoynte & chuse Edward Wylke, to be register of the bayle's accompte & other busynes & w^r^tyngs belongyng vnto the sayd towne, and he to haue for his paynes & fee for exersysyng of his office, x^s.^

"Also, we will & ordeyne that eu~y teñnte of the bodye corporate of the towne of wisbyche shall consent & pay vnto the baly their rents due vnto ye same inhabitaunts at their p'fyxed day or daies of paym^t^ expressyd in ther indentures accordyng to ye true intent & meanyng of ther seyd leases upon payne of forfytur of their seyd lease; and also y^t^ the baley shall distreyne for the rent vnpayd, & to have for eu~ry dystrene y^t^ he shalbe compelled to take for ye rent behynd, iiij^d.^

"Also, we will and ordeyne that an inventerye shalbe mayd of all man~ of ymplem^ts^ belonging to the bodye corporate of ye towne of wisbyche before mychaelmesse next, upon payne of xx^s.^

"Also, we wyll and ordeyne accordyng to the tenore of the kyng's ma~ties patente that noyne be chosen to be of ye tenne but suche as be wise, discreyt, sobre, & most substancyall men, inhabytyng w^th^in the sayd towne, xl^s.^ by the yere ou~ and aboue all charge."

Agreeably to one order of this meeting we find an inventory of implements in the next entry.

"An inventorye of all man^r^ of implements belonging to ye body corporate of wisbyche remanying in the towne hall chamber.

"Pewther dyshes & platters xxviij pec^s.^

"ij long great spytts for ye kytchyn chymley

"a corselyt compleyt bought of Mr. R. Balom, Esqer.

"one halman ryvyt, viz., ye breyst & ye backe

"one coyt of playt & iij Jacks

"a bowe & halff a shyff of arros, viz., xix wth a cayse for them, iij bylls and a skulle."

"viij syds of wyndowes late standyng in y[e] hall wyndowes."

Though the charta of King Edward was of so simple a character, it was only by slow degrees, and by the exercise of powers, if not at variance at any rate unrecognised in that Charta, that the full development of the corporate government was effected. The earliest feature which the proceedings of the body manifest, and, indeed, the only sort of proceedings which are entered for several years, is the decision of controversies between townsmen. This feature cannot be said to be at variance with the provisions of the Charta, as the parties coming before the "Ten Men" generally agreed to submit to their decision; so that their proceedings can only be viewed in the light of arbitrations, in which the "Ten Men," as being the "more honest and discreet" of the town, were selected as judges. Had either party questioned the decision of the Ten, the latter had no official power to enforce their judgments; and there were, doubtless, many cases in which this power of dissent was exercised.

The following entries will illustrate the peculiarity of these earlier portions of the corporate history:

"*Wisbeche Villa:* The assemblye & metying of the Ten Men of y[e] body corporate of y[e] Toune aforsayd for certayne affayrs touchyng y[e] busynesses & appeteynying to y[e] sayd corporation y[e] xx day of Apryll .. & in y[e] comon hall of y[e] sayd Towne, & of others y[e] inhabitants of y[e] most best, wysest, & substantialest of y[e] sayd Towne, beyng called for y[e] appeasyng of such controversyes as doe aryse or grow betwene any of o[r] neyghbours contrarey to y[e] dutye of Christyans, &, therfore, to be appeased; for as yt ys truly sayd: *Concordia res parve crescunt, Discordia magne dilabunt;* and thys day accordyng to o[r] former order as brethren in vnitie appoynted, to dyne at y[e] howse of o[r] neyghbour."

"In primis, a matter dependyng in controversey in the comon lawe w[th]in the Isle, betwene Symon weston, smythe, playntyffe, & thom~s andrewe, tayloure, defendant, concernyng an action of the cayse,[1] and by bothe their assents & consents put vnto the order, det'mynacon, & fynall judgem[t] of Robert Skortred, &c., to order and det˜myne the same controu˜sy; and we callyng borthe the sayd p'ties before us, and also heryng borthe the forsayd p'ties what they culd sey, & also p'ceyvyng their greytte aunsweres[2] & replicacons and vewing the matter in all respects accordyng to equytye, Justice, & good conscience, have det'myned, Judged & awarded, in maner and forme herafter following, that ys to say, that the forsayd p'ties shalbe lovers and fryndes hereafter, where as either of them have offended the other any kynd of wyes by wordes, that they shall forgyff frelye the same from the bottome of their harts, and shalbe lovers & fryndes hereafter: and for thermore yt ys agreed by vs the forsayd arbytratours that the sayd thom's andrewe shall content & pay in hand vnto the sayd Symon weston, in suche recompence of his charge which he haithe spent in the lawe, the sum off iij[s.] iiij[d.] p[d] and quyte a sit get.[3]

The disputes which in this manner came before the Corporation were such as now are commonly decided by the local magistrate. In 1569 there is one "touchyng the worowing of stayne shepe," and, in 1570, "touching an action of trespasse for the estray of a mare into a stack of hay;" in 1572, "touchyng stayne reed caryed away by the salt wort[r] of mychelm's last;" and in December the same year, "touchyng the hyryng of a house standing in the newe M'ket of wisbyche." In April, 1574, "a matter dependyng in controu˜sy for stayne reconynge, debts, debate, & demands, & other thyngs, being stuff of household in pawne," which was decided in the subjoined manner: "We, the arbytrators.. have.. awarded y[t] the def. shall content, paye, & delyu˜ vnto y[e] playntiff a Ryssyt gowne to make his wyff a cassok, and also xxx[s.] of lawful money of yngland." We give one more illustration of this primitive method of "going to law:" "xxviij

(1) We suspect we have mistaken this word, as the writing of many parts of these Records is not very readable.

(2) So we read it. (3) Perhaps "assuaged."

day of october, 1579. Md., that a matter in controu˜sy depending in sute between henry fawsyt, sadler, playntyff, & John hebletwayte, sadler, def., touchyng stayne iniuryes, wrongs, vexacons, & p'turbacons moved between them, aswell for bying of saddletres, as for vnkyndness & other quarrells, and by medyacon of frendes, of borthe their mutuall assente & consent, put by them to the hearyng, det'mynacon, and judgem[t] of hughe M˜gesson, &c., to order and det'myn all the sayd controu'syes depending betwen them, and that the end and det'rmynacon thereof be made by sayd arbytrators before candle˜s next coming aft[r] the dayt hereof, and yt is further concluded and agreed by borthe their co'sents that yff the forsayd arbytrators can not agre, then they to stand to the order and judgem[t] of John Colvyl, esquyer, to ende and det'myne the same." This apparently difficult dispute was decided in the following manner, as appears by a later entry: "We the arbytrators callyng before us borthe the said sadlers, and hearyng borthe their complayntes and aunsweres, and consideryng their causes indifferently, have awarded.. as followeth: first, we do award and judge that the said p'ties shalbe hereaft[r] lovers and fryndes, and that the one shall relesse and discharge the other.. and that they shall acquyt all matters what soever moved or depending betwen them.. from the begynnyng of the world vnto this p'sent day, being the 25 of January, 1579, and that John hebletwhight shall pay for the wyn he sent for, and also for ij pottes of beare."

The meetings of the "Ten" were held at this time on the first Tuesday of the month; and for twelve years—1564 to 1576—we meet with no other entries than such as we have just given specimens, and a yearly agreement between the "Ten Men" and a number of their fellow-townsmen to dine together "at our neighbor's," after the duties of regulating the scales of justice were finished. The number who thus met was generally between thirty and forty; and it was, doubtless, in those days of slow-paced intelligence, the point where the news and events of the month were canvassed and circulated, The form of these agreements is too quaint to be omitted:

"*Wisbech. infra Insul: Elien: in Com: Cantebr:*" This booke made the xxij day of november, in the eleventh yere of the reign of our most dreade sou'aign ladye Elizabeth ... by the advice and consent of the tenne men of the bodye corporate... and off dyu~s other w^r^shippfull and of the best, most discreyt, wise, the most s'bstancyall and honest men of the same towne of Wisbyche, to the honore, laude, and prayse of almyghtye god, and also for the good gouvverm^t^ of the comonwelthe of the sayd toune, and also for the avoyding of stryff, contencon, & debat between p'tye & p'tye, and also for the encrease of amytye, love, and concorde, to be had and contynued hereafter emongest the inhabitants, yt ys concluded, condescended, and agreed, the day and yere above wrytyn, by the tenne men of the body corporate, by the advise and consent of other thynhabitaunts aforesaid, whose names be hereunder wrytyn, that they and eu~y off them shall assemble and mete together in the comon hall of wisbyche this p'sent tuysday, being the xxiij day of november, for the onely purpose and effect in this p'sent booke aboue declared, and so monthly eu~y tuysday next aft^r^ following; duryng one hole yere next aft^r^ following in the same comon hall, and afterward to dyne together at suche place as shalbe agreed vpon by consent, and eu~y man to pay for his dinner iiij^d.^ and no more, and who so ever shalbe lacking any day of this o^r^ assemble at the den^r^ to pay iiij^d.^ as well as yff he were p'sent, and he y^t^ shall refuse thus to do to be crossed and put out as noyne of the companye aft^r^ward." Thirty-two names are subjoined to this agreement, and upon every occasion the names of the absentees are written after some such entry as the following: "M^d.^ payd to the goodwyff lord for our den~s this p'sent day, and their was absent of the c'mpany at den^r^ these men whose names be here vnder w^r^ytyn."

On some occasions there are no controversies for their arbitration, which are generally entered with a high degree of satisfaction, as in the following: "Md. that this p'sent tuesday being the xxiij of november, there was no matter or cause of controu˜sy dependyng betwene any p'son or p'sons of o[r] neighbours to o[r] knolege, so that all causes of controu'sy warre well appeased, thanks be gyven to almyghty god for the same, and for all other of his singular benyfytts bestowed upon us. *Laudes deo.*"

In 1586, in consequence of a scarcity, the "Ten" and their companions resolved to depart in one instance from their ancient custom, "by consent for y[e] vyttuyll now dere at thys p'sent dyner to pay for thys tyme vj[d.] a pe˜, & that this be no p'sydent."

These regular proceedings are broken in 1576 by another feature of the corporate power—that of putting out apprentices; the first of whom there is any mention was this year bound, and the agreement is entered as follows: "Md. that this p'sent tuysday, the xij of february, 1576, et a° xix° dm Regne Elizabeth, the tenne men of the bodye corporate of the towne of wisbyche, wth the advyse and consent of M[r] vycar and others, have by one consent put John Shamn, son of Rob[t] Shamn, late of wisbyche, glover, of thage of xi yeres, unto thom's tompson of wisbyche, EE brynck, husbandman, from the day hereof vnto thage of xix yeres, and the sayd thom's tompson to fynde hym meate, dryncke, lynnyn, and wollen, as well in sycknesse as in healthe, during his hole t'me, vsyng hym honestlye, and to bryng hym in y[e] Trade or occupacon w[ch] he nowe vsethe or hereaft[r] shall vse and exersyn, in consideracon whereof the forsayd tenne men and others have gyven vnto thom's tompson in hand xiiij[s.]"

Thenceforth the duties of the Corporation increase rapidly, or at any rate a variety of duties are entered in the Records which do not appear in the earlier portions of those documents. It is certain, however, that more transactions than appear upon their books were entered into in the earlier periods of their history, as we do not meet with any items of expense, except the charge of their dinners, which apparently they paid for themselves. Yet, at this time, they had a regular income of, perhaps, £200 a year—at any rate, the rental of upwards of six hundred acres of land, besides messuages and other property. The following miscellaneous payments of the same date as the above apprenticeship will show us how part of their funds was at this period disbursed:

"Md., thom's edward delyu'ed & payd this p'sent day vnto y^{e} tenne men xlv$^{s.}$ and payd to thom's baldyng to occupye wthall, and to bryng yt agane vpon y^{e} first sonday in lent next, vj$^{s.}$ viij$^{d.}$

"It., more payd to John byrde y^{t} he layd forth, ix$^{s.}$

"It., to Edmund the belman for a q~ter wayges due at chrystmesse last ij$^{s.}$

"It., to M'garett brown to kepe the chyldren y^{t} she hathe in her custodye to buy thyngs wthall, ij$^{s.}$

"It., to carye a boy of M'che home again wthall, iiij$^{d.}$

"It., to Jean burye to heale iij skauld heads of iij boyes, ij$^{s.}$

"Item, to gregory laborne, to bryng y^{e} same in agayne accordyng to the statute, to occupye wthall for a monthe, xii$^{d.}$

"It., to father bede, iij$^{d.}$

"It., to a pore lame woman, iij$^{d.}$

"Itm., to thom's adam, wyff, &c., xij$^{d.}$

"It., to myles tompson, lying in syck by the space of iij weeks, iij$^{d.}$

"It., to thomas yne and Goynot the pore fole, iij$^{d.}$

"Two angells put into y^{e} chest by thom's crosse."

We here perceive that in addition to the arbitration of disputes, and the putting forth of apprentices, the Corporation had become money-lenders, the keepers of orphan children, and furnished money for healing sickness. We have rather a peculiar instance of the latter function, illustrated in a record a few years after the present:

"M$^{d.}$ y^{t} y^{e} 20 of June, 1592, henry Edmunds dyd p'myse to cure one who ys kept w^{t} M'garette Browne, hevyng a sore legge, for w^{h} paynes he ys to have x$^{s.}$ yf he doe heale y^{e} s^{d} sore legge—viz., in hand 3$^{s.}$ 4$^{d.}$, vpon lykyng of y^{e} healyng 3$^{s.}$ 4$^{d.}$, and vpon full healyng 3$^{s.}$ 4$^{d.}$ for y^{e} full, and yf it be lyked well of y^{e} healyng to gyve more, yf yt be worth yt and dothe contynew wholl."

In 1588 another function appears to have devolved upon them, but the following entry of 1594 gives the most detail of this new province of the Ten:

"All y^{e} orphans' stock for y^{e} poore, put forth at all Saynts, 1594, ys as afore, 280$^{li.}$ 9$^{s.}$

"Itm., more rem^{r} of y^{e} Towne stocke put forth for p'fytt, and some rem$^{\sim}$ in debt w^{t}out p'fytt, all 79$^{li.}$ 15$^{s.}$

"Md., y^{t} Mr Styrman dyd accompt thys p'sent day for y^{e} money wch was taken out of y^{e} mony letten at xii$^{d.}$ y^{e} li., out of eu$^{\sim}$y li. 1$^{d.}$, for y^{e} sm. of xvij$^{s.}$; wch sayd sm. was deuyded amongest y^{e} x men, viz. to eu$^{\sim}$y of them for y^{r} dynners; for y^{r} paynes accordyng to Bar. Edwards gifte, x$^{d.}$ wch s^{d} dyn^{r} & 6$^{d.}$ a pece was allowed y^{e} 4 of us. 1594: More for y^{e} paynes accordyng to Ric. Best's gifte, v$^{s.}$, wch sd v$^{s.}$ and 2$^{d.}$ a pz more was destributed to eu$^{\sim}$y of y^{e} x men alyke, except M^{r} wylks, 8$^{d.}$, wch was bestowed in wyne, and v$^{d.}$ more on y^{e} company, and so y^{e} rekenyng ends."[1]

From this period we find the Corporation engaging in such duties as the above extract exhibits rather extensively; we meet with little or no controversy, the arbitration of which in a few years after this time seems to have ceased in the "comon hall." The manner of using orphans' money may not be very clear in the extract we have given, but we learn from after proceedings that in one of the instances above quoted it was left with the Corporation trust under the following circumstances: £120 was left by Bartholomew Edwards, the profit of which, then estimated at £8 per cent., was to accumulate till his youngest child attained the age of fourteen, when £100 was to be repaid to the widow. The profit of £20 was to be distributed to the poor, and, should the child die, the £20 was to remain to the poor for ever. This continued twelve years, during which time one of the children died, and the £20 fell to the poor. Also two hundred marks were bequeathed to "Barth: hys sonne & Lucretia hys daughter at ye seuall ages of xvij years, or day of marriage, and y^{t} yf they both chaunce to dye before y^{t} tyme,

(1) Corporation Records, v. ii.

xxx li. of ye same shall remayne for eur to ye poore." The principal sum which came into the hands of the Corporation as an orphan trust was £500 for the daughter of Robt. Gyrden. The manner of putting it out to use was by the lending it in small sums on bonded security. Thus we find such sums as £4, £5, &c., lent to different persons, and in the following extract we learn the manner in which the profit of this £500 was disposed of:

" A note of ye receyving in of ye p'fytt of ye fyve hundred powndes wch were put forth by ye Tenne men from ye xx of August, 1593, vntyll ye xx of August, 1594, for viij li. to eu~y hundred, and of ye paymt of ye sayd p'fytt or bestowyng of yt, accordyng to ye last wyll of Rot. Gyrdyng, made in ye comon hall of ye sayd town ye xxi day of October.

" Itm. Red of John Neapes for p'fytt of l li. for one year, iiij li.."[1]

The receipts amounting, in various small sums, to £40 in all, which were disposed of:

" Md. Yt yr was payd to John Holland, vyccar of walpool, and to ye churchwardens of Wallpool St. Andrew's, out of ye forsayd p'fytt, accordyng to ye last wyll of ye forsayd Ro. Gyrdyng, for wch yr ys an acquytance in ye Towne chest, ye sm. of v li.

" Itm. more payd to ye late wyffe of Wm. Hall, out of ye sayd p'fytt, v li.

" Itm. more payd to ye x men yt were elected at all saynts, 1593, for yr paynes, iij li. iij s. viij d., and destrybuted to ye poore in october, 1594, ye sm. of xxxiij s. iiij d., all ye v li.

" No. ye remn in ye bayley's hand wch ys to be payd to ye chyldren of franck and coley, v li.

" No. yt ys other xx li. ys letten forth wt ye v li. as aftr appereth, & xx s. p'fytt of ye same ys to be allowed for & toward ye bryngyng vp of Elizabeth, ye daughter of John Gyrdyn, yerely, & ye stock to rem~ in ye custody of x men, to her vse accordyng to ye forsayd last wyll."[2]

The class of friendless and portionless orphans was also

(1) Corporation Records. (2) Ibid.

now become a constant matter of concern to the Corporation, as it appears this division of pauperism had not, in Wisbech at least, come within the statute of Elizabeth:

"Stuffe remayning in y^{e} hands of widowe herbye wch was John lows, one olde cou~lett $viij^{d.}$, iiij paynted curtayns $xvj^{d.}$, one olde red chest $xij^{d.}$, one olde mattresse $xij^{d.}$, more remaynyng viij yerds of cloth $iiij^{s.}$. Y^{t} y^{e} same day yt was agreed y^{t} y^{e} widowe herbye should have all y^{e} goods as ys abousayd, beyng now in her hands, so as she doe suffytiently kepe w^{t} meate, drynke, & clothe, one Jane Skortred, of thage of v years, and dischardge y^{e} Towne of her, wch yf she doe not, then y^{e} Towne to have y^{e} goods agayne, or y^{e} valow as they be now pryced abousayd.

"We put forth Johanne Reyr to be kept w^{t} Beatrix Browne for $vj^{d.}$ eu~y weeke tyll maydaye next, out of Coxsen's mony, & theye to have out of y^{t} mony a payr of shoos, a payr of hoses, & ij smocks.

"1593. Edward peake consented for & in consideration of a coate to be bestowed vpon M'gery lynde at y^{e} cost of y^{e} Towne, y^{t} he shall kepe y^{e} sayd chylde from may next tyll may 1595, for $xx^{s.}$, quarterly to be payd $v^{s.}$"[1]

The duties which the Corporation seem to have undertaken were those of auditors or treasurers—for it is not very apparent which—of the churchwardens' accounts and of the surveyors of highways, or menworks, as they were then called:

"Y^{e} xxx day of october, 1589. Itm. y^{e} same day was ex~m~ed y^{e} accompts of wyllm. day & Robert lynde, surveyors of menworks in a° dm 1588, & then they yelded y^{t} they had collected in all $vij^{li.}$ $iiij^{s.}$, and they layd forth as appeareth in all $iij^{li.}$ $xiiij^{s.}$ $viij^{d.}$, so they have remaynyng in y^{r} hands $xlix^{s.}$ $iiij^{d.}$, wherof Ro. lynde hathe p^{d} $xvj^{s.}$ $iiij^{d.}$ for pavyng certayn comon place in y^{e} Town."[2]

In 1594 a portion of the duties of these surveyors is expressed:

"Y^{e} surveyors of y^{e} menworks yielded y^{r} accompts, & then

(1) Corporation Records. (2) Ibid.

they had collected in all v$^{li.}$ xvj$^{s.}$ xj$^{d.}$, so rests in y^{r} hands iiij$^{d.}$, & y^{r} ys to be collected of Mr. Wylks iiij$^{s.}$, besyde of dyuers others as by y^{r} books appereth, and more they are to collect of eu~y fronter and suche as dreyne by y^{e} g^{t} channell of wch ys of new amended by y^{e} chardge of y^{e} mony collected in y^{r} accompt, so y^{t} y^{e} chardge of xx$^{s.}$ shalbe borne by them y^{t} dreyne by y^{t} channell."[1]

Besides these offices, they had engaged in a similar spirit the management of the affairs of the churchwardens, not only of their own town, but also of Wisbech St. Mary's and Guyhirn, as is manifest in the following extract:

"31 Oct., 1603. Md. some of vij$^{li.}$ ix$^{s.}$ was allowed to y^{e} churchwardens of Wisbech St. Maries towards repair and re-edyfyinge of their churche... by the consent onely of the Tenne men, as a benevolence, at the earnest sute of the said church wardens.

31 July, 1604. 'At wch tyme yt was agreed that Thomas Whyle & Wm. Okeherd, Church wardens of Wisbech St. Maryes, was allowed their expenses of their yeare of Church-wardens, amounting to the some of xiij$^{li.}$, to be paid by the Balye for this yeare. And y^{t} is in full payment of xxv$^{li.}$ xij$^{s.}$ vij$^{d.}$, w^{t} the some of xj$^{s.}$, to be paid by Mr. Pepys at Mich^{s}."[2]

Next year we find an order for £7 to be paid to the churchwardens towards their charges and expenses; and, some years afterwards, the following record occurs:

"It was agreed that if the Churchwardens for the next yeare shall exceed in their expenditure upon the p'vision in bread & bear the some of x$^{s.}$, or at St. Maries the some of xx$^{s.}$, that no allowance be made thereof."[3]

These various duties which had gradually grown upon the Corporation, and which they appear to have assumed rather as a body in whom authority was specific though its direction was, according to the charta, limited; and, therefore, assuming that the charta was intended as a means of the good government of the town, they did not scruple at engagements which probably appeared to them to be beneficial.

(1) Corporation Records. (2) Ibid. (3) Ibid.

The funds at their command are not very clearly accounted for; but it appears they had, in 1595, accumulated a surplus sum which they laid out in the purchase of land.

Another purchase, which was made about six years afterwards, involved the Corporation in some difficulties, and they were sued for King's service, or rather for the money for which such duties had been commuted. They pleaded the Charta, and, as appears, with success; but some doubts seem to have called forth the wish, with certain parties, for its renewal, which is first touched on in the Records in the following manner:

"June 11th, 1604. It was agreed that Edward Buckworth, Esquire, Willm. Wilks, and Nicholas Sandford, gent., shall have the Charta of the Corporation to carry upp to London, there to take advice concerning the confirmation of the said Charta, and altering the course of the election to be made by the freeholders inhabiting the said towne, and havinge there a family, or the greater number of them."[1]

This resolution does not appear to have been executed, or, at any rate, executed with success; and two years afterwards the Charta became "in question" concerning the purchase we have named, which is thus recorded:

"29 Jan., 1606. It was agreed... that as the Charter was in question concerning Hart's Land, late purchased by the Towne, it is sent upp by Mathias Taylor, and he hath promised to take the afores^{d} Charter, and to return the same safe & undefaced to the inhabitants... 5 March. Mathias Taylor delyv~ed into the Towne chest the Charter of the Corporation... and also v peces of evidence concerning Hart's land in Walpole, for the wch landes the Inhabitants was sued for service to the Kinge, and the said service was avoyded in Exchequer by pleading y^{e} Charter; and the record was entered in the Exchequer; and so the said Charter and evidences were redelyvered safe and undefaced... The chardges of the sute, pleadinge, and travaile about the same buysynes amounted unto ix$^{li.}$ xxi$^{d.}$ expended by the said Mathias Tay-

(1) Corporation Records.

lor, wch some was agreed and appointed by the Tenne then to be paid."[1]

Many of the Corporation charters were renewed by King James, who appears in most instances to have given more individual privilege to the Corporate body, and weakened the privilege of the people, and thus united to his own interests the most responsible parties. This was done with a greater degree of effrontery by his grandson, Charles II. Wisbech appears to have been anxious for a renewal of the Charta, as we have seen in 1604, and that anxiety is again shown in 1610, heightened perhaps by the dispute in which the purchase of the Walpole land had involved the Corporation a few years before.

"2 Nov., 1610. It was ordered that the Charter concerning the Town Lands shall be dd ore to Wm. Wiles, &c., to be carried upp to London, and to be renewed to the best p'fitt of the Inhabitants, as their learned Counsell in Law shall devise, or advise, for the better benefitt of the more peaceable and quiett election, and to add unto the same, if it be renewed, full power & authority for the purchasing of Lands and Tenements to valew of iij, iiij, or v pounds p. anno, and the election to be made by freholders and ou~ and above $x^{li.}$ by y^e yere."[2]

The former Charta, as we have shown, recognised every householder "maintaining a family" as an elector, and thus gave the suffrage as much of the democratical character as has been exercised under the English Constitution. But this approach to universal suffrage seems to have entailed serious difficulties on the election, as we may infer from the above extract, for it is there stated that one reason for renewing the Charta was the obtaining a "more peaceable and quiett election," and this the Corporation intended to effect by limiting the franchise to freeholders of £10 and above "by ye yere." Such an alteration would have had the effect of converting the most democratic body almost to an autocracy, as only a very small portion of the town—when £10

(1) Corporation Records. (2) Ibid.

was as much as £50 now—could have been electors, and the Corporation would doubtless have almost been self-elected. It is true, in the course of time, the diminution of money value would have greatly democrised so autocratic a law, yet it may be doubted whether a great and irremediable evil might not have been inflicted on the affairs of the town before this reaction had been effected. As it was, the law officers of James, though certainly not disinclined to despotic alterations in liberal institutions, appear to have over-ruled so sweeping a change, and limited the franchise to 40s. freeholders instead of £10; and thus, by purging the election of its baser portions, still preserved a democratic character in it which every year had the effect of increasing.

By the Charta of Edward VI. the Ten Men were to be of the "better, more honest, and more discreet inhabitants;" under that of James they were to be of the "better, *more opulent*, honest, and discreet *Burgesses*." The day of election was altered from the 1st to the 2nd of November, and the body corporate, formerly called the "tenne men," now received the loftier designation of Capital Burgesses. The only other material alterations effected in this Charta were the limiting the elective power to freeholders of 40*s*. yearly value, being householders, and a provision that in default of an election on the 2nd of November, the Capital Burgesses should elect ten men on the 3rd of November.[1] There is still no recognition of a Town Bailiff.

The following entries from the Records are all the further information we find on this subject:

"The accompt of Tho. Crosse beinge cast upp and exam~d for chardges layd out and expended by him for the renewing of the charter amounted to the some of 193li. 19s. 3d., wch sume was agreed by ye company to be allowed him wth the p'fitt therof at our Lady next, or els some order to be be taken for the same.

"26 Feb., 1610. The same day Wm. Wiles, &c., dd in the

(1) Suspeximus of the Charta of James I., affixed to a translation of the Charta of Charles II., by the Rev. J. Jackson, M.A.

old charter, committed to them in truste concerning the Towne landes, as also the new Charter lately renewed for the more quiett & peceable election of the Tenn Burgesses called Capitall, for one whole year, for the disposing of the Townes buysinesse and affaires."[1]

The following miscellaneous extracts illustrate the powers and dealings of the Corporation better than commentary:

"16 June, 1609. The Company did allow unto Wm. Langstaff his bill he had expended in his office of Constableshipp, viz., the sume of xxij$^{s.}$

"26 Oct., 1609. It was ordered that wheras warrant was sent from the Commissioners of Ely towards the finishing of a shire house for payment of vj$^{li.}$, that the sayd sume of money should be pd by the Town bailiff.

"2 Nov., 1609. It was ordered that Tho. Pack should pay unto Richard Atkyns of Well the sume of ix$^{li.}$ being the remaynder of x$^{li.}$ p'missed him for a book of Sewers dd into the Town chest to the use of the Inhabitants, wherof he hath rec. xx$^{s.}$ in hand, and so remanes ix$^{li.}$ to be pd unto him, wch sayd sume was pd him the same day.

"27 Nov., Item., the same day was allowed by the company to And^{o} Myrgeson, towards the relief of his wyf, being grievously visited with sycknesse and five children, v$^{s.}$

"Item., to be distributed to the pore people, according to the guyfte of the most excellent prince Edward the sixth of famous memory, uppon fryday next, according to the charter, iij$^{li.}$ xv$^{s.}$" The following year this gift is thus distributed: "to the toun watch l$^{s.}$, to the Brink x$^{s.}$, to Guyhirn v$^{s.}$, to Murrow v$^{s.}$, & to Maries v$^{s.}$

"1610. ordered, that there should be a vice for a Glasier to draw lead in bought at the chardge of the Tenn Capitall

(1) The three Charters of Edward, James, and Charles, are still in pretty good preservation, though somewhat broken and creased from being folded up for so many years. The Great Seal is almost all gone from that of Charles, and is very much broken on that of Edward. The head of Edward's charta is decorated with the Tudor emblems; that of James is quite plain; but that of Charles contains his portrait, and is otherwise highly embellished and painted. It would not ill become the Corporation to preserve their Charters in a more perfect manner by framing them, and placing plate glass over them; they would then be an ornament to their chamber and be much more effectually preserved from the influence of time.

Burgesses... and the same to be lent unto Wm. More towards the relief of his wyff and children, p'vided always the same be at y^{e} Towne's s'vice.

"Allowed Ro. Atkyn for cutting of the yce in y^{e} porte at the Sluice that the water might passe into y^{e} Grate ryver, the sume of xviij$^{d.}$

"4 Aprill, 1614. The Capytall Burgesses did agree that the towne Bayliffe shall give presentlye unto the overseers of the pore of Wisbech Saint Peter's, towards the releif of the pore people of the same parish, v$^{li.}$

"8 Maii, 1620. Ordered, that the baylife should paie into the hands of Mr. Willyam Wills the some of v$^{li.}$ towards the charge to be expended in his journey to London for the country about the business of the undertakers, and about the state of the Copyholders and the butchers' shambles."[1]

It is not seen by the Records when the charge of the House of Correction was assumed by the Corporation, but that they had the control of this division of good government as early as 1620 appears by the following extracts:

"11 Dec., 1620. The Companye did agree that the Towne shall lend the house for a house of Correction, and to wall yt about wth a wall of brick.

"19 July, 1621. The Company did appoint the Baylife to pay to Thos. Wilcock, Keeper of the House of Correccon, the sume of xxx$^{s.}$ for one qu^{r} of a yeare, to be ended at Michaelmas next."[2]

By a later entry it appears, however, that they only paid part of this salary:

"3 June, 1624. The Ballife delyvered into the Towne's handes one acquittaunce from Richard Gayes, Maister of the House of Correction, for his halfe yeare's stipend, to be ended at the feast of Saint Michaell the archangell, paid him beforehand, vj$^{li.}$ xiij$^{s.}$ iiij$^{d.}$

"Memor., that iij$^{li.}$ p'cell of the said halfe yeare's stipend is to be paid againe by the countrye."[3]

Other expenses, being melancholy items in the distribu-

(1) Corporation Records, vols. 3 and 4. (2) Ibid, v. 4. (3) Ibid.

tions of justice, entering into the same department, are also accounted for:

"3 Oct., 1622. Itm., the Bailye appointed to paie to J. Edwards, for hanging the felons, $ij^{s.}$ $iij^{d.}$

"Oct., 1623. The chief Constable... did paie into the hands of the baylife the some of $iij^{li.}$ and $x^{s.}$ being money collected of the countrye, wherof $xvi^{s.}$ is for the Captain's Dyett, and the resydue for the chardges of the new Gallows, made in the yeare of our lord, 1622."[1]

We have seen, by the renewed Charta, that there was a provision made by which the former Capital Burgesses had the privilege of election when that duty was omitted by its natural possessors, the freeholders. In 1621 this clause came into operation, the Burgesses having failed to elect on the 2nd of November, and the omission is thus noticed in the Records:

"1621. Memorandum, that the Companie of the Ten Capitall Burgesses that were the $form^r$ yeare did meete at the Towne hall, the 3 of November, 1621, and forasmuch as the Burgesses of Wisbech did fayle in the election upon the secund of this November, Therefore, the said Ten Capitall Burgesses did newly elect these p'sounes whose names are hereunder written to be the Tenne Capitall Burgesses for this yeare following, according to the $teno^r$ and true meaning of the pattente graunted by our sovereign Lord James, by the grace of god, King, &c., unto the Burgesses of Wisbeche."[2]

This omission again occurred in the years 1623, 1624, 1625, 1626.

The Corporation complained of the want of quiet and order while the election was in the hands of the body of the inhabitants: they had now succeeded in sifting the dirty and, we should suppose, quarrelsome members from that body, and, if we may trust in the following item, there were very few electors left to raise a disturbance; or they were secured by temperance from over-excitement.

(1) Corporation Records, v. 4. (2) Ibid.

"2 Nov., 1617. Paid for bread, beare, & fier, at the hall upon the election day for the electors, iij[s.] iij[d.]"

But the electors increased in numbers yearly, and fifty years seem to have made a great difference both in their numbers and the liberality of the Corporation:

"8 Nov., 1671.

	L.	S.	D.
Ordered to pay Mr. Casinghurt's bill for wine	1	0	0
——— Mr. Whindell's	1	13	0
——— Simpson & Warner for cakes	0	12	0
——— Robeny for cakes	0	12	0
and to Wm. Tennard for cakes	0	12	0
and to Mr. Rich[d] Harrison for tobacco & pipes one whole year	0	12	4
and to Rob[t] Poulter, Glesse, & Burtone for beare	0	3	10
	5	5	2"[1]

Seven years after, disturbance was again creeping into the election, and these cakes and wine were apparently accused of having some share in the disorder. In January, 1678, the following is entered:

"Forasmuch as the expendinge Cakes, wine, & ale for the genrall Recepcon of the freeholders at every electon of the Capitall Burgesses y[e] second day of November yearely, hath pr'ued of inconveniancye to y[e] Townshipp by retarding y[e] electon, and hath many times contrary to the first intencon growne an unavoidable & an irregular distribucon, and sometimes p'duced quarrellings & vndecent language in the neighbourhood, itt is ordered that noe such p'vision be hereafter made, untill y[e] Capitall Burgesses for y[e] time being order y[e] contrary in their Judgm[t], and the rather because the next elecon will fall out upon a Sunday."[2]

But the Burgesses were unused to dry voting, and the new abstinence apparently sat very uneasily upon them. They endured it once, but on the 1st of November, 1780, the subjoined order restored the old privilege:

(1) Corporation Records, v. 4. (2) Ibid.

"Whereas, by an order of the Capitall Burgesses of the 6th January, 1678, the findinge Cakes, Wine, & Ale for the freeholders att the election was taken away by reason of sevrall disturbances and irregularityes which happened att the p'cedent election, besides other reasons, .. men˜ced and was to continue untill ye Capitall Burgesses for the tyme being should order ye contrary; now ye said Capitall Burgesses, for some other reasons, and in expecting that such disturbances will not hereafter happen, doe hereby order that the p'sent Town bayliffe make p'vision as formerly hath bene used, not exceeding ye sume of Eight pounds, and take care of an orderly and decent distribution of itt."[1]

So this yearly debauch continued, and in 1757 it had reached to such a height that we find that "twenty-five gallons of wine and no more" were ordered on the occasion. But on the 5th of November, 1767, the Corporation came again to the resolution of stopping it, and apparently with more effect than on the previous occasion:

"Whereas, a custom some years since prevailed in the Corporation of Wisbech Saint Peter's of giving cakes to such of the Burgesses as should attend pursuant to the Charta at the election of Capital Burgesses; now, therefore, we the Capital Burgesses, having well considered the same agreement, and being sensible of the evil thereof, and that the money so spent in cakes may be much better apply'd and more for the interest of the Corporation, hereby promise and agree to and with each other, and to and with the Burgesses, that we will not upon any account whatsoever revive the custom .. but will from time to time oppose the same whenever moved."[2]

It appears from the above that the custom had been already abolished in 1767, but as twenty-four gallons of wine were ordered, in 1758, it must have been some time in the nine years' interval between these dates. It does not appear that it was ever again revived.

Besides the provision which we have seen the Corporation

(1) Corporation Records, v. 5. (2) Ibid, v. 6.

made it a custom to bestow upon the Bishop of Ely while he resided in the town, they were early in the habit of presenting him with a sum of money on his primary visitation to the town,—a custom which continued till 1813. In 1619 it was ordered " that the Bayliffe should paie into the hands of Mr. Taylor, to the use of my Lord of Elye, the some of vij$^{li.}$ xvj$^{s.}$ for recognition money;" and, six months afterwards, " xxxiij$^{s.}$ iiij$^{d.}$, besides the money formerly appointed," is ordered to be paid to him. In 1676 the amount is increased to twenty guineas, " not doubting but his Lord'pp will have and continue his favour and kindness to this Townshipp and his Tenants." In 1775 the Bishop, Edmund Keene, refused this offering; and having visited the Corporation in their hall, he entered the following memorandum of the circumstance in the Records:

" The matter relating to the present of a purse of gold which the Corporation of Wisbech St. Peter's used to make to the Lord Bishops of Ely, on their coming to their Town Hall, having been considered by me, and it appearing to have been antiently given by way of recognition money on the Bishop's first coming to Wisbech, I thought it proper to give my opinion of the case under my hand, and to signify that as this present was made to me at my primary visitation, I do not expect any such acknowledgment from the Corporation at this or any future time. *(Signed)* EDM. ELY."[1]

In 1813 a purse of twenty guineas was presented to Bishop Sparke, which he appears to have accepted; but since that date we believe the custom has been discontinued.

Notwithstanding the poor law had been long firmly established, the Corporation still—as we have seen in several quoted instances—continued to relieve the poor; and they generally contributed some considerable sum to relieve the town of its portion of poor-rate. On the 18th of March, 1673, we find £100 contributed for this purpose; in 1686 £32; and in various other ways the contributions of the Corporation tended to relieve this burden. In 1622 they

(1) Corporation Records, v. 6.

appear to have entered into a scheme for employing the poor by preparing hemp and weaving it into cloth, as these extracts show:

"29 Oct., 1621. 60 bush. of coals for the poore, xx$^{s.}$

"20 feb., 1622. There was deliv'd by Thoms. Love, which is left in the towne hall vj boulte of cloth conteyning in toto ix score and three yards, and also 46 pounds of towe, w^{h} cloth doth cost the towne in hempe, wth the bunching, hickling, spinyng, and weaving, viij$^{li.}$ ij$^{s.}$ 4$^{d.}$

"Memorandum, the baylife hath paid to Willm. Pearson for x stone of hempe to set the poore on woorke, xl$^{s.}$ iij$^{d.}$

"Itm., the ballife hath received of Mr. Buckworth for cloth, xxxviij$^{s.}$ iij$^{d.}$

"Itm., y^{e} ballife appointed to pay to Witcocke to be by him paid to weavers and woorkfolk about cloth, iiij$^{li.}$

"1624. The Ballife charged by him selfe wth money receyved for yarne, towe, and cloth, wch was made of hempe bought by the Burgesses to sett the poore at work the yeare past, xxxvj$^{li.}$ viij$^{s.}$"[1]

This was followed, in 1764, by apparently a spinning school and an establishment, "with a parson to sett the poore on workes," in which, after a note of sundry agreements, we are told "the burgesses are to send the children to school the first month to be taught to spin," and "that the Towne bayliffe pay and reimburse the overseers of the poore such moneys as they have disbursed in finding spindles, reeles, and other materials for ye manufacture, and in paying ye women y^{t} teach."

"22° Feb., 1680, to pay for the stamp and 180 badges p'vided for ye poore."

The election of 1657 must have been a proud one for the town, for on that occasion we find the name of "the Right Honble John Thurloe, Principall Secretary of State," among the list of Capitall Burgesses, and the form of entry runs as follows: "to have power and authority to demise, sell, and lett their lands, Tenem^{ts}, and hereditam^{ts} belonging to the

(1) Corporation Records, v. 4.

said Towne of Wisbech, accordinge to the Letters Patente granted them the nine & twentyeth day of Julye, in the yeare of our Lord, 1658, by his highness Oliver, late Lord Protectr of England, &c., unto the Burgesses aforesaid."[1]

Charles II. had not long assumed the government before there was another general movement in the country, instigated by the despotic principles of that monarch, for the renewal of the charters of incorporation.[2] This movement which has been commonly considered an artful contrivance to subject the liberal opinions generally prevalent in those institutions to surveillance, was for the second time unable to make any material inroad into the free and well-working Corporation of Wisbech. A party, however, seems to have been formed in the town on this occasion who put the freedom and leading principles of the Charta in extreme peril; but, happily, though seemingly so much more formidable than the party which was formed to diminish the liberty of the Charter when it was renewed by James, they were capable of effecting much less, and the Charter of Charles remained to the town with even more privileges than that of James. The following extracts from the Records afford us sufficient notions of the proceedings to effect this object:

(1) Corporation Records, v. 4.

(2) "All hope of a return to the original principles of borough freedom was destroyed by the patronage extended by the Stuarts to every corruption that would favor the despotism of the prerogative. A fine field for undermining the spirit of the commons was presented by the state of the boroughs, which, by oppressive acts under the mask of law, were induced to submit their liberties to the king, with petitions to have them confirmed. In the new charters which were granted by James I. power was assumed of dictating every detail of the internal polity of the boroughs, and of nominating the persons who were first to exercise the several offices under the new charter, and to form the common councils with authority to assess local taxes, although not the representatives of the commonalty. Where the public voice was not sufficient to counteract this fraudulent policy of the crown, it was invariably exercised to destroy popular rights, to encourage political corruption.... Wherever it could be attained, the Corporations were made self-elected, or *close*, as it is expressively termed, as a portion of the progressive design to enslave the whole nation to a government equally *close* and unsanctioned by its voice; though, where powerful communities still enjoyed the rights of their ancestors, they frequently resisted these influences to a considerable extent. .... These measures were pursued with undeviating perseverance during the continuance of this dynasty; and it was a sweeping attempt to subvert the remaining liberties of the boroughs, begun by the *Quo Warrantos* of the 35th Charles II., that greatly contributed to the happy expulsion of the Stuart family."—*Origin of Municipal Corporations, in Westminster Review*, v. xxii., p. 429.

"April 20th 1668. Att a meeting in the towne hall, there being present the major part of the Capitall Burgesses, it is taken into consideration the sad consequences that may insue by renewing our Charter, as is intended by some, to be Capitall burges for ther lives, contrary to the priviledges of our freeholders in our ould charter, it is therefoor agreed upon by us Capitall burgesses whose names are under writen, wth the consent of many able freeholders, that John Neale, Towne Balife, dow apose the proceedings, and indevor to bring the sayd premisses to a hering befoor suche as may determin the controversy, (wee hope for the good and benefit of our toun,) and it is further ordered that the sayd John Neale, towne baliff, be alowed out of the towne stocke all suche sums of mony as shall be layd out for the renewing our Charter, or in apposing any that shall indevor to deprive us of ours and the freeholders' privileges mentioned in our ould Charter. witnes our hands the day and year above writen.[1]

"*(Signed)* James Edwards, John Neale, James Whinnell, John Marshall, being the major part of the Capital Burgesses."[2]

On referring to the election in the previous November, we find the names of Anthony Buckworth, Anthony Balam, Anthony Fisher, Simon Loake,[3] John Marshall, jun., and Thomas Edwards, besides the four that signed the above protest. There are, it will be perceived, but four names to this protest, and yet they call themselves the major part of the Capital Burgesses, who were ten in number. We can only take this statement as meaning that the major part of the Capital Burgesses were favorable to the opinion then ex-

(1) The above appears, from the spelling and other significant marks, to have been entered into the Records by a person somewhat illiterate. The writer was apparently Richard Harrison, a grocer of the town at that period, who appears to have made the entries in the books for a series of years. He was for many years a member of the Corporation, and when a Town Clerk was first proposed, or rather a Corporation Clerk, he strongly protested against the measure,—doubtless believing his syntax and orthography clerkly enough. He appears, however, to have been a man of honest straightforward purpose.

(1) Corporation Records, v. 4.

(3) Probably the same Simon Loake as bequeathed a silver tankard to the Corporation, which is still filled on "Mayor's day" with bishop, from which the members drink success to the new mayoralty.

pressed; and as we find John Marshall, jun., and Thomas Edwards among the remaining six Capital Burgesses, we suppose them to have been also favorable, and the former to have been the son of John Marshall there mentioned, and Thomas Edwards, perhaps, the son or brother of James Edwards. It is rather significant that the four persons who appear to have promoted this illiberal alteration in the Charter do not appear to have taken any further part in the proceedings of the Corporation during the year, and that they were all deservedly turned out of the hall on the next election day, while the patriotic band who battled for their old privileges were returned at the head of the poll, if we may draw such a conclusion from the position of their names in the minute of their election. This very forcibly testifies the feeling of the town upon the proceeding of Anthony Balam and his three followers, and shows that the spirit of liberty, which has been such a predominant feeling in the public disputes of England in every age, was as well understood and as boldly contended for in Wisbech during the tyranuy of the Stuarts, as in places of greater consequence and more historical celebrity. It was only, however, after the manifestation of the public feeling in the election, that the Corporation, though the major part of them were liberal, found themselves able to act with effect; yet, immediately after that *purge*, we find them bravely contending against their tyrants.

"November 5th, 1668. Whereas his Majesty hathe beene gratiously pleased to grantt to the burgeses of Wisbeche his warrant to his aturny generall for the renewing oure Charter, the town Balife is ordered to goe to London and renew oure Charter, with as many preveledges as may be inserted by law for the good and benefit of the towne."[1]

The "life Capital Burgesses" managed, however, to obstruct proceedings, as the subjoined entry denotes:

"1st Feb., 1668. John Neale, towne balife,... hath provided acording to our directions, and hath by y[e] assistance of the towne's solesetare, brought oure Charter before the Lord

(1) Corporation Records, v. 4.

Keeper, but ther being a cavett and petition put in to stope oure proceedings, we canot proceed, but have procured a day of hearing the 26th of Febbury; therefore, now the sayd burgeses dow order the afoorsayd John Neale to gow to London and tacke with him boathe oure Charters, and retayne suche counsell as he shall think fitt... befoar my Lord Keepp: or any other parson or parsons whatsoever... and also dow order the towne balife to provide in the renewyn of Charter as now it is drawn upp and aproved of by the Councell, unlesse the Lord Keeper shall thinke fitt to altar it."[1]

The petition appears to have been overruled, and justice again triumphed. On the 9th of April is an order for "oure solesitor to deliver oure Charter into the hands of Thomas bond the caryar;" and the following minute closes this subject:

"Be it remembered this 20th day of Aprill, 1669, John Neale, Towne Balif, delivered into the Comon hall oure Charter, granted... from his most exelent majesty King Charles the seckond."[2]

The following refers to articles which are now unknown:

"1695. It was agreed that the Town Balife doe pay forthwith the money due for King Wm. & Queen Mary's Picktures, now in the Towne Hall."[3]

In judging the acts of the Corporation so many years after their commission, we own to holding an unfair advantage. We know the right and wrong now, because we see them in their effects. It is very different to foresee and aftersee. In the latter case an idiot may philosophise; in the former truth of opinion is rare and difficult to be obtained. It is these facts which ought to make us regard with more consideration such memorials of perverted judgment as we now and then meet with in these Corporation Records; among which the following must certainly be classed:

"July 13th, 1719. Whereas, it has been represented... that near two thousand acres of salt marsh land, belonging to y[e] parish of Sutton... are about to be imbanked, we, being apprehensive that it will be destructive to the naviga-

(1) Corporation Records, vol. 4. (2) Ibid. (3) Ibid, v. 5.

tion and trade of the Port, do resolve to petition the Parliament... for an act to prevent the imbanking it." And further: "The Town Bailiffe shall pay fifty pounds, when required, towards ye charge of preventing any damage to our Port or navigation, by imbanking any marshes." And £200 is ordered to be borrowed, about three months later, for the same unworthy purpose.

In 1752 we meet with an instance which bears the appearance of fraud in the Town Bailiff—Mr. John Garland. He refused, on the termination of his office, to give up his books and the writings and records that were in his keeping. The Corporation, therefore, after due notice, commenced an action against him; but it was not until four years and three months—in February, 1756—that the matter terminated, apparently by compromise. Mr. Garland makes the following admission:

"Wheras I, John Garland... have been the occasion of a long and expensive suit in the Court of Chancery between the Burgesses of Wisbech and myself. Now I do hereby agree—1st. That I will, within three months next... pass a fair and regular account of all my transactions, &c. 2nd. That within three months I... will deliver up... all the deeds, writings, &c., now in my custody. 3rd. That I will pay the full costs of the suit."[1]

On these conditions the Corporation agreed to put an end to the suit.

We meet with one more instance, not of the same kind as the above, but apparently as dishonorable:

"Oct. 26, 1778. As it appears that our late Town Bailiff, Richard Colvile, Esq., did, before passing of his accounts with the Corporation, prevail on several of our tradesmen, workmen, and others who had demands on the Corporation, to sign discharges for the several sums owing to them on his giving them his promissory notes, and our tradesmen and others are likely to become great sufferers by the failure of the said Richard Colvile,—Resolved, that this mode is dis-

(1) Corporation Records, v. 6.

graceful, and very detrimental to the credit of the Corporation, and ought not to be followed by any of our Town Bailiffs for the time to come."[1]

1774. Previous to this period the Corporation had employed large portions of their resources, upon which they had borrowed various sums of money, for constructing the Bridge, the Workhouse, the Crane, and other necessary public works. They had by degrees abandoned many of the old charges which they had allowed to be imposed upon them—such as, contributing largely to the expenses of the churchwardens and overseers, and relieving the poor,—as they had doubtless gradually formed more necessary and important demands on their resources, in the increasing wants of the town, in wharfage and public buildings. But as, for these capital purposes, they only possessed very inadequate funds, they could only meet their demands by lopping away all expenses, except such as their duties compelled them to pay. Under these circumstances there was no method for them to adopt when any great work was to be done or any large improvement in the town contemplated, than that so frequently adopted since, of borrowing money on the credit of their estates, paying the interest, and reserving a small sinking fund for a gradual liquidation of the debt. They had resorted to this method of raising money in building the Bridge, but had found the debt had increased so much beyond the means of a speedy payment, that some other method must be resorted to in order to remove it. A Committee was, therefore, appointed to investigate the finances and suggest some plan of speedier liquidation; and after this scrutiny they reported that in 1760 the bonded debt was £1750, which had since been reduced to £1411 12*s.* 2*d.*, making a reduction of only £348 7*s.* 10*d.* in fifteen years, while £846 9*s.* interest had been paid in that time: unless, therefore,—the Report suggests—the Corporation alter their present mode of meeting their liabilities, they will not be able in fifty years or more to discharge their debts. They,

(1) Corporation Records, v. 6.

therefore, recommended £1000 to be raised by annuities on lives at £10 per cent. for ages of 60 years, and £11 per cent. for 65 years and upwards; which suggestion was afterwards adopted, apparently with satisfactory results.

1818. The transactions of the Corporation had at this period become, as it were, fixed. By suits at law, and other means, they had become fully acquainted with their powers and liabilities; and having gradually seceded from duties unattached to their capacity, and merely assumed, as charities or otherwise, they had now become guardians of the river from Wisbech to the sea, superintendents of the various charities, trustees of the various estates, and providers for the comfort, convenience, and commerce of the town. These objects—the settled province of their rights and their labors—they appear to have performed with perfect integrity. The popularity of the election never allowed its members to corrupt their authority; there was so constant and so healthy a change in the Ten, that time and security—the common fosterers of corruption—were both guarded against by the provisions of the Charter. There is no fact in the history of the Corporation which speaks more powerfully for the general integrity and complete independence, because complete honesty, of that body, than the readiness with which, at the request of the Burgesses in 1818 to allow their accounts to be published yearly, they acceded to the request. It was an instance of too much disinterestedness to be passed over as a common concession, and it eventually became an example which, in remodelling the municipal laws, the country considered worthy of adoption.

But though the general principles on which the Corporation acted were so unimpeachable, we have had occasion to show that a mistaken judgment has frequently led them into errors,—a failing, however, in keeping with the most perfect institutions in the world. At other times it has been disturbed by different kinds of foes, among which the principle on which Mr. James Hill and Mr. Wilkin opposed it deserves notice.

The Test and Corporation Acts, by which all persons were excluded holding office in Corporations, unless they had received the sacrament according to the rites of the Church of England within twelve months of their election, had long been considered tyrannical by the Dissenters, and as the Constitution of England permits the manifestation of feeling against its unpopular acts, the Dissenters had in various ways shown their opposition to this injudicious measure. Modern instances show us that even an actual defiance of an unpopular law has been attended with beneficial results to the oppressed, and has led to its removal; and this form of opposition, which in its milder moods is termed agitation, is now the popular mode of demonstrating public opinion when in opposition to elected opinion as it exists in the House of Commons.

1819. Mr. Hill, one of the most uncompromising of Dissenters, whether for the sake of giving more odium to an unpopular cause, or in the vain hope of evading its provisions, caused himself to be nominated as a Capital Burgess on the 2nd of November, 1819, and, on being rejected by twelve to five, demanded a poll. The event proved his election by votes, but Mr. Hill having refused to answer whether he had received the sacrament according to law, the eleventh election—the Rev. Jeremiah Jackson—entered a protest against Mr. Hill's election, and claimed the tenth place in the Hall. This being the only legal method in the case, Mr. Jackson was of course declared a legal Capital Burgess. Two other instances, of similar character, occurred in the Corporation proceedings in 1821 and 1822, but each time with of course a similar result. The offensive act was repealed in 1827, and the Hall was consequently freed of disturbances of this nature.

1823. Public improvements have at various times imposed such burdens on the funds of the Corporation as at times to rendera serious revision of their accounts necessary. This happened, as we have seen, in 1774, after the Bridge was built, and was removed by an adoption of annuities; in 1823 the building of the Custom House, the providing of Cattle Markets, and the building of the Corn Exchange, though some years previous, had so diminished the resources of the Capital Burgesses, that they found themselves obliged to make another formal inquiry into their affairs, in order to save themselves from a yearly increasing debt. Upon the report of the committee upon this subject it appeared that the yearly expenditure, including annuities, interest of bond debts, salaries, lamps, watchmen, &c., amounted to £2399 1*s.* 11½*d.* To meet this, there was the rent of 754 acres of land, the crane, and the proceeds of the fairs and markets, amounting to £1919 6*s.* 9*d.*, leaving a yearly deficiency of £479 15*s.* 2½*d.* The committee recommended a partial alleviation of this excess by reducing the lamps, scavengers, and watchmen, and by further anticipating an increase of the proceeds of the markets, but they recommended a "wise frugality" as the only sure means of relieving present difficulties and preventing the increase of embarrassments.

In 1833, after the settlement of the nation from the fever occasioned by the Reform agitation, the ministers began to look for some of the benefits of that act in a thorough remodelling of the Corporations of the kingdom. By their Charters these Corporations had become most unequal and unmanageable bodies; the alterations of corrupt kings and the influences of time and property acting with a variety of power on various kinds of privileges, had, in many instances, become, instead of benefits, burdens to the people; while their functionaries had become public masters where they should have been public servants. Under these circumstances, thorough reform, which should place the whole system under the some code, was resolved on. But, preliminary to this, it was necessary to know the present condition of the Corporations and their mode of distributing their funds. For this purpose a Commission was granted, which was strenuously resisted by several Corporations. Wisbech, however, very willingly rendered an account of her transactions; and the Town Bailiff reported "that he had reason to believe that the various explanations given were considered creditable to the Capital Burgesses and satisfactory to the Committee."[1] Wisbech—though from the purity of its old Chartas it required less renovation than almost any other corporation in the kingdom—was strenuous and decided in its approval of of the new Municipal Bill; to which, by public meetings, hall resolutions, and petitions, it lent all the aid in its power; and as the plan of remodelling the corporations approximated in some measure to that so long acted on with success in Wisbech, its fervor in the cause brought a proof, with every opinion expressed, in favor of an open and intelligible system of municipal legislation.

Though the bill was endangered by several alterations attempted by the Lords, it finally triumphed; and, on Monday the 28th day of December, 1835, the old Charta went out of operation, the town was divided into two wards, was denominated a borough, and the homely Town Bailiff and Capital Burgesses were succeeded by a more aristocratic body of Mayor, Aldermen, and Councillors.[2]

Upon the realisation of this measure the Council sent an address of gratitude to the King, in which they said: "In doing this we venture to state to your Majesty that we, as a Town Corporate, do not derive from the measure advantages to the same extent which it is intended to confer on other towns, in consequence of a peculiarity in our old Charter

(1) Corporation Records, v. 4.

(2) The following is a list of the first election with the number of votes:

North Ward.		*South Ward.*	
Henry Leach (Ald., 1st Mayor)	119	T. Dawbarn (Ald.)	97
Henry Morton (Ald.)	118	J. R. Weatherherd (Ald.)	65
Charles Jecks (Ald.)	107	T. S. Watson	83
James Usill (Ald.)	93	J. Brewin	80
C. Metcalfe, Jun.	137	R. Clarke	79
J. Rumball	93	J. Lilley	65
J. Maule	82	C. Boucher	64
H. M. Usill	81	Joseph Groom	63
W. G. Jackson	77	N. Walker	61
W. Jecks	76	W. T. Cleeve	56
R. F. Pate*	71	H. Leach	55
John Bellamy	61	H. Ollard	45
R. Ward	60		
W. Exley	60		

* Mr. Pate declined serving, and paid £25 fine.

which had already embraced, to a considerable extent, the principle of popular controul recognised by the new law."

By the Municipal Act various alterations were made in the proceedings of the Corporation. They were prohibited from taking fines on granting leases of their estates; the administration of the Charities was taken out of their control and put under the superintendence of an independent body called Trustees, who were, however, chosen by the Councillors; the particular affairs were invested in Committees; and the act provided for a permanent local magistracy, selected from the ranks of the Corporation,—the Mayor and ex-Mayor being always added to the number.

The old Charters, as we have seen, constituted a minimum Burgess to be a freeholder of 40*s*. annual value. The new act conferred this privilege on occupiers of houses and shops rated for three years to the relief of the poor, if residing within seven miles.

The new act disqualified all persons in holy orders, or being a minister of a dissenting congregation, from being Councillors.

One third of the Council, or six members, go out of office annually, so that, unless chosen Aldermen, the Councillors must be re-elected every third year.

The act also gave power to the Council to appoint a Coroner and a Recorder, and hold independent Sessions,—the Magistrates of the Borough having no control in county courts of Sessions. The abstract of accounts, which had been voluntarily published yearly since 1818, now became compulsory. It also annulled exclusive trading, which had grown to a violent evil in some boroughs, though Wisbech had fortunately never attained this ungracious privilege.

Another feature, not perhaps altogether introduced by the Municipal Act, though the unpopularity of it has generally been attributed to that measure, was a Borough-rate. The affairs of the Corporation had, for many years previous to the Municipal Act, been gradually showing the necessity of other resources than those which were at command. Upon a calculation, it was found that the rate of expenditure over the income would probably amount to £540 3*s.* 3*d.*; and if to this an expensive police establishment were added, it would probably be much increased. A Lighting and Watching Rate of about 1*s.* in the pound has, consequently, been regularly levied since.

Officers.

The *Town Clerk*, who was first employed in the Corporation in 1679, as appears by the following record: "y[e] 9 of February, 1679. Ordered y[t] whereas there is a great want of a Town Clarke for y[e] entring in of orders into y[e] Town books and making y[e] leases and bonds (according to y[e] will of Mr. Rob[t] Holmes, a good benefactor, who gave to a clarke 2*s.* every bond makeing), that Rob[t] Cockson be y[e] Town Clarke for this year for p'forming y[e] abovesaid businesses."[1] One name at the foot of this record stands as dissenting from it; it has, nevertheless, been constantly filled since that date. The duties are to issue summonses, attend the council meetings and their committees, record proceedings, &c. The salary is now £45, to which £15 as clerk to the Subcommissioners of Pilotage, and £25 as clerk to the Charitable Trustees, are added. There are also certain other fees attached to the office—as the making out of indentures and leases—which add, though not considerably, to the yearly amount.

Town Chamberlain. This officer was appointed on the passing of the Municipal Act. His duties are to keep the rental of the estates, and view them twice a year, to see that the covenants of the leases are observed; to collect and pay bills; to prevent nuisances; superintend works; &c. His salary is £50 per annum.

Town Inspector. This officer was first appointed after the passing of the Town Act in 1810. The duties are principally to keep the streets clear of casual encroachments and prevent nuisances. The duties of this office are now undertaken by the Police. The cost of it is about £20 per year.

(1) Corporation Records, v. 6.

Beadle. This officer is wholly attached to the Corporation as their servant and general officer. At first, as is apparent in the following Record, it was united with the office of Scavenger: "8 Nov., 1621. The company did enterteyne John Showne to serve the office of Scavenger and beadle, and he to have for his fee xij^d. p. weeke, and a coate, and his yeare to begynne at hallowmas lasst, 1621."

Crier, or Bellman, appears to be one of the most ancient offices in the Corporation. In 1576 we find a quarter's wages to the Bellman, 2*s*. In 1609 a coat is ordered for "old father Parker the belman." On October 28th, 1678, it is ordered "that ye Toun Bayliffe agree w^t a Bellman who shal begin his rounds at nyne of ye clock in ye evenynge, continue walking ye streets till break of daye, be soe employed till May-day next;" and in 1680 there is an order that "John Walpoole have a dogg to goe aboute as Belman, as cheape as one can bee procured, and that the Toune Baylife take care to buy him a coate and a pair of Bootes." There appear to have been intermissions in this office; for, seven years later than the last Record, we read that "it is ordered that the Toune Balife doe pay the Bellman his sallery att Candlemas next, and y^t that office from that time forward cease." When it was again renewed we do not learn; but it has now been an uninterrupted office in the Corporation, at any rate, for a hundred years. His salary, with that of Beadle and Hall Keeper, is £43 15*s*.

Watchmen are also very ancient officers of the Corporation. The first time we meet with the name in the Records is in 1618, when "yt was ordered that the Bayliffe should pay to William Woodes, Taylo^r, in consideracon of his losse susteyned by ymprisonm^t upon a strooke wch he gave in the performance of his office, being a watchman, the party stricken being in danger of deathe, vj^s. viij^d." In 1774 the following orders are issued: "it is agreed that Robert Bingham and Thos Towler be night bellmen at the weekly wages of six shillings each during their good behaviour, and that they be continually watching the streets every night, with each of them a Bell, from eleven o'clock in the evening to four the next morning, and during that time ring their bells, call the hour, wind, and weather, every five minutes at least." To frighten thieves, in those days, seemed a plan preferable to detecting them. As late as 1828 two superintendents of watchmen were appointed, who were ordered to carry cutlass, pistol, and dark lantern, and each watchman to carry a lantern, rattle, and bludgeon. This office is now vested in the Police force.

The *Police* force consists of a Superintendent, a Sergeant, and six officers. They supplanted the old constabulary force in 1836, and the annual cost of their establishment amounts to about £600.

Sales.

The Charters which have successively realised the privileges of the Corporation have all granted power to that body to "demise, sell, or exchange estates," and of this power, in producing public improvements, the Corporation have at various times availed themselves. It was not, however, till late in their history, and during the era when most public improvements have been effected, that the privilege of selling was exercised to any extent. One of the first instances we meet with was in 1801, when it was resolved to sell "the Three Tuns public house, and the several houses, shops, granaries, stables, and buildings, extending from the Market Place to the river, for the redemption of the Land Tax payable for the several estates belonging to the Corporation." This estate had been left by John Crane, in 1651, "one half of the revenue to amend the schoolmaster's wages of the Free School, and the other moiety to be laid out to buy corn and firing for the poor." About five and thirty years after the sale, in 1837, it became questioned whether it had been legally made, and the Charity Commissioners, which had been appointed to overlook such matters, instituted an inquiry into the mode and power of sale. This investigation was by no means satisfactory to the Commissioners, and they signified to the Corporation that "from the slight information hitherto afforded, the Board are led to fear that the sales were not authorised and were not properly made," and they further threatened that "unless full information were supplied, they would feel themselves bound to submit the case to His Majesty's Attorney-General." The Corporation stated in reply, "That the property consisted of houses, stables, and buildings, let at the time of the sale in ten lots to eight tenants, at rack rents amounting to £66 12*s*. per annum, out of which some charges were payable by the Corporation for Land Tax, Insurance, and Repairs;" and they further stated that "the Corporation does not maintain the validity of the sales, but considers the property was sold with the best intentions." The case was placed in the hands of the Attorney-General, and it was ultimately decided by the Court of Chancery that the Charity was entitled to the full benefit of the devise, deducting the Land Tax and cost of maintaining the wharf.

Another small sale was effected in 1837 of two roods of land in Eastfield, near the Horseshoe, and a piece of ground in the Old Market used as a slip-way to the river. After gaining the consent of the Lords Commissioners of the Treasury, the two roods were sold for £95, and the slip-way for £303.

In 1839, the old station-house was sold for £160; and the cobble-house, about which we have already recorded a conflict—for £120.

The only other sale we have to record was that of the Bell Inn, which was sold in 1842, to be removed for a material improvement in one of the approaches of the town, and a widening of the river. As only part of the Bell was required for this improvement, the Corporation first made their agreement with the Master in Chancery—it being a Charity Estate—for the purchase of the whole for £1200; of which purchase-money one third was agreed to be paid by the Surveyors of the Highways, and the rest in equal proportion from the General Purpose and Port Funds. To this is to be added the enfranchisement by the Bishop. But as it was expected to realise a considerable part of the amount by the sale of a portion of the ground and the materials of the old buildings, the sum to each party would be less than a third of the whole purchase-money. On this re-sale of part of this estate, it made £805 with the materials, and the two tenements adjoining £100, thus reducing the real purchase of the Corporation to £295, to which £400 to the Bishop for enfranchisement being added, made the purchase £695, and £68 10*s.* 11*d.* expenses.

Purchases.

These have more than compensated for the sales, which, it will be seen, have not been losses, but rather translations of cumbersome property into improvements. The first purchase we meet with is in 1595, which is preserved in the following record:

"1595. Item, payd for ye expenses of James Saylebank, John Rogers & hys wyffe, Robert Adam & hys wyffe & wyne, ye 29 & 30 of September, at Lynne, in going to Mr. Justice Goodyer, to have ye fine acknowledged in full of ye land wch we p~chased of ye forsayd Rogers, as y^{t} we p~chased of Robert Adam, for ye use of the Toune.

Item, for ye forradge of us and o^{r} horses	0	0	4
Item, for one quarte of wyne afore supper & o^{r} supper, & wyne, & sugar	0	4	10
Item, for a quarte of wyne, & sugar, & cakes in ye mornyng	0	0	11
Item, for o^{r} dynners & iij quartes of wyne and sugar	0	5	10
Item, for o^{r} horse meate, and gyven to ye chamberlayne & others	0	0	18
Item, p^{d} to Mr. Herett for ye double fine, ye precipe, & concord	2	8	4
Item, p^{d} to hym towards suyng forth ye same . .	0	36	8
Item, p^{d} & gyven to Roger's wyffe	0	20	0
Item, p^{d} & gyven to R. Adam's wyffe	0	10	0
Item, for o^{r} passage at ye brydges	0	0	3

Item, more I p^{d} at London towards suing forth
& fines 0 20 0
Item, more towards p'te of my chardges
Item, more I p^{d} for ye fyne when I took yt forth 0 23 4"

In 1610 the Corporation made another purchase in Walpole, for which the inhabitants of Wisbech were afterwards sued for service to the King. In consequence of this a deputation was sent to London with the Charta, and the service was overruled. But the entries on this subject are so brief and mysterious that we are left without accurately knowing either the extent or the precise situation of the purchase.

In 1625 the following is noted: "Memorandum, the Bayliffe hath paid for 17 acres of land purchased of Falkner Traunce, gent. in Elme, viz., paid to John Marshall, gent., 23$^{li.}$ 6$^{s.}$ 8$^{d.}$, & to the said Falkner Traunce 70$^{li.}$ paid in all, lxxxxiij$^{li.}$ vj$^{s.}$ 8$^{d.}$."

We do not meet with any other purchases till 1809, when the Nag's Head Estate, a public-house, &c., standing on the site of the present Exchange Hall, was purchased for the purposes of that building and a Cattle Market, for £1700.

In 1811 some vaults for the purposes of the edifice then building for a Fish Market, now used as an Engine House, were purchased for £200.

In 1820 some premises called Darlow's premises, which projected very much upon the foot of the Bridge, on the most dangerous side of that dangerous crossing, were purchased by the Corporation for £840, and re-sold after providing for a wider descent on the South Brink.

In 1841 the Corporation purchased part of the Anchor Inn for £470; and the Bell purchase and partial re-sale we have already noticed.

Resources.

The resources of the Corporation are from the rental of 716 acres of land, from a Borough Rate—from the proceeds of the Crane and Cattle Market—and from 3*d.* per ton charged on all vessels entering the Port of Wisbech. The average income from these sources for the last ten years—1837-1846—has been respectively as follows:

	£.	s.	d.
Rental	1968	9	0
Borough Rate	364	5	0
Crane and Wharf	176	0	0
Cattle Market and Exchange Hall	437	18	9
Port Dues	1526	4	9
	£4472	17	6

making the net income about £4500 per year; but there has been a considerable increase in the last item during the past two years, so that the income at present is about £5000 per year.

Expenditure.

The rentals of estates, and borough rates, are appropriated to general purposes, such as the salaries of the public officers, the police establishment, the lighting and cleansing the town, public works, elections, interest of debts incurred in borrowing money for public improvements, and a small payment to the Grammar School. The Crane is now partly liable to a heavy debt of £5000, incurred in the improvement of the wharf and rebuilding of the Crane, completed in 1846. The Cattle Market income is expended on certain annuities granted on lives for raising the funds to make that improvement; but these are now nearly all passed away, so that this estate is now comparatively free of liability.[1] The Port Dues are appropriated to salaries of Harbor-masters and other officers connected with the river, the furnishing and keeping buoys and beacons in repair, wharfing and piling the river, and keeping the channel between Wisbech and the sea open and free.

Present State of the Finances.

These are not in a bad state at this time, though there are one or two heavy debts still charged upon the funds. There is a charge of upwards of £6000 upon the Estates, and

(1) The Sheep Market has been within the last year newly penned.—*October*, 1847.

£5000 upon the Crane and Wharf, to which £15,000 upon the Port Dues will soon probably be added.[1]

We think, on an impartial view of the Corporation of Wisbech, from its foundation by Edward VI. to the present day, it will be found to have erred in its judgment and to have mistaken in some instances its proper functions; but these instances are happily so rare, that they are completely overwhelmed by the good it has conferred on the town, and the prosperity that has sprung up, if not in consequence of its effects, at any rate in accordance with them. We have not to regret, as many greater towns have, the loss of estates, the perversions of their purposes, an involved and inextricable series of transactions that have frittered away great properties into bankruptcy. On the contrary, the estates of the Charta of Edward VI. exist in augmented proportions at the present day; and, by a wise and scrupulous use of the funds yielded by those estates, not only have the establishments of the town been preserved, but charities of various kinds have been yearly distributed out of them; the town has been kept in a state of cleanliness and health; the expenses of

(1) 1847. An act was passed this year empowering the Corporation to borrow a further sum of £15,000 upon the Port Dues. The object of this bill is to make certain improvements in the river, not specified in the act but understood to be more systematic wharfage than has at present been provided for the shipping. The act, however, is a mere permission for the borrowing of money—the purpose to which that money is to be applied being invested in higher powers than the Corporation. The act recites "that it shall be lawful for the Mayor, &c., of Wisbech.... to borrow and take up at interest any sum in their discretion, not exceeding the sum of £15,000 in the whole, to be at any time upon the credit of the duties [Port Dues of 3d. per ton] and to mortgage.... them to any person who shall advance on them the said sum." A yearly sum of £300 is to be appropriated to a sinking fund, and further sums of £15000 are authorised to be raised if expedient. But in the spending of this money the act provides "that it shall not be lawful.... to construct any work below high water mark at ordinary spring tides without the previous consent of the Lord High Admiral .... and where any work shall have been constructed, it shall not be lawful for the Mayor, &c., at any time to alter or extend the same without obtaining.... the like consent.... and if any such work shall be commenced or completed contrary to the provisions of this act it shall be, lawful for the Lord High Admiral, &c., to remove the same.... at the cost of the Mayor, &c., and Corporation. And it is further enacted that nothing in the act shall authorise the execution of any work not already authorised." Under such conditions the use of the £15,000 may be well doubted, and the policy of borrowing what we cannot spend upon securities hardly able to bear it seems a practical delusion, which like fishing in a tub requires a large portion of imagination to make the labor remunerative. When this bill was passed the Port Dues were 9d. per ton—6d. appropriated to the Nene Outfall debt, and 3d. to Port and Harbor purposes. But the 6d. tonnage had only a few hundreds to clear off, and in June last it ceased. The opportunity was therefore offered of retaining part of this 6d. tonnage and thus facilitating whatever improvements might be contemplated, repaying the capital speedily, and

watching and lighting have been defrayed; and such great improvements as the Cattle Market, the Bridge, the Custom House, and the Market Place have been erected and provided for.

We do not suppose, however, there has been a better humanity in the history of the Corporation of Wisbech so much as a healthy poverty, and a direct control in the people. Had the spirit of the old Chartas been suffered to evaporate in the alterations of the Stuarts, we should probably have seen Wisbech under the new Municipal Act with few of the antiquated inconveniences of the seventeenth century removed from its public thoroughfares; we should probably have seen its streets unpaved, and its foot-ways unslabbed; the Market-hill might hardly have got beyond its cobble-stones; whale-oil might have cast its yellow glimmer from the street-lamps; the Cattle Market might still have triumphed in the public thoroughfares; we should, perhaps, have crossed the river by a wooden bridge, and have had neither a Custom House, nor an Exchange; but may be we should have had the Castle standing, which would have almost consoled even for such a series of other antiquarianisms. Happily, however, the Corporation stood firm in the hour of trial, and, by preserving itself pure, cast a lasting obligation on all the inhabitants who have fixed on Wisbech as their home.

doing an effective work. But the Corporation had some very tender regards for the shipping which they contended had great difficulties to overcome; its burdens were heavy, the Railways were sapping into the sea trade, and threatened every year to operate more destructively on its interests. These are the arguments of well meaning imbecility, or of men who use their tongues to conceal their thoughts. If the bill was intended to do good, the good would result in better security to the shipping, and a large and effective work is better than partially-matured, ill-contrived, and blunderingly-executed half measures. This, however is yet an unacknowledged principle in Wisbech, and the 3d. dues, yielding something less than £2000 per year, are to be burdened with a loan of £15,000. The interest of £15,000 will be £600, which, with £300 sinking fund, and £200 salaries, leaves something less than £900 per year for "opposing bills in parliament," "stoning and repairing Woodhouse Marsh Cut," maintaining buoys and beacons, and other heavy charges connected with the port. We have an illustration, which we forbear detailing here, of the ruinous policy of the half measures so dear to pettifogging legislators in the history and cost of Woodhouse Marsh Cut; and when the Corporation begin to threaten a renewal of schemes of the same calibre, they are undeserving of that support which schemes, in which private interests and dogmatic prejudice do not interfere, ought to command. The cost of carrying this bill through Parliament was £1030—a fair per centage on an amount which we may spend when we get leave to do so.

CHAPTER V.

THE CHURCH.

IT is rather remarkable that the churches of the Fens in England are among the most beautiful which the country affords; and the two Cathedrals which are situated in this district are each of the first class, and bear remarkable points in which they yield to no similar buildings in the world. The finest fen church—Boston—is perhaps altogether the finest church in the kingdom, and it is only in the magnificence of its tower and the size of its other parts that the church of Walpole St. Peter's yields to it. Leverington, Walsoken, Upwell, Outwell, and Walton churches, all in the immediate neighbourhood of Wisbech, have each especial claims on admiration, and are generally characterised by specimens of architecture of an independent and admirable character.

[illegible]

FROM THE [illegible]

[illegible]

The Church of Wisbech, though apparently the principal foundation of the kind in the district, has in some respects been less fortunate than either of these churches; for though it displays very varied specimens of architecture, it is neither so pure nor so rich in Norman character as Walsoken Church; it has no such graceful and perfect specimens of the Early English as Walton shows, both in its ruins and its glory; its Perpendicular character cannot compete with that of Walpole; and its internal fittings, far from being able to compare with those of Upwell, which are so perfect in convenience and beauty, seem thrown together by the genius of disorder and absurdity. Still it is not wholly despicable; and though it contains nothing of even second-rate architecture, it contains much of an interesting character. The form of the Church is nearly a square, in which two naves and two aisles are comprised. There are two projecting chancels to the east—one on the north side being longer than that to the south. It bears all the evidence of having undergone a process of continual patchwork, yet some portion of its original features have through every change been preserved. One part of it, indeed, is still composed of ancient rubble-work, looking almost as original and rough as the herring-bone masonry of the Saxons, but with even more disorder than is apparent in that primitive style. But in the coarse walls which this work exhibits we see windows all characteristic of the rude taste of higher styles,—efforts at form and grace sadly defeated. But, generally, an unpolished taste prevails over every part of the building, which, by the coarse renovations of eight hundred years, seems as if it had been put together by unskilful workmen out of the second-hand fragments of various churches. We are struck with this particularly in looking at the west end, where the eave of the south aisle is surmounted with a heavy moulded parapet that presses even on the arch of the window, while the corresponding aisle to the north, which is of stone while the other side is rubble, has no moulding at all. On the south side of the great south aisle window a Decorated buttress terminates some feet beneath the roof of the church; while, on the corresponding side to the north, a plain rubble-formed Norman buttress with scarcely any projection terminates under the eave. Between these points, agreeing neither in height nor character with either, is another buttress, oddly formed of stone and stone-faced rubble, placed on one side, or rather pushed out by an awkwardly constructed turnpike-stair, which forms the centre of this end of the church, and terminates in a blunt lantern. There is also another Decorated buttress on the south side of it, producing a crowd of projections with neither purpose nor art in them. The windows, which in this division are rather of a loftier character than those in other parts, display in two corresponding situations an elaborate Decorated specimen with flowing lines filled in with quarterfoils, and a Perpendicular flat-arched specimen with plain trefoil lights and a transom punctured with multafoils. These contrasts and disagreements do not, nevertheless, produce such an ill effect as might be anticipated. While the rubble was plastered, with great strips peeled off showing the elementary work beneath, the effect was very unprepossessing; but the recent scaling which the walls have undergone has removed a great portion of this poverty of effect.

The south aisles, two years ago, were lighted by ten windows, three of which in the clerestory were plain deal casements painted white. These have now been removed, and superseded by three of a Decorated character. The lower windows of this portion of the church, which almost fill the compartments between the buttresses, are perfectly flat-headed; and the porch, which is on this side, is of the Decorated period, but so heavy in its construction that it might be cut down into Norman without losing the solidity so necessary to that style; and, with the singular delight in disorder so manifest in every portion of this church, the window that lights the parvise over it is on one side, close under the eave. A portion of moulding is inserted on each side in the ridge, as if it had sunk into the coarse rubble beneath it.

The south chancel is lighted by three Perpendicular windows, two of which claim some merit for taste and proportion.

We think, however, the east end presents the best features of the Church in their best position. There is no rubble-work on this face of the edifice, nor are there any really bad lines or ungraceful workmanship. The grouping is good, of that kind which painters delight in, and all the best features of the building show themselves here unassociated with those corruptions of style and taste so manifest in every other part. The two chancels form the foremost feature, and their diverse styles, the unequal pitch of their roofs, and their unequal lengths, only constitute so many broken outlines which form the elements of the picturesque; while the bold well-developed tower, rising between the gables, and immediately over the chapel—now the vestry—filling the corner between the chancels, and agreeing in era only with that part of the building, constitutes as imposing a group of architecture as could possibly be combined out of materials by no means of foremost character.[1] The crosses which terminate the chancel gables ought not to be omitted; that on the north chancel is especially rich, and at the same time uncommon.[2] There is, however, one lamentable blot upon the otherwise agreeable effect of this end of the church. The baseness of the mason and the plasterer have shut out of view every part of the east window of the south chancel, except its moulding, and thus it stands, with graceful outline under a gracefully pitched roof, a dead blank space, that ought to have been the eye and light of the building.[3]

(1) This is the point we have selected for our view, which, however, requires the removal of the ugly brick wall, and the opening of the chancel window, to give full effect to the architecture.

(2) This cross, which was sadly dilapidated by age, has been recently replaced by a new one of the same form and dimensions in every respect. It was executed by Mr. J. S. Swansborough, and presented to the church by that gentleman. The original now ornaments the vicar's garden.

(3) The carelessness, if not impiety, of former times has permitted the most shameful innovations of private vanity to obtrude itself in prominent places in our churches and cathedrals. But, perhaps, the most wanton and inexcusable have been such examples as the present case, where a tasteless monument has been placed over a fine window, whose mullions are probably used to fasten this cumbrous piece of marble. Did we now pray for the

The north side of the Church contains nothing remarkable but the tower, which is the best and only perfect feature in it. This, it must be confessed, if not among the best examples of the Perpendicular style, is but little inferior to them; and its inferiority is rather of date than of workmanship. The period of its erection is evidently that in which the debasement of the style began to be predominant. The windows are small and confined, the ornaments slightly cut, and there is a predominance of shields, heraldry, and emblems, —features which mark its date as hardly anterior to an age when these forms became the principles of style. The proportions, however, are good and bold, the buttresses well developed, and the eight battlemented pinnacles with which the tower terminates only want depth and decision of workmanship to make them models of style.

The interior of the Church contains many elements of sublimity and beauty, without being either sublime or beautiful; there is space—but, instead of adding to the grandeur of the edifice, it only serves to make its want of grandeur more legible; there is diversity of style, but instead of being an interesting study, it seems rather the diversity of convenience than taste, and produces the effect of some of those clumsy buildings which second-hand architects put together out of the remains of better and nobler constructions. There is a double nave, divided by a row of columns; but this feature, noble in itself, seems here to want development. We are not certain that it had not as much length when it was only half the breadth—a proportion much more suitable to its construction than the present bloated absurdity. The windows—those divisions of the edifice which in most other churches constitute at once its color and its dignity—are here cramped up in corners, pushed out of sight by galleries, left to obscurity behind staircases. The organ hides one principal window, and galleries either perfectly shut out or

souls of the rich, and institute obits for them, the vanity of putting up memorials and filling them with the record of unpractised virtues would have its purpose; but it seems wholly inexcusable to let the monument of one who has left nothing worthy of remembrance shut out an elegant necessity of a public building.

cross the middle of the rest. Now, however degenerate in style or rough in execution these portions of a church may be, this neglect or contempt of order and of their service can never be palliated. There are twenty-six windows to the aisles and the nave, of which only the eleven belonging to the clerestory can be seen from the inside otherwise than by glimpses. But when we turn from these architectural deformities to the arrangements by which they have been doubly degraded, the want of order, almost of decency, strikes us at every point. The nave and aisles occupy a space of nearly 3000 feet, and this extent is so portioned into pews, many of which have the appearance of small parlours, and are unwarrantably claimed by individuals, that only an inadequate portion of the population is accommodated, while the space is so over-occupied that the transit from one part of the church to another is very ill preserved. The pews are elevated about eighteen inches above the floor of the church, which, combined with their high construction, gives the interior the appearance of a collection of confessionals, in which the penitents were anxious to hide from every eye their mortified countenances. The base of every column in the church is hidden under the baize on the seats of these hereditaments of aristocratic humility, and the only palliation that is felt for this crowded and inconvenient arrangement is the sight of a greater crowd and more inconvenience above it. On turning the eye upward nothing is seen but piled and hanging galleries, with which all the comfort, sound, and beauty of the church, which the lower arrangements have not destroyed, are wholly extinguished. Galleries, the invention of a late period in church history, are the most unmanageable of architectural forms. Their use, therefore, when they cannot be avoided, should be very sparingly adopted. But the successive constructors of Wisbech Church have exhausted space in order to establish their connection. We have galleries one behind another, and galleries one above another, till we are reminded of a theatre in the succession of tier over tier almost to the roof.

The architectural details are scarcely more satisfactory than the arrangements and the architectural impression. The north side is the oldest, and contains, in the row of pillars which separate the north aisle from the north nave, undoubted remains of an original church. The small size of the round pillars, their lowness, and the plain round recessed arches and chamfered capitals tempt us to believe them Saxon, did not the zig-zag moulding in one of them, and a kind of attempt at intercolumniation in two of them, give a Norman, almost a Transition, preponderance to our notions, which is further increased by an arch at the opposite end, gives us a specimen of the period when the Norman was becoming anglicised.

The division between the two naves is by a row of five pillars, dating in the Perpendicular age. They are without capitals, and have lost the little character they ever had by being partly boxed up in pews and smothered with paint and whitewash. Of the pillars which separate the south nave and south aisle it is almost impossible to speak, as you have to grope in the bottom of pews, and hunt along obscure galleries, to find them at all. They do not honor architecture much after they are discovered, but seem to belong to the Decorated division by their bases and capitals.

The chancels are of different lengths, the north extending twenty-seven feet further to the east than the south chancel. The north chancel, which alone is used for chancel purposes, has recently undergone some wholesome alterations, and the improvements which they have effected in its character and appearance only make us the more regret that means or inclination cannot be found to restore other parts of the church in the same manner. We are not sure that the effect of the double nave and double chancel would not, under a good system of restoration, be imposing, and give an unique as well as an extended character to the edifice. The arches by which the chancels communicate with the church, though belonging to one description of style, are very different in elegance and workmanship.[1] That connected with the south is much more elegantly moulded and far more perfect in form than the corresponding arch to the north, which is stunted, roughly worked, and heavy, compared with its light and elegant associate. These chancels are separated by three arches of the Decorated period, and the walls are well covered with monuments, of which two on the north wall and one over the south chancel door are the most striking. In the east end of the north chancel is perhaps altogether the finest window in the church, whether its style or proportions be considered. It consists of five lights of the early Decorated lancet form, with cinquefoil heads. A small portion of this window is filled with stained glass; and, till lately, all of it, except this part, was blocked up. The opening and glazing of it have disclosed one of the most beautiful parts of the church, while the removal of the white and yellow wash from the walls and pillars, and re-roofing the whole with timber-work, have given a decency and elegance to this part of the church which no other part can lay claim to. The removal of the gallery, which, against all precedent, use, and convenience, was placed under the north chancel arch, thereby shutting the sight of the altar completely away from all parts of the church except its immediate vicinity, is another newly completed improvement, whose good effect is likely, we hope, to be only a precedent.

The altar is reached by three steps, and in its right wall the late improvements have disclosed a piscina and water-drain. The altar table is carved after the manner called Elizabethan. There are also the remains of three misereres under the north wall, which have been mutilated, but one which is still nearly entire seems to have a carved head as its sub-ornament.

It is the habit of the age to divide ecclesiastical architecture into different styles, and on the faith of a number of

(1) On the south side of this arch, probably originally forming its capital though now shamefully cut away to form gallery pews, is the remains of an admirable niche groined with a flower boss. This is all we were able to trace of it, the rest being hidden by the boarded floor of the pew.

examples to form a kind of chronology by the prevailing mode with which the different parts of a church are executed. Though this rule is founded in truth, truth does not always prevail in it; and we should find the recognised rules of Gothic architecture would soon involve us in a mist of contradiction, did we attempt to regulate the age of different parts of the church by the style or the approaches to style which it manifests. The separation of styles,—as Early English, Decorated, and Perpendicular, which are at present the three great recognised phases of Gothic architecture,—being a mere modern classification, without any decided ancient authority to support it, or any actual chronological sequence to authenticate it, must often involve in difficulties any authority that depends on the mere evidence of construction for his dates. If, for instance, we were to make its style and construction the records of the age of different parts of Wisbech Church, we should be reduced to somewhat such sequence as the following. The earliest portion of the Church is certainly that forming the division of the north aisle and nave. The date of this division of the edifice seems to be about the middle of the twelfth century; but the mean half-wrought character of the style—the plain sharp-edged arch and the chamfered heading which is alone resorted to on four of the arches, while on another there is a chevron ornament, but so unskilfully wrought that the workman had to nip up one of his points in order to make the proper fitting of the arch, would almost induce the idea that the style was very imperfectly understood when this part was built. This, indeed, would appear to be the case, not with the age, but merely with the architect of Wisbech Church, as from other parts connected with this portion we incline to the opinion that it was built late in the Norman period. The next date appears to be the portion of the Church where the original tower stood, and which is now occupied by the organ. One of the arches which supported the tower still remains: it belongs to the period immediately following that we have appropriated to the round arches of the nave, and is decidedly Transition.

The other remains of this tower, which are still seen externally in two flat, rubble, and long and short work buttresses, must be attributed to the same period.[1] The north chancel, both the chancel arches, the south porch, the columnar separation between the south nave and aisle, both aisles, and the clerestory windows above, appear to belong to the fourteenth century, or Decorated period.[2] The south chancel and the columnar separation of the naves appear to belong to the fifteenth century, or early Perpendicular period; while in the tower and the vestry we see the sixteenth century, or late Perpendicular period. But if we attach ourselves dogmatically to style, we should be obliged to show that, while the lower portion of the tower gives much evidence of the fourteenth century, or Decorated style, in its construction, the upper portion contains perfect evidences of the sixteenth century. Now, the date of the tower is pretty well ascertained to belong wholly to the last period. We are, therefore, left to the idea that in Gothic works the architect frequently for convenience, or for taste, reverted to older styles in order to produce his effects; and, therefore, that several former methods of building were sometimes adopted in one edifice, in order to cheapen the construction, or heighten the effect, according to taste. Unless this conclusion be adopted, we must believe that the tower of the church was two centuries in building, and that the north and south aisles were constructed a century before the naves were covered in. This latter conjecture is not so unlikely, however, as it

(1) It is remarkable, and little known, that the ruins of the original tower of the Church still remain in the false roof between the top of the organ and the leads. By the remains of this interesting relic the tower appears to have fallen. A small mean window is left, but only the most wretched construction and poverty appear in all its parts. The turret staircase, by which the lantern on the west end is reached, is the original turret staircase of this tower, and the wall which separates the organ-gallery from the gallery of the south nave is probably the original wall of the old tower.

(2) Three clerestory windows, executed by Mr. Swansborough, have been lately substituted in lieu of the old deal casement windows which formerly degraded this part of the church. They are, of course, no argument in chronology, though they are in style accordant with the other parts of the clerestory.

appears at first sight. If the original west tower fell, as its ruins appear to denote, the slope of the ruins seem to indicate that it must have fallen on the nave, and crushed it; and so the naves and the present tower belong to the same style, though not precisely the same date, the latter being later: the arches of the nave may have been a subsequent erection to their aisles. If this was the case, we must attribute the fall of the tower to the fourteenth century, if we may trust the early character of the style of these columns; but, if so, the church must have remained nearly a century without a steeple.

The Church contains altogether thirty-four windows, one of which is yet filled up. Twenty-two appear to belong to the Perpendicular period, and eleven to the Decorated style, which style must be considered in other respects the leading style of the church. Fourteen of the Perpendicular windows are square headed, and generally of three trefoil-headed lights, sub-divided near the top into six small plain heads; only four are surrounded with a slight label moulding. The great west Decorated window before alluded to is divided into five lights; the mullions, dividing from the line of the spring of the arch, spread across the window, producing an easy flowing tracery, almost wholly occupied with quarterfoils. Two of the south clerestory windows are of small elegant proportions, of two trefoil lights, with a trefoil between the head of the lights and the point of the arch. The Decorated windows of the north chancel are similar in character, but of larger dimensions. Only one of the Perpendicular windows has a transom, which is battlemented.

We have said that the Church is principally built in the Decorated style. This is especially apparent in the south aisle and north chancel, which are completely identical, as is the separation between the chancels. There is one internal feature, however, that remains to be noticed, which, like many other features of this church, cannot be ranked as either elegant or ornamental. The wall of the north chancel is placed six feet beyond the line of the pillars of the north nave and aisle. The effect of this disorder is to make the aisle apparently advance into the nave, and, on the contrary, to cut off six feet of the chancel from the view when seen in a line from the opposite extremity of the church. Had there been but one chancel to the church, and a similar advance been made by the south aisle into the nave, the disagreeable effect now so apparent would have been avoided, and somewhat of uniqueness might have been obtained, as well as a greater breadth of chancel. A contrivance, in harmony with nothing but the clumsiness of this design, has carried a Decorated pillar from the Norman pillars to the chancel-wall, and in order to draw the last clerestory window more into line with the rest, the segment of an arch is stretched over this Decorated pillar and in front of it, on which the window is carried. Nothing but the most perverse blundering can be appealed to for such injuries to consistency. The intention of the architect in the first instance was evidently to increase the area of the chancel, and it might have been the intention to pull down the north aisle and rebuild it uniform with the south, in which case it would doubtless have been carried back the six feet which now project so unseemly into the nave.

Much of this Church is built of rubble, which is only very loosely cemented together. In several instances it will be seen that this rude and imperfect construction of the walls has been injurious to the arches of the windows, and has apparently yielded to pressure. It seems a singular circumstance that these half-secure walls should have been so tested with weight, as they are, from galleries, &c., in the interior of the church. On the recent removal of the gallery stretching across the north chancel, it was found to be in a very insecure state, though from the small distance of the walls in which its beams were inserted, and from two iron supports which bore it in front, it must have had more provision for security than any other gallery in the church. If this gallery was insecure, what must be the state of the galleries over the south aisle, where one is lifted over the other, and a great part of the weight of both is thrown on a half-secure rubble wall? The pillars which run through the lower of these galleries give evident tokens of weakness, and not without reason, when we consider that their original construction is weak, that they have been half cut away to form these galleries and pews,—that, besides the clerestory wall, they have been recently loaded with three heavy stone windows in lieu of three comparatively light though disgraceful casement windows. Such united circumstances have twisted these pillars variously out of the perpendicular, and it would be no very marvellous circumstance if the galleries they support, should they be suffered to remain, were on some occasion to be precipitated into the church. If that be a true canon in architecture, that nothing is perfectly secure which does not seem so, these galleries are beyond doubt without the pale of moderate insurance.

There were formerly three chapels, if not more, in the church. These were dedicated to the Virgin, St. Martin, and the Holy Trinity. That of St. Martin is best authenticated, and was the portion of the church now appropriated to the baptistry. The font here is exceedingly plain, being merely four small columns clustered round a heavy central pillar, and is probably attributable to the thirteenth century. This chapel was originally endowed with lands, for a priest to say masses for the souls of the founders; and here, in 1495, Bishop Alcock held an ordination. "Under James I. the messuages and lands belonging to Saint Martin's chantry, and four acres of lamp land, were granted to L. Johnson for forty years."[1] In 1670 we find the following recorded on the same chapel: "Ordered, the Town Bailiff pay Mr. John Grouse the sume of five pounds out of the thirty pounds payd by Mr. Jaggard for the arrears of a rent charge of $11^{s.}$ $3^{d.}$ a yeare proceeding out of the lands late of the chantry of St. Martin's in Wisbech... which rent charge is to be payd yearly towards y^{e} repaires of y^{e} Church of Wisbech for ever.[2]" How these lands have been since appropriated we

(1) Watson. (2) Corporation Records, v. 4.

know not, but nothing of the sort appears to remain for the above specified purpose. Another chapel occupied the place of the present south chancel. A screen parted it from the church at the chancel arch, which some inconsiderable remains still existing lead us to believe was of Decorated work. In this chapel the piscina of the Decorated age still remains; and here, also, under one of the three perpendicular windows within the chapel, is a kind of desk, on which was formerly placed *Foxe's Book of Martyrs*, in three volumes. Nothing of the books remains, but an inscription carved in wood over the shelf is as follows: "Robert Gooderidge, son of James Gooderidge, Blacksmith, borne in Wisbeach St. Peter's, deceased at London one Easter day, in the yeare 1635, and gave by his last will and testament $8^{ll.}$ to buy theise threc books of marters, and to have them set in y^e church of Wisbeach aforesaid, which was performed according to his will in y^e yeare of our Lord, 1636." This is not the only donation of the kind which has been given to Wisbech, and probably to the Church, as appears by the following entry from the Corporation Records: "y^e xi January, 1592. $M^{d.}$ y^t there was payd to y^e x men by Wydow Pull & Wydow Rechell $xl^{s.}$ for to buye y^e book of y^e martyrs, gyven and bequeathed by y^e last wyll of John Megytt, & ys comytted to y^e hands of Tho. Edwards to buye y^e same... I bought y^e booke wch cost $57^{s.}$"[1] The third chapel was probably the building attached to the church, and now used as a vestry. There are no internal relics to identify this purpose, but it is fully evident that it was erected as a chantry, or chapel. It is an elegant specimen of the late Perpendicular period, though, from the circumstance of being attached to two sides of the church, it has only an east and a south front. These are beautiful enough to excuse a detailed description. It is 22 feet long by 24 wide, and is surmounted by an embattled parapet, round which the coping is continued, and is lighted by two windows to the east and the south. That on the south side is square-headed, and its label is blended with the

(1) Vol. 1.

moulding which traverses both sides of the chapel. It is divided by a heavier mullion in the middle into two parts of three lights each, and above it, on both sides, runs an ornamental cornice, divided into ten square compartments on the south side and twelve on the east, each of which contains a flower, arms, or a monogram on a shield. The cross keys and cross swords, and cross of St. Andrew, are repeated on each front. The knife and cleaver, sword between two wheels, cup and wafer, and the three crowns—the arms of the Isle of Ely—and the Tudor rose are the principal figures occupying the other shields, except one monogram, which from its being repeated three times on the east front, and once on the south, must be considered more than usually important. It consists of the letter B, through which, forming its first stroke, runs a line crossed at the top almost like T; after the B there is on each monogram, in Old English, **ur**, and either by the side or below, a round piece of brickwork, seeming to indicate a well. There can be little doubt that the meaning of this monogram is T. Burwell. It is repeated, we have said, four times, but on the east front it is raised above the parapet on the centre merlon, in order, we suppose, to mark its importance. On referring to the proceedings of the Guild we find the name of Burwell constantly occurring either as alderman, or inquisitor, or some other officer, from 1469 to 1518, and as the date of this building may be safely placed about 1500, we have no doubt it was erected by one of this family as a chantry for his soul, or a chapel for the holy offices of the Guild. The Burwells appear to have been persons of property from the distinguished places they held for so long a time in the Trinity Guild. The east side of the chapel rises in the middle so as to form a low pediment, and the window in this front, instead of being flat-headed, is a depressed arch of five lights. Each merlon of the battlement is ornamented with a small rose.

The steeple is the last and most perfect part of this irregular building. It is built, as we have said, in the late Perpendicular style, when it was verging on debasement, and it thus discovers some of the weakness of its style. It is, however, built wholly of stone, of very solid construction, but is only 96 feet high. A string-course of quarterfoils with a central flower is carried round it near the bottom, and another about three parts up. This is principally composed of shields, except to the north, which being the front of the tower, it is there adorned with the arms of England, the emblems of St. Peter and St. Paul, the arms of the Isle of Ely, and other heraldry and devices. There is no other attempt at ornament in the lower stories, which have thus a very naked appearance,—not, however, offensively so. The lower window has rather a Decorated character, but those of the ringing and bell chambers have the battlemented transom. It is in the upper part that the principal attempts at decoration have been made. Above each belfry-window is a central device held by an angel under a groined canopy, and supported by two smaller angels on each side. The devices to the north and west have been cut away to make room for the clock-face, leaving only the canopy remaining; but on the south side it is apparently the letters I. H. S., which is also repeated on the pinnacle of each face. To the east this central figure is a cup or a font, we are not certain which. Col. Watson calls it the cup and wafer, but we doubt whether this be correct. It appears to us to be rather a covered font, and is doubtless an emblem of the sacrament of baptism. Situated around this central figure, on each front, are four other designs upon a kind of shield. On the north are the letters T. R. under coronets, and the arms of the see of Canterbury, and those of the Bishop of Ely. The cross keys, cross swords, St. Catharine's wheels, and a pilgrim's scrip suspended from a staff, and four limpet-shells, form the devices of the east front. On the west are the lamb and book, and three unknown arms. On the south the cup and wafer, three cups, St. George's cross, and a shield, make up the twenty devices which adorn the upper part of this steeple. Above these devices runs a third string-course, or cornice, formed of shields, flowers, and the emblems of St. Peter and

St. Paul, and upon this rise the eight pinnacles beautifully panelled and supported by sixteen battlemented buttresses, pierced and otherwise ornamented. The pinnacles terminate with small crocketted spires. Some of this work is very slightly cut, which, together with the preponderance of armorial bearings, mark the decline of an architecture which was becoming too proud and personal to retain the character of simple devotion with which in earlier periods it was peculiarly marked. The founders and officials of the edifice are marked in stronger characters than its purposes, and it was no wonder that under such a system the faith which had become so subordinate to vanity and ostentation soon became weak enough to be readily overthrown. The Reformation followed close after the style was introduced which is so conspicuous in the tower of Wisbech Church, but with the Reformation, unfortunately, only a general ruin of style in architecture succeeded. It happens that a few memorials remain of the construction of this tower, though all record is lost of the construction or alteration of any other part of the church. The first Record we meet with is in the year 1520. From this memorial, which is an extract from the will of one Robert Smith, who otherwise bestowed much upon the church, it appears that the building was not then begun, which will mark its erection as very late in the late Perpendicular period: "Itm, I gyve & bequeth to y^{e} buyldyng of y^{e} stepull of y^{e} Chyrche of Wysbeyche xx^{ti} li., v$^{li.}$ y^{e} begynnyng of y^{e} buyldyng of y^{e} seid stepull, and wthin half a yere next aft^{r} yth other v$^{li.}$, and x$^{li.}$ wthin halff a yere next aft^{r} yth, so that the hole xx^{ti} li. be payd wthin a yere when the seid stepull is begann to be made or buyldyd wth the fyrst money." Whether this donation incited the immediate building we know not, but it appears from an entry five years later that it was then begun: "1525. It is agreyd & ordeynd y^{t} of vij$^{li.}$ iij$^{s.}$ iiij$^{d.}$ wyche was in y^{e} hands, y^{r} shall v$^{li.}$ of it remayned to y^{e} use of y^{e} gyld, & iij$^{li.}$ xliij$^{s.}$ iiij$^{d.}$[1] shalbe pd to y^{e} buyldyng of y^{e} stepull." Thirteen years after this entry it

(1) So in the Record, but evidently a mistake; iij$^{s.}$ are probably meant.

still seems to have been unfinished, for in 1538 we meet with the two annexed Records:

"That Katyn Wynde gaue iiij$^{li.}$ resideu of Cresses vi$^{li.}$ at the asseynemen^{t} of M^{r} alderman & his brethren to the vse of the steple.

"That the Alderman & xij of his Brethryn hath assigned Willm. Salibank to pay to the makyng of the Steple the iiij$^{li.}$ the which he hath in his hand upon an obligacon made this p'sent yer and borowyd of the same gild till Cristmas."

It thus appears that the erection of this part of the church was not completed till the Reformation had actually commenced. We may, therefore, consider the work to have been lucky in its period, for, had it been delayed a few more years, it is very uncertain whether it would have been erected at all. While church property was undergoing the changes that now began to agitate the country, men had too many personal concerns and too many misgivings to advance money for the decoration of a form of religion which appeared to be in the convulsions of death. The puritanic rage which succeeded these convulsions was as fatal to all art, and when architecture did recover a little from the depression of fifty years, it had grown as it were childish, and frittered upon vain ornaments and trumpery toys that high and noble spirit which had formerly scaled the air and mounted, like the feelings it was intended to enshrine, heavenward.

There are four entrances to the church; one under the tower, which is the principal entrance, is highly enriched with grotesque sculpture. Externally is a deeply-cut moulding, within which is a series of lizards, birds, and a deep hollow; to this succeeds another moulding, and within that, bounded by an internal moulding, is carved foliage. This entrance appears to have been always the principal one, if we may trust the high effort of decoration, compared with any other part of the edifice, which the doorway displays. Though apparently under the tower, it is distinct from it, and not only belongs to an earlier style, but is inserted in the wall of the church, to which this tower is merely attached.

It is now, unfortunately, so filled with white-wash, that its decoration is very little noticed.

The south doorway is of good shape, and deeply under-cut in its free uniform mouldings, which are without capitals. Of the unshapely porch in which it is placed we have before spoken. There are two entrances from the south.

The pulpit is placed against the second pillar from the north chancel. It is panelled and ornamented with heavy carving of a late date. Cherub-heads, the dove, the celestial crown, and other emblems, combined with some open foliage-work, are its principal features, in which it consorts with the organ, though in the latter the accessories appear more appropriate.

The organ was built in 1789 by Mr. Green, of London, at a cost of £500. It had been preceded by one set up in 1711 by C. Quarles, of Cambridge. It consists of three instruments,—the great organ, choir, and swell,—containing altogether twenty-one stops, of which the great organ contains ten stops:

Two open Diapasons	Fifteenth
Stop Diapason	Sesquialter
Principal	Cornet
Twelfth	Two Trumpets

The choir organ has five stops:

Stop Diapason	Flute
Dulciana	Fifteenth
Principal	

The swell organ has six stops:

Stop Diapason	Cornet
Open Diapason	Trumpet
Principal	Hautboy

The best stops are the diapasons of the great organ, which are exceedingly sweet and tender in tone;[1] but the reed stops, consisting of the principal, twelfth, fifteenth, and trumpets, are very inferior. The organ has also the defect of

(1) It is said these stops were intended by Mr. Green for the organ of the Chapel Royal at Windsor, which he was building simultaneously with the present; but, finding them fit so well in the Wisbech organ, he resolved to place them there.

having no pedal pipes, the pedals merely serving to open pipes in the great organ. If pedal pipes were added, with the modern and beautiful stop the Cremona, its powers, which are still considerable, would be much increased and improved; and it cannot be considered otherwise than a great pity that these additions are not made to this instrument. With these and a few other alterations, at comparatively small cost, the organ would rank among the best in these parts. In chorus the organ is superior to St. Margaret's at Lynn, and that of the Cathedral at Peterborough, which is loud and metallic in tone.[1] The service of the Church of England requires, in its pure form, essential use of the organ. It is almost mockery to hear the high poetry with which the ritual abounds torn to pieces by a hundred voices and babbled into jargon, while the loftiest anthems and services lie neglected. The Church of England service arranged for devotional music as well as devotional words, has, by the lax notions of modern times, degenerated into a cheap and slubbering system, which leaves scarcely any effect on the hearer, who naturally grows inert to the same formula repeated in the same manner day after day and year after year. This want of interest would even become prevalent were the repetition connected with one settled form of music, though Mozart or Palestrina were its author. How much more so must it become when linked with a horrid, indiscriminate gabble? The old masters of the English church saw this defect in set forms, and wisely united the liturgy with a variety of anthems, chaunts, and services, that there might be an eternal variety of character connected with the same sentiments, and thus a youthful blood be continually instilled into the old frame of public worship. A generation, however, that reverences devotional forms more than devotional feelings, has allowed the church service to degenerate

(1) It is probable that the sum of £200 would make these additions, and otherwise rank it high among its class of instruments. It is therefore, a pitiful economy to keep a good instrument imperfect for so small a sum, when its outlay would afford so much gratification to all lovers of music in its power and purity. The organ at Peterborough will soon redeem its character, as £300 are about to be expended upon it.

into monotony; and it is to be feared that unless some more vigorous opinions replace the present apathetic ones, the church will, in the end, deservedly lose more power and privilege than it will be willing to part with.

Before the erection of the present organ it is doubtful whether any regular organist was employed. At any rate, on the erection of this instrument, an application was made to the Corporation for a yearly grant as a salary to him, which they consented to fix at £40. This was subsequently raised to £50. and was paid by the Corporation till the election of the present organist, Mr. Jones, whose salary is obtained by voluntary contributions.[1]

The monuments of the Church are numerous and various, but only one of them of a high ecclesiastical character. They are mostly mural. The one referred to claims the first attention, not only for its antiquity, but for the art which has been employed upon it. It is a brass, and commemorates the death of Thomas de Braunstone, who was Constable of the Castle, dying in 1401. He is represented in armour under a Decorated canopy, and wears the conical cap, or bascinet without a vizor, having a camail or neck guard of chain. The arms are protected by brassarts, and the hands, which are clasped in the attitude of prayer, are fastened by leather gauntlets with gads. The body is covered with a surcoat, or perhaps the close-fitting guipon of the age, quite plain, to which hangs a sort of fringe, with the highly ornamented belt across the hips, to which a sword in a figured sheath is attached on the left side, and a dagger on the right. The legs are protected by greaves, the pointed shoes are covered with sollerets; and rowelled spurs complete the costume of the figure. He is represented as treading on a lion, the general emblem of the triumph of the Christian, and around the slab is this inscription: "*Cy gist Thomas de Braunstone jadis Con*estable du Chastel de Wisebeche qi moruit le vyngt

(1) It may be worthy of note, as a characteristic of the times, and of the esteem in which the church service in its higher forms is held, that Mr. Jones is at present obliged to solicit his salary from door to door.

MONUMENT OF SIR THOMAS DE BRAUNSTON, ST PETER'S CHURCH WISBECH

Published by Richd Walker Bridge Foot, Wisbech.

septisme iour de Maii l'an de nostre seignour Mil. CCCC primer. De lalme de qi dieu per sa grace ait mercy. Amen."[1] The portion of this inscription in *Italic* is now gone, as are also the entire canopy and pinnacles, the handle of the dagger, and two shields which occupied the spandril between the canopy and pinnacles. Our engraving represents a portion of the canopy remaining, as well as the entire inscription, but our plate was engraved from one in *Lyson's Magna Britannia*, which was taken about forty years since, when so much of the brass was yet in existence. Abundance of these brasses were torn up and sold to copper-smiths and tinkers at the Reformation, till Queen Elizabeth issued a proclamation to prevent it, which was only very slightly attended to.

There is evidence of another slab partly inlaid with brass in the church. It is seen near the pulpit, where the forms of two small figures, now almost worn away, appear to have formed the bed of former brasses.

The most ambitious monuments in the church are two in the north chancel of a similar character. That nearest the altar is of marble, and is erected to the memory of a benefactor of the town—Thomas Parke. It consists of two large-sized figures—a man and a woman—kneeling before a low desk, the representation, it is probable, of Mr. Parke and his wife. On the end of the desk another female kneeling figure is sculptured. Two Ionic columns of black marble, placed on each side, support the arms of the wife and the husband, and the husband's arms are repeated on the topmost centre of the monument. The figures are kneeling on cushions—the man being bare-headed and habited in armour—the apron armour of the time of James I. The female wears a broad-brimmed hat, crimped frill, and flowing garment. Both have their hands clasped in attitude of prayer. On the upper part of the monument lies a skeleton supported on brackets. The inscription tells us that Mr. Parke "was born of a

(1) "Here lies Thomas de Braunstone, at one time Constable of the Castle of Wisbech, who died the 27th day of May, 1401; the soul of whom God in his grace have mercy on. Amen."

worthy family in ye county of Huntingdon, who through the blessing of God and his own endeavours rose to an ample estate, was Justice of the Peace for ye Isle of Ely for many years, and ye year before his death he was High Sheriff of ye county of Cambridge and Huntingdon, and out of those blessings gave good relief to the Poor in his life time, and by his last will many large legacies to charitable uses.[1]"

The other monument of a similar style is of less costly material and poorer workmanship. It is of stone, erected to the memory of Mathias Taylor, and consists, like Parke's monument, of two figures, a man and a woman, facing each other, kneeling before a low desk placed between them. They are blackened; the man has a scull-cap, and the woman a flowing head-dress, and each wears flowing garments. Two Corinthian pillars bear the arms of the figures, which are three times repeated on the monument. It was formerly much gilt. The inscription, cut in black on a faded gold ground, informs us that Mr. Taylor died in 1633, aged 67,—that he was brought up a linen draper, and obtained a large estate by trade, and was chosen capital burgess of the town,—"and of the number without any dislocation continued to his dying day. Also he had the constableship of the castle conferred on him, and by the space of twenty years before his death he was made justice of the peace and quorum under his majesty in the isle of Ely."

On the south wall is a monument to Caroline Burrough, wife of Henry Burrough, vicar. She died in child-bed in 1651. The inscription is surmounted by a figure of a weeping child, gracefully carved in marble: he is leaning on a broken column, and pointing to an urn surrounded with a chaplet.

A monument to Wm. Rayner, over the altar, consists of a well-designed bas-relief figure of Commerce, seated in a feminine attitude, and looking on two inverted cornucopias. Mr. Rayner died in 1831.

(1) Both Mr. Parke and his wife will be found as donors to the town in our account of the Charities.

In this chancel there are also monuments to the memory of Thomas Fox, Rear Admiral, who died in 1763. A marble tablet surmounted with naval emblems.

Captain Wm. Hanner, who died in 1746.

Alexander Fraser, M.D., who died in 1836.

Steed Girdlestone and family, 1843.

Elizabeth Rayner, 1820.

Hannah Jobson, 1803.

Rev. W. Coldwell, 51 years vicar of the church, 1702.

In the south chancel, whose walls are pretty well covered with monuments, are six to the memory of the Southwell family, who for a series of years occupied the castle. Their monuments are all mural,—of the obelisk form,—and of marble. The achievements of this family, eight in number, were formerly placed on the east wall of this chancel, but they have been recently removed, and the royal arms, which used to occupy the upper part of the arch between the chancel and nave, has been placed here.

The only monuments betraying either taste or art, are two erected to the Southwells. One to Henry Southwell, who died in 1762, represents two bassi-relievi figures standing beside a monument,—Hope pointing upwards, and an angel, expressively sculptured, bearing the arms of the deceased.

A finer is erected to the memory of John Southwell, who died in 1771. An angel is represented weeping over an urn, and on the opposite side is a small exquisite figure of Cupid with an inverted torch.

The largest of these monuments is that to the memory of Edward Southwell, who died in 1748, and now covers the space formerly occupied by the east window. It has more of the joyous than the pathetic emblems about it, being covered with wreaths and garlands such as we rather associate with Pan or Bacchus than with the "bony skeleton." They would have been more appropriate as a memorial of the sorrow of the heirs to the estate of the dead than of his widow "for one of the best of husbands."

Over the south door is a monument to Edward Southwell, who died in 1787. It is the work of Nollekens, and consists of a perfect figure of Hope. The face is gracefully thrown heavenwards, and while the left hand rests on the anchor, the right is spread sympathetically with the pure expression of the features. Its poor position prevents this beautiful work from being well seen, but it is worth some trouble to examine that face, which idealizes all that a Christian can desire. Who would believe that a niggard miser could dream himself into such morsels of pure form and expression as are displayed in this fine work?

This chancel also contains mural monuments to

Mrs. Amy Worrall, 1795.	Ralph Archbould, 1837.
Edward Southwell, 1792.	Isaac Young, 1763.
Mrs. Frances Southwell, 1779.	Anne Leach, 1838.
Mrs. Robinson Ward, 1842.	Isaac Gann, 1763.

The floor of this chancel is nearly paved with monumental slabs, among which may be noted that which commemorates the death of Nicholas Sanford, before alluded to. He was descended, it is said, from an ancient and religious house of Sandford Hall, Shropshire. He died in 1636, aged 75, and if we may trust the testimony of this slab,

"He was
A patterne for townesmen whom we may enrole,
For at his own charge this towne hee freed of tole."

In a former division of this work we have had occasion to notice the great storm and inundation which overwhelmed Wisbech and Marshland in 1613. A memorial of this event was preserved in several of the churches which had suffered most grievously, and that in Wisbech formerly occupied the east wall of this chancel, now occupied by the large monument of the Southwells. It was as follows:

"To the immortal praise of God Almighty, that saveth his people in all adversities—Be it kept in perpetual memory, that on the feast of All Saints, being the 1st November, in the year of our Lord 1613, late in the night, *the sea* broke in, through the violence of a north-east wind meeting with the spring tide, and overflowed all Marshland, with this town of Wisbech, both on the north side and the south, and almost the whole hundred round about, to the great danger of men's lives, and the loss of some. Besides the exceeding great loss which these countries sustained through the breach of banks and spoil of corn, cattle, and houseing, which could not be estimated.

"The next year following, *i.e.* the year of our Lord 1614, upon the 23rd day of March, this country was again overflowed with the *fresh waters*, which came down in such great abundance, through the extraordinary great snow that fell that year in January and February, that not only this town, whereof the south side only was lost, but the greatest part of the grounds within the South Eau Bank in Holland, from Spalding to Tidd St. Giles, was drowned, and almost wholly ost for that year.

"Moreover, a great part of Marshland, from their bank called the Edge, between their towns and the Smeeth, to the new Podike, was lost through divers breaches between Salter's Load and Downham Bridge. In conclusion, many towns in Norfolk, confining with Marshland, and most part of this whole Isle of Ely."

"D. O. M. S.

O frugum fœcunda domus nimiumque beata,
  Si male vicinis non premereris aquis.
Quas, tu cum sedeas, imis in vallibus, a te
  Quis prohibere undas, ni deus ipse potest?
Scilicet in fluctus nequicquam tenditur agger,
  Atque infida suo sedet arena mari.
Quod si te impietas, fraudes, scortatio, fœdus,
  Commaculant, ab aquis cur velet ista deus?[1]

"Posuit Joshua Blaxton in theologia Baccalaureus & hujus ecclesiæ dignus vicarius."

(1) "O fruitful fane! too happy wouldst thou be,
Wert thou from dread of inundation free,
When floods shall menace this low marshy plain,
'Tis God alone their fury can restrain.

There are three monuments on the wall of the north clerestory:

To Elizabeth, daughter of Col. T. Hardwicke, 1816.

Robert Hardwicke, upwards of fifty years magistrate for Norfolk and Cambridge, died 1836, aged 83.

Marie Gynn, 1811.

The north aisle has monuments to

W. Moore, 1802. Jane Edwards, died 1832.

In the south aisle:

Theophilus Buckworth, died 1698.

Robert Harris, Apothecary, 1722.

Dr. Massey, who died 1773. And

James Smith, whose monument, consisting of a marble tablet in a Gothic frame of stone, is the only ecclesiastical memorial, with the exception of that of the Constable, which the church contains. His character is appropriately condensed in the following inscription:

"THIS MONUMENT
IS ERECTED TO THE MEMORY OF
JAMES SMITH,
WHO CONDUCTED AN EXTENSIVE SCHOOL IN THIS TOWN
FOR NEARLY FORTY YEARS.
HE WAS AN EFFICIENT INSTRUCTOR,
BENEVOLENT IN THE EXERCISE OF HIS VOCATION,
UNREMITTING IN HIS EXERTIONS FOR THE IMPROVEMENT
OF THOSE COMMITTED TO HIS CHARGE,
AND EVER SOLICITOUS FOR THEIR FUTURE WELFARE.
ONE HUNDRED AND EIGHTY-SIX OF HIS PUPILS,
BY A VOLUNTARY AND EQUAL SUBSCRIPTION,
HAVE RAISED THIS TESTIMONIAL
OF THEIR GRATITUDE TO HIM AS A TEACHER,
AND THEIR RESPECT TO HIM AS A FRIEND.
HE DIED DECEMBER 2ND, 1835, IN THE 62ND YEAR OF HIS AGE."

In the baptistry are several monuments:

Peter E. F. Mason, 1713.

In vain its banks the rising waters brave,
In vain the sand repels the foaming wave;
But should foul crimes thy sacred walls disgrace,
In help divine thy trust how canst thou place?"

Translation in Watson's History.

Alice Watson, 1808, the mother of Col. Watson, and granddaughter of Alice Jermy, descended from John Jermy, Knight, by Margaret, one of the daughters and co-heiresses of Roger Bigott, Earl of Norfolk and Earl Marshal of England, *temp*. Edward II.[1]

Charles Vavazor, who died 1750; a monument of variegated marble with wreaths of flowers.

Thomas Wood, who died 1759.

Sir Philip Vavazor, 1796, who was knighted by George III. on carrying up the address on the coronation.

James Watson, who died in 1841.

Lastly, that of Col. Watson, of white marble, with the following inscription:

"SACRED TO THE MEMORY OF WILLIAM WATSON, ESQ., F.A.S.,
LIEUTENANT-COLONEL OF THE CAMBRIDGESHIRE LOCAL MILITIA,
DEPUTY LIEUTENANT AND CHIEF BAILIFF OF THE ISLE OF ELY.
HIS DEATH TOOK PLACE AT RICHMOND, IN SURREY,
ON THE 31ST DAY OF MARCH, IN THE 64TH YEAR OF HIS AGE,
AND HIS REMAINS WERE INTERRED IN A VAULT
BENEATH THIS TABLET, ON THE 8TH DAY OF APRIL, 1834.
IN LIFE THIS AMIABLE MAN
WAS HONOURED AND BELOVED BY ALL CLASSES,
AND IN DEATH LAMENTED.
IN HIM THE POOR NEVER WANTED A FRIEND,
THE EMBARRASSED AN ADVISER, THE GOOD A PATTERN.
HIS FAITH WAS ENTIRELY BUILT UPON THE MERITS
OF THE SAVIOUR'S ATONEMENT,
AND THE EVIDENCE OF IT WAS DAILY VISIBLE
IN THE CONSISTENCY OF A HOLY LIFE."

The Corporation Records contain various notices respecting the church which will enable us to elicit some of the former customs relating to this edifice. In the proceedings of the Guild we have a variety of notices of it, but none of them are of very general interest, being chiefly orders for certain formalities to the priests, and decorations of the altar, of which that body had one or more devoted to their service. The first mention that is made of it in the general accounts of the Corporation is in 1595, when there is a memorandum

(1) Watson's Wisbech.

that "Thomas Edwards yelded hys accompt . . . for y^{e} repayr of y^{e} new selyng & other thyngs in y^{e} Church & at y^{e} Church his Receypts was $lxxxvij^{li.}$ $x^{s.}$ $vij^{d.}$, hys payments $lxxxix^{li.}$ $viij^{s.}$ $iij^{d.}$, so rests to him $i^{li.}$ $xvij^{s.}$ $ix^{d.}$"[1] It appears from various entries that the communion wine was formerly found by the Corporation: "The Balye shall paye for wyne spent at the comunion, in the year 1604, $xxj^{s.}$ $viij^{d.}$"[2] The Reformation drove most of the ancient embellishments from worship,—the images, paintings, and rich traceries, which, dedicated to the holiest purposes, had become highly instrumental in controlling and subduing the mind, were all abolished by this sweeping alteration. But Henry VIII. had proclaimed himself supreme head of the church, and in submission to this royal edict, though it was not generally adopted till his successors, churches began to be ornamented with the royal arms. The virgin and child, and the holy legends, and the sacred histories, and the moral pictorial representations of the early struggles of Christianity, were supplanted by the lion and the unicorn. Images were broken, niches were hacked, the ornamental tracery which had as it were made the stone intelligent was obliterated with plaster and whitewash. But, in lieu of this, personal vanities were retained; arms and shields were permitted; and in almost every church the royal escutcheon was exhibited as a symbol at once of defeated Popery and of the king's supremacy in church as well as state:

"27 May, 1605. It was agreed that Robert Buckstone shalbe $forthw^{h}$ paid fower pounds . . . for the emblazoning and furnishing the king's ma^{ty} armes in the P'rsh church of Wisbeche. And whereas there be some defects in the same armes, yt ys further agreed (the same being p'fected as was formarly covenented) that then the said Mr. Buckstone shall have further allowed the some of $xx^{s.}$"[3] In 1607 there is a yearly allowance of £10 to the vicar, that he may provide a preacher, which is ordered to be continued "at the discretion of the Tenn;" and, in 1609, five shillings are ordered to be

(1) Corporation Records, v. 2. (2) Ibid, v. 3. (3) Ibid, v. 3.

paid, being a "quarteridg for ringing of the Bell at viij of the clock and fower in the morninge." In 1625 there is £60 ordered to be paid for church repairs. In 1616, £10 is noted as paid for paving the church. It was also customary for the Corporation to pay the parish clerk till 1690, when the following order is made: "It was agredd upon the sallary of $15^{li.}$ formerly pd Mr. Tho. Bell, the clarke of the Parish, should cease, & noe sallary or allowance to be pd to any succeeding clarke by the Towne Bailiff." This order is followed, two years afterwards, by the following: "Agreed upon, y^t y^e order made y^e 21 of November, 1690, be & is hereby reversed, & y^t ye sallary of five pounds p. ann. for ye reading of morning prayer, wch has been allowed out of ye town stock time out of mind, be hence forth continued & pd." The sexton is only once mentioned, in 1680, when it is "ordered to p'vide John Buckley, the sexton, a decent gown to attend the vicar of Wisbech and other ministers, who shall preach, to the pulpitt from time to time, the decent fashion and makinge whereof we refer to the direccon of Mr. Coldwell, o^r present vicar."[1]

The tower contains ten bells, and a set of chimes. Previous to 1823 there were only eight bells, when the whole were re-cast, and two fresh ones were presented by Dr. Jobson, the vicar.[2] The oldest of the former peal was dated 1566. In

(1) Corporation Records, v. 4.

(2) The new casting was opened on Friday, the 19th of December, 1823. The tenor bell weighs 21 cwt. 2 qrs. 15 lbs., and the whole peal 5 tons, 2 qrs. 5 lbs.

The following are the inscriptions on the bells:—

1st and 2nd.—Wm. Dobson, Downham, Norfolk, Fecit, 1823.

3rd.—Fear God and Honour the King.

4th.—Long live King George the Fourth.

5th and 6th.—Abrahamus Jobson, S.T.P. Vicarius, me Dono dedit, A.D., MDCCCXXIII.

7th.—Prosperity to the Town of Wisbech St. Peter, 1823.

8th.—LAUDO DEUM VERUM; PLEBEM VOCO; CONGREGO CLERUM; DEFUNCTOS PLORO; PESTEM FUGO; FESTA DECORO. 1823.

9th.
In wedlock's bands all ye who join,
With hands your hearts unite;
So shall our tuneful tongues combine
To laud the nuptial rite.

10th.—Abraham Jobson. Vicar; Wm. Swansborough and T. Moore, Churchwardens; William Dobson, Founder, 1823.

I to the church the living call,
And to the grave do summon all.

1615 we find the following regulations ordered to be observed in ringing the great bell: "Whosoever shall desire to have the greate bell in the steeple ronge out eyther in his sicknesse or otherwise, except in ringing a peale or peales, shall pay for the same so ofte as it is ronge out, the sume of iij$^{s.}$ iiij$^{d.}$ wherof xvj$^{d.}$ to be allowed for the ringinge, and ij$^{s.}$ to y^{e} use of y^{e} Towne, to be received by the towne baylife for y^{e} tyme beinge." From this extract it would appear that the Corporation had then very absolute control in the regulations of the church, to which they had perhaps a right, as it appears that the principal burden of providing for the church, which is now vested in the inhabitants, was undertaken by them. The next extract, which dates upwards of fifty years afterwards, shows that a church rate was then levied: still we perceive that the Corporation had not given up their contributions towards the support of the establishment: "1671. Ordered, the charge of new casting and hanginge the great bell of Wisbech be defrayed by the Town baylife out of the common stock of the Townshipp, for the general ease of the inhabitants in theire Church rate."[1] In 1662 we meet with another item which deserves extract: "Ordered, that the Towne bayliffe doe cause a close bedd & bedsted to be sett up in the Churchsteple for the Belman, for ringing the 4 of the clock bell in the morning;" and in the same year it is ordered, "that morninge prayer be read in the parrish church of Wisbech St. Peter's as of ancient time the same hath bene, after the tollinge of the bell att six a clocke in the morninge."[2]

"Wisbech is one of the oldest possessions of the church of Ely. In 1232 the living was a rectory, and valued at fifty marks,[3] twenty years before the first endowment of the vicarage; the Bishop of Ely being the patron of it. The old coucher book of Ely is said to prove that the church of Wisbech had in the year 1251 a tenth part of the money paid to the bishop for the agistment of stock. In 1252 Hugh de Northwold, Bishop of Ely, appropriated the church of Wisbech to the convent of Ely, and endowed the vicarage with

(1) Corporation Records, v. 4. (2) Ibid. (3) £33 6s. 8d.

all the small tithes.[1] And in 1275 Hugh de Balsham made a second endowment,[2] and assigned to the monks of Ely certain tithes of corn between the banks of Wisbech and the fields of Leverington, the rectory-house, and the house belonging to Kilhus chapel, and half the tithe of hay of the demesne; and he ordained that the vicar should have all the arable land belonging to the church, and the whole tithe of corn, hay, &c., from the fields and pasture grounds between the bank of Wisbech and the parish of Elm, and also the moiety of the tithes of all the demesnes, &c. When a taxation of the revenues of the clergy by Pope Nicholas took place in

(1) "The first endowment is as follows: To all the faithful in Christ to whom these presents shall come, Hugo de Norwold, by the grace of God, bishop of Ely, sendeth health in the Lord:—Know ye, that Mr. John de Cadamo, appointed parson of the church of Wisbech in our presence, hath given and granted to our beloved Mr. William de Norwold, the vacant vicarage of the aforesaid church of Wisbech, with all its appurtenances, reserving to himself the tithes of flax and wool; he also yielded to the same the foldage and piscary; also the tithe of all lambs, cheese, and butter; of geese, calves, pigs, and all the oblations and revenues of the whole altarage; also the manors, as well of the vicarage as of the chapel, which is from the fosse of the castle to the sea, and as far as it returns towards Elm. He also granted to the same (saving the tithes) two acres of land near the manor of the vicarage, and all the tithes of the mills, and the land he bought of the convent of Spinctus, (Spinney) for the service of the chapel, to hold of his favor. In testimony whereof we have, with the consent of the said Mr. John, caused our seal to be set to this present deed. Given at Downham upon the day of exultation of the Holy Cross, and in the year of our Lord 1252."

William de Norwold was bound to find a lamp burning before the high altar continually, from vespers until the whole service by night and day was finished.

(2) "The second endowment is as follows: To all the faithful in Christ to whom these presents shall come, Hugo, by the grace of God, bishop of Ely, sendeth health in the Lord:—Know ye, that the church of Wisbech being vacant, of which the collation doth of full right belong to us, we have assigned certain issues and profits belonging to the said church to the monks of Ely, for a certain use, viz., the tithes of corn between the bank of Wisbech and the fields of Leverington; the farm of the rector, with the farm of Killhus, and the granges standing thereon; the homage, with the whole yearly revenue of the same church, and a moiety of the hay of the land belonging to our manor, in the name of the parsonage. We, desirous of having regard to the burthen of William de Norwold, *vicar of the said church*, have resolved and ordained, that the *said vicar* and his successors, shall have and receive, in the name of the vicarage, the arable land belonging to the said church; the tithe of corn, hay, pasture, and fisheries, and all tithes whatsoever proceeding from the fields, meadows, pasture, or pasture grounds, between the bank of Wisbech and the parish of Elm, together with a moiety of the tithe of hay of the land belonging to our manor, and all the tithe of the hay of the said parish; saving always to the said vicar and his successors, all the profits of *Altarage* of the church of Wisbech, with the tithe of wool and flax, and all other yearly profits belonging to the same church, with this exception, that if the said lands, from which the monks receive the tithes of corn, shall be overflowed with waters, the said monks shall receive the tithes of flax, hay, and pasture, proceeding from off the said lands; and the said vicar and his successors, and the said monks, shall bear the charges of repairing the chancel in their proportions. In witness whereof our seal is affixed to these presents. Given at Downham, on the eve of the blessed apostle James, in the year of our Lord 1275.—By altarage is meant the tithes of wool, lambs, calves, pigs, and other small tithes, with the offerings due."

the year 1291, (sixteen years after the second endowment), the valuation appears by the exchequer as under:

	£.	s.	d.
Ecclesia de Wisbech	26	13	4
Vicaria ejusdem	6	13	4

"Disputes afterwards arising between the monks of Ely and the vicars of Wisbech, an appeal was made to John Fordham, the then bishop, to settle the same, who determined such disputes by an award, dated 1st October, 1420, which fully established the vicar's claim to tithe in its full extent.

"The high fen, containing 4387 acres, was not at the time of the endowment between the banks of Wisbech and the fields of Leverington, but Bishop Morton by his new leam from Peterborough to Guyhirn altered the course of the river, and made new banks. After the high fen, from being common and waste land, became drained and inclosed about the year 1664, it then for the first time produced corn, the tithe whereof was claimed by the dean and chapter, who have since enjoyed it.

"Several of the vicars, for many successive years, were contented to receive certain compositions for their tithes; but in the year 1803 the vicar instituted a claim, and made a formal demand of all the tithes in kind of the grass lands, and of all other vicarial tithes arising within the parishes of Wisbech St. Peter and Wisbech St. Mary, which he first submitted to the owners and occupiers of lands, who, however, set up a modus for exemption from such tithes. The parties, therefore, became at issue in the Court of Exchequer, and after a suit which lasted nearly five years, the claim of the vicar to tithe in kind was established; so that the vicarage is now estimated at £2000 per annum, and upwards.[1] while the rectory, which is in the hands of the dean and chapter of Ely, (and originally of the greater value), is not more than £1200.[2] The vicar has in his gift the chapel of Guyhirn, worth about £100 per annum."[3]

(1) Now estimated at £2500.

(2) The rectorial tithes are derived from about 11,000 acres. They were appropriated to the dean and chapter by Bishop Balsham, 1275. (3) Watson, pp. 244-247.

The VICARAGE, WISBECH

To the REVEREND HENRY FARDELL M.A. Vicar of Wisbech

The vicarage, which is an extensive modern building comprising spacious and beautiful apartments, is beautifully situated on the south side of the church. The grounds and gardens about it, which do not comprise more than four acres, are laid out with great taste. There are, besides, forty-seven acres of glebe land attached to the living, lying dispersed in four pieces.[1]

The churchyard, which is large, has for four years been disused as a burial-place. This had become absolutely necessary from its crowded condition; having, previously, been almost the sole burial-place for a gradually increasing population. Many years, however, before this resolution was adopted, it had been entertained; but a dispute having arisen between the parish and the vicar concerning their mutual rights, provided a new piece of ground were purchased, the half-completed contract for a new burial-ground was about fifteen years before it was finally settled. It was so far settled previously, however, that several acres of ground separated from the old churchyard by the vicarage and grounds, were purchased, and in 1832, about ten years before it was generally used, it had become the burial-spot of persons who died of the cholera during that year: at length the over-crowded condition of the old churchyard caused a general feeling that some new spot must be adopted for interment, and after a little more dispute the difference between the parish and the church was settled amicably, In 1840 the burial-ground was consecrated by Bishop Allen, and thenceforward the old churchyard was given up, except as a family burial-ground. The new ground, conveniently situated and tastefully laid out, has since been ornamented with an admirable service chapel, in the Early English style of architecture. This small edifice we need not say is a perfectly integrant specimen of style so far as the architecture is concerned, for it was designed by Professor Willis, and built under the directions of the late Mr. Basevi. It is thirty feet long by sixteen broad. Over the entrance, which is by a finely-moulded

(1) Watson's Wisbech.

well-proportioned doorway, is a small six-foiled window in a deep pointed arch, and a bell-turret raised on a small pedimental ledge set transversely to the roof, and rising above it. At the south end are three lancet windows, merely splayed in the interior. These, as well as the window over the door, are filled with beautiful stained glass. The lancet windows represent the crucifixion in the centre, with the Virgin in the right-hand light, and St. John in the left. In a vesica piscis, over the crucifixion the resurrection is represented, and, beneath, Christ bearing his cross. The angel, the winged lion, winged bull, and eagle,—emblems of the four evangelists,—are represented over the right and left hand figures. In the hexafoil over the door three saints, two angels, and the dove, are pourtrayed in the foliations, and Christ in the centre. There are also two other slits filled with stained glass. Though there is, perhaps, some slight departure from the style in introducing personal figures in stained glass connected with Early English architecture, we cannot wish these beautiful specimens were removed for the mere geometrical figures which are generally connected with this style. The floor of the chapel is of encaustic tiling, and there is a small carved lectern for reading the service.

This slight but elegant construction was raised by the proceeds of a very popular bazaar in 1843, under the patronage of the Earl and Countess of Hardwicke, and under the immediate direction of the vicar, the proceeds of which were further augmented by a subscription at the church after full cathedral service there; by a picture exhibition at the Court House; and by a concert at the Theatre, and a ball afterwards. Upwards of £800[1] were raised in this manner, for it

(1) The following statistical account was published at the time:

	£.	s.	d.
Taken at the Bazaar—In Gold	337	0	0
——— ——— ———In Silver	243	6	10
——— ——— ———In Notes	65	0	0
By Mrs. Fardell after the Bazaar	44	15	6
Queen Adelaide	10	0	0
The Earl of Hardwicke	20	0	0
Hugh Jackson, Esq.	20	0	0
The Dean and Chapter of Ely	50	0	0
Collection at the Church	53	14	7
Concert	40	0	0
	£883	16	11

exclusive of the proceeds of the Ball, Picture Exhibition, and other donations.

was enjoyed as a general fete and recreation, to which all the neighbourhood flocked with right hearty enthusiasm. It was perhaps, one of the most popular holidays which Wisbech ever enjoyed; and its purpose being for a permanent benefit and ornament to the town, can never be remembered otherwise than pleasingly.

When the trees which are planted over this cemetery get sufficiently shady, they will add much to its quiet and retired beauty. The tendency of the present age to give these last resting places natural and attractive aspects can only be looked on as an improvement upon the taste of former days, when the centres of towns were chosen as burial-spots, and the most culpable neglect rendered them places rather of disgust than of veneration.

Chapel of Ease.

Wisbech now contains about 10,000 inhabitants; and, as its population has been increasing for a series of years, the parish church—though aided by galleries, and seats in every imaginable corner—is only estimated to hold 1800 persons. Much of this space, is certainly unwisely frittered away upon large roomy seats, which are claimed as heritages, and very inadequately filled: yet the most prudent arrangement of a single edifice could hardly accommodate its proportional of the present population. This deficiency had long been felt; and, in 1826, the erection of a chapel of ease was seriously entertained, especially as Dr. Jobson, then vicar, offered to endow it "by the conveyance in fee simple of a real estate exceeding in value £5000."[1] So generous an offer was quickly responded to. The subject was entered on enthusiastically. The erection of the edifice—estimated at £7500 was proposed to be defrayed by shares of £50 each, to be repaid by the letting of sittings: £6000 was quickly raised by this means, and the building was entrusted to Mr. Wm. Swansborough as architect. It happened, unfortunately, that the period of erecting this chapel was a period

(1) Watson. This estate now yields about £400 per year.

in which the true principles of Gothic architecture were very ill understood. The enthusiasm which has followed up this interesting study of late years into its remote retirements—wresting every secret from it, and opening up all those conveniences and decorations which it had formerly compelled into subjection—was then unknown. If, therefore, Mr. Swansborough erred both in its construction and the style of this building, we must remember that his errors were the errors of his time. Few erections of this period can be referred to as worthy of imitation. The form adopted in this edifice is that of an octagon, with an elongation of its eastern side for a chancel, and an elongation of the lower story of its west front for a porch. A hexagonal buttress rises from each corner, and is carried above the roof, and terminates with a Tudor crocketed pinnacle. The porch is surmounted by a battlement, and flanked by an angular buttress which is carried up and terminates with a crocketed pinnacle. A string-course, unmarked by any peculiar style, divides the blank wall between the two stories into which the edifice is divided, and upon the roof is an open battlement formed of archets and quatrefoils. The architect placed an octagonal lantern upon the roof, and rising to the height of twenty-six feet above it, but the difficulty of providing adequate support for such a feature in such a situation made it fall into comparatively early decay; and, in 1846, the chapel-wardens came to the resolution of removing it, and substituting the present low embattled termination in lieu of it. This latter feature was designed by Mr. Buckler, and is merely a battlement perforated with quatrefoils, and surmounted with pinnacles, looking like a coronet on the edifice. The chapel is built of brick, faced in some parts with stone, and in others with plaster. It cost altogether about £10,000.

Perhaps it would be difficult, even among the absurdities of its day, to find a building combining so many and such remarkable examples of bad construction. The styles here collected together are about the worst examples of each, while the material is varied from white brick to stone, and from stone to plaster, in such a manner as to make meaner their natural mean association. With a neighbourhood abounding in good examples of church architecture, not one true principle is adopted; but wretched errors are gathered together as if to warn us how much money it may sometimes require to make form and style ridiculous. There is an octagon at Ely, and there is an octagon at Wisbech. The octagon at Ely is the praise of the world; the octagon at Wisbech is fortunately unknown, except to its inhabitants. The octagon at Ely, built by a pure artist upon the highest principles of beauty, was not able to bear a lantern of the same materials as its other parts. It was not, therefore, surprising that the lantern of Wisbech, built in remote imitation of it, gave early signs of weakness, especially as the Wisbech architect ventured on heavier materials than the Ely architect. Alan de Walsingham was unable to counterbalance the weak effect of a broken arch: this work was notwithstanding considered an aerial beauty, an elegant weakness, whose grace was more worthy of admiration than of imitation. No other architect ventured in the same track, though nothing, had it been successful, could have been better adapted for chapter-houses than the octagon and lantern. It is dangerous even for good architects to imitate a beauty where there is only a single example of it, since we may fairly conjecture that its singularity is its difficulty. The architect of the chapel at Wisbech had no such misgivings; and, without Alan de Walsingham's buttresses, he aspired to raise Alan de Walsingham's lantern in the air. The recent removal of this feature of the edifice showed how he accomplished his work. He made the sides of slate, the window frames of iron, the crockets of composition, and the pinnacles of wood; these he stuccoed over, and merely fastening his work to the roof with nails, by this means secured his lantern for sixteen years. Sixteen years are not much for a building, even a modern one; it is proportionally less for even a weak part of a church; but sixteen years must be considered an extraordinary age for such a piece of architecture as that we are now considering. It gave signs of decay for a year or two before it was removed, which was in 1846, and the present low construction was substituted, which is a better specimen of Mr. Buckler's taste than the Museum.

The interior of the chapel is hardly capable of more defence than the exterior. Its construction, though tending to draw the congregation round the speaker, is so mismanaged, that in some parts of the chapel, where the hearers are nearest the pulpit, it is with difficulty the words of the preacher can be distinguished. Two or three perceptible voices, glancing from different faces of the chapel, cross one another, and render either reading or preaching in such parts indistinct. The gallery looms over the floor of the chapel, making its paltry proportions appear less. The architect, in consequence of his unfortunate design, was obliged to place the pulpit in front of the chancel arch, thereby hiding all that part of the chapel from view; and sundry long cracks in this part give threatenings, before the edifice is twenty years old, of instability.

The chapel contains an organ of thirteen stops, built by Nicholson at a cost of £170, and erected in 1836. The general sittings are let at from ten to twelve shillings each per year: there are, besides, a number of free sittings. Service is performed here morning and evening.

We must not omit to mention a recent donation to the chapel by G. M. Lefever, Esq. It consists of an ancient metal chasing of the Ascension, and seems to be the copy of a picture by one of the early painters. The Redeemer is floating in the clouds bearing a banner with the cross. Soldiers in armour are beneath, one of whom is rushing forward, and another, shielding his eyes from the glory, endeavors to trace the progress of the Saviour through the clouds. The whole has been gilt and enclosed in a gothic frame, and now forms a very appropriate altar-piece to the chapel. Beneath the chasing is the following inscription:

"Presented to the Chapel of Ease for ever, by George Micklefield Lefever, Esq., the 30th day of September, 1847."

CHAPTER VI.

THE DISSENTERS.

THAT diversity of opinion so observable among mankind, especially upon theological and metaphysical subjects, became more prominent at the Reformation, when the right of private judgment in matters of religion, was recognised, and an examination of the Scriptures inculcated as a personal duty. This new privilege developed itself to a great extent during the reign of Charles I., when political rancour blended with polemical bitterness inflamed the passions of the people, till it issued in the death of the king and the overthrow of the church and monarchy. As might have been expected, the disputes which led to such a catastrophe were not only aggravated by that event, but greatly extended; hence, during the Commonwealth, the nation seemed to have been formed into a great debating society, in which the most extravagant opinions were advocated by sects which quickly disappeared to make way for others still more extravagant. The Restoration, which hushed for a time the turmoil of party, was far from healing the wounds which charity had received during the long reign of bitterness and strife. The Episcopalians, reinstated in all their power and emoluments, attempted the suppression of those opinions to which they attributed all the calamities that had befallen the constitution. With this view the Act of Uniformity was promulgated, compelling all ministers of the church to subscribe to certain articles on pain of losing their preferment. This arbitrary enactment tended only to defeat the object it was designed to promote, as by its operation two thousand ministers relinquished their livings rather than subscribe to the obnoxious articles, and who, on leaving the church, carried with them the sympathy of the people into almost every town in the kingdom, where meeting-houses were built, in which by their pathetic appeals to the people upon their privations they propagated more effectually the principles which it was the intention of the Act of Uniformity to suppress. Among the sects of this period the Presbyterian was the most important, both for its numbers and its wealth, as may be inferred from the size of their meeting-houses, some of which remain to the present time, though occupied by congregations professing doctrines differing widely from those of their founders. The sites chosen for these meeting-houses show the odium that attached to dissent from the established creed, as they are generally found in yards or lanes, removed from public observation. Even those built after the Revolution of 1688, which gave increased protection to dissenters from the church, were not in the situations usual in the present day, for though the law had cast its shield over them, public opinion still looked upon them with dislike, the expression of which the dissentients sought to avoid by retirement. The Presbyterian meeting-house in this town, which was built during the period at which we have glanced, was situated in a yard in Upper Hill Street, in which is now carried on the business of a currier. The Baptist meeting-house was in a situation still more obscure, being in what was called Place's Yard, accessible only by a narrow passage; while the Unitarian Chapel, originally built by a congregation of Baptists, shows that its founders avoided rather than sought observation. The times, however, have so far changed that dissenters from the church no longer shrink from public view, but erect their places of worship in situations as conspicuous as their circumstances will admit. In Wisbech, therefore, the more popular denominations are clustered together in the Crescent, a part of the town in which the wealthier classes reside.

In describing more particularly the various denominations which have established themselves in the town, we have thought advisable to allow each to speak for itself through its minister or leader. In doing this they are noticed according to what appears to be the priority of their claims to antiquity. The following account, furnished by Wm. Peckover, Esq., of the religious society with which he is connected, will be read with interest.

SOCIETY OF FRIENDS.

The Society of Friends was established at Wisbech in the time of the Protectorate, and (although, for many years past, few in numbers) has continued here ever since that period. About the years 1663 and 1664 the members suffered much persecution for their attendance of their meetings and refusal to take oaths, in common with their brethren in other parts of the kingdom, and the following extract from their records bespeaks the arbitrary spirit of those times:

"John Inds, late of Ely, was taken with several other Friends from a peaceable meeting on the sixteenth day of the second month, 1663, and sent to Wisbech Gaol, where he was kept prisoner for the space of three whole years."

Their meeting-house on the North Brink, which appears to have been originally two cottages, was converted to its present use in 1711. A burial-ground is attached, in which a grave, with the initials and date (I. S., aged 88—1742) planted over it in box, marks the burial-place of Jane Stuart, said to have been a natural daughter of King James II.[1]

An ancient burial-ground, situate in the parish of Walsoken, still belongs to the Society of Friends, but it has not been used for that purpose since the year 1711.

(1) The following account of Jane Stuart is extracted chiefly from the *Monthly Magazine* of February, 1810. Jane Stuart, supposed to have been a natural daughter of King James II., after renouncing the world and the splendour of courts, resided at Wisbech in Cam-

GENERAL BAPTISTS.

The Baptist Chapel, situated in Ely Place, belongs to the Society of General Baptists; so called from their maintaining the doctrine that Christ died, not for a part only of the human race, but that he is the propitiation for the sins of the whole world. The rise of this society in Wisbech is not known; it is probable that it originated during the time of the Commonwealth, about which period the General Baptists were numerous and active in various parts of Cambridgeshire. A number of persons of this persuasion appear to have met for worship, and to have supported the cause for some time without being regularly organised into a church. Mr. John Milles, one of the leading friends, wrote, February 20th, 1655, to the church at Fenstanton, at that time numerous and flourishing, giving an account of the congregation, and earnestly entreating them to send faithful messengers "to do the work of the Lord, and to administer his ordinances to those amongst them whose hearts were free and ready to embrace the truth." John Denne and Edmund Mayle were sent in April, and received a hearty welcome from the friends. In September of the same year they paid a second visit, and at the request of the congregation ordained elders and dea-

bridgeshire. It is to be regretted that few memorials remain of her; but two ancient and respectable inhabitants, now deceased, "have related to the writer of this the following incidents: When she first came she sought employment by standing, as is usual at this day with laborers who want work, at the foot of the bridge, where in hay-time and harvest the farmers resort every morning to hire. She selected for her abode a cellar in a part of the town called the Old Market, where she spun worsted, to dispose of which she regularly had a stall on the market-day. Being once thus employed, she recognised by the arms and livery a coach and attendants going to the principal inn, (the Rose and Crown,) near to which her stall stood, upon which she immediately packed up her worsted, retired to her cell, and carefully concealed herself. The owner, who was said to be the Duke of Argyle, endeavoured to find her, but without effect. She constantly attended, when in health, the meeting of the Society of Friends in Wisbech, was humble and exemplary in her conduct, well esteemed by her neighbours, invariably avoided all conversation relative to her family connexions, and when in the freedom of intercourse any expression inadvertently escaped leading to an inquiry, she stopped short, seemed to regret having disclosed so much, and silenced further research. She read the New Testament in Greek, but even this circumstance was discovered accidentally by an unexpected call."—Another account mentions that she told two ministers of the Society of Friends who called upon her, that she enjoyed such contentment and peace, that she would not leave her cell and spinning-wheel to be Queen of England. She had been at most of the European Courts, particularly the Hanoverian and Prussian, and she mentioned she had often played with the Pretender on her knees, when he was a little white-headed boy.

cons, chosen by and from amongst themselves. About thirty years afterwards in the year 1686, James Marham, who had been the instrument of raising a General Baptist Church at Holbeach, removed to Walpole Bell, in the neighbourhood of Wisbech. He had not been settled in the place three weeks before the parish officers waited upon him requiring him to attend the established church, or appear before the justice and rector to answer for his neglect. Marham adopted the latter alternative, and was closely examined by the magistrate and the clergyman for upwards of four hours. The result not proving satisfactory another day was appointed for the conference; meanwhile, the proclamation for liberty of conscience was issued, and the rector declined to engage further in the matter. The same week Marham opened his house for preaching. In time a church was formed, which, at the Revolution in 1688, numbered about thirty members. It is highly probable that before the close of that century the congregations at Wisbech and Walpole were united in one society, which eventually was denominated from the market-town, rather than from the hamlet. In the year 1697 the General Baptists built a meeting-house at Wisbech: it was situated in Place's Yard, near the canal. Mr. Henry Place, a woollen draper in the town, accommodated them with the ground. The present chapel was erected in 1803; the gradual increase of the congregation has rendered repeated enlargements necessary: it will now seat from seven to eight hundred persons. A plot of land in Crescent Passage was purchased for a burial-ground in 1823, over part of which was erected in 1836, the commodious building belonging to this society, in which the Sabbath School is taught, and occupied during the week by the Girls' British School.

The Rev. Joseph Freestone, known as the author of "Encouragement for Travellers to Zion," and other publications, was the minister from 1783 to 1799, when he removed to Hinckley. He was succeeded, in 1802, by the Rev. Joseph Jarrom, who continued for more than thirty years the able and devoted pastor of the church, and for many years conducted an institution belonging to the denomination for educating young men for the ministry. His friends have erected a neat marble tablet to his memory in the chapel, and a monument in the General Cemetery, containing the following inscription:

ERECTED
as a Memorial of the
REV. JOSEPH JARROM
who was thirty-three years
PASTOR OF THE
BAPTIST CHURCH, ELY PLACE,
and twenty-five years
THEOLOGICAL AND CLASSICAL TUTOR
of the General Baptist
ACADEMY.
—o—
His unaffected piety,
robust intellect, sound judgment,
extensive learning and profound
knowledge of the Scriptures,
eminently qualified him for the
offices he sustained; while the
gentleness of his deportment,
the kindness of his disposition,
the wisdom of his counsels, and
the transparent integrity of his
character, caused him to be
universally esteemed and
venerated.
HE WAS BORN
October 7th, 1774,
AND DIED
September 5th, 1842.

The present minister is the Rev. James Carey Pike, who commenced his stated labours in November, 1837. A valuable institution was established by this congregation in 1818, called "The Christian Fund," for providing relief in time of sickness. It is formed on the most liberal and unsectarian basis. At the last annual report there were 254 members, and an accumulated fund of upwards of £1300.

INDEPENDENTS.

Castle Square Chapel, which stands at the west entrance to the Crescent, is occupied by a congregation of Protestant Dissenters of the Independent denomination. The foundation stone was laid by the present pastor, the Rev. William Holmes, formerly of Old College, Hoxton, on the 4th of May, 1818. It has three galleries, and a basement appropriated to the use of the Sunday School connected with this place of worship. It is capable of accommodating 700 persons, its average attendance being between five and six hundred, and the members of the church are at the present time nearly 200 in number. The chapel, and also the adjoining dwelling-house, designed as a residence for the minister, were built by voluntary contributions, at a cost of upwards of £2000. In order to the entire removal of the expense incurred, £110 have been raised by the congregation in the course of the past year. There are two branch congregations of the Independents in the villages of Gorefield and Wisbech St. Mary's, in each of which a small place of worship has been erected, and the religious services are conducted by a Home Missionary, who is sustained in part by the villagers among whom he labours, they contributing one moiety of his stipend, and the parent church and congregation at Wisbech the other. Flourishing Sunday Schools exist at each of those places.

The doctrinal sentiments of the Independents harmonise for the most part with the articles of the Church of England, but in their ecclesiastical polity and discipline they materially differ. They reject all creeds and confessions drawn up by the wisdom of man—regarding the bible, and the bible alone, as the standard of their faith and practice. They acknowledge no allegiance to diocesan bishops or synods, but declare that "one is their Master, even Christ, and they all are brethren." They administer baptism to those who make a credible profession of faith in Christ, not having previously received it, and also to their infant offspring, but dispense with the sponsor's vow. They allow those only who are received into Christian fellowship with their community to partake of the Sacrament of the Lord's Supper, and do not acknowledge any persons as regular members of their society until certain delegates appointed for that purpose are satisfied of their piety, and that their conduct adorns their Christian profession.

BAPTISTS.

There is a society of Baptists who have a neat chapel for public worship in Upper Hill Street. Being as much isolated from the other denominations as the Society of Friends, this society does not come under the name of either General or Particular Baptists. They baptise by immersion such as make a creditable profession of faith in Jesus Christ; and they believe that the scriptures teach the doctrine of eternal and unconditional election, while the scriptures make it equally plain that it is the will of God that all men—in the broadest sense of the term "all"—should be saved, and come to the knowledge of the truth. They maintain, also, that no person who is not walking in obedience to the commandments of Jesus Christ has a right to presume he is in a state of salvation. This society formerly occupied the chapel in Deadman's Lane, and in the history of Wisbech published by Mr. Watts, in 1834, its establishment is carried back to the year 1722; but when the Unitarian doctrines began to be preached in that chapel in 1792, by the late Mr. Richard Wright, in order to avoid contention about the chapel, those who objected to the Unitarian doctrines separated from the rest, and built their present chapel in Upper Hill Street, where they have since continued to meet for worship. Their number, as to those who stand in the particular relation of membership, is about 80, but the congregation assembling in their chapel for public worship is about 300. They have a small cemetery for the dead, neatly laid out with shrubs and flowers, in New Walsoken.

CALVINISTS.

This religious body met for several years in a large room known by the name of the "Wool Hall," but in 1837 the friends built their present place of worship, called "Zion Chapel." The congregation consists of from 80 to 100, about 40 of whom are members. The present minister, Mr. Edmund

Wilkin, officiated for many years alternately at Wisbech and Guyhirn, but now confines his labors to Wisbech.

The founder of this denomination appears to have been David Culy, the son of a French refugee, who fled from France, it is supposed, about the time of the revocation of the Edict of Nantes. We learn from traditionary accounts that he commenced preaching at Guyhirn and other places in the Isle of Ely about the time of the Revolution of 1688, when he composed his hymns, which were published in parts in 1692-3-4. Being only a laboring man, his style and bold manner of preaching roused the attention of the authorities, and he was summoned to appear at the Sessions' House, Wisbech, to answer for himself, touching the doctrines he preached; but, after a long hearing, he was acquitted. Some time afterwards he was taken by the press-gang down to Lynn, and put on board the tender lying there, when he commenced singing hymns, which species of exercise so annoyed the officers and crew that they put him on shore, and he found his way back to the Isle of Ely, where his friends resolved on making him a freeholder to protect him against a repetition of this kind of persecution. The piece of land purchased for this purpose was in Hobbs' Lots, and was known for many years as Culy's Lot. After this time he left the Isle of Ely, and settled at Billingham, in Lincolnshire, where he died, and was buried in an obscure corner of the churchyard of that village.

UNITARIANS.

The meeting-house in Deadman's Lane, occupied by this denomination, was erected on a piece of ground purchased in 1692 by Joseph Brown, William Rix, and others, for the use of a congregation of Baptists in Wisbech who held the doctrine of eternal election; but as this is the only tenet mentioned in the original deed, it is not easy to see wherein they differed from other denominations in the town and neighbourhood. The above-named Mr. Rix, who officiated as minister, appointed Samuel and Jacob Norris and others a new trust, after which little is known till about 1776, when Mr. Richard Wright and Mr. Fisher were joint ministers of the congregation. Shortly after this Mr. Wright introduced some notions about the sonship of Christ which led to much discussion, and ultimately to a division, one party adhering to Mr. Wright and the other to Mr. Fisher, who established the congregation in Upper Hill Street, now under the care of Mr. Robert Reynoldson. Mr. Wright then avowed himself an Unitarian, and was for several years employed as a missionary under the direction of the "London Unitarian Fund Society" to spread the doctrines held by that body in various parts of the kingdom. In consequence of this engagement he gave up his charge at Wisbech, where he had raised a considerable number of hearers, by whom he was much respected. For several years after his resignation the congregation was left without a regular minister, and the attendance materially decreased: in 1816 it began to revive, and continued so till 1840, since which time it has gradually declined. Mr. M. A. Moon is the present minister.

WESLEYAN METHODISTS.

This society takes its name from John Wesley, Fellow of Lincoln College, Oxford, who, with George Whitfield and other members of the same University, formed a society for reading the scriptures and prayer about the year 1729, which, from the strictness of its rules, obtained for them the name of Methodists. Soon after they commenced itinerant preaching, and both Wesley and Whitfield embarked for America, where they were eminently successful in making converts. On their return to England a difference arose between them about the doctrines taught by Calvin and Arminius, which led to a separation, and distinct societies were formed under the names of their respective founders. Whatever might be the comparative merits of these two great men, the superiority of John Wesley has been evinced in that system of discipline he established among his followers, under which they have kept together and increased in number beyond all modern example. Their introduction into this town and their present state is furnished by one of the congregation.

The first Methodist preachers who visited Wisbech were Mr. Ashmead and Mr. Charles Kyte, from the Lynn Circuit; this was about the year 1789. The market-place was their first place of worship, where they preached amidst showers of stones and mud. About 1795 they rented a barn, called "Bell's Barn," opposite Gaol Lane, very near to those cottages recently erected by Mr. Cook. After occupying the barn for some time they purchased the old thatched building in Deadman's Lane, now occupied by Mr. Adams as a school, where they continued to preach till 1803, when they removed to the situation they now occupy in the Crescent. In 1812 they commenced a Sunday School, which was for a considerable time the only one in the town. In 1835 the chapel was taken down and considerably enlarged. The number of persons comprising the congregation is about 600: the chapel is capable of accommodating about 1000. The number of children upon the books of the Sunday School is 127; viz., 74 boys, and 53 girls.

PRIMITIVE METHODISTS.

This society professes to restore Methodism to what it was in the days of Wesley. They originated in Yorkshire about twenty-seven years ago under the leadership of Hugh Bourn and others, who by their zeal and perseverance succeeded in establishing a conference, district meetings, and circuits, and extending their labors to almost every part of the kingdom; and such has been their success that they now number nearly 90,000 members. They visited Wisbech about 1824, and for some time preached in obscure rooms, or in the open air: in 1838 they purchased Providence Chapel, in New Walsoken, where they now meet, which will accommodate nearly 400 persons. Connected with the chapel is a room in which a Sunday School is taught; the number of children under instruction amounts to 160 of both sexes.

CHAPTER VII.

PUBLIC AND OTHER CHARITIES.

PERHAPS few towns in the kingdom have more largely participated in the charitable bequests of pious and benevolent individuals than the town of Wisbech. In noticing these bequests we shall not enter upon the question of their effects upon the habits and conduct of those classes whom it was the intention of the donors to relieve. Upon this philosophers are divided in opinion; but, while human nature remains the same, and the experience of mankind accords with the Scripture declaration, that "it is more blessed to give than to receive," the number of givers and receivers will be little affected by the conflicting speculations of political economists. It may, however, be necessary to notice the errors into which the unreflecting are apt to fall when comparing the charitable feelings of past ages with the present. In casting their eyes over the charitable institutions of Wisbech, they perceive that by far the greater number were founded prior to the eighteenth century; hence, they too hastily conclude that the benevolent feelings have given way to those more selfish and mercenary. This change, however, when properly inquired into, will be found to be more apparent than real, and that the balance in favor of the present age greatly preponderates. In proof of this view of the subject it will be sufficient to refer to the establishment of schools in every town and village throughout the kingdom, in many of which the children are clothed as well as taught, and encouraged in their studies by those who furnish the means of "training them up in the way they should go." The numerous associations and societies that have been formed during the present century to ameliorate the condition of humanity, not only at home but abroad, loudly testify that charity still holds a place in the human breast; and, as if to show how strong this feeling is in the English people, the wants and woes of Ireland seem to have been permitted; for there can be no doubt that the magnitude and variety of those benevolent efforts—in which the people of Wisbech heartily joined—are without a parallel in the history of the world.[1] We now proceed to notice the various bequests that have, from time to time, been made to the town of Wisbech for the relief of poverty under its various modifications.

Those of an early date are necessarily involved in considerable obscurity, being transmitted from the Guild of the Holy Trinity, who, prior to the Reformation, were the guardians and administrators of the various charities belonging to the town. As early as 1476 an order is made for "all the buildings of the Guild to be repaired where defective, and principally a certain new building called the Almshouses." From this and some other incidental notices in the public Records it has been concluded that the Almshouses here referred to are those which formerly stood on the north side of the church, known by the name of King John's Almshouses, and which were taken down in 1832 to widen the street at that point.

Mrs. STURMYN gave, in 1610, to the Capital Burgesses £100 to erect a Market-house, and also £100 to erect four Almshouses for aged persons to live in. With this latter

(1) The subscriptions at Wisbech for the Scotch and Irish, in 1847, amounted to upwards of £1000.

sum four houses were erected on the piece of ground on which the old House of Correction and Shire Hall now stand. In 1810, being much decayed, they were taken down, and six other Almshouses erected by the Capital Burgesses on a site near the church, opposite the National School for Boys, on which is the following inscription: "These six Almshouses were erected by the Burgesses of the Town of Wisbech, A.D. 1813."

In 1631, Dr. HAWKINS, who was a native of Wisbech, and died in London, by his will gave £300 for erecting certain Almshouses, which were situated near to those erected 1813 by the Burgesses of the town. In 1834 it became a question with the Corporation whether the site upon which Hawkins's Almshouses stood could not be sold at a rate that would be advantageous to the charity. After some discussion it was resolved to expose them for sale by public auction, which was accordingly done. With the proceeds of this sale new buildings were erected for the accommodation of twelve poor persons, by the Capital Burgesses in 1835, on a piece of ground near the gate leading to the Church Cemetery. A stone in the centre of the building contains the following inscription: "Hawkins's and King John's Almshouses were rebuilt by the Burgesses of Wisbech, anno domini, 1835. Henry Leach, Esq., Town Bailiff."

Mrs. MAYER'S Asylum is an institution of a higher class than those already described, and evinces not only the benevolent intention of the donor, but also the honorable feeling of Hugh Jackson, Esq., who was appointed residuary legatee and executor of Mrs. Mayer's will. The late Mrs. Judith Mayer, of Wisbech, by her will, dated May 20th, 1811, and who died in the month of September following, gave to Robert Walpole, Esq., and Hugh Jackson, Gent., £500 to be laid out in the erection of an asylum to be called after her name, "for the reception of such poor persons in Wisbech as may happen to be afflicted with palsy, rheumatism, gout, blindness, or any other complaint, to render them objects of compassion; and to the Capital Burgesses, the Vicar, and Churchwardens, the sum of £1200 in trust to apply the dividends (except £5 towards keeping such building in repair) for the benefit of such poor persons whose bodily afflictions and meritorious conduct rendered them fit objects. She also gave £400 further—making altogether £2100—the interest of one-half of the said £400 to be distributed among such of the poor of Wisbech as the Capital Burgesses, Vicar, and Churchwardens should deem proper objects; and the interest of the other half to be expended in the purchase of coals for the persons dwelling in the other almshouses. The humane intention of the testatrix in this noble bequest was in danger of being defeated, as by the Statute of Mortmain of 9 Geo. II., c. 36, the will became void, and a question arose as to whom the several sums of £500 and £1200 belonged,—whether to her next of kin, or to her residuary legatee, Hugh Jackson, jun., Esq., of Wisbech, and it being found that the latter was of right entitled to them, he generously determined to fulfil Mrs. Mayer's intentions. Accordingly, he erected five comfortable tenements, at an expense of £744, which he conveyed to trustees, and endowed with £1120 Five per Cent. Annuities, purchased with the £1200 after payment of the legacy duty of ten per cent. The names of the trustees were John Goddard Marshall, Esq., of Elm, the Rev. Jeremiah Jackson, of Wisbech St. Peter's, (now of Elm), and Robert Gaye, of Wisbech St. Peter's, Gent. In this case we have a striking example of generous feeling, which adds to the interest of the institution; and though, strictly speaking, it does not come under the designation of a public charity, yet it is virtually such, as the trustees have evinced the same benevolent and enlarged feelings that prompted the original foundation of the charity.

Besides the almshouses referred to above, there are five situated at the back of the Crescent, in the lane leading from the Churchyard to Deadman's Lane, built and endowed by Mr. Joseph Medworth, who purchased the Castle estate, and built upon it the range of houses called the Crescent. The inmates (five poor women above 50 years of age) were appointed by Mr. Medworth himself during his life, but after his decease the duty of appointment was vested in certain trustees named in his will.

There formerly existed other Almshouses, which have been pulled down, and are no longer appropriated to their original purposes; but, from the character of the Ten Men as managers of the public charities, there is reason to conclude that none of these buildings have been diverted from their original object without an equivalent.

The sum of £3 15*s*. is annually distributed under the charter of Edward VI. amongst the poor. Under the administration of the Ten Men this was called the "Town Bailiff's Gift."

BERTHO EDWARDS gave by will, in 1583, the interest of £10 to be distributed yearly to the poor by the Ten Men.

JOHN STREGYTT gave by will, in 1592, £2 to buy the Book of Martyrs.

WILLIAM SCOTREL, in 1626, gave by deed 12 acres of land in Wisbech St. Mary's, the rent to be paid to the churchwardens of Wisbech St. Peter's, and to be distributed by them in relieving the most necessitous poor of this place.

THOMAS PARKE, Esq., in 1628, gave by will his house in Ship Lane, called the Bell Inn,[1] with all the buildings

(1) The Corporation were desirous of purchasing the Bell Inn and two tenements adjoining to improve the road and the river; the Charity Trustees were willing to sell them. An order was made by the Court of Chancery on the 18th April, 1842, enabling the Trustees to sell to the Corporation for £1200. They conveyed the premises for that price, by deed dated 22nd July, 1842, to Wm. Peckover, Esq., as a Trustee for the Corporation (the premises being copyhold). The Corporation then re-sold part of the site and all the materials

thereto belonging, to provide shoes and hose for the poor of Wisbech for ever. He also gave 28 acres of land in Elm to increase the stipend of the master of the Grammar School.

ROBERT LOVICK, in 1635, gave six acres of land in Terrington St. John's, to pay £3 10*s.* for preaching seven sermons between Easter and Whit Sunday.

ETHELDRED PARKE, the widow of Thomas Parke, gave 5 acres of land in Wisbech, out of the rents of which 13*s.* 4*d.* was to be paid for a sermon on the 2nd of November, the residue to provide gowns for three poor women annually. She also gave 15 acres of land in Emneth, out of the rents of which £7 was to be paid yearly for sermons on saint days.

JOHN CRANE, who was a native of Wisbech, but practised as an Apothecary at Cambridge, was a man esteemed for his extensive benevolence. He gave at his death £3000 for charitable uses, in which several towns, including Wisbech, largely shared. By his will, dated June 26th, 1651, he gave a certain inn called the Black Bull,[1] in Wisbech,

of the buildings, the purchaser giving bond to remove the buildings and throw open the unsold part of the site. The gross cost of the improvement was as follows:

			£. s. d.
Purchase-money and interest thereon			1203 18 10
Fine and fees on admission of a Trustee for the Corporation			99 8 10
Enfranchisement of the Estate			290 11 8
Expenses			91 10 7
			1685 9 11
Towards which was received for sale of materials and part of site		905 0 0	
Rent after purchase		16 10 0	
Bank interest		0 9 0	
		921 19 0	
Leaving the net cost only £763 10*s.* 11*d.* which was thus raised:			
The Corporation, from General Funds	254 10 4		
The same, from Port and Harbour Fund	254 10 4		
The Surveyors of the Highways	254 10 3		
		763 10 11	
			1685 9 11

Out of the purchase-money of £1200 the Charity Trustees, under the order of the Court, paid their costs of the proceedings relative to the sale, which amounted to £130 8*s.* 10*d.*—and under the same order they invested the residue—£1069 11*s.* 2*d.*—in the purchase of £1062 17*s.* 11*d.* Stock in the new £3 10*s.* 0*d.* per cent. Annuities, which are now reduced to £3 5*s.* 0*d.* per cent.

(1) Now called the New Inn.

with outbuildings thereto belonging; "the one half of the revenue to amend the schoolmaster's wages of the Free School, and the other moiety to be laid out at the best time of the year to buy corn and firing to be given to the poor of the same town about Christmas, or New-Year's-Day." He also further enjoins his executors "to buy sixty pounds a year of good land, or tenements, so as the tenants may have a good pennyworth to pay willingly their rent ... And I desire my executors to take good heed in the letting it in good honest men's hands, and able men, as feoffees in trust, or as they shall think safest to be bestowed. I think Wisbech men very safe: the ten men corporate of Wisbech, or as my executors shall think best." He then gives instructions that the rents shall be applied during every five years successively to the University of Cambridge, and the towns of Wisbech, Cambridge, King's Lynn, and Ipswich. The £60 are "to be lent freely to three young men to help to set them up, they putting in good security to pay it back to the ten men, or others in trust, at the twenty years' end; and that then it be lent to other three men in like order, they putting in good security to repay it at the twenty years' end." And he further declared in his will that when the rents should form a fund larger than was required for such loans at the stipulated times, that it "be given and bestowed upon honest poor men that be in prison for debt, or old women, or the relief of poor men in want, or to relieve them out of prison for debt, desiring them intrusted in this business, as they will answer it before God, that they relieve the most honest, godliest, and religious persons, men and women, that have lived well, and had a good report, being fallen into decay by some extraordinary occasion, and not to give it to dissembling hypocritical persons." He also gave 40s. to each town where the money was bestowed "to have a sermon that year to invite other men to do the like."

The money was laid out in the purchase of an estate at Fleet, in Lincolnshire, consisting of 181A. 3R. 37P., the rents of which are appropriated to the University of Cambridge and the four towns mentioned in the will in equal proportions, the town of Wisbech receiving the rents every fifth year. The first payment of such rents and profits to the Ten Men corporate of Wisbech was made in 1660, at which time the property was let at £62 per annum, from which £4 2s. having been deducted for taxes allowed to the tenants, there remained £57 18s. applicable to the purpose intended. Of this money 40s. were paid for the commemoration sermon, and the remainder was lent on August 26th, in that year, in two sums of £20 each and one of £15 18s., to three young men of the town towards setting them up, for the term of twenty years without interest. As the rents came into the possession of the Capital Burgesses in their turn, they were applied in sums of £20 until the stock so employed amounted to £200, which from that time to this has been transferred from hand to hand, and is now on loan to ten several persons, pursuant to the will of the founder.

Since the repeal of the law for imprisonment for debt, that portion of the funds applicable to the relief of poor men from prison is now applicable to other purposes, and the surplus is distributed in sums varying from 5s. to 20s. during the month of February, among persons who have fallen into decay, and other classes, according to a list revised annually.

LORD VISCOUNT SAYE and SELE, in 1656, gave £100, the interest to be expended annually in providing clothing for poor people.

WILLIAM HOLMES gave by will, in 1656, £200 to be lent, in sums of £10 for three years without interest, to poor tradesmen. He also gave £400 to be invested in land for the maintenance of two scholars at Magdalen College, Cambridge. This sum was expended in the purchase of 40 acres of land at Holbeach, which, at that time, produced a rent of £20 per annum, but is now let on lease at £80 per annum. The balance in the treasurer's hands, on the 1st of September, 1847, was £230, and the amount of the Magdalen

College Fund was £169. There was also the sum of £70 outstanding on seven notes of £10 each.

There is one scholar at College at this time who receives the benefit of this bequest; as there had been no appointment for several years previously, the funds had increased considerably, so that it became a question with the Trustees whether the whole should be given to one, or additional appointments be made, and apportion the income among them. It was, however, considered doubtful whether they could make any of the proposed alterations without the sanction of the Lord Chancellor, in whose court it was formerly ordered: "That all future unappropriated funds shall be invested in the Three per cent. Consols."

Secretary THURLOE, in 1658, gave £150, the interest to be applied towards putting out poor children apprentice; he also gave £50 to purchase books for the church library, and £50 towards making a road "from the corn market to the little sluice."

RICHMOND GIRLING, in 1658, directed that £2, out of the rents of certain lands in Stradbroke, Suffolk, should be distributed every tenth year among the poor of Wisbech. This will be due in 1848.

Mrs. MIDDLECOAT, in 1658, gave £2 yearly for six sermons on Wednesdays in Lent.

Mr. HENRY PIERSON, in 1664, gave the greater part of his books to the church library.

RICHARD ROYCE, in 1669, gave 16 acres of land in Wisbech Fen, the rents to be applied to the purchase of a piece of plate for the church, and afterwards to purchase annually clothing for poor widows.

ALICE THROCMORTON, in 1678, gave the interest of £25 to be expended in clothing for poor people.

The BISHOP of ELY, in 1695, gave the Shambles' estate to provide clothing for the poor. The Shambles were taken down in 1810, and £500, the produce, invested in the funds.

RICHARD LOAKE bequeathed £100; the interest to be applied in clothing five poor widows or housekeepers.

Mrs. ELIZABETH VINCENT, by will in 1717, left £2 each yearly to three poor widows of Wisbech.

Mrs. ELIZABETH WRIGHT, a native of Wisbech, was a liberal benefactress to the poor. By her will, dated 29th January, 1729, she gave estates of the value of £400 per annum; £12 of which she directed should be applied to the benefit of the Charity School for Girls, which sum has since been increased—by the authority of the Court of Chancery—to £40 per annum; and the profits of the messuage and premises near the Bridge, amounting to upwards of £60 per annum, to be applied to the benefit of the Charity School for Boys. Her estate in Sutton, containing about 40 acres, she gave for the exclusive benefit of "honest necessitous women, that have lived in good credit and reputation, and attend at church." The unappropriated funds arising from her other estates are placed at the discretionary disposal of the trustees,[1] and are devoted to any benevolent object that presents itself

(1) In 1847 this charity was distributed in the following manner:

	£.	s.	d.
Annual Rent of House near the Bridge to the Boys' Charity School........	60	0	0
Additional Sum given under decree of Court of Chancery to Boys' and Girls' Charity Schools	60	0	0
For Sermons annually in Wisbech Church on St. Barnabas and St. Paul's days	2	2	0
To 10 widows of good reputation, who attend church, 40s. each	20	0	0
To 40 ditto, 20s. each	40	0	0
To 50 ditto, 10s. each..	25	0	0
To 5 aged men, 20s. each	5	0	0
To 10 ditto, 10s. each	5	0	0
To 152 poor families 7s. 6d. each	57	0	0
To 192 ditto, 5s......	48	0	0
Attendants' remuneration	1	5	0
Gratuity to one boy leaving National School Annually	5	0	0

The following are the Trustees who have the management of this Charity: Rev. Jeremiah Jackson, Elm; Rev. Henry Fardell, Wisbech; James Usill, Esq., Wisbech; Wm. Goddard Jackson, Esq., Wisbech; John Bellamy, Esq., Wisbech.

to their notice. This charity is distributed annually about Christmas.

In 1793, JOHN BAXTER, by his will, gave to his wife the use of all his real and personal property during her life, and, after her decease, he directed that the same should be divided among her children; and, in case she died without issue, he empowered his executor to sell all his property to the best advantage, and deposit the money, amounting to £1386 capital stock, in the English Funds; after the death of the executor—who was allowed to enjoy the interest during his life—he left the following instructions for its disposal: "I give and bequeath to the Capital Burgesses of Wisbech Saint Peter's all the interest arising from such property.... for the uses hereinafter mentioned: that is to say, to allow annually ten pounds each to such poor old man or woman, as far as my property will allow, totally incapacitated from labour, as shall be by them thought fit and proper objects, and with this injunction, that they shall constantly attend divine worship every Sunday, and should they not punctually and strictly attend to this desire, to discontinue the charity to such person or persons so neglecting or refusing to comply with the same." The relief afforded by this charity is, perhaps, more felt than any of the others—with the exception of Mrs. Mayer's—as it lightens the pressure of poverty and smooths the descent into the grave. There are eight poor persons who now receive the proceeds of this charity.

Mrs. JANE BELLAMY, widow of John Bellamy, Esq., gave by will £200, and directed her executors to apply it to any charitable purpose which they might deem most worthy; it was, therefore, applied to the Charity School for Boys.

GEORGE SWAINE, Esq., in 1829, gave £400 Three per Cent. Consols, the dividend to be expended in body linen for the poor.

Mrs. ELIZABETH STEVENS, in 1838, gave by will £500, the interest to be distributed annually among poor widows in sums of one pound each.

STEED GIRDLESTONE, Esq., in 1841, purchased £100 stock in the Three-per-cent. Consols in the names of the Charitable Trustees, and directed that the interest should be annually expended in providing a dinner on Christmas Day for poor families in the town of Wisbech, each family to receive seven pounds of beef. He reserved the right of nominating twelve families yearly during his life, and the trustees to nominate others as far as the dividends would allow.

In addition to the various public charities already noticed, are several associations for the promotion of specified objects. Among these are the *Little and the Great Dorcas Charities*, which are chiefly supported by annual subscriptions and donations, and are managed by committees of ladies. Subscribers receive a certain number of tickets, in proportion to their subscriptions, which they distribute among such poor persons as are thought proper objects. The holders of tickets are allowed to select such articles of clothing as may be required, for which they pay only half the value. This method of distribution was deemed more favorable to the promotion of industrious habits among the recipients, and the benefits may be estimated by an extract from the Annual Report of 1847, by which it appeared that "550 Garments of various kinds, and 4670 yards of flannel, calico, prints, &c., had been disposed of to 580 poor persons." The late Dr. Jobson paid over to the Corporation £1000, the interest of which he directed should be given to this charity.

The Grammar School.

At what period the Wisbech Grammar School was established is involved in some obscurity, although the name of Jacob Cresner, as master, occurs so early as 1446. The probability is that the Guild supported a Grammar School among its other charities, as all religious houses prior to the Reformation were schools of learning, in which the neighbours that desired it might have their children taught grammar and church music. But the obscurity which hangs over this institution in its foundation and early progress was dispelled by the charter granted by Edward VI. in 1549, which ordains "that there should be in the town of Wisbech a school or place of learning for the instruction of boys and young men in grammatical knowledge and polite learning, and also a schoolmaster learned in the Latin and Greek languages, and imbued with virtuous morals, to the end that he, the boys, and young men whomsoever thither resorting and coming together, in grammatical knowledge and the Greek and Latin tongues should freely without any exaction institute, teach, and imbue, and that he a salary and stipend of twelve pounds from the inhabitants of the aforesaid town should annually have and receive, as by the letters patent among other things therein contained more fully doth appear." The time at which this charter was given being favorable to the extension of learning, we find that many persons were induced to contribute by gifts of money or lands to this object. It is stated in the old Records that William Bulman gave a plot of ground for the school-house in 1549, the same year in which the charter of Edward VI. was granted; and, afterwards, laws were enacted to enable persons to give lands for the benefit of the public schools in which were taught the Latin and Greek languages and the principles of the Reformation. As might have been expected, several individuals in Wisbech and its vicinity evinced their zeal in the cause of religion and learning by liberal bequests. Thomas Parke gave by will in 1628 twenty acres of land in the parish of Elm for the use of the schoolmaster; and, in 1657, John Crane left a moiety of an estate called the Black Bull "to amend the schoolmaster's wages."

The charter granted by Charles II. confirms that of Edward VI., and adds "that the schoolmaster shall be elected by the Capital Burgesses, with the consent and approbation of any other ten inhabitants of the said town, having voices in the election of the Capital Burgesses, and the Bishop of Ely for the time being, from time to time, for ever, shall have the visitation, reformation, and correction, as well of the schoolmaster, as of the school aforesaid." The arrangements for giving efficiency to the school have disappointed the expectations of those for whose benefit the school was established. The cause of this has been variously accounted for, and the remedies for the evils complained of have been as diversified as the parties complaining. Some have contended that Grammar-schools, however much adapted to the times in which they were established, have become in a great measure obsolete, and ought to be remodelled to meet the requirements of the altered condition of the population. This has been felt in many towns where Grammar-schools exist, and efforts have been made to effect a change in their constitution, but uniformly without success. A free Grammar-school has been defined by the highest legal authorities to be an endowment for teaching the learned languages, or Greek and Latin, and for no other purpose, unless the founder has prescribed other things to be taught besides grammar. This legal meaning of the term Grammar-school has been fixed by various judicial decisions, and it is quite established that if the founder merely expresses his intention to endow a Grammar school, it must be an institution for teaching Latin and Greek only; and so tenacious is the Court of Chancery in its adherence to this principle, that in cases where the funds have been diverted to other purposes it has been ordered that the founder's intention must be carried out, no matter the length of time during which it has been disregarded.[1]

Besides the bequests of Thomas Parke and John Crane, William Holmes, of the city of Exeter, directed by deed £400 to be laid out in the purchase of lands, partly for the poor and partly for two scholars at Magdalen College, Cambridge; and by his will, dated April 2nd, 1656, he directed

(1) See the case of *Attorney General v. Earl of Mansfield*, 2 Russ. 501.

that the money should be appropriated to the scholars only. An estate was purchased at Holbeach, in Lincolnshire, in 1641, which at that time was let for £20 per annum; the present rent is £86. The first two scholars were elected in 1647 and sent to Magdalen College agreeably to the directions in Mr. Holmes's will. Ten pounds continued to be paid to each of the two scholars that were elected till 1758, when some irregularities took place which led to an action being brought against the Capital Burgesses to compel them to fulfil the trusts under the will. It was decided "that the arrears of rents, &c., be paid into the Court of Chancery to be invested in Three-per-cent Bank Annuities, and that future unappropriated funds be invested in like manner, and that the interest and rent of the estate be applied in conformity with the directions contained in the deed."

Among those who have enjoyed the advantages of this institution may be mentioned the Rev. Thomas Grainger Hall, who, on proceeding to Magdalen College, applied himself to his studies with so much assiduity as to attain the rank of fifth wrangler, and was elected a fellow of his College. He is now Professor of Mathematics at King's College, London.

The Rev. J. Jackson, rector of Elm-cum-Emneth, held the office of Head-master for a period of twenty-three years, the duties of which he discharged in a manner highly creditable to himself and beneficial to those placed under his charge. Upon his resignation in 1826, the Rev. J. R. Major, M.A., of Trinity College, Cambridge, was elected Master; but after a few years residence in Wisbech he was appointed to the honorable and lucrative office of Head-master of King's College, London. He was succeeded, in 1831, by the Rev. G. Thompson, B.A., who is the present Master.

Several men of eminence have been educated at this school among whom may be mentioned Thomas Herring, D.D., Archbishop of Canterbury; the Hon. Charles Dalrymple Lindsay, late Bishop of Kildare; Thomas Clarkson, the well-known philanthropist, and others.

The Boys' National School.

From the nature and constitution of grammar schools, as defined by courts of law, it is evident that they were not intended for the instruction of the great body of the people; and it was not until the beginning of the eighteenth century when the systems of Bell and Lancaster were first introduced to public notice, that so desirable an object was deemed practicable. The method of instruction pursued at this school is that suggested by Dr. Bell, and is intended to instruct the children in useful knowledge and the principles of the Christian religion as taught by the established church. The first stone was laid July 16th, 1811, and the building will accommodate 250 boys; the number usually attending varies from 200 to 220. Although bequests had been previously made by many benevolent persons,[1] it is to the exertions of Dr. Jobson, Mr. Edes, and other contemporary philanthropists that this town is indebted for the erection of the above school.

The Girls' National School.

Is situated in Lower Hill Street, and is indebted for its erection and endowment to the same benevolent individuals as the school for boys. The finances are in a very prosperous state, owing to the endowments having been chiefly invested in land, which has greatly increased in value during the last fifty years. From the report published in April, 1848, we learn that the balance in the treasurer's hands amounted to £161 8*s.* 5*d.*, and that the number of children under instruction was 164.

(1) Legacies, &c., to the National Schools.—Joseph Taylor, Esq., £200; Fleetwood, Bishop of Ely, £26 17*s.* 6*d.*; Edwd. Bangor, £40; Lady Trafford Southwell, £100; Rev. Dr. Jobson, £100; the interest to be equally divided between Boys' and Girls' Schools. Mrs. Jane Bellamy, £20: Frances Southwell, £20; Thos. Roberts, £50; John North, £15; Valeny North, £10; Ellen Ainger, £15; Henry Edwards, £20; Ellen Spelman, £20; Anthony Lumpkin, £10; — Shepherd and — Bromley, Esqs., £27; Wm. Rayner, £100; the interest to be paid to the Boys' School, excepting £9 to the Girls' School. The Rev. A. Jobson and J. Edes, Esq., gave £500 each which was invested in 23A. 1R. 19P. of land in Leverington, the rents to be applied to the Girls' School. Mrs. E. Wright, as we have previously stated, was also a liberal benefactress to these institutions. In addition to these bequests, there are also annual subscriptions and donations to a considerable amount.

The British School.

This school was established in 1840 by several benevolent individuals belonging to various religious persuasions in the locality, for the purpose of affording a sound and scriptural education to children in this town and neighbourhood at the weekly charge of two-pence each. The school is perfectly unsectarian in its character and operations, and is supported by the children's pence and by the voluntary contributions of persons belonging to the various religious bodies in the town. Since its formation 1040 children have enjoyed the benefits of the institution. There are now 204 boys on the books.

A school for girls was established in 1834 upon the same principles as the school for boys. It is held in the Union School-room, at the back of the Crescent. At present there are 203 girls on the books, who each contribute three halfpence weekly. The school is supported by annual subscriptions and donations, by the sale of work, and by the children's pence.

Infant School.

This building, which stands in Deadman's Lane, was erected by Mr. James Hill to carry out a system of training similar to that proposed by the well-known Robert Owen, but, failing in his object, it was purchased for the accommodation of an Infant School supported by members of the Established Church and various denominations of Dissenters. At present there are about fifty children, from two years and a half to six years of age, who are placed under the system of training recommended by Mr. Wilderspin.

A Sunday School, in connection with the church, had been conducted for some years by several pious ladies at their own expense, when the late Dr. Jobson, observing the salutary effects produced by their laudable exertions, gave £500 to the Corporation, and directed the interest to be applied to the education, on the Lord's Day, of poor boys and girls resident in the town—the school to be under the direction of the Capital Burgesses, Mrs. Wright's Trustees, and the subscribers to the National School. This school is at present conducted in a building in Deadman's Lane. As the children attending the National Schools are instructed on Sundays by their respective teachers, the attendance at this school is not so large as might be expected. Besides these there are classes for adults, which meet in the vestry under the care of competent teachers, so that the number receiving instruction on Sundays is very considerable.

There are also Sunday Schools in connection with the Baptist, Independent, Wesleyan, Primitive Methodist, and Unitarian congregations, which are numerously attended, and are gratuitously instructed by teachers belonging to the respective societies.

CHAPTER VIII.

ANCIENT AND MODERN BUILDINGS.

THESE buildings are more of the useful than the ornamental character. Antiquity, except in its most humble forms, seems to have neglected Wisbech; and our narrative of the history of ancient buildings will be confined to such erections as the Bridge, Alms-houses, Corn-cross, the Poor-house, and the Gaol. There is, however, one building—or the remains of one—entitled to previous consideration, which seems formerly to have been the adjunct to an edifice of importance. It is at present used as a cellar, and is situated under the house and shop of Mr. Dieppe, in the Market-place. This subterranean apartment has a groined ceiling of an arch and an intersection, supported at the sides on carved brackets. The intersection of the ribs and the centre of the arch are marked by bosses, one of which somewhat resembles the tudor rose, and another bears a face—apparently a female with a ruff round her neck. There is a small grated window at one end, and towards the other there are the remains of a turnpike staircase. This relic of architecture—apparently ecclesiastical—seems to belong to the fourteenth century, though for what purpose it was used, or to what building attached, it is useless now to conjecture. It is situated in the portion of the town which has, apparently, always been

Drawn by J. C. Sammons. Engd by John Mottram.

VIEW OF THE NORTH BRINK, WISBECH,

FROM THE ARCH OF THE BRIDGE

This Plate, Engraved at the Expence of William Peckover Esq. is Respectfully Inscribed to him

by his obliged Servants THE AUTHORS

Published by R. Walker, Wisbech [illegible]

central; for, in its vicinity the Guild Hall was built, and the Market, though called New in contra-distinction to the Old Market, bears that name in our earliest documents.

The BRIDGE.—Two bridges are spoken of in the earlier portion of the history of the town—one called Walsoken Bridge, and the other New Bridge or Great Bridge. Walsoken Bridge seems to have been mutually repaired by Wisbech and Walsoken, but the new bridge was a constant matter of dispute—Wisbech endeavoring to lay some of the burden of its preservation on the higher parts of the country, and these parts as anxious to elude the tax. We find mention made of this bridge at very early periods; and, in 1326, the following document furnishes not only a record of its existence but of the means adopted to keep it in repair:

"The King to the right rev. father in Christ John by the same grace bishop of Ely greeting: Know ye, that at your request, in aid of amending and repairing the bridge of your town of Wysebeche, which is decayed and broken, as we are informed, we have granted to you, that from the 26th April ensuing to the end of three years then next following, to be fully completed, ye take by the hands of those in whom ye confide, of things for sale coming to the town, or to the market of the said town, the customs following, that is to say, &c."[1]

These customs were levied on hay, horses, corn, &c. By the presentments of its condition, which at various times were made, we learn that the Bishop of Ely was liable for a considerable portion of its repair, as he is the party generally mentioned in the earliest documents. In 1426 all the lands in the Old Market were commanded to repair. In 1533 the Bishop and the North Side were charged with it; and in 1571 the Bishop and the Hundred. In 1583 the charge of the Bridge is stated at £51 4*s.* 10*d.*, of which the Queen's part was £33 8*s.* In 1586 the Bishop was ordered to pay one-third of the expense of keeping the Bridge in repair.

(1) Extract from the Records of the Court of Chancery, preserved in Tower of London. —*Quoted by Watson.*

On the in-corporation of the town, the Burgesses undertook part of the expense of repair. In 1608 a note is made of £9 10*s.* having been paid for timber to repair the Bridge; and an order is given for a further payment of £8; which is followed, three months after, by a note of £36 6*s.* 5*d.* having been allowed for the same purpose. This action, however, appears to have involved the Corporation in a sort of liability, for, in 1612, we are told the town was indicted for not mending the Great Bridge. The decision of the dispute is not mentioned; but it appears to have been so far successful that the town had only to bear a portion of the charge. In 1627 three items, amounting to £3 5*s.*, are mentioned for timber, planks, and workmanship used about the Bridge and Sluice. In 1637 a memorandum is made of a treasurer appointed by his Majesty's justices for receiving all such sums as are to be levied within the Hundred for new making the Great Bridge; and in 1651 £100 are ordered by the Burgesses to be paid for the same purpose. In 1667 "it is ordered that the Town Balliff dow maike a bricke wall att the Bridge foote, and on the other side of the Bridge foote, withe posts & deals, and that he see to mend the bridge where it is decayed.... provided that this be no president for the future to mend the bridge."[1] In 1668, under the same precautions, £4 10*s.* are ordered to be paid to the same purpose, "and it is further ordred that the burgeses will beare the charge of sute in bringing in Elme and the two townes of Well to contrybute to the mayntang the bridg as formarly they have done."[2] In 1679 the repair of the Bridge was again disputed, and the Town Bailiff is ordered to prefer an indictment in the Court of King's Bench, or some other regular way, against the Hundred, for not repairing it. Two years afterwards we learn that the dispute was still in action, for one of the Capital Burgesses is ordered "to take some care in searching into

(1) Corporation Records, v. 3.

(2) Col. Watson mentions, on the faith of the ancient records in the Bishop's registry, "that the men of Wells were bound to furnish five boats to transport the bishop and his suite from Wisbech: and if the five boats were not sufficient, that the men of Wisbech were to supply the residue necessary."

ye p'cesse in the sessions of peace or assizes upon the presentm^t for repairing the towne bridge, and thereupon to use some course for the p'venting the levieing the issues upon the towne."[1] Two years after this, in 1683, it is ordered that the "p'sent Towne Balif take speedy care to buy such timber as shall be wanting to repaire the towne bridge on behalf of the Bishop of Ely, the country, and themselves."[2] A fortnight after certain persons are ordered to repair, for which they are to have £109 and the old timber. We do not learn any further on this subject till after a lapse of fifty years, when, in January, 1738, "John Addey, carpenter, did agree to repair and keep in repair the Great Bridge in Wisbech (that is to say) the starlings, timbers, floors, and rails, after the rate of eighteen pounds each year, debarring extraordinary accidents that may accrue from the violence of waters, shipps or barges breaking loose and breaking or destroying the starlings, piers, or bruns of the said bridge."[3] From this date the Corporation of Wisbech seem to have taken the reparation of the Bridge on themselves. We meet with no further disputes upon the subject; and, notwithstanding their precautions against precedent, their liability to repair would seem to have been substantiated and confirmed. About twenty years after the last date, the Bridge had become so far out of repair as to need a new one; for, in October, 1756, "the present state of the Bridge being taken into consideration, it was agreed that the same was in a very ruinous condition, and ought to be taken down. It was also resolved that a new bridge should be built, and that the same should be built of stone. That the said bridge be of one arch, and that it be built where the old one now stands."[4] The corporate resolutions were followed by a public meeting to gain the opinion of the inhabitants upon borrowing, upon the mortgage of their lands, a sufficient sum of money to execute the work. £1200 were voted for the purpose without dissent, which was afterwards increased to £1600, and finally to £1750. "Oct. 21, 1757. Whereas a plan and

(1) Corporation Records, v. 3. (2) Ibid. (3) Ibid. (4) Ibid.

elevation of a stone bridge has been this day delivered to us by George Swaine and John Sharman; now we do agree to take the opinion of James Burrough, Esq., Master of Caius College, Cambridge, touching the height and width thereof, and if, in his opinion, the arch agreeable to the plan is a part of a circle likely to stand and answer the purposes of a bridge, then we do agree to proceed thereupon."[1] The new bridge was thenceforward commenced, and a floating bridge was provided while it was building "from the shoar near the Workhouse to the opposite shoar."[2] Certain sums were laid for passing by the bridge, and an additional horse-boat was provided to ply from the White Hart to the opposite side. The first stone was laid in June, 1758, in which was inserted the following inscription: "*Ex ligneo surrexit lapideus, A.D.* 1758. *Esto perpetuus.*" This latter benediction is in great danger of violation, as the narrowness of its construction,—which only allows of one vehicle to pass over at a time,—the steepness of the ascent, and the abruptness of the turn on the south side, have rendered it an extremely dangerous bridge ever since it was erected; and it has been successively threatened with destruction at every proposed improvement in the river. Considered as a work of architecture it is ornamental, solid, and well constructed. The arch is elliptical, of seventy-four feet span, and its situation at the termination of the Brinks—almost the whole of which it commands—is very ornamental to each side of the river. The whole expense of its erection appears to have been about £2250, as an additional £500 was borrowed in consequence of some unforseen and untendered works connected with it.

The GUILD HALL.—Of this building, which in many places is a highly ornamental edifice, generally in the ecclesiastical style of architecture, there are no remains at present in Wisbech. We are certain, however, of the former existence of such a place, from the frequent mention made of it

(1) Corporation Records, v. 6. (2) Ibid.

in the Guild proceedings. There are no notices there which enable us to form any opinion of the kind of building which existed at any period during the existence of the Guild, except in a single instance, when, in 1173, two hundred reed are ordered to be purchased for repairing their hall—a fact which at this day gives us very mean notions of its condition. It was not without pretensions, as in 1379 a sum of money is advanced for "ornamenting the hall." It was called the common hall as well as Guild hall, and was probably used by the incorporated body for their proceedings, after the dissolution of the Guild; and, if so, it will have been situated on the site of the present Grammar-school. In 1658 John Crane gave £100 for "building a Town House, and £30 towards repairing of the house where the Capital Burgesses meet.[1] This money was expended in erecting an additional room at the back of the Grammar-school, wherein, till 1810, the Capital Burgesses met.[2]

The GRAMMAR-SCHOOL.—The school-room in this building is in fact the ancient Town Hall, and from certain slight remains in its interior we have proof that the present plain and meagre apartment is only the dilapidation of one of more pretension and interest. There are the remains of slight embattled work in stone still left in the west end, which seems to have belonged to the transomed windows of some work of the Perpendicular age, and a series of carved stone brackets on each side, show that the room was formerly ornamented with an open timber roof. Now, however, six plain circular-headed casement windows, a ceiled roof, and plastered walls, remind us of none of the features which should belong to a public building devoted to the service of an ancient Corporation. Here, until the passing of the Municipal Act in 1835, the annual nominations and elections of the Capital Burgesses were held. The uproarious scenes which were then here enacted—the bantering at noon and the chairing at midnight—the repetition of old griev-

(1) Corporation Records, v. 6. (2) Watson.

ances and their hearty dispensation—are things of mere recollection, and the ancient hall with its porch and battlemented gable is now wholly abandoned as a public building. It is situated in a line with the High Street; the easy alteration of removing it and carrying the street through the premises at the back of it, would convert a narrow, roundabout, inconvenient entrance of the town into a roomy, direct, and ornamental one. At different times, therefore, it has been entertained to remove the Grammar-school premises, and carry the street directly forward to Lynn Road; but obstacles, some created by the town, some by the disputes of property, have hitherto prevented the realisation of this measure. But the readiness with which it might be done, and the old inconvenient nature of the buildings to be removed, render the scheme one probable to be perfected on some future occasion.

CORN MARKET-HOUSE.—In 1619 a house of this description appears to have been erected, from which we may infer that though the fen was then in the distressed condition which preceded the first general drainage, a considerable quantity of corn was grown in the neighbourhood of Wisbech, and sold in its market. The first notice of this building is in an entry dated the 10th of February, when "it was agreed that Andrew Pausey of Spaldinge .. Carpenter, should sett upp one house in the corne m'rkett 20 foot in breadth and 40 foot in length, and he to have for every foot of tymber 10ᵈ· the foot, being the guyfte of Mrs. Styrman, as apyointed by her last will and testament: the scantlinge of wᶜʰ tymber is in a bill of particulars betwene him and the burgeses, wᵗʰ his m˜ke annexed unto the same." Other persons were ordered "to slat the house in yᵉ corn m˜kett at lvjˢ· the rood.... as Mr. Edmonson his house is nʷ slated in all poynts." In September, 1615, the building appears to have been completed, and "the burgesses uppon a metinge did measure both the depth and breadth of the house in the Corn M˜kett for the roof, and there was by measure at xvj foot and a half to the rood, the sum of six roods and sixteen foot, allowing the depth of the roof to be xx^{ty} foot, and the length thereof to be xlj foot and a half, the wch at lvj$^{s.}$ the rood comes to the sume of xvij^{li} xij$^{s.}$ ij$^{d.}$" The work, however, appears to have been left unfinished, as in the following February the "Company" took advice for "procedinge agaynste him for not fynyshinge the worke."[1]

CORN CROSS.—There appears to have been another building erected under this name in 1665, about fifty years after the former, which could hardly have come to ruin in that time. The first notice of it is an order for Anthony Fisher, Esq., to "wayte upon the Lord Bishop of Ely to knowe his pleasure where the seed house shall be buylte, and to obteyne a copy for the same." The work appears to have remained in hand three years, as, in 1667, we learn that £7 16*s.* 8*d.* was paid to the Bishop; and in August, 1668, John Louen is ordered to sett the buter crosse with rayles and banisters of freestone round abovte, accordinge to the patern now sett." A further record states that "for setting the staires of the seed cross on the outside and enlardging the same 8 foot or longer, and p'viding it wth hard polished stone and rubble, shall have over and above the former contract the sume of fifty pounds, wch said former contract was three hundred sixty and five pounds." In 1669, the year after its erection, a sudden express was sent to the contractor "to acquaint him that ye newe Corn Market Crosse is in very great danger by ye ddfault of ye timber and stone worke." In 1671 40*s.* are allowed for "paines and cost about the 4 dyalls of the New Crosse." We hear no more of it till 1705, when it is ordered to be stripped. This appears to have been only for repair, as it is eighty years afterwards that the Town Bailiff is ordered to employ proper persons immediately to take it away for the purpose of erecting a crane "upon or near the place where the present Corn Cross stands,"[2] which appears to have been the crane only recently removed.

(1) Corporation Records, v. 3. (2) Ibid.

SHAMBLES.—The Shambles were a comparatively early erection in the town. They are first mentioned in 1595, when "Thomas Edwards yelded hys accompt of ye Shambles, and then all by hym rec. for ye same ; towards ye buyldyng was hys receypts ye s~m of lxxxjx^li.^ x^s.^ viij^d.^ and hys payments civ^li.^ vij^s.^, so rests to hym xiv^li.^ xvj^s.^ iiij^d.^"[1] They were let at the yearly rent of £7 10*s*., but subsequently the price was advanced 20*s*. as appears from the following: 13 April, 1610. The companie was contented to let the Butchers Shambles for one yeare to William Skortred for viij^li.^ x^s.^ the yeare ... p'vided allways y^t^ the Towne Butchers shall have theare stalls for viij^s.^ iiij^d.^ the yeare, and to let to strangers such as shall remane unletten att the ratte of viij^s.^ iiij^d.^ And p'vided allwayes that William Skortred, nor any for him, shall not let any of the stalles, as well the Town butchers as the countrye butchers, not for above iiij^d.^ a market day."[2] In 1619 they appear to have come into dispute with the Bishop of Ely, and the Town Bailiff is ordered to pay £20 to the Bishop, "that his Lo^pp^ shall relinquish his clayme in the butchers' shambles, and that he will be pleased to graunt the same to the Corporacon by copy of Court Rolle, and wilbe pleased to let his tenants have a favorable tryall in law whether the fines be certaine or uncertaine," taking no advantage of them if they prove uncertain, but "take such reasonable fines as he takes of other men's lands." The trial issued in substantiating the Bishop's claim. These Shambles remained standing till 1811, when, on £20 paid to the Bishop for enfranchisement, and £300 to the trustees, they were pulled down without reconstruction.

WORKHOUSE.—This edifice was first built in 1720-2. "Nov. 14th 1720. It was agreed that the Town Bailiff do cause 260,000 of bricks to be made for the use of the town, in order to build a Workhouse, ye bricks to be made on 3 acres of town land." A year elapsed in this work, when the Corporation resolved "that a Workhouse about 110 foot square,

(1) Corporation Records, v. 2. (2) Ibid, v. 3.

in a place called ye Hors Fare, be Built, and y^t in order thereto the Town Bailiff may procure upon ye Town seal a sum of money not exceeding one thousand pounds." This sum was increased eleven months afterwards [October, 1722,] by another thousand pounds borrowed in the same manner. This continued to be the house that "held the parish poor," till the passing of the recent Poor Law Act, when it was sold for £1700, some time after the erection of the Union Workhouse on Lynn Road.

GAOL.—The first notice we find of a building of this kind is in 1620, when "the Company did agree that the Town shall lend the house for a house of Correction, and to wall it about wth a wall of brick." What house is here meant is uncertain. There must, however, have been a prison here before the above date, as we read of persons committed to it in the time of the plague, and it is very probable that Wisbech has always been a seat of justice. Some part of the castle was allotted, it is supposed, as a common prison, the assize being held in the mote hall of that building; and the governor was responsible for the safety of the felons, as two of them—Sir Andrew Ogard in 1452, and Sir James Hobard in 1494,—were fined £5 each for the escape of felons. When the castle fell into decay the Capital Burgesses, who then first it appears assumed the maintenance, or partial maintenance, of this establishment, set apart two tenements as a house of correction or confinement. They also paid the keeper's salary, which in 1624 was £13 6s. 8d., but received, as appears by an after item, £6 of the above sum from the country. In 1616 ten thousand bricks are ordered to be delivered at the "towne house of correction," for which the Town Bailiff was to allow "for every thousand xv^s. viij^d."[1] In 1681 the rights of the town suffered invasion in this matter, as the following Record exemplifies: "Wheras att the last assizes for the Isle of Ely there was a pe~tion p'ferred to ye Judge by the Capitall Burgesses and Inhabitants

(1) Corporation Records, v. 3.

of y[e] Townshipp, concerninge the Townshipp's right to the house now and for some years past used as a Gaole in Wisbech, the matter of which pe~tion was referred by y[e] Judge to the consideration of sevrall Justices of the Peace to treat with the Townshipp, w[ch] has taken no effect."[1] The petition is, therefore, ordered to be re-presented, and should the matter receive no settlement, that the town be allowed to argue their rights "as by counsell they shalbe advised." It is not recorded how this question was finally settled, but we may perhaps infer from the following record that Wisbech established its right, as it seems to have retained the right of repair: "Nov. 6, 1720. Agreed, that the Town Bailiff, as soon as he conveniently can, order the Gaole yard to be inclosed by a good wall, for airing y[e] Prisoners, and do other necessary repairs, and to give notice that the rent of the Gaole from Lady day next is not to be less than fourteen pounds p. annum, to reimburss our great charge in repairs."[2] The Burgesses' right to this building, which they seem to have taken some pains to confirm, was called in question again in 1757, when the Clerk is ordered to search and arrange all writings and documents in a methodical order, that the evidence may be laid before "the gentlemen of the hundred of Wisbech and the north part of the hundred of Witchford, in order to prove the Burgesses' right to the Gaol." From this time, however, the right of the Corporation seems to have been dropped, and the next notice that is taken of this subject is in 1807, when application appears to have been made by the Isle authorities for a portion of ground occupied by almshouses, on the South Brink, for the purpose of erecting a new Gaol and Sessions' House. This application was complied with, and the premises at present only occupied as a Sessions' House were then built, from a design by Mr. West. The treadmill, an adjunct of the building, was erected in 1823.

The CUSTOM-HOUSE was erected in 1801 on the site

(1) Corporation Records, v. 2. (2) Ibid, v. 3.

of the old Cross and Custom-house. This cross was used for the sale of butter, of which, while the fen was unsusceptible of high agricultural purposes, and much of it could only be used as summer or grass land, great quantities were sold at Wisbech. Indeed, butter[1] and linseed oils seem at this time to have been the staple commodities of the place, and to have held the same rank in its market as wheat does at the present day. Gazetteers have still an affection for these obsolete commodities, and Wisbech is almost universally represented in their pages as the market of butter and oils "pressed from seeds at mills in the neighbourhood."[2] This old cross was removed, as we have said, in 1801, and the present edifice was erected, consisting of rooms raised on open arches of rustic work, which was formerly used as a wool repository, but is now, though of very inadequate dimensions, appropriated as a butter and poultry market. The customs of this port were never very great, though they have materially increased of late years, in consequence of the great quantities of timber which have been imported for railway purposes. In 1845 the customs amounted to £7000; but in 1847 they had increased to £25,000.

BOY'S SCHOOL.—This is a plain building near the church, claiming no consideration, except for its purpose. It was built in 1811 on a spot then occupied as a pound for cattle.

GIRLS' SCHOOL.—This is a building of more pretension than the Boys' School, and the room is ample.

EXCHANGE HALL.—This was built in 1811, immediately after the passing of the Town Act, by which the Burgesses obtained the right of forming a cattle market, and in various other ways improving the town. The site of the Exchange Hall was then occupied by a public-house called

(1) "8000 firkins of butter have been exported in one year to London."—*Watson.*

(2) Brookes's Gazetteer.

the Nag's Head. It was built somewhat after the manner of the Custom-house, being two second-story rooms raised upon five open arches in front, which front is built of freestone, with the town arms in a small parapet pediment above. The lower story was at first fitted up with stalls as a Corn Exchange, which stalls were let at £3 3*s.* per year, but the buyers and sellers soon mutually deserted this public system of doing business, and preferred a more free and easy method of bargaining than the restriction of stallage offered. It, therefore, happened that very soon after the Corn Exchange was erected, its purpose was superseded, as the farmers and merchants preferred the open hill in front of the Exchange to the accommodation of its walls, and there a considerable portion of the Saturday corn business was formerly transacted. The corn trade, however, which has increased so materially within the last fifteen years, is now almost wholly transacted privately in the counting-houses of the merchants. The Corn Exchange retained its character, though deserted as an Exchange, till 1831, when the lower apartment, or proper Exchange, was let for one pound per year for five years, the hirer agreeing to "fit it up at his own expense as a room for public and other meetings, assemblies, the performance of concerts, delivery of lectures, public exhibitions, respectable auctions, public library, or bazaar, to the satisfaction of the Capital Burgesses." Since this date it has been used exclusively for the above purposes, and has been, as a public room, a great accommodation to the town. The annual election of Councillors has been held here since the passing of the Municipal Act. It occupies an area of nearly 1600 feet. The rooms above were hired of the Corporation till 1836 by a company of gentlemen as News and Billiard-rooms, but after the great increase of numbers which the Corporation received by the Municipal Act, it was found impossible to accommodate them in their former apartment in the Custom-house, especially as a civil power became attached to the municipal, and rooms were needed for magisterial as well as for council business. Under these circumstances the old Corporation room was resigned for a News-room, and the rooms of the Exchange Hall were fitted as a Council Chamber and Magistrates' Room, or Town Hall. There is also a smaller apartment used as a muniment room and library. The larger room is fitted up with an oblong council-table, and contains two valuable portraits, one of Dr. Jobson, executed by Strutt, at a cost of 30 guineas, and the other of Thomas Clarkson, the most celebrated of the natives of Wisbech. This is a fine picture of a fine nervous old man, whose keen eye and energetic features almost tell of one who was able by indomitable zeal to shame mankind of his crimes, and make justice prevail over interest. It was executed by S. J. Lane, at a cost of eighty guineas, raised by subscription.

THEATRE.—This is a wretched building, but so situated among back lanes and back yards that its wretchedness is in private, as such things ought to be. It is merely four bare walls and a roof, painted and boxed in the interior into a tolerable illusion. Still, wretched as it is, it is too pretending for the poor fallen amusement for which it is appropriated; and it is now oftener opened to the auctioneer than to the heroes of the buskin. It was built in 1793, and for fifty years it was annually visited by the Lincoln Company, under the late Mr. T. Robertson, and latterly under his widow. But, within the last ten years, the visits of the company, through the difficulties of their profession, began to suffer slight intermission; and, after two years' interruption, the Theatre was opened this year—1847—by the Norwich Company, whose success was anything but satisfactory. This is not a place to discuss the cause of the rapid decline of popularity which the drama has suffered of late years. But it may be briefly intimated that the above building, however it may be now deserted, is not likely to be wholly abandoned. The drama is no more dying, as many pretend, than the oak is dying when it sheds its leaves in autumn. It is based too firmly on the nature, and the senses, and the feelings of mankind ever to be overthrown either by commerce, art, or prejudice. The noblest men that ever lived have consecrated it in a hundred immortal forms, and their detractors are to them only "as the gourd compared with the cedar." When France forgets Moliere, and Spain Calderon, and Germany Schiller, and England Shakspere, and all of them forget Sophocles, the drama may perish—but not till then.[1]

BATHS.—The most lamentable object of desertion in Wisbech, after all, is the Baths. This building was erected in 1826 at an expense of £700, by shares of £10 each, but has never given the remotest prospect of remuneration to the shareholders, and it now stands, with its windows broken and its door-way never open, a libel on cleanliness. It is surprising that Englishmen, who so generally despise the dirt of foreigners, should in the most material and healthy particular of cleanliness be beneath almost every foreigner, and second only to the Bushmen and the Esquimaux.

UNION WORKHOUSE.—This building, which was erected after the passing of the New Poor Law Act in 1835, is the Poor-house for twenty-two parishes. It is built in an ornamental manner on Lynn Road. The external walls of the building form a square, which is internally divided into two oblong courts by a line of building carried from the centre of the front parallel with the side walls. It is calculated to accommodate 600 persons, and consists internally of a board-room, two school-rooms, waiting hall, dining hall, register room, receiving wards, shoemaker's and tailor's shops,

(1) Those who denounce plays and playhouses, may perhaps be induced to read what the Reverend Sydney Smith, a clergyman of the Church of England and a Canon of St. Paul's, has written upon their resolution :—"Where is every feeling more roused in favor of virtue than at a good play? Where is goodness so feelingly, so enthusiastically learnt? What so solemn as to see the excellent passions of the human heart called forth by a great actor animated by a great poet? To hear Siddons repeat what Shakspere wrote! To behold the child and his mother,—the noble and the poor artisan,—the monarch and his subjects,—all ages and all ranks convulsed with one common passion, wrung with one common anguish, and with loud sobs and cries doing involuntary homage to the God that made their hearts! What wretched infatuation to interdict such amusements as these! What a blessing that mankind can be allured from sensual gratification, and find relaxation and pleasure in such pursuits!"—*Miscellaneous Works.*

THE BRITISH SCHOOL, WISBECH.

This Plate engraved at the expense of Algernon Peckover, Esq is most respectfully inscribed to him by his obliged Servants. THE AUTHORS

Published by R. Walker, bridge foot Wisbech, 1848

two sick wards, two hospitals, ten sitting rooms, twenty-three bedrooms, four clothing stores, two oakum sheds, kitchens, &c. The style adopted is that called Elizabethan, though Stuart architecture would perhaps more appropriately denominate its degenerate degeneracy. The centre and wings are of three stories, the rest of the front is of two. The centre, which is pedimented, surmounted with a bell-turret, is almost wholly occupied by a pointed window, not so depressed as the style warrants. A clock awkwardly occupies the upper part of the window, which is flanked by two octangular buildings with plain deeply-splayed windows, the upper of which are surmounted with label mouldings on, carved brackets. The wings are flat and pedimented, with two windows with label mouldings and mullions. The rest of the front has a small pediment raised on the parapet over every window. There is also a neat lodge in the same style next the road, and a wide clean gravelled path, and evergreens which fill the considerable space in front, gives the whole rather the appearance of an opulent private mansion than a parish poor-house.

The BRITISH SCHOOL, of which we are enabled, by the kindness of one of its principal supporters, to give an engraving, was erected, with a commodious house for the master, in 1840, at a cost of nearly £2000, of which £160 were granted by the Lords of Her Majesty's Committee of Council on Education; the remainder was supplied by the liberality of friends of various religious denominations. The building is well calculated for its purpose, but our engraving gives a better idea of its architecture than a description would do.

The NEW GAOL is nearly opposite the above-named building. It is built after the manner of the model prison at Pentonville, consisting of two wings and a grand corridor, with a system of yards behind. The architect was the late Mr. Basevi, who, in the morsel of architecture incorporated in the front, has combined some of those high principles which he has so nobly developed in nobler works. The idea follows the occasion,—a small pediment surmounting the slightly advanced centre,—the plain dentil ornaments of the cornice,—the rough-hewn vermicular stone forming the arched entrance and basement,—and the two massy windows,—are so many principles whose junction seems to intimate as much as Dante's frightful line: "*Lasciate ogni speranza, voi ch' entrate.*"

The NEW CRANE was erected in 1845, in conjunction with the new wharf on which it stands. The Old Crane had for many years given uneasy signs of its decrepitude, and the bank beneath it kept gradually shelving into the river, which at that point was narrowed till in floods it almost became a cataract. The purchase of the Bell Estate and part of the Anchor Inn, the formation of the Wharf, and the erection of this New Crane, are the most spirited works which have been done of late years by the Corporation, though not the most politic. But, after completing the wharf and railing it in strongly as well as ornamentally, and building an ambitious looking warehouse for craned goods, it was hardly in accordance to fence the crane in with a plain deal partition as an invitation to bill-stickers. The crane warehouse is built with red brick faced with stone. On the town side it has two exceedingly heavy stone buttresses bearing the cross keys at the top; on the river side these are of brick. On the roof an elevated rusticated look-out is erected of wood, carrying a flag-staff from which the corporation flag is suspended on rejoicing days. The building has the unique feature of a double cornice.[1]

(1) The foundation-stone of this building was laid on the 24th of October, 1845, by John Whitsed, Esq., M.D., Mayor, who delivered the following appropriate address on the occasion:

"GENTLEMEN OF THE CORPORATION,

"It is a source of pride and pleasure to me, that, in my official capacity as Mayor of Wisbech, I should be deputed by you to lay the first stone of what may be deemed a very important work; and I hail with peculiar satisfaction the prospect thence resulting of great convenience and advantage to our Port and Harbour. When, as fellow-townsmen, we look back to the years which are gone, and compare our past with our present condition, surely we have ample cause to rejoice at the immense increase which has taken place in respect of

THE NEW CHURCH AND WHARF, WISBECH.

MUSEUM.—This building is only just finished. A museum was established in Wisbech in 1835, by a few gentlemen attached to the study of realities, and it made such good progress that though a large room was hired, sufficient we should have supposed for the accumulation of Wisbech for many years, it had been for some time too small to afford an adequate display of the collection of fossils and minerals, birds and other objects of natural history, implements and ornaments of savage life, and mediæval antiquities, which had been collected.[1]

our trade and commerce. Though much of this increase may be fairly ascribed to the zeal and enterprise of the merchants and traders of our port, it should, nevertheless, be borne in mind that great facilities have been afforded through the improvement of our navigation towards the sea, in the completion of that stupendous work, the Nene Outfall,—a work of engineering skill, labour, and ability, unparalleled in the history of this country. I say unparalleled, gentlemen, since it is believed there is no other work of the kind to be compared with it; hence, how great, how distinguished a tribute of honour is due to those by whom it was achieved! Our present undertaking, though inferior in point of magnitude, still constitutes another link in the chain of improvements. Were our resources greater, gentlemen, doubtless we had endeavoured to accomplish more; but even the limited outlay we resolved upon, by giving additional scope to our river for the accommodation of shipping, together with increased facilities for landing and warehousing of goods, I trust will not only prove of immediate advantage to the port, but lead also to further—let us hope, indeed—signal improvements. In fine, gentlemen, the stone, which under your direction has been laid this morning, may be regarded as one step towards the realization of the continued and permanent welfare of the Town and Port of Wisbech. I pray that God may speed the work."

(1) The following is a summary of the contents of the Museum:

MAMMALIA.—Several British and foreign animals.

ORNITHOLOGY.—Upwards of five hundred birds, two thirds of which are local specimens, including some very rare ones, as the Osprey, Hoopoe, Bohemian Waxwing, Bustard, Spoonbill, Honey Buzzard, Egyptian Goose, Bewick's Swan, &c.

ICHTHYOLOGY.—Upwards of sixty specimens, principally of a local character, including fresh and salt-water fish; among them the Opah, or King-fish, caught at Hunstanton, the Sturgeon, the Blue Shark, &c., and the finest specimen of the head and saw of the Saw-fish in the world.

ERPETOLOGY.—Several curious specimens of reptiles.

ENTOMOLOGY.—A collection of British and foreign butterflies and moths, and upwards of three thousand beetles.

CONCHOLOGY.—A choice collection of British and Foreign shells, numbering several hundred, and many of them scarce specimens.

MINERALOGY.—A small but interesting collection, presented by various parties.

FOSSILS.—A very interesting collection. Among them, remains of the Beaver, from Chatteris, Littleport, and Sutton Fens; lower jaw of the Wild Boar, from Feltwell Fen; vertebræ of Saurians, &c.

BOTANY.—Several thousand specimens of dried plants, arranged according to Smith's English Flora.

ETHNOLOGY.—A series of implements of warfare, dresses, ornaments, models, &c., from North-west America, South Sea, and other islands.

ANTIQUITIES.—Etruscan, Egyptian, Roman, and Early English Curiosities and Antiquities, such as vases, figures, swords, utensils, &c. Among the most interesting may be mentioned a fragment of sculpture from Herculaneum; three mediæval bricks found at Wisbech; and a fine carving in white marble of the Burmese idol Ghaudama.

This accumulation of antiquities, and of natural objects, induced the subscribers in 1846 to make an effort towards building an edifice for their preservation. They were in better hope of succeeding, as a Literary Society existed in the town, which had gradually formed a collection of several thousand volumes, ill provided with a library of general convenience. It was thought, therefore, if the interests of the Literary Society could be induced to conjoin with those of the Museum, the united bodies—especially as they comprised the principals of the town—might raise money sufficient to build an appropriate place for the accommodation of each. An attempt was made, upon this plan, by £25 shares, and in a short time the requisite number of shares was raised, which amounted to £2500. The building we are about to describe was the result. It was designed by Mr. Buckler, whose name and the name of his father have long been honorably connected with Gothic architecture. The style adopted for the Museum must be generalised as the Tuscan, the feeblest and coldest of the classic styles; and the building, which is fitted into a space long vacant between the Churchyard and the Crescent, consists of two stories surmounted by cornice and architrave of a compounded character, being somewhat Doric, somewhat Ionic. The wings, which are slightly advanced, are together about three times the breadth of the centre, which is filled by a retired portico. The windows, of which there are five in front—two in each wing and one over the entrance—are, in three instances, nearly square; the rest are in about the proportion of one to two. The library windows are in the proportion of one to three. They are all surmounted with an ill-proportioned cornice supported on heavy brackets.

Mr. Buckler is an architect of character, but his character has been gained rather in the school of romantic than of classic architecture. The severe rules and severe proportions of the latter are evidently treated with some small degree of freedom in the above building, so that it may be termed the romantic rather than the pure classic. But it was, perhaps, impossible to have made classic proportions pure in a situation which admitted only, without great violation of taste, a certain height with a certain length. These proportions, unfortunately, were no proportions at all, admitting only the effect of flatness without sufficient length to give it force. Still there are some principles admitted into this building which, but for the high character of its designer, might have been passed in silence. The wings are the principal feature of the building, occupying four-fifths of the whole front, and the windows, which so inadequately occupy this feature, only catch attention by their disproportionate breadth. The entrance, which is formed by two three-quarter Tuscan columns flanked by two antæ, seems shrinking behind the wings, and thus the feature which of all others requires boldness, decision, and grace, bears only a character of feebleness and weakness. In fact, proportion, grace, and dignity are wholly wanting; and bad as the style is, it is only followed impurely.

The internal arrangements of the Museum, which are of course more important to its purposes than the mere external proportions, are good and complete. They consist of the Museum, having a gallery round it and lighted from above; this occupies the whole right wing, and is 70 feet by 26. The lecture-room and entrance-hall occupy the front—the library and committee-rooms the left wing. There are extensive cellars beneath the building, as well as the curator's residence.

THE MARKET-PLACE.—This portion of the town is centrally situated, and well adapted for its purpose. It forms a parallelogram of 380 feet by 94, of which 310 by 37 are appropriated to the stallage, and the rest as thoroughfare. The stallage portion is slabbed on the portion intended for passengers, and cobble-paved where the stalls stand. It was completed in this form in 1811 at a cost of £1170;[1] £300 of

(1) 1811 must be considered a year of great public spirit in Wisbech; for the Cattle Market was purchased and made, the Corn Exchange built, the Fish-market built, and the Market-hill paved by the Corporation during this year.

which was paid out of the highway rates, the rest by the Corporation.[1] The Market-place seems to have formerly boasted far greater dimensions than at present, for "the whole space from the bridge to the present market-place was called the new market, and old title-deeds describe all the property from the bridge to the church to be abutting on the new market, without any distinction of the High Street or any other place."[2] In 1549 it appears to have been paved, for in an account already quoted we find an item "for pavyng of the M~ket place, and for Raggestone, sand, & workmanshippe of the same, $xvij^{li.}$ $ij^{s.}$ $ij^{d.}$" In 1570 the following curious fact is mentioned at a Session of Sewers. Speaking of Crab Marsh bank, a presentment continues: "which bank from Crabmersh gate was decayed in Bishop Goodrick's time, and part thereof carried (by consent of the Bishop) for the pavement of the market place in Wisbeche, and part by Mr. Wm. Bloomfield, for making of a windmill there."[3] This was, perhaps, at the paving with ragstone just before quoted, for though there is twenty-one years' difference in the dates, the presentment speaks of it as a past event performed in Bishop Goodrick's time, who held the see of Ely 1534-1554. There seems, at this period, too, to have been a windmill on the same spot, showing that the term Market Hill was perhaps one of literal meaning in those days. It must, also, have been very open. There was probably nothing between it and the castle but the moat and a few cottages "on the castle dyke." In 1592 the butchers' shambles were erected at the church end of the Market-place, and here the Sessions' House stood, though whether built at this time, or afterwards, is uncertain. In 1638 "the towne baliffe was appoynted to pay unto William Harvie his bill of laying out in repaire of the backside and getting upp the pumpp on the Markett hill, and other layings out, $iij^{li.}$ $xvij^{s.}$"[4] In 1664 there is another order for paving the Market-hill, "and that the well there be disannulled." In 1753 there is an order to lay down a substantial iron grate, "where the Crying stone lately

(1) Watson. (2) Corporation Records. (3) Dugdale, p. 338. (4) Corporation Records.

stood, in the Market place, for carrying of the waters," and December 3rd, 1764, there is an order for the third time for paving the Market-place at the expense of the town estates, and an order likewise for the Town Bailiff "to cause four dials to be erected on the oblisk" in the same place. Here, too, as well as the buildings already mentioned, the cage and stocks were placed, as appears by the following entry, preparatory to the last paving of this place in 1811. "Resolved, that the Town Bailiff do cause the Obelisk standing in the Market-place to be sold by auction as now standing, and to be taken down, and that he request the magistrates to give an order for the taking up and removal of the cage and stocks adjoining the old shambles."[1] There was also, originally, a market-cross, for in the same account which informs us of the first paving of the hill with ragstone, we find an item "for lead, tymber, and workmanshippe of the crosse in the M^kett place iiij$^{li.}$ iij$^{s.}$ iiij$^{d.}$"[2]

Wisbech appears to have been always a market-town, or at any rate we have no record that leads us to infer that it was ever otherwise. A market is mentioned in 1332. There is a portion of the town called the Old Market, situated on the side of the river opposite to the present market, but it is not certainly known whence this name was derived, though, from the open space which it still maintains, there is every reason to believe the term under which it is at present known is not inappropriate. There is a law of the Commission of Sewers in 1436 which commands that all who "held land in the *old market* of Wisbech should contribute to the repairs of the bridge,"[3] which shows that it was at that date unused as a market-place, or at any rate that there was a more recently established market in the town. It may, perhaps, be not unjustly inferred that the Saxon town was chiefly if not wholly on the north side of the river, and that centrally in this town the market would be held; but that on William the Conqueror founding the castle on the south side of the river, in order more completely to command the fen, the

(1) Corporation Records. (2) Ibid, v. 3. (3) Dugdale.

town, as in most instances during the feudal ages, clustered under the defences of the castle, and the market and the fairs were held under its walls. There used to be a pond in the Old Market, and a May-pole, for in 1679 it is ordered, "that ye Towne Baylife take care to gett a well maide & a pumpe sett downe in ye olde Markett, nere where ye maypole stood, & also an other well maide & pumpe sett nere the white crosse."[1]

The Corporation hold the fairs and markets by lease of the Bishop of Ely, and pay an annual fee farm rent of £5 6*s*. 3*d*. for the same. The tolls of the market were let in 1845 for £153 per annum, in 1819 for £85.

CATTLE MARKET.—This market was held in the public streets till 1811, when after the passing of the Town Act the Corporation immediately prepared to rid the streets of such a nuisance, and at the same provide more adequate accommodation to the cattle market. In the old view of Wisbech which accompanies this work the cattle-pens will be seen occupying the North Brink, so that at this period market-day must have presented on a smaller scale somewhat the appearance of the bullock fair on the 12th of August. In 1806 it was contemplated to remove the Cattle Market into the Old Market and Pickard's Lane, but as the Town Act began to be immediately after thought of, it was resolved to wait the event of it before any alteration was commenced. The first Cattle Market, which is the part south of Pickard's Lane, occupies a space of nearly half an acre. In 1827 it was found that this space was inadequate to the accommodation required, and as a piece of ground comprising rather more than half an acre, immediately opposite, on the north of Pickard's Lane, offered for £500, it was purchased. Further additional accommodation was afforded in 1838. The tolls, which are let for three years, were let in 1845 for £287 per year.

(1) Corporation Records.

CHAPTER IX.

THE NENE OUTFALL.

ALTHOUGH an improved outfall had been recommended by several engineers early in the seventeenth century, it was not until 1720 that an attempt was made to carry it into effect. This project of making a new cut from the river's end to a place called Peter's Point was ably planned by Charles Kinderley, and, when all but completed, the works were demolished by a misguided multitude, under the impression that they were protecting the interests of the Wisbech navigation, and it was not till 1775 that the works were resumed and completed. During this long interval the drainage of the district depending upon the Wisbech river for the discharge of its waters was in the most unsatisfactory state, as indicated by four breaches of bank from 1763 to 1770, and as many reports by eminent engineers during the same period. The completion of Kinderley's Cut after a protracted struggle of half a century, though productive of important advantages to the drainage and navigation of the river Nene, was upon a scale too limited for these advantages to be permanent. It was, however, valuable as establishing the principle for which its projector had long contended, viz.,—"that the chief obstruction to the discharge of the waters lay at the outfall." The establishment of this great principle by an experiment so unequivocal and satisfactory, while it directed attention to the root of the evil, pointed to further efforts in the same direction as the means of its removal. This was of the greater importance, as it was soon found that the immense sand-banks immediately below the cut, which had been partly cleared away by its operation, had begun to accumulate to such an extent as to cause, so early as 1804, great anxiety to the owners and occupiers of land draining by this outfall; while the Wisbech navigation was in a state equally unsatisfactory.

At this period the districts draining by the Nene depended upon the working of about sixty windmills, which, owing to the uncertainty of the power that moved them, were frequently at fault when most wanted, entailing upon the cultivator of the soil great losses, and occasionally blasting his prospects by breach of bank and consequent inundation. Nor was agriculture the only interest that suffered. The Wisbech navigation and trade were in an equally deplorable condition. Ships of large burden could no longer reach the town, and had been exchanged for a humbler class of vessels, from 40 to 60 tons burden, and even these were frequently neaped within a few miles of the town for two or three weeks, and sometimes even for a longer period. Sutton Wash had therefore become the port—if exposed sand-banks deserved the name—where the larger class of vessels took in and unloaded their cargoes, at an immense risk and expense to the merchant who carried on his business under circumstances so unfavorable.[1] To give some idea of the delay, expense, and risk, to which the trade of Wisbech was at that time subject, it may be stated that vessels carrying from 80 to 100 tons of coals unloaded into barges or lighters at the Wash-way, which with the barge freight to Wisbech amounted to 4*s.* 6*d.* per chaldron, or about 3*s.* 6*d.* per ton. In like manner, corn exported from Wisbech was taken in barges to the Wash-way, and there delivered to the outward-bound

(1) See "*Considerations on the Principles of Mr. Rennie's Plan for the Drainage of the North Level,*" by Tycho Wing, Esq.

vessels, at a charge of 6*d.* per quarter for wheat, and 3*s.* per last for oats. To increase the anxiety, these tedious operations could only be carried on during particular states of the tides, and a few hours too late might cause a delay in the sailing of a vessel of eight or ten days. Pilots were also required for the whole distance between Wisbech and the Eye, the charge from the town to Kinderley's Cut being 7*s.* 6*d.*, and from thence to the Eye it was proportioned to the draught of the ship, at the rate of 2*s.* per foot; and when the channel was bad, the barges were obliged to meet the ships in the Eye, on which occasions an extra freight of 12*s.* 6*d.* each barge was charged.[1]

This being the state of the drainage and navigation, it might well cause anxiety in those who were exposed to such periodical losses, besides being at times kept in a state of alarm for the safety of the banks which stood between them and ruin; while the merchant and the mariner who were engaged in a trade so hazardous, must have been in a constant state of excitement. Such were some of the circumstances under which the Corporation of the Bedford Level issued their instructions to Mr. John Rennie "to report his opinion on the Wisbech outfall and the drainage of the extensive washes lying between the two branches of the Nene, as also the North Level, &c." Having made the necessary surveys, he published his Report in 1814, and, by the importance of its facts and the clearness of its deductions, it attracted the attention of every person interested in the drainage or navigation of the district. The levels which were taken by Mr. Rennie showed that between Wisbech Bridge and Gunthorpe Sluice—a distance of about five miles and three quarters—the fall was only six inches, but

(1) A case in illustration of this occurred to one of our oldest merchants which is related by him as follows. "Having an order for about a thousand quarters of wheat from a house at Liverpool, I chartered a Lynn vessel for the purpose, there being none of this class at that time belonging to Wisbech. The wheat was sent down into the Eye in barges carrying about ten lasts each, and as it was the winter season, there was so much danger and delay, that the captain threatened to leave without the cargo. However, after about four weeks' delay, the vessel was laden, the barges being at times knocked against the ship's sides, and the spray finding its way among the wheat."

from Gunthorpe Sluice to Crabhole—a distance of about five miles and a half—the fall was thirteen feet. From these remarkable facts Mr. Rennie concluded that "it is, therefore evident that the high shifting sands which lie between Gunthorpe Sluice and Crabhole form one of the great bars to the discharge of the waters of the Nene, and of course to the general drainage of the lands depending upon this river." He then proceeds as follows: "It is not necessary to give the opinions of the many able engineers who have written upon the subject. The levels prove so incontestably where the obstruction lies that little reasoning is required. If the outfall of the Nene is to be effectually improved, it must be by a new channel from the mouth of Kinderley's Cut to the level of low water in the bay.... and no place seems so eligible, both in point of distance and depth of water, as Crabhole." In connection with the outfall he recommended also that the river should be deepened and enlarged as far as the Horseshoe at Wisbech, a cut from thence to Rummer's Mills, and from thence to Peterborough, and certain improvements through the town of Wisbech. The Report detailing this magnificent scheme was favorably received by the parties with whom it originated, but it became a question for grave consideration with many whether the land could sustain such an addition to its burdens as the tax that would be necessary to carry it into effect. But, while this question was being discussed by the various parties affected by the measure, the peace that followed the battle of Waterloo, in 1815, so completely deranged the finances, commerce, manufactures, and agriculture of the country. that every thing was forgotten in the distress that ensued. After a struggle unparalleled in history the country seemed to sink through exhaustion, in which the fens suffered severely. The wet harvest of 1816 still further aggravated the burdens pressing upon this part of the country, so that it is not surprising that the new scheme of drainage should have lain dormant till 1818, when the plan was revived with increased energy.

At this juncture the project of establishing a direct communication between the counties of Lincoln and Norfolk, by a bridge and embankment across Sutton Wash, was brought forward under the leadership of Lord Wm. Bentinck, who, after distinguishing himself abroad in the service of his country, threw his talents and energies into this new field of enterprise, which had for its object an immense addition to the agricultural and commercial importance of the district, as well as an increased facility of internal communication. As chairman of the Bridge Committee his efforts were incessant, and though his movements excited the alarm of some parties opposed to the scheme, their tendency was to advance its claims among the more reflecting. He also strove to conciliate the various conflicting interests by personal interviews, correspondence, and public meetings, at which he explained the various bearings of the combined plan upon the interests of individuals, particular districts, and the country at large.

At the same time the Bedford interest, under the direction of Tycho Wing, Esq., were maturing their plans, which were laid before a meeting convened at Wisbech, on the 10th of October, 1820, at which the Marquis of Tavistock—the present Duke of Bedford—presided, and which was attended by the most influential persons in the neighbourhood, and by gentlemen representing the various districts affected by the measure. After a clear statement, by Mr. W. G. Adam, the Duke of Bedford's agent, of the objects contemplated by the promoters and the means of carrying them into effect, resolutions in favor of the plan were unanimously adopted, and a subscription entered into to meet the preliminary expenses. The influence of this meeting upon the minds of the promoters of the measure was such as to encourage them to anticipate its speedy execution as all but certain. The large sum, however, that the execution of the plan involved created dissensions among the conflicting interests, so that when the report of the committee appointed at the meeting at Wisbech in 1820 was taken into consideration by a meeting held at Peterborough in November, 1821, at which the Duke of

Bedford presided, it was deemed advisable, "That, as the merchants and inhabitants of Wisbech did not concur in that part of Mr. Rennie's plan which recommends a cut from the Horseshoe to Rummer's Mill, the meeting should forbear coming to any decision upon the mode of executing that part of the works, in the confidence that some plan may yet be suggested that will reconcile the interests of all parties." Instead of these hopes being realised, dissatisfaction with the plan spread still further among parties in Wisbech and the neighbourhood, and in the April following a memorial to the Bedford Level Corporation was got up, and signed by most of the respectable inhabitants of the town and district. In this memorial the distressed state of the country, and particularly the difficulties of the agriculturists, were pleaded as reasons for delaying the execution of a plan that involved so enormous an expense at a time when, to use the language of the memorialists, "the capitals of the farming occupiers are daily diminishing, and many of that most respectable class have become absolutely ruined since the month of November last, and their effects sold under distresses for rent and taxes, and executions for debts, and that other proprietors have been absolutely obliged to sacrifice a portion of their estates to enable them to defray the payments of the county charges and other burdens on their property." The concluding paragraph runs thus: "That your memorialists, the merchants, traders, and others interested in the prosperity of the town of Wisbech, most humbly represent to your honorable Board, that the peculiar situation of the port of Wisbech will not admit of the tonnage duty proposed, and, if laid, the greater part of the present trade and commerce will be drawn from the port of Wisbech, to the serious injury of your memorialists and others interested therein." These glowing statements, after due allowance for the usual coloring admitted into such documents, may be taken as some apology for the determined opposition of the memorialists to the measure then pending.

Although many of the mercantile and trading classes had joined the agriculturists in signing the memorial, yet there were others who from their pursuits were more favorably disposed towards a scheme that promised so great an improvement to the navigation. Accordingly, a meeting of the merchants, traders, and other inhabitants of the town of Wisbech, took place on the 5th of May, 1824, for the purpose of considering what effect would be produced on the trade of the port by the adoption of either of the two plans brought forward for effecting alterations in the river Nene between Wisbech and the sea. At this meeting Wm. Rayner, Esq., presided, and resolutions favorable to the large scheme were unanimously passed.[1] But while these friendly sentiments were expressed by the mercantile interest of the town, discontent was acquiring strength among the agriculturists, who were led on in their opposition by some of the most extensive landowners in the neighbourhood. On the day previous to the meeting called by the promoters of the plan on the 10th of May, 1824, at which Lord Wm. Bentinck had been advertised to preside, a letter signed "*A Fenman*," addressed to

(1) At this meeting the following resolutions were passed:

"That the plan for deepening and improving the river from Wisbech to Gunthorpe Sluice, and making a new cut from Gunthorpe Sluice to Crabhole, would, if executed, be highly beneficial to the trade of the port and navigation of the river,—as it would then be navigable for brigs and vessels of large burden during spring tides, and that the small vessels which at present can approach the town during spring tides only, would be able to navigate at all times; and that the whole risk, expense, and delay attending the transhipment of merchandise at Sutton Wash would be altogether avoided; and that vessels, their cargoes, and the lives of seamen, would be far more secure in the harbour at the town of Wisbech, than exposed to the rough gales and heavy seas which so frequently prevail where they at present anchor.

"That in fixing as a maximum 1*s.* per chaldron on coals, and 1*s.* per ton on every other kind of merchandise, the merchants and shipowners of Wisbech are of opinion that a greater aggregate amount would be raised than would be produced by a higher rate of taxation; and they trust they are not too sanguine in anticipating that, from the improvement likely to be effected in the drainage of the surrounding country, the recovery of many thousand acres of land from the sea, the great increase in the trade, wealth, and population of the town, from the great facility given to navigating the river and the security of the harbour,—the annual amount of tonnage collected, even at these rates, will ere many years equal, if not exceed, the amount calculated to be produced by the tax of 2*s.* per ton.

"That a bridge across the contemplated new cut would under any modification be an impediment to the ingress and egress of vessels; yet, on the event of such a bridge being absolutely necessary, care should be taken that it be a drawbridge, and formed on the best possible principle, and the drawing it up regulated in such a manner that no delay to the passage of vessels be occasioned beyond what may be utterly unavoidable."

the landowners in the hundred of Wisbech, was extensively circulated, urging the agriculturists to resist a measure "which, if passed into a law, would reduce them to the condition of laborers upon the land which had been their own." Every one, therefore, that wished to protect himself from such wholesale ruin, hastened to the place of meeting, which, long before the hour appointed, was full to overflowing. The noble chairman, after stating the object of the meeting, and giving an outline of the plan and the mode proposed to raise the necessary funds for carrying it into effect, was followed by other speakers in explanation and support of the measure, who were scarcely heard amid the murmurs and interruptions of an audience that had assembled not to listen, but oppose whatever might be brought forward by the promoters. Accordingly, when an amendment to the resolutions was put, a forest of hands was held up, while the original resolutions had not more than a dozen supporters. His lordship, who no doubt felt mortified in being thus thwarted in a favorite object, intimated to the meeting that though they could, by withholding their assent, prevent or delay the execution of that part of the plan by which they would have been the most extensively benefitted, they could not hinder the promoters of the bridge and embankment from carrying their plan into effect, as they were determined, should the general scheme be rejected by that meeting, to apply for a separate bill in the next session of parliament.

This victory was soon found to be a barren one, as all parties felt that neither drainage nor navigation was improved by the decision. Notwithstanding all that was said at the meeting by the opponents of the measure about efficient drainage and an excellent navigation, and the strong recommendations "to let well alone," we find the following notice placed on the books of the Wisbech Corporation in the February succeeding: "The necessity of removing obstructions from the river."[1]

(1) On this occasion the late Steed Girdlestone, Esq., whose character stood high both in the Town and neighbourhood, and whose opinion was entitled to great respect, suggested

It was fortunate however for the districts draining by the Nene, as well as for the navigation of Wisbech, that in the face of all this opposition, the leaders in this magnificent project persevered to carry out Mr. Rennie's plan in its leading features. At a Meeting of the North Level Commissioners held at Thorney, in July, 1825, resolutions in favor of the scheme were adopted; and it was proposed that, if the opposition of the town of Wisbech still continued, the Commissioners should avail themselves of the alternative proposed by Mr. Rennie of a cut from Shire Drain to Lutton Leam, by which, also, they would obtain an inland navigation from thence, by the Dog and Doublet, to Peterborough and up to Northampton. Thus Wisbech was reminded of what it might lose by a protracted opposition, as there were other means of getting rid of its waters besides bringing them to Wisbech; and it also threatened the diversion of a considerable portion of the trade into another channel. But though Wisbech was thus warned of her danger, conciliation and co-operation with her merchants and traders were still sought after. Hence we find, Lord Wm. Bentinck, in November, 1824, soliciting the aid of the Wisbech mercantile classes in furnishing their share of the means necessary to bring the plan before parliament; and though he met with a refusal on this as on former occasions, he still persevered, and in

to the Corporation (of which he had been long an influential member) a plan for the removal of these obstructions, and for other improvements in and near the town, which he communicated to the Common Hall assembled—He introduced these suggestions by expressing his attachment to an improved outfall upon the most comprehensive plan, and regretting the failure of that which had been submitted to public discussion, and which had excited so much warmth and jealousy on the part of the landed interest in the neighbourhood; and then proceeded to recommend: "To ease the bend of the river opposite Messrs. Watson and Usill's brewery by cutting a new channel from the Toll Bar through Mr. Lumpkin's house—adding an arch to the Bridge, and taking down two or three houses adjoining it on the north side—to straighten the Horse Shoe—to confine and deepen the channel, where necessary, to Kinderley's Cut, and from thence to South Holland Sluice, or any other point that may be thought desirable."—The expenses he estimated at £30,000, and suggested a plan by which the funds be raised. But without entering into the merits of a plan originating with an individual who, though highly respectable, made no pretentions to engineering skill, it is no imputation on his character to say that twice the sum proposed would have been insufficient to complete the works sketched in the suggestions. The plan, however, was cordially entertained by the Corporation, entered upon the Records, a vote of thanks to the author was recorded, a meeting appointed to take it into consideration, and a copy of the letter was sent to each of the members for his perusal.

September, 1825, he repeated his application in a letter addressed to the Town Bailiff, in which he pointed out the advantages that would arise to the trade of Wisbech by co-operating wlth the North Level Commissioners and Bridge Committee in carrying both plans into effect; "which measure," observed his lordship, "forms part of the two greatest improvements of which the outfall of the Nene is susceptible, and which the daily increasing deterioration of the navigation stands so much in need of." To explain these points still further, he proposed a conference with the parties on an early day at Wisbech, and named the first day of October, or any other day that might suit the convenience of the Wisbech gentlemen.

These conciliatory efforts seemed to produce little effect on the people of Wisbech, who, though they had heard of large vessels coming up to the town, had no experience of a better navigation, and appeared content with the craft to the sight of which they had become familiarised, and with a trade carried on chiefly by means of barges and lighters. Indeed, this class of vessels had, by long custom, acquired something like vested rights, so that when a larger vessel occasionally visited the port, it was looked upon as an intruder. Besides, it was sometimes a question with the merchant whether he was not increasing his risk when he employed a larger vessel, as it rendered it more uncertain when she would reach her destination. Under such circumstances, the improvement of the navigation was to the greater part of those engaged in the trade of Wisbech a matter of indifference or dislike. Beset with these difficulties, the great measure made little progress during the year 1825, but in the following year increased efforts were made by the Bridge Committee to carry their object, and as the chief difficulty lay in the expense involved in executing Mr. Rennie's scheme, Lord Wm. Bentinck suggested "whether, if instead of continuing Kinderley's Cut to the Wash, where there is a fall of only thirteen inches, they executed the first part of Messrs. Rennie and Telford's plan, between the Wash and Crabhole, where there is a fall of twelve feet, and thereby gaining the real outfall," the object would not be more easily obtained. A meeting of the Bridge subscribers was held at Lynn on the 28th of February, 1826, at which it was resolved, "That steps be taken to introduce a bill into parliament and carry it through both houses. This was followed by a meeting of the North Level Commissioners, at Thorney, on the 2nd of March, when the injurious effects of the Bridge and Embankment as a separate measure, as pointed out by Mr. Telford and Mr. Chapman, were taken into consideration, and resolutions adopted to oppose the bill in parliament. At the same time the meeting approved of an abridged plan recommended by Messrs. Telford and Rennie, of making a new channel from the site of the proposed bridge to Crabhole, at an estimated expense of £86,715, as a measure in their opinion highly beneficial to drainage and navigation. On the same day a petition to parliament against the bill was got up at Wisbech, and also a memorial to the Lords Commissioners of the Admiralty and other influential bodies, imploring their assistance in opposing the bill in all its stages.

But while these hostile proceedings were going on, a friendly conference was proposed and agreed to between the Bridge Committee and that of the North Level proprietors. At this conference, which was held at Mr. Adam's chambers in London, on the 11th day of March, 1826, it was resolved: "That it is expedient to execute the plan of forming a channel from the end of Kinderley's Cut to Crabhole, together with the Bridge and Embankment at Sutton Wash, as one united measure. That, to carry this measure into effect, application be made forthwith to Messrs. Jolliffe and Banks, to ascertain for what sum and upon what terms they would execute the united plan; and that negotiations be opened with the proprietors of South Holland, for the purpose of inducing them to contribute a sum of money proportionate to the benefit the lands in that district would derive from the measure, towards the execution of the work. That Mr. Adam and Mr. Tycho Wing be requested to negociate with the trade of Wisbech and Peterborough, and the proprietors of land in Wisbech Hundred, and other parties, for the purpose of inducing them to contribute a sum proportionate to the benefit they will respectively derive from the execution of this important work. That these parties be requested to appoint committees to act on their behalf at the next conference; and that Mr. Adam be requested to invite the several committees to assemble as soon as the result of the foregoing negociations can be ascertained, the committee for the Bridge and Embankment now agreeing that the committee on the bill shall not proceed to business before the Easter holidays."

The above resolutions having been laid before a meeting of the Corporation, merchants, traders, and other inhabitants of Wisbech, on the 22nd day of March, it was resolved: "That this meeting will concur in the plan of forming a new channel from Kinderley's Cut to Crabhole, provided that all parties interested contribute their fair proportion of the expense, and provided that no charge be made upon this town or port, or the navigation thereof, for the intended bridge and its embankment, or any of the works connected therewith;" and a suggestion having been made by Mr. Wing on behalf of the North Level, "that the charge and expense of the said new channel and the banks thereof shall be undertaken by that Level on having reasonable contributions from all the other parties in this measure," it was resolved: "That if the several other parties interested shall contribute their proper and reasonable proportion, this town and port will consent to a tonnage of 6*d*. per chaldron on coals, and 6*d*. per ton on other goods, in aid of the work; or that they will allow a sum not exceeding £30,000 to be raised on their tonnage duties, and will consent to a duty of 6*d*. per chaldron and ton towards defraying the interest of the sum to be so raised, the surplus of the said last mentioned duty—if any, after the payment of the interest—to be applied as a sinking fund for the discharge of the principal, and after the payment thereof that tonnage duty to cease; provided that if the said tonnage duty of 6*d*. shall be insufficient to pay the principal so raised and the interest thereof, the deficiency shall be charged upon and made good by the North Level; and provided that no further or future charge whatever shall be made upon the trade or navigation of this town or port for making and maintaining the said channel, or the banks thereof, or any other works whatever, from the upper end of Kinderley's Cut to Crabhole, or from thence to the sea."[1]

At this meeting a committee was also appointed to attend a conference of the interested parties that was to be held in London on the 7th of April following, and which met at Mr. Telford's house. After resolving—"That it is expedient to make a new channel from Gunthorpe Sluice to Crabhole, if sufficient funds can be provided for that purpose," an estimate by Messrs. Jolliffe and Banks and Mr. Telford being laid before the conference, it was agreed on the part of the North Level to raise this sum, and to take the execution and maintenance of the works upon themselves, on condition that they receive of

	£.
The Town of Wisbech	30,000
The proprietors of Wisbech Hundred	15,000
———————— South Holland	10,000
St. Edmund's, St. James', and St. Mary's. .	5,000
	£60,000

It was also resolved: "That the lands and marsh vested in the Bedford Level Corporation, together with the marsh farm, also vested in the Bedford Level Corporation, and such proportion of any other lands and marshes as may be obtained as compensation for reclaiming such other lands, be applied to reimburse the North Level any sum expended by them in the execution of the proposed works exceeding the sum of £48,000, to discharge the current expenses of maintaining the said banks, and to form a fund of £30,000 for the maintenance thereof."

(1) It is apparent from this proviso that the Wisbech Corporation had no idea of the great increase in the trade of the port which would ensue on the opening of the Nene Outfall. The North Level Commissioners rejected the proposal as inadmissible, notwithstanding their anxiety to forward the work.

The final adjustment of differences of the parties interested took place at a conference held at the Caledonian Hotel, London, on the 10th of April, 1826, which soon led to the completion of that part of the great plan suggested by Lord W. Bentinck, and sanctioned, with a few amendments, by Messrs. Rennie and Telford. On it being proposed to throw additional expense and responsibility on the North Level, so impressed were the proprietors of land in that district with the importance of the measure, that they agreed to undertake the risk of executing and maintaining this great work upon the conditions before stated.[1]

Opposition to the measure having been in a great measure neutralised by the conference that had taken place in London, and it being supported in Parliament by facts and arguments of the most cogent nature, the bill received the royal assent on the 14th of June, 1827. The act having been obtained, steps were taken for the execution of the works with all convenient dispatch, and a contract was concluded with Messrs. Jolliffe and Banks, the celebrated contractors, for the sum of £110,000. Being provided with a large stock of implements suited to such vast undertakings, the necessary preparations were soon made, and the work commenced in August, 1827, and proceeded until about the same period in the following year, when from the nature of the soil and other circumstances observed by the contractors, the attention of the engineers was again required to meet the new difficulties that had arisen. The cause of these difficulties was the deviation from the line originally laid down by Messrs. Rennie and Telford, which was considerably more inland than that sanctioned by the Nene Outfall Act, and which had been given up in the progress of the bill through Parliament

(1) The Committee deputed by the Corporation of Wisbech seem to have been among the last to withdraw their opposition, as appears from the following entry of their report in the Records, on the 30th October, 1826: "Although your committee were unable to effect a successful opposition to the bill, so as to defeat it altogether, they trust their endeavours will not be considered wholly unavailing, as they fully anticipate that the advantages to be obtained to the trade of Wisbech by the proposed improvement of the navigation of the river to deep water on such moderate terms will considerably outweigh the disadvantages to be apprehended from the opening of the communication between the counties of Lincoln and Norfolk, by means of the bridge and embankment across Sutton Wash.

in favor of a cut through the open sands, as being less expensive. This line, the contractors suggested, being more inland than that under contract, would be exposed to less risk and difficulty to the Commissioners; and though it was considerably longer than the one in progress, they offered to execute it on the same terms. This proposition being submitted to the engineers they cordially approved of it, as it was straighter, more inland, and would correspond better with the upper limb of Kinderley's Cut, thereby offering greater freedom to the flux and reflux of the tide and the discharge of the drainage water, and that it would require a much shorter artificial embankment across the present channel to turn the river into its new course. "Under all these circumstances," say Messrs. Rennie and Telford, "we have no hesitation in recommending that this variation and extension be adopted, more especially as Messrs. Jolliffe and Banks undertake to execute the work of the same form and dimensions, and completed in all respects agreeable to the terms of the present contract, without any additional charge." This deviation meeting the approbation of all parties concerned, an act was obtained to sanction it in the following session of Parliament, and the work proceeded, under the personal superintendence of Mr. Jolliffe, until June, 1830, when having nearly completed the embankment, he engaged, in addition to his own large force, the assistance of the neighbouring farmers, with their teams, and by a grand effort forced the waters from their old course.

As the contractors had calculated that the flux and reflux of the tide would scour out from four to five feet of the bottom, some disappointment was experienced on finding that it became rather deteriorated. In fact, the ebb was so directed into the large bay between the embankment and the upper end of Kinderley's Cut, where the new channel commenced, that much of its scouring power was lost, and hence it became imperative to construct a dam across the old channel at this point, to throw the whole force of the ebb through the new cut. The experiment was eminently successful, as not only the four or five feet upon which the contractors had calculated were scoured out, but nearly twice that amount. The effect of the opening of the cut on the bridge—which had been constructed previous to the letting in of the water —was prodigious, and became to the proprietors an object of extreme anxiety, as it was in danger of being washed down. To prevent this, immense quantities of stone were thrown in, a practice which has continued ever since, to the prejudice both of drainage and navigation, as there is a fall of from two to three feet occasioned by this ridge of stones; besides, the water precipitated over it at the ebbing and flowing of the tide, has scooped out holes on each side of the bridge from 28 to 30 feet deep at low water. The effect of these holes is to create a series of eddies, especially on the flowing of the tide, so as to render a vessel almost unmanageable, under which circumstances serious accidents have frequently occurred, occasioning damage to the vessel, or the bridge, and sometimes to both. To show how far this scour proceeded beyond the calculations of the engineers employed, it may be stated that a sluice constructed immediately above the bridge, at an expense of £4000, for the purpose of warping up that part of the old channel which lies above the embankment, was never used, as the channel became so low that the tide seldom or ever reached the sill; this occasioned some disappointment, as, besides the expense of erecting the sluice, the lands intended to be improved by its operation remained comparatively sterile and valueless. This extraordinary scour rendered it necessary to protect the banks of the new channel with stones, amounting in quantity to 100,000 tons, at an expense of £32,214. As a set-off against this, however, was the immense saving in the excavation, which, had it been performed by manual labor, would have amounted to double what it actually cost.

The following are the dimensions of the new cut:

Width of top at Crabhole	300 feet.
———— bottom	250 —
Depth	24 —

At the upper limb of Kinderley's Cut these dimensions[1] are reduced to 190 feet at top, 140 feet at bottom, and 24 feet in depth.[2]

Here, then, was a river of sufficient capacity to discharge the waters of the district for which it was intended; but, in order to derive the full benefit of this improved outfall, it was necessary to adapt the internal drains to this new state of things. Accordingly, the North Level Commissioners, who had been the chief promoters of the great scheme, lost no time in availing themselves of the advantages to be derived from its completion. A bill was therefore introduced into parliament in 1830, which, after a feeble opposition, passed into a law in 1831, and the works were commenced forthwith. A new sluice was constructed for the discharge of the waters of the Level into the Nene Outfall, the sill of which was laid eight feet deeper than the one by which it formerly drained into the old channel. The width of water-way of the old sluice was 17 feet, that of the new 36 feet. In connection with this sluice a main drain is formed extending to Clow's Cross, a distance of eight miles and a quarter, eight feet deeper than the Old Shire Drain for which it was substituted, and in capacity more than six times as large.[3] From Clow's Cross the new drainage diverges by two separate

(1) "The dimensions originally set out by the engineers were 80 feet in width of bottom at Crabhole, diminishing gradually to 60 feet at the junction with Kinderley's Cut."—*Compendium of Expenditure on the Nene Outfall, by Tycho Wing.*

(2) The following is an abstract of the whole expenditure to July, 1831:

	£.	s.	d.
Expense of obtaining Acts of Parliament	8,788	10	0
Purchase-monies for land and premises taken for the Cut	14,045	15	0
Messrs. Jolliffe and Banks's contract	110,000	0	0
Ditto for extra work and charges allowed by the engineer	22,314	1	1
Contribution to North Level Sluice by Act of Parliament	2,000	0	0
Soiling, seeding, and flagging banks	3,504	9	7
Stoning sides of Cut	32,214	1	2
Berths for vessels	914	1	10
Salaries of clerks, engineers, and superintendents	2,105	16	2
Solicitors' charges for preparing securities for loans, &c., and printers, stationers, and other miscellaneous payments	2,283	19	3
Interest on loans and advances	2,545	13	7
	£200,716	7	8

(3) Memoir of Nene Outfall and North Level Drainage.

lines, called respectively the New South Eau and the New Wryde, which receive on their courses the waters from every district of the North Level, including Newborough, Borough Fen, and Great Portsand. These new branch lines are as superior to the old ones as the new main drain is to the Old Shire Drain; and when the works were opened in 1834, their efficacy was found to surpass the most sanguine expectations of the promoters.

The works having been thus finished to the entire satisfaction of the parties interested, a meeting was held at Thorney, when it was resolved, "That, on the 23rd of May, 1834, they should invite Tycho Wing, Esq., to a public dinner at Wisbech, to present to him a public tribute of their esteem for the part he had taken in conducting the works to so successful a termination, and that the leading gentlemen connected with the Great Level be invited to meet him, for the purpose of viewing the works just completed." Accordingly, there assembled on the morning of that day a large party from all parts of the Great Level, who embarked at Wisbech in a vessel provided for the occasion; and, as the day was fine, there was an opportunity of viewing every part of the Nene, as they glided down to the lower part of the new cut which had been named "Tycho Wing's Channel."

In passing through Kinderley's Cut, many reflections crowd into the minds of those acquainted with its history, as it may be considered the germ from which sprung those magnificent works, the completion of which it was the business of the day to celebrate. Near this spot the new North Level Sluice is situated, with its firm masonry and ample arches, through which might pass, if necessary, the waters of the Nene; and when it is borne in mind that the sill of this sluice is eight feet lower than the former one, some idea may be formed of its efficiency as an outlet to the waters of the North Level. From this point the river stretches in a straight line to Sutton Bridge, where the pleasure we had experienced suffered some abatement. This bridge is a great drawback from this noble undertaking. How it was placed in such an awkward position would be difficult to conjecture, had we not been told that it was to save the contractors from £4000 to £5000 by carrying the embankment to a more convenient point on the Norfolk side. What a paltry economy that injures an important navigation almost to this amount annually! But if it were asked to what this blunder is to be attributed, the answer would be, to the petty jealousies then existing among the parties concerned in the undertaking—jealousies which produced supineness in some who should have watched with vigilance those interests which they were bound to protect. The error, however, has been committed, and must remain a serious obstruction to the navigation of Wisbech while the bridge stands. Before attempting to pass through, we found it necessary to drop the anchor and throw out lines on each side of the vessel, and, by the tedious process of warping, were enabled to pass safely through, after a delay of nearly an hour. Having passed the bridge, we observed a long line of the larger class of vessels delivering their cargoes, which, but for this obstruction, might have proceeded up to Wisbech. Contrasting this with the time when the smaller vessels were exposed on the open sands near this spot, and the larger ones to the violence of the elements at a great distance from the shore, we could not help admiring the talent and enterprise which had conferred such immense benefits upon the country. We were particularly struck with that stupendous work—the embankment across this dangerous estuary, over which an army might now pass in safety.

On receiving Mr. Wing on board, the party proceeded to view the lower part of the cut which had been named in honor of Mr. Wing, and soon after returned to Wisbech.

A dinner was provided for the party in the Girls' National School, at which Sir Culling Eardly Smith presided, when Mr. Wing was presented with the tribute of respect, consisting of a handsome silver epergne weighing 480 ounces. On one of the tablets is a basso relievo view of the river, the Nene Outfall, and the North Level works; on the second, the inscription ; and on the third, the arms and crest of Mr. Wing. Seated on the base are three figures: first, a female figure supporting a plan, compasses, and rule, with other instruments, indicative of the science of surveying, at her feet; second, a male figure of an excavator resting on a spade; third, a figure of Ceres. A foliage pillar supports six branches for lights, with a chased vase in the centre for flowers. The inscription is as follows:

Presented to
TYCHO WING, ESQUIRE,
Of Thorney Abbey, in the County of Cambridge,
By Owners and Occupiers of Lands, and other persons chiefly
interested in the North Level and adjoining Districts,
AS A PUBLIC TRIBUTE,
expressive of their acknowledgment and unqualified admiration
of the foresight, judgment, activity, and perseverance,
exhibited by him in the preparation, progress, and completion
of the
NENE OUTFALL AND NORTH LEVEL WORKS,
which are already displaying results highly beneficial to the
Agriculture and Commerce of the surrounding Country,
and which mainly owe their successful accomplishment to his
well-tempered and unremitting exertions.
23d May, 1834.

Woodhouse Marsh Cut.

Having noticed the various steps by which the Nene Outfall and the North Level works were brought to completion. with the various causes which facilitated or retarded their progress, and some of their splendid results, it may be useful to glance at a work which, though greatly inferior, is of some importance to illustrate the difficulties connected with works of drainage, and the impolicy of undertaking them excepting under the direction of competent engineers, and with sufficient funds for their completion.

Immediately above Kinderley's Cut the river took a most circuitous sweep towards the Norfolk side, which subjected vessels to much inconvenience and delay, and it was proposed to make a new channel in a line with Kinderley's Cut. The opinions of several engineers were taken, whose estimates of the expense varied from £800 to £7000. The cost being so uncertain and the means of the Corporation very limited, the work was postponed from time to time for want of funds; and, but for the agricultural distress that prevailed in 1827, it is doubtful whether it would have been undertaken. In that year the great uumber of able-bodied laborers thrown upon the Poor Rate, led to a conference between the Select Vestry and the Corporation, at which it was arranged that they should contribute jointly to the cost of the work, and operations were commenced forthwith. Like other works, however, undertaken under such circumstances, it proceeded by fits and starts through parts of the years 1827, 1828, and 1829, encountering occasional disasters from high tides and floods, when, after expending between £2000 and £3000, the following resolution was entered upon the Corporation books: "That the works at Woodhouse Marsh be suspended for want of funds." In the following year, Messrs. Jolliffe and Banks being consulted as to whether £400 would be sufficient to complete the work, they replied in the negative, and it was abandoned to the mercy of the elements, acquiring the name of "The Paupers' Cut," which it is likely to retain. But though the joint operations of the parish officers and the Corporation were so unfortunate, there were still those interested in the navigation of the river who entertained hopes of completing that which had thus been abandoned. At the election of Capital Burgesses in November, 1830, a majority favorable to the completion of the work was returned, and one of the first motions put upon the books for discussion had this for its object. It was eventually resolved: "That the opinion of an engineer be obtained, with estimates of the probable expense."

Mr. Wm. Swansborough, a resident engineer, estimated the expense of completing the cut at £800, and in case of a dam being necessary, £300 additional. The Corporation also consulted Mr. Cubitt, whose estimate differed little from that of Mr. Swansborough. Being thus fortified by the opinion of an engineer who had acquired considerable celebrity by works at Lowestoff a few years before, operations were soon after commenced under the superintendence of Mr. Swansborough. As the funds of the Corporation were very low at the time, the work progressed but slowly during the summer, and an irruption of the tide, towards the end of the year, damaged it to a considerable extent, which so exhausted the funds, that it became necessary for the promoters of the scheme to furnish the means themselves for carrying on the work. During the following summer the cut was sufficiently excavated by manual labor, as to warrant the attempt of constructing a dam to force the waters into the new channel. In the progress of this part of the work difficulties multiplied to an extent which none of the engineers anticipated, as the construction of the dam, which they had estimated at £300, was actually contracted for at £1000; and the contractor, after spending that amount, abandoned the work in despair, leaving it in a worse state than when he began, as the flux and re-flux of the tide over the materials thrown in to form the dam had gulled holes on each side to the depth of twenty to thirty feet. In this emergency Mr. Cubitt was called in, who recommended that the dam be constructed with sand-bags, according to a plan which he described. Operations went on in conformity with his directions for several days without any progress being observed. On the contrary, the workmen were of opinion that the part of the river where they were letting down the sand-bags became deeper, which puzzled them to account for, until a number of empty bags were picked up floating below Sutton Bridge, which fully explained the mystery. The sand had oozed through the pores of the bags, which, being thus deprived of their gravity, floated down with the current.

All being again confusion and disaster, the opponents of the measure anticipated a triumph in its failure, which was considered all but certain. In this dilemma, it became a question of grave consideration with the Corporation whether the works should not be abandoned altogether. While this was strongly urged by one party in the hall, it was contended by the promoters that, as a large sum had been expended in the attempt to construct a dam, it would be more advisable to spend £500 or £600 more to complete the work, than to leave the materials that had been thrown in at an expense of several thousand pounds as an obstruction to navigation, and which would require a far greater sum to remove. The question being decided in favor of proceeding, no time was lost in making the necessary preparations for another attempt, and the promoters had learned from former disasters that nothing but solid materials and a large force could be of any avail, under the circumstances that had arisen through the scour occasioned by the opening of the Nene Outfall. Application was accordingly made to Mr. Tycho Wing to allow a quantity of stone that was being sent down from Wansford to secure the banks of the new channel, to stop at Woodhouse Marsh. This was readily granted, though with considerable inconvenience to the works below, with which he was more particularly identified. A large quantity was thus stopped to be applied as emergency might require. On the morning of the 7th of May, 1832,—everything being prepared for the trial,—three gentlemen,[1] who had taken a lead in promoting the scheme. went down to the works to witness the operations, and with the determination to get the dam closed, if possible, before they returned. In addition to the regular laborers, the assistance of several farmers with their teams was procured, and the work progressed with great spirit till tide-time, which happened about noon, when the dam was so far advanced as to allow teams to pass along the top from one side to the other in apparent safety. But, at this critical moment, the elements seemed to conspire once more to frustrate the attempt. A gale, which had blown from the northwest during the morning, increased with the rising of the tide, and added four or five feet more than had been calculated upon to its height. The dam, so hastily constructed, was but ill adapted to resist this extraordinary pressure and tumult of waters, and began to give way, and in a few seconds the whole was laid prostrate by the raging elements, while those who had beheld its progress during the morning

(1) The gentlemen here referred to were Messrs. William and Charles Jecks, and Mr. N. Walker, the writer of this account.

with satisfaction, stood almost petrified on witnessing this instant demolition of their favorite work, which but a few minutes before they had looked upon as all but completed.

The superintendent and workmen, giving up all for lost, adjourned to dinner, while the members of the Corporation remained gazing upon the desolation before them, exposed to the bitterness of a storm that seemed more like November than May. However, when the tide became stiller, as it approached high water, it occurred to them that with promptitude the dam might yet be taken before the strength of the ebb. Accordingly, all hands were summoned to their posts, and after considerable reluctance, even on the part of the superintendent, operations were resumed with increased vigor, and before the ebb acquired its strength, the waters were forced into the new channel, the bed of which was six feet above that of the old one. At first the waters found their way but slowly through this new course, but in a short time they acquired the force of a mountain torrent, tearing up the soil with tremendous power, and in a few hours the cut was completed so far that the gentlemen who had come down to witness the operations, had the pleasure of seeing two vessels sail through before they left the spot, and this undertaking, which had caused so much anxiety and expense, completed, without interrupting the navigation for a single tide. This result was the more gratifying, as an application to the Court of Chancery had been talked of by the opponents of the measure a few days before, when appearances were less promising. An error in setting out the line when the work was undertaken occasioned considerable expense afterwards to correct, as through fear of injuring the Newton bank, which at the lower end of the cut approaches near to the river, the engineer gave it a slight inclination to the Norfolk side, which made the current set in with such force in that direction, that in a short time it gulled out a bay which required considerable expense to fill up, and as the ebb continues to set in on that side, it requires constant care to prevent a recurrence of a similar breach. However, by training and stoning for several years after the opening of the cut, it has been brought into a state to answer the purposes of navigation. The cut itself has also been stoned, and the foreshores trimmed, and at the upper end the training has been carried on for several hundred yards, and is intended to be continued onwards to the town of Wisbech.

The effect of the opening of the Nene Outfall upon the river was extraordinary, and in the town of Wisbech it added from ten to twelve feet to its depth, solely by the scour occasioned by the lowering of the outfall. This was a result as unexpected as it was beneficial, Mr. Rennie having, in his Report in 1814, estimated the expense of deepening the river from the lower end of Kinderley's Cut to the Horseshoe below Wisbech, at £44,544. This was exclusive of deepening the river through the town up to Rummer's Mill, which was estimated at about £12,000, making the gross amount £56,544. In point of saving, therefore, the advantages were immense, as the excavation of from ten to twelve feet by manual labor would have amounted most probably to the full sum mentioned in Mr. Rennie's estimate. The saving in expense, however, was small in comparison with the advantages which it conferred on the navigation of the port. There were no longer to be seen vessels of small dimensions detained within a few miles of the town for weeks together, disappointing the hopes and wasting the property of the merchant who had risked it on a navigation so precarious. Commerce under such circumstances partook too much of the nature of gambling to be profitable, as great losses were frequently sustained by delay, damage to cargoes, and other contingencies, necessarily connected with such a navigation. The shipowner was also in a position equally hazardous, as his vessel suffered more from lying on a sand-bank than in pursuing her voyage in deep water; besides, the crew must be fed and paid when thus detained as well as when engaged in more active and profitable service.

The state of things commencing with the opening of the Nene Outfall forms a striking contrast to the above. Instead of the uncertainty of former times, a vessel can now sail with the utmost regularity, and may safely calculate on the passage from Wisbech to the sea offering no obstruction to her voyage. Besides, three voyages to Wakefield or London can now be performed in the time that two formerly required, or it may perhaps be nearer truth to say two instead of one, as it is well known that vessels frequently make the voyage to and from Seaham in the course of a week, though of a much larger class of vessels than those formerly trading to the port. Even these larger craft are not delayed for want of water, being able to get up at any period of the tide. This facility of communication was soon apparent in the increase of the tonnage, which rose from 55,040 in 1829 to 63,180 in 1830, the year in which the Nene Outfall was opened, and continued to increase till 1847, when it reached 167,443.

As improvements, however, may be purchased too dear, it will not be out of place to inquire whether those effected by the Nene Outfall have not been of this description. It appears from the various documents which we have examined that above £400,000 have been expended on the works, the greater part of which fell upon the land. In pursuing the inquiry, therefore, the drainage naturally presents itself as the first in importance. The Nene Outfall cost about £200,000, of which the land contributed £170,000, the North Level quota being £140,000. In addition to this the internal drains cost £150,000, making an aggregate of £290,000 besides the expense of maintaining the whole of the works. This at the time had a formidable appearance, and few agriculturists in the districts affected by the measure believed it possible to bear up under the burden it would impose. So early, however, as 1834, the gentlemen who assembled from all parts of the Great Level, to pay a tribute of respect to the man who had by his talents and perseverance conducted the works to a successful issue, vied with each other in setting forth the advantages which had even then resulted from the works; and, in 1837, Mr. John Peck, of Parson Drove, on the completion of the internal drains of the district with which he is more particularly connected, observed, on his health being drunk: "Perhaps it may be said a great deal of money has been expended; I admit it, and even more than was at first expected; but the end will prove that our capital has been well employed, and that it will pay abundant interest to us and to our children. When we look back and see what has been done in the last few years, it appears like a dream;—all the waste lands of our country made fertile—the lowest of the low well drained, even in the wettest winters—and the Grand Sluice we have opened this day will more than compensate us for all our trouble and expense." And on another occasion, when the same gentleman was presented with a piece of plate as an acknowledgment of his services in the drainage of the country in 1834 and 1835, every speaker spoke in the most glowing terms of the advantages which had accrued from the completion of the works to the owners and occupiers of land in the district. To show that these were not mere words of course, or flattery of individuals, it was stated in evidence before a committee of the House of Lords, so lately as 1848, by Tycho Wing, Esq., "that the value of land in some parts of the North Level had increased 100 per cent., and in some cases more." And it is well known that land, that might have been bought twenty years ago for £5 per acre, would now bring from £60 to £70. These facts show that the proprietors have the most substantial reasons to be satisfied with their bargain, as they must have been already more than repaid for their great outlay.

The next in importance is the Corporation of Wisbech. £30,000 was considered at the time a large sum, and serious doubts were entertained whether the trade of the port could bear it. But the debt has been liquidated without the outlay on the part of the Corporation of a single shilling. Besides, the trade of the port has by its operation been more than trebled, and when all the collateral advantages of a trade so extended are taken into account, Wisbech has good cause to be content with the advantages she has gained by the Nene Outfall. In corroboration of this, since the opening of the Nene Outfall the timber trade has increased tenfold, and may, when the contemplated improvements are completed, be indefinitely extended; and other branches of trade may be increased in a similar proportion.

Of all the parties to the scheme the Bridge Company have been the least successful, for though they succeeded in improving the communication between the eastern and midland counties, they failed in making it pay, and as this is the chief feature in all business concerns, it may be pronounced so far a failure; and now that railways have come into competition with it, the prospects of the shareholders are still more discouraging. But, notwithstanding its failure as a speculation, it may be ranked among those national works of which the country has reason to be proud, and which, in addition to affording a safe and easy passage across a dangerous estuary, has been the means of gaining from the sea a large tract of valuable land, above 3000 acres of which have been enclosed, and an equal quantity is in progress of formation. Taking the whole plan into account, with its results, all parties have ample cause to be satisfied, more especially with so large an addition to the means of subsistence.

CHAPTER X.

BIOGRAPHY.

THIS is a chapter in the history of Wisbech which may be soon dismissed, since few names of any importance have been connected with the town, nor have any opulent families settled in its neighbourhood. Neither should we have considered it an agreeable task to have enumerated the dusty genealogy of half a dozen aristocratic families distinguished only by the possession of an old house and a long rent-roll. History is getting too ponderous a machine to be loaded with such useless lumber as these genealogical family histories, which secure all the immortality they deserve on their escutcheons and their epitaphs.

1340. The first name belonging to the town, or apparently so, is that of John de Wisbeche, who was connected with the construction of the Lady Chapel or Chapter House of Ely Cathedral, one of the triumphs of Gothic architecture. Hewas one of the monks of the monastery, and is recorded to have had the "oversight" of the work, which Stephenson conjectures was overseer under Alan de Walsingham,[1] to whom the design is generally attributed. The same authority informs us that he held the office of Custos Capellæ B.

(1) Stephenson's Continuation of Bentham.

Mariæ, from the time the chapel was begun to his death, which happened July, 1349, during the great plague, about which time the chapel was nearly finished.[1] He was buried in the chapel.[2] It is recorded in the life of Bishop Montacute that while John de Wisbech dug the foundations of the Lady Chapel *with his own hands*, he discovered, among other things, a brass pot full of money, with which he paid the workmen's wages as long as it lasted.[3] Among the artisans employed on this chapel a William de Wisbech is named, at 20*d.* a week and a robe of eleven shillings value. It thus appears that this famous building, now converted into a parish church of Ely, and, though in dilapidation and crowded with ugly pewing, the admiration of taste, was somewhat indebted in its construction to Wisbech architects—the first and the last time that such, we believe, have been connected with anything tolerable in the art.

1469. Another monk, bearing the same name of John de Wisbech, is recorded at this date as Abbot of Croyland. He was first Prior of Freiston. He built the infirmary and great granary at Croyland, and did much towards completing and beautifying the abbey. He completed the state apartment and gave a house to the chamberlain, to pay four shillings on Christmas-day annually, *quatenus ad reparationem conventus in eorum munitionibus.* He also built convenient apartments in Buckingham Castle, Cambridge, for the scholars of this house to sleep and study in. Amongst other things, he obtained from the Pope a bull to allow the eating of meat in Lent. His improvements of Crowland were the last previous to the Reformation. He died 19th November, 1476.[4]

JOHN MORTON, Bishop of Ely, though not a native of Wisbech, appears to have resided here for some time during

(1) Stephenson's Cont. of Bentham, p. 221. (2) Bentham.

(3) Leland's Collectanea ab Bentham.

(4) Watson's Wisbech, Thompson's Boston.

his holding the see of Ely, which was from 1478 to 1486. We have already had occasion to notice different portions of his history. The work of drainage, called after him, will not easily allow his name to perish in this district, and he will not the less live in literature from the incidental scene in Shakspere's Richard III., where he is introduced, though the passage is only a transcript of the annals of the day. As Cardinal of the Church of Rome, Archbishop of Canterbury, and prime adviser of Henry VII., he has so many other reasons for being remembered, as a statesman, a churchman, and a benefactor.

1616. JOHN THURLOE, Esq., has become famous, less from his individual talents, than from the important period with which he was connected. Characters that would have passed off without notice in the unpeculiar annals of monarchy, have, by their connection with a daring experiment on the constitution of England, become characters of interest, and in somewise of esteem. Thurloe was one of these. He is connected with Wisbech merely by residence here, by purchasing the castle, and by being the only man the inhabitants ever had an opportunity of electing to parliament. He was the son of the Rev. Thomas Thurloe, rector of Abbot's-Roding, in Essex, where he was born in 1616. He was educated for the law, and in 1645 was made one of the secretaries to the Parliamentary Commissioners at Uxbridge. In March, 1650-1, after the execution of Charles I., with which he declared himself unacquainted, he attended the Ambassadors to the United Provinces as their secretary. In April, 1652, he was made Secretary to the Council of State, and in December, 1652, Secretary of State to the Protector. In 1654 Thurloe was made one of the Masters of Lincoln's Inn, and in the same year Receiver of the Foreign and Inland Postage. In September, 1656, he was returned a member of Parliament for the Isle of Ely, in which office he detected the conspiracies of the Fifth-monarchy men. In 1657 he was made one of Cromwell's Privy Council, and in

November following a Governor of Charter House. In Februarp, 1658, he was invested with the Chancellorship of Glasgow. Thurloe continued in office during the Protectorate; but, though attainted of high treason by Charles II., he was acquitted, and even more than once solicited by the king to engage in his administration, which he always declined. He died suddenly at Lincoln's Inn, in February, 1668. Cromwell probably owed some of the virtues, with which his partisans delight to cover him, to Thurloe. Thurloe appears to have had a higher sense of legal right and justice than his master. He induced Cromwell to resort to the ordinary course of law in trying conspiracies against the government, rather than pursue his enemies through the tyrannical forms of the High Court of Justice. The leaders in the army, however, entertained a violent dislike to Thurloe, and in 1658 nearly succeeded in inducing him to quit his position and emoluments. This, however, he was not permitted to do. He was highly esteemed by Richard Cromwell, but his advice was, notwithstanding, slighted on the most important act of the administration of the second Protectorate. The Protector dissolved the parliament against the advice of Thurloe, and was soon precipitated from his eminence.

Wisbech seems to have highly esteemed its distinguished resident. The inhabitants built a gallery for him in the church, elected him a Capital Burgess, and would have made him their parliamentary representative. He returned their good-will with a charitable donation for putting out apprentices, which is still applied to its specified purpose.[1]

1716. THOMAS HERRING, Archbishop of Canterbury, was the son of the Rev. John Herring, rector of Walsoken, and was educated at Wisbech Grammar School.[2]

(1) A fine portrait of the Secretary, copied by Mr. R. Browning, from an original in the possession of the Thurloe family at Norwich, has been lately presented to the Museum by Daniel Gurney, Esq., of Runcton. It is placed in the lecture room, and represents Thurloe in his younger days.

(2) Watson's Wisbech.

He does not seem to have been celebrated for anything except being an archbishop, which in itself is a very questionable title to remembrance, much more posthumous celebrity.

1729. SIGISMUND TRAFFORD, author of an essay on draining, particularly of the Bedford Level.[1]

1752. The Rev. BROCK RAND, rector of Leverington and Newton. He was an antiquary of a useless kind, and collected a list of the incumbents of the dioceses of Ely and Norwich, which formed a quarto volume consigned to Corpus Christi College, Cambridge, but it is now lost.[2]

1770. HENRY BURROUGHS, D.D., vicar of Wisbech and prebendary of Peterborough, was the author of sermons, which were printed at a private press of his own.[3]

1780. CHARLES LINDSEY, Bishop of Kildare, was the younger son of the Earl of Balcarras, and was educated at Wisbech School. He was vicar of Wisbech from 1787 to 1795, when he accompanied his brother-in-law, the Earl of Hardwicke, to Ireland as his chaplain and private secretary. He was afterwards made Bishop of Killaloe, and subsequently of Kildare, which see he held till his death in 1846. He accumulated a large fortune.

ABRAHAM JOBSON, D.D., was made vicar of Wisbech in 1802, from which date to his death in 1831 he bestowed on the town such a series of benefactions as has made him perhaps its most munificent donor. On obtaining the vicarage of Wisbech, which was then compounded at about £700 per year, he made a formal demand of all the tithes in kind of the grass lands, against which the owners and occupiers set up a modus for exemption. After a suit of nearly five years the vicar's claim was established, so that the income was raised to about £2000 per annum. It is, however, for

(1) Watson's Wisbech. (2) Idem. (3) Idem.

his charities that he will be gratefully remembered, and these were principally bestowed on education and the church. In the former list must be comprised £500, which he gave towards the establishment of a Boys' Charity School, and £100 towards the same kind of establishment for Girls. He also gave £500 for establishing a Sunday School connected with the church. In the church he made various expensive alterations, which, if not improvements, served the purpose of increased accommodation so much demanded there. Among these must be mentioned the second gallery over the north aisle, and half the cost of the north aisle gallery. He new ceiled the church, and was at half the cost of new glazing the windows. He also erected fresh pews, and transformed and altered the old ones. To Doddington, March, and Benwick, he gave £100 each, the interest of which he directed to be employed for providing religious books for the poor. But the greatest and last act of beneficence of his life was the endowment of the Chapel of Ease, which he effected by conveying in fee simple a real estate exceeding £5000 value, the rents and profits of which now amount to about £400 a-year. Besides this he took twenty shares in the undertaking, amounting to £1000. These various benefactions have connected his name with the best interests of Wisbech, and will preserve it among its Cranes and Wrights.

In 1823 various of the inhabitants, emboldened by his many donations, entered into a subscription for his portrait, which now adorns the Town Hall.

THOMAS CLARKSON has achieved a national—a universal reputation. He was born at Wisbech on the 28th of March, 1760, at the Grammar School, of which his father was at that time master. When he was six years old his father died, and he removed from the Grammar School to reside with his mother in the house at the bottom of High Street, now occupied by Mr. Ollard, surgeon. He received his early education at the Grammar School, from whence he was removed to St. Paul's School, and afterwards to St.

John's College, Cambridge. Here he distinguished himself in 1784 by gaining the prize Latin essay. This success induced him to try for the same prize the following year, which was on a subject that scattered the seeds of all his future toils and fortunes :—"*Is it right to make slaves of others against their will?*" While diving into books, and gathering facts for his essay, he became daily more absorbed in his subject; and the more painfully it affected him, the more eagerly he pursued it. He left no suggestion untried to gain a fuller acquaintance with the negro condition, and every thought which entered his mind, constantly employed on one object, was immediately noted down. For this purpose, he always had a light in his bed-room, that any idea which might occur in the sleepless watches of the night might not pass unrecorded. "It is impossible," he remarks, in his *History of Slavery*, "to imagine the severe anguish which the composition of this essay cost me. All the pleasure I had promised myself from the contest was exchanged for pain, by the astonishing facts that were now continually before me. It was one gloomy subject from morning to night. In the day I was agitated and uneasy; in the night I had little or no rest. I was so overwhelmed with grief that I sometimes never closed my eyes during the whole night, and I no longer regarded my essay as a mere trial for literary distinction. My great desire now was to produce a work that should call forth a vigorous public effort to redress the wrongs of injured Africa." The essay was successful, and Clarkson, having quitted the University, went to London to seek a publisher of it in a translated form. In this search he was introduced to Joseph Hancock, one of the Society of Friends, and by his means he now became acquainted, for the most part personally, with the small band of philanthropists who were already engaged in exposing the cruelties of the slave-trade, and of whose exertions he had not till now heard. His scheme of depicting the crime of slave-dealing and arousing the public against it, was thus unexpectedly forwarded by the assistance of William Dillwyn, and especially of Granville Sharpe, by whose exertions in the cause of the negro Simmons the celebrated British apothegm, that the slave who sets foot on English ground is free, had been extracted from the twelve judges.

He now, therefore, began to work in earnest. He sought information everywhere—by travelling and conversing with partisans and enemies: he applied to influential persons, and commenced that process of active agitation which, since his day, has become almost a fourth power in the state. By these actions he succeeded in securing Wilberforce, the member for York, whose attention was first called to the subject by Clarkson; and by the means of Wilberforce the measure was introduced into parliament in 1787,—two years after Clarkson had first undertaken the subject. In the mean time, he continued to keep the public attention on the subject: Wilberforce had undertaken to keep it before the eyes of the senate, but Clarkson undertook to agitate the kingdom; and, with this view, he gave lectures, got up meetings, and drew swarms of sympathisers in all the great cities to his cause. In the course of this mission he travelled over England, and visited France during the heat of the Revolution. His friends entreated him to conceal his name on this perilous journey; but, confiding in the majesty of his intentions, he refused all concealment, and boldly proclaimed his cause and his name as he went. He had an interview with Louis XVI., already the phantom of a king; was befriended by Necker and Lafayette, introduced to Petion, Brissot, Vergniaud, the "*Societé des Amis des Noirs*," and was presented with the privilege of citizenship. He was also publicly honored with a seat in the French Assembly during the discussion which Mirabeau, at his instance, moved, and which resulted in the abolition of all slave-trade bounties. Clarkson returned to England; and "for seven years," he says, "I had a correspondence to maintain with four hundred persons. I had some work or other to write annually for the cause. During this time I had travelled more than 35,000 miles in search of evidence, performing a great part of these journies in the night. All this time my mind had been incessantly on the stretch upon one subject only, for I had no leisure to attend to my own concerns. The various instances of barbarity that had frequently come under my notice had vexed, harassed, and afflicted me. The wounds thus inflicted had been deepened by the cruel disappointments I had so often experienced by the reiterated refusal of persons to give their testimony after I had travelled hundreds of miles in quest of them."

All these pains and exertions were repaid by the final triumph which Clarkson achieved. In 1801 the bill was passed for the total abolition of the Slave Trade, but it was not till 1807 that it became the law of the land. Thus was the first great triumph achieved. There still remained, however, the greatest evils behind,—an extensive foreign slave-trade, and an enslaved population in the isles. To repress the one and emancipate the other was now the object of Clarkson. But the war which Europe had now for some years carried on prevented any effective means being used on foreign evils, so that Clarkson was obliged to confine his attention to Britain. However, on the peace he visited Paris, and had an interview with the Emperor Alexander at Aix-la-Chapelle in 1818, to whom he showed several articles of African manufacture, and otherwise interested him in the negro cause.

In 1833 he had the triumphant satisfaction of witnessing the passing of the Slave Emancipation Bill. But age was now pressing on him, and his last public appearance was in 1840, at the Anti-Slavery Convention in London.

For several years before his death, which happened in September, 1846, he had been principally confined to his sitting-room, where, since 1840, he wrote a commentary on the New Testament, except the Book of Revelations.

He was presented with the freedom of the City of London, and his bust was placed in Guildhall; and "not long before his decease," says a relative," a very gratifying tribute was paid to his public virtue and merits by a subscription for his portrait set on foot at his native town of Wisbech, where an admirable likeness of him was placed in the Town Hall."

He has been celebrated by Brougham, Darwin, and Wordsworth. The latter has dedicated one of his fine, but rugged sonnets to his honor.

"Clarkson! it was an obstinate hill to climb;
How toilsome—nay, how dire—it was, by thee
Is known: by none, perhaps, so feelingly.
But thou, who, starting in thy fervent prime,
Didst first lead forth that enterprise sublime,
Hast heard thy constant voice its charge repeat,
Which out of thy young heart's oracular seat
First roused thee. O true yoke-fellow of time,
Duty's intrepid liegeman—see the palm
Is won, and by all nations shall be worn!
The blood-stained writing is for ever torn.
Thou henceforth wilt have a good man's calm,
A great man's happiness. Thy zeal shall find
Repose at length, firm friend of human kind." *March*, 1807.

Clarkson's publications are: "Essay on the Slavery and Commerce of the Human Species, particularly the African," 1786—"On the Impolicy of the African Slave Trade," 1788—"On the Comparative Efficiency of the Regulation or Abolition, as applied to the Slave Trade," 1789—"Letters on the Slave Trade and the State of the Nations in those Parts of Africa contiguous to Fort St. Louis and Goree," 1791—"Three Letters to the Planters and Slave Merchants," 1807—"The Portraiture of Quakerism," 3 vols., 1807—"The History of the Abolition of the Slave Trade," 2 vols., 1808—"Memoirs of the public and private Life of William Penn," 2 vols., 1813—"On Negro Improvement and Emancipation," 1823. Besides these, Clarkson contributed largely to the *Philanthropist*, a quarterly publication, in the early part of the century. His last years were embittered by an indirect attack on his exertions by the sons of Wilberforce—one of whom is the present Bishop of Oxford—who arrogated the whole merit of abolition to their father. This indiscreet mode of filial piety was answered by Clarkson in a small pamphlet commentary on the work, and highly resented by the public as a mean and unworthy arrogance, and highly unjust to the greater name of Clarkson.

WILLIAM GODWIN was born at Wisbech on the 3rd of March, 1756. His father was a dissenting minister here, and he was educated at the dissenting college at Hoxton. After quitting college Godwin took charge of a congregation near London, and afterwards at Stowmarket, in Suffolk; but at the end of five years—in 1782—he renounced his profession, and applied to literature. In his first work we see how far he had already advanced beyond the narrow boundaries of sectarianism, and with what a free, almost a frolicsome, spirit he assailed opinions dear to the bigotry of his party. His first work was "Sketches of History in Six Sermons," which was followed by contributions to the "New Annual Register." These writings had already given him a name. The principles he adopted were the broadest spirit of liberalism, which had at this time, in the course of four years, progressed all over Europe, and in France had changed from speculative theory to practice, and from practice to that wonderful madness which Europe has yet been unable to reconcile with any philosophy or any other political phenomena. But, in every other country in Europe, though they shared not in the realities which France was experiencing, a section of men arose strongly attached to the measures of France, and hailed even her murders and her intoxications as the preparation for nobler things—the cropping of extraneous branches, in order to increase the abundance and the size of the fruit. Godwin was of this class, and the popularity of these notions at the time secured him £700 for his next work, "The Inquiry concerning Political Justice and its Influences on general Virtue and Happiness." It was published in 1793, and the singularity of some of the principles adopted in it affords a good criterion of the kind of ideas which the French Revolution had encouraged. The experience of fifty years has somewhat cooled these kind of speculations, or rather altered their tendency; and we can now hardly reconcile the bold doctrines it administers with the judgment of a man of philosophic thought. It is a philosophical inquiry into the origin and progress of those ideas which generally result in selfishness, and to show how much more rational, happy, and beneficent it would be to disburden ourselves of this exclusive system, and adopt no distinctions but those which nature has provided—the distinctions of intellect. In pursuit of this chimera Godwin analyses innate principles, the principles of society, property, opinion, and other branches of his subject, gradually advancing notions which the wildest dreams of Rousseau never indulged, till mind predominating over matter is to supersede all the labor of the hands, and even the appetites themselves become obsolete. "If intellect can be exerted over all other matter," he says, "why not over the matter of our bodies?—in other words, why may it not supersede death?"

Such theories could never hope for listeners except during a period of universal delusion, and the celebrity of the work which propagated them is only a conclusive evidence that the madness of France had inoculated England. Godwin wrote in sincerity. The simplicity of his character was no less marvellous than its daring spirit of speculation. These boldly-argued doctrines were neither madness nor probabilities to him, but mere fore-shadows of inevitable destiny. Nor were they founded upon a narrow and partial knowledge of mankind; for his next work—"Caleb Williams"—which appeared about a year afterwards, has established his reputation over all the world in this respect. It is only just to Godwin to say that the extravagant notions of his "Political Justice" were the fever of his immaturity, as well as portions of the fevered character of the age. He entertained them only a year or two after the publication of the "Political Justice;" for, in 1799, in a preface to his "St. Leon," he says: "Some readers of my graver productions will, perhaps, in perusing these little volumes, accuse me of inconsistency; the affections and charities of private life being everywhere, in this publication, a topic of the warmest eulogium, while in the 'Inquiry, &c.,' they seemed to be treated with no great degree of indulgence and favor. In answer to this objection all I think necessary to say on the present occasion is, that for more than four years I have been anxious for opportunity and leisure to modify some of the earlier chapters of that work in conformity to the sentiments inculcated in this."

"Caleb Williams" is in many respects the most extraordinary novel in any language. The hint of it was taken from the popular tale of Blue Beard. It was founded on a chapter of the "Political Justice," and was intended to show how the present state of society, by its falsehoods and its rigid respect for wealth and influence, may hunt innocent poverty into degradation, while guilty power may sustain its position and influence. Godwin in this powerful novel has forgotten his theories in the marvellous use he has made of his knowledge of human nature. The story is simple. Falkland murders his neighbour: Caleb Williams, the servant of Falkland, learns the secret, and thus becomes a constant object of suspicion to his master, who, to preserve his own name pure, lays the guilt on Williams, and pursues him as a murderer through the country. The power of Falkland's character, and the dissection which it undergoes in the course of the novel, have been the theme of universal admiration. Colman adopted the story for his play of the "Iron Chest;" and in the extraordinary acting of Kean this creation of Godwin's, though only in reflected light, became a double favorite with the country. Shortly after the publication of this novel, the early reformers,—Holcroft, Thelwall, and Horne Tooke,—were thrown into the Tower on a charge of high treason. Godwin belonged to them in every respect "save their bonds;" and on their trial Judge Eyre, in his charge to the grand jury, proclaimed principles so offensive to our author, that he answered them in "Cursory Strictures," which eventually, it is said, led to the acquittal of the prisoners. In 1797 he married Mary Wolstonecroft, author of the "Rights of Women," but who died about a year after the marriage, having given birth to a daughter, who afterwards became Mrs. Shelley. Godwin, in 1799, published "St. Leon"—a novel that will reach the same posterity as "Caleb Williams," though its human interest is inferior to the elder performance.

"Caleb Williams" and "St. Leon" evidently cost their author great thought and labor. Lord Byron once asked him why he did not write a new novel. Godwin was then old, and he replied it would kill him. "And what matter," said Lord Byron, "we should have another 'St. Leon.'" It may be imagined what are the adventures of "St. Leon," when they are accompanied by such securities as the following: "I have in my possession the choice of being as wealthy as I please, and the gift of immortal life." He subsequently produced three other novels, "Fleetwood" in 1804, "Mandeville" in 1817, and "Cloudesley" in 1820, none of which sustain the reputation of his earlier works. After the death of his wife Godwin wrote the "Memoirs of her Life," and in 1801 "Thoughts on Dr. Parr's Spital Sermon," in which he defends his opinions against the attacks of that dogmatic churchman and others. In 1803 he produced a "Life of Chaucer," in two quarto volumes, an author of whom we scarcely know anything except his actual existence. Godwin has eked his story on conjecturally, catching at every slight incident for a long dissertation or description. This method of writing a life without materials naturally raised a great outcry against it. Sir W. Scott reviewed it with asperity in the "Edinburgh Review." It has, however, been the model for a recent life of Shakspere. Charles Knight, with as little material as possible, has produced as voluminous a biography of the Bard of Avon. Previous to this last work our author had adventured his reputation in the perilous straits of the drama. In 1800 he produced "Antonio, or the Soldier's Return," which was hooted from the stage. "Mr. Godwin," says Sergeant Talfourd, "sat on one of the great benches of the pit, unmoved amid the storm. When the first act passed off without a hand, he expressed his satisfaction at the good sense of the house: 'the proper season of applause had not arrived;' all was exactly as it should be. The second act proceeded to its close in the same uninterrupted calm; his friends became uneasy, but still his optimism prevailed; he could afford to wait; and although he did at last admit the great movement was somewhat tardy, and that the audience seemed rather patient than interested, he did not lose his confidence till the tumult arose, and then he submitted with quiet dignity to the fate of genius too lofty to be understood by a world as yet in its childhood." In 1807 he re-entered the same field with "Faulkner," but with the same want of success. In 1824-28 he published his "History of the Commonwealth," in four large volumes, which has become a text-book for those who look on the Protectorate as regeneration. The reputation of this work has been constantly progressing, and the opinion of 1847 is much more in accordance with its principles than that of 1827. He has, of course, represented Cromwell as a hero, and the master men of that age as master men for all ages. Though, perhaps, it misleads less than those histories which are written to make Cromwell infamous, it certainly oversteps the modesty of nature, and allows too little of human alloy to enter into the composition of the actions of the Roundheads. The Independents, who ultimately succeeded in beheading Charles and carrying the Revolution to its extremities, are represented as a race of almost pure virtue, and their system is lauded for its "generous spirit of toleration and fearlessness of sects," and as demanding "no other liberty for itself than it is willing to yield to all others." Yet this was the sect that robbed England of its amusements, persecuted the drama, destroyed social intercourse, abolished the liberty of the press, stabled horses in churches, purged the parliament, beheaded the king, and raised their leader to the pinnacle of power in the face of the self-denying ordinance. Beside this contribution to the political history of that age, Godwin wrote the "Lives of Edward and John Philips, Nephews and Pupils ot Milton," whose memoirs throw a certain degree of light on the literary history of a very obscure literary period. In 1820 he engaged himself against "Malthus's Essay on Population;" but here he misestimated his strength. His book was condemned at the time, and experience has shown its fallacy; while Malthus has gained celebrity with age. During the latter years of his life he produced his "Thoughts on Man," and the "Lives of the Necromancers," neither of which added to his fame. In the latter part of his life Godwin enjoyed a sinecure office of £100 a year under government, which was bestowed on him by the Whigs. He died in 1836, aged 80.[1]

Godwin has had violent detractors and violent friends. He lived in those times when Whig or Radical principles, which have come to be the ruling principles of the nation, were invigorated by persecution and rendered strong enough by the infatuation of their enemies to overpower them. The state trials and persecutions, Judge Eyre, and Lord Eldon, and Castlereagh, were the real precursors and promoters of Reform, Catholic Emancipation, Free Trade, and the Maynooth Grant. Though he never suffered personal abuse himself, he always belonged to the party who had some martyr at the stake. However, he lived to see his cause triumphant, and the arch-enemies of his opinions fall by death or minorities into the hinder ranks of the state. Enemies or friends have only borne one opinion on his literary merits, which we may appropriately close this sketch by illustrating. "He has now," says Dr. Maginn, an inveterate Tory, "taken his place in our world of authors; and we incline to think that 'Caleb Williams' and 'St. Leon' are the only books of his which will be remembered. His mind is

(1) We subjoin a chronological list of Godwin's works :—

Sketches of History in Six Sermons, 1782. Enquiry concerning Political Justice, and its influence on general virtue and happiness, 1793. Things as they are, or the Adventures of Caleb Williams, 3 vols., 1794. Cursory Strictures on the Charge delivered by Lord Chief Justice Eyre to the Grand Jury, Oct. 2, 1794. The Enquirer, Reflections on Education, Manners, and Literature, in a series of Essays, 1796. Memoirs of (Mary Wolstonecroft) the author of a "Vindication of the Rights of Women," 1798. St. Leon, a Tale of the 16th century, 4 vols., 1799. Antonio, a Tragedy, 1801. Thoughts occasioned by the perusal of Dr. Parr's Spital Sermon, being a reply to the attacks of Dr. Parr, Mr. Mackintosh, and others, 1801. The History of the Life and Age of Geoffrey Chaucer, 2 vols. 4to, 1803, 2nd Ed. 4 vols., 1804. Fleetwood, or the New Man of Feeling, 3 vols., 1805. Faulkner, a Tragedy, 1807. Essay on Sepulchres, 1809. Lives of Edward and John Philips, nephews and pupils of Milton, 1815. Mandeville, 1817. An Inquiry concerning the Power of Increase in the Numbers of Mankind; being an answer to Mr. Malthus's Essay on that subject, 1821. History of the Commonwealth, 4 vols., 1824-28. Cloudesley, 1830. Thoughts on Man. Lives of the Necromancers, 1834. Besides these, Godwin was the author of various school-books, published under the name of Baldwin.

not productive,—therein singularly differing from that of Sir Walter Scott, with whom alone as a novelist of power he of all our contemporaries can be compared. There is a want of invention even in his best books, and we can believe the current story that 'Caleb Williams' was written to illustrate a system, or to prove that a novel might be composed without reference to the passion of love."[1] "Caleb Williams," says a writer in the *Edinburgh Review*, "is probably the finest novel produced by a man—at least, since the 'Vicar of Wakefield.'.... It has been translated into most languages, and it has appeared in various forms on the theatres not only of England, but of France and Germany. There is scarcely a continental circulating-library in which it is not one of the works which most require to be replaced. Though written with a temporary purpose, it will be read with intense interest and with a painful impatience for the issue long after the original circumstance which produced its original composition shall cease to be known but to those who are well read in history. There is scarcely a fiction in any language which it is so difficult to lay by."[2] The same writer thus adverts to the personal history of Godwin. "All observations on the personal conduct of a writer, when that conduct is not of a public nature, is of dangerous example; and, when it leads to blame, it is severely reprehensible. But it is but common justice to say that there are few instances of more respectable conduct among writers than is apparent in the subsequent works [to the 'Political Justice'] of Mr. Godwin. He calmly corrected what appeared to him to be his own mistakes; and he proved the perfect disinterestedness of his corrections by adhering to opinions as obnoxious to the powerful as those which he relinquished. Untempted by the success of his scholars in paying court to the dispensers of favor, he adhered to the old and rational principles of liberty, violently shaken as these principles had been by the tempests which had beaten down the neighbouring erections of anarchy. He continued to seek independence and reputation with that various suc-

(1) Fraser's Magazine, 183. (2) Vol. 25—Article, "Milton's Nephews."

cess to which the fashions of literature subject professed writers, and to struggle with the difficulties incident to other modes of industry, for which his previous habits had not prepared him. He has thus, in our humble opinion, deserved the respect of all those, whatever may be their opinion, who still wish that some men in England may think for themselves, even at the risk of thinking wrong; but more especially of the friends of liberty, to whose cause he has courageously adhered."

WILLIAM WATSON, Esq., F.A.S., must not be omitted in a notice of the individuals who have given celebrity to Wisbech; for, although he was not born in the town, his long residence, and his singular exertions for the benefit of the place, entitle him to be distinguished among the best of its recent benefactors. His first public effort in Wisbech was as a banker. This business, however, proved unfortunate: he was obliged, by the fluctuating circumstances of public credit, to suspend payment; but with the promise to discharge his obligations if time were allowed him. This promise he faithfully fulfilled, paying not only his liabilities, but the interest on the time during which his payment had been suspended. This honorable conduct was acknowledged by the gratitude of his creditors, who subscribed him a handsome silver-gilt cup. Mr. Watson afterwards established himself successfully as a brewer, which business he followed till his death. In 1807, when the volunteer system was filling the country with local soldiers, Mr. Watson entered enthusiastically into the spirit of the day, and afterwards volunteered to extend his services to the whole country. He was rewarded with the honor of Lieutenant-Colonel, which he retained till his death. But, in 1827, the work which will hand his name locally to posterity was published. This was a "History of Wisbech," most carefully and industriously compiled from every resource obtainable. It also contains a very satisfactory account of the neighbourhood, and is embellished with nineteen very neat engravings, and comprises 700 pages. In 1833 his health began to decline, and he died in 1835.

CHAPTER XI.

MISCELLANEOUS.

PERHAPS nothing serves so well to preserve the features of a town as pictures. No kind of description will render us such perfect notions of its condition and of the changes which have come over its external features. Pictures, though they only arrest a single moment of time on its way to oblivion, yet that moment properly embalmed does more service to our knowledge than a volume of theory and reasoning. We have learnt, in the extracts from records which have been given in the course of this work, that the town must, like every other town, have undergone such essential alterations, that every hundred years have served to make it almost a new town. These changes are very slow in towns which have no external means of traffic; but in places where the current of manufacture or commerce is constantly chafing, the old boundaries are speedily swept away. If, therefore, we are anxious to discover the general features of towns two or three hundred years ago, we ought not to seek them where business is active and the inhabitants have ready intercourse with distant places, but in those situations where life flows in quietude, and the fret and toil of business are almost unknown. Every traveller must have remarked that, as he withdraws from the coast, he meets with more and more examples of old English life and architecture; till, in some places, towards the centre of England, he is almost constrained to believe himself transported into a former age.

Few towns, however, can perhaps boast such a vast difference in its leading features as Wisbech in the course of a century. We will take the view of it as it appeared in 1756, which accompanies this work, as our datum, and we shall there find that (apparently) only three buildings of the picture are the same as at the present day; these are Dr. England's house, the last house on the South Brink, and the church tower. At the foot of the bridge, and partially covering the church tower, is the castle. Both Brinks were open to the river, and on the south side the bank shelved into a watering-place. On the north side of the bridge a shed stands, and near it a stand used then for shoeing horses. Where the present Exchange Hall stands we see the sign of the Nag's Head. The old wooden bridge—which appears to have had the advantage over the present one of being level with the street—forms a central object, and along the North Brink we see the pens and protection posts used to keep the cattle from the houses on a market-day, for at this date the cattle market was held in the public streets. The houses stretching from the Bridge to the Old Market have suffered modern alterations, but we do not know that they are otherwise improved. The original copper-plate from which this old print was struck is now, we believe, in the possession of Mr. Rumball. It was engraved at the expense of Dr. Massy, who in his chariot, with his servant on a bob-tailed horse before him, forms a conspicuous object in the foreground of the print. The present bridge was erected immediately after the date of the engraving, and the old wooden bridge was then blocked out of the copper, and a representation of the present structure substituted. In this new edition of the print (which is, of course, the one in Mr. Rumball's possession) the trees lately felled on the South Brink, near the old Gaol, are shown surrounded with a kind of trellis-work. Our print was engraved from a very good impression in the possession of Mr. W. Chamberlin.

Drawn by A Peckover Esq[r]

Engraved by James Mitchell

THE NORTH BRINK.

LOOKING WESTWARD.

This Plate, Engraved at the Expence of M[rs] Shewell of Rushmere, Suffolk, is most Respectfully Inscribed to her by her Obliged Servants, THE AUTHORS.

Published by Rich[d] Walker, Bridge Foot, Wisbech, 1847.

It would have been exceedingly interesting, had we been able to retrace the town back with as much authenticity as this print permits us, to more remote times, when the chief houses were probably thatched, and presented the gable-ends of their high-pitched roofs, or their projecting upper stories, in the true style of the Elizabethan period, when beam-work and plaster were so contrived as to exclude the comfortable and secure the picturesque. We have seen that, at one period, there appears to have been a windmill on the Market Place, and there does not seem to have been at that time any houses between the Market Place and the Castle. The ditch intervened, and on this deceitful foundation some of the houses of the Crescent are built, and (partially) the new Museum. It is a great pity we have no view of the Castle in its original state. The view which remains, though bearing the name of a castle, is merely a private residence, and would be more properly called a hall than a castle. It was built by Secretary Thurloe as his country residence, and appears to have had none of the appliances of a castle. The building of the Conqueror, if it was ever generally used as a place of defence, must have been a building of a very different character, and would perhaps be somewhat in keeping with the stern defensive building which is to be traced on the Castle seal, though this is not likely to be a representation of the edifice; but a mere symbol of the kind of authority by whom it was used. In the Old Market a pond and a maypole seem to have been conspicuous objects, and a white cross was fixed on the North Brink, where the Low is now situated. The part of the town now called Bridge Street was only partially built on before the Protectorate, for Col. Watson tells us that "the houses from the spot where the bridge now stands to High Street on the side leading to York Row, and in front of Deadman's Lane, were not erected until the Protectorate of Cromwell." It has been sometimes thought that Deadman's Lane formerly formed part of the castle-ditch, an opinion which its former vicinity to that building makes by no means unlikely.

It appears that, little more than a hundred years ago, the streets of the town were unpaved, in the modern acceptation of that term. Col. Watson, on the information of Mr. James Stanroyd, an aged inhabitant, who died shortly afterwards, states that the streets were covered with loose silt, so that planks were obliged to be laid across High Street in winter, lest foot-passengers should be mired in passing from one side to another. An open sewer ran on the north side of High Street, with three little bridges over it, and posts by the side of the street for fastening horses. The earliest paving was by cobbles next the houses in 1740, which, in 1750, was followed by the same kind of pavement in the centre, leaving the gutter running down the middle, and the overhanging houses probably dropping nearly into it.

At the end of High Street, next the "Rose and Crown," the common sewer was exposed, part only being covered over of sufficient width for passengers to cross. This covering consisted of flag stones, on which steps were raised, with a wall having a front towards the Market Place, about three feet high; on these steps the town-crier ascended, and leaning against the wall delivered his public notice, which caused that spot to have the appellation of the "Crying Stone."[1] The same authority informs us that a very old building was situated upon the Market Place, somewhere near the front of the shop now occupied by Mr. E. Ground. It had some carved wood in front, as of a man felling an ox, and an inscription in Saxon characters.

Some of the old English sports—often, unfortunately, sports which derived their gusto from the agonies of desperate animals—had formerly their days of celebration here. In this category bull-running must be included. It took place on Shrove Tuesday—a day famous for the number and the cruelty of the sports of which it was the anniversary. The bull was let loose from the building last described, and the animal was prevented from getting away by an ambuscade of waggons or other vehicles. About 55 years ago, a Magistrate, the Rev.

(1) Watson, p. 394.

Drawn and Eng.d by W. Taylor, from an old Print in the possession of J. W. Chamberlain

VIEW OF WISBECH AS IT APPEARED IN THE YEAR *1756*

To G. M. Lefever Esq. this plate is respectfully inscribed by his obliged servants *The Authors*

Published by Richard Walker, Wisbech 1846

Thomas Sheepshanks, whose name deserves commemoration, succeeded in abolishing it. Wisbech had also its races, an amusement she has now resigned to Gorfield Green and Lake's End. These races appear to have been of some pretension, for Col. Watson notices that in 1775 a purse of £50 was run for. The Colonel gives an interesting extract from the travels of Baretti, who had come on a visit to Wisbech Castle on an invitation of the owner, and describes the sport with great spirit; for though he treats Wisbech rather scurvily, and says he was tired of it in less than a week, the bustle of the races, the theatre, the public balls, and public suppers and assemblies, which were all combined during the second week of his visit, made the time pass "without perceiving how it went." He gives an account of two stands, from which the more select and especially female portion of the company witnessed the races, which were, he says, "scaffoldings of timber, twelve or fourteen feet high, and large enough to contain 600 or more persons." The gentler sex he describes as being smitten with the enthusiasm of their lords, and, unable to resist the general mania for betting, "wagered amongst each other for a pot of coffee, so many pounds of tea, chocolate, or some other little thing." The ball which followed pleased him as much as the races, which seem to have lasted a week. They were run every other day; for on the intervening days, he says, "the evening was spent in the theatre, a wretched place, where certain poor devils of players represented some comedy or tragedy—causing perhaps more laughter in tragedy than in comedy."[1]

These recreations are now wholly forgotten, and the only period devoted to amusement is during Lent, when the Mart is held. This annual fair is held by sufferance, or rather custom—there being no grant or charta for its establishment, and it seems merely to have originated as a resting place between Lynn Mart and Stamford Fair. Lynn Mart, which was established by a charter of Henry VIII., is proclaimed on the 14th of February, lasting by law only six days, and

(1) Watson.

Stamford Fair always happens at Mid-Lent. As therefore Lent is a moveable fast, and the Mart here occupies the entire interval between the termination of Lynn Mart and Mid-Lent, this saturnalia sometimes continues five weeks, and during that period all the noise that can be tortured out of drums, dulcimers, lungs, trumpets, organs, and cymbals, serve to enliven, if not to gratify. There is no doubt this festival had its origin with Lynn Mart in the reign of Henry VIII., of which it appears to have been an off-shoot, and we may see in its establishment at Lynn a little of that rancorous spite which Henry had then engendered towards Catholicism. The Catholics allowed none of their recreations to intrude upon the holy part of Lent; but Henry, as if to show his contempt of the religion he had so lately supported, gave Lynn an especial charta for the holding of one of the most riotous of assemblages during that season.

The utility of marts and fairs is now almost wholly superseded; and those of Lynn and Wisbech have degenerated into a mere gathering of freaks of nature, "harlotry players," dirty exhibitions, conjurors, wild beast, and ragamuffin life in all its gipseyism. When there were few or no shops, and private families as well as religious fraternities resorted to annual fairs for their annual necessities, fairs were important features in the national system. In such ages the great fairs of Stirbridge and Peterborough had their origin; but Lynn and Wisbech Marts came in a more degenerate age, and though they were formerly, especially Lynn, extensively resorted to for business, they seem never to have attained the commercial importance which that of Peterborough manifests even at the present day. When its period is short, however, Wisbech Mart still presents an active scene; but it is doubtful whether the rapid change which society seems now undergoing, may not in a few years sweep it out of existence. All institutions of a purely fanciful or holiday character are looked upon as thriftless idleness by an age that values itself on lengthening, not abridging time, and giving to minutes the value of hours. Amusement gains little mercy from so industrious a generation. There are, however, other fairs attached to Wisbech, which, although coming within the description of business fairs, cannot boast the popularity of the Mart. There are two fairs for horses, and one for bullocks. The former have degenerated within the memory of the living, but the last-named has maintained its character with sufficient regularity. It is held in the streets, and is sometimes the means of a considerable change of stock. On consulting Gazetteers and Almanacks, we are enlightened with three other fairs attached to Wisbech—as for Hemp and Flax, Saturday before Palm-Sunday, Saturday before Whit-Sunday, and August 1st; but the celebration of these is almost if not wholly confined to the pages which announce them. They are unknown to the majority of the inhabitants; a generation is gone since any transactions in an amount worthy the name of a fair was made in Wisbech. Formerly, when these articles were largely grown in the neighbourhood, they used to constitute commodities of considerable traffic, but the traveller may ride over the whole Fen without now finding an acre of either—commodities of a richer and more lucrative description having superseded these vegetables of a colder and more impoverished character.

Allied to fairs, and in some sort partaking of the nature of a pleasure fair, is the Statute, held annually a week or two before Michaelmas. It is a custom purely attached to the agricultural districts, and is still sustained here with a spirit beyond the generality of institutions of so primitive a character.

One of the peculiarities of the times is the prevalence of Literary and Scientific Societies; but in proportion as the age has advanced such societies from cities to towns, and from towns to hamlets and villages, Wisbech seems to have gone back, or only to have made abortive efforts at their establishment. One Literary Society has indeed existed since 1781, and has now accumulated a library of several thousand volumes. But although the population of the town has doubled—intelligence according to the hacknied vanity of the age trebled—

every attempt to establish another on a more liberal principle has failed. Every member on admission into this Society pays £2 2s., and an annual subscription of £1 1s., and they have recently by a compact with the proprietors or Trustees of the Museum procured a large room as a Library in that building. The books being of that miscellaneous description which pleases general readers cannot be expected to be very select, though by an almost universal renunciation of novels and romances, works of a more permanent character than would otherwise have been received have accumulated. We have a more unsatisfactory record to make of Mechanics' Institutes or Scientific Societies. At the latter end of the last century, a Society supported by a few inquirers flourished for twenty-five years, and died at the very era when Scientific Societies were growing into a rage. Three other Societies based on principles of Science—the Scientific Society in 1834, the Mechanics' Institute in 1836, and the Wisbech Institution in 1837, have all been overcome by want of patronage in the same cause. We do not know that Wisbech has acted in any way absurd in this. The idea of Science for the people is one of those airy dreams so common to the age, and so unsubstantial. Science is not for the people, and it may be doubted whether Wisbech, with no Scientific Society, is not as far advanced in Astronomy, Chemistry, and Natural Philosophy, as other towns which have had all the advantage of profound lectures and well-supported establishments. Science is no more to be learned in the lecture-room, or by mere societies, than farming or cabinet-making. Science only differs from the common working crafts in that it requires as much hand labor, and an infinitely greater labor of the brain. A chemist must work like a blacksmith, a geologist like a stone-breaker, an anatomist like a butcher. Scientific Societies may popularise a science, as they have done geology and chemistry, by exhibiting the fiction-like facts of the one, and the necromantic brilliancies of the other; but these are only sports or lures; and he who expects a science to be composed of such materials, would believe with as much rationality the

Drawn by F. Baxter — Engraved by James Mitchell

THE NEW GENERAL CEMETERY & CHAPEL.

narratives of the old travellers, who represented their countries as glittering with diamonds and gold. The last-named society, the Wisbech Institution, expired in 1845, after having lived eight years. It was established under good auspices—town and country hasted to become members—and for a time it bore the appearance of prosperity. But after flourishing four years, and languishing four years, its property was sold by auction, and no other institution of the character seems likely to take its place.[1]

Were Englishmen of a less political character, there would be more chance for its Literary and Scientific Societies. But the intervals of business are so well filled with political study that the higher arts have little chance, and are abandoned to their professors, or a minor portion of society. Bonaparte called England a country of shopkeepers—he would scarcely have been in error if he had called it a country of statesmen. It is not, therefore, surprising that among all the rise and fall of Literary and Scientific Societies, a news-room should have flourished in unabated vigor, and still continues to exist with even renewed life.

Other societies, as the Humane Society for restoring persons near drowning, the Dorcas Society for providing clothing to the poor, and the Female Friendly Society with the same philanthropic purpose, give a creditable colouring to the humanity of the town, and are supported with spirit.

General Cemetery.

In an enumeration of the public objects of Wisbech worthy of visit and description, the General Cemetery must not be passed over. For many years previous to its establishment, the Church yard, the sole public burial place, had become so crowded, and even infectious, that it was the shame of the

(1) This account was written before the agitation of a new society had commenced, which may now [January, 1849] be considered as established. It is based upon the true English principle of a Scientific Society, being a compound of news and nature; the former of which, to an Englishman, is as necessary a relish to the latter as salt to meat, or grumbling to a bargain. We do not write blamingly. Men have a right to be instructed and gratified in their own way, and societies of greater towns than Wisbech have been obliged to unite news with science in order to maintain themselves. This society has been named the Scientific Institution.

town, and an object of disgust rather than of veneration, even to those whose generations had been interred there. Animated by these considerations, a company of gentlemen endeavored in 1836 to purchase a piece of ground by the establishment of a company of shareholders of £5 each. After a little time, a very appropriate piece of land was purchased—consisting of 3 acres, 2 roods, 3 perches—for £950, subject to an annuity of £17 during the life of the original proprietor. 210 shares of £5 each, held by 85 shareholders, were quickly obtained for the purchase, and immediate steps were taken for making the ground ornamental, and fitting it for interments. It is situated on the west side of the river near the Leverington Toll Bar. In 1840 it was vested in the hands of 21 Trustees, and enrolled in the High Court of Chancery.

The principle of its establishment is the most liberal. Churchman or Dissenter of any sect may be interred according to his own peculiar ceremonies without any restraint or interference.

After the purchase had been completed, which was an extremely favorable one, the Committee of Management set about laying out the ground in an ornamental manner, planting evergreens and other shrubs and trees, and in short making the place more like a pleasure garden than a receptacle for death. The example of Pere la Chaise, at Paris, and of Kensall Green and Highgate Cemetery, in London, had perhaps incited this ambitious feeling ; but whatever it might be, the public have received an essential benefit in an almost public garden, where the beauties of vegetation, arranged and cultivated by art, may be enjoyed.

Not satisfied with these exertions, the Committee in 1848 came to the resolution of erecting a Chapel for reading the funeral service, and for other public business connected with the Cemetery, as well as a gate-house for the residence of the overseer of the ground. A very neat Chapel, from a design by Mr. Adams, has accordingly been erected, being partly brick-work, partly plaster, and partly stone. The style is classic. There are four Roman pilasters in front with two niches, and an entrance in the same style. Five pilasters divide the sides, between which are four recessed arcades. The entrance is reached by a flight of six stone steps. It forms a very pleasing as well as necessary addition to the beauties of the ground.

The monuments scattered over the Cemetery are, considering the effect of prejudice in a small country town, various, and more tasteful than might be expected. The broken column erected to the memory of Mr. Southwell, the vase on the substantial pedestal to the memory of the Rev. Joseph Jarrom, the marble to the memory of Mrs. Fairy, the marble headstone and iron railings to the memory of Mr. Reeve, and the marble vase to Mr. Frederick Veall, are so many departures from common church-yard memorials as to demand the particnlar notice we have given, and show how we may depart with grace from the beaten path on which our ancestors have for so many years erected their monotonous absurdities.

Harmonic Society.

Among the very few institutions of Wisbech which have maintained their character, and supported themselves upon the very uncertain strength of public spirit, the Harmonic Society stands conspicuous. This Society was founded in 1821, and to this present day, with few fluctuations of spirit or interest, has maintained its place, and performed its promises to its members and the public. It was established by ten persons at the "Arms Tavern Inn," was subsequently removed to the "Unicorn," and now meets weekly at the "Rose and Crown" for the practice of vocal and instrumental music. The objects of the Society are to give to the friends of its members a concert, originally three times a year, but now only twice. The concert was for many years entirely performed by its members—instrumental and vocal parts being wholly local. But the original members being removed, or incapacitated, or otherwise rendered unfit for public exhibition, and none or few of the younger being adapted to take their places, the Society found itself obliged to engage foreign aid; and singers from Peterborough, Ely, Cambridge, and Norwich, have since been successively engaged, the novelty of whose performances, and generally the respectability of their powers, have given, as it were, a new impulse to the interest excited by the Society; but, unfortunately, at a serious outlay of its funds. The members of this Society are limited to forty, who pay 6s. a-year subscription, but the funds of the Society are materially augmented by the admission of Honorary members at 20s. each, who are not subject to fines as the general or 6s. members. The members have three tickets each for distribution among their friends at each concert, which is sometimes crowded to the extent of 300 or 400 persons. Each concert costs from £15 to £20.

The property belonging to the members now amounts to £300, in consequence of which in 1843 the Society was enrolled in the legal manner. During its existence the net receipts have amounted to £1125. The officers are annually elected, and consist of Leader, Treasurer, Librarian, and Secretary.

Canal Company.

The latter part of the last century was distinguished by a canal mania almost as wild and sanguine as the railway mania of 1845. The astonishing success of the few canals that had been made previous to 1790, and especially that of the Duke of Bridgewater, between Manchester and the Mersey, fired speculators; and in 1791, England was threatened with as many canals as would have made it into a mere woof of waters. From this period to 1796, forty-eight of the hundred canals which intersect the country were projected, besides many others which were unable to pass through their parliamentary campaign. Wisbech imbibed the mania of the day. There was at that time no direct water communication between the port and the internal parts of the fen, as well as the neighbouring villages of Upwell, Outwell, &c. At a period, therefore, when all men were speculating in water conveyance, it was conceived that if a canal of six miles were made to the Old Nene, at Outwell, the merchandise of Wisbech, by the communications of the latter river, might traverse the fen in any direction, and some of the monopoly of Lynn be superseded. The idea was followed up with the spirit of speculative times. A meeting was called in 1792; shares of £100 each were eagerly taken by the inhabitants, as well as by many speculators from the midland counties; and, in 1794, an act for the work was obtained. The £100 shares were, however, found insufficient for the work, and were afterwards raised to £120, and the canal was completed. But this undertaking, so sanguinely begun and executed, was doomed to the fate of many such other designs. The public obtained a benefit, the shareholders a misfortune. The traffic was wholly insufficient to pay any interest on the outlay, and as year by year went, the proprietors saw their £120 shares gradually lose their value: for sixteen or seventeen years nothing was paid on them; and at length, in 1837, their estimated purchase was not more than £5 per share. This distressing state of affairs had been partly introduced by the Company being obliged, in 1836, to borrow a large sum for the erection of a new sluice at Wisbech, but was chiefly, as it proved, the proper effect of exorbitant dues. The shareholders felt that the time was come when they must make an effort, or die. Adversity teaches men wisdom. They reduced their rates, and in accordance with their newly-adopted principle, induced the Corporation of Wisbech to make a reduction of 2*d.* per ton on the coals carried on the canal, by which the Corporation left themselves, in reality, but 1*d.* tonnage. The new scheme succeeded, The shares rose year by year, till they have now reached par, and the last distribution of interest was after the rate of seven per cent., with a residuary fund for expenses. The canal is six miles long, is crossed by six bridges, and has two sluices on it. The last instalment of the debt on the new sluice at Wisbech was paid in 1843, and a renewal of dividend commenced May, 1845, and has hitherto been regularly continued. The following view of the tonnage on coals will afford an idea of the rapid increase of traffic since the dues were reduced.

	TONS.		TONS.
1838 - - - -	2508	1844 - - - -	16,002
1839 - - - -	3893	1845 - - - -	11,913
1840 - - - -	3534	1846 - - - -	16,099$\frac{1}{2}$
1841 - - - -	7350$\frac{1}{2}$	1847 - - - -	23,040$\frac{1}{2}$
1842 - - - -	10,077$\frac{3}{4}$	1848 - - - -	29,561$\frac{3}{4}$
1843 - - - -	12,141$\frac{3}{4}$		

The Canal and Nene Trust

is composed of a joint Committee of Trustees of the Wisbech Canal and the River Nene Commissioners. The chief duty of the Trust is to secure a good navigation from Outwell Sluice to the Ouse at Salter's Lode.

Steam Towing Company.

The long interval of twelve miles between Wisbech and the sea has always been an impediment to the navigation of large vessels up to the town, and has often greatly hindered the progress of smaller ones. While the old river remained obstructed with sands, none but the smallest craft attempted to go beyond the Washway; lighters performed the rest. But since the opening of the Nene Outfall, and the consequent accession of trade—greater vessels and more of them crowding into the port for some ten or twelve years after that event—it was found extremely inconvenient to trust to the slow and laborious hauling of a horse. It was conceived by some persons, of more imagination than judgment, that a steam-tug would do better service than the old system, and pay its shareholders well. The scheme was projected, and shareholders of £20 each were soon found. But one steamer proved insufficient: another was provided; and, subsequently, a third. The wear and destruction incident to this class of vessels has, however, never given the shareholders any remote hopes of interest for their outlay, nor is there any prospect, like the canal, that a turn of fortune, through reduced charges, will elevate the shares to par.

CHAPTER XII.

THE NEIGHBOURHOOD.

THE neighbourhood of Wisbech has few objects of interest except its churches. It has, indeed, a large amount of Roman embankment, but this feature we have already noticed in an earlier part of this work. The embankments which may be considered Roman are those which now at some distance from the river serve to mark its former course, or that of some other river. The embankment running for some distance nearly parallel with the present channel, and designated "Mount Pleasant," evidently marks the route of a channel which took a very different direction from the present one. Its course may be traced along the fields towards Walsoken, and thence towards Elm and Emneth. Fragments enough to identify the windings of the stream occur at intervals between these places, and show that this was the direction of the channel of the river when the Ouse discharged itself by Wisbech, and the original course of the river had not been altered, to the subsequent flooding and detriment of the country. It thus appears, by the direction of these embankments, that the Ouse formerly discharged its waters near the present Horseshoe, and at this point it is probable the Nene and the Ouse formed their junction.

Another rather interesting feature of the neighbourhood is the water which remains in various parts of Walsoken, called "the Gool." Whether this was formerly a lake, or merely a gull formed by the breaking of the banks, can hardly at this distance of time be determined. But, if we consider the distance which intervenes between these pools of water, we can hardly attribute it to any breakage of the bank, but must incline to the idea that there was formerly a large fresh-water lake in this part, which the value of land in its situation has caused successive generations industriously to fill up.

WISBECH ST. MARY'S,

though not the nearest village to Wisbech, demands our notice from its being in the same parish, and from its claim to being the mother church of St. Peter's. It is about two miles and a half north-west of St. Peter's, and is a small straggling village, with nothing remarkable either in its history or its condition. The church consists of a plain square tower with a small leaden spire, and a nave, which are altogether unremarkable for any architectural features. A sect of Dissenters formerly existed in this parish, which seems to have arisen and died like the gourd. The following account, from the Appendix to "Bentham's Ely," has preserved them from total oblivion. "The Culimites were so called from their founder, one David Culy, who lived about the time of the Revolution, and was, as I've been informed, a native of Guyhirn, (a hamlet of Wisbech St. Peter's) most of the inhabitants of which place became his followers, and many also from Wisbech St. Mary's, Outwell, and Upwell, until at length his flock, from very small beginnings, was increased to 700 or 800. But since his death, which happened about 1718, it has been continually on the decline, and is now so much reduced, that according to the account returned in by the Churchwardens, there are not above fifteen families of this sect remaining in the diocese of Ely, who all dwell in Wisbech St. Mary's and Guyhirn. David Culy's doctrine differed very little from that of the Anabaptists, to which sect he originally belonged." Population 1931, in 1841.

GUYHIRN

is a village or rather hamlet of the parish of Wisbech, situate about four miles and a half beyond Wisbech St. Mary's. It has a small endowed chapel realising about £100 per annum to the incumbent, who is appointed by the vicar of Wisbech. When this country was subjected to its former deluges, and the breakage of banks and the casualty of heavy rains were calamities that reduced the land to a number of islands, and insulated the inhabitants one from another, it became necessary to provide places of worship on the spots where the settlements had been made; that is, on the spots which, during such events, formed the islands of the waste. In this manner the chapel of Guyhirn, a chapel at Murrow, a chapel in Pigge's Drove, and a chapel in an unknown spot which is called in the old documents Kilhus or Kilhusing, were erected. None of these, however, except that of Guyhirn, is at present existing. We have seen, in the reply of the Guild to the articles of Edward VI.,[1] how they describe the cause of the foundation of the chapel of Corpus Christi at Murrow. "The chapel of Corpus Christi was there set and founded nigh unto the high fendyke, forasmuch as the said high fendyke being in distance from the parish church four miles or more, and being a very painful and noisome way, and commonly also unsound, so that the inhabitants adjoining is not able neither to ride nor go to their church . . . In consideration that the said high fendyke might be continually and for evermore better maintained, the said chapel of Corpus Christi was set and founded." This document, which explains the foundation of Corpus Christi, gives us a clue to the foundation of the others, situated in the same part of a perilous country, and established at a time when the religious thraldom of the people was politicly attended to, and made the means of their control, and the exaltation of the proudest

(1) Page 299.

and most successful establishment which has ever yet appeared in the world. Population 332, in 1841,

LEVERINGTON

is divided into two townships—Leverington St. Leonard's, and Leverington Parson Drove. "In Bloomfield's Collectanea there is mention made of a license granted for celebrating divine service in the chapel of Richmond Manor in Leverington, granted in 1390."[1] This manor of Richmond was held by John de Chardeleigh in the fifteenth century, and it then appears by a presentment that its value was one hundred shillings above reprize. Another manor in Leverington, called Fitton Hall, was held by John Everard, and was of the value of £6 per annum.

There was formerly a decoy for catching wild ducks in this parish, but drainage has so reduced the waters of the fens that these birds are now comparatively rare, though formerly so abundant. The decoy of Leverington used to be particularly productive. At present there are but few left in the fens.

There used also to be an extensive common in this parish, which was inclosed by Act of Parliament a few years since, and it is now blended in the contiguous farms. The policy, to say nothing of the law, which incloses and appropriates these common pasturages to the opulent according to his opulence, instead of making the poor some provision out of them, may be doubted. Leverington Common, while it existed, formed a considerable part of the means of many poor families, who lost their necessities by the inclosure, while those who obtained the portion that belonged to these poor people could well have spared it. The inclosure of commons is without doubt beneficial, their appropriation unjust. Neither the king, the lord of the manor, nor the landowner, are such legitimate proprietors of these wastes as those who have derived part of a mean subsistence from their overstocked pastures. There were means sufficient to give

(1) Watson.

the poor the advantages of commons after their inclosure; but the letter of those laws which, however unjustly, tend to feed the overfed, is never disputed where the latter have to legislate on their own cause.

Leverington has ambition. It boasts a Town Hall, and yearly elects an officer who is called a Town Bailiff, though there is no charter or legal foundation for the office. But the former opulence of the inhabitants of Leverington has left it some considerable charities, amounting to about three hundred pounds annually, which are secured in the hands of trustees, and this body selects one of its members yearly as the distributor and active agent in their dispensation, who is called Town Bailiff. £30 of this money is given to a schoolmaster for the education of poor children.

Leverington possesses one of the most beautiful churches in a district abounding with beautiful churches. It was found, during the recent restorations which this edifice has undergone, that the foundations of the church are exceedingly high; so that the building may almost be said to be placed on the surface of the ground. It consists of a tower surmounted by an elegant spire, nave, aisles, chancel, and a chapel. The prevalent style is Perpendicular, though there are elegant examples of the Early English in the tower and of Decorated at the east or chancel end. The south side was almost entirely rebuilt in 1843. The aisles and nave are separated by twelve perpendicular arches, six on each side, and the nave is surmounted with a modern roof of open wood-work without any particular character. The windows attached to this portion of the church—22 in number—are all in the same style, and the eastern part of the north aisle which was formerly divided from the nave by a screen, and formed a chapel, is ornamented with a very beautiful window of its period, having various remains of stained glass in a state of wretched misusage: several figures of Jewish kings, each with a scroll in his hand, may still be traced.[1] Here,

(1) Former observers have, however, preserved a better record of the figures than can be furnished now. Cole, in his M.S., tells us that one of the figures is the Virgin, with the

also, is the rather uncommon remnant of the Roman church, a credence-table. It is of stone, and is battlemented at the top. A piscina near it marks sufficiently the former uses of the spot.

The chancel contains one very bold Decorated window, lately erected, and four others of an inferior character. Small portions of painted glass, the plunderings of some forgotten window of the edifice, are scattered about these lights with little other effect than to make us regret their original desecration. On the north side of the chancel is a chapel filled with monuments, some of which—to the Swaine family—are good. Here, also, is a credence-table of the same character as that already mentioned, and a very beautiful piscina near it. This chapel is separated from the chancel by three Decorated pillars bearing two arches.

We must not leave the interior of this interesting church without noticing the font—one of the beauties of Perpendicular design, though of inferior workmanship. It is of oolitic stone, octangular, and from every face a saint or bishop stands in good relief, beneath niches ornamented with crockets and pinnacles. Round the foot, at every side, is a flower or other ornament of its period.

The tower and spire is, however, the triumph of this edifice, and wherever seen, as a land-mark over the wide fen, or half hidden in its surrounding trees, it is always a pleasing object,—the thin spire, beautifully diminished, almost melting into the sky of which it seems to form a part. The base of the tower is Early English, not of the highest character, but by no means despicable, or worse than it occurs in country churches generally. Towards the upper part the style

Saviour in her lap, bearing the following legend:

"Lady, lead us well fro harm,
"To him y'at lay ded in ye barm."

Another legend was formerly there, though the figure it implored is gone:

"Ju, fro sine make us fre,
"For John's love we baptised be."

The following legend was formerly inscribed on the chancel window, according to Cole's M.S.

"Orate pro anima Johis Aylestone, rector istis ecclesiæ, qui hanc fenestram fieri fecit, et edificavit hunc cancellum, 1429."

assumes a Decorated character, and the octangular spire is Decorated, and entirely of stone. Between the foot of the spire and the angles of the tower are four castellated turrets, a poor and unworthy substitute for pinnacles. The tower has four stories, and contains a peal of five bells, and with the spire, reaches 162 feet in height.

On the south side of the church is one of its most remarkable features—a fine porch of the Decorated period. It is supported by six buttresses, four of which have niches in them, and seem formerly to have contained statues. These buttresses terminate at the angles in plain but not misappropriate pinnacles. The pitch of the roof is high, and along the slope of the pediment a range of crockets, and along the ridge a fine pierced flowing work, give great additional beauty to the porch. Over the entrance is a small pinnacled and crocketted window, with a niche of similar character over it. This window lights a small parvise, now disused, and sadly deformed with rubbish. But the neglect it has suffered has not destroyed its original and singular beauty. It is about twelve feet square. The roof of stone is supported by stone arches. But the very high pitch of the roof evidently made the architect doubt whether the lancet form of arch he would be obliged to use would adequately support the building. To avoid, therefore, this weak method of construction, he inserted a ring of stone beneath the angle of the roof, and carried his arch up to its under surface, thereby giving a greater span and strength to the arch, and a more secure support to the roof, since the ring and arch each pressing on the roof give it four points of support intead of two. Leverington, in 1841, contained 1954 inhabitants.

PARSON DROVE,

included in the parish of Leverington, is situated four miles from it, and owes its origin apparently to one of those chapels of which we have formerly spoken; for, in an old document, it is stated, as a reason for its foundation, "that the way and passage to and from Leverington was troublesome and dangerous in time of winter." The license for celebrating divine service in Parson Drove chapel was transferred from Leverington Chantry Chapel in 1469 by Bishop Gray. The church—for it has now assumed that more imposing title—is dedicated to St. John the Baptist. It is a mean but not inconsiderable structure, with a poor tower containing five bells.

"The estate belonging to this chapel consists of a messuage and 141 acres of land, which were vested after the Reformation in feoffees, for the maintenance of the chaplain, together with 11 acres 3 roods since allotted in respect of the said messuage. Some mismanagement or misconversion took place in regard to the application of the rents of this estate"[1] in the reign of William III., and an inquisition was held upon it at Wisbech in 1698. It appeared that in 1690 the chapel-warden received the rents, then amounting to £64 10*s.* 2*d.*, but refused to make out an account of the employment of it, except of £20 to the minister. The inquisition ended with confirming and describing the powers of the trustees with regard to the letting of the land and the disbursement of its profit.

Through this parish runs the great North Level drain, and here is one of its most considerable sluices, called Clow's Cross. This sluice, which is constructed on the principles of strength and adaptation, is placed at the junction of the North Level system of drainage, and where a considerable portion of fen water is discharged into the main drain. It has always been a point of importance, and here was formerly a stone cross, but whether to mark the division of the counties of Cambridge and Lincoln, or to indicate its other importance, is unknown. The drain which Clow's Cross regulates cost the North Level proprietors £120,000.

There was anciently a hermitage or chapel at a part of this parish which retains the ancient name of Trokenholt. This Trokenholt is mentioned as one of the boundaries of the estate which King Wolfere gave for the endowment of Peter-

(1) Watson, p. 473.

borough Cathedral, and is mentioned in his charta of 664. It was given by Nigel, Bishop of Ely, to the Abbey of Thorney in 1169, and is there mentioned as a hermitage. It had formerly belonged to the church of Ely, "it being expressed in a very ancient letter that this church enjoyed it for 191 years."[1] In the earlier period of the church it seems to have suffered the common calamities of that establishment, since it lay for 111 years in a state of desolation, after having been overrun by the Danes. "Afterwards, for 139 years, the Abbot of St. Benedict enjoyed it; of whom Edwin gave permission to one of his monks of the name of Trokenholus to live as a hermit in the place called Endewicke; so the place laid aside its ancient name, and from that time forth was called Trokenholt, which has been continued to the present time."[2] Nigel probably transferred this property from Ely to Thorney by virtue of his office as Chancellor to Henry II., an office which it has been said he never held; but the above fact seems to intimate him to have had more state power than that of Bishop, since he could not as Bishop alienate the property of his own church, but was fully competent to do so as Chancellor. Trokenholt is a wide bleak fen, productive indeed, but with no other recommendation to a civilised being. As a hermitage it must have been highly advantageous when its cold black acres were only relieved by reedy shallows and wide lakes of mallard-haunted waters.

By the will of John Bend, 1593, who left a messuage and sixteen acres of land to the poor of Parson Drove, the proceeds of this estate, now amounting to £100, are distributed annually to the poor who have not received parish relief for six years, on New Year's Day. Population in 1841, 828.

ELM

is a neat and ancient village situated about two miles south of Wisbech. It is mentioned in the same early charta of King Wolfere with Wisbech, and had then the "great river"

(1) Watson. (2) Watson, p. 477.

passing through it which now runs by Lynn. In Doomsday Book it is called *Helle.*

Elm has probably diminished in its importance from very early ages; at any rate it has diminished in very recent times. It is singular, that previous to the present improvements in the drainage and cultivation of the fens, when they were liable to winter floodings, and reed and osiers, or at best flax and hemp, instead of wheat or other corn, were their produce,—when, indeed, over the majority of the waste, no arable cultivation could be pursued at all, but the sodden pastures were reserved for the feeding of an inadequate number of cattle in summer;—while this depressed state of things prevailed in the fens, Leverington, Newton, Tid St. Giles, Elm, Emneth, and Outwell, could boast their manors, their manor-houses, their titled residents, and all the pomp and hospitality of the owners of great estates. But, with the improvement of the fen lands, this kind of residents all departed; and their deserted mansions, now converted into farm-houses, or left to ruin, would persuade a hasty observer that the country has gone back instead of pushing forward. They fled with the wild duck, the bittern, and the heron; and we cannot but think that the sport afforded by the wild winter birds which flocked to these parts may have had some influence in retaining its aristocracy in the vicinity of so much desolation.

The manor of Elm formerly belonged to the Bishop of Ely, and was held of his capital manor of West Walton.[1] Coldham, Benford, and Hanstead, are other manors which occur in old writings, or still retain their designatien. Coldham is of the last class. The original manor-house was pulled down in 1793, and a farm-house erected on its site. It was here that the dam was constructed in the reign of Edward I. by Walter de Langton, Bishop of Coventry and Lichfield, which caused so many presentments for damages, and proved of such terrible importance to the fens.[2] It now belongs to the Peyton family.

(1) Watson. (2) See page 99.

Needham Hall was taken down in 1804; and, as usual with these old manorial residences, a farm-house was built near its site. "The old mansion was of brick, with a porch in front, and a court-yard walled round. The length of the building was 108 feet, adorned by fifty-two windows, with two large wings, bearing a similitude to the Roman letter E, of three stories in height, with bay windows on the first and second stories. Two spacious oak staircases led to each wing: several of the rooms were twenty feet square, and upwards of twelve feet high. The entrance-hall was forty feet by twenty, supported by a row of six oak pillars, beautifully carved, on stone pedestals. In the hall was an extensive fire-place, over which was a curiously carved coat of arms in a shield."[1] Here, it appears, during the great Civil War, Oliver Cromwell was lodged one night—not in a bed, but on the kitchen table. The table is preserved: it is "of oak, of one solid piece." Col. Watson, in his History, remarks, that at the date of that book, (1827) there was living at Elm a person far advanced in years, who well remembered his grandfather saying, "that when he was a boy, he saw Oliver Cromwell and his troops pass by the avenue leading to this hall, and that the person then inhabiting the mansion offered to Cromwell his best bed, which he declined, observing, that perhaps the next day he should have to sleep in the open field: therefore, in preference, he chose to pass the night on the table. Such of the officers as could be accommodated were supplied with beds; the rest of the troops took shelter in the outbuildings and premises."[2] Cromwell's head-quarters are said, further on, to have been at a building called Nine Chimney House, at Emneth. A six-pounder cannon ball and the remains of a bomb-shell were found in the walls of the hall when it was pulled down.

This parish has yielded considerably to the numismatic antiquary. In taking down Needham Hall, in 1804, several coins of silver and brass, and eleven of copper, were disco-

(1) Watson, p. 506. (2) Ibid

vered in the foundations. Several were unintelligible, but two of the size of a shilling—1569—were found.[1]

The church, though possessing few features that attract, is still a pleasing building. The tower belongs to the Transition period, between Norman and Early English. It has four stories. In the lowermost is a circular-headed doorway, with Early English mouldings, splayed with three slender pillars. In the second and third stories are, on each side, three Early English lancet arcades, partly occupied with lights, and the upper story has a round-headed window. The tower is flanked with octangular buttresses, which terminate in battlemented octangular pinnacles. It contains five bells.

On the south side of the church is an Early English doorway, splayed with two pillars; and on the north side is a Perpendicular porch, placed before a fine Early English arch, splayed with three isolated pillars, and four pilasters or half pillars.

The clerestory contains twenty lancet Early English Transition windows, ten on each side,—and the aisles are lighted by nine Decorated and five Perpendicular windows. The chancel has a very mean Perpendicular window to the east, and four Early English side lights.

The aisles and nave are divided in the interior by six Decorated arches on each side, above which an elaborate Perpendicular roof of open wood-work is the most attractive portion of the interior of the edifice. The carving is not very good, but plentifully ornamented with angels and tracery, so as to give a fine effect to a very ill-pewed church.

(1) In 1785, in a field in Waldersea, an earthen pot, containing a considerable number of small copper Roman coins, chiefly of Valentinian and Arcadius, were ploughed up. In 1813, in making a trench in the garden at Needham, three silver pieces were dug up, one bearing the head of John of Gaunt, another of Brutus, and the third of Mercury. Some more modern English coins were found in a pond in 1818. A tesselated pavement and pieces of richly sculptured stone were dug up near the hall, and in 1825 a lachrymatory, probably belonging to the old mansion, was dug up by some laborers. "About 1713, not far from a tumulus in Elm, an urn full of Roman brass coins, most of them of Victorinus and Tetricus, was taken up; and a Roman altar, twenty-six inches high and fourteen broad, is said to have been found in the same place. Also coins from Gallienus down to Gratian were found in this parish."—*Watson.*

The font is a very small marble of Italian work. The church contains some good monuments of opulent persons who have lived in the neighbourhood.

We have notices of two chapels in this parish; one, St. Christopher, near Berryal, which is mentioned by Dugdale,[1] and another dedicated to St. Giles, which "appears to have been formerly surrounded by a moat."[2] It was situated about a quarter of a mile to the south-east of the church. In the year 1250, Nicholas, Archdeacon of Ely, granted to Walter de Tylneye and his heirs leave to build a chapel on his own premises *in the marsh* at Elm, provided the family attended divine service in the mother church on the six principal festivals of the year.[3]

The benefactions to the poor are considerable. Seven acres were given, in 1563, by William Maynard; sixteen acres by William Payne, in 1597; six acres by Thomas Coward, in 1674; four acres by Thomas Adams, in 1697; two acres by Thomas Jenkinson, in 1757. Besides these, twenty-two and a half acres, a house, and barn, were given in 1689, by Thomas Squire, to provide a schoolmaster. Sixty acres as common right, situated in a field called Crowmere, have also been bestowed on the poor. Every house or cottage had formerly a right to 3,000 hassocks from this estate, and no cattle were allowed to be pastured on it. It is now let by auction, and its proceeds distributed in coals and flour. The value of the living is about £800 per year. The population in 1841 was 1742.

Elm is a pleasing village. It is prettily shut up among trees, and displays a neatness which the irregularity of the place by no means deteriorates. The remains of Elm Leam, formerly an important sewer for drainage, are still visible, but the course which the "great river" took, that "goeth to Elm and to Wisbech," is now quite obliterated, though it is considered to have been near that taken by the present Wisbech and Outwell Canal.

(1) Watson, p. 348. (2) Ibid. (3) Ibid.

EMNETH

is a hamlet in the parish of Elm, and has a chapel, or rather church, dedicated to St. Edmund. "It is larger than most parish churches, having a nave and north and south aisles, and a chancel. In the chapel are several monuments. At the east end of the south aisle, enclosed with iron rails, is a sumptuous one erected altarwise, on which lie the effigies of Sir Thomas Hewar and his lady at full length, and at their feet that of a child, their son, who died young. Over this monument is a canopy of marble, supported by pillars of the same material. On the summit of the canopy are shields, with the arms of Hewar and Oxburgh. It was erected in 1617 by Nicholas Stone, master mason to James I., who had £95 for it. Also opposite, against the south wall, is a neat mural monument, on the summit whereof is 'Hewar, 1586.'"[1]

In this parish stood Hagbeach Hall, an old building with tall chimneys and many gables, ornamented with what the Scotch call corbie-steps. It had also an old-fashioned porch with pinnacles; and being quadrangular, inclosing a small court, was a commodious and picturesque building with fine grounds around it, and all the requisites of an aristocratic mansion. But, by some unaccountable perversion of taste, for which we have already endeavoured to account, this hall was taken down in 1806, about the era at which the other halls in the neighbourhood were deserted. The gateway, consisting of two stone pillars, still stands to mark the entrance of the former grounds of the hall. The building belonged, when taken down, to the Peyton family, who had, however, not possessed it for more than forty years. It had for three hundred years before, been in the possession of the Hewar family, and was probably built by one of the Hakebeches, whose names occur in the early history of the fens in connection with their drainage.

At the extremity of Emneth stood, a few years since, an old thatched bilding, with gabled wings and moulded win-

(1) Watson.

dows. It was called Emneth Lodge, and attracted general attention from an enigmatical inscription which it bore:

M A N I N M I R T H A A E
M E R S E A I N M I N D F O R M E S A R E I S
T R E S A R W H E N M I R T H I S A T E N D

which is thus rendered:

Man in mirth have
Mercy in mind, for mercy is
Treasure when mirth is at end.

The house rebuilt on the site of the old lodge still retains the above inscription. The population of Emneth in 1841 was 1065.

WEST WALTON

lies about three miles north of Wisbech. It is supposed to derive its name from the embankment or wall of the sea which runs through the parish. Walton has, notwithstanding the protection of this wall, suffered frequent inundations of the sea, some of which have been attended with severe losses of property and life. At the Doomsday survey it was noticed as having seven salt works, an article of manufacture very important in those early times, but which the extensive mines in Cheshire and other places have completely banished from modern manufacture.

Several manors are mentioned as being in this parish. One was very large, and extended into Walpole and Walsoken. It belonged, as was the case with most of these large manors, to the church. On the dissolution of the monasteries it was bestowed on the Duke of Norfolk, whose treason afterwards caused it to revert as a forfeiture to the crown. It was afterwards possessed by Lord Coleraine, and passed from him to the Townshend family. The church of Ely possessed a manor here, and another manor called "the Marshes" was possessed by the Colville family. Lovell's manor was possessed by the family of Kepps.

The church at Walton is its most attractive antiquity. Though now in a state of wretched desolation—the effect of long misusage and the want of proper renovations at the proper time—it renders in every part a perfect notion of what it was in its days of perfection. The tower, which first meets the eye of the stranger as he turns the road that leads to the church, attracts his notice, not less for its beautiful workmanship than for its standing insulated from the church. The Italians frequently detach their bell-towers, but it is far less customary in England. It is a very fine specimen of Early English workmanship, verging on Transition, and consists of three stories, the lowermost of which is a doorway, splayed with four pillars and mouldings, and enriched with the dog-tooth ornament; two pedimented niches flank the arch of this entrance. The second story is occupied on each side with an arcade of three lancet arches, and the bell-chamber is lighted by four windows of two lights each, beneath an arch of two mouldings, forming with the window a splay of four banded pillars. Octangular buttresses support the angles, which are covered with blank lancet arches. A Perpendicular parapet and pinnacles inadequately finish this otherwise fine specimen of Gothic architecture.

From four angular arches to be seen in the upper story of the tower, it would almost seem as if the architect had intended to raise a spire on the top, which would have finely finished the enriched tower beneath. There are five bells in this chamber.

The principal external object on the south side of the church is an Early English porch of fine but dilapidated workmanship and design. The arch is surmounted by corbie-steps, and it is supported by octangular buttresses with blank lancet arches, and terminates in a blunt-pointed pinnacle. The entrance beneath this porch is finely splayed with arches, and the sides of the porch are filled in with blank arcades. There is a similar entrance to the north, but without the porch.

The interior presents many ruinous but interesting features of departed magnificence. Among these a window in the south aisle attracts the first attention, from the truth of its form and the purity of its workmanship—an elegant compound of Early English grace. It consists of two lancet lights under a moulded arch, with a quatrefoil above the lights. The internal mouldings are ornamented with the dog-tooth, while the external shafts have the rose and a five-leaved flower. The capitals are finely undercut foliage.

There are five pillars and two responds on each side of the nave, which support equilateral Early English arches, and are surrounded with four Purbeck marble shafts, banded in the centre, with capitals of bold open foliage. The clerestory over these arches is pierced with seventeen small archets of the same period as the rest of the building, eight of which contain lights. Here the industry of the present incumbent (Rev. E. Blencowe) has lately disclosed six original paintings, seemingly of geometric figures, &c., and apparently in a style almost coeval with the church.

The aisles have nothing remarkable except their width, which is nineteen feet and a half in the south and twenty-one feet in the north aisle.

The chancel is but a ruin. There are four sedilia on each side the altar, and a fine chancel arch. The arches of the nave formerly extended into this part of the church, and probably were screened off into chapels; but they have been filled up. Some open seats, with carved Perpendicular finials, just serve to show us how the church was formerly furnished.

A beautiful tomb of Purbeck marble, representing a recumbent figure of a monk under an Early English canopy, and trampling on a dragon, has been conjectured to be the monument of the founder of the church. It has only been lately restored to its proper place, having been broken to fragments and distributed over the parish: but the zeal of Mr. Blencowe has gathered up these detriti, and united them together; and though he has failed in completing the monument, he has probably brought to light all that remains of a tomb which was perhaps broken up at the Reformation.

But, after all the ruined beauty we have seen, the west end strikes the observer most regrettingly for the havoc that time, neglect, and spoliation have together wrought on what was originally a brilliant specimen of style, and a noble entrance to a noble building. A large circular arch spans the nave, deeply splayed with five Early English mouldings, which spring from foliaged capitals, and are supported by five insulated pillars. Octagonal turrets, perhaps somewhat similar to those of the south porch, sprang from the sides, and a double dog-tooth and a four-leaved flower run between the mouldings. Within this arch two Early English lancet arches, with Purbeck shaft, divided the entrance into two parts, as at Ely, Lichfield, Peterborough, &c., and added much to the style and character of the entrance, which when the arch was colored and gilded, of which it yet shows tokens, must have been very imposing.[1]

There is a record in the north aisle of the drowning of 1613, similar to that at Wisbech, recounting the state of one of their most terrible inundations.

The parish consists of two incumbencies, one in the patronage of the crown, the other in the Townshend family.

There is a free school, but the charities of Walton are few, realising only about £60 per annum. There are also nine almshouses. The population in 1841 was 954.

OUTWELL

is situated on one of those higher fertile spots in the fens which have always been habitable. It is, accordingly, an ancient place, and has contributed to the possessions of the church. It is of Saxon origin, and belonged to the abbey of Ramsey according to Doomsday-book, which describes it as containing sixteen borderers with lands valued at five shillings per annum. It was granted to Edmund Beaupre, of

(1) It would be unfair to conclude a notice of Walton Church without adverting to the praiseworthy exertions of Mr. Blencowe, the present co-incumbent, by whose endeavours the old tomb has been recovered, the walls cleaned and scraped in some parts, the Purbeck shafts of the nave cleaned of miserable whitewash, the west entrance thrown open, and other expensive and laudable efforts at restoration effected.

Beaupre Hall, by Henry VIII., on the dissolution of the monasteries. A hermitage dedicated to St. Christopher, with a chapel belonging to it, as well as Mullicoat Priory, were in this parish. The last-named religious house was very ancient, having been founded in the time of the Saxons.[1] Mullicoat is frequently mentioned in the old presentments on questions of drainage, but does not appear at any time to have been a very considerable establishment. There are no remains of the edifice standing, nor is it precisely known where it was situated. Had it been an opulent establishment, the ecclesiastical elegance and strength with which monks were proud of ornamenting their abbeys and priories, would probably have preserved some remains of it. The inundations to which the lands attached to the Priory were subject, by reason of the imperfect drainage of the times when it flourished, kept it, however, poor, and finally overwhelmed it. It lingered with gradually diminished resources till it was unable to support one monk, when it was united to the Priory of Ely by Henry VI. The lands are now in the possession of the Dean and Chapter of Ely.[2]

At Outwell the Wisbech Canal forms its junction with the old Nene. There are two bridges over the river nearly in a line with each other. One is called the Norfolk, the other the Isle Bridge.

There are two manors in Outwell, the ancient proprietors of each of which have representative chapels in the church. One called Bardolph belonged to the Fincham family, and was sold at the latter end of the last century. The other, the Beaupre manor, formerly belonged to a family of that name, to whom it descended by marriage from Gilbert de Beaupre, in the reign of Henry I. Beaupre Bell, one of the descendants of the family, was a singular character. He "was educated at Westminster School, afterwards admitted of Trinity College, Cambridge, and soon commenced a genuine and able antiquary. He made considerable collections of church notes in his own and the neighbouring counties, all

(1) Watson, (2) Ibid.

which he bequeathed to the college where he received his education. Beaupre Bell had many singularities, hardly allowing his son necessaries, and suffering his house to be much dilapidated. He had five hundred horses of his own breeding, many above thirty years old, unbroke, which he allowed to come into the very hall, then uncovered."[1] The Bells married into the family of the Greaves, who married with the Townleys, and the hall and manor are now the property of Richard Greaves Townley, Esq., of Fulbourn. The hall yet partly exists. The dilapidations suffered by Beaupre Bell were partially repaired by Mr. Greaves. In its original state it consisted of an ancient gateway with octangular battlemented turrets, a pedimented wing with angular buttresses running into a sort of spire, and a range of building between extending on the other side of the gateway. Two smaller projections of a similar character to the wing were situated between it and the gateway, and a series of tall thin chimneys were the chief characteristics of the edifice. The wing is now gone, and much of the building between it and the gateway, which is still standing. It is now the residence of the Rev. Wm. Gale Townley.

The benefactions of Outwell are eight acres of land in Elm; eleven acres and a house in Outwell; twenty-one acres in Exmore Drove, Upwell; three acres in Emneth. These produce about £70 per year.

The church is dedicated to St. Clement, and is a very interesting building. It is entered on the south by a groined porch, and may be generally referred to the Perpendicular period, of about, perhaps, the fourteenth century. The arches of the nave, of which there are five on each side, are octangular, with clerestory windows of the same period above them. The north aisle door, of oak, is covered with finely-carved Decorated work, which from exposure exhibits much decay. It has been partly imitated in the beautiful doors of Upwell church. The chancel is lighted to the east with a very graceful Perpendicular window, containing some remains

(1) Watson.

of painted glass: it was, probably, once filled with it. There are two other windows in the chancel with little character about them. This part of the church is otherwise very plain. The remains, however, of the original Perpendicular screen, above which the Holy Rood was formerly placed, makes up for this deficiency, since this feature in church architecture is comparatively rare. It is a painted oak screen, filled with Perpendicular tracery. A chapel, situated to the north of the chancel, and connected by an arch and screen with it, is lighted by three Perpendicular windows, one of which contains some good remains of painted glass, representing Moses and Aaron.[1] The chapel is otherwise plain and uninteresting. It contains, however, a singular oak chest, banded with iron hoops, and fastened with seven padlocks, and was once, perhaps, the treasure chest of the church. Another chapel projects like a transept from the north aisle, and was formerly the burial-place and probably chantry of the family of Fincham. The roof alone now contains any remains of the former splendour which sometimes adorned these places of intercession for the souls of the departed. This part of the chapel is elaborately though not very skilfully carved, and consists of Perpendicular open work, whose beams rest on carved brackets with angels with expanded wings between. The whole retains good traces of the ancient paint and gold with which it was covered.

The south aisle is lighted with Perpendicular windows, three of which are of extraordinary expansion. Two of them light a small chapel, formerly appropriated to the Beaupre family, and dedicated to St. Mary. It is separated from the chancel by a depressed arch and railing, has a chequered marble floor and an enriched carved oak roof, which extends along the aisle, from which the chapel is separated by an iron screen. There is a low blocked arch in the south wall, which seems to have been a monument whose effigy is bricked up or removed. The upper part of the east window of the chapel contains the remains of some very rich painted

(1) Watson.

glass, being figures of the Almighty, St. Lawrence, St. Anthony, St. Edmund, &c. Against the south wall is an old monument of Purbeck marble, which seems to be about the fourteenth century, without inscription or date. Another monument, of the year 1567, has been placed upon it. It is partly of alabaster.

The Beaupre Chapel forms the most interesting portion of the exterior of the church. At the base a string of enriched quatrefoils, and the two elegant but depressed Perpendicular windows we have named, with buttresses bearing shields, form its principal characteristics.

The tower is short and unpeculiar. It contains a ring of six bells. On the north side of the church are some very peculiar and unmentionable gargoyles, and the east end has an enriched basement of quatrefoils and an embattled parapet. The length of the church is seventy-eight feet. Near the pulpit is a small brass eagle.

There are in the parish of Outwell two schools which may be considered as free, the scholars paying only the nominal sum of a penny per week. They are attached to opposite interests, one being supported by Dissenters, the other by the Church, and principally the Rector of Upwell, the Rev. W. G. Townley. That supported by the church is a new and comfortable building, well fitted up, and perfectly adapted to its purpose. It has an adjoining school-house for the master, and is divided into two portions, for the accommodation of both sexes. Population, 1252, in 1841.

UPWELL

forms with Outwell one continued village or street about four miles long, with the old Nene between it. Though now a considerable village its importance relatively to the country must be considered as diminished, since it is recorded that, in 1202 the abbot lord of the manor had a market-place, and "King Henry VI. granted to the Bishop of Ely and John Abbot of Ramsey one common and open market weekly,

Engraved by W. Taylor.

INTERIOR OF UPWELL CHURCH.

[illegible] ENGRAVED AT THE EXPENSE OF THE REV.[D] WILLIAM GALE TOWNLEY, RECTOR [illegible] RESPECTFULLY INSCRIBED TO HIM BY HIS OBLIGED SERVANTS

THE AUTHORS

[illegible] Wisbech [illegible]

with a fair yearly on St. Peter's day.[1] In this parish was a priory of Gilbertines, being a cell to Sempringham, in Norfolk, which was founded in the reign of King John. Martmound priory, founded by Richard I., was endowed by him with 300 acres in Upwell and Outwell, to support the prayers of three priests. It continued to the dissolution of the monasteries.[2]

The rectory, in the patronage of Richard Greaves Townley, Esq., is one of the richest in the kingdom, being fixed at £6000 a-year under the general Commutation Act, though valued in the king's books at £16.

The benefactions to the poor consist of several small bequests, amounting to £35 in money; a quantity of land, variously situated, amounting to about 20 acres, and the rents of four messuages. There are five almshouses for five poor widows, who receive ten bushels of coals each at Christmas, given by James Lee, Esq.

The present rector, the Rev. W. G. Townley, has here, as at Outwell, established a free school.

Upwell has many good houses, and with a population of 4891,[3] may be considered almost more than a village. The length, however, without breadth which the houses occupy, being about three miles, leaves its extremities as remote as separate villages, and is very inconvenient, and destructive of that communication and improvement which so many houses and population compactly situated would command.

The church is of large dimensions, consisting of a nave of six bays with north and south aisles, and a chancel of good proportions. The tower, at the west end of the north aisle, is the most ancient portion of the structure: it was built at two periods, an octagonal belfry-stage having been added in the fourteenth century to the original square tower which was erected early in the thirteenth century. It contains six bells, and was until lately crowned with a leaden spire about forty feet in height, the timber of which was so much decayed as to render removal necessary. This was accomplished in

(1) Watson, p. 547. (2) Ibid. (3) In 1841.

1842. The church itself was almost wholly rebuilt in the fifteenth century. The walls on the sides and at the angles are sustained by buttresses, and pierced with windows of handsome design. An ample height was given to the clerestory, which is lighted by pointed windows: the parapets throughout are embattled, and the roofs covered with lead. The principal side entrance to the church is towards the north, by a groined porch of handsome design, with a room over. There is a staircase at the south-west angle of the chancel, surmounted by an open bell-turret of elaborate design.

The chancel is distinguished by a roof of lofty pitch. The side windows are ancient: the mullions and tracery of the original east window having been destroyed by a storm, were replaced by the present design.

The interior is very imposing. The nave, which is light and expansive, is separated from the aisles by four pillars with responds on the north side, and four towards the south. These pillars are of the most graceful proportions, consisting of a small shaft and capital in the soffit of the arch, surrounded by the elegant slightly-cut mouldings of the style. The arch itself is equilateral, and of a plain character. A small shaft without capital runs between the mouldings of the pillars, and carries the pendants of the roof, which are of oak. A flat arch is thrown from side to side. The tie-beam is enriched and battlemented, and is connected with the rafters by a series of trefoil arches, which also fill the spandril of the arch. Midway between this part of the roof, and immediately over the clerestory windows, an angel of carved oak, with expanded wings, projects from the wall plate, with a carved cherub on each side of it. These elegant features have worthy associates in the furniture of the church, a neglected portion of ecclesiastical architecture, which has here been well provided. The pews have oak doors, with enriched panels and quatrefoils, and are surmounted by elaborate finials. A gallery runs along the north aisle of the church, partly concealing the beautiful pillars to which it is attached.

The carving on this gallery is in the Perpendicular style, while that on the lower pews is of a Decorated character. The pulpit is a very choice specimen of the carver's art. It is octangular, and surrounded with richly wrought panels, well filled with tasteful tracery. The sounding-board has a domed top, embellished with tracery and crockets, and is surmounted by a cross. A beautiful statuette of St. Peter, to whom the church is dedicated, stands at the foot of the hand-railing, and forms an excellent and appropriate finish

The arch is plain and springs abruptly from the walls. The roof of the chancel is of oak, not less elaborate than that of the nave; an angel beneath each hammer-beam forms a bracket, the roof being without any tie-beam, as in the nave. There are four windows in the sides, but the chief object of attraction is the painted glass of the east window, which is of a highly wrought and admirable character. When we look at the beautiful manner in which three highly artistic paintings have been copied in the three principal compartments, we are inclined to forget how much more recent it is in style than the architecture of the church dictated. The windows consist of three lights, the centre being nearly three times as wide as those on the side. Above the point of the arches formed by these lights a flat arch is introduced, over which are six smaller compartments, surmounted by a pierced quatrefoil. The central compartment is occupied by a copy of Guiseppe Ribera's (commonly called Spagnoletto) celebrated painting of the Deposition from the Cross.[1] The figure of the body of our Lord exhibits painful fidelity, and the tearful eyes of his mother, who kneels over him with clasped hands and looking up to heaven, are in

(1) Lanzi, speaking of this picture and of Ribera's imitation of Caravaggio, says: "In emulation of him he painted at the Certosini that great Deposition from the Cross which alone, in the opinion of Giordino, is sufficient to form a great painter, and may compete with the works of the greatest luminaries of the art." The original picture is now above the altar in the chapel Tesoro in the church of San Martino at Naples. Mr. Townley is said to possess a replica, or repetition of the work, by the same artist. Lord Arundel, at Wardour Castle, claims to have the original; the Neapolitans do the same. The late Mr. Seafer, an admirable judge, who cleaned and repaired Mr. Townley's picture, pronounced it genuine. It was bought at Naples in 1830.

every respect expressive of the deepest sorrow. Mary Magdalene is kissing the feet of her Lord; and St. John, raising the body from the ground to wrap it in the winding sheet, turns a face of commiseration on the afflicted one of Mary. Joseph of Arimathea stands in the back ground; and two cherubs descending through the gloom complete the composition of this powerful performance. Spagnoletto's love of violent contrast makes this picture well suited for representation on glass, and this love has here been lavishly, though not imprudently, indulged. Of the two side compartments, that on the left is filled with the celebrated picture of Christ bearing the Cross, of which the original is in the chapel of Magdalen College, Oxford; and that on the right with the picture of Christ revealing himself to Mary in the garden, from the picture by Raphael Mengs, in the chapel of All Souls College, in the same University. In the compartments of the tracery are introduced the scriptural emblems of the brazen serpent, the flowing rock, the falling of the manna, the tables of the law, the bible, the cloven tongues, and the crowns of immortal life.

The font is a beautiful specimen of the fifteenth century. It is octangular, with angels on each face holding shields. The pillar on which it stands is carved with shields and canopies.

The following inscription in the south wall of the church records with minuteness the alterations which have been effected in it during the last ten years.

"This church was fitted up in its present manner, the roof of the nave and north aisle thoroughly repaired, the south entirely renewed, the walls underpinned and flag stones laid between the buttresses, the interior stuccoed, the north gallery added and the west enlarged, in the years 1836-37-38, by faculty obtained in the Ecclesiastical Court at Norwich, towards which the sum of £300 was raised, under sanction of the High Court of Chancery, upon the estate of William Fox, left for the repairs of this church. At the same period the chancel roof was entirely renewed, the stone screen and parapets added. During the whole of these extensive repairs, be it recorded, to the credit of the respectable inhabitants of Upwell, that they forsook not the assembling of themselves together on the Sabbath. In the year 1842, the exterior of the church was stuccoed, stone battlements added, the spire—found to be in a dangerous state—removed, the east window—blown out by a hurricane—restored, and composed to receive the designs represented on the glass. In the same year an enlargement of the churchyard took place. The whole was surrounded by walls, and that part adjoining the public street surmounted by iron railing; the gates brought from Peterborough Cathedral, and the vases from Wanstead House, were presented by Richard Greaves Townley, Esq., the patron."

Pope has said that

"Who builds a church to God, and not to fame,
Will never mark the marble with his name."

Mr. Townley seems to have had this couplet in his mind when he penned the above inscription, in studiously withholding his own name. It is, however, well known that all the improvements, except the two mentioned in the inscription, were defrayed out of his own purse, and that they cost him several thousand pounds.

WELNEY,

consolidated with Upwell for ecclesiastical purposes, lies near the Old Bedford river, and is about three-quarters of a mile from the New Bedford, whose wash is crossed at this point by a road made in 1826. Welney owes much to its rector, Mr. Townley. He exerted himself much in making the new road, and in 1824 erected over the New Bedford river a handsome suspension bridge, at an expense of more than £3000, by which the low road between Ely and Wisbech was perfected. Connected with this, a new turnpike, ten miles in length, through Littleport to Mildenhall, has been opened.

Welney is in possession of one of the most munificent charities in the county. In the year 1555, Mrs. Margaret Venall, of Mildenhall, in the county of Suffolk, left 21 acres of land for charitable and useful purposes. In 1661, William Marshall, of Lincoln's Inn, bequeathed nine pieces of land in Upwell and Welney, to the amount of 749 acres, whose proceeds are disposed as follows:—

One third of the profits go to the repair of the chapel and bridge in Welney, that the inhabitants may with facility attend divine service.

One third is directed to be distributed towards relieving poor widows and putting and binding out poor infants apprentices.

One third is to be expended on repairing the highways.

These charities are now united in one trust, under provisions of the High Court of Chancery, in accordance with the view of the testators; but as they much increased in value, and were more than sufficient for their bequeathed purposes, application was made in 1805 for a more extensive appropriation of them; which resulted in the Court ordering that the residue, after the will of the donor had been fulfilled, should be expended on a Charity School for the use of the poor, to be held in the vestry, and be called the "Charity School of William Marshall."

The small population of Welney, and the comparative great amount of this benefaction, notwithstanding the subsequent appropriation, left an accumulative surplus for other purposes. "The chapel in which service was performed had, previous to 1848, become time-worn and unaccommodating, and it was conceived that the overplus of these charities could not be more appropriately applied than in the erection of a new and more convenient place of worship. It was, therefore, ordered, under similar direction, that a church, with school-rooms and master's house, together with six almshouses for poor widows, should be built; and they were erected accordingly, from designs and under the superintendence of Messrs. Buckler and Son. The church, consisting of nave and chancel, is in the later Early English style, fitted up with open seats for 400 persons, with a western gallery for 120 children. It is built of carr stone, which has a very good effect. The pulpit and font are of Caen stone, the former very beautiful in design and workmanship. An east window, painted by Wilmshurst and presented by the rector, representing Faith, Hope, and Charity, in the centre compartment, the Queen's arms and those of East Anglia introduced very judiciously into the side lights, give an admirable tone and finish to the whole."[1]

(1) In a sermon preached by the Rev. W. G. Townley, on the consecration, 11th of August, 1848, he thus adverts to the window: "I am myself responsible for the designs which appear in the east window, and taking Faith, Hope, and Charity for my ground-work, have purposely connected the throne with the altar, not only because I consider their mutual safety to be dependent on each other, and believe, with good Bishop Horn, that whenever

Welney had a population of 996 in 1841.

In the vicinity of Welney is one of the peculiarities of the fen—the Wash or receptacle left by Sir. C. Vermuyden for relieving the overflooded rivers. This Wash contains 5200 acres. In summer it has the appearance of a fine grassy plain, and is then well stocked with cattle; and should the spring prove favorable, a large crop of hay, somewhat inferior in quality, is often obtained from it. There are three roads over this Wash—two in the south, and one in the north. The waters being frequently several feet deep, the roads are marked by posts or willows. The crossings in the south at Mepal and Sutton are very narrow, but the Wash is here of considerable depth. The crossing on the north, which is at Welney, is about three-quarters of a mile broad, but its shallowness renders it more easy of transit in time of flood than the narrower roadways in the south. The Old Bedford river is crossed by a cast-iron bridge; the counter-drain or delph, which runs beside it, is crossed by a wooden one; but the New Bedford river, on the opposite side of the Wash has the elegant suspension bridge we have alluded to erected over it.[1] Mr. Townley exacts a moderate toll from both passengers and carriages over this bridge. There was formerly only a ferry at this place, and as it is the line of road between Wisbech and Ely, being nearer by seven miles than the road by March, the advantage of a bridge in lieu of a ferry—before railways were in operation—may be readily

'the day fatal to one of them shall come, in their deaths they will not be divided;' but because throughout the whole of the Old Testament, after the institution of the Kingly Government, they were intimately connected."

(1) "The bridge is one hundred and ninety-one feet long, and in breadth fourteen feet; the platform or road of the bridge springs two feet in the centre, and five feet six inches above the general level of the bank, with a neat iron railing five feet high, and three feet walk on each side for foot passengers. The bridge is supported by four principal suspending chains, driven twelve feet into the ground, riveted end to end, and properly secured by coupling plates and bolts of proportional strength, with perpendicular suspenders supporting the lower bars, on which the beams of the bridge rest; the suspension rods are of different lengths, being nineteen in number on each side. The foundation of the structure consists of sixteen strong piles of timber to each of the two piers, driven twenty-one feet in the solid bed of gravel. A large iron plate, fixed twelve feet in the ground, forms a sort of bed called the anchor, through which the chains run, and to which they are fastened. The piers of the brickwork are twelve feet high, and the cast-iron piers twenty-one feet, making in all thirty-three feet from the foundation to the top of the pier."—*Watson.*

imagined. Notwithstanding this advantage the traffic was never likely to pay the expense of the erection; the work must therefore be considered one of those public benefactions which are unfortunately rare, but which will connect Mr. Townley's name, in two or three other instances, with posterity.[1]

WALSOKEN

seems to have bequeathed nothing of much importance to historical inquiry. It had formerly a manor called the Marshes, from the family of De Marisco says Col. Watson, but which would be readily solved by a hasty inquirer in the fact of it having been originally marsh. We have already noticed the several large inundations which have at times almost swept this parish away, and at a period when such were prevalent, this manor must have often been a marsh. Like most of this kind of property, we may trace it back to the church. Another manor called Popenhoe, larger than that of the Marshes, existed in this parish. It was given to the Abbey of Ramsey by Ailivin Duke of the East Angles. It was given by Henry VIII. as Walsoken manor, with the rectory, to Sir Thomas Wriothesly and Sir Richard Southwell, and has since passed to various proprietors.

(1) From the time of making the Hundred-foot river there was no road, no direct communication between one part of Welney and another. The Bedford Level Corporation, on application, declined to restore it, and left to an individual that which they should have done themselves. Some years previous to the application a ferry had been provided by subscription; this, however, being found incommodious, led eventually to the present bridge, held under a ninety-nine years' lease from the Bedford Level Corporation. The effect of the railroad crossing the Hundred-foot about two miles and a half from the bridge has materially diminished the traffic. The lessee applied to the Corporation, who, with consistent liberality, refused to entertain the question. "*To the Hon. the Corporation of the Bedford Level. The Memorial of the Rev. Wm. Gale Townley.* Sheweth,—That your memorialist, having in the first instance strongly urged upon your honourable Board the propriety of restoring the communication between those parts of the Isle of Ely, severed by your predecessors in cutting the Hundred Foot River, did, on your refusal, at his own great risk and expense, erect a Suspension Bridge over the said river, in his own parish of Welney, your honourable Board having granted him a lease of the banks for the term of ninety-nine years, at the same time restricting the amount of tolls. And whereas, with your permission, the Eastern Counties Railroad Company have crossed the Hundred Foot River, within three miles of your memorialist's bridge, to his great prejudice, thereby dimishing by one-half the traffic,—your memorialist having no claim upon the railroad company, who came forward, like himself, as public improvers, seeks compensation at your hands, and trusts to your taking his claim into consideration, upon the common principle of equity between landlord and tenant. Your memorialist has the honor to subscribe himself, yours faithfully, W. GALE TOWNLEY."

Walsoken derives its principal importance from its vicinity to Wisbech. The village itself, which is about a mile and a half to the north of Wisbech, is a poor place, with a very few inhabitants. The portion of the parish, however, which adjoins Wisbech is pleasant and populous, containing about 2000 inhabitants, with excellent houses along its main street, or road. This part of Walsoken has been principally built in the present century, and it is chosen as a residence, not only for its pleasant country aspect immediately adjoining the town, but for a certain leniency of rates, which give it the advantage over its older and more expensive ancestor. There are extensive remains of embankments in this parish, besides large mounds which have the appearance of tumuli.

The church is the only important object in the parish. It bears the architecture of various ages, beginning at the Norman, *circa* 1100, and ending with the Perpendicular, *circa* 1400. Externally it is not very imposing, as the tower seems completed in a style inferior to its commencement, and is finished with a heavy spire, inadequately relieved with the small stunted pinnacles which terminate the angular buttresses. Almost all the windows are Perpendicular, those in the aisles being mostly flat-headed. The clerestory, containing in all fourteen Perpendicular windows, is battlemented and pinnacled between each pair of windows, with a sacristy bell to the east. The roof was formerly of a much higher pitch. There is a porch on the south surmounted with a good cross. The vestry, which is attached to the south side of the chancel, seems formerly to have been a chapel. There is also a doorway of the Transition period attached to the south aisle. The tower in its two lowermost stories contains beautiful Transition, lancet, and trefoil arcades, with a round-headed doorway splayed with Early English mouldings and three pillars. The third story, which occupies nearly half the height of the tower, is traversed by vertical bands, between which and reaching about half their height is a plain lancet arcade of not much elegance. The upper story has four Perpendicular windows. The tower is flanked with octangular buttresses, and is battlemented at the top.

The interior has many claims on the attention of those interested in the progress of church architecture. The nave is Norman, being the most interesting specimen of the style in Norfolk, except Norwich Cathedral. There are six pillars, alternately round and hexagonal, on each side, and two responds. The arch moulding towards the nave is zig-zag, with a zig-zag soffit. The roof of oak is of the Perpendicular period, with angels on the transome beam and niched figures on the bracket. The tower communicates with the church by a lancet arch, and at the other extremity of the nave, communicating with the chancel, is a beautiful and celebrated specimen of Transition work. Cotman has given this arch in detail in his etchings of Norfolk antiquities, and it has otherwise engaged the attention of antiquaries. The arch springs from six banded pillars, and has a soffit exquisitely worked with zig-zags and ornamented with a kind of cusp, which stands out from the under face of the arch. There are the remains of the old carved oak seats and miserere in this part of the church. There is an aisle on each side of the chancel which have formerly been chapels, having their screens remaining. The screen which separates the chapel from the south aisle is attached to a Decorated arch, and is a very rich specimen of Perpendicular work. The interior of the chapel contains an exquisitely carved oak roof. On the north side is another chapel, much larger than the southern one, but with less remains of former beauty about it. Some stained glass in the windows seem to show that a colored window formerly ornamented this division of the church.

This church contains the remains of the ancient fittings, which have been cut and converted into modern pewings. The old oak carving, still visible on these oak seats, is of a higher character than usual, and the finials are beautifully wrought. The arm-rest of the seat was ornamented with a standing figure of a beast, a bird, or a man, and two or three interesting specimens of this elegant but not very common feature are preserved. The ends of the seats towards the aisles and nave seem to have been ornamented with a carved niche containing a figure, and though a specimen or two appears to remain, they are so boarded up as to be altogether out of observation.

The last object we shall notice in this church is the font—a famous and beautiful example of highly decorated Perpendicular work. It is octangular, and is formed of hard oolitic stone. Each side has a carved groined niche, with crocketted ogee arch and expanded finial, behind which is a sort of cusp work in very good taste. Seven of the niches are occupied with the sacraments of the Catholic Church, and the eighth contains the crucifixion. The base is occupied with eight standing figures, also in groined niches, with crockets and finials, and above is a series of angels, eagles, and other decorations. The whole forms as enriched a specimen of its period as is to be found. Round the base is this inscription: "Remember the soul of S. Hoynter, and Margaret, his wife, and John Beforth, chaplin."

Walsoken had formerly its guilds, and a chapel apparently belonging to one of them was situated near the Gull, about three-quarters of a mile east of the church.[1]

The population in 1841 was 2562.

"NEWTON

is a small village, four miles north of Wisbech. The church, which is dedicated to St. James, is a decent structure, with a nave and side aisles, a spacious chancel, and a neatly paved floor. The tower has six bells, which were cast in 1786 at a cost of £98 6*s.* 9*d.*, and they weigh 38cwt. 3qrs. 2lb. The north aisle is said to have been erected by the Colvile family, and that to the south at the expense of Jeffrey Wantling, who espoused the Parliamentary cause in the time of Cromwell. The east end of the north aisle is railed off, and incloses a burial-place of the Colvile family, about eighteen feet deep: but, notwithstanding the many years the family

(1) Watson.

lived here, there is not a monument in the church to them; and even this part where they buried is in a manner unpaved. Two ancient brass helmets, which appear to have been formerly much decorated, still remain there, with two escutcheons, which seem as if there had been heretofore some care taken about the burial-place of the family. In 1527 one Wm. Thornborough gave 20*s*. to buy a canopy for the high altar. Five arches support the roof of the building, which has been once highly ornamented, the remains of gilding being still to be seen. Over the arches are painted several sentences of scripture. The pulpit and reading-desk are neat. The windows have been formerly decorated with painted glass, remnants of which were preserved till lately, especially on the south-east side, in which were two figures, and a scroll from their mouths: *Orate pro animabus—Colvile.* A large arch at the east end divides the chancel from the nave, with a screen, which, if entirely taken away, would add considerably to the general good effect of the interior. The altar, on three steps, is railed in. In the middle aisle are several very ancient monumental stones, now defaced, some of which appear to have been originally ornamented with brass. There is one dedicated to Ann, daughter of Richard Stone, Knt., with the following inscription:

Cætera magnificis ditescant templa sepulchris;
Nostra satis ditas ossibus, Anna, tuis.[1]

"The communion plate belonging to the church is very handsome, and was given by the Bishop of Ely in 1674. It consists of a gilt flagon, a gilt chalice and cover, and a gilt patin. The flagon holds three quarts, and stands about eight inches high.

"The living is in the gift of the Bishop of Ely, and is valued in the king's books at £18 14*s*. 8½*d*. It is worth about £1200.

"The manor of Newton continued in the Colvile family from nearly the Conquest till 1792, when it was sold by

(1) Others may magnificently adorn the place of the tomb;
Ours is enriched enough by thy bones, Anna."

Robert Colvile, Esq. The founder of this family came over with William of Normandy, and received the reward that was usually bestowed by William on his followers in confiscated lands. They did not figure importantly in any of the national scenes of the middle ages, and were among the Tory adherents of Charles I.

"In the reign of Henry IV., Sir John Colvile founded a college in the parish of Newton, and had a patent to endow it with £40 per annum. The ancient endowment was as follows: *Collegium perpetuum quatuor Capellanorum, quatuor Clericorum, et decem pauperum, et quorum quidem, Capellanorum unus esset magister sive custos.*[1] It was called the college of St. Mary by the sea coast. One of the chaplains, who served in the parish church, had £5 6*s.* 8*d.* per anuum, the other 100*s.*; the clerks 40*s.* 4*d.*; and the poor men, who lived in a house called the Bede House, 6*d.* per week each and clothes. The first statistics given by the founder are dated 18th June, 1411, in which the college is commanded to pray for the soul of the founder, and of Emma, his wife. There are no remains of this college, but the site is well ascertained to be near the old Roman bank, adjoining the rectory-house towards the west. After the Reformation the lands of this college or chapel were annexed to the rectory.[2] The Colvile family kept up a residence at Newton Hall from the time of Henry III. to 1792, about five hundred years. The old hall was a low building of many gables, like two or three houses set lengthwise and crosswise one with another. It was pulled down in 1792, and a farm-house was erected on its site. There are no public benefactions in the parish."[3]

Population in 1841, 183.

(1) A college of four Chaplains, four Clerks, and ten poor men, of whom one of the Chaplains should be master or overseer.

(2) The lands of Newton Rectory lie in the parishes of Newton, Parson Drove, Wisbech St. Peter, Wisbech St. Mary, Elm, Walsoken, West Walton, Emneth, and Tid St. Giles; containing together 398 acres.

(3) Abridged from Col. Watson.

"TID ST. GILES,

is a village adjoining Newton, and lies at the most northern extremity of the Isle of Ely. It borders in part upon the shire drain, which divides the county of Cambridge from Lincolnshire. The church, dedicated to St. Giles, is a rectory in the deanery and hundred of Wisbech, and stands rated in the king's books at £21 13*s*. It is a neat structure, with a square embattled tower, containing a ring of five bells, and stands about fifty feet from the body of the church at the east end, which is very unusual. The pillars of the nave incline to the west, which induce some persons to suppose that a tower did once support that end of the church. The altar stands on an eminence of two steps, but is not railed in. The chancel is of modern erection, built about seventy years since, when particular attention was given to discover whether the present tower was ever connected with the church, but the foundation showed no marks that any former building ever existed to unite the tower therewith. The roof has several projecting figures of angels and saints, rudely carved in wood. At the foot of the altar steps, exactly in the middle, was an old grey marble with the half figure of a priest in brass on it, but no inscription. The nave is separated from the chancel by a screen. In the middle aisle of the church is a gravestone with a large cross on it, and the following fragment of an inscription in old Gothic characters all round it, which appears to belong to the thirteenth century, though it bears no certain evidence of exact date; such part of it as is perfect is: '*Orate pro anima dni John' Fysner—— aie de ppiciet. Amen.*' In the windows of the north aisle used to be some old painted glass, and in the same aisle are two ancient slabs, appearing to have once had figures in brass. The Bishop of Ely is patron of the living, which, by Pope Nicholas's taxation, was charged at £42. The font is entitled to notice, being of the later Gothic style, octagonal, and richly ornamented with tracery, carved with emblems of the passion, and arms of the see of Ely. Nicholas Breakspear is said to have been curate here, who, for planting Christianity in Norway, was made a cardinal, A.D. 1154, and afterwards became pope, under the name of Adrian IV. The manor in the fourteenth century was in the ancient family of Colvile, before named in the account of Newton; and afterwards, in the year 1637, came by purchase into the Trafford family. This manor was sold in the time of the great rebellion in 1648, to one Davies for £472 11*s.*; but afterwards reverted to the family of Trafford. The benefactions to the poor consist of thirteen acres and three roods of land, left by Robert Brigstock, in 1667; and of fifteen acres bequeathed by Matthew Wren, Esq., in 1672. These united charities are let by auction every seven years, and the proceeds distributed twice every year to such poor and deserving people as have lived without parochial relief since the distribution of the previous dole."[1]

Population in 1841, 863.

WALPOLE ST. PETER'S.

The name Walpole, which has become famous in English literature and English history, is supposed to be derived from the Latin word *vallum*, a wall, and perhaps *pelagus*, the sea, —the vast sea-bank which bounds it to the west being of course signified in this not very authentic interpretation.

Walpole is mentioned in Doomsday Book, and formerly contained eight manors: 1. Lovell's. 2. Ely and Walpole Eldred. 3. Marshe's or Colvile's manor. 4. Walpole. 5. Rochford. 6. Denver. 7. Prior of Lewes. 8. Pannel's. Of these, Colvile's manor alone retains its name. The second, seventh, and eighth, were possessed by the church, the rest by distinguished families, who seem to have left an ostensible memorial of their property in these parts in the church.

The church of Walpole St. Peter's is the finest parish church in this district, and it is one of the noblest village churches in the kingdom. Indeed, in purity of style and elegance, there are few ecclesiastical structures of any kind that surpass it. The style is Perpendicular of the fifteenth

(1) Abridged from Col. Watson.

century. It consists of a tower, nave, aisles, and chancel, of large proportions. There are two entrance porches of different character. That on the north is smaller and plainer than that to the south. It has angular buttresses and sloped battlements, whose merlons are filled in with quatrefoils. and shields. The porch to the south is much more elegant: it has a parvise over it, which is lighted by a window, on each side of which is a niche, supported by griffins holding a shield and cross keys on one side, and lions holding a shield and cross swords on the other, indicating the dedication of the church to St. Peter and St. Paul.[1] The interior of the porch is richly groined with elaborate bosses. There are six very large aisle windows on each side the church, with corresponding arches along the nave, and two other similar east and west windows in each aisle. There are twenty-six clerestory windows in all. There are no less than eleven large chancel windows besides. When it is remembered that these windows are of uniform date, and very large, occupying nearly all the space between buttress and buttress, the internal effect of the church may be conceived. It is as if the entire building were built on pillars—the walls seeming actually transparent with so many lights. The chancel is very long: it has a series of sedilia on each side in the form of elegant niches, and the ancient seats in this portion of the church retain the old paintings of saints with which they were originally ornamented. The altar is nobly reached by a flight of twelve steps. Under this part of the church was, perhaps, formerly the vault of the founder; it is now opened, and become a thoroughfare under the church. It still, however, retains its elegant groined roof, depressed Tudor arch, and a variety of bosses, of which there are three prominent in size, bearing the cross keys and cross swords, with the Tudor emblem—the portcullis—in the centre of the vault. The east end is surmounted with a fine cross and

(1) "Over the entrance of the south porch are the arms of Godard and Denver, and between them Godard and Denver quartered."—*Watson*. Godard and Denver were families united by marriage, who held large possessions here in the thirteenth and fourteenth centuries.

pinnacles, and there is a beautiful open pinnacle over the chancel arch, in which the sacrist's bell still hangs. The ornaments which fill the battlements, with which the whole church is surmounted, are a small panel trefoil and shields. The moulding beneath is filled in with roses, heads, flowers, &c. The tower is the same in style as the church. It has three stories, is battlemented like the church, and of stone.

There was formerly much painted glass of saints, &c., in the windows of the chancel, the greater part of which was removed forty years ago.[1]

The font, which is covered with a carved canopy in oak, bears a date hardly decipherable, but seemingly of the fifteenth century. It is nearly plain. A brass eagle is used for reading.

The living, which is worth about £1400 a-year, is in the gift of the crown. It was in the presentation of the see of Ely till the reign of Elizabeth.

Population in 1841, 1335.

WALPOLE ST. ANDREW'S.

This living is in the gift of the Townshend family, and is worth about the same as Walpole St. Peter's.

John Dacot, vicar of this parish, in 1502 left the following curious clause in his will relating to this church. "John Dacot, vicar, wills to be buried on the north side of this church, before his hall,[2] and gives thirty stone of lead to the church-work, and a suit of vestments of white damask, branched with angels of gold or lily pots, like the red suit in the said church, and a cow to the parish."

The church of Walpole St. Andrew's is Perpendicular in style like St. Peter's, but is in every respect inferior. It is of brick, plastered over, and contains nothing worthy of particular mention except a painting over the altar of the entombment of Christ. There are five bells in the tower.

In the year 1809 £1000 were expended in repairing this

(1) Watson.

(2) The site of Dacot Hall is now the residence of Mr. Charles Boon.

church, at which time a new window was placed at the east end.

There were formerly several chapels in Walpole, of which the only record remaining is in the terriers; several lands still retain the names of the chapels to which they once belonged.

1. The chapel of St. Katharine, which appears to have been situated on the west of East Drove, between March Lane and Reeve's Lane.

2. Chapel of St. Edmund. The new chapel erected by Mr. Moore, the rector of Walpole St. Peter's, is near the site where stood this ancient building. It probably belonged to the Rochford family, to whose hall it was contiguous.

3. Chapel of St. Thomas. This is now a farm-house in East Drove. In the neighbourhood of this chapel was the guildhall of St. Thomas.

4. Chapel of St. Mary, at the Fen-end, which was situate on East Drove, about half way between Casto Dyke and the Smeeth-gate.

5. Chantry of St. James and St. Peter, which was near St. Peter's church, where the old poor-house stood.

6. Chapel of St. Helen's, at Cross Keys.

Walpole stretches far about, and its two churches—the least of which is more than sufficient for its immediate population—lie within a quarter of a mile of each other. But, two miles east of St. Peter's, and two miles north-east of St. Andrew's, the parishes again become populous, and places of worship have been provided in each of these parts, chiefly by the present incumbents of the respective parishes. That attached to the church of St. Peter's is an ambitious and rather ornamental edifice, situated near the side of the road which leads to Lynn. It was built in 1844, and is somewhat questionable in point of taste. The building consists of a nave, apse, and vestry, and is built in the heavy Norman style. The nave is 42ft. 6in. long, and the apse is 16ft. by 14ft. It has a high pitched roof, and a bell-cote, in which are hung two bells. There are eight small round-headed windows in the nave, and it is seated after the manner of the 14th century. An arch, eight feet wide, divides the chancel from the nave, and to the south of this arch a stone pulpit, communicating with the vestry, projects from the side wall. A font of large dimensions for so small a chapel occupies a considerable portion of the building at the entrance. A cornice beneath the roof is highly painted, and inscribed with eight verses of the Te Deum in Latin—a piece of vanity; since, if it is intended to be of any other use than that conveyed by the mere form of a series of letters, it should certainly have been in a language which the audience could read: and who expects ploughmen and rustics to be able to decipher college erudition? It is time to use as little Latin as possible when we have a tongue that will express all its ideas to thousands, where the classic tongue would not instruct tens. The circular apse is the most ambitious part of this chapel. It consists of a stone altar table, with four lights over it, occupied with glass painted with figures of Christ, St. Peter, St. Catherine, and St. Edmund, to whom the chapel is dedicated. There are the piscina and sedilia ready, should the church at any future time return to its Roman principles.

The chapel in connection with St. Andrew's, at the other extremity of the parish, is wholly without ornament or ambition, and has only just been erected.

The population in 1841 was 565.

Charities.

1. Butler's charity, of 37a. 1r. of land and four cottages, was left by Robert Butler, in 1630, to poor widows who have been born in the township of Walpole, and resident in the parish of Walpole St. Peter ten years at the least, and have been but the wife of one husband. The rent of the above land is applied to the maintenance of four women, who occupy the cottages, and receive 3*s.* 6*d.* weekly, a chaldron of coals annually, and a blue cloth gown once in two years.

2. There are twenty-seven acres of land, unknown by whom and when left, called Town Bailiff land, the rent of which is applied to the repairs of the church ways; this rent is received by the churchwardens.

3. Dole Land in Walpole St. Peter's, consisting of a house and 12a. 1r. of land, which have since received in addition, by the inclosure of Marshland Smeeth and Fen, 27a. 1r. 7p. making a total of 39a. 2r. 7p. let for the annual rent of £81. It is also unknown when or by whom this land was left, or for what particular purpose. The rents are received by the churchwardens, and annually distributed amongst the most industrious poor, and such as maintain their families without parochial relief; the amount according to the size of the respective families.

4. Dole Land in Walpole St. Andrew's: this consists of one messuage, one cottage, and 23a. old inclosed land. By the marsh inclosure (the award of which is dated 1789) it received an addition of 26a. 2r. 22p., and by the inclosure of the smeeth and fen (award dated 1803) it received 7a. 1r. 17p. of smeeth, and 27a. 3r. 20p. fen, making a total of 84a. 3r. 19p. and in 1810 let for the annual rent of £152 10*s*. The land is divided into portions of one acre each, and let to the poor of Walpole St. Andrew's at a reduced rent.

5. A public free school is established for the instruction of the children in the parishes of Walpole St. Peter's and St. Andrew's. This was formerly kept over the south porch of St. Peter's church; but in 1813 a new school-room was built by voluntary contribution. The master's salary is paid by the rent of fifty-six acres of land, left by Anthony Curton in 1706, situated in Terrington St. John's.[1]

(1) Abridged from Col. Watson.

APPENDIX.

SKETCH OF THE GEOLOGY OF THE FENS.

CONTRIBUTED BY MR. H. M. LEE.

In examining the surface deposits of the great level of the Fens, the geologist finds that they are composed principally of silt in the marsh lands, of peat or turf in the fen lands, and occasionally of gravel.

The first is principally the result of the accumulation of detritus brought by the tides from the Norfolk and Yorkshire coasts, by which the Wash, assisted by the system of warping and embanking, is so rapidly being converted into dry land.

The peat is formed by the decay of vegetable matter in a damp atmosphere, and where water is stagnant. As we may suppose from the number of trees found in it,* remains of animals which inhabited its formerly extensive forests are not uncommon, and consist of the bones of deer, wild boars, oxen, beavers, &c.

The gravel generally occurs in insulated masses, and as it afforded the advantages of dry building ground, and supplies of water, we find most of the fen towns, churches, &c., have been built upon it. At March and Elm, near Wisbech, it contains numerous shells in a good state of preservation, and of species common on the Norfolk coast, such as Cardium Edule, Mactra Subtruncata, Tellina Solidula, Ostrea Edule, Cyprina Islandica, Turritella Terebra, Purpura Lapillus, Littorina Littorea, Buccinum Undatum, Natica Glancinoides; but at Whittlesea, Chatteris, &c., it appears to be totally devoid of them. Shells derived from the oolite deposits of Northamptonshire frequently occur, but I believe the most interesting fossils which have been found in it are fragments of the jaws and the teeth of an extinct species of elephant (Elephans Primigenius) found lately at Whittlesea, and now in my collection.

The boulder clay, brown clay, or Till of geologists, also occurs in a few places, consisting, as usual, of clay with large fragments of chalk and other rocks, and containing the fossils of the strata from which these have been derived. There can be little doubt that it was produced by the rush of large bodies of water, occasioned by the sudden elevation of land beneath the sea.

These deposits belong to the post-tertiary or recent epoch of geology, and as the tertiary beds have no representative in this district, we must seek the next newest formations belonging to the secondary deposits, in the southern and eastern borders of the Fens. The uppermost of these is the chalk, which is found in the neighbourhood of Cambridge, forming the Gog-Magog Hills, and extends by Newmarket, Downham, and Castle Acre, to the sea at Hunstanton. It is divided into the UPPER CHALK, containing flints and numerous remains of marine shells, zoophytes, and fish; and the LOWER CHALK, devoid of flints, but rich in fossils. The latter bed is that most developed, and is well known under the name of clunch, from its supplying the material for nearly all the lime used in this part of the country. I have obtained from it, at Isleham, near Newmarket, numerous teeth and vertebræ of fish, a few zoophytes, and a great variety of shells.

Below the lower chalk at Hunstanton is found the CHALK MARL, as in the southern counties, and containing a very singular sponge (Spongia Paradoxica) in great abundance; but this bed is wanting at Cambridge, where there occurs below the chalk a thin bed of UPPER GREENSAND, only a few inches thick, but remarkable from its containing numerous nodules of a dark colour, composed principally of phosphate of lime, along with numerous fossils, of which I have collected the following:—Terebratula Biplicata, Terebratula Obtusa, Terebratula Elongata, Terebratula Subrotunda, Terebratula Semiglobosa, Terebratula Dimi-

* See "Physical Characteristics" of this Work.

diata, Avicula Gryphæoides, Gryphæa Conica, Plicatula Inflata, Plicatula Pectinoides, Inoceramus Concentricus, Solarium Ornatum, Solarium Conoideum, Belemnites Minimus, Ammonites 2 species, Orbitolites 1 species, Stems of Zoophyte, Carapace of Crab (Corystes) Bones, Vertebræ, and teeth of Sharks, teeth of Saurocephalus Striatus, teeth of Icthyosaurus Campylodon. Below the Upper Greensand lies the GAULT, a blue clay 150 or 200 feet thick, but from which, I am informed, few fossils are obtained. This clay is represented at Hunstanton cliff by the RED CHALK, which is only 3 or 4 feet thick, but contains in great abundance Terebratula Biplicata and Belemnites Minimus, fossils characteristic of the gault in the south of England and in France, along with Spongia Paradoxica and a few other fossils. It is through the gault at Cambridge that the Artesian wells are bored, the bed which underlies it, the LOWER GREENSAND or IRON SAND, yielding an abundant supply of water. The latter deposit comes to the surface a few miles from Cambridge, is abundant at Ely, Downham, &c., and forms the lower part of Hunstanton cliff. It is provincially called "Car-Stone," is used for building, and the repairs of the roads, and it also affords supplies of water and dry building ground. A great part of the glass manufactured in England is made from the white sand of Sandringham, near Lynn, which belongs to this deposit. The only fossils which are generally found in it in this part of England, are Pecten Quadricostatus, Trigonia Clavellata, and a little wood.

Below the Iron Sand, we find the KIMMERIDGE CLAY, differing but little in mineral character from the gault, a name applied provincially to all our blue clays. It is best seen at the large clay pit at Ross Hill, near Ely, where part of it displays a laminated structure, and contains large nodules of blue argillaceous limestone, which are often traversed by fissures or cracks filled with calcareous spar, commonly called "fossil water."

A very interesting "Fault" (or dislocation which interrupts the continuity of the strata, occasioned by a convulsion of nature) is displayed at the same place, by which part of the Kimmeridge Clay, and the thin bed of lower greensand above it have been elevated, according to Professor Sedgwick, 150 feet above their usual levels. The ridge caused by this Fault is the original Isle of Ely, the last rallying post of the Saxons against their Norman conquerors. This deposit at Ely is also exceedingly interesting, from the organic remains which it contains; those in my collection are Gryphœa Virgula; Ostrea Deltoidea; Trigonia Clavellata; Ammonites, 4 species; Belemnites, 1 species; Pliosaurus Brachydeirus,* teeth, vertebræ, paddle bones, &c.; Plesiosaurus, vertebræ; Icthyosaurus, vertebræ. In the southern counties and in Yorkshire, a bed of limestone called the CORAL RAG, is found below the Kimmeridge Clay, but the only trace of this deposit (interesting from its having been a Coral Reef, similar to that now forming on the Australian coast) is at Upware, a few miles from Cambridge, where it extends for about a mile. Excepting that locality, the Kimmeridge Clay passes imperceptibly into the OXFORD CLAY, on which the greater part of the Great Level is based. It is a stiff blue clay, generally several hundred feet thick, and is of great importance to agriculturists, as the system of "Gaulting" or claying the Fen land with it, forms one of the richest and most productive soils in the kingdom.

From the numerous organic remains which are dispersed through its whole extent, there can be no doubt that the Oxford Clay was gradually deposited in a deep and tranquil sea. The following is a list of the fossils which I have obtained from it, the localities being Whittlesea, March, and St. Ives:—Terebratula Inconstans; Terebratula, 3 other species; Avicula Echinata; Gryphæa Dilatata; Ostrea; Nucula; Tellina; Arca; Venus; Astarte; Trigonia Costata; Panopea Gibbosa; Serpula, 3 species; Pleurotomaria, 1 species; Rostellaria, 1 species; Ammonites Callovicensis; Ammonites Gulielmi; Ammonites Duncani; Ammonites Lamberti; Ammonites Cristatus; Ammonites Exaratus; Ammonites, 7 other species; Belemnites Anomalus; Belemnites Hastatus; Claws of Crab (Astacus); Icthyosaurus, vertebræ, tooth, &c.; vertebræ, paddle bones, &c., of Plesioaurus; wood bitumenized.

On approaching the western side of the Fens, we come to a slightly elevated tract of country, and on examining beneath the surface soil, we find that the Oxford Clay is no longer found, but a succession of limestones, clays and sands. These belong to the LOWER OOLITE FORMATION, which extends from Yorkshire, by Lincoln, Stamford, and Peterborough, to the Dorset coast. It is also a marine deposit, and in many localities (Stamford, Peterborough, &c.) contains numerous fossils, principally shells. To it belongs the "Ketton Stone," which has afforded a valuable supply of building material for centuries; and the "Collyweston Slates," the latter of which abound in shells, and occasionally yield fossil plants and teeth of fish. One of its beds, a coarse limestone called the "Cornbrash," abounds with fossils, especially at Stilton, where I have obtained from it numerous shells

* Remains of the Pliosaurus, which was a gigantic marine reptile, with some resemblance to the Crocodile, and supposed to attain the length of 40 or 50 feet, are rare, having only been found in a few localities of the Kimmeridge Clay.

(principally Terebratula), teeth of fish, bones of Saurians, &c. With the exception of the Post-tertiary, I have already stated that these deposits, (of which I much regret that the foregoing is so imperfect a sketch) belong to the secondary formations; they are all of marine origin, and have been formed in the same gradual manner that deposits are now taking place in our estuaries and round our coasts. They nearly all contain distinct fossils, none of which are of existing species; many of the genera even to which these are referred are extinct, and those having living representatives are generally inhabitants of the warmest parts of our planet.

To those unacquainted with the discoveries made of late years by geologists, this may be matter of surprise and incredulity, but a careful perusal of any good work on the science will prove to them that geology is established on a sure footing, and that the remark of one of the most eminent of philosophers, Sir John Herschel, is not undeserved when he states that "Geology in the magnitude and sublimity of the objects of which it treats, undoubtedly ranks in the scale of the sciences next to Astronomy."

The Names of such of the ALDERMEN of the Guild of the Holy Trinity in Wisbech, from its Foundation, 2d Richard II., 1379, to its Dissolution, 29th Henry VIII., 1540: and of such of the TOWN-BAILIFFS as are noticed in the Records, from the Incorporation of the Town, in the third Year of the Reign of King Edward VI.

ALDERMEN OF THE GUILD OF THE HOLY TRINITY.

The records commence 2d Richard II. A.D. 1379.

The accountant's expenses in respect to the guild are the first transactions stated, after which there is a lapse of forty-four years, until

2d HENRY VI.

	A.D.
John Lambe	1423-1431
Nicholas Outclark	1432
—— Sutton	1436-1443
John Masse	1445-1460

EDWARD IV.

John Masse	1461-1467
William Calowe,	1468-1474
Martin Andrew, in absence of W. Calowe	1475
William Calowe	1476-1478
Robert Dygby	1479-1482

EDWARD V.

Robert Dygby	1483

RICHARD III.

Robert Dygby	1484

HENRY VII.

Robert Dygby	1485-1489
John Burwell	1494-1495
Robert Tooke	1499
John Burwell	1502
Willm. Gatesend	1503-1505
Dr. Rd. Wyatt, vicar	1506-8

HENRY VIII.

Dr. Richard Wyatt	1509-11
Nicholas Style	1512-1514
William Ladd	1515-1516
Thomas Wythe,	1517-1520
Richard Rede	1521-1523
Alexander Balam	1524-1525
Lawrence Daniel	1526-1527
Alexander Balam	1531-1539

The act of parliament for dissolution of monasteries, passed in 1540

EDWARD VI.

John Proctor	1547

His majesty, in the third year of his reign, granted a charter of incorporation, with power to elect, on every 1st of November, ten of the more honest and more discrete inhabitants, "maintaining a "family," to have the care of the several affairs of the town, &c. And by such charter the following ten men were nominated in 1550, viz.

Henry Goodrick, Esq.
Richard Everard, Esq.
John Sutton
Nicholas Fordham
John Proctor
Thomas Crosse
William Beste
William Perte
Robert Scorterede
Thomas Bocher

TOWN-BAILIFFS.

ELIZABETH.

Richard Best, gent	1564
Thomas Crosse	1565-1566
Robert Cooper	1577
John Williamson	1578
Thomas Pierson	1585-1586
John Ladd	1587-1591
William Sturmyn	1594
James Saylebank	1596
Robert Tipping	1597
J. Saylebank, 2d time	1598
William Wilkes	1599
Thomas Crosse	1600
Robt. Tipping, 2d time	1601
Thomas Crosse	1602

JAMES I.

Nicholas Sandford, gent	1603
Thomas Crosse	1604
Thomas Pigge	1605
William Edwards	1606
Matthias Taylor, Esq.	1607
John Sandford, gent.	1608
John Warner	1609
Thos. Crosse, 6th time	1610

The king, in the eighth year of his reign, granted his letters patent, for incorporating the inhabitants; under which charter the first town-bailiff appointed was Anthony Fisher, gent. 1611

Thomas Pigge 1612
Thomas Edwards 1613
Thomas Parke, esq. 1614
Thos. Pearson, gent. 1615
John Marshall 1616
Thomas Proctor 1617
Thomas Williams 1618-1621
William Twells 1622
Thomas Williams 1623
The like, 6th time 1624

CHARLES I.

Ed. Buckworth, esq. 1625
Nicholas Sandford, gent 1626
Matthias Taylor, esq. 2d time 1527
Thomas Girling, gent. 1628
The like 1629
Anthony Fisher 1630
Arthur Taylor 1631
James Whynnall 1632
Thos. Pigge, 3rd time 1633
John Day 1634
Thomas Swaine, Edward Crosse remainder of the year 1635
John Wilson, gent. 1636
Edward Crosse 1637
William Edwards, jun. 1638
Matthias Taylor, Thomas Pigge remainder of the year 1639
Robert Edwards 1640
Thomas Pierson 1641
Everard Buckworth, esq. 1642
Nicholas Sandford 1643
John Daniel 1644
William Fisher, esq. 1645
Henry Ferrour, gent. 1646
John Marshall 1647
Nich. Sandford, 3d time 1648
William Edwards, sen. 1649

COMMONWEALTH.

John Wilson, gent. 1650-53
Anthony Balam 1654
Robert Twells 1655
John Wilson, 6th time 1656
William Fisher, esq. 1657
James Edwards, gent. 1658-9

CHARLES II.

Wm. Walsham, gent. 1660
Robert Stevens 1661
John Wilson, 7th time, Nicholas Sandford remainder of the year 1662
James Edwards 1663-5
Anth. Buckworth, Esq. 1666
John Neale, gent. 1667-68

This king renewed the town charter, whereby the ten men were to be called "Capital Burgesses," and to be elected every 2d November, under which last charter the first town-bailiff elected was

John Marshall, gent. 1669
Thomas Edwards, esq. 1670
Robert Vaughan, gent. 1671
James Whinnel 1672
John Coxen 1673
The like and John Neave 1674
Richard Harrison 1675
Thomas Flanner 1676
John Marshall, 4th time 1677
Simon Loake 1678
James Whinnel 1679-83
Philip Easinghurst 1681
John Bellamy 1682
Jonas Brown 1683
Daniel Walker 1684

JAMES II.

William Fox, gent. 1685
Oliver Brown 1686
Henry Medow 1687

WILLIAM AND MARY.

William Fox, 2d time 1688
Henry Laughton 1689
William Tunnard 1690
James Marshall, sen. 1691
William Allen, gent. 1692
Richard Loake 1693
John Twells, esq. 1694
John Barker, gent. 1695
Joseph Taylor 1696
Robert Gynn 1697
James Whinnel, jun. 1698
The like, 2d time 1699
Edward Bellamy, esq. 1700
Richard Loake, 2d time, on his decease, Joseph Taylor, 2d time 1701

ANNE.

Thomas Cock, gent. 1702
Richard Bladwick 1703
Robert Twells 1704
Lawrence Banyer 1705
Nathaniel Kinderley 1706
Richard Loake 1707
William Stevens 1708
John Kelsall, esq. 1709
Rev. John Bellamy, clk. 1710
John Middleton, gent. 1711
Edward Crosse 1712
Henry Longstae 1713

GEORGE I.

Anth. Lumpkin, gent. 1714
Samuel Vine 1715
John Marshall, jun. esq. 1716
Rev. T. Cole, clk. vicar 1717
Anthony Lumpkin 1718
John Horncastle 1719
James Anthony 1720
Thomas Spire 1721
Richard Taylor, esq. 1722
John Cuthbert, gent. 1723
Thomas Towers 1724
Henry Bull, D.D. vicar 1725
Edward Southwell, esq. 1726

GEORGE II.

Henry Southwell, gent. 1772
James Lowry 1728
Jacob Norris 1729
Charles Vavasor 1730
James Anthony, esq. 1731
Richard Taylor, gent. 1732
Robert Hemus 1733
John Thompson 1734
Thomas Marlow 1735
William Flanner 1736
Robert Gynn 1737
Samuel Massey 1738
Isaac Young 1739
Thomas Woods 1740
John Bellamy 1741
Edmund Cobb, esq. 1742
Edward Southwell, esq 1743
William Esekiel Flanner 1744
Charles Browne 1745
Robert Wensley 1746
William Long 1747
Joseph Barwick 1748
Edward Southwell, esq. 3d time 1749
Rev. Henry Burroughs, clerk, vicar 1750
John Garland, gent. 1751
David Waite 1752
Robert Wensley, 2d time 1753
Thomas Berrier 1754
Henry Southwell, esq. 2d time, 1755
Samuel Massey, M.D. 2d time 1756
Isaac Young, gent. 1757
John Bellamy 1758
Jeremiah Hancock 1759

GEORGE III.

William Marshall, gent. 1760
Sir Philip Vavasour, knt 1761
Edward Warmoll, gent. 1762
Hugh Maplesden 1763
John Southwell, esq. 1764
John Thompson, gent. 2d time 1765
George Swaine 1766-7
Thomas Chapman 1768
Robert Colville, esq. 1769
Sir Philip Vavasor, knt 2d time 1770

John Waite, gent. 1771
Henry Burroughs, LL.D. 2d time 1772
Wm. Skrimshire, gent. 1773
Joseph Hancock 1774
Rev. John Warren, D.D. vicar 1775
Richard Colville, esq. 1776
John Mayer, gent. 1777
Thomas Fawsett 1778
Robert Kilby 1779
Thomas Newman 1780
William Skrimshire 1781-2
Robert Stevens 1783
James Bellamy 1784
William Smalley 1785
Rev. T. Sheepshanks, A.M. 1786
Mann Hutcheson, F.S.A 1787
Robert Hardwicke, esq. 1788
William Rayner 1789
Hon. and Rev. Charles Lindsay, A.M. vicar 1790
John Mayer, gent. 2d time 1791
Josiah King Life 1792
John Edes, esq. 1793
Robert Kilby, gent. 1794
William Clark 1795
Rev. Cæsar Morgan, D.D. vicar 1796
Rev. William Walker 1797
John Swansborough 1798
Abraham Hardy, gent. 1799
William Skrimshire, esq. 4th time 1800
Chas. Laughton, gent. 1801
Hugh Jackson, jun. 1802
Charles Metcalfe 1803
William Watson, esq. 1804
James Watson, gent. 1805
James Bellamy, 2d time 1806
Robert Hardwicke, esq. 1807
Steed Girdlestone, gent. 1808
Joseph Medworth 1809
William Jump 1810
Rev. Abraham Jobson, D.D. vicar 1811
William Rayner, esq. 2d time 1812
Rev. Jeremiah Jackson, 1813
John Edes, esq. 2d time 1814
Hugh Jackson, jun. 1815
Ralph Archbould, gent. 1816
Edmund Ward 1817
H. J. Nichols, esq. 1818

GEORGE IV.

Robert Hardwicke, esq. 1819
W. Swansborough, gent 1820
W. Watson, F.S.A. 1821-2
Steed Girdlestone, esq. 1823
J. R. Weatherhead, gt. 1824
James Usill, esq. 1825
William Orton, esq. 1826
C. Boucher 1827
Abraham Usill, 1828
Henry James Nichols 1829

WILLIAM IV.

Thomas Steed Watson 1830
Robert Dawbarn 1831
Henry Ollard 1832
Harley Matthew Usill 1833
Henry Leach 1834

MAYORS.

Henry Leach 1835
John R. Weatherhead 1836
Thomas Dawbarn 1837
Henry Morton 1838
Henry Leach 1839
Thomas Steed Watson 1840
Thomas Stear 1841
James Usill 1842
Charles Metcalfe, jun. 1843
John Whitsed 1844
William Stevens 1845-6
Henry Leach 1847-8
William Stevens 1849
William H. Ward 1850

VICARS OF WISBECH.

CATHOLIC.

William de Norwold 1252
Dr. Rogers 1338
John Bolin 1349
William de Newton 1384
John Judde or Rudde . . . 1401
John Ockham, LL.D. . . . 1422
William Abyinton . . . . ——
John Clampain 1448
John Warkworth, D.D. . . . 1472
William Gybbs 1473
William Doughty, LL. D. . . 1494
John Wyatt 1503
Robert Cliffe, LL.D. . . . 1525
John Cheesewright . . . . ——
William Lord 1537
William Hande 1544
Henry Ogle 1549
Hugh Margesson, A.B. . . . 1554

PROTESTANT.

Matthew Champion 1587
Joshua Blaxton, B.D. . . . 1613
Thomas Emerson 1615
Edward Furnis, A.M. . . . 1630
William Coldwell 1651
John Bellamy, A.M. 1702
Thomas Cole, A.M.* 1714
Henry Bull, D.D. 1721
Henry Burrough, LL. D. . . 1749
John Warren, D.D. . . . 1773
James Burslem, LL. D. . . . 1779
Hon. and Rev. C. Lindsay, A.M. 1787
Cæsar Morgan, D.D. . . . 1795
Abraham Jobson, D.D. . . . 1802
Henry Fardell, A.M. . . . 1831

CHIEF BAILIFFS OF THE ISLE OF ELY.

1294	Robert de Scadeworth		Jordan de Daventre	1725	Charles Clarke, Esq.
	Roger Abynton	1501	John Burgoyne	1726	Edward Patherick, Esq.
1308	Ralph de Norwich	1516	Edmund Wyngfield	1749	Thomas Gooch, Esq.
1329	John Bosse		Thomas de Inglethorpe	1753	Francis Wyatt, Esq.
1445	Roger Davy	1546	Thomas Meggs	1770	William Ward, Esq.
1459	John Ansty		Sir John Huddlestone	1783	Thomas Gotobed, Esq.
	John Mesanger	1600	Thomas Heton, brother	1791	Francis Bagge, Esq.
1468	William Curson		to Thos. Edwards, Esq.	1822	William Watson, Esq.
	William Michell	1661	Wm. Wren, brother to	1831	Spelman Swaine, Esq.
	Matthew Christian	1698	Thomas Edwards, jun.		

CONSTABLES OF THE CASTLE OF WISBECH.

William Justice	1246	Sir Thomas Grey	1476
Simon de Dullingham	1262	Sir Thomas Hobard	1489
Richard de Halstead	1308	Walter and Miles Hubbard	1525
Thomas de Bramstone	1401	Thomas Megges, Arm.	1531
Sir John de Rochford	1403	Sir Richard Cromwell	——
Sir John de Colvile	1410	William Chester, sen., Esq.	1605
Sir Andrew Hoggard or Ogard	1446	Matthias Taylor, Esq.	1633

MASTERS OF THE GRAMMAR SCHOOL.

1446	Jacob Cresner	1669	George Frisney	1749	John Clarkson, Clerk
1548	Henry Ogle	1678	Francis Fern, M.A.	1766	Richard Oswin, Clerk
1564	Mr. Rastall	1690	Thos. Johnson, M.A.	1796	Martin Colcher, Clerk
1580	Thomas Lowthe	1697	Thomas Carter	1803	Jeremiah Jackson, M. A
——	John Power	1727	John Newson, Clerk	1826	J. R. Major, M.A.
1630	William Frisney	1731	Richard Foster, Clerk	1832	G. Thompson, B.A.

NOTE.—CATHOLIC CHAPEL.

In particularising the Dissenters and their places of worship, we inadvertently omitted the Catholics, whose history has been sent us in the following remarkable words:—"In the summer of 1840 a carpenter's workshop in New Wisbech was hired and fitted up as a Catholic Chapel, and on the 11th of October of the same year it was opened for divine service by the Rev. John Dalton, of Lynn. There is no priest for this mission, but a regular service is performed every first Sunday in the month, supplied either from Lynn or Peterborough." It seems almost superfluous to make any remark on this short but forcible account. It suggests much; but we must restrain comment on such fallen grandeur. The former cost of the robes of its priests was more than their incomes now. The golden and silver ornaments wrought upon the stole by the delicate fingers of queens and princesses, cost more than the whole establishment and officers as it exists now in Wisbech. Yet this humble taper of Catholicism is so much greater than its former darkness here. From the Reformation to 1840 we have no knowledge that the Catholic dared to offer a single prayer in public in Wisbech. His faith was a dead, almost a forgotten form of belief. But the singular principle of regeneracy which Catholicism possesses has caused the seed, like the corn from the lapping of the mummy, to re-sprout and grow, and we know not—for what can we know of such things?—that it may not like the mustard-seed, "which is the smallest of germs, become the greatest of herbs, so that the birds of the air come and lodge in the branches thereof." We believe the establishment of a chapel at Wisbech chiefly succeeded through the exertions of Mr. Mantegani, of Lugano, in Italy, and who has for many years been a resident and tradesman in Wisbech, and the principal supporter of the chapel.

Wysbeche, in the Isle of Ely, in the County of Cambridge (1547.)	A Schedule of the Possessions which fell into the hands of our Lord King Edward VI. by the grace of God, &c. by reason of certain Acts of Parliament begun at Westminster on the 4th November, in the first year of his reign.

No.	Where situated.	Consisting of: Messuages.	Consisting of: Gardens.	Quantity: In separate Parcels.	Quantity: Total.	Rent per annum. £	s.	d.	Value to purchase £	s.	d.	In whose tenure.
1	Wisbech in the fields.			20			23	0				Thomas Drabbe
	Ditto			4			8	0				Martyn Pierson
	Ditto			11			16	0				Thomas Tooke
	—— in Flatmore			3			5	0				William Sallabank
				2½			4	2				John Martynson
	Wisbech in the fields.			8			11	8				Robert Tego
	Ditto			50			43	4				Thomas Crosse
	Ditto			8			17	8				John Proctor
	Ditto			19½			31	0				Robert Skotred
	Ditto	1		7			10	0				Alan Jekin
	Ditto			11			10	0				Edward Arthor
	Ditto			28			29	4				John Knight
	Ditto			30			48	0				H. Adams, alias Stephynson
	Ditto			20½			44	0				Radolph Rychardson
	—— in Bridgecroft ..			10			20	0				William Sallabank
	Ditto			4			4	0				Richard Doddynge
	—— in the fields			14			7	0				Paul Appleyard
	Ditto			30½			22	6				Agnet Warner
	In free socage	1		5			12	0				Robert Osborne
				2½			6	0				Catherine Wynd
				3½			4	1½				John Reyner, senior
		1	1				13	4				William Peyrte
				10			7	2				William Peyrte
	Guild of the Holy Trinity of the town of Wysbeche aforesaid....			3			4	1				John Martynson
				9			8	0				John Austen
				10			20	0				Richard Lorde
				1½			2	8				Agnet Robynson
	In free socage			18			22	4				Nicholas Pierson
				6			11	5				Robert Ballam
	Wisbech in the town.	1	1				10	0				Thomas Drabbe
					349½	23	2	5½	462	9	2	.. At 20 years' purchase.
		4	2	......	......	1	3	4	11	13	4	.. At 10 years' purchase.
2	Leverington	1	1				4	4				William Chandwell
	In free socage											
	In the fields			36		2	15	0				William Thompson
	Ditto.......... ..			2½			16	0				William Chandwell
	Ditto...............			14			14	0				Ditto
	Ditto...............			53		3	4	0				John Tegoe, junior
	Ditto..........			8			14	0				William Bryon, Gent.
	Ditto			13½		1	3	0				Thomas Tooke
					127	9	6	0	186	0	0	.. At 20 years' purchase.
		1	1	......	......	0	4	4	2	3	4	.. At 10 years' purchase,
3	Newton, and a moiety of a fishing gate in free socage			7¾			4	0				Simon Trone
4	Tidd			6			16	8				John Fynn
5	Elm			7			6	0				Thomas Palmer
6	Emneth			40		3	19	8				Thomas Pyckarde
7	Walton.............			9		1	0	0				John Shepherd
					69¾	6	6	4		6	8	.. At [illegible]0 years' purchase.
8	Walpole in free socage	1	1				13	4				Edward Wylkes
	In the field			40		3	10	0				Henry Gooderike
	Ditto....			39		2	10	0				Edward Wylkes
					70	6	0	0	120	0	0	.. At 20 years' purchase.
		1	1	......	......	0	13	4	6	13	4	.. At 10 years' purchase.

RECAPITULATION.

WHERE SITUATED.	MESS.	GARD.	ACRES.	CLEAR RENTAL.	£. s. d.	YEAR'S PURCHASE.	£. s. d.
No. 1.—Wisbech - - - - - - - -			349½	of Land - -	23 2 5¼	at 20 years' purchase	462 9 2
Ditto - - - - - - - - -	4	2		Messuages - -	1 3 4	at 10 years' purchase	11 13 4
No. 2.—Leverington - - - - - -			127	of Land - -	9 7 0	at 20 years' purchase	186 0 0
Ditto - - - - - - - - -	1	1		House - - -	0 4 4	at 10 years' purchase	2 3 '4
Nos. 3, 4, 5, 6, and 7, Newton, Tid, Elm, Emneth, and Walton - -			69¾	of Land - -	6 6 4	at 20 years' purchase	126 6 8
No. 8.—Walpole - - - - - - - -			70	of Land -	6 0 0	at 20 years' purchase	120 0 0
Ditto - - - - - - - - -	1	1		House - - -	0 13 4	at 10 years' purchase	6 13 4
	6	4	616¼	Carried forward	46 16 9¼		915 5 10
Deduct Reprises as on the following side - - - - -					18 13 7		
					28 3 2¼		
Other reprises to the poor - - - £3 15 0							
Schoolmaster - - - - - - - - 10 6 8					14 1 8		
Clear annual value - - -					£14 1 6¼		
Reprises - - £18 13 7							
Other outpayments 14 1 8							
Total £32 15 3 at 20 years' purchase - - - - - - -							654 15 0
The Consideration paid for the Charter, being 20 years' purchase on the clear sum of £14 1 6¼ was							£260 10 10

	per ann. £.	s.	d.	£.	s.	d.
The clear Rental as on other side brought forward				46	16	9
Particulars of the Rents, Outgoings, and Annual Payments out of such Possession, as follows:						
The Lord Bishop of Ely, as of his Manor of Wysbech........	3	17	9			
The Dean and Chapter, as of the Manor aforesaid	0	13	9			
Galfred Norman	0	2	0			
Rectory of Wysbech	0	7	10			
Nicholas Meggs	0	11	8			
Darville..	0	6	2			
Godfred Colville, Esq.	0	0	8			
Robert Bushey..	0	0	6			
Richard Everard, Gent.	0	2	3			
Lady Mary, as of the aforesaid Manor	0	2	1¾			
Richard Hunstone	0	7	0			
John Reppes	0	1	1			
Christopher Langholme, Esq...............................	0	1	1			
Simon Trone	0	0	1½			
John Fynn	0	0	2			
—— Haggard	0	5	1			
	6	19	3			
Rents going out of the Lands and Tenements aforesaid, for the Repairs of the Shores, Banks, and Annual Payments of the late Fraternity, to the Bailiff of the Hundred of Wisbech, in each year certain	10	14	4			
To the Fee of the Bailiff, or Collector of the same	1	0	0			
				18	13	7
				£28	3	2½
Memorandum—Out of the Possessions of the Guild was yearly distributed in relief to the Poore of the same Towne, the sum of	3	15	0			
Also out of the said Possessions was yearly paid the Schoolmaster for his Wages, the sum of	10	6	8			
				14	1	8
Clear Annual Value				£14	1	6½

My Lord Protector's Grace, upon the suyte of the Byshop of Ely, was then pleased that the Inhabitants should be allowed the sums as of the King's Majesty's gyft, making together £28. 3s. 2½d.

Therefore, deducting these charges from the above annual value, £46. 16s. 9½d., there would remain a clear income of £14 1s. 6½d.; which, valued according to the rate in the before-going schedule of possessions, amounts to £260 10s. 10d.—the consideration paid for obtaining the charter. And the king's majesty discharged the purchaser of all incumbrances, except leases and covenants in the same, and except the rents above mentioned. The purchaser was to have the yssues from Michaelmas last, and to be bound for the woodd;—the lead, bells, and advowsons excepted.

(Signed) Richard Sakevyleth.
Wa. Mildemaye.
Robert Keylkey.
per Thomas Wreeme

In order to draw a comparative view of the possessions of the guild, and the actual quantity of land at present enjoyed by the Corporation, the following statement is subjoined.

By the before-going schedule, it is shown what possessions of the guild fell into the hands of king Edward VI. which his majesty re-granted to the inhabitants of Wisbech by his charter, for the purposes therein mentioned, which appears in the recapitulation to have consisted of six messuages, four gardens, and 616¼ acres of land, by estimation. Upon a personal view, taken in the year 1822, of all the lands then and now belonging to the body corporate, by the then town bailiff, it appeared that their property in houses and lands consisted of one messuage, and 716A. 1R. 39P. of land, as follow:

Possessions of the Guild re-granted to the Inhabitants by the Charter of King Edward VI.				Actual quantity of Land on a view made and taken thereof by the Town-Bailiff in 1822.				
Where situated.	Mess.	Gard.	Lands Arable & Pasture. ACRES.	Messuage.	Garden.	Lands. A.	R.	P.
In Wisbech	4	2	349½			355	1	2
— Leverington	1	1	127			138	3	17
— Newton, a fishing cote, &c.*			7¾					
— Tidd St. Mary's ..			6			6	0	0
— Elm			7			44	2	0
— Emneth			40			40	0	0
— Walton			9			17	0	3
— Walpole	1	1	70	1		114	3	17
	6	4	616¼	1		716	1	39

	A.	R.	P.
Since the period of king Edward's Charter, several Allotments in Wisbech Fen have been set out to the capital burgesses, in right of their Messuages, &c. amounting to	47	0	0
Also, under the Walpole Inclosure and Marshland Smeeth and Fen Acts, several other allotments, amounting to	28	3	17
The Capital Burgesses also purchased in Studmoreholme Field and West Newfield, in Walpole, in the year 1596	30	0	0
Ditto, in Walton, in 1820	2	2	0
There have also been set out for the Capital Burgesses, certain allotments in Walton, containing	8	0	3
Which accounts for an increase of	116	1	20

After the valuation of the possessions of the late guild, his majesty Edward VI. was pleased not only to re-grant the said guild estates, but to elevate the town of Wisbech into a CORPORATION, confirming the same to the inhabitants by virtue of the following Charter.

CHARTER OF THE TOWN OF WISBECH.

3d Ed. VI. A. D. 1549. EDWARD the Sixth, by the grace of God of England, France, and Ireland, King, Defender of the Faith, and on Earth of the English and Irish Church, Supreme Head, to all to whom these present letters shall come, greeting:— KNOW YE that we, as well for the sum of two hundred and sixty pounds, ten shillings, and ten pence, of lawful money of England, into the hands of the Treasurer of our Court of our Augmentation and Revenues of our Crown to our use, by our beloved Henry Gooderick, Esquire, Richard Everard, Esquire, John Sutton, Nicholas Fordham, John Prokter, Gentlemen, Thomas Crosse, William Beste, William Perte, Robert Skorterede, and Thomas Bocker, Yeomen, inhabitants of the Town of Wysbyche, within the Isle of Ely, in our

* The fishing cote, and seven acres and three roods of land in Newton, are not at this time in the possession of the burgesses, nor does it appear among their recorded proceedings how this right or the land has been alienated.

County of Cambridge, well and truly paid; and at the instance of the Reverend Father in Christ, Thomas, Bishop of Ely, who for certain urgent causes and considerations for the general advantage and common benefit of the Isle, us moving and exciting,—do will, and of our knowledge and mere motion, also by the advice of our most dearly beloved Uncle and Counsellor, Edward, Duke of Somerset, the Guardian of our Person, and of our Kingdoms, Dominions, and Subjects, Protector, and of other our Counsellors, for ourselves our Heirs and Successors, by these presents have granted to the inhabitants of the Town of Wysbyche aforesaid, that the said inhabitants of the said Town of Wysbyche from henceforth may and shall be in fact and in name, one Body and one Community of themselves for ever incorporated, by the name of the Inhabitants of the Town of Wysbyche, within the Isle of Ely, in the County of Cambridge; and the said inhabitants of the Town aforesaid, by the name of the Inhabitants of the Town of Wysbyche, within the Isle of Ely, in the County of Cambridge, we have by these presents incorporated, and a Body Corporate for ever to remain, really and fully have created, established, ordained, determined, declared, made, and constituted by these presents; and that they may and shall have perpetual succession; and that they may have a Common Seal to be serviceable for transacting their affairs; and also that they should be by the same name persons fit and capable in law to acquire, take, receive, and have, as well of us the Messuages, Lands, Tenements, Meadows, Feedings, Pastures, and all and singular other things in these our letters patent expressed and specified, as from all other persons whomsoever, and any other person whatsoever, Manors, Lands, Tenements, and Hereditaments whatsoever, to have and to hold of our successors for ever. And also of our special favour, and of our certain knowledge and mere motion, also by the advice aforesaid, and for the causes and considerations above mentioned, we have given and granted, and by these presents do give and grant to the said inhabitants of the Town of Wysbyche, within the Isle of Ely, in the County of Cambridge, all those our Messuages, Lands, Tenements, Meadows, Feedings, Pastures, and Hereditaments, wheresoever situated, lying and being in the Towns, Fields, and Parishes of Wysbyche, Leverington, Newton, and Elm, in the said County of Cambridge, and in Tyde St. Mary's, in our County of Lincoln, and in Emnethe, West Walton, and Walpole, in the Country of Marshland, in our County of Norfolk, which are or late were in the separate tenures or occupations of Thomas Drabbe, Martin Person, Thomas Tooke, William Salabanke, John Martinson, Robert Tego, Thomas Crosse, John Prokter, Robert Scortred, Alan Jekyn, Edward Archure, John Knight, Hamon Adam alias Stephynson, Ralph Richardson, Richard Dodyng, Paul Appuliarde alias Applyarde, Agnes Warner, Robert Osbourne, Katherine Wynde, John Rayner, senior, William Perte, John Austyne alias Augustyne, Richard Lorde, Agnes Robynson, widow, Nicholas Peerson, Robert Balam, Gentleman, William Thomason, William Chadwell, William Dryver, John Tego, junior, William Bryan, Gentleman, Thomas Toke, Simon Trone, John Fyn alias Fyne, Thomas Palmer, Thomas Pyckarde, John Sheparde, Edward Wilkes, and Henry Goodrick, Esquire, or any of them, or any of their assigns; also all Reversions whatsoever of all and singular the Premises, or any parcel thereof, and the Rents and annual Profits whatsoever, reserved upon any demises and grants made of the Premises, or of any parcel thereof, which said Messuages and other Premises lately belonged or appertained to the Fraternity or Guild of the Holy Trinity of Wysbyche aforesaid, and to our hands lately amongst other things came, and ought to come, by virtue of a certain Act of Parliament in the first year of our reign on that occasion, amongst other things declared and provided; and which said Messuages and other Premises, with their appurtenances, are now extended to the clear annual value of twenty-eight pounds, three shillings, and twopence farthing; to have and to hold all and singular the said Messuages, Lands, Tenements, Meadows, Feedings, Pastures, ando ther Hereditaments, and all other the Premises, with the appurtenances, to the said inhabitants of the said Town of Wysbyche, and to their successors for ever, to the proper use and behoof of the said inhabitants and their successors for ever, to be holden of us, our heirs and successors, as of our Manor of East Greenwich, in our County of Kent, in socage, and not in capite, viz. by fealty only, instead of all services, rents, and demands whatsoever; and also we have of our special grace, and by the advice aforesaid, given and granted to the said inhabitants of the said Town, all Issues, Revenues, and Profits of all the said Messuages, Lands, Tenements, and other Hereditaments, from the feast of St. Michael last past, howsoever proceeding or accruing, by the hands of the tenants and occupiers thereof to be paid, to be holden to the said inhabitants of our special gift, without any reckoning or any other thing from henceforth to us or our heirs to be rendered, paid, or done; And further we will, and by these presents, for us, our heirs and successors, have granted to the said inhabitants of the said Town of Wysbyche, that the inhabitants of the said Town there maintaining a household, or so many of them as shall be willing, on the first day of November which will be in the year of our Lord one thousand five hundred and fifty, lawfully and without damage, may assemble in a certain house in the said Town of Wysbyche, commonly called the Common Hall, and there, by themselves or the major number of them the said inhabitants of the said Town there maintaining a household, and then present in the said house, to nominate and choose ten men of the better, more honest, and more discreet inhabitants within the said Town of Wysbyche, and there maintaining a family, to the intent and purpose that the said ten men so nominated and elected, and the survivors of them hereafter from time to time, until the first day of November which will be in the year of our Lord one thousand five hundred and fifty, shall have full power and authority to grant and let to farm for the inhabitants of the said Town, in the names of the inhabitants of the said Town, by indentures or indenture, one part thereof to be sealed with the Common Seal of the inhabitants of the Town aforesaid, the Manors, Lands, Tenements, and other Hereditaments of the inhabitants of the said Town, or any parcels or parcel thereof, at their pleasure, for the term of twenty years, or for a less number of years, and to reserve upon every such grant and demise the old rent or more, and to consent for all the inhabitants of the said Town, for such grants and demises within the said time to be made; also from the aforesaid first day of November in the aforesaid year of our Lord one thousand five hundred and fifty, until the first day of November in the year of our Lord one thousand five hundred and fifty one, to have the care and administration of all the Manors, Lands, Tenements, and other Hereditaments of the aforesaid inhabitants, and of their matters and affairs whatsoever; and also during the same time to repair, overlook, and manage the Manors, Lands, Tenements, and other Hereditaments, for the common benefit of the said inhabitants.

Then follow certain clauses, empowering the inhabitants, maintaining a family, to meet on the first of November, to elect ten men maintaining families, who, being so elected, are to have authority to let to farm, by indenture, for twenty or a less number of years, the lands and hereditaments before mentioned, for the inhabitants of the said town, and in their names; and who are to have the care and administration of all such lands and of their affairs, and to manage them for the common benefit of the inhabitants: such ten, on being elected, not to remain, unless within one year after being elected, they shall be elected anew;—with licence for the inhabitants to acquire and enjoy other messuages, &c. to the value of £100, or under the same value; to implead in any action, and to lease, grant, sell, and exchange such lands. And for the good government and administration of the lands, the ten men are empowered to meet and summon so many and such of the more discreet and honest men there maintaining families, for the purpose of consulting about their matters and affairs touching the public good; with a clause, that a schoolmaster, with a salary of £12. should be provided,—the bishop of Ely to be visitor; and a direction that the said inhabitants, and their successors, should distribute amongst the poor annually £3. 15s. and maintain such and the like sea shores, banks, and streams, as the guardians and brethren of the late guild ought and were accustomed to do. Henry Goodrick, Richard Everard, Esquires, and eight others, are then nominated to be the first ten to execute all matters to the first day of November 1550;—with the following conclusion:

We will also, for the consideration aforesaid, and by the advice aforesaid by these presents have granted to the said inhabitants of the aforesaid Town of Wysbyche, that they may and shall have these our Letters Patent, under our Great Seal of England, in the appointed manner made and sealed, without fine or fee, great or small, to us in our Exchequer, or elsewhere, to our use in any manner to be rendered, paid, or done, so that express mention of the true annual value, or of the certainty of the Premises, or any of them, or from any other gifts or grants by us, or by any our next progenitors to the aforesaid inhabitants of the said Town of Wysbyche, before these times made, in these presents be not made by any statute, act, ordinance, provision, or restriction, to the contrary thereof made, set forth, ordained, or provided, or any other thing, cause, or matter whatsoever in any wise notwithstanding:—In testimony whereof we have caused these our Letters to be made Patent. Witness ourself at Westminster, the first day of June, in the third year of our Reign.

By the same King,

CONTHWETT.

BIRTHS, DEATHS, AND MARRIAGES,

Collected from the Parish Registers of the Church of Wisbech St. Peter.

Year.	Baptisms.	Marriages	Burials.	Year.	Baptisms.	Marriages	Burials.	Year.	Baptisms.	Marriages	Burials.	Year.	Baptisms.	Marriages	Burials.
1558	25	7	—	1631	79	32	120	1704	97	37	214	1777	130	45	101
1559	39	13	43	1632	115	25	95	1705	131	40	170	1778	125	42	186
1560	48	22	40	1633	104	31	97	1706	120	49	166	1779	96	38	188
1561	46	16	50	1634	109	25	110	1707	134	49	176	1780	93	37	200
1562	57	12	33	1635	123	23	114	1708	146	65	195	1781	92	43	186
1563	48	14	31	1636	114	24	84	1709	137	43	133	1782	119	49	175
1564	55	11	36	1637	123	37	121	1710	121	54	118	1783	115	50	181
1565	34	18	46	1638	107	28	248	1711	132	43	150	1784	114	54	178
1566	53	23	39	1639	82	33	169	1712	128	47	111	1785	142	40	79
1567	43	18	26	1640	95	40	129	1713	144	48	121	1786	121	40	143
1568	47	23	84	1641	124	32	124	1714	145	48	138	1787	119	59	108
1569	39	15	55	1642	120	34	128	1715	151	46	134	1788	145	62	140
1570	44	21	50	1643	151	19	106	1716	150	45	150	1789	156	53	131
1571	43	14	42	1644	99	34	121	1717	185	45	139	1790	161	55	142
1572	52	10	38	1645	115	26	73	1718	130	28	202	1791	161	57	135
1573	50	14	52.	1646	99	48	76	1719	145	39	270	1792	167	58	127
1574	45	16	59	1647	116	36	77	1720	135	51	272	1793	168	55	183
1575	44	17	54	1648	89	35	101	1721	133	70	152	1794	178	52	133
1576	58	21	48	1649	116	37	81	1722	169	54	181	1795	137	41	153
1577	51	12	59	1650	103	33	135	1723	181	55	184	1796	148	36	160
1578	63	26	42	1651	143	37	127	1724	169	46	196	1797	146	78	134
1579	60	26	44	1652	125	6	182	1725	166	49	178	1798	169	59	164
1580	57	25	30	1653	130	42	78	1726	163	43	160	1799	150	57	122
1581	64	19	31	1654	110	48	140	1727	148	48	309	1800	159	60	140
1582	64	27	51	1655	127	49	115	1728	126	69	207	1801	171	32	236
1583	55	32	62	1656	129	14	148	1729	139	60	158	1802	130	64	182
1584	62	38	95	1657	99	33	193	1730	126	46	168	1803	184	56	144
1585	45	25	67	1658	67	17	182	1731	152	56	150	1804	188	65	138
1586	67	20	72	1659	121	26	180	1732	164	38	179	1605	162	37	115
1587	65	34	205	1660	136	17	100	1733	144	50	151	1806	161	69	105
1588	64	33	97	1661	118	22	136	1734	134	37	157	1807	168	53	159
1589	77	27	74	1662	123	21	135	1735	147	37	147	1808	158	59	174
1590	78	32	147	1663	114	36	142	1736	142	32	222	1809	139	55	163
1591	53	40	158	1664	153	22	209	1737	124	30	198	1810	156	57	133
1592	83	33	177	1665	113	31	118	1738	120	40	150	1811	158	55	130
1593	79	33	95	1666	132	21	187	1739	126	25	130	1812	168	60	110
1594	63	44	67	1667	116	21	181	1740	131	35	168	1813	168	60	83
1595	96	26	108	1668	109	22	179	1741	106	61	201	1814	188	63	117
1596	92	18	102	1669	116	19	226	1742	101	41	135	1815	185	57	139
1597	64	18	99	1670	121	36	181	1743	113	38	136	1816	174	58	87
1598	98	23	108	1671	116	34	178	1744	94	37	115	1817	203	57	155
1599	86	26	96	1672	143	28	196	1745	110	26	126	1818	176	66	129
1600	78	22	73	1673	146	20	127	1746	111	27	117	1819	206	66	131
1601	89	37	64	1674	116	34	162	1747	97	45	183	1820	198	69	111
1602	82	22	107	1675	138	18	119	1748	98	33	156	1821	201	60	133
1603	96	32	64	1676	125	20	152	1749	92	26	131	1822	245	57	176
1604	67	35	96	1677	132	26	162	1750	106	36	98	1823	211	80	176
1605	83	41	119	1678	117	24	168	1751	72	38	112	1824	311	79	147
1606	76	26	94	1679	84	37	170	1752	112	36	119	1825	245	72	145
1607	88	34	82	1680	111	23	207	1753	103	23	89	1826	209	53	147
1608	94	30	84	1681	96	22	143	1754	67	33	103	1827	264	76	261
1609	86	25	101	1682	112	28	149	1755	121	38	154	1828	264	81	186
1610	96	21	119	1683	110	29	102	1756	104	41	182	1829	264	65	154
1611	96	32	108	1684	116	22	107	1757	107	22	160	1830	266	66	129
1612	86	17	114	1685	85	31	95	1758	114	29	119	1831	259	69	160
1613	83	26	95	1686	133	37	142	1759	115	27	140	1832	242	67	267
1614	77	24	89	1687	91	56	119	1760	125	42	101	1833	188	71	155
1615	63	21	128	1688	94	21	113	1761	102	41	107	1834	183	79	162
1616	44	37	146	1689	80	31	117	1762	125	34	153	1835	185	67	138
1617	82	47	105	1690	83	22	103	1763	102	48	183	1836	187	63	178
1618	67	32	88	1691	121	11	180	1764	123	48	185	1837	221	60	214
1619	86	24	78	1692	89	33	123	1765	133	41	94	1838	149	75	158
1620	89	36	91	1693	106	26	165	1766	144	39	102	1839	109	53	156
1621	94	21	67	1694	81	34	118	1767	122	41	190	1840	104	52	148
1622	86	26	76	1695	114	35	144	1768	126	34	158	1841	155	81	141
1623	62	30	123	1696	107	26	134	1769	145	43	127	1842	136	75	201
1624	92	23	94	1697	129	31	102	1770	151	35	109	1843	106	63	183
1625	66	25	98	1698	135	22	101	1771	124	38	132	1844	105	56	121
1626	77	30	87	1699	128	25	132	1772	134	53	124	1845	103	65	135
1627	66	36	82	1700	141	32	127	1773	118	43	149	1846	149	69	160
1628	102	17	62	1701	121	29	137	1774	139	35	112	1847	154	71	157
1629	88	31	71	1702	136	32	158	1775	120	40	114	1848	478	78	190
1630	86	41	121	1703	138	36	152	1776	152	19	98				

CORPORATION REVENUE.

Year ending 1st Sep.	General Purposes. Rents.			General Purposes. Borough Rates.			Cattle Market. Rental.			Port & Harbour. Receipts from Tonnage.		
	£	s.	d.	£	s.	d.	£	s.	d.	£	s.	d.
1836	1146	0	0				230	5	0	1082	17	11
1837	1986	12	0	222	9	9	368	0	0	1356	15	0
1838	1956	15	4	664	15	7	456	1	0	1245	0	0
1839	2033	9	2	480	13	8	425	0	0	1213	19	9
1840	1922	1	8	230	17	7	426	2	6	1373	11	3
1841	1888	17	6	358	13	11	416	2	6	1450	14	6
1842	1949	13	3	364	2	1	445	10	0	1428	7	0
1843	2070	19	6	364	19	4	460	10	0	1517	1	0
1844	2150	10	6	376	6	7	450	10	0	1567	8	9
1845	2304	10	0	396	6	0	436	0	0	1995	19	6
1846	2398	0	0	377	9	10	421	10	0	1949	2	9
1847	2250	3	9	385	6	9	427	16	0	2093	0	9
1848	2425	17	3	387	9	10	437	11	0	1988	6	3
1849	2272	14	3	381	18	1	452	5	6	1751	10	0

CORPORATION RECEIPTS AND EXPENDITURE.

The following summary of one year's Accounts (1848-49) of the Corporation will give an idea of the manner in which the revenues are disbursed:—

GENERAL PURPOSES.

Receipts.

	£	s.	d.
Balance from the Treasurer, 1st September, 1848,	232	2	7
Rents,	1589	0	9
Borough Rates,	359	16	2
Dividend,	3	0	0
Principal paid off	281	16	9
Crane,	110	0	0
Fines on Convictions	2	2	6
Miscellaneous,	29	1	9
Balance due to Treasurer, 1st September, 1849,	106	19	4
	£2713	19	10

Payments.

	£	s.	d.
Salaries,	£185	16	6
Rents, Rates, Taxes, & Insurances,	64	1	6
Police and Constables,	473	8	0
Lighting and Cleansing,	153	7	2
Administration of Justice,	33	11	10
Public Works,	289	9	11
Charities,	139	5	8
Municipal Elections,	25	10	6
Printing, Advertising, & Stationery,	39	14	11
Law Expenses and Clerks' Disbursements,	56	6	10
Interest,	322	5	5
Sinking Fund,	800	0	0
Annuity,	48	10	10
Grammar School,	14	0	0
Pumps and Engines,	33	0	1
Miscellaneous,	35	10	8
	£2713	19	10

CATTLE MARKET.

Receipts.	£	s.	d.	Payments.	£	s.	d.
Rent and Arrears, . .	£431	9	10	Annuity, ...	£52	8	6
Lettings of Exchange Hall,	5	0	0	Taxes, Insurance, and Cleansing,	18	8	0
				New Sheep Pens, . .	17	10	0
				New Doors, &c., . .	30	9	1
				Gravelling and Repairs, .	35	17	6
					154	13	1
				Balance transferred to General Purposes Account, .	281	16	9
	£436	9	10		£436	9	10

PORT AND HARBOUR.

Receipts.	£	s.	d.	Payments.	£	s.	d.
Dues on 140,120 Tons at 3d.	£1751	10	0	Balance and Poundage,	£101	7	4
Extra dues on Foreign Vessels,	15	16	6	Salaries, ...	140	0	0
Rent of Ship Yard, . .	1	0	0	Rent of Buoy House and Look Out,	18	7	6
				Works, ...	602	9	0
				Parliamentary Proceedings (on account),* . . .	665	9	6
				Nene Valley Drainage, .	110	6	7
				Interest, . . .	100	3	0
				Printing, Advertising, and Miscellaneous, . . .	26	12	0
					1758	14	11
				Balance Due from Treasurer,	9	11	7
	£1768	6	6		£1768	6	6

* £545 paid in 1848.

NENE IMPROVEMENT.

Receipts.	£	s.	d.	Payments.	£	s.	d.
Dues on 152,262 Tons at 3d.	£1903	5	6	Poundage, . . .	£ 38	2	6
Principal borrowed on Mortgage of Dues, . .	3500	0	0	Nene Outfall Commissioners, 1st instalment of £14,000, payable to them under the Nene Improvement Act,	4666	15	4
				Solicitor's Bills, . .	79	7	6
				Treasurer for interest and commission, . . .	19	10	3
				Printing, Advertising, &c. .	8	0	11
					4811	14	6
				Balance due from Treasurer,	591	11	0
	£5403	5	6		£5403	5	6

NENE IMPROVEMENTS.—ENGINEERS' REPORTS.

Since this Work was commenced, several important plans and alterations, connected with Wisbech, have either been agitated or come into operation, whose history may be briefly sketched in a note. Without detailing the disputes of Railway agitation, which have resulted in the passing of an Act for a line to Spalding, connected with the Eastern Counties line, with a small branch line to Sutton Bridge, we may recur to the Nene Improvement Bill passed in 1848. This Bill, which had become necessary in consequence of a threatened decay of the Nene Outfall and of the North Level Drainage, proposed:

1. To remove Cross Keys Bridge, and erect another better adapted to both drainage and navigation.
2. To remove the bends and contractions of the channel between Wisbech and the Cross Keys Bridge.
3. To improve the channel through Wisbech, so that a better water-way and better berthage for shipping might be obtained.
4. The promotion of Upland Navigation.
5. The drainage of the Washes above Wisbech.

The question of this Scheme, which most interested Wisbech, was the third, which was proposed to be accomplished by cutting a new channel and locking up the old one for a wet dock. The statement of Mr. Stephenson in his report, contains some important facts on this point:—

"The next great barrier to the free passage of the waters, is at the town of Wisbech and its bridge, in which there is, in a distance of a mile and a half, a fall of three feet, or at the rate of two feet per mile. This simple fact is conclusive of the existing obstruction, and the question is, how can it best be removed? Is it possible so to enlarge and improve the present channel, by the removal of the bridge, and by widening, deepening and wharfing, to give the necessary facilities at a reasonable cost;—or must a substitute for the present channel be found by a new cut, such as recommended by Mr. Rennie, or some modification of it?

"The sectional area of waterway at low water is,—

At the North Level Sluice - - -	721	superficial feet.
2¼ miles above North Level Sluice - -	367	,,
Opposite Haley's Dockyard - -	362	,,

"While, in the town, we have only—

Near the Wisbech Canal Sluice - -	100	,,
At the new Crane Wharf - - -	86	,,
Opposite Harrison's Granary - -	100	,,
At Wisbech Bridge - - -	105	,,
And at Phillips's Brewery - - -	105	,,

"And, as a comparison of widths, at low-water level there is,—

At North Level Sluice - - -	120	lineal feet.
At 2¼ miles above North Level Sluice -	118	,,
Opposite Haley's Dockyard - - -	83	,,
At the Canal Sluice - - - -	70	,,
At the new Crane Wharf - - -	43	,,
At Harrison's Granary - - -	40	,,
At Wisbech Bridge - - -	44	,,
And near Phillips's Brewery - - -	59	,,

"These figures sufficiently show an extreme irregularity and contraction through the town of Wisbech, particularly when coupled with the fact, that a greater sectional area and a larger width exist in several points above; and the great fall of two feet per mile from Phillips's Brewery to the Horseshoe Corner, while the average fall of the river is under seven inches per mile, is easily accounted for. To equalize the bed of the river through the town of Wisbech, without regard to other objects of improvement, would therefore require its being lowered about three feet, which alone would be perilous to the bridge, and even more to the buildings on either side of the harbour; but the contemplated measure of a much more extended drainage and navigation above, necessarily requires a vastly greater increase of the sectional area,—to be achieved only by increased width and depth.

"To widen the channel would involve the reconstruction of the bridge (in itself perhaps no insuperable difficulty), and the pulling down of the valuable granaries and other business premises overhanging the river,—a matter of serious cost, and attended with inconvenience and difficulty, which I do not well know how to meet; for even if the pecuniary question could be satisfactorily disposed of, I do not see how the business of the town could be continued in its present *locale*, but by such an encroachment on the houses fronting Market-street [Old Market?] as would in fact amount to almost their entire demolition, and the erection of new warehouses on the site so cleared.

"Again, by deepening the river to any beneficial purpose, although the buildings might possibly be preserved, great risk to them would be incurred, and an expensive wharfing on each side of the harbour for almost its whole extent, would be absolutely necessary; and, in addition to all these difficulties, there would still remain the obstruction to the discharge of the floods caused by the absorption of so much of the sectional area by vessels lying in the harbour, which would of course tell the most at low water, when the freest outlet is required for drainage.

"Taking all these circumstances into consideration, and saying nothing of the crooked course that would still remain, I can come only to the conclusion *that a sufficient water-way for the combined purposes of navigation and drainage, cannot, at any reasonable cost, be attained along the present course of the river through the town of Wisbech, and that a new channel is therefore necessary to the fulfilment of the objects contemplated.* This channel, as referred to above, was suggested by the late Mr. Rennie to extend from Rummer's Mill to the Horseshoe Corner, a distance of about three miles and a half in the straight line, which would be a very complete measure; but, with all deference to that justly high authority, I am of opinion that such a work would be too costly in proportion to the advantage gained, and that a more limited work, not however differing in principle, would answer every practical purpose; especially as, since his day, the Nene above Wisbech has been relieved of all the waters of the North Level, and in truth is little more than the outlet of the upland waters passing through Peterborough Bridge, the accession below being only the drainage of Moreton's Leam Wash and the districts of Waldersey and Redmoor.

"The New Cut I recommend, which is not a new suggestion, extends from Phillips's Brewery above the town to the Horseshoe Corner below it, and is about a mile and a quarter long."

To this suggestion the Corporation became opposed, and they commenced a Parliamentary warfare against the measure. The opposition, which cost about £1600, was futile—the bill was passed; but the portion of it relating to the New Cut and the Wet Dock, was dropped on account of an insufficiency of funds to carry out the work. The removal of Sutton Bridge, and the improvements of the river below Wisbech, are the only portions of the bill at present in operation. Wisbech was made to contribute £14,000 to the work, which involves about £30,000.

The works were immediately commenced after the passing of this bill, and a new bridge at Sutton is now in the course of erection (December, 1849). The conservation of the river nearly to the Horseshoe at Wisbech is placed in the hands of Commissioners. These improvements augur a new if not an increased shipping trade to Wisbech. A barque, the "Mungo Park," the first that ever penetrated so far as Wisbech, discharged her cargo of deals here in the autumn of 1849; and since then one has been built in the town by Mr. Cousens. She is called the "Richard Young," and was launched November 17th, 1849.

But another scheme quickly succeeded this. The rise above Peterborough is subject to extensive inundation, and consequent great loss of crops, attended with much local disease, arising from miasma. To remedy this, the noblemen and gentlemen, having estates or interest in the district, met at Northampton in the spring of 1849, and a plan, involving the improvement of the river from Northampton to Wisbech, was proposed. Here the obstructions of Wisbech were again the principal points of grievance and dispute; but, after several meetings, Mr. Rendel was employed to report on the subject, and for that purpose traversed the whole valley of the Nene. His instructions and suggestions, with respect to Wisbech, were as follows:—

"'In approaching the town of Wisbech, the Committee are anxious to express their desire to avail themselves of the concurrence and assistance of the Corporation in an earnest effort to accomplish this great undertaking. They wish to provide effectually for its town and harbour the same benefits which they equally desire for all portions of the River. Impressed with the conviction that mutual support will confer mutual advantages, and that a zealous and united co-operation betwixt all parties concerned can alone give confidence and security to the various proprietors on the banks of the Nene, they wish you to report upon the best mode of effecting the discharge of the upland waters through the town of Wisbech, if practicable, and, if not, in what other way the discharge thereof may be effected; and to report, also, on the relative expenses and advantages of the respective plans.'

"'At this extreme point of your observations the Committee express the hope that some plan may be recommended for improving the course of the River at Wisbech, which will meet the wishes of the Corporation; that the River will be made subservient to the commercial enterprise of the inhabitants, and the utmost advantage taken of the improvements seaward of the town.'

"It is beyond all question essential to the economical carrying out of any extensive scheme of improvement in the Nene, so to provide for all the existing interests, as to insure the greatest possible amount of unanimity. In this respect the concurrence of the town of Wisbech in a general measure is most desirable, and there is every reason to expect that the inhabitants will respond to the strong wish of the Committee, to continue the River-course through the town, if possible. After a most anxious attention to this question, I am of opinion that limiting the alterations to what are necessary for carrying off the upland waters, and for the restricted Fen district now left for drainage by the Nene, it will be possible to make its present channel through Wisbech sufficient for that object, and that having the assistance of the authorities and influential inhabitants of the town in acquiring the necessary property for the works, the cost would be considerably less than in making a great diversion of the River, and the adjunct works thereby involved. To assist me in my investigation of this part of the business, I have been furnished by the town authorities with a variety of plans, reports, estimates, &c., and, though I consider none of these now applicable, I think it proper to state that Mr. Telford's plan bears the nearest resemblance to the scheme I consider the most suitable. I must, however, be understood that I do not think it possible to decide on any positive plan till the whole scheme can be laid down, and that the extent to which I now offer an opinion is only that it is not necessary for efficient drainage to divert the course of the River from the town—that it will be better for the town of Wisbech to retain it, but to have it efficiently improved, seeing that thereby the flood waters will less interfere with the ships lying in the harbour—that less damage will be sustained by the bed of the River, and consequently to the wharfs and warehouses on its margin—and, finally, that the Navigation down to the sea, will be preserved at a greater and more uniform depth than at present. These are all objects in which the town of Wisbech is vitally interested, and should it lead, as doubtless it will, to an increase of shipping business up the country, it will still further augment the trade of the Port."

These suggestions, so completely opposite to those of all other engineers who have agitated this question, can only be considered as politely escaping the question. Mr. Rendel has not decided what is the best course, but which is the most agreeable to prejudice. It needs not the engagement of engineers to decide on such questions, but to show the very best plan for the end in view, which, with Rennie, Stephenson, Walker, and others, as authorities, we may safely decide to be a new Cut at the back of the present crooked unimprovable channel. However, the poor funds which the scheme could alone command, and its great expense, seems to have nipped it in the bud. The following is Mr. Rendel's recapitulation and estimate:—

"First.—That the Valley above Peterborough may be freed from all but winter floods, and its low lands placed from two to four feet above the ordinary level of the water in the drains, by the removal of some of the Mills—the remodelling of the Navigation—the formation of efficient waste weirs—and the construction of proper back drains.

"Second.—That such a system of drainage is quite compatible with, and in fact facilitates irrigation.

"Third.—That if a greater amount of drainage is required, it may be obtained by the sacrifice of the Navigation and greater number of the mills, but that I cannot recommend such a course.

"Fourth.—That to the extent named, viz., a drainage of two to four feet, the works required will greatly improve the Navigation and the mill property where it is retained.

"Fifth.—That to make the river below Peterborough a suitable conduit for the upland waters, and relieve Whittlesea Wash from floods, its channel must be deepened and enlarged.

"Sixth.—That I do not think it would be a judicious expenditure of money, or beneficial to the general interests, to incur a large outlay on this part of the River for the sole object of improving the navigation.

"Seventh.—That so restricting the River improvements it is not necessary or desirable to divert its course through the town of Wisbech, assuming the authorities and inhabitants of that town to facilitate a liberal improvement of the old channel.

"Eighth.—That the works contemplated would give from four to five feet rise of spring tides at Peterborough, and make a good seven feet Navigation to the city, giving to its sewers two to three feet more fall than at present.

"Ninth.—That the probable cost of the required works above Peterborough

will be		£140,000
Below Peterborough		230,000
Making a total of		£370 000
The gross area of flooded lands—		
Above Peterborough	13,140	acres.
Below ditto	3,300	,,
	16,440	,,
Waldersea and Redmore districts	7,166	,,
Total	23,606	,,

"And Tenth.—That until a complete Engineering Survey of the whole Valley is made, no definite plan or estimate for the works can be settled."

SECRETARY THURLOE.

The following letters, which we have received through the kindness of Wm. Peckover, Esq., at the very moment of sending the last sheet to press, refer to an event of some interest in the history of Wisbech. We have traced whatever is known of the connection of Secretary Thurloe with Wisbech in the text of this work. The letters subjoined relate to another circumstance—his election as a Member of Parliament in 1656 for the Isle of Ely, which election appears to have taken place at Wisbech.

"Right Honourable,—Indeed, Sir, my ayme in going to Wisbech was but to have conferred with the Commissioners—and many of the Gentlemen I thank them, met me there, as doctor Stave and collonell Castle, with captain Pitchford from the south part, Mr. Farrer, coll. Diamond, & coll. Underwood from the parts of Wisbeech and Whittlesey; and finding the business of the elections to be the only thing they had to discours there, and that they were devyded much about the place, as also that some of them had expressed their desires for myselfe to joine with your honour, I judged it most advyseable to do least in it but to hasten to Lynn, where I had appointed to settle some business the next day, whether Mr. Sheldricke and Mr. Clapthorne follows, and there againe I was drawne most unwillingly into the debate of the place of election, wherein I was more passive than in the former resolutions of Ely; for my judgment ledd me to that as the fittingest place for that isle and that which would have given most general satisfaction, because the last was at Wisbeech; and besides I did thynke then that it would something reflect uppon your honour to confine it to Wisbeech.

"Finding that resolution disgusted very much those about Wisbeech, as judging it was a design in col. Castle to putt a blott upon yourselfe, and not well accepted of the midland part neither, and being convinced of my former mistake of the sherriffe of the county having noe jurisdiction in that point there I fledd for it, before my resolution was had more then to leave it to Mr. Clapthorne."

"Bury, Aug. 15, '56."

"Right Honorable,—I received yours of the 23rd inst. at Wisbech, Thursday last, by the hands of Mr. Edwards your bailiffe.

"In my way to Wisbeech I was met by young Mr. Fisher and with a complement from the Capt. his Father to lodge at his house; but consulting your honour's letter and Mr. Edwards's, I judged it was not adviseable to engage till I could be assured what the Capt. would do as to standing.

"So I went to Mr. Sheldrack's, and there meeting with Col. Underwood, Col. Castle, Lieut-Col. Diamond, Mr. Glapthorne, doctor Stanes, Mr. Ferrer, Mr. Coldwell, with some others; consideration was had of what was fit to be done as the case stood, capt. Fisher having prepared the people of all parts to serve him in the election, and having also provided inns for their reception. That meeting issued in this resolution, to wait till the next day to see what the appearance of the country would be, and every man to try his utmost, and some of them with myself put upon the discoursing of capt. Fisher, which accordingly was done; and meeting the next day after dinner to compare notes, we found capt. Fisher so strongly engaged that he would not recede by any means—yea so violent in it that your own interest seemed to be called in question by him to myself and others, resolving to dispute the first election with you if it came to a pole, which could not have been avoided by any third man standing: also that by himself and instruments making use of my being a stranger; as also your own Town of Wisbeech either engaged for him or else standing neuter.

"These things duly weighed, it was agreed as best, we not being able to controul his election, he might be let alone.

"Feltwell, Aug. 28, 8 at night, Thursday, 1656."

"By Mr. Hill who had been at Wisbeech to find me, I understand your honour and Mr. Fisher is chosen for the isle.

"Feltwell, Aug. 29, 56, nyne in the morne."

TONNAGE OF THE PORT OF WISBECH FROM 1805 TO 1849.

	TONS.		TONS.
1805	29,242	1828	66,162
1806	29,816	1829	55,040
1807	28,313	1830	63,180
1808	35,416	1831	71,037
1809	32,128	1832	78,322
1810	34,954	1833	81,778
1811	46,243	1834	86,618
1812	45,340	1835	92,844
1813	43,110	1836	86,631
1814	42,584	1837	108,540
1815	38,995	1838	99,600
1816	46,611	1839	97,119
1817	51,860	1840	109,885
1818	64,191	1841	116,058
1819	52,621	1842	114,268
1820	62,030	1843	121,364
1821	52,191	1844	125,395
1822	60,140	1845	159,678
1823	64,611	1846	155,931
1824	70,000	1847	167,442
1825	70,320	1848	159,065
1826	44,095	1849	152,262
1827	41,552		

POPULATION RETURNS.

First Census taken about 1676	1705	In 1821	6515
In 1801	4710	In 1831	7223
In 1811	5309	In 1841	8530

The present population of Wisbech is supposed to amount to 10,000, and including the suburb of New Walsoken, to nearly 12,000.

INDEX.

SECTION I.—THE FENS.

CHAPTER I.—PHYSICAL CHARACTERISTICS.

CHAPTER II.—POLITICAL HISTORY.

CHAPTER III.—HISTORY OF THE DRAINAGE.

CHAPTER V.—THE SOUTH LEVEL.

CHAPTER VI.—THE NORTH LEVEL.

CHAPTER VII.—THE MIDDLE LEVEL.

SECTION II.—THE TOWN.

CHAPTER I.—GENERAL HISTORY OF WISBECH.

PRINTED BY RICHARD WALKER, BRIDGE-FOOT, WISBECH.

Ingram Content Group UK Ltd.
Milton Keynes UK
UKHW021834240323
419150UK00005B/190

9 781015 602038